PHILIP'S

STREET ATLAS

UNRIVALLED DETAIL FROM THE BEST-SELLING ATLAS RANGE*

NAVIGATOR® CORNWALL
& PLYMOUTH

www.philips-maps.co.uk

Published by Philip's, a division of Octopus Publishing Group Ltd
www.octopusbooks.co.uk
Carmelite House
50 Victoria Embankment
London EC4Y 0DZ
An Hachette UK Company
www.hachette.co.uk

First edition 2022
COREA

ISBN 978-1-84907-572-5

© Philip's 2022

This product includes mapping data licensed from Ordnance Survey® with the permission of the Controller of Her Majesty's Stationery Office. © Crown copyright 2022. All rights reserved. Licence number 100011710.

*Philip's Navigator – Britain's bestselling road atlas in its category. Data from Nielsen Bookscan.

**All streets named in the source Ordnance Survey dataset at the time of going to press are included in this Philip's Street Atlas.

Printed in China

CONTENTS

II	**Key to map pages**
IV	**Route planning**
VIII	Major administrative and Postcode boundaries
1	**Key to map symbols**
2	**Street maps** at 1¾ inches to 1 mile
104	**Street maps** at 3½ inches to 1 mile
148	**Street map of Plymouth city centre** at 7 inches to 1 mile
150	**Index** of towns, villages, streets, hospitals, industrial estates, railway stations, schools, shopping centres, universities and places of interest

T0329493

Key to map pages

80	Map pages at 1¾ inches to 1 mile
112	Map pages at 3½ inches to 1 mile
148	Map pages at 7 inches to 1 mile

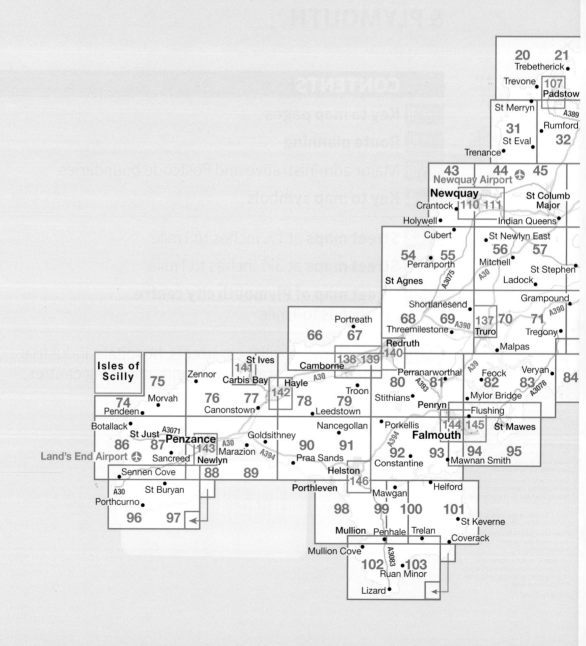

Trebetherick 20 21
Trevone
107 Padstow
St Merryn
A389
31 Rumford
St Eval 32
Trenance

43 44 45
Newquay Airport
Newquay
Crantock 110 111 St Columb Major
Holywell Indian Queens
Cubert
St Newlyn East
54 55 57
Perranporth Mitchell
St Stephen
St Agnes A3075 A30 Ladock
Grampound
Shortlanesend 71
68 69 A390 137 70 Tregony
Threemilestone Truro A390
Redruth Malpas
66 67 140
Portreath Perranarworthal A39 Veryan
Camborne 138 139 80 81 Feock 82 83 A3078 84
St Ives 141 Mylor Bridge
Zennor Carbis Bay Stithians Penryn Flushing
Isles of Scilly 75 Hayle A30 Troon 144 145 St Mawes
76 77 142 78 79 Leedstown Falmouth 94 95
Morvah Canonstown Nancegollan Porkellis 92 93 Mawnan Smith
Pendeen Goldsithney 90 91 Constantine
Botallack St Just A3071 Penzance Praa Sands Helston Helford
86 87 143 Marazion A394
Land's End Airport Newlyn Porthleven Mawgan 98 99 100 101 St Keverne
Sancreed 88 89 146 Coverack
Sennen Cove Mullion Penhale Trelan
A30 St Buryan Mullion Cove A3083
Porthcurno 96 97 102 103
Ruan Minor
Lizard

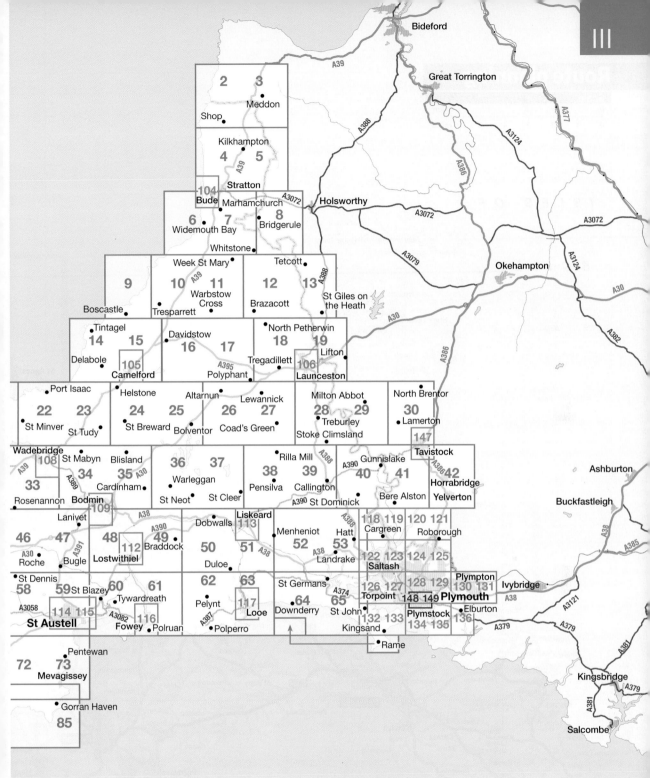

Bideford

Great Torrington

Meddon
Shop
2 3

Kilkhampton
4 5
Stratton
104
Bude Marhamchurch
Holsworthy
6 7 8
Widemouth Bay Bridgerule
Whitstone

Week St Mary Tetcott
9 10 11 12 13
Boscastle Warbstow Brazacott St Giles on
Tresparrett Cross the Heath

Okehampton

Tintagel Davidstow North Petherwin
14 15 16 17 18 19
Delabole Lifton
105 Tregadillett
Camelford Polyphant 106
A395 Launceston

Port Isaac Helstone Altarnun Lewannick Milton Abbot North Brentor
22 23 24 25 26 27 28 29 30
St Minver St Breward Coad's Green Treburley Lamerton
St Tudy Bolventor Stoke Climsland

Wadebridge St Mabyn Blisland Rilla Mill Gunnislake Tavistock
108 36 37 38 39 40 41 42 147
33 34 35 Warleggan Pensilva Callington Bere Alston Horrabridge
Rosenannon Cardinham St Neot St Cleer St Dominick Yelverton
Bodmin 109 St Dominick

Lanivet Liskeard 118 119 120 121
46 47 48 49 50 113 Menheniot Cargreen Roborough
Roche Bugle Braddock Dobwalls 52 53 Hatt
Lostwithiel Duloe 51 Landrake 122 123 124 125
St Dennis Saltash
58 59 60 61 62 63 St Germans 126 127 128 129 Plympton
St Blazey Tywardreath Pelynt 117 St Germans Torpoint 130 131 Ivybridge
114 115 116 Looe 64 65 148 149 Plymouth
St Austell Fowey Polruan Downderry St John Plymstock
132 133 134 135 136
Kingsand Elburton

Pentewan Rame
72 73
Mevagissey

Gorran Haven
85

Ashburton

Buckfastleigh

Kingsbridge

Salcombe

Scale
0   5   10   15   20   25 km
0   5   10   15 miles

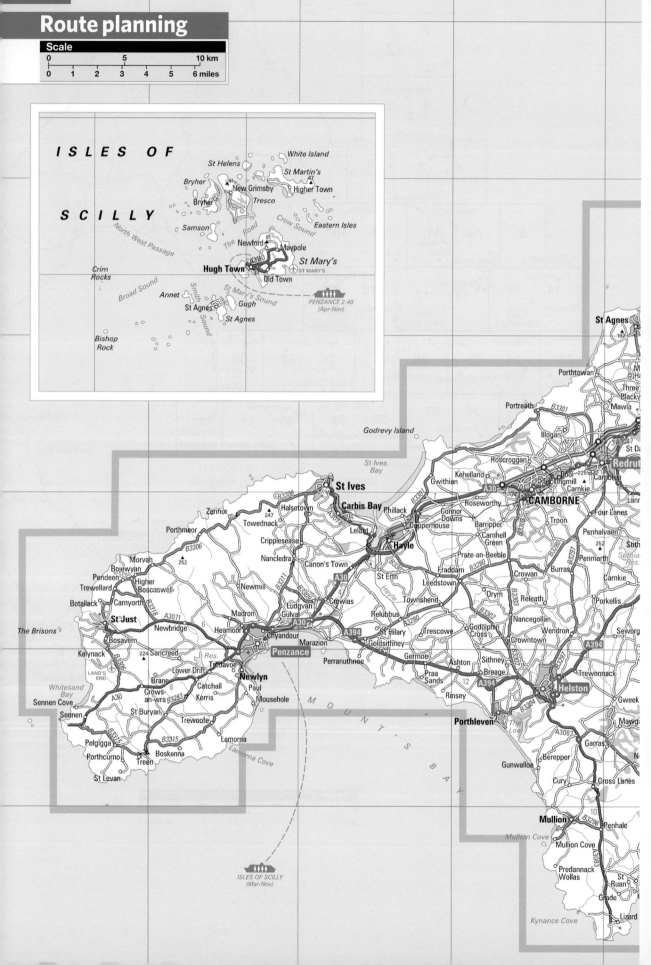

Scale

0		5		10 km
0	1	2	3	4	5	6 miles

I S L E S   O F

S C I L L Y

White Island

St Helens

Bryher · New Grimsby · St Martin's 47

Bryher · Tresco · Higher Town

North West Passage · Samson · Crow Sound · Eastern Isles

Crim Rocks · The Road · Newford 51 · Maypole

Broad Sound · A3110 · St Mary's · St Mary's Sound · Hugh Town · Old Town · ST MARY'S

Annet · Smith Sound · Gugh · St Agnes · St Agnes

PENZANCE 2:40 (Apr-Nov)

Bishop Rock

St Agnes · 192

Porthtowan · M...

Portreath · B3301 · Mawla · Blackw... · Three...

Godrevy Island · Illogan · A3047 · St Da... · Redrut...

St Ives Bay · Roscroggan · Pool · 225 · Cambre... · Carnkie

Gwithian · A30... · A3047 · CAMBORNE

St Ives · B3306 · Kehelland · Tuckingmill · Troon · Four Lanes

Zennor · Halsetovvn · Carbis Bay · Phillack · Connor Downs · Roseworthy · Barripper · Penhalvaen · 252 · Stith...

247 · Towednack · Lelant · Hayle · Carnhell Green · Praze-an-Beeble · Crowan · Burras · Carnkie · Penmarth · Stithia... Res.

Porthmeor · Cripplesease · Canon's Town · St Erth · Fraddam · B3280 · Leedstown · Townshend · Drym · B3303 · Releath · Porkellis

Morvah · B3306 · 252 · Nancledra · A30 · 4 · Crowlas · Townshend · Godolphin Cross · Nancegollan · Wendron · Seworg...

Bojewyan · Higher Boscaswell · Newmill · Ludgvan · Crowlas · Relubbus · B3280 · Crowntown · A394

Pendeen · Trewellard · Madron · Gulval · St Hilary · Trescowe · 9 · Sewor...

Botallack · Carnyorth · Heamoor · A30 · Chyandour · Marazion · Goldsithney · Germoe · Ashton · Sithney · Breage · Trewennack · Helston · Gweek

St Just · Newbridge · 6 · Penzance · Perranuthnoe · Praa Sands · Rinsey · 12 · A394 · Gwee...

The Brisons · Bosavern · Sancreed · Res. · Tredavoe · Newlyn · Paul · Mousehole · Gunwalloe · Garras · Mawg...

Kelynack · B3306 · 224 · Lower Drift · Catchall · Kerris · MOUNT'S · Berepper · N...

LAND'S END · Brane · Crows-an-wra · B3283 · Trewoofe · Cury · Cross Lanes

Whitesand Bay · Sennen Cove · A30 · St Buryan · Lamorna · Lamorna Cove · BAY · Predannack Wollas · St Ruan · A3083

Sennen · Polgigga · B3315 · Boskenna · Mullion · B3296 · Penhale · Grade

Porthcurno · Treen · Mullion Cove · Mullion Cove · A3083 · Lizard

St Levan · Porthleven · B3304 · The Loe · A3083 · Kynance Cove

ISLES OF SCILLY (Mar-Nov)

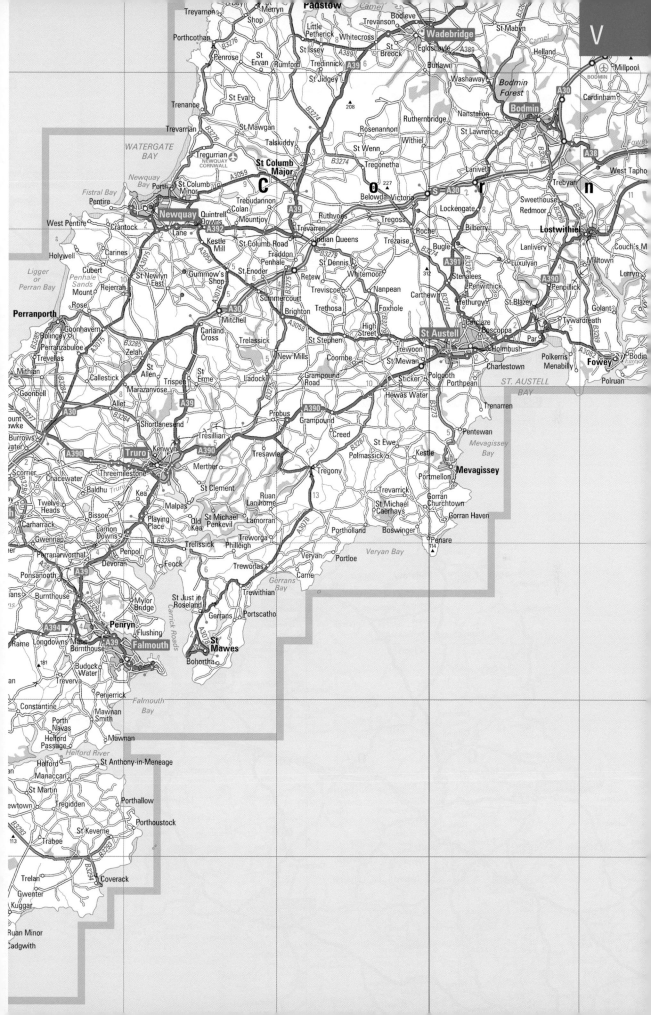

Scale

0 5 10 km

0 1 2 3 4 5 6 miles

BUDE BAY

Hartland
Higher Clovelly
Philham
Milford
Eddistone
Woolfardisworthy
Elmscott
Tosberry
South Hole
Hartland Forest
Alminstone Cross
Welcombe
235
Meddon
Ashmansworth
Gooseham
Woolley
156
Eastcott
Youlstone
West Putford
Morwenstow
Dinworthy
A39
Shop
Bradworthy
Woodford
Bradworthy Cross
Kilkhampton
14
Alfardisworthy
Sutcombe
Coombe
Venn Green
Stibb
Soldon Cross
Holsworthy Beacon
Flexbury
Poughill
Hersham
Chilsworthy
Bude Haven
Stratton
Grimscott
Pancrasweek
Bude
Launcells
A3072
A388

St Genny's
Poundst
Tregole
Trewint
Rosecare
Crackington Haven
Widemouth Bay
Mil
Trevalga
Beeny
Tresparrett Posts
260
B3263
Marshgate
A39
Tresparrett
Lesnewth
Otterham
25
Boscastle
Trevalga
Bossiney
Tintagel
308
Trewarmett
Davidstow
Tremail
Treknow
B3263
Trewassa
13
Trebarwith
B3314
Trelash
Hallw
Treligga
Rough Tor 400
Delabole
Crowdy Res.
Valley Truckle
Camelford
Brown Willy 420
Helstone
Garrow Tor 331
Coddа
St Teath
Bol
Port Isaac Bay
Port Isaac
Treveighan
Michaelstow
18
Port Quin
Port Gaverne
B3266
10
New Polzeath
Pendoggett
A39
St Breward
Padstow Bay
Trelights
Trelill
Row
Trebetherick
Polzeath
St Endellion
Bradford
Port Quin Bay
Port Quin Bay
St Minver
Trewethern
St Tudy
Wenfordbridge
Blisland
Crugmeer
Pityme
St Kew
Temple
Trevone
Rock
B3314
Chapel Amble
St Kew Highway
Colliford Lake
Constantine Bay
Constantine Bay
St Merryn
Camel
Bodieve
St Mabyn
Treyarnon
Shop
Trevanson
Wadebridge
Helland
Camel
Padstow
Little Petherick
Whitecross
Eglostown
A389
268
Maidenwell
Porthcothan
B3276
St Issey
St Breock
Burlawn
Millpool
Penrose
St Ervan
Rumford
Tredinnick
A39
Washaway
Bodmin Forest
Warleggan
Trenance
A389
St Jidgey
208
Bodmin
Cardinham
St Neot
Trevarrian
B3276
St Mawgan
Ruthernbridge
Nanstallon
Mount
Watergate Bay
Talskiddy
Rosenannon
St Lawrence
Ley
Tregurrian
Newquay Cornwall
St Columb Major
St Wenn
Withiel
Tregonetha
Lanivet
Fowey
West Taphouse
East Taphouse
A390
Newquay Bay
Porth
St Columb Minor
A3059
CORNW
Trebudannon
B3274
227
Victoria
S A30 2
Trebyan
Braddock
Pentire
St Columb Minor
Colan
Belowda
Sweethouse
11
astral Bay
Newquay
Quintrell Downs
Mountjoy
Ruthvoes
Tregoss
Lockengate
Redmoor
B3359
Crantock
Lane
Trevarren
Roche
Bilberry
Lostwithiel
Carines
Kestle Mill
Indian Queens
Trezaise
Bugle
Lanlivery
Couch's Mill
Bocaddon
Rejerrah
St Columb Road
Fraddon
Penhale
St Dennis
Whitemoor
312
Stenalees
Penwithick
Luxulyan
Milltown
Lerryn
Lanreath
St Newlyn East
Gummow's Shop
Retew
Nanpean
Carthew
Trethurgy
Penpillick
A390
Treviscoe
Trethosa
Foxhole
St Blazey
Golant
St Veep
Penpoll
Mitchell
Summercourt
Brighton
High Street
Boscoppa
Penpillick
Tywardreath
Lanteglos Highway
Carland Cross
A3058
St Stephen
Trewoon
St Austell
Holmbush
Par
Polkerris
Bodinnick
Trelassick
New Mills
Coombe
St Mewan
Charlestown
Menabilly
Fowey
Zelah
St Allen
St Erme
Ladock
Grampound Road
Sticker
Polgooth
Porthpean
St Austell Bay
Polruan
Trispen
Marazanvose
Aller
A39
Probus
Grampound
Hewas Water
Trenarren
B3284
Shortlanesend
Tresillian
Creed
Pentewan

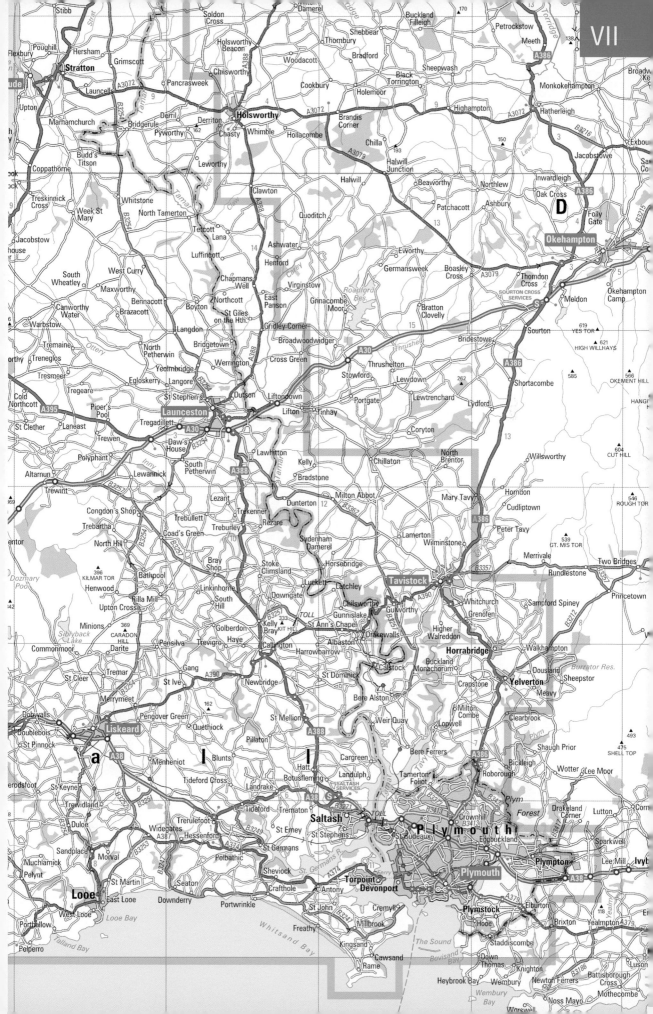

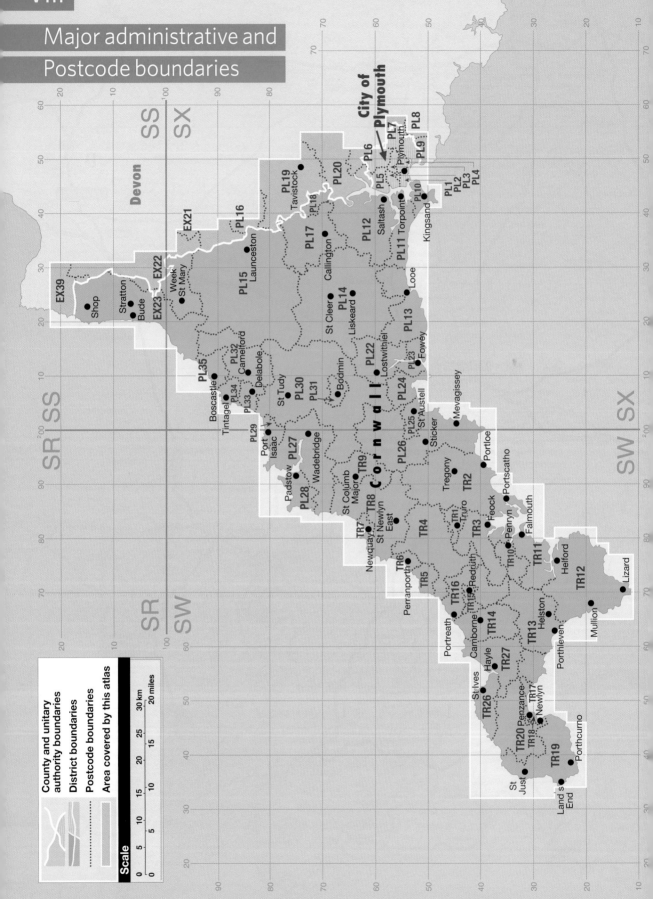

City of
Plymouth

Devon

Cornwall

Scale

County and unitary
authority boundaries
District boundaries
Postcode boundaries
Area covered by this atlas

0   5   10   15   20   25   30 km
0   5   10   15   20 miles

Key to map symbols

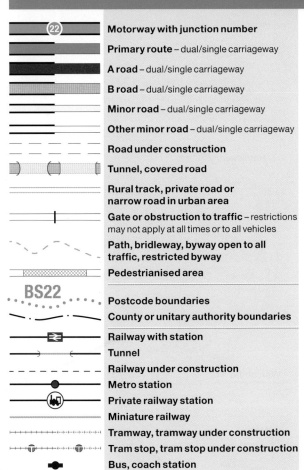

	Motorway with junction number
	Primary route – dual/single carriageway
	A road – dual/single carriageway
	B road – dual/single carriageway
	Minor road – dual/single carriageway
	Other minor road – dual/single carriageway
	Road under construction
	Tunnel, covered road
	Rural track, private road or narrow road in urban area
	Gate or obstruction to traffic – restrictions may not apply at all times or to all vehicles
	Path, bridleway, byway open to all traffic, restricted byway
	Pedestrianised area
BS22	Postcode boundaries
	County or unitary authority boundaries
	Railway with station
	Tunnel
	Railway under construction
	Metro station
	Private railway station
	Miniature railway
	Tramway, tramway under construction
	Tram stop, tram stop under construction
	Bus, coach station

	Ambulance station
	Coastguard station
	Fire station
	Police station
	Accident and Emergency entrance to hospital
H	Hospital
+	Place of worship
i	Information centre
	Shopping centre, parking
P&R PO	Park and Ride, Post Office
	Camping site, caravan site
	Golf course, picnic site
Church ROMAN FORT	Non-Roman antiquity, Roman antiquity
Univ	Important buildings, schools, colleges, universities and hospitals
	Woods, built-up area
River Medway	Water name
	River, weir
	Stream
	Canal, lock, tunnel
	Water
	Tidal water
58 87 246	Adjoining page indicators and overlap bands – the colour of the arrow and band indicates the scale of the adjoining or overlapping page (see scales below)

The dark grey border on the inside edge of some pages indicates that the mapping does not continue onto the adjacent page

The small numbers around the edges of the maps identify the 1-kilometre National Grid lines

Enlarged maps only

	Railway or bus station building
	Place of interest
	Parkland

Abbreviations

Acad	Academy	Meml	Memorial
Allot Gdns	Allotments	Mon	Monument
Cemy	Cemetery	Mus	Museum
C Ctr	Civic centre	Obsy	Observatory
CH	Club house	Pal	Royal palace
Coll	College	PH	Public house
Crem	Crematorium	Recn Gd	Recreation ground
Ent	Enterprise	Resr	Reservoir
Ex H	Exhibition hall	Ret Pk	Retail park
Ind Est	Industrial Estate	Sch	School
IRB Sta	Inshore rescue boat station	Sh Ctr	Shopping centre
Inst	Institute	TH	Town hall / house
Ct	Law court	Trad Est	Trading estate
L Ctr	Leisure centre	Univ	University
LC	Level crossing	W Twr	Water tower
Liby	Library	Wks	Works
Mkt	Market	YH	Youth hostel

The map scale on the pages numbered in green is 1¾ inches to 1 mile
2.76 cm to 1 km • 1 : 36 206

The map scale on the pages numbered in blue is 3½ inches to 1 mile
5.52 cm to 1 km • 1 : 18 103

The map scale on the pages numbered in red is 7 inches to 1 mile
11.04 cm to 1 km • 1 : 9051

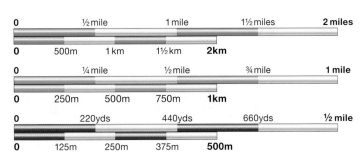

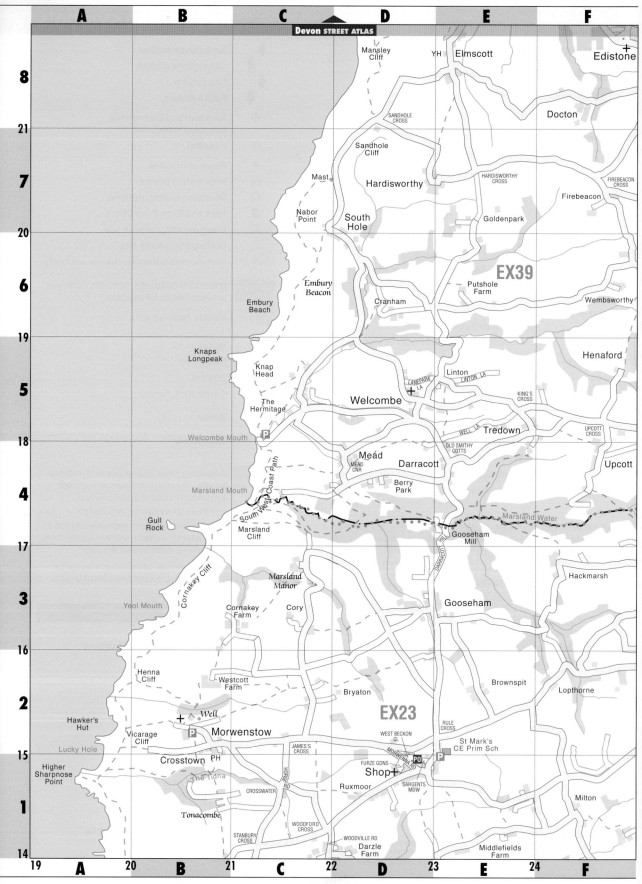

Scale: 1¾ inches to 1 mile

Devon STREET ATLAS

A **B** **C** **D** **E** **F**

8
21
7
20
6
19
5
18
4
17
3
16
2
15
1
14

Mansley Cliff
YH
Elmscott
Edistone

SANDHOLE CROSS
Docton

Sandhole Cliff

Mast
HARDISWORTHY CROSS
FIREBEACON CROSS

Hardisworthy
Firebeacon

Nabor Point
South Hole
Goldenpark

EX39

Embury Beacon
Cranham
Putshole Farm
Wembsworthy

Embury Beach

Knaps Longpeak
Henaford

Knap Head
Linton
LINTON LA

LANEPARK LA
KING'S CROSS

The Hermitage
Welcombe
WELL LA
Tredown
UPCOTT CROSS

Welcombe Mouth

OLD SMITHY COTTS
Upcott

Mead
Darracott

MEAD CNR

Marsland Mouth
Berry Park

South West Coast Path

Gull Rock
Marsland Cliff
Gooseham Mill
Marsland Water

DARRACOTT HILL
Hackmarsh

Cornakey Cliff
Marsland Manor

Yeol Mouth
Cornakey Farm
Cory
Gooseham

Brownspit
Lopthorne

Henna Cliff
Westcott Farm
Bryaton

Hawker's Hut
Well
EX23

Vicarage Cliff
RULE CROSS

P
Morwenstow
WEST BECKON CL
St Mark's CE Prim Sch

Lucky Hole
Crosstown PH
JAMES'S CROSS
MORWENNA RD
PO
P

Higher Sharpnose Point
FURZE GDNS
Shop

HORSE RD
Ruxmoor
SARGENTS MDW

The Tidna
CROSSWATER

Tonacombe
WOODFORD CROSS
Milton

STANBURY CROSS
WOODVILLE RD
Darzle Farm
Middlefields Farm

19 **A** **20** **B** **21** **C** **22** **D** **23** **E** **24** **F**

4

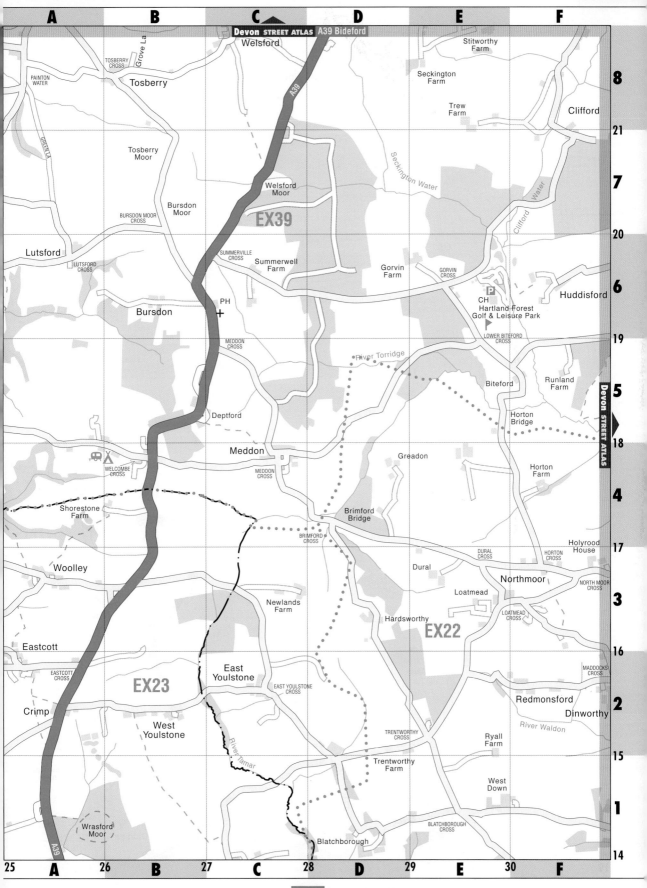

Scale: 1¾ inches to 1 mile

0   ¼   ½ mile
0   250m 500m 750m 1 km

A   B   C   D   E   F

Devon STREET ATLAS A39 Bideford

Welsford

Stitworthy Farm

TOSBERRY CROSS

PAINTON WATER

Tosberry

Seckington Farm

Trew Farm

Clifford

8

21

GREEN LA

Grove La

Tosberry Moor

Bursdon Moor

7

Lutsford

BURSDON MOOR CROSS

Bursdon Moor

Welsford Moor

EX39

Seckington Water

Clifford Water

LUTSFORD CROSS

SUMMERVILLE CROSS

Summerwell Farm

Gorvin Farm

GORVIN CROSS

20

Bursdon

PH

Gorvin Cross

Hartland Forest Golf & Leisure Park

CH

P

Huddisford

6

MEDDON CROSS

LOWER BITEFORD CROSS

19

Deptford

River Torridge

Biteford

Runland Farm

5

WELCOMBE CROSS

Meddon

MEDDON CROSS

Greadon

Horton Bridge

Horton Farm

18

Shorestone Farm

Brimford Bridge

BRIMFORD CROSS

Dural

DURAL CROSS

HORTON CROSS

Holyrood House

17

4

Woolley

Newlands Farm

Hardsworthy

Loatmead

Dural

Northmoor

NORTH MOOR CROSS

3

Eastcott

EX23

East Youlstone

EAST YOULSTONE CROSS

EX22

LOATMEAD CROSS

16

EASTCOTT CROSS

MADDOCKS CROSS

Crimp

West Youlstone

River Tamar

TRENTWORTHY CROSS

Ryall Farm

Redmonsford

Dinworthy

River Waldon

2

Trentworthy Farm

West Down

15

Wrasford Moor

A39

BLATCHBOROUGH CROSS

1

Blatchborough

14

25   A   26   B   27   C   28   D   29   E   30   F

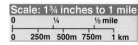

Scale: 1¾ inches to 1 mile

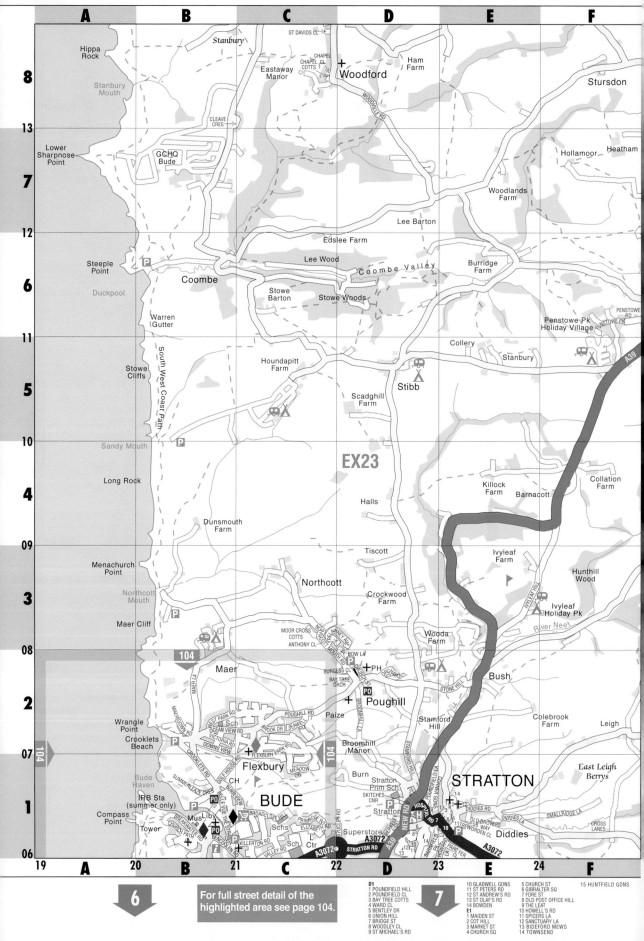

For full street detail of the highlighted area see page 104.

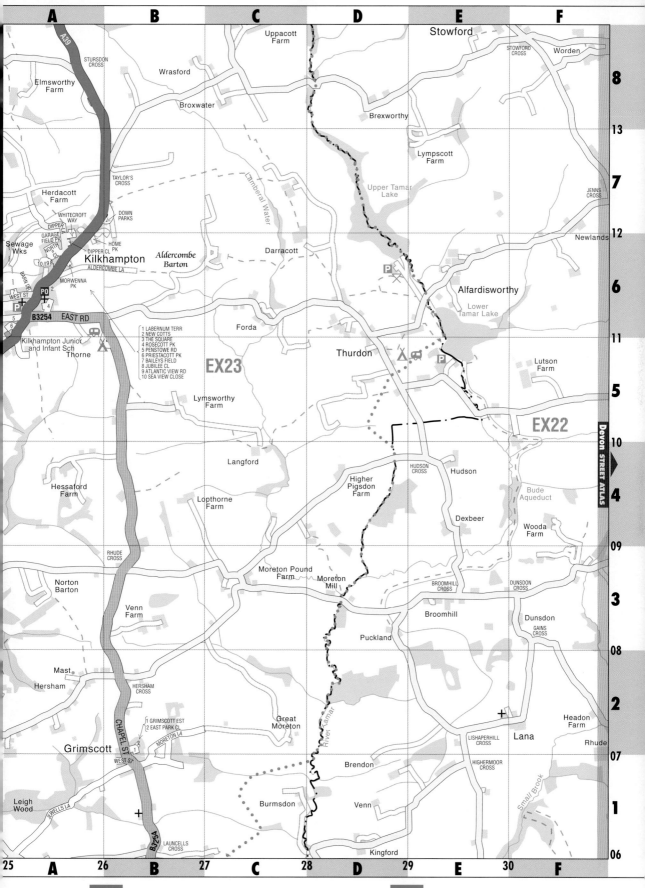

Scale: 1¾ inches to 1 mile

0   ¼   ½ mile
0   250m 500m 750m 1 km

Stowford

Uppacott
Farm

Wrasford

Broxwater

Brexworthy

Elmsworthy
Farm

STURSDON
CROSS

Stowford
Worden

Lympscott
Farm

Upper Tamar
Lake

JENNS
CROSS

Herdacott
Farm

TAYLOR'S
CROSS

DOWN
PARKS

Darracott

Newlands

WHITECROFT
WAY

HOME
PK

Alfardisworthy

Kilkhampton

Aldercombe
Barton

Sewage
Wks

Lower
Tamar Lake

MORWENNA
PK

Forda

EAST RD

Thurdon

Lutson
Farm

Kilkhampton Junior
and Infant Sch
Thorne

EX23

1 LABERNUM TERR
2 NEW COTTS
3 THE SQUARE
4 ROSECOTT PK
5 PENSTOWE RD
6 PRIESTACOTT PK
7 BAILEYS FIELD
8 JUBILEE CL
9 ATLANTIC VIEW RD
10 SEA VIEW CLOSE

Lymsworthy
Farm

EX22

Langford

HUDSON
CROSS

Hudson

Higher
Pigsdon
Farm

Bude
Aqueduct

Hessaford
Farm

Lopthorne
Farm

Dexbeer

Wooda
Farm

RHUDE
CROSS

Norton
Barton

Moreton Pound
Farm

Moreton
Mill

BROOMHILL
CROSS

DUNSDON
CROSS

Venn
Farm

Broomhill

Dunsdon

GAINS
CROSS

Mast

Puckland

Hersham

HERSHAM
CROSS

Headon
Farm

Great
Moreton

Lana

Rhude

LISHAPERHILL
CROSS

Grimscott

1 GRIMSCOTT EST
2 EAST PARK CL

River Tamar

Brendon

Venn

HIGHERMOOR
CROSS

Small Brook

Leigh
Wood

CHAPEL ST

Burmsdon

Kingford

4

For full street detail of the highlighted area see page 104.

Scale: 1¾ inches to 1 mile

0   ¼   ½ mile

0   250m   500m   750m   1 km

Ebbingford Manor

Efford Beacon

HIGHER WHARF

Lynstone

LYNSTONE RD

Bude Canal (dis)

River Neet

05   104

Upton

UPTON MDWS

MARINE DR

COUNTY RD

7

Phillip's Point

Hotel

Phillips Farm

104

Higher Longbeak

Lower Longbeak

P

Salthouse Cottage

PH

BRAMBLE CL

1 ATLANTIC CL

2 CRESCENT CL

MADEIRA DR

ASHTON WLK

BRANDON WLK

Widemouth Sand

P

Widemouth Bay

Black Rock

LEVERLAKE RD

COMBE LA

Wanson Mouth

MARINE DR

01   P   PH

Widemouth Farms

Foxhole Point

South West Coast Path

Wanson

EX23

A39

P

Penhalt Cliff

Millook Haven

Wanson Water

00

Millook

Trevisick

BANGORS EST 1

BUTTERCUP FIELD 2

Bangors

Cancleave Strand

Millook Common

Poundstock

VICARAGE LA

Cemy

Trekennard Farm

Dizzard Point

COAST RD

Trebarfoote

Chipman Strand

Long Cliff

Bynorth Cliff

Trevoulter Farm

Treskinnick Cross

99

Mast

Dizzard

COAST RD

The Den

1

Cleave Strand

Tregole

A39

98

15   A   16   B   17   C   18   D   19   E   20   F

10   11

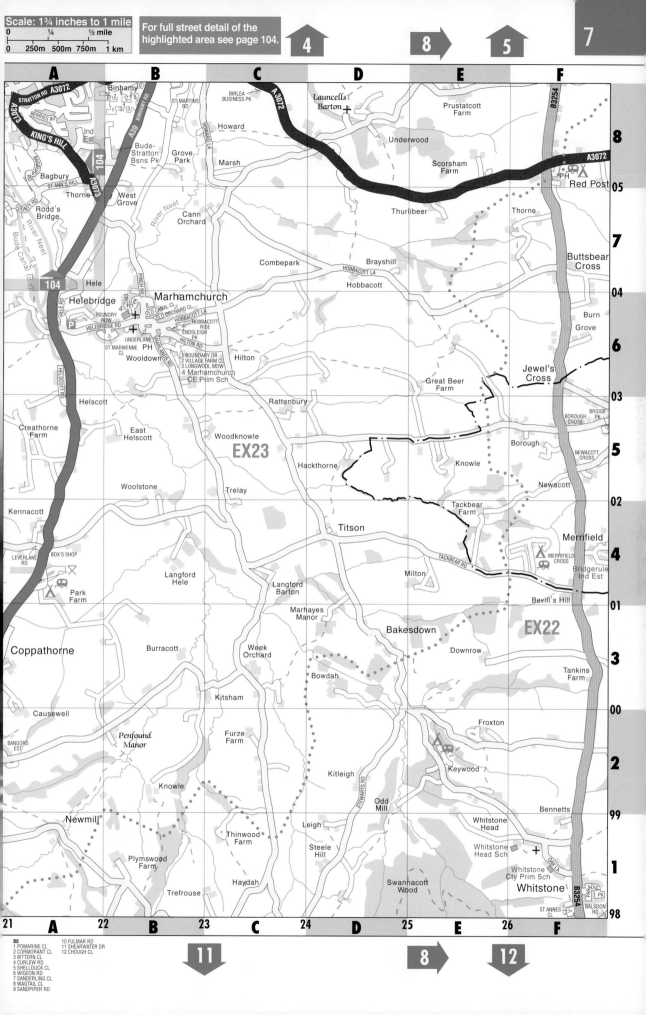

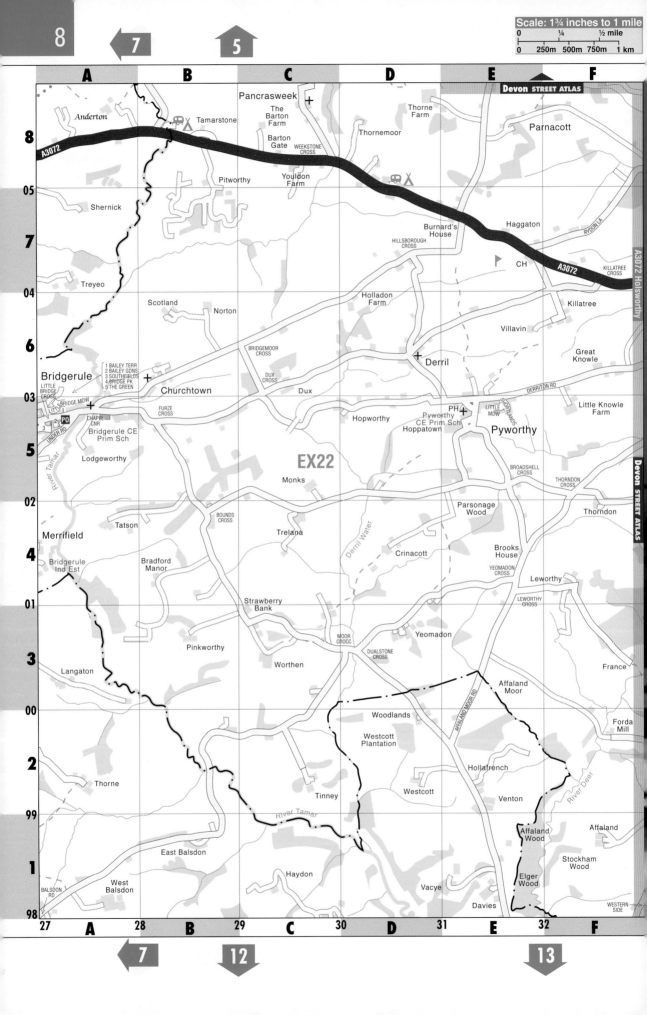

Scale: 1¾ inches to 1 mile

0 ¼ ½ mile
0 250m 500m 750m 1 km

| A | B | C | D | E | F |

8

97

Cambeak

7

96

6

95

Voter Run

EX23

High Cliff

5

Rusey Beach

94

Rusey Cliff

Buckator

Gull Rock

4

93

Beeny Sisters

Fire Beacon Point

Seals Hole

South West Coast Path

Beeny Cliff

Beeny

Trebyla Farm

B3263

3

92

Mus of Witchcraft

Pentargon

Hillsborough

Tremorle

Penally Point

Penally Hill

VALENCY ROW

Penally Terr

Penally House

Trewannett

2

Meachard

PENALLY HILL

PENALLY CT

Tresuck

PL35

Newmills

Harbour

THE HARBOUR

Water La

P

Willapark

MARINE TERR

Visitor Ctr

PENALLY CT

River Valency

91

Forrabury

Mast

FORE ST

Boscastle Com Prim Sch

Trafalgar Farm

Short Island

Grower Rock

NEW RD

B3263

PO

B/OTT's LA

Home Farm

MINSTER RD

Trebiffin

1

Firebeacon Hill

Ladies Window

Boscastle

UNDER RD

GREEN LA

B3266

Trewold

Long Island

Welltown Manor

TINTAGEL RD

BARN PARK RD

PARADISE RD

HIGH ST

B3266

MOUNT PLEASANT

WILLAPARK VIEW

Trevalga

GIBBS

Paradise House

90

B3263

| 07 | A | 08 | B | 09 | C | 10 | D | 11 | E | 12 | F |

10 DUNN ST

C1
1 PENTARGON RD
2 EGLOS VIEW
3 TREFLEUR CL
4 LANGFORDS MDW
5 FORRABURY HILL
6 CLOVER LANE CL
7 WHITE SMOCK MDW
8 DOCTORS HILL
9 GUNPOOL LA

C2
1 HOLLOWELL HO
2 BRIDGE WLK
3 THE OLD MILL

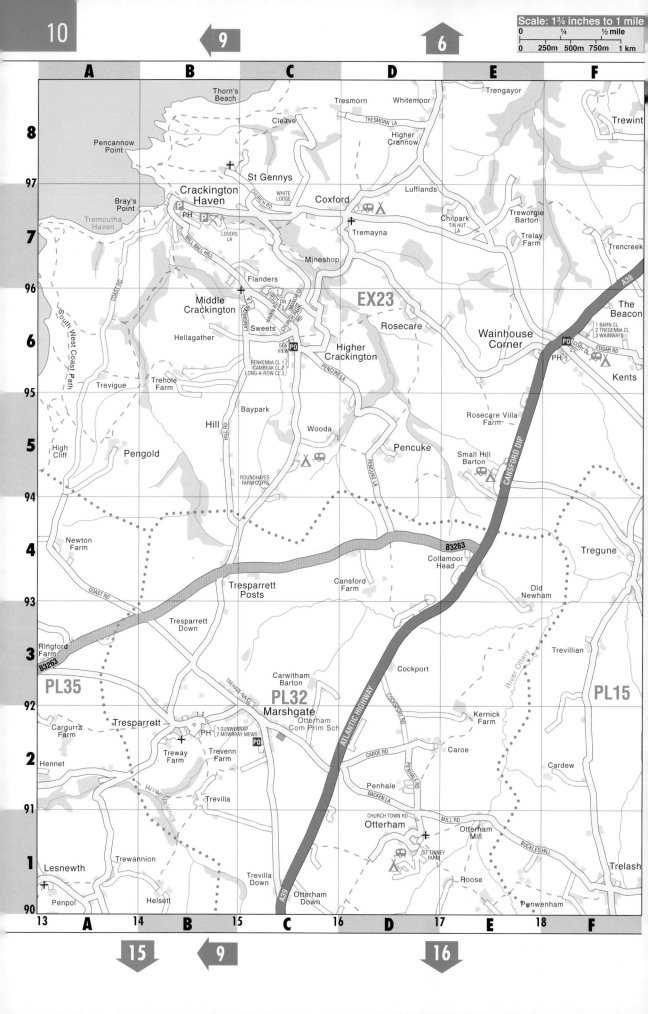

A   B   C   D   E   F

8

97

Thorn's Beach

Tresmorn   Whitemoor   Trengayor

Trewint

Pencannow Point

Cleave

TRESMORN LA

Higher Crannow

Bray's Point

St Gennys

Crackington Haven

CHURCH RD

WHITE LODGE

Coxford

Lufflands

Treworgie Barton

Tremoutha Haven

P
PH
P

Chilpark
TIN HUT LA

Trelay Farm

Trencreek

7

LOVERS LA

Tremayna

MILL BALL HILL

Mineshop

EX23

The Beacon

96

Flanders

Middle Crackington

LADY DR
JANEY RD
MANOR CL
CHURCH PARK RD

Rosecare

Wainhouse Corner

1 BARN CL
2 TREGENNA CL
3 WAINWAYS

PO

Hellagather

Sweets

SEA VIEW
PO

Higher Crackington

Kents

EDGAR RD
CORY CL

PH

6

COAST RD
LANSWEATH

PENKENNA CL 1
CAMBEAK CL 2
LONG-A-ROW CL 3

PENCURLA

95

South West Coast Path

Trevigue

Trehole Farm

Baypark

HILL RD

Wooda

Rosecare Villa Farm

High Cliff

Hill

Pencuke

Small Hill Barton

5

Pengold

ROUNDHAYES FARM COTTS

CANSFORD DIP

94

Newton Farm

B3263

Tregune

4

COAST RD

Tresparrett Posts

Cansford Farm

Collamoor Head

Old Newham

93

Tresparrett Down

Cockport

Trevillian

River Ottery

3

Ringford Farm

B3263

PL35

TREHAZE-NA CL

Carwitham Barton

PL32

ATLANTIC HIGHWAY

COCKSPORT RD

PL15

92

Marshgate

Otterham Com Prim Sch

Kernick Farm

Cargurra Farm

Tresparrett

PH

1 2

1 GUNWENNAP CL
2 MOWBRAY MEWS

PO

Caroe

Cardew

2

Hennet

Treway Farm

Trevenn Farm

Trevilla

CAROE RD

PENHALE RD

Penhale

BACKEN LA

91

River Valency

CHURCH TOWN RD

Otterham

MILL RD

Otterham Mill

BUCKLES HILL

Trelash

1

Lesnewth

Trewannion

Trevilla Down

Otterham Down

ST TINNEY FARM

Roose

Penwenham

90

Penpol

Helsett

13   A   14   B   15   C   16   D   17   E   18   F

A39

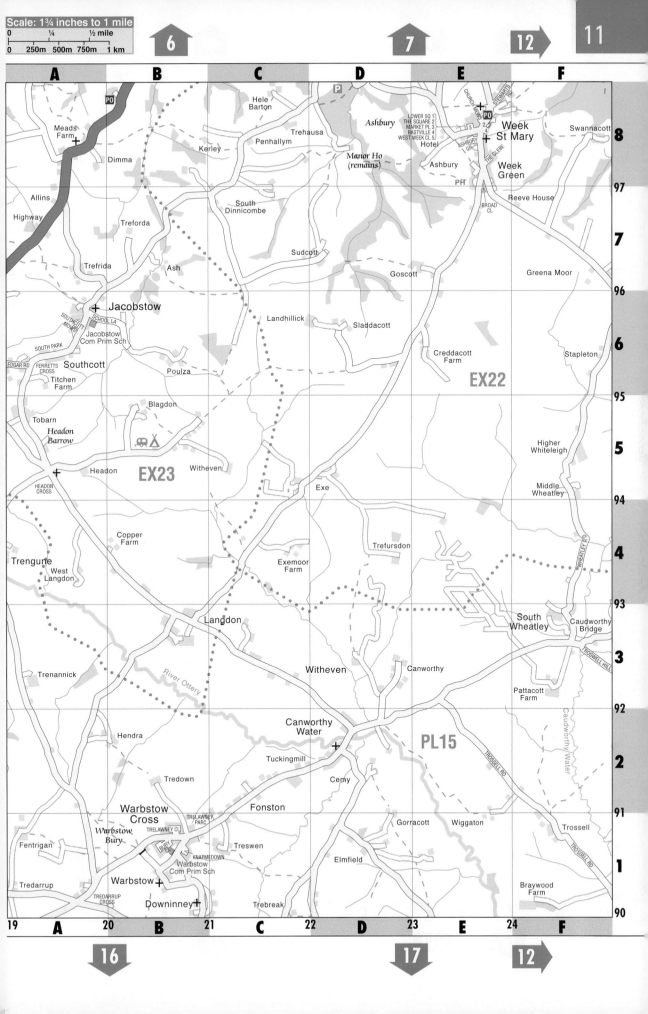

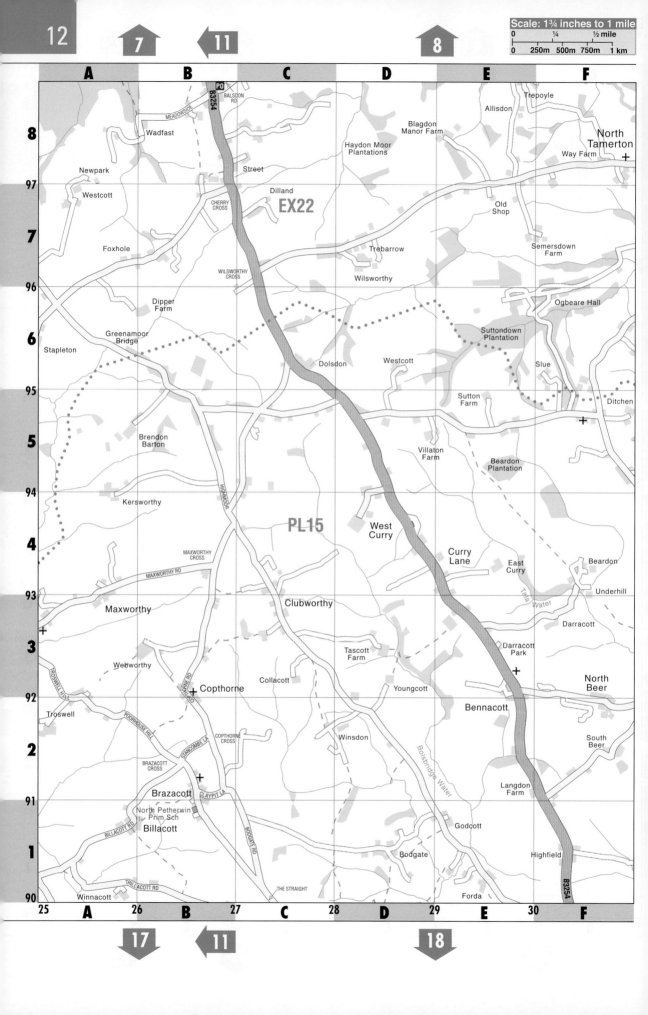

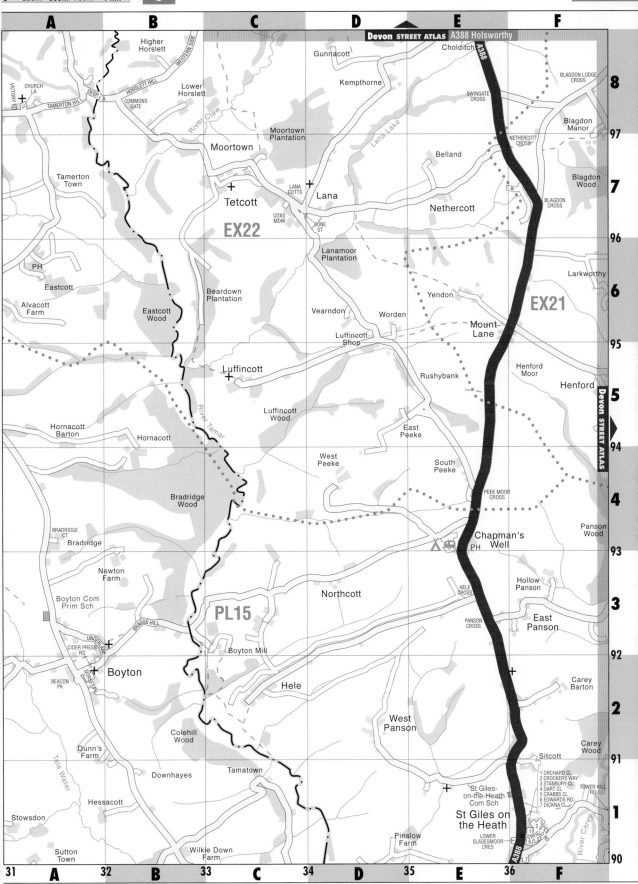

Scale: 1¾ inches to 1 mile

0   ¼   ½ mile
0 250m 500m 750m 1 km

Devon STREET ATLAS A388 Holsworthy

Devon STREET ATLAS

Higher Horslett
WESTERN SIDE
HORSLETT HILL
Lower Horslett
VICTORY RD
CHURCH LA
DEER LA
TAMERTON HILL
COMMONS GATE

Gunnacott
Cholditch
A388
BLAGDON LODGE CROSS

8

Kempthorne
SWINGATE CROSS
NETHERCOTT CROSS
Blagdon Manor

97

Moortown Plantation
Lana Lake
Belland
Blagdon Wood

7

Tamerton Town
Moortown
Tetcott
Lana
LANA COTTS
Nethercott
BLAGDON CROSS

EX22
COXS MDW
BONE ST

96

PH
Eastcott
Beardown Plantation
Lanamoor Plantation
Yendon
EX21
Larkworthy

6

Alvacott Farm
Eastcott Wood
Vearndon
Worden
Mount Lane
Henford Moor
Henford

River Claw

River Tamar

Luffincott Shop

95

Hornacott Barton
Luffincott
Rushybank
Henford

5

Hornacott
Luffincott Wood
East Peeke
South Peeke
River Tamar

94

Bradridge Wood
West Peeke
PEEK MOOR CROSS
Panson Wood

4

BRADRIDGE CT
Bradridge
Chapman's Well
PH
Hollow Panson

93

Newton Farm
Northcott
HELE CROSS
East Panson

3

Boyton Com Prim Sch
BRIGGS HILL
UNDERLANE
PANSON CROSS

CIDER PRESS RD
Boyton Mill

92

BEACON PK
DORSET PK
Boyton
Hele
West Panson
Carey Barton

2

Dunn's Farm
Colehill Wood
Carey Wood

Tala Water
Downhayes
Tamatown
Sitcott

1 ORCHARD CL
2 CROCKERS WAY
3 STANBURY CL
4 DART CL
5 CRABBS CL
6 EDWARDS RD
7 DICKNA CL
TOWER HILL RD

91

Hessacott
St Giles-on-the-Heath Com Sch

Stowsdon
Pinslow Farm
St Giles on the Heath
LOWER SLADESMOOR CRES
A388
River Carey

1

Sutton Town
Wilkie Down Farm

90

31   A   32   B   33   C   34   D   35   E   36   F

9

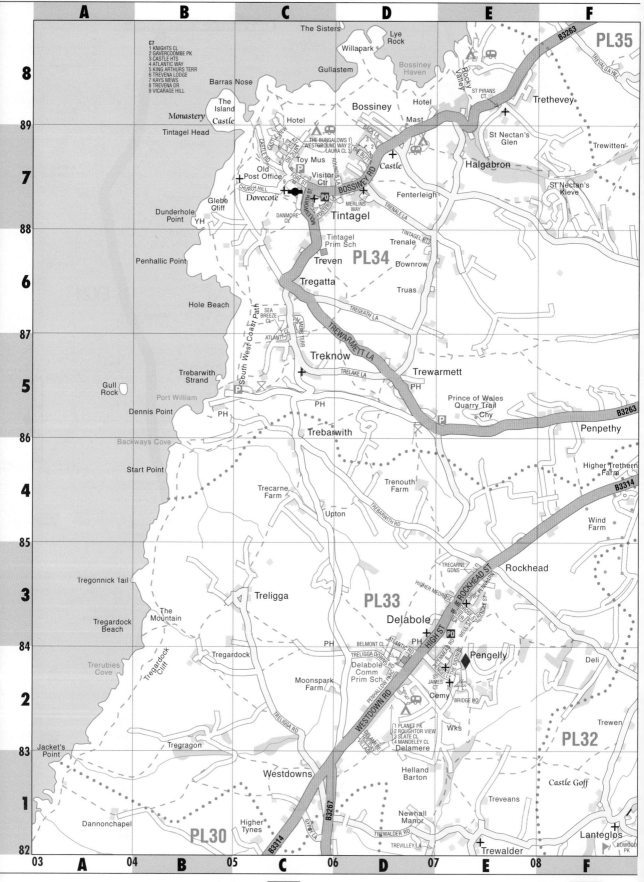

A   B   C   D   E   F

PL35

The Sisters
Willapark
Lye Rock
Gullastem
Bossiney Haven
Rocky Valley
St Pirans Ct.
Trethevey

Barras Nose
The Island
Castle
Monastery
Tintagel Head
Hotel
Bossiney
Hotel
Mast
St Nectan's Glen
Trewitten

C7
1 KNIGHTS CL
2 GAVERCOOMBE PK
3 CASTLE HTS
4 ATLANTIC WAY
5 KING ARTHURS TERR
6 TREVENA LODGE
7 KAYS MEWS
8 TREVENA DR
9 VICARAGE HILL

THE BUNGALOWS 1
WESTGROUND WAY 2
LAURA CL 3
THE BUTTS
BACK LA
Castle
St Nectan's Kieve

Old
Post Office
Toy Mus
Visitor Ctr
CHURCH HILL
Dovecote
DANMORE CL
FORE ST
ST THOMAS RD
BOSSINEY RD
ROUND'S LA
PO
MERLINS WAY
TRENALE LA
Fenterleigh
Halgabron

Glebe Cliff
YH
Dunderhole Point
Tintagel
Tintagel Prim Sch
Trenale
TINTAGEL HTS
Downrow

Penhallic Point
PL34
Treven
Trenouth
Truas

Hole Beach
Tregatta
TREGEATH LA
Trewarmett

South West Coast Path
SEA BREEZE CL
PALMERS TERR
ATLANTIC
TREWARMETT LA
Treknow
TRELAKE LA
Prince of Wales Quarry Trail
Chy

Trebarwith Strand
P
PH
Trebarwith
P
B3263
Penpethy

Gull Rock
Dennis Point
PH
Port William
Higher Trethern Farm

Backways Cove
Trecarne Farm
Trenouth Farm
B3314
Wind Farm

Start Point
Upton
TREBARWITH RD

Tregonnick Tail
Treligga
PL33
TRECARNE GDNS
HIGHER MEDROSE
ROCKHEAD ST
Rockhead

The Mountain
Delabole
CHY PENKARN
MEDROSE
TRENDLE ST
PH
HIGH ST
PO
Pengelly
Deli

Tregardock Beach
Tregardock
BELMONT CL
ATLANTIC RD
TRELIGGA DOWNS RD
WATER
PENMEAN RD
THE SIDINGS
ST JAMES CT
PL32

Trerubies Cove
Tregardock Cliff
Moonspark Farm
Delabole Comm Prim Sch
PENHALLOW PARC
Cemy
BRIDGE HO
Wks
Trewen

TRELIGGA RD
WESTDOWN RD
1 PLANET PK
2 ROUGHTOR VIEW
3 SLATE CL
4 MANDELEY CL
Delamere
Helland Barton
Treveans
Castle Goff

Jacket's Point
Tregragon
GYPSY LA
Westdowns
PL30
Newhall Manor
Lanteglos
BOWOOD PK

Dannonchapel
Higher Tynes
B3267
B3314
TREWALDER RD
TREVILLEY LA
Trewalder

03   A   04   B   05   C   06   D   07   E   08   F

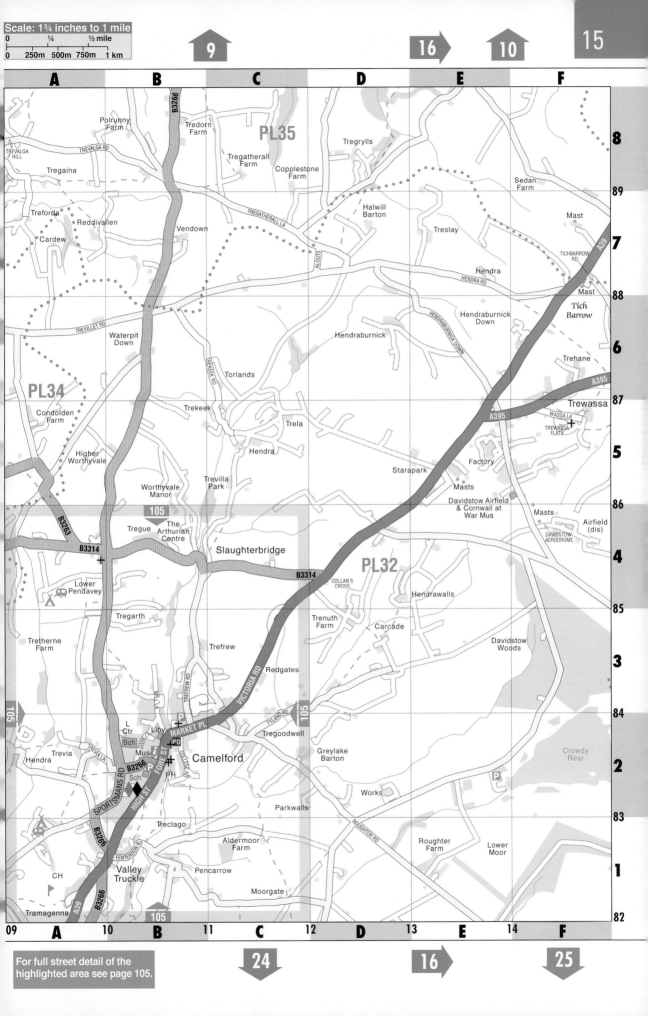

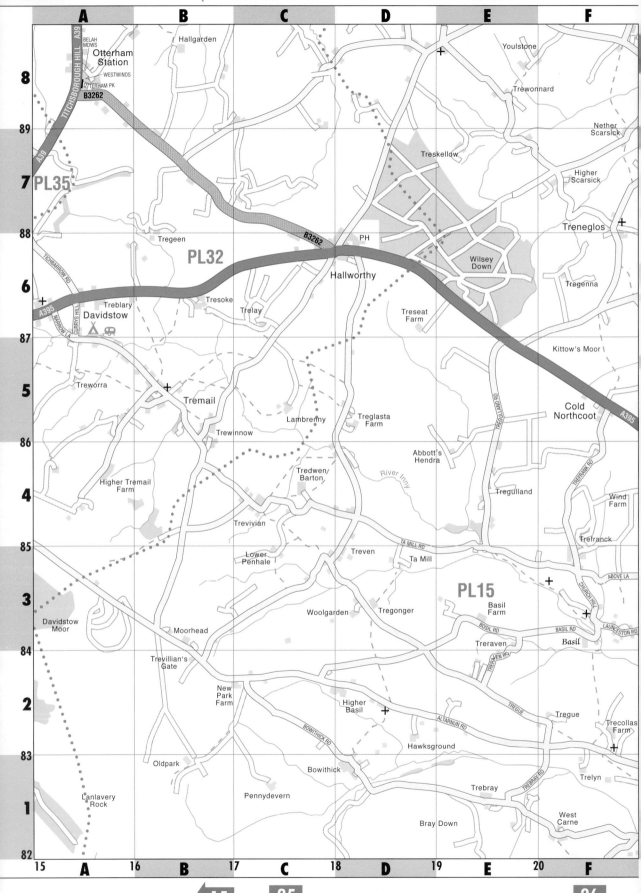

15 10
11

Scale: 1¾ inches to 1 mile

0   0½   0¼ mile
0   250m   500m   750m   1 km

A B C D E F

BELAH
MDWS
Otterham
Station
WESTWINDS
OTTERHAM PK
B3262
Hallgarden
Youlstone
Trewonnard
Nether
Scarsick
Higher
Scarsick

PL35

B3262
Tregeen
PL32
PH
Treskellow
Treneglos

Hallworthy
Wilsey
Down
Tregenna

Davidstow
Treblary
Tresoke
Trelay
Treseat
Farm
Kittow's Moor

Treworra
Tremail
Lambrenny
Treglasta
Farm
Abbott's
Hendra
Tregulland
Cold
Northcoot

Trewinnow
Wind
Farm

Higher Tremail
Farm
River Inny

Trevivian
Trefranck

Lower
Penhale
Tredwen
Barton
Treven
Ta Mill
TA MILL RD
Above La

PL15

Davidstow
Moor
Moorhead
Woolgarden
Tregonger
Basil
Farm
Treraven
Basil

Trevillian's
Gate
BOSIL RD
BASIL RD
LAUNCESTON RD

New
Park
Farm
Higher
Basil
ALTARNUN RD
Tregue
Trecollas
Farm

BOWITHICK RD
Hawksground
Trebray Trelyn

Oldpark
Bowithick
TREGUE
TREBRAY RD

Lanlavery
Rock
Pennydevern
Trebray
West
Carne
Bray Down

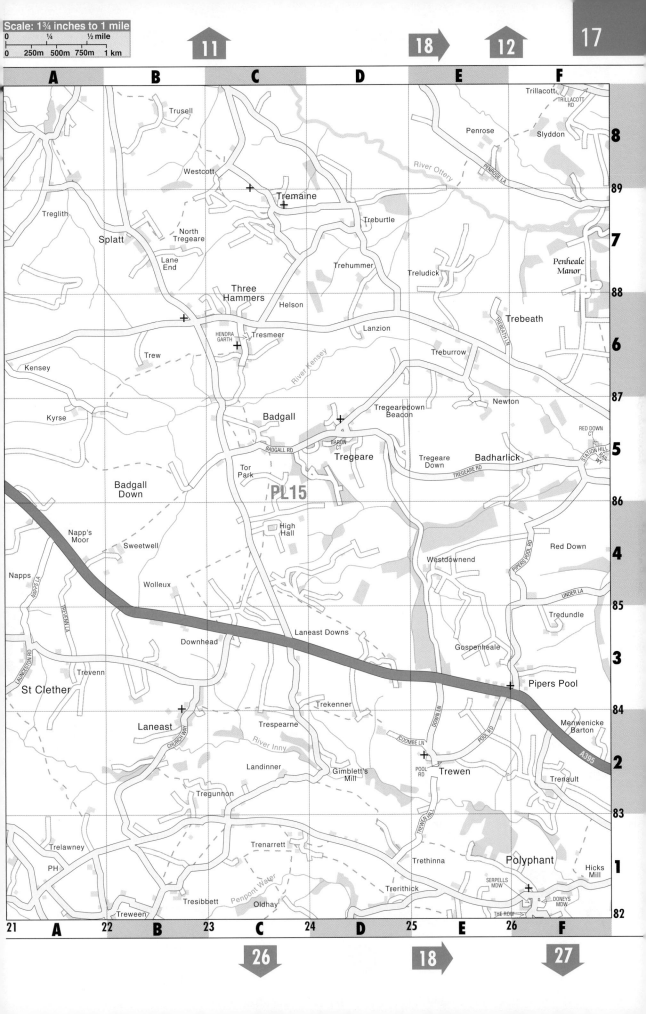

A   B   C   D   E   F

8

Trillacott
TRILLACOTT RD

Penrose   Slyddon

River Ottery   PENROSE LA

89

Trusell

Westcott

Tremaine   Treburtle   Penheale Manor

7

Splatt   North Tregeare

Lane End   Trehummer   Treludick

88

Three Hammers   Helson   Trebeath

TREBEATH LN

Treglith   Tresmeer   Lanzion

6

HENDRA GARTH   River Kensey   Treburrow

Trew   Newton

Kensey   RED DOWN CT

87

Kyrse   Badgall   Tregearedown Beacon

STATION HILL

5

BADGALL RD   BARON CT   Tregeare   Badharlick

Tor Park   Tregeare Down   TREGEARE RD

86

Badgall Down   PL15

Napp's Moor   High Hall   Westdownend   Red Down

PIPERS POOL RD

4

Sweetwell   UNDER LA

Napps   Wolleux   Tredundle

NAPPS LA   85

TREVENN LA   Laneast Downs

Downhead   Gospenheale

LAUNCESTON RD   3

Trevenn   Pipers Pool

St Clether   Trekenner   84

Laneast   Trespearne   DOWN LN   Menwenicke Barton

CHURCH WAY   COOMBE LN   POOL RD

River Inny   Trewen   A395   2

Landinner   POOL RD   Trenault

Gimblett's Mill

Tregunnon   TREWEN HILL   83

Trenarrett   Trethinna   Polyphant

Trelawney   Hicks Mill   1

PH   SERPELLS MDW

Trerithick   DONEYS MDW

Tresibbett   Oldhay   THE ROW   82

Treween   Penpont Water

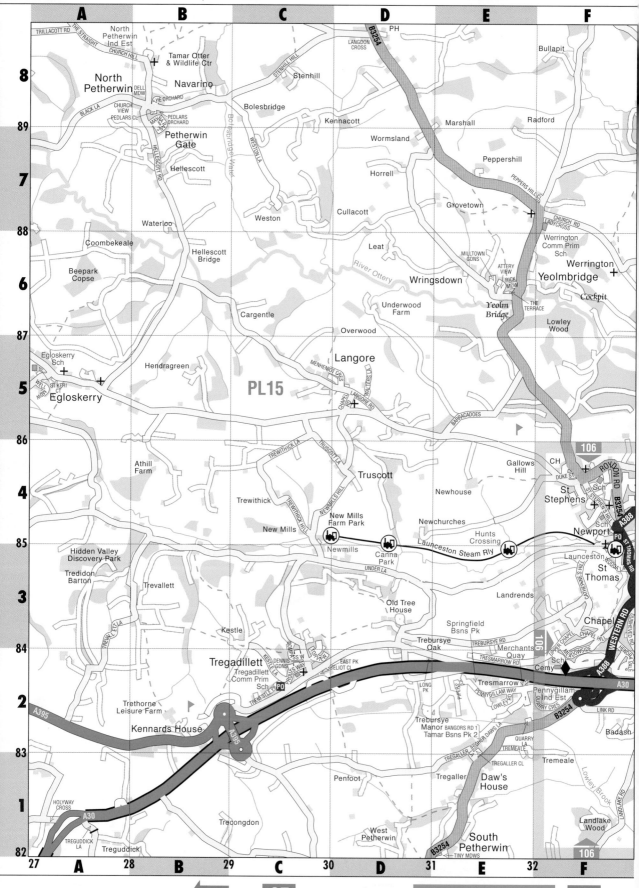

17 12
13

Scale: 1¾ inches to 1 mile

0   ¼   ½ mile
0   250m 500m 750m 1 km

A   B   C   D   E   F

8

89

7

88

6

87

5

86

4

85

3

84

2

83

1

82

TRILLACOTT RD   THE STRAIGHT   North Petherwin Ind Est
CHURCH HILL
Tamar Otter & Wildlife Ctr
North Petherwin   Navarino   Stenhill Hill   Stenhill   PH   B3254   Langdon Cross
DELL MDW   THE ORCHARD   Bolesbridge   Kennacott   Marshall   Radford   Bullapit
CHURCH VIEW   PEDLARS CL   PEDLARS ORCHARD   Petherwin Gate   Wormsland   Peppershill
BLACK LA   HELLESCOTT RD   Hellescott   Weston   Horrell   Grovetown   PEPPERS HILL CL   CHURCH RD   Werrington Comm Prim Sch
Waterloo   Cullacott   LADYCROSS   Werrington
Coombekeale   Hellescott Bridge   Leat   MILLTOWN GDNS   Yeolmbridge   Cockpit
Beepark Copse   Wringsdown   ATTERY VIEW   RICK MDW   THE TERRACE   Lowley Wood
Egloskerry Sch   Hendragreen   Overwood   Langore   Yeolm Bridge
WELL MDW   ST KERI CT   Egloskerry   PL15   MENHENIOT CRES   WALTERS HILL   CHAPEL RD   LANGORE RD   BARRACADOES   106   CH   ROYDON RD
Athill Farm   TRUSCOTT LA   Truscott   Gallows Hill   DUKE ST   St Stephens   B3254   A388
Trewithick   NEWPORTS HILL   Newhouse   Sch   Newport
TREWITHICK HILL   New Mills   Newchurches   Hunts Crossing   Launceston Steam Rly   PO   St Thomas
Hidden Valley Discovery Park   New Mills Farm Park   Newmills   Canna Park   Launceston Wood La
Tredidon Barton   Trevallett   UNDER LA   Landrends   St Thomas
Kestle   Old Tree House   Springfield Bsns Pk   Chapel   CHAPEL HILL   WESTERN RD
DENNIS GDNS   Trebursye Oak   TREBURSYE RD   Merchants Quay   UPPER CHAPEL   MEADOWSIDE   A388
Tregadillett Comm Prim Sch   PO   PRYORS WAY   EAST PK   ELIOT CL   TRESMARROW RD   Cemy   106
Tregadillett   TREKESTLE W   Tresmarrow   QUARRY CRES   Pennygillam Ind Est
Trethorne Leisure Farm   LONG PK   PIPERS CL   PENNYGILLAM WAY   LOWLEC   Badash
A395   Kennards House   A395   Treburse Manor   Tamar Bsns Pk 2   BANGORS RD 1   HIGHER DAWS LA   QUARRY   LINK RD   B3254
TREGALLER LA   TREMEALE   Tremeale   LANDLAKE RD
Penfoot   Tregaller   TREGALLER CL   Lowley Brook
HOLYWAY CROSS   A30   Tregongdon   Daw's House   Landlake Wood
TREGUDDICK LA   Treguddick   West Petherwin   South Petherwin   106
B3254   TINY MDWS

27   A   28   B   29   C   30   D   31   E   32   F

17   27   28

For full street detail of the highlighted area see page 106.

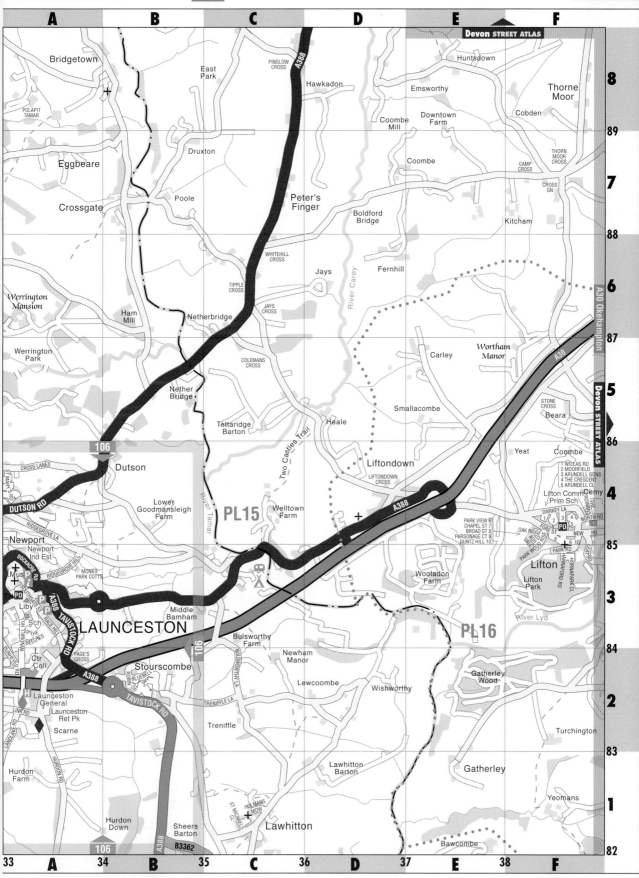

Scale: 1¾ inches to 1 mile

| 0 | ¼ | ½ mile |
| 0 | 250m | 500m | 750m | 1 km |

13

Devon STREET ATLAS

A   B   C   D   E   F

Bridgetown

POLAPIT TAMAR

Eggbeare

Crossgate

East Park

Druxton

Poole

Werrington Mansion

Ham Mill

Werrington Park

Netherbridge

Nether Bridge

Dutson

Lower Goodmansleigh Farm

Newport

Newport Ind Est

Dutson Rd

Ridgegrove La

MONKS PARK COTTS

Middle Bamham

LAUNCESTON

Stourscombe

Tavistock Rd

Launceston General

Launceston Ret Pk

Scarne

Hurdon Farm

Hurdon Down

Sheers Barton

B3362

PINSLOW CROSS

A388

Hawkadon

Peter's Finger

WHITEHILL CROSS

TIPPLE CROSS

Jays

JAYS CROSS

COLEMANS CROSS

Tettaridge Barton

PL15

Welltown Farm

Two Castles Trail

River Tamar

Bulsworthy Farm

Newham Manor

Lewcoombe

Treniffle

Lawhitton

Holmans Mow

St Michaels Cl

Huntsdown

Emsworthy

Coombe Mill

Downtown Farm

Coombe

Boldford Bridge

River Carey

Fernhill

Heale

Liftondown

LIFTONDOWN CROSS

A388

Smallacombe

Carley

Wortham Manor

Wooladon Farm

Wishworthy

Lawhitton Barton

Thorne Moor

Cobden

THORN MOOR CROSS

CROSS GN

CAMP CROSS

Kitcham

A30 Okehampton

A30

STONE CROSS

Beara

Yeat

Coombe

1 WILLAS RD
2 MOORFIELD
3 ARUNDELL GDNS
4 THE CRESCENT
5 ARUNDELL CL

Lifton Comm Prim Sch

Cemy

DARKEY LA

PARK VIEW 6
CHAPEL ST 7
BROAD ST 8
PARSONAGE CT 9
DUNTZ HILL 10

Lifton

Lifton Park

River Lyd

PL16

Gatherley Wood

Gatherley

Turchington

Yeomans

Bawcombe

Devon STREET ATLAS

8

89

7

88

6

87

5

86

4

85

3

84

2

83

1

82

33   A   34   B   35   C   36   D   37   E   38   F

For full street detail of the highlighted area see page 106.

28

29

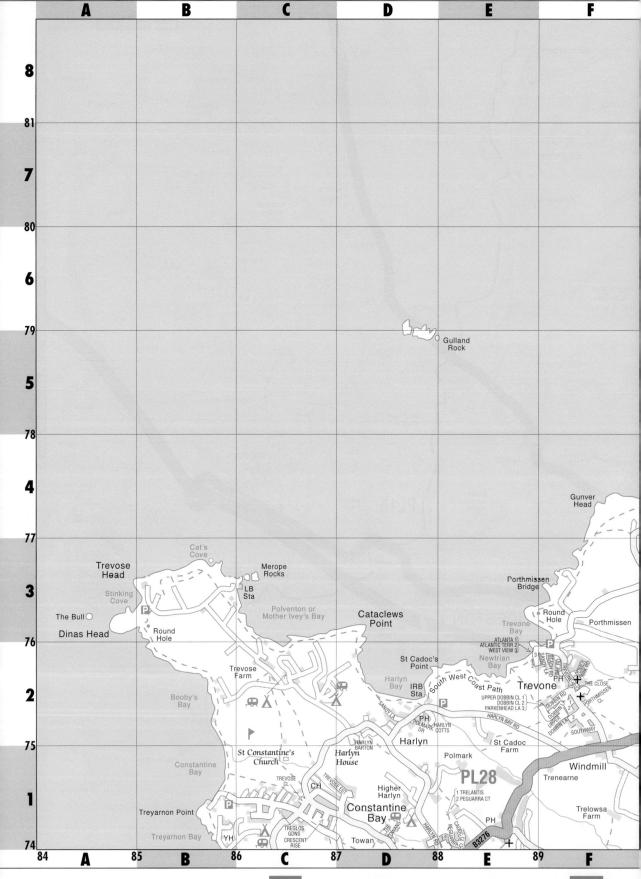

A B C D E F

8

81

7

80

6

79

Gulland
Rock

5

78

4

Gunver
Head

77

Cat's
Cove

Trevose
Head

Merope
Rocks

Porthmissen
Bridge

3

Stinking
Cove

LB
Sta

Round
Hole

Porthmissen

The Bull

Round
Hole

Polventon or
Mother Ivey's Bay

Cataclews
Point

Trevone
Bay

Dinas Head

ATLANTA 1
ATLANTIC TERR 2
WEST VIEW 3

76

St Cadoc's
Point

Newtrian
Bay

Trevone

Trevose
Farm

Harlyn
Bay

IRB
Sta

South West Coast Path

UPPER DOBBIN CL 1
DOBBIN CL 2
PARKENHEAD LA 3

THE CLOSE

2

Booby's
Bay

SANDY LA

PH
POLMARK
DR

HARLYN
COTTS

HARLYN BAY RD

SOUTHWAY

75

HARLYN
BARTON

Harlyn

St Cadoc
Farm

St Constantine's
Church

Harlyn
House

Polmark

Windmill

Constantine
Bay

TREVOSE
CL

CH

Higher
Harlyn

PL28

Trenearne

1

1 TRELANTIS
2 PEGUARRA CT

Trelowsa
Farm

Treyarnon Point

Constantine
Bay

Towan

PH

Treyarnon Bay

YH

TREGLOS
GDNS
CRESCENT
RISE

THE TOWANS

HARLYN RD

CADOC
CL
PEGUARRA

B3276

74

84   A   85   B   86   C   87   D   88   E   89   F

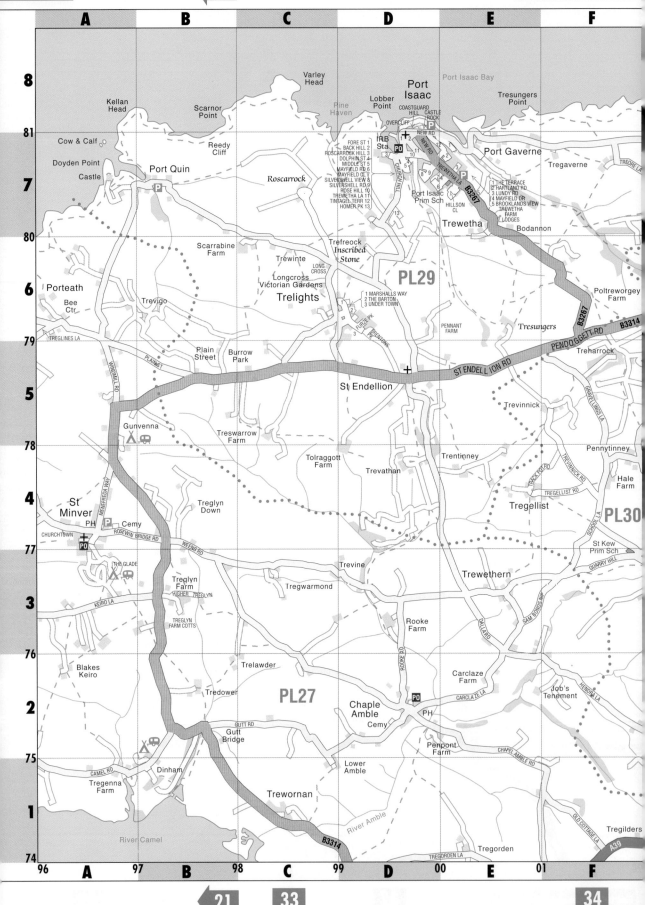

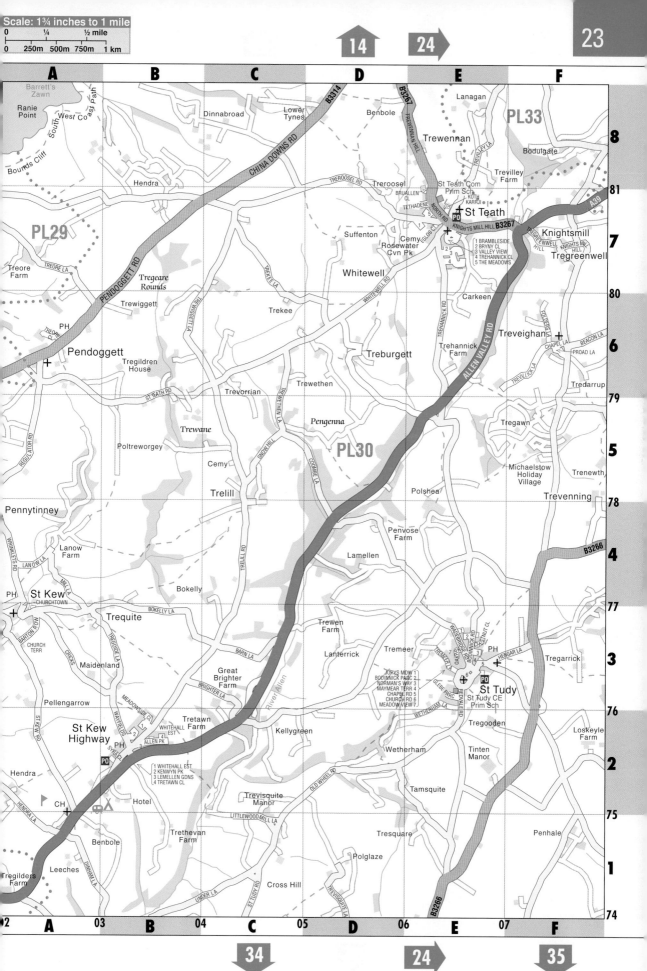

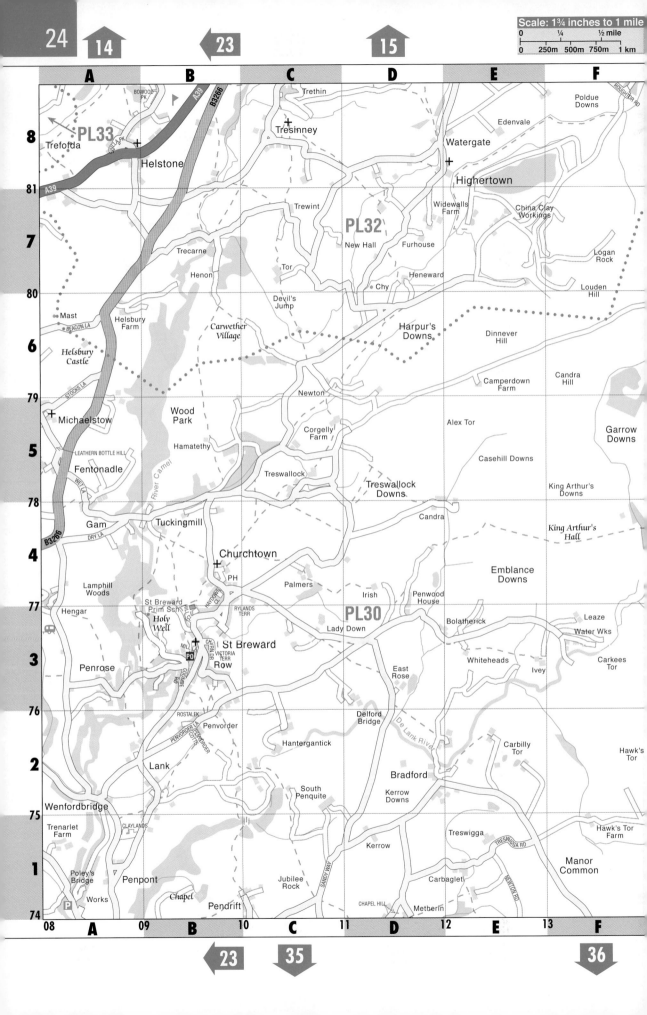

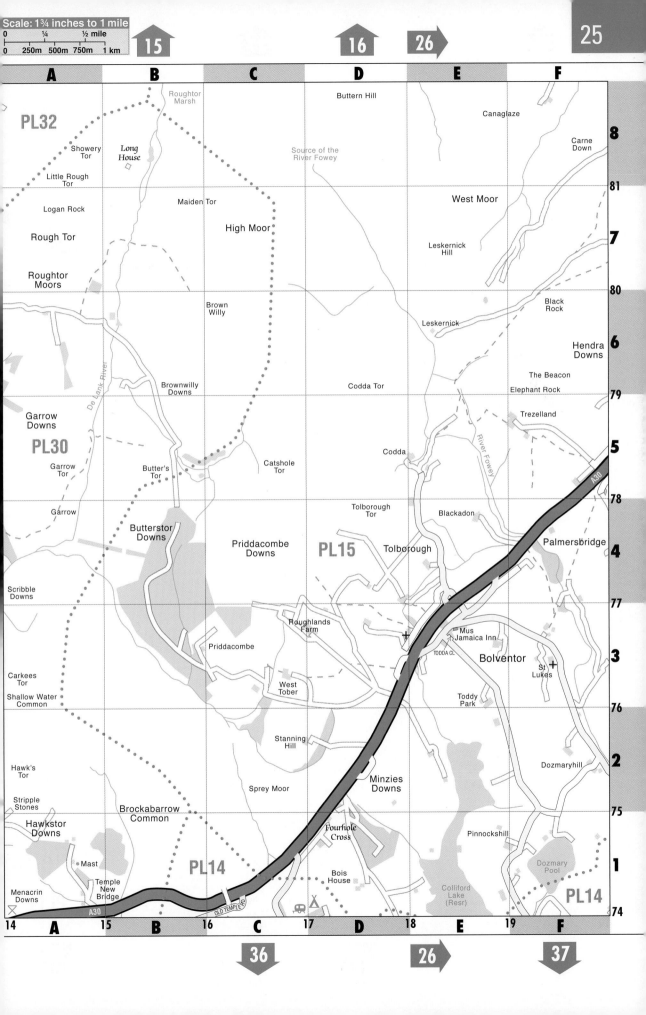

A   B   C   D   E   F

PL32

Buttern Hill

Canaglaze

Roughtor Marsh

Source of the River Fowey

Showery Tor   Long House

Carne Down

Little Rough Tor

Maiden Tor   West Moor

81

Logan Rock

High Moor

7

Rough Tor

Leskernick Hill

Roughtor Moors

Brown Willy

80

Brownwilly Downs

Leskernick

Black Rock

6

De Lank River

Garrow Downs

Codda Tor

Hendra Downs

PL30

The Beacon

Elephant Rock

79

Codda

Trezelland

Garrow Tor   Butter's Tor

Catshole Tor

5

Garrow

Tolborough Tor   Blackadon

78

Butterstor Downs

Priddacombe Downs

PL15

Tolborough

Palmersbridge

4

Scribble Downs

Roughlands Farm

Mus Jamaica Inn

77

Priddacombe

TODDA CL   Bolventor

Carkees Tor

West Tober

Toddy Park   St Lukes

3

Shallow Water Common

76

Stanning Hill

Hawk's Tor

Dozmaryhill

2

Stripple Stones

Sprey Moor

Minzies Downs

Brockabarrow Common

75

Hawkstor Downs

Fourhole Cross

Pinnockshill

PL14

Dozmary Pool

1

Mast

Bois House

Temple New Bridge

OLD TEMPLE

Colliford Lake (Resr)

PL14

Menacrin Downs

A30

74

14   A   15   B   16   C   17   D   18   E   19   F

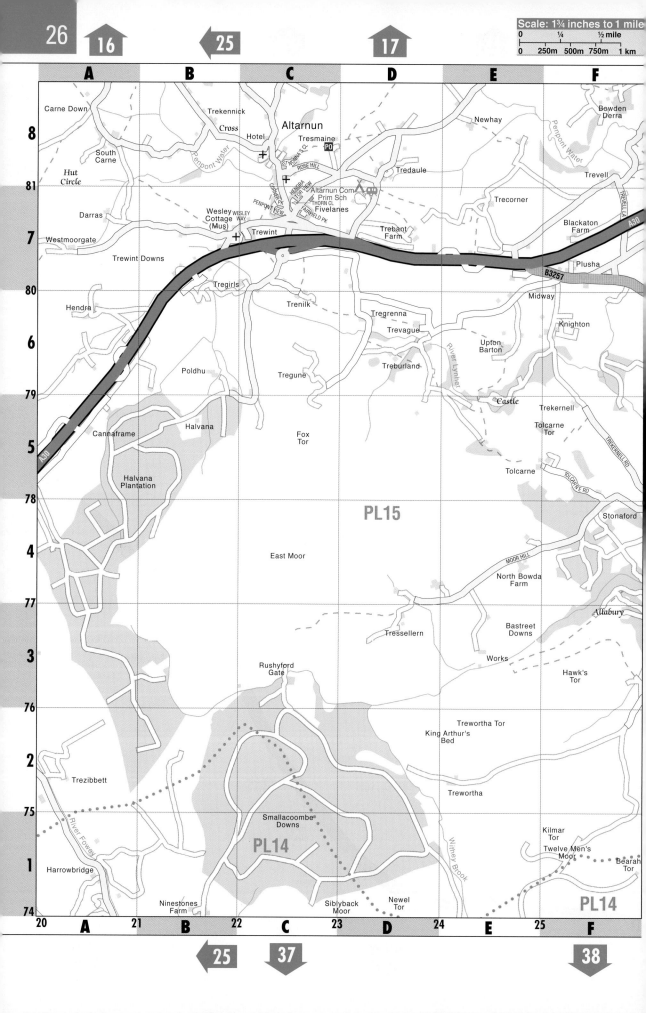

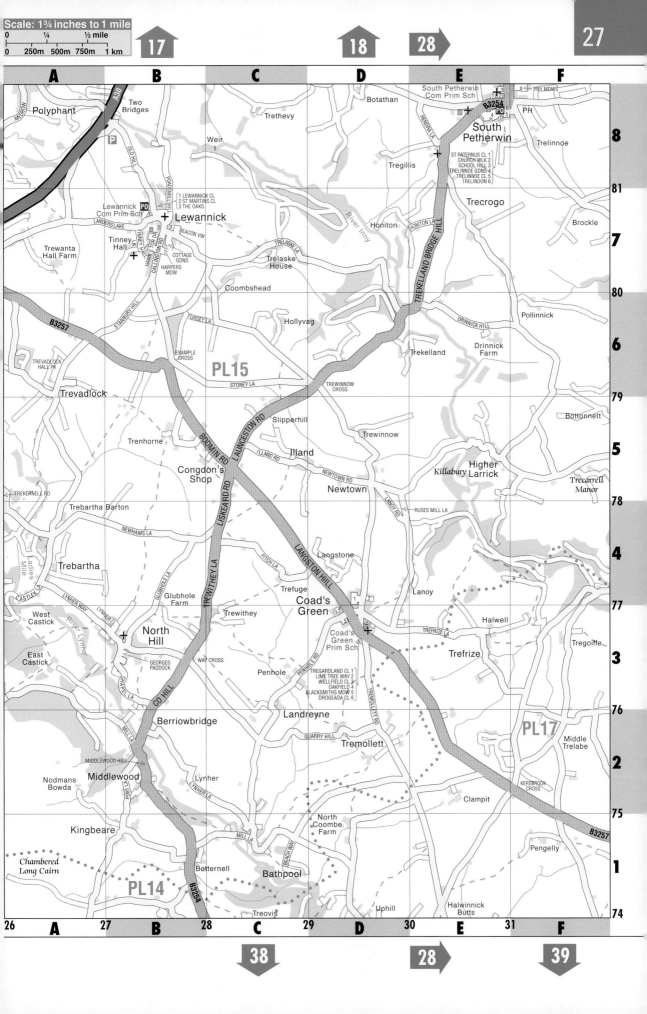

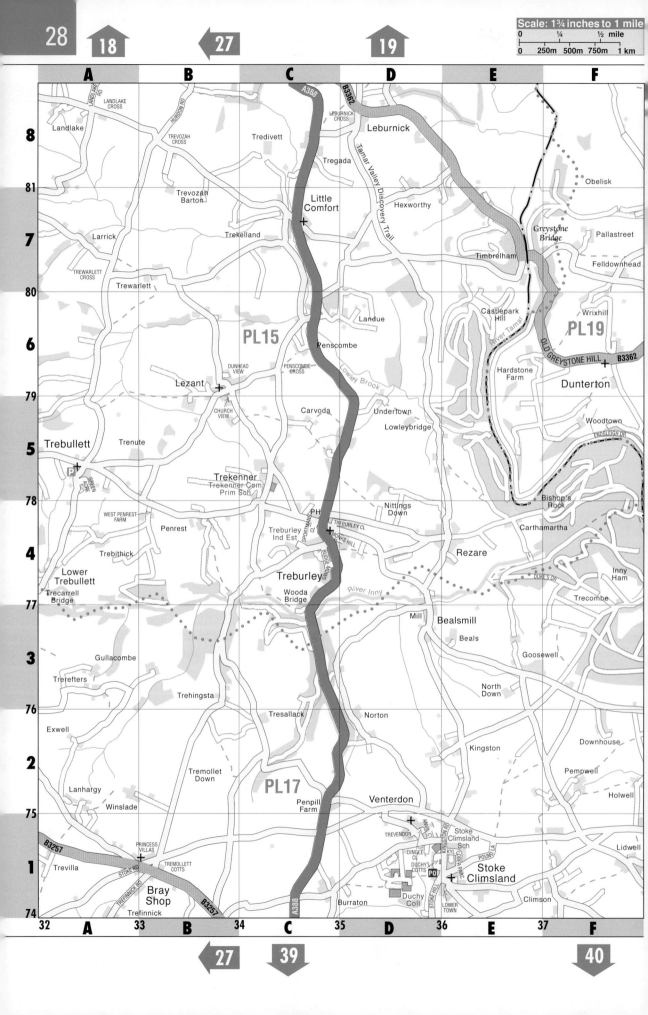

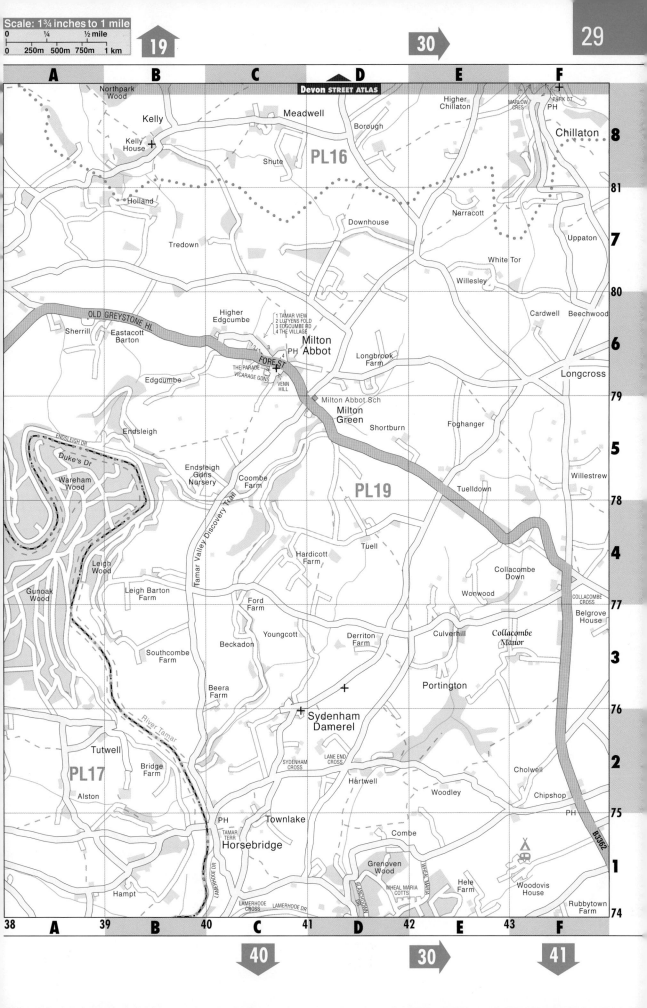

A   B   C   D   E   F

Devon STREET ATLAS

Northpark Wood

Kelly

Meadwell

Borough

Higher Chillaton

MARLOW CRES

PARK OT

PH

Chillaton   8

Kelly House

Shute

PL16

81

Holland

Downhouse

Narracott

Uppaton   7

Tredown

White Tor

Willesley

80

OLD GREYSTONE HL

Higher Edgcumbe

1 TAMAR VIEW
2 LUTYENS FOLD
3 EDGCUMBE RD
4 THE VILLAGE

Milton Abbot

Longbrook Farm

Cardwell   Beechwood   6

Sherrill

Eastacott Barton

FOREST

PH

Longcross

79

Edgcumbe

THE PARADE
VICARAGE GDNS

VENN HILL

Milton Abbot Sch

Milton Green

Shortburn

Foghanger

Endsleigh

ENDSLEIGH DR

Duke's Dr

Wareham Wood

Endsleigh Gdns Nursery

Coombe Farm

PL19

Tuelldown

Willestrew   5

78

Tamar Valley Discovery Trail

Leigh Wood

Hardicott Farm

Tuell

Collacombe Down   4

Gunoak Wood

Leigh Barton Farm

Ford Farm

Wonwood

COLLACOMBE CROSS   77

Youngcott

Derriton Farm

Culverhill

Collacombe Manor

Belgrove House

Beckadon

Southcombe Farm

Portington

3

Beera Farm

Sydenham Damerel   76

Tutwell

SYDENHAM CROSS

LANE END CROSS

Cholwell   2

PL17

Bridge Farm

Hartwell

Woodley

Chipshop

Alston

Townlake

Combe

PH   75

B3362

PH

TAMAR TERR

Horsebridge

LAMERHOOE DR

Grenoven Wood

WHEAL MARIA COTTS

Hele Farm

Woodovis House   1

Hampt

LAMERHOOE CROSS   LAMERHOOE DR

BLANCHDOWN

WHEAL MARIA

Rubbytown Farm   74

Scale: 1¾ inches to 1 mile
0   ¼   ½ mile
0   250m 500m 750m 1 km

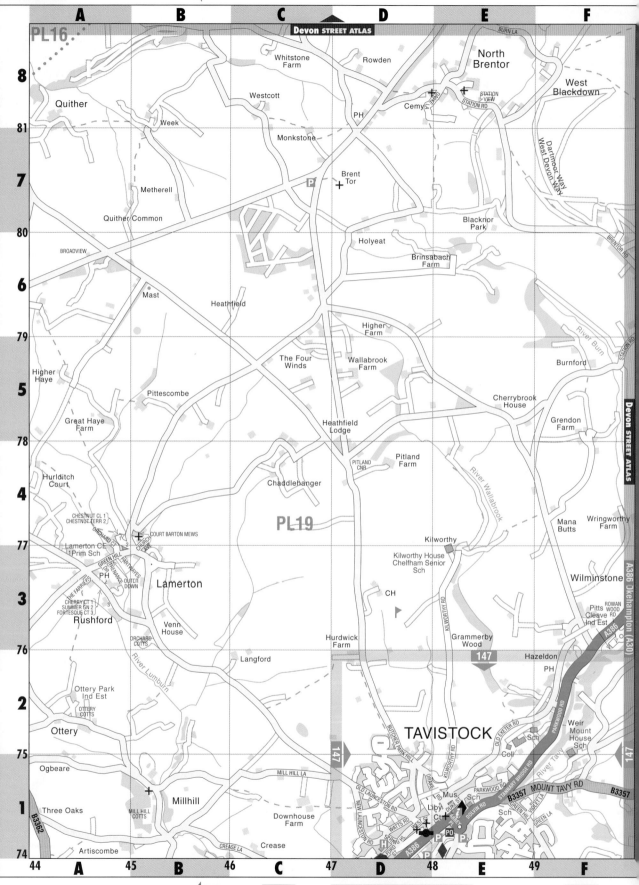

Devon STREET ATLAS

PL16

A **B** **C** **D** **E** **F**

8

Quither

Whitstone Farm

Rowden

North Brentor

West Blackdown

Westcott

PH

Cemy

STATION VIEW

STATION RD

BURN LA

81

Week

Monkstone

Metherell

Brent Tor

Dartmoor Way
West Devon Way

7

Quither Common

Blacknor Park

BROADVIEW

Holyeat

Brinsabach Farm

BRENTOR RD

80

6

Mast

Heathfield

Higher Farm

River Burn

79

Higher Haye

The Four Winds

Wallabrook Farm

Burnford

5

Pittescombe

Cherrybrook House

Grendon Farm

78

Great Haye Farm

Heathfield Lodge

Hurlditch Court

PITLAND CNR

Pitland Farm

River Wallabrook

Mana Butts

Wringworthy Farm

4

CHESTNUT CL 1
CHESTNUT TERR 2

Chaddlehanger

PL19

Kilworthy

77

ORCHARD CT

Court Barton Mews

Lamerton CE Prim Sch

GREEN HILL

PARTWAYES

CHURCH LA

OUTER DOWN

Kilworthy House
Chelfham Senior Sch

Wilminstone

A386 Okehampton (A30)

PH

THE FARRIERS

CHERRY GN 1
SUMMER GN 2
FORTESCUE CT 3

Lamerton

CH

ROWAN WOOD RD

Pitts Cleave Ind Est

3

Rushford

Venn House

ORCHARD COTTS

Hurdwick Farm

KILWORTHY RD

Grammerby Wood

Hazeldon

PH

147

76

River Lumburn

Langford

2

Ottery Park Ind Est

OTTERY COTTS

Mill Hill La

147

Weir Mount House Sch

BUTCHER PARK HILL

OLD EXETER RD

PARKWOOD RD

STANNARY BRIDGE RD

River Tavy

TAVISTOCK

Sch

Coll

147

75

Ottery

Ogbeare

NEW LAUNCESTON RD

OLD LAUNCESTON RD

DRAKE RD

KILWORTHY RD

PARKWOOD RD

B3357

MOUNT TAVY RD

B3357

GREEN HILL

1

Three Oaks

Millhill

MILL HILL COTTS

Downhouse Farm

Crease

WATTS RD

DOLVIN RD

Mus

Liby

Ct

Sch

PO

P

P

B3362

Artiscombe

CREASE LA

A386

PO

Sch

74

44 **A** **45** **B** **46** **C** **47** **D** **48** **E** **49** **F**

29 41 For full street detail of the highlighted area see page 147. 42

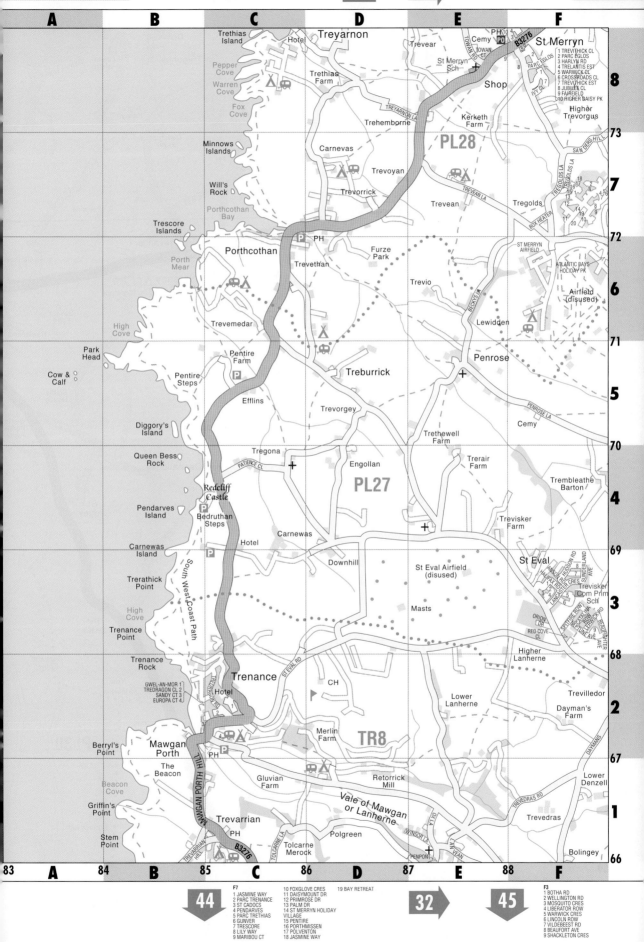

Scale: 1¾ inches to 1 mile
0   ¼   ½ mile
0   250m 500m 750m 1 km

20   32

A **B** **C** **D** **E** **F**

Trethias Island
Hotel
Treyarnon
Trevear
St Merryn Sch
Cemy PO
B3276
St Merryn

1 TREVITHICK CL
2 PARC EGLOS
3 HARLYN RD
4 TRELANTIS EST
5 WARWICK CL
6 CROSSROADS CL
7 TREVITHICK EST
8 JUBILEE CL
9 FAIRFIELD
10 HIGHER DAISY PK

Pepper Cove
Warren Cove
Trethias Farm
Shop
Higher Trevorgus

Fox Cove
Trehemborne
Kerketh Farm

8

73

Minnows Islands
Carnevas
PL28
SANDERS HILL

Will's Rock
Trevoyan
Trevean LA
Tregolds

7

Porthcothan Bay
Trevorrick
Trevean
Tregolds

Trescore Islands
P PH
Furze Park
St Merryn Airfield

72

Porth Mear
Porthcothan
Trevethan
Trevio
ATLANTIC BAYS HOLIDAY PK

High Cove
Trevemedar
Airfield (disused)

6

Park Head
Pentire Farm
Lewidden
Penrose

71

Cow & Calf
Pentire Steps
Treburrick
PENROSE LA

Efflins
Trevorgey
Cemy

5

Diggory's Island
Tregona
Trethewell Farm

70

Queen Bess Rock
PATIENCE CL
Engollan
PL27
Trerair Farm

Redcliff Castle
P
Trembleathe Barton

Pendarves Island
Bedruthan Steps
Carnewas
Trevisker Farm

4

Carnewas Island
Hotel
Downhill
St Eval

69

South West Coast Path
St Eval Airfield (disused)
Trevisker Com Prim Sch

Trerathick Point
Masts

3

High Cove
RED COVE CL

Trenance Point
Higher Lanherne

68

Trenance Rock
Trenance
ST EVAL RD
Trevilledor

GWEL-AN-MOR 1
TREDRAGON CL 2
SANDY CT 3
EUROPA CT 4.
Hotel
Lower Lanherne
Dayman's Farm

2

Berryl's Point
Mawgan Porth
Merlin Farm
TR8

67

The Beacon
PH
Gluvian Farm
Retorrick Mill
Lower Denzell

Beacon Cove
Vale of Mawgan or Lanherne

Griffin's Point
Polgreen
Trevedras

1

Stem Point
Trevarrian
PH
Tolcarne Merock
Bolingey
Penpont

MAWGAN PORTH HILL
TREVARRIAN HILL
B3276

66

83   A   84   B   85   C   86   D   87   E   88   F

44   32   45

F7
1 JASMINE WAY
2 PARC TRENANCE
3 ST CADOCS
4 PENDARVES
5 PARC TRETHIAS
6 GUNVER
7 TRESCORE
8 LILY WAY
9 MARIBOU CT

10 FOXGLOVE CRES
11 DAISYMOUNT DR
12 PRIMROSE DR
13 PALM DR
14 ST MERRYN HOLIDAY VILLAGE
15 PENTIRE
16 PORTHMISSEN
17 POLVENTON
18 JASMINE WAY

19 BAY RETREAT

F3
1 BOTHA RD
2 WELLINGTON RD
3 MOSQUITO CRES
4 LIBERATOR ROW
5 WARWICK CRES
6 LINCOLN ROW
7 VILDEBEEST RD
8 BEAUFORT AVE
9 SHACKLETON CRES

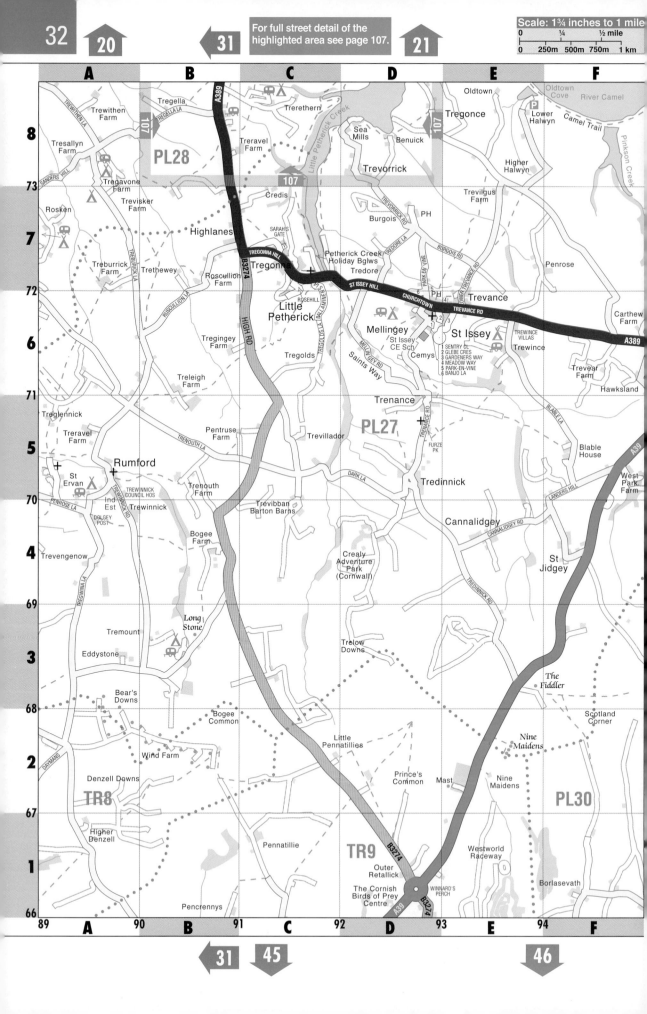

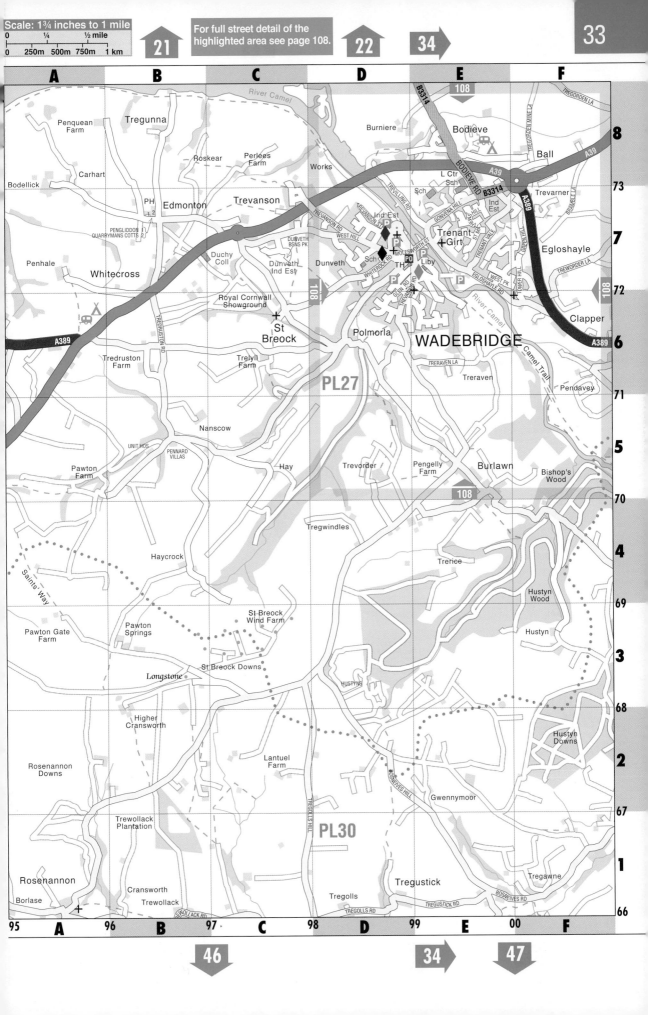

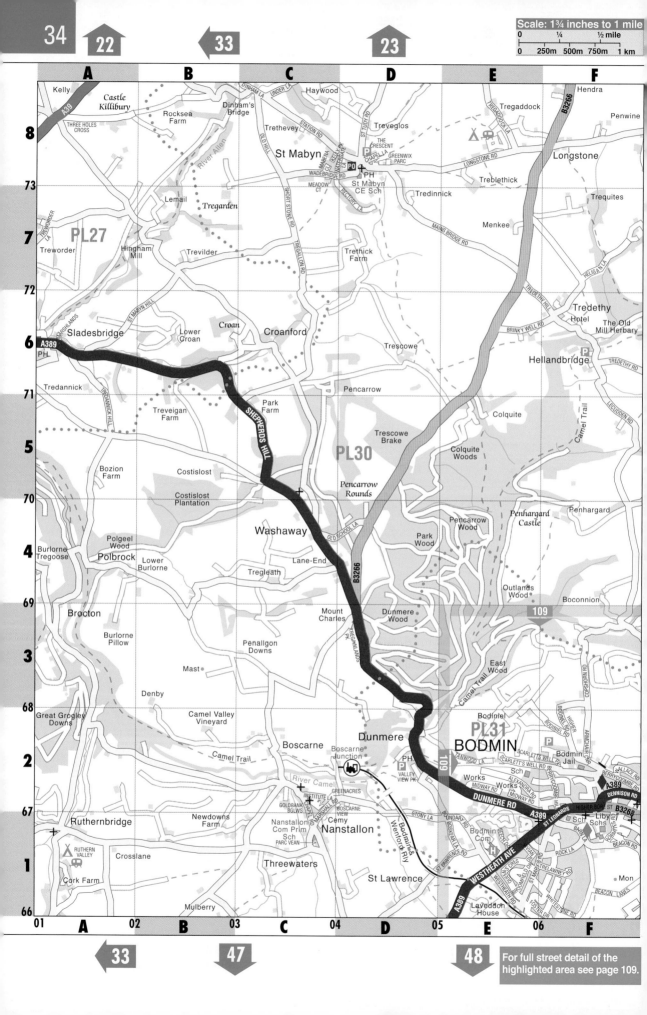

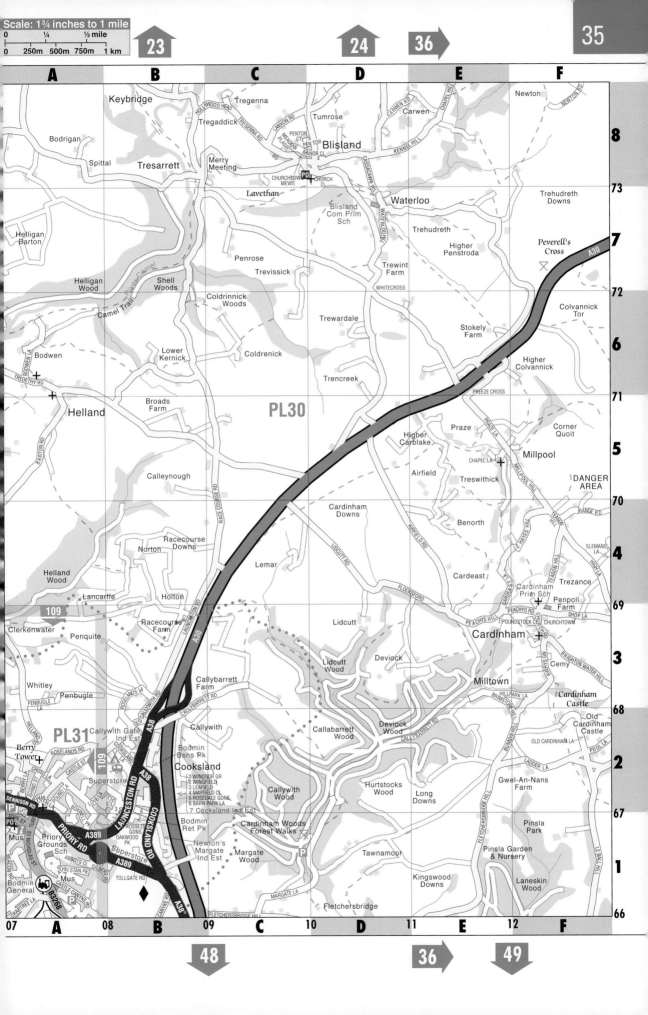

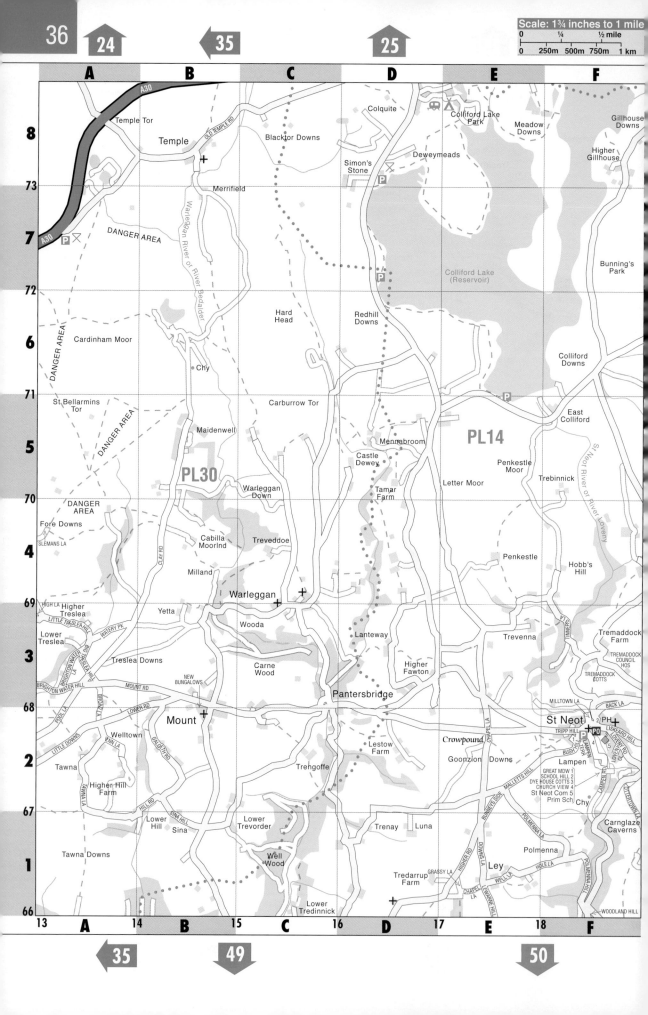

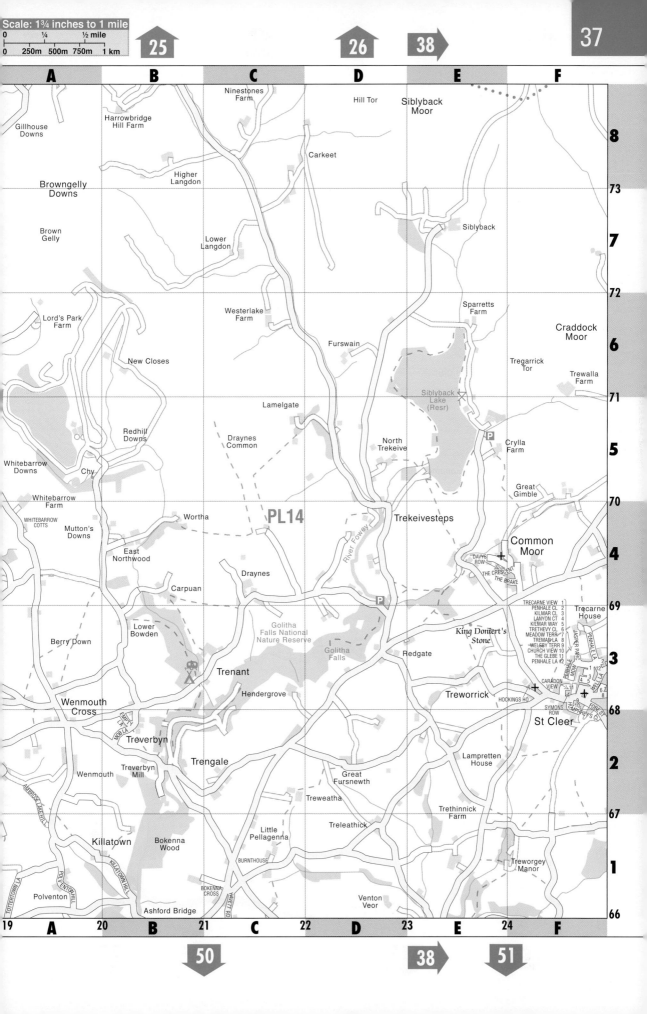

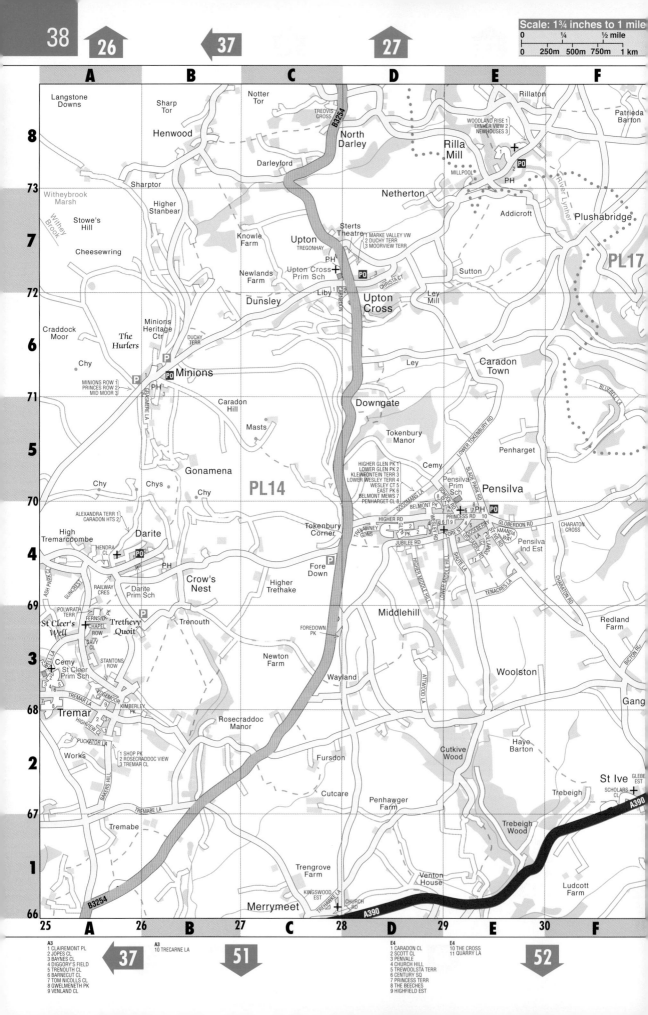

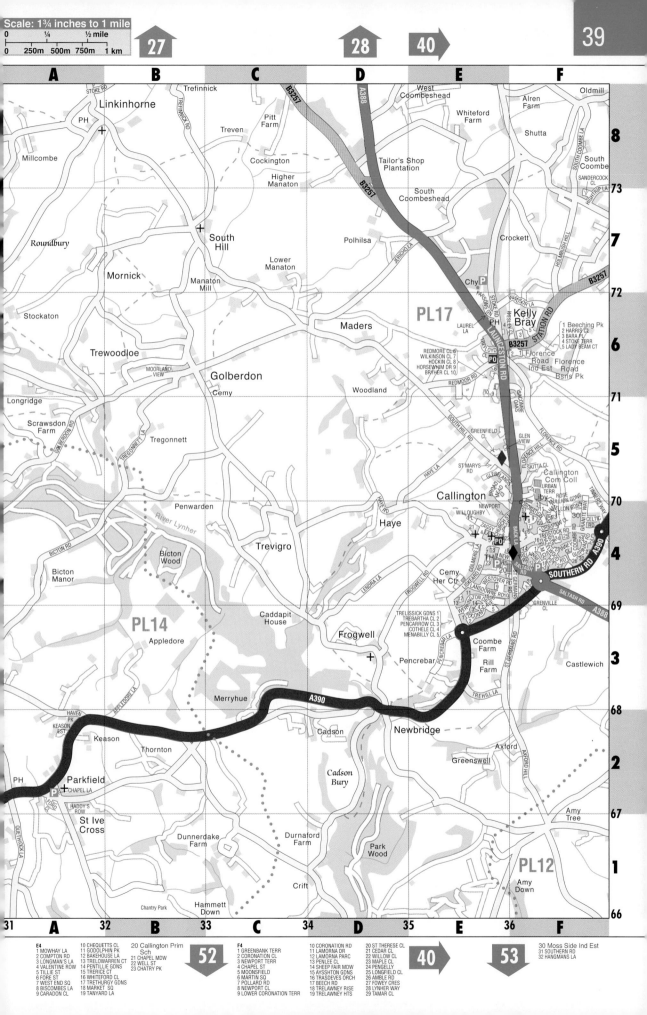

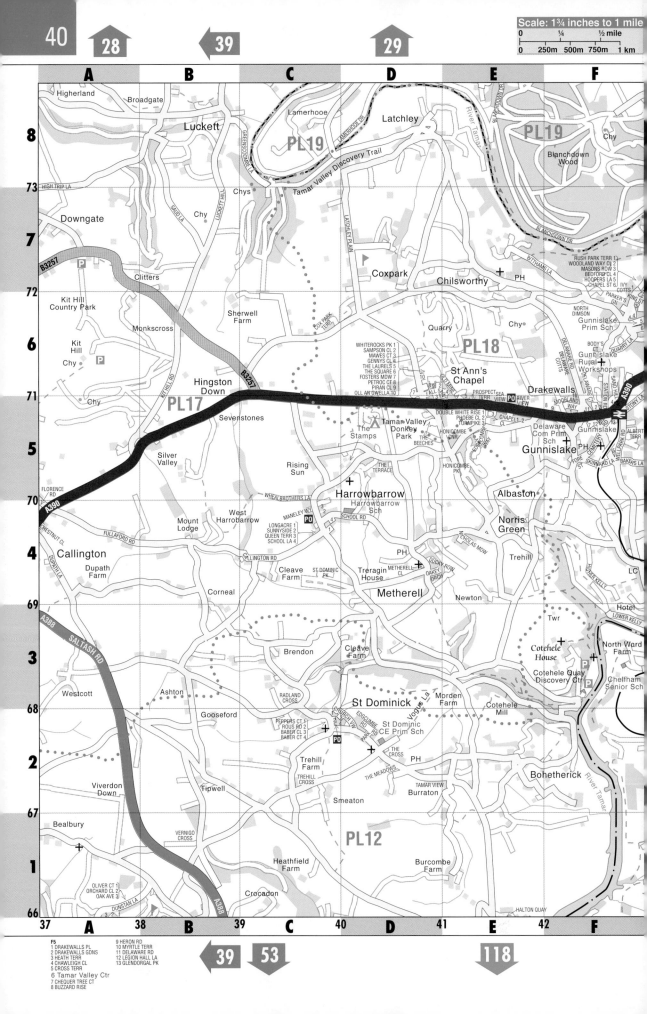

Scale: 1¾ inches to 1 mile

0   ¼   ½ mile
0 250m 500m 750m 1 km

8
Higherland
Broadgate
Luckett
Lamerhooe
Latchley
PL19
Chy
PL19
Blanchdown Wood

73
HIGH TRIP LA
Chys
Tamar Valley Discovery Trail

7
Downgate
Coxpark
Chilsworthy
PH
RUSH PARK TERR
WOODLAND WAY CL 2
MASONS ROW 3
BEDFORD CL 4
HOOPERS LA 5
CHAPEL ST 6
IVY COTTS 1
KING ST 2
B3257
P
Clitters

72
Kit Hill Country Park
Sherwell Farm
Quarry
Chy
NORTH DIMSON
Gunnislake Prim Sch
PARKER'S GN
Monkscross
PL18
BODY'S CT
Gunnislake Rural Workshops
QUARRY LA

6
Kit Hill
Chy
P
WHITEROCKS PK 1
SAMPSON CL 2
MAWES CT 3
GENNYS CL 4
THE LAURELS 5
THE SQUARE 6
FOSTERS MDW 7
PETROC CT 8
PIRAN CL 9
OLL AN GWELLA 10
St Ann's Chapel
Drakewalls
A390

71
Chy
Hingston Down
B3257
PL17
Sevenstones
PROSPECT TERR
SEA VIEW
PO
RIVER VIEW
DOUBLE WHITE RISE 1
PHOEBE CL 2
TURNPIKE 3
CHAPEL 1.2
MOORLAND WAY
Delaware Com Prim Sch
PH
Gunnislake
ALBERT TERR
BAKERS LA

5
Silver Valley
Rising Sun
The Stamps
Tamar Valley Donkey Park
THE BEECHES
HONICOMBE CNR
HONICOMBE PK
Gunnislake
Albaston

70
FLORENCE RD
A390
WHEAL BROTHERS LA
West Harrobarrow
MANELEY WY
PO
Harrowbarrow
Harrowbarrow Sch
SCHOOL RD
THE TERRACE
Norris Green
Trehill
LC

4
CHESTNUT CL
Callington
Dupath Farm
Mount Lodge
LONGACRE 1
SUNNYSIDE 2
QUEEN TERR 3
SCHOOL LA 4
ST DOMINIC PK
PH
Treragin House
METHERELL CL
DUCKY ROW
OAKEY ORCD
Newton

69
DUPATH LA
DUPATH LA
Corneal
ELLINGTON RD
Cleave Farm
Metherell
NICHOLAS MDW
Hotel
LOWER KELLY

3
A388
SALTASH RD
Westcott
Ashton
Brendon
Cleave Farm
Twr
Cotehele House
North Ward Farm
Cotehele Quay Discovery Ctr
P
Cheltham Senior Sch

68
Gooseford
RADLAND CROSS
Morden Farm
Cotehele Mill
CHURCH LW
EDGCUMBE RD
St Dominick
PEPPERS CT 1
ROUS RD 2
BABER CL 3
BABER CT 4
PO
St Dominic CE Prim Sch
PARK RD
Vogue La

2
Viverdon Down
Tipwell
Trehill Farm
TREHILL CROSS
THE CROSS
PH
THE MEADOWS
TAMAR VIEW
Burraton
Bohetherick
River Tamar

67
Smeaton

1
Bealbury
VERNIGO CROSS
Heathfield Farm
PL12
Burcombe Farm

66
A388
DUNSTAN LA
OLIVER CT 1
ORCHARD CL 2
OAK AVE 3
Crocadon
HALTON QUAY

A 37 B 38 C 39 D 40 41 E 42 F

F5
1 DRAKEWALLS PL
2 DRAKEWALLS GDNS
3 HEATH TERR
4 CHAWLEIGH CL
5 CROSS TERR
6 Tamar Valley Ctr
7 CHEQUER TREE CT
8 BUZZARD RISE
9 HERON RD
10 MYRTLE TERR
11 DELAWARE RD
12 LEGION HALL LA
13 GLENDORGAL PK

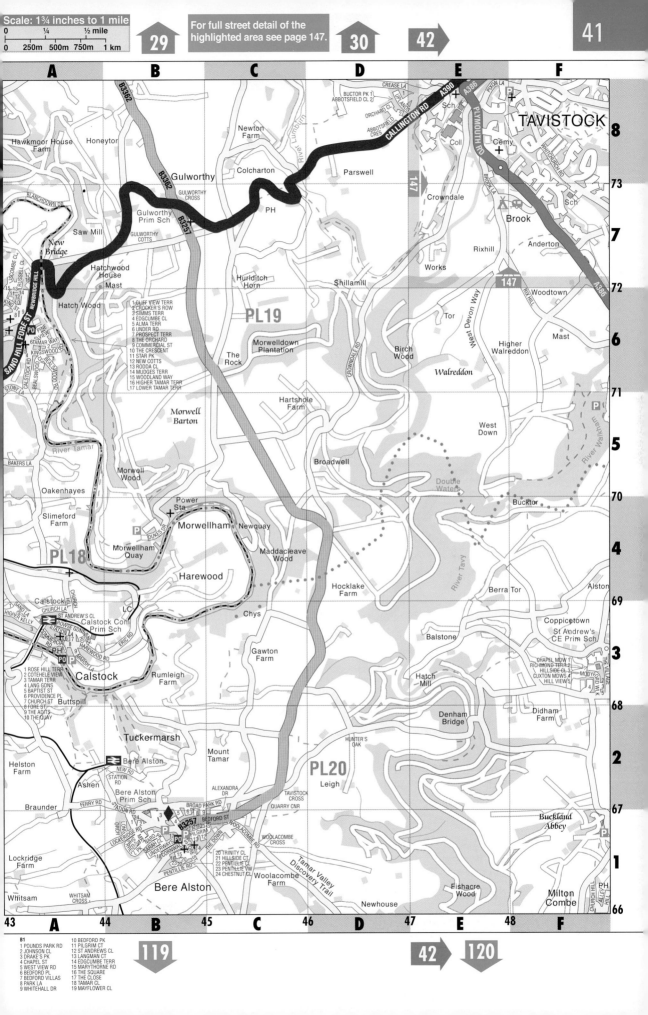

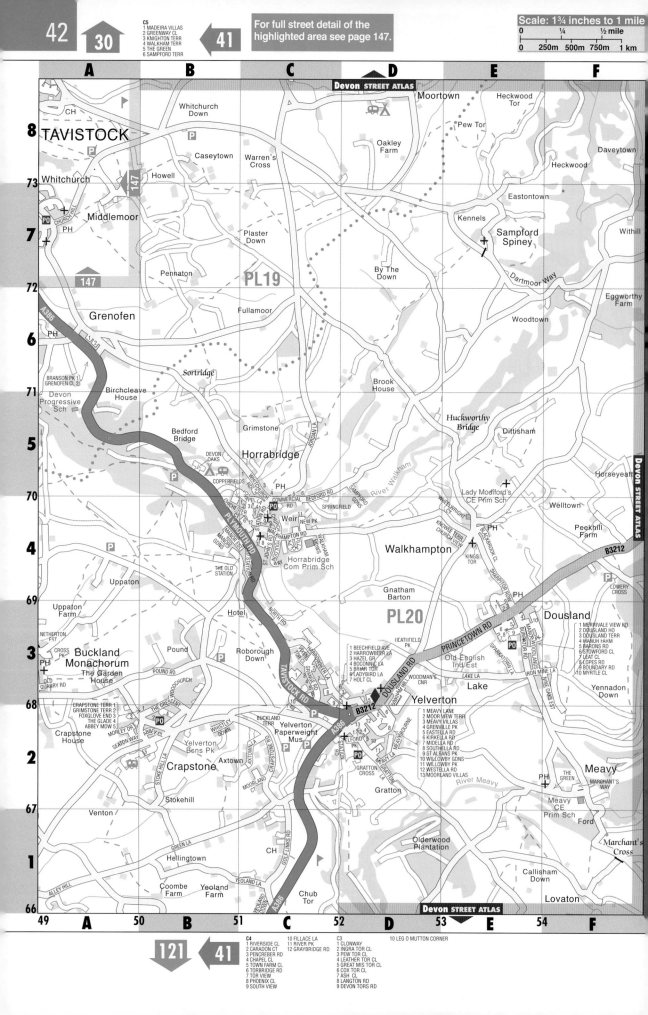

A   B   C   D   E   F

8

65

7

64

6

Towan Head

63

110

P

Gazzle

5

Hotel

Fistral
Bay

P

Fistral
Beach

62

LB
Sta

HEADLAND RD

DANE RD

NEWQUAY

CH

Cemy

TR7

CROSE

TOWER RD

ST GEORGES RD

P

CRANTOCK ST

+

The Goose

ESPLANADE
RD

ESPLANADE RD

PH

Pentire
Point East

PENTIRE RD

MOUNT
WISE

P

4

Pentire
Point West

Pentire

PH

P

Pentire Ave

PENTIRE CRES

PENMERE DR

CITY

GANNEL RD

STRET CARADO

NIANCE DR

A392

The
Chick

Vugga
Cove

Ferry P
(summer only)

PENTIRE RD

TREVEAN WAY

Kelsey
Head

Porth
Joke

Crantock
Beach

110

P

Penpol

PENPOL HILL

The
Gannel

61

Hotel

West
Pentire

Crantock

BEACH RD

PH

GREEN LA

+

VOSPORTH HILL

TREPELVICH RD

South West Coast Path

PENPOL HILL

Trevella

Treringey

3

South West Coast Path

P

WEST PENTIRE RD

GUSTORY RD

Treago
Farm

TREAGO RD

PENTIRE GN

ST
CARANTOC
WAY

HALWYN
AVE

PO

HALWYN RD

+

Trevella
Park

60

Cave

The
Kelseys

P

Wheelgate
House Sch

Trevowah

TREVEMPER RD

Carines

110

2

Holywell
Bay

Carter's or
Gull Rocks

Dunes

Lewannick

Cubert
Common

TR8

COMMONS RD

59

Penhale
Point

Holywell
Beach

Holywell

TREGUTH
CL

CAMP RD

RHUBARB HILL

CH

CL GOLDEN DR

Treworgans

LEWANNICK RD

WESFT RD

Carevick

Treworthal

A3075

Penhale
Camp

GUN HILL RD

CAMP RD

PH

CENTRAL RD

HOLYWELL RD

CURLEWS

Trevornick

SEA VIEW LA

Tresean

Cemy

Cubert
C P Sch

Trenissick

1

Cave

Hoblyn's
Cove

Ligger
Point

DANGER
AREA

Holywell Bay
Fun Park

TREVAIL
COTTS

Trevail

CHYNOWEN
PARC

HOLYWELL RD

CHYNOWEN LA

PH

58

75   A   76   B   77   C   78   D   79   E   80   F

55 ▼

44 ▶

For full street detail of the
highlighted area see page
110.

Scale: 1¾ inches to 1 mile
0   ¼   ½ mile
0   250m   500m   750m   1 km

A   B   C   D   E   F

8

Strasse Cliff

South West Coast Path

Tregurrian Hill

Tregurrian

Cemy

B3216   TOLCARNE LA

Newquay Airport

LONG LA

NEW RD

65

Watergate Bay

Hotel

P   P   Beechcombers

MARBEIN COTTS

Newquay Cornwall Airport

Penvose Farm

7

Tregurrian or Watergate Beach

WATERGATE RD

Mast

Higher Trewince

Penvose Farm

64

Zacry's Islands

THE WILLOWS 1
COASTLINE CT 2
TREVELGUE CT 3
HIGH ATLANTIC 4
SPINDRIFT 5
ISLAND POINT 6

Trebelsue Farm

Twr

Aerohub Business Park

LIME CL

6

Trevelgue Head

Flory Island

Hotel

TREVELGUE RD

Trevelgue

Tregustick Farm

Water Tower

A3059

63

110

Caves

Whipsiderry

Penrose

Tregenna

CH

Treloy

Treissac Farm

5

Newquay Bay

Lusty Glaze

PORTH WAY

ALEXA

Porth

111

St Columb Minor

PARKENBUTTS

Coll

PRIORY RD

RIALTON VITS

Trebarber

Melancoose

Porth Resr

62

Caves

Aquarium

NARROWCLIFF

CHESTER RD

GLAMIS RD

HENVER RD

Acad

Cemy

RIALTON RD

Rialton Barton

P

4

Liby

Acad

Newquay

MOUNT WISE

Acad

TRETHELLAN RD

ROBARTZ

HILGROVE RD

TR7

Sports Ctr

Newquay Tretherras Sch

PO

Gusti Veor

A3058   A3059

NEWQUAY

Trewollack Farm

TR8

East Penhill

Colan

61

Trenance

A3058

L Pk

LC

TRERICE RD

ISLAND

Gusti Vean

QUINTRELL RD

Sch

111

Lowertown

Treninnick

Trencreek

LC

Chapel

Quintrell Downs

Bejowan

3

TREVEMPER RD

A392 GANNEL RD

Treloggan Ind Est

Lane

LC

QUINTRELL DOWNS

Quintrell Downs

PH

EAST RD

Lady Nance

Superstore

WEST RD

PO

A3058

A392

60

Trevemper

A3075

A392

Trevithick Manor

PH

Trevilley Court Farm

Manuels

Trethiggy Farm

BRIDLE WAY

PH

Coswarth

2

Penhallow

River Gannel

Higher Trevilley

TAYLORS LA

Legonna

Kestle Mill

Kestle

Trevean

59

110

Sewage Works

Gwills

111

TRERICE HOLDINGS

Trevarthian

Tregonning

1

A3075

Trerew Farm

Tregair Farm

Polgreen

Trerice

Trewerry Mill

Tresillian House

A3058

DairyLand Farm World

58

A   B   C   D   E   F

81   82   83   84   85   86

For full street detail of the highlighted area see pages 110 and 111.

Treringey Round

Rosecliston Park

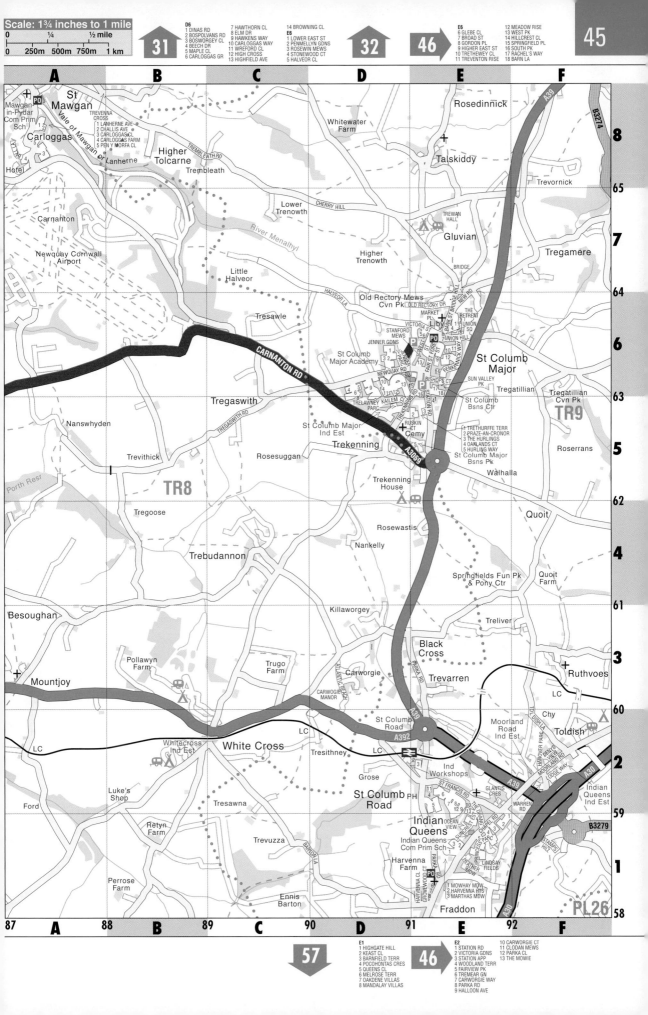

Scale: 1¾ inches to 1 mile

0 ¼ ½ mile

0 250m 500m 750m 1 km

A B C D E F

8 Retallack | Spirit of the West | Killeganogue Farm | Great Skewes | Treliver

65 | Penhellick | Pengelly | Higher Polgrain | St Wenn | St Wenn Sch | PL30 | Lanjew

Tremayne | Rostigan Hill | Trenance

7 | Gypsy Corner Rd | Lancorla Farm | Rostigan | Prince Park Rd

Tregurtha Farm | Hotel

64 | Trevithick East Farm | Reterth Farm | Criftoe | Tregonetha | Demelza | Hendra

Criftoe Rd | Lower Kernick

6 | Lower Trewolvas | Dennis Farm | Kernick Rd | Brynn Mill

63 | Tresaddern | Tregonetha Downs | Brynn Hill | Little Brynn

Castle Down | Saddle Rock | Belowda Beacon | Chy

5 | TR9 | Castle-an-Dinas Fort | Castle Farm | Chy

62 | Providence | Higher Trenoweth | Belowda | Victoria | PH

Castle Rd | Lane End | Beacon Rd | A30

4 | Ennisworgey | Black-acre | Castle Rd | LC | Penstraze La | B3274

61 | Treburdon Dr 1 | Rock View Pard 2 | Hermitage Rd 3 | Fibsleigh Pk 4 | Tremodrett Rd 5 | Mayfield Rd 6 | Springfield Way 7 | Tregarrick Rd 8 | Marshall Cl 9 | Shikes Way 10 | Queens Cl 11 | Farrow/Fordh 12 | Finsbury Ri 13 | Tregarrek Cl 14 | Foxglove Cl 15 | Tregoss Moor | Pentre Cl | Victoria Rd

Screech Owl Sanctuary | Pendine | Tregoss Rd | Tregoss | Tregoss M | Roche | Thornton Cl | Parkwoon | Harmony Rd | Harmony Cl | Chapel Rd | Fore St

3 | LC | Fuller Re | Eastbourne Rd | B3274

60 | Moorland Rd | A30 | Pitsmingle Hill | Harmony Moor | Roche Com Prim Sch | PO | Trezaise Rd | Higher Trerank Rd

2 | Gaverigan Manor | Goss Moor National Nature Reserve | Toads Hole | PL26 | Enniscaven | Trerank | St Michaels Wy 1 | Church Town Cl 2 | Angarrack Ct 3 | Dukes Ct 4 | Trerank Moor | Plas Jowan

59 | B3279 | Penrose Veor | Gothers | Coldvreath | Reskill Rd

1 | Domellick Hill | Domellick Cnr | Carne | Chy | Gothers Hill | Roseveare Mobile Home Pk | Cleers | New Rd | Coldvreath Rd

Domellick Farm | Carne Hill | Merna La | St Dennis | Gothers Hill | Pine View 1 | Windy Ridge 2 | Chateau Cl 3 | Rocklake Dr 3 | Cleers Hill | Tip | China Clay Works

Rectory Rd | Church Hall Rd | Cemy

58

93 A 94 B 95 C 96 D 97 E 98 F

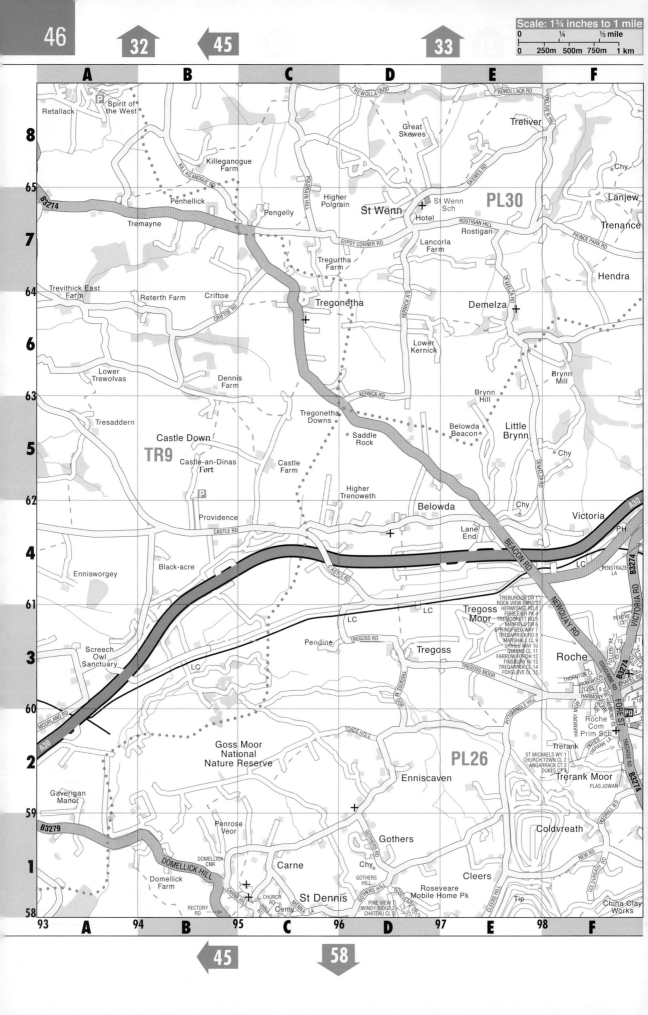

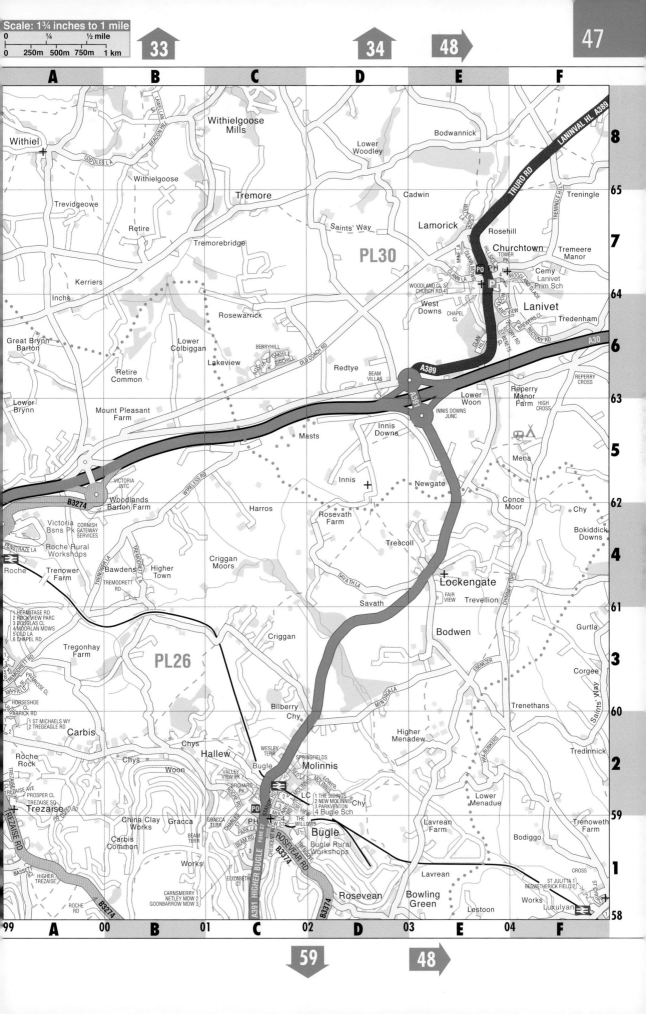

D8
1 PAARDEBURG RD
2 LUCKNOW RD S
3 Walker Lines Ind Est
4 Carminow Rd Ind Est

Scale: 1¾ inches to 1 mile

0   ¼   ½ mile
0   250m   500m   750m   1 km

A B C D E F

8

A389
Laveddon Mill
Kymsland
Little Kirland
Trekillick Farm
Kirland
Bawden Rd
Gladstone Rd
Crabtree La
Bodmin & Wenford Rly
Coll
College Green
PL31
Halgavor Farm
Kirland Bower
Hawke's Bridge
L Ctr
Turfdown
Sunny Bank
Fletchersbridge
Crem
Castle Canyke
Castle Canyke Rd
Beatrice Av
Norman Way
Lucknow Rd 3
Carminow Cross
Respryn Rd
A38
A30
Colesloggett Halt
Bodmin & Wenford Rly

109

65
Stephen Gelly
Lidcutt Farm
109

7
Tremabyn
Kirland Bower
Oak Ford
CH
The Fairways
Halgavor Plantation
Bazley's Plantation
Little Cutmadoc Farm
Tregullon
Tretoil Hill
Treliggon Bottoms

64
Treliggon
Tretoil
Cemy
Hart Wood
Cutmadoc
Bodmin Parkway

6
A30
St Ingunger La
Treffry
Foxpark
Treffry La
Trebyan Bsns Pk
Lanhydrock House & Gdns
Newton
Great Wood
P
Waterlake
Bofarnel

63
St Ingunger Farm
Fenton Pits
Mast
Trebyan
Ford Farm
Coombe Farm
Works
Brownqueen Wood
112

5
Trebell Green
Lesquite Farm
Tredinnickpits
Maudlin
Coombe La
Woodlands Farm
Brown Queen
Slip Wood
River Fowey

62
Bokiddick
Wilderness Trail
Creney Farm
Sweetshouse
Bridge Hill
Sturta La
Turnpike B3268
Black La

4
Higher Trevilmick
Helman Tor
P
PL30
Boslymon
Boslymon Hill
B3269
Leadenhill Wood
Restormel Castle
Restormel Farm
Barngate Farm
Bodmin Hill
Restormel
Restormel Manor

61
Lowertown
Red Moor
Redmoor
112
Hillhead
PL22

3
Breney Farm
Bodwen Farm
Saints' Way
Crift
Ruzza
Chark La
Chark
Penquite
Terras Hill
LOSTWITHIEL
Poldew Wood
Poldew
Restormel Rd
CH
Cott Rd

60
Roseney Farm
Crift Downs
Streigh Farm
Iron Bars
Penhale
Polgassick Farm
Victoria
Penknight
Mus
PO
LC
NORTH ST
Lliddicoat Rd
A390
Lostwithiel
B3268

2
Luxulyan Quarry
Tregantle
Pennant Hill
Lanxon Cres
Thomas Bullock Cl 2
PH
Lanlivery Prim Sch
Uplands
Penknight La
Edgcumbe Rd
Scrations
Crewell
Castle Hill
Cark La
Quay's Rd
Cemy
Rosehill
Lanwithan
Maddery Moor
Shirehall Moor

59
Treganoon
Lanlivery
Puddle
Pelyn
Mast

1
Luxulyan
Middle Greadow
Trethew
Sandyway Wood
A390
B3269
Castle

58
1 ST JULITTA
2 ST SULIEN
Luxulyan Sch
PO

05 **A** 06 **B** 07 **C** 08 **D** 09 **E** 10 **F**

For full street detail of the highlighted area see pages 109 and 112.

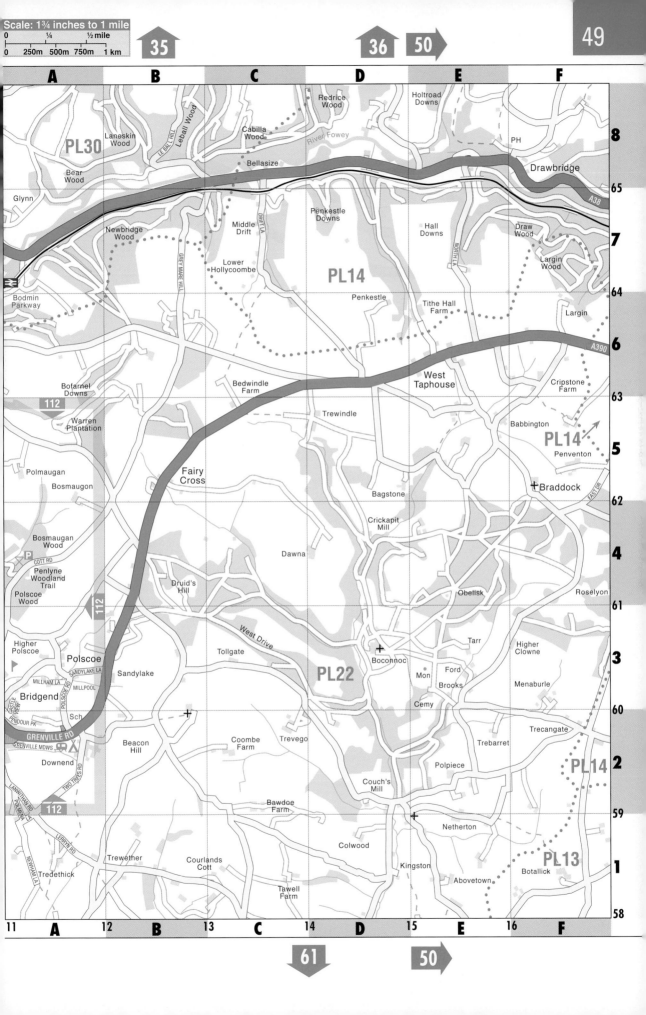

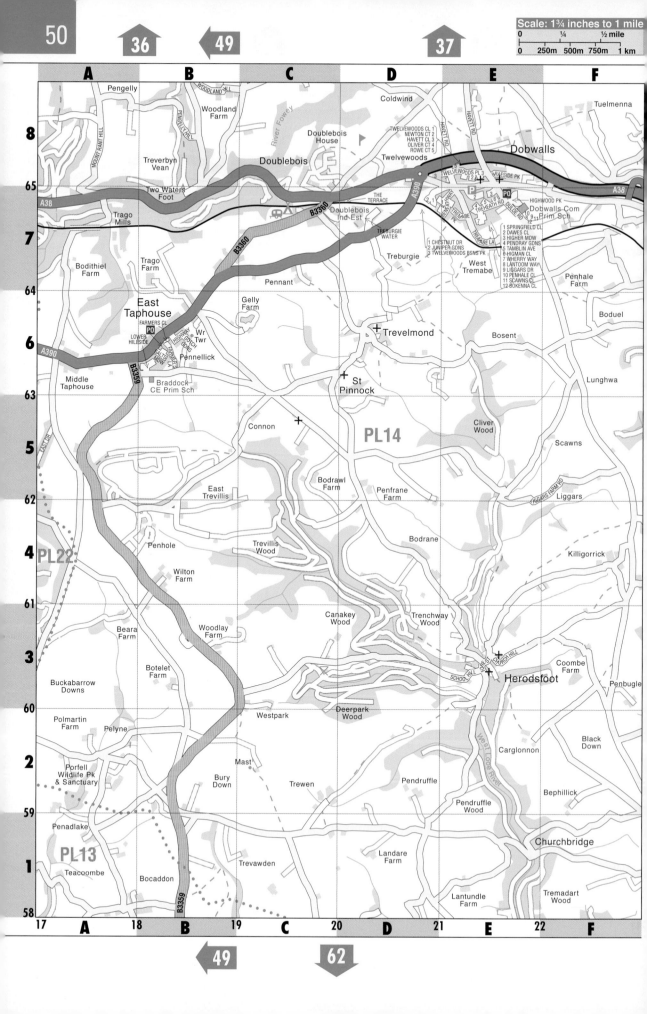

A B C D E F

8

Pengelly

Woodland Farm

WOODLAND HILL

Coldwind

Tuelmenna

Treverbyn Vean

River Fowey

Doublebois House

Twelvewoods

TWELVEWOODS CL 1
NEWTON CT 2
HAVETT CL 3
OLIVER CT 4
ROWE CT 5

Dobwalls

65

Doublebois

Two Waters Foot

A38

B3360

THE TERRACE

A390

Doublebois Ind Est

TWELVEWOODS PL 3

BRAESIDE PK

P

PO

Highwood Pk

Dobwalls Com Prim Sch

A38

Trago Mills

Treburgie Water

Treburgie

1 SPRINGFIELD CL
2 DAWES CL
3 HIGHER MDW
4 PENDRAY GDNS
5 TAMBLIN AVE
6 HIGMAN CL
7 WHERRY WAY
8 LANTOOM WAY
9 LIGGARS DR
10 PENHALE CL
11 SCAWNS CL
12 BOKENNA CL

64

Bodithiel Farm

Trago Farm

Pennant

1 CHESTNUT DR
2 JUNIPER GDNS
3 TWELVEWOODS BSNS PK

West Tremabe

Penhale Farm

7

B3360

East Taphouse

FARMERS CL
PO
LOWER HILLSIDE

Gelly Farm

Trevelmond

Bosent

Boduel

6

A390

Wr Twr

Pennellick

HIGHWAY
GOTCH GDNS

St Pinnock

Cliver Wood

Lunghwa

63

B3359

Middle Taphouse

Braddock CE Prim Sch

PL14

5

EAST DR

Connon

Bodrawl Farm

Scawns

62

East Trevillis

Penfrane Farm

Liggars

IGGARS FARM RD

4

PL22

Penhole

Trevillis Wood

Bodrane

Killigorrick

61

Wilton Farm

Canakey Wood

Trenchway Wood

3

Beara Farm

Woodlay Farm

Herodsfoot

Coombe Farm

Penbugle

SCHOOL HILL

TACH HILL

60

Buckabarrow Downs

Botelet Farm

Westpark

Deerpark Wood

West Looe River

Carglonnon

Black Down

Polmartin Farm

Pelyne

Mast

Pendruffle

Bephillick

2

Porfell Wildlife Pk & Sanctuary

Bury Down

Trewen

Pendruffle Wood

59

Penadlake

Churchbridge

PL13

1

Teacoombe

Bocaddon

Trevawden

Landare Farm

Lantundle Farm

Tremadart Wood

58

17 A 18 B 19 C 20 D 21 E 22 F

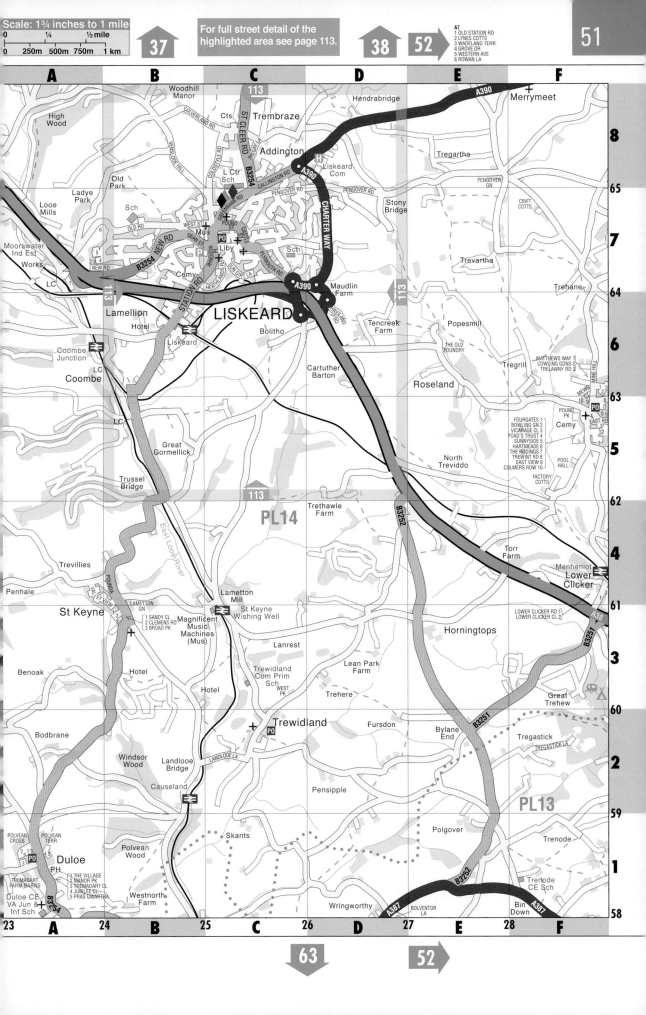

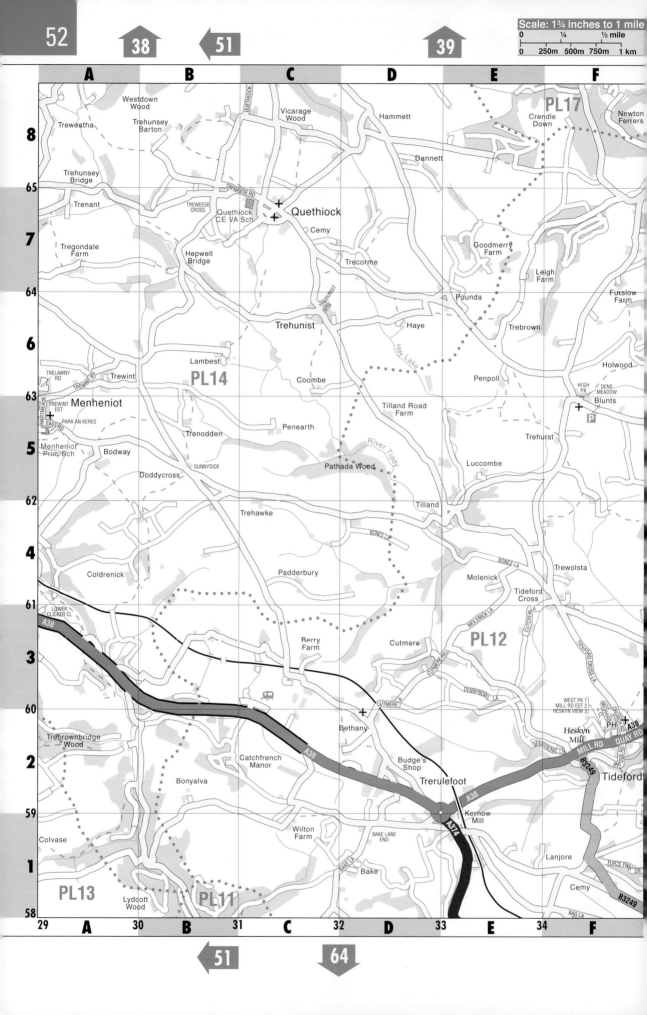

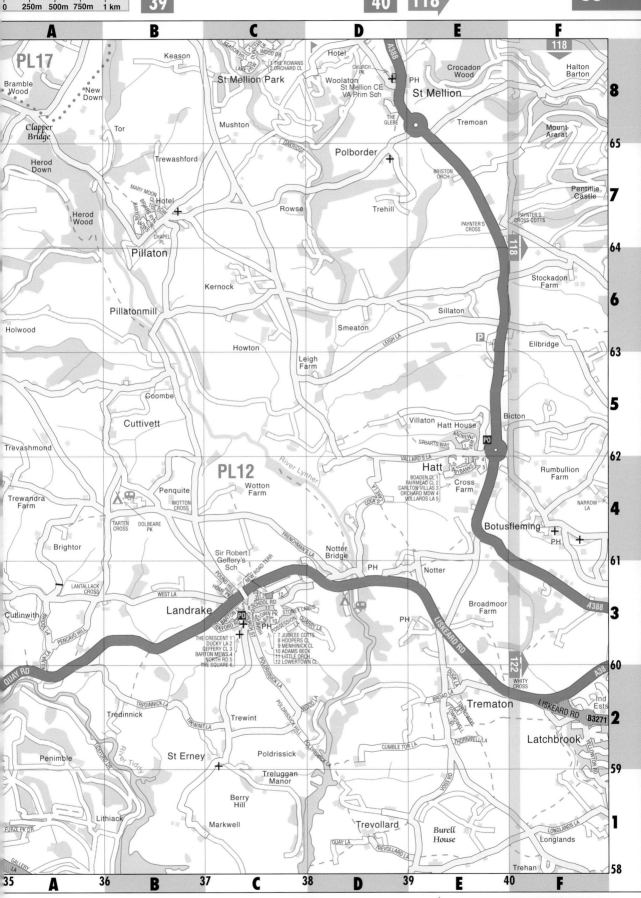

PL17

Bramble Wood

Clapper Bridge

New Down

Keason

St Mellion Park

KEASON HILL

LAKE VIEW

WOOD DR

1 THE ROWANS
2 ORCHARD CL

Hotel

Woolaton

St Mellion CE VA Prim Sch

CHURCH PK

PH

St Mellion

Crocadon Wood

Halton Barton

Herod Down

Tor

Mushton

OAKRIDGE

Polborder

BRISTON ORCH

Tremoan

Mount Ararat

Trewashford

Mary Moon Hotel

BRIAR'S RYE

THE ROW

BARTON MEWS

CHAPEL PL

Pillaton

Rowse

Trehill

PAYNTER'S CROSS

118

Pentillie Castle

Herod Wood

Kernock

Sillaton

PAYNTER'S CROSS COTTS

Holwood

Pillatonmill

Howton

Leigh Farm

LEIGH LA

Smeaton

Stockadon Farm

Ellbridge

Coombe

Cuttivett

PL12

River Lynher

Wotton Farm

Villaton

Hatt House

Bicton

Trevashmond

Penquite

WOTTON CROSS

STUARTS WAY

ANDREW

PO

VALLARD'S LA

Hatt

Rumbullion Farm

Trewandra Farm

TARTEN CROSS

DOLBEARE PK

COCK'S LANE LA

WYBANKS

BOADEN CL 1
FAIRMEAD CL 2
CARLTON VILLAS 3
ORCHARD MDW 4
VOLLARDS LA 5

Cross Farm

NARROW LA

Brighton

LANTALLACK CROSS

FRENCHMAN'S LA

Notter Bridge

PH

Notter

Botusfleming

PH

Cutlinwith

BRIDGE LA

PENCAVO HILL

WEST LA

HOME PK

POUND HILL

NEW ROAD TERR

Sir Robert Geffery's Sch

Landrake

BARTON RD

BEFORD RD

PO

SCHOOL RD

WINDSOR RD

TOWN PK

POSSESSION

STONEY LANDS

QUARRY LA

PH

Notter

PH

LISKEARD RD

Broadmoor Farm

A388

Quay RD

KILNA LA

TREDINNICK LA

THE CRESCENT 1
DUCKY LA 2
GEFFERY CL 3
BARTON MEWS 4
NORTH RD 5
TRE SQUARE 6

7 JUBILEE COTTS
8 HOOPERS CL
9 MENHINICK CL
10 ADAMS BECK
11 LITTLE ORCH
12 LOWERTOWN CL

POLDRISSICK LA

POLDRISSICK HILL

POLDRISSICK LA

DUCK LA

BROAD LA

Trematon

WHITY CROSS

122

A38

LISKEARD RD

Ind Ests

B3271

Latchbrook

FELLDOWN RD

Tredinnick

TREWINT LA

Trewint

River Tiddy

St Erney

Poldrissick

TILHEDRA DR

CUMBLE TOR LA

VOSS RD

THORNWELL LA

TOWNSEND

THORNHILL LA

Longlands

LONGLANDS LA

FURZE PK DR

Penimble

Lithiack

Markwell

Treluggan Manor

Berry Hill

QUAY LA

Trevollard

TREVOLLARD LA

Burell House

Trehan

GALLERY LA

35 36 37 38 39 40
65 122

For full street detail of the highlighted area see pages 118 and 122.

A   B   C   D   E   F

8
57
7
56
6
55
5
54
4
53
3
52
2
51
1
50

69   A   70   B   71   C   72   D   73   E   74   F

Shag Rock
Shafts (dis)
Cligga Head
Cligga Workshops 1
ST GEORGE'S TERR 2
CLIGGA HEAD IND EST 3
B3285
Shafts (dis)
Hotel
TR6
Hanover Cove
Anchor
South West Coast Path
Airfield
ST GEORGE'S HILL
Bawden Rocks
Green Island
Trevellas Porth
Trevaunance Cove
Cross Coombe
Chy
Trevellas
Newdowns Head
New Downs
Trevaunance Cove
Chy
Heritage Trail
Blue Hills
Trevellas Coombe
Blowinghouse
St Agnes Head
Crams
Chy
Shafts (dis)
PH
Wheal Kitty Workshops
Perran View Holiday Pk
TR5
Carn Gowla
Trevaunance Cl
Wheal Kitty
Mithian Sch
Higher Bal
Chy
Peterville
Barkla Shop
PH
Tubby's Head
Chy
B3285 GOONLAZE
Mithian
St Agnes Beacon
St Agnes Prim Sch
Liby
Chy
B3277
St Agnes
Goonown
PROMISED LAND
Mus
Beacon Farm
Chy
Cemy

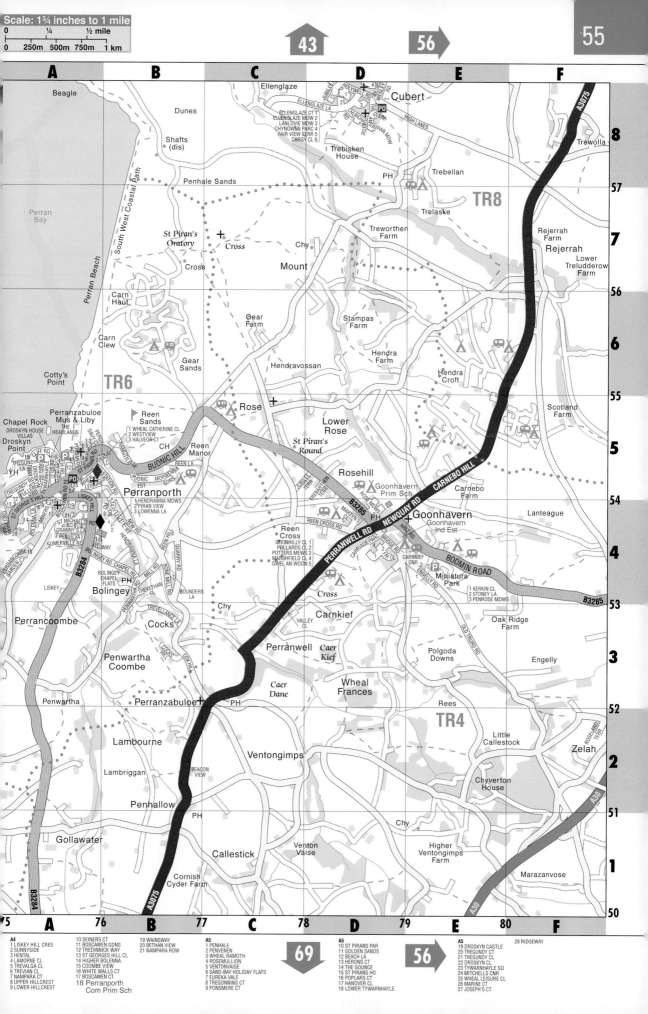

A   B   C   D   E   F

Beagle

Dunes

Shafts
(dis)

8

Penhale Sands

57

Perran
Bay

7

St Piran's
Oratory

Cross

Cross

Mount

Chy

56

Carn
Haut

Gear
Farm

Stampas
Farm

Hendra
Farm

Hendra
Croft

6

Carn
Clew

Gear
Sands

Hendravossan

55

Cotty's
Point

TR6

Perranzabuloe
Mus & Liby
THE
HEADLANDS

Reen Sands
1 WHEAL CATHERINE CL
2 WESTVIEW
3 HALVEOR CT

Rose

Lower
Rose

Scotland
Farm

5

Chapel Rock
DROSKYN HOUSE
VILLAS
Droskyn
Point
YH

Budnic Hill

Reen
Manor

CH

St Piran's
Round

Rosehill

Goonhavern
Prim Sch

Carnebo
Farm

Lanteague

54

Perranporth
1 HENDRAWNA MDWS
2 PIRAN VIEW
3 LOWENNA LA

Reen
Cross

GOONHILLY CL 1
POLLARDS CL 2
POTTERS MEWS 3
MARSHFIELD CL 4
GWEL AN WOON 5

Goonhavern
Goonhavern
Ind Est

1 KERKIN CL
2 STONEY LA
3 PENROSE MDWS

4

B3284

Bolingey
CHAPEL
FLATS
PH

Cross

Carnkief
CNR

Miniatura
Park

BODMIN ROAD

Oak Ridge
Farm

B3285

53

Perrancoombe

Cocks

Chy

Carnkief

VALLEY
CL

Perranwell

Caer
Kief

Polgoda
Downs

Engelly

3

Penwartha
Coombe

Caer
Dane

Wheal
Frances

Rees

TR4

2

Perranzabuloe

PH

Ventongimps

Little
Callestock

Zelah

Lambourne

Chyverton
House

Lambriggan

BEACON
VIEW

Penhallow

PH

Chy

51

Gollawater

Venton
Vaise

Higher
Ventongimps
Farm

Marazanvose

1

Callestick

Cornish
Cyder Farm

50

5   A   76   B   77   C   78   D   79   E   80   F

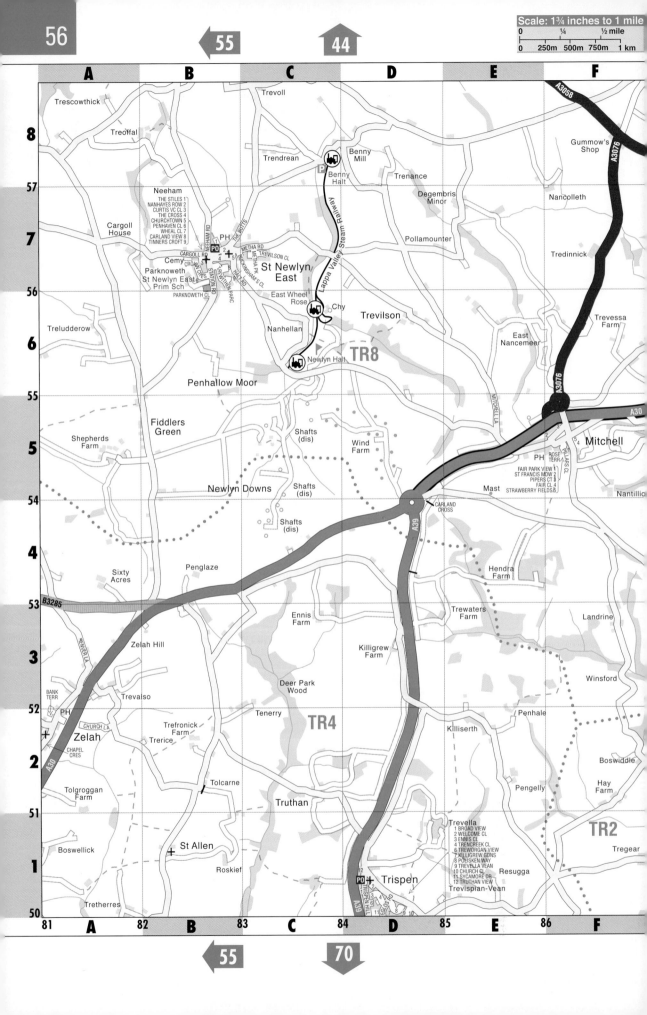

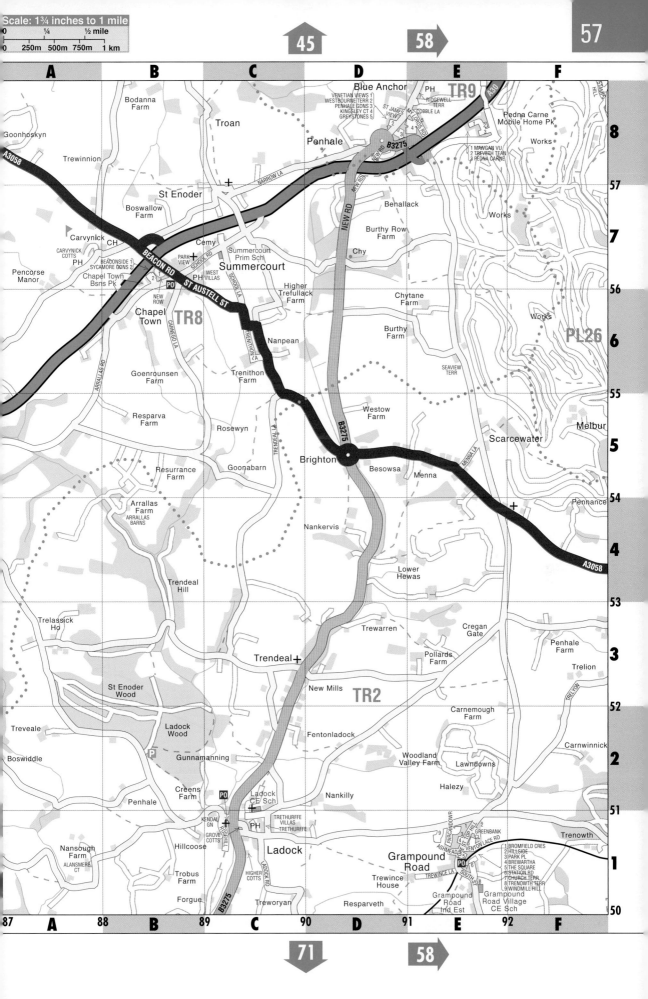

A   B   C   D   E   F

8   57   7   56   6   55   5   54   4   53   3   52   2   51   50

Goonhoskyn

Bodanna Farm

Troan

Blue Anchor

PH

TR9

VENETIAN VIEWS 1
WESTBOURNE TERR 2
PENHALE GDNS 3
KINGSLEY CT 4
GREYSTONES 5

ST JAMES
VIEW

RIDGEWELL
TERR

COBBLE LA

MT LORD RD

Pedna Carne
Mobile Home Pk

Works

Penhale

B3275

NEW RD

1 MAWGAN VU
2 TREVETH TEAM
3 PEDNA CARNE

Trewinnion

St Enoder

NARROW LA

Benallack

Works

Carvynick

CH

Boswallow Farm

NEW RD

Burthy Row
Farm

Works

CARVYNICK
COTTS

PH

BEACONSIDE 1
SYCAMORE GDNS 2

BEACON RD

Cemy

SCHOOL RD

PARK
VIEW

Summercourt
Prim Sch

Chy

Chytane
Farm

Pencorse
Manor

Chapel Town
Bsns Pk

ST AUSTELL ST

PH
WEST
VILLAS

Summercourt

SCHOOL LA

Burthy
Farm

Works

PL26

Chapel
Town

NEW ROW

NEW
ROW

PO

TR8

CARNEGO LA

Higher
Trefullack
Farm

Nanpean

TRENITHON LA

SEAVIEW
TERR

ARRALLAS RD

Goenrounsen
Farm

Trenithon
Farm

Resparva
Farm

Rosewyn

TRENDEAL LA

Westow
Farm

B3275

Scarcewater

MENNA LA

Melbur

Resurrance
Farm

Goonabarn

Brighton

Besowsa

Menna

Pennance

Arrallas
Farm

ARRALLAS
BARNS

Nankervis

Lower
Hewas

A3058

Trelassick
Ho

Trewarren

Cregan
Gate

Penhale
Farm

Trendeal
Hill

Trendeal

Pollards
Farm

Trelion

St Enoder
Wood

New Mills

TR2

Carnemough
Farm

TRELOW

Carnwinnick

Treveale

Ladock
Wood

P

Fentonladock

Woodland
Valley Farm

Lawndowns

Boswiddle

Gunnamanning

Nankilly

Halezy

Penhale

Creens
Farm

PO

Ladock
CE Sch

PH

TRETHURFFE
VILLAS
TRETHURFFE

PARCANDOWR

Trenowth

KENDAL
GN

GROVE
COTTS

RISEHILL

Hillcoose

Ladock

Grampound
Road

9

GREENBANK
CL

ASHMEADS

ST TOP HILL

VENTON LACE RD

1 BROMFIELD CRES
2 HILLSIDE
3 PARK PL
4 BREWARTHA
5 THE SQUARE
6 STATION RD
7 CHURCH TERR
8 TRENOWTH TERR
9 WINDMILL HILL

Nansough
Farm

ALANSMERE
CT

Trobus
Farm

HIGHER
COTTS

LADOCK RD

Trewince
House

PO

SOUTH ST

TREWINCE LA

Grampound
Road Village
CE Sch

Forgue

B3275

Treworyan

Resparveth

Grampound
Road Ind Est

57
46

Scale: 1¾ inches to 1 mile
0 ¼ ½ mile
0 250m 500m 750m 1 km

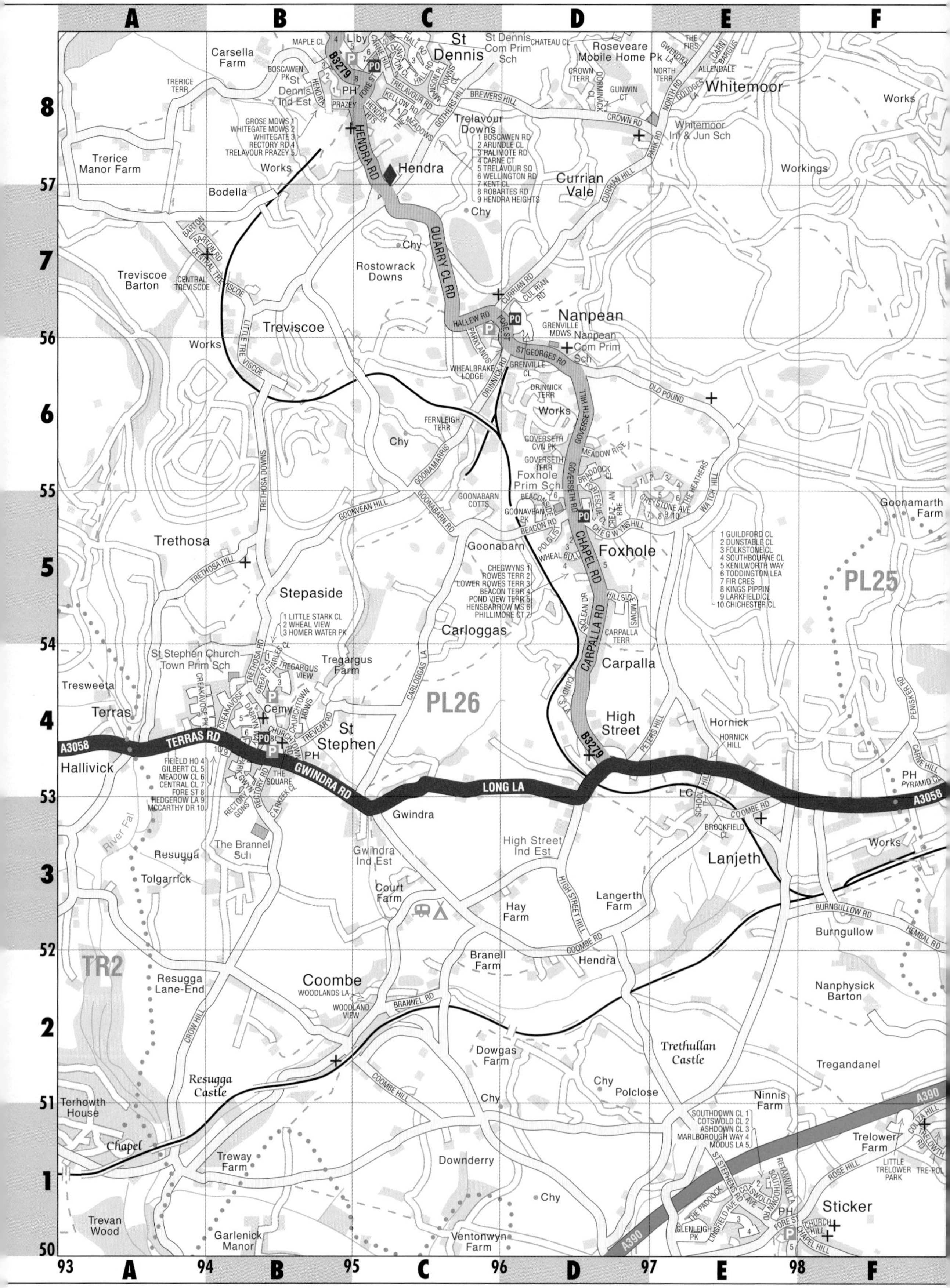
A
B
C
D
E
F
8
7
6
5
4
3
2
1
57
56
55
54
53
52
51
50
93
94
95
96
97
98
Carsella Farm
St Dennis
St Dennis Com Prim Sch
Roseveare Mobile Home Pk
Whitemoor
Whitemoor Inf & Jun Sch
Works
Trerice Manor Farm
St Dennis Ind Est
Trelavour Downs
Hendra
HENDRA RD
B3279
BREWERS HILL
CROWN RD
Curran Vale
Workings
Bodella
Chy
QUARRY CL RD
Rostowrack Downs
Treviscoe Barton
Treviscoe
Nanpean
Nanpean Com Prim Sch
Works
Fernleigh Terr
OLD POUND
Goonabarn
Foxhole
Foxhole Prim Sch
CHAPEL RD
Trethosa
Stepaside
Carloggas
CARPALLA RD
Carpalla
St Stephen Church Town Prim Sch
Tregargus Farm
Tresweeta
Terras
PL26
PL25
Goonamarth Farm
High Street
Hornick
A3058
TERRAS RD
GWINDRA RD
LONG LA
St Stephen
Hallivick
Gwindra
High Street Ind Est
Lanjeth
The Brannel Sch
Resugga
Tolgarrick
Gwindra Ind Est
Court Farm
Hay Farm
Langerth Farm
Burngullow
BURNGULLOW RD
TR2
Resugga Lane-End
Coombe
Branell Farm
Hendra
Nanphysick Barton
BRANNEL RD
Dowgas Farm
Trethullan Castle
Tregandanel
Resugga Castle
Chy
Polclose
Ninnis Farm
Terhowth House
Chapel
Treway Farm
Downderry
Trelower Farm
A390
Trevan Wood
Garlenick Manor
Ventonwyn Farm
Sticker

57
72

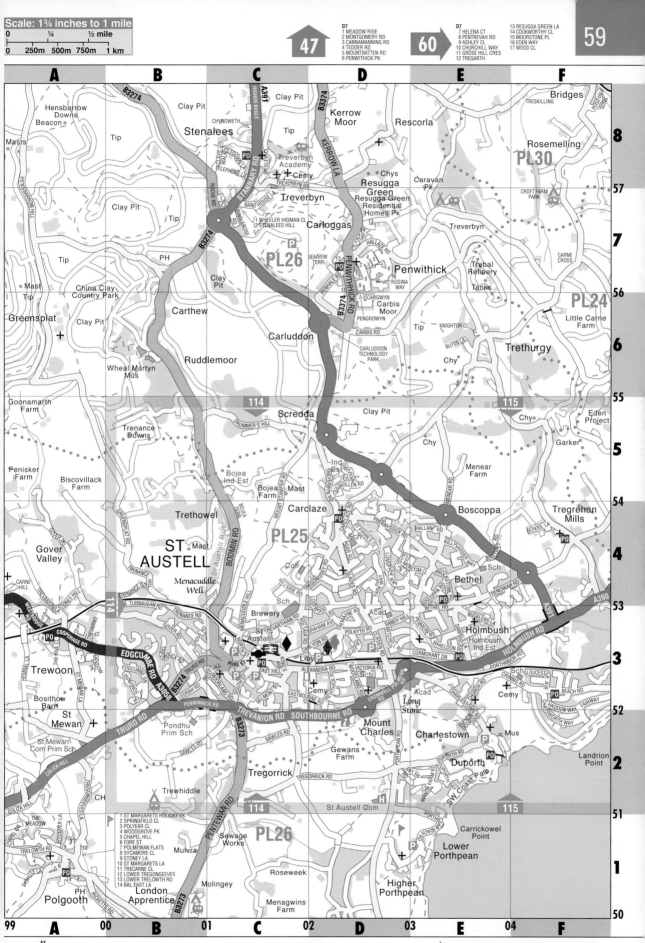

Scale: 1¾ inches to 1 mile

0   ¼   ½ mile
0   250m 500m 750m   1 km

D7
1 MEADOW RISE
2 MONTGOMERY RD
3 CANNAMANNING RD
4 TEDDER RD
5 MOUNTBATTEN RD
6 PENWITHICK PK

47

D7
7 HELENA CT
8 PENTREVAH RD
9 ASHLEY CL
10 CHURCHILL WAY
11 GROSE HILL CRES
12 TREGARTH

13 RESUGGA GREEN LA
14 COOKWORTHY CL
15 MOORSTONE PL
16 EDEN WAY
17 WOOD CL

60

59

A   B   C   D   E   F

Bridges
TRESKILLING

Hensbarrow
Downs
Beacon

Masts

Clay Pit

HIGHER BUGLE

A391

Clay Pit

B3374

Kerrow
Moor

Rescorla

Rosemelling

PL30

8

Tip

B3274

Clay Pit

Stenalees

CHYNOWETH

Tip

KERROW LA

Caravan
Pk

CROFT FARM
PARK

57

Clay Pit

Treverbyn
Academy

Cemy

Treverbyn

Resugga
Green
Resugga Green
Residential
Homes Pk

Treverbyn

CARNE
CROSS

7

Tip

RICHE RD

B3274

PH

BAND HOUSE LA

1 WHEELER HIGMAN CL
2 STENALEES HILL

PL26

P

SEAVIEW
TERR

Penwithick

Trebal
Refinery

Tanks

56

Mast
Tip

China Clay
Country Park

Carthew

Clay
Pit

B3374

Carbis
Moor
PENGROWYN

Tip

KNIGHTOR CL

PL24

Little Carne
Farm

Greensplat

Clay Pit

Ruddlemoor

Carluddon

CARBIS RD

Chy

BUTTS LA

Trethurgy

6

Wheal Martyn
Mus

CARLUDDON
TECHNOLOGY
PARK

Chy

55

Goonamarth
Farm

114

ScreDda

Clay Pit

Chy

115

Eden
Project

Garker

5

Trenance
Downs

DRUMMER'S HILL

Chy

Penisker
Farm

Biscovillack
Farm

Bojea
Farm

Bojea
Ind Est

Menear
Farm

54

Trethowel

Carclaze

Boscoppa

Tregrehan
Mills

SCHOOL LA

PO

4

Gover
Valley

PL25

Mast

Coll

Bethel

A390

53

CARNE
HILL

St
AUSTELL

Menacuddle
Well

Sch

Brewery

Acad

Holmbush

HOLMBUSH RD

Holmbush
Ind Est

3

Trewoon

114

EDGCUMBE RD

A3058

Truro Rd

PENWINNICK RD

TREVANION RD

SOUTHBOURNE RD

Liby

Cemy

Acad

Cemy

PO

BEACH RD

52

St Mewan

B3273

Pondhu
Prim Sch

SAWLES RD

Mount
Charles

Long
Stone

Charlestown

Mus

Landrion
Point

2

St Mewan
Com Prim Sch

THE
MEADOW

CH

Trewhiddle

Tregorrick

TREGORRICK RD

Gewans
Farm

Duporth

SW Coast Path

1 ST MARGARETS HOLIDAY PK
2 SPRINGFIELD CL
3 POLYEAR CL
4 WOODGROVE PK
5 CHAPEL HILL
6 FORE ST
7 POLMEWAN FLATS
8 SYCAMORE CL
9 STONEY LA
10 ST MARGARETS LA
11 TRECARNE CL
12 LOWER TREGONGEEVES
13 LOWER TRELOWTH RD
14 BAL EAST LA

114

St Austell Com

115

Carrickowel
Point

Polgooth

PH

London
Apprentice

Mulvra

PL26

Sewage
Works

Molingey

Roseweek

Menagwins
Farm

Higher
Porthpean

Lower
Porthpean

1

50

99   A   00   B   01   C   02   D   03   E   04   F

73

60

For full street detail of the
highlighted area see pages
114 and 115.

A3
1 TREMEWAN
2 TREVANION RD
3 ST ANNE'S RD
4 HEMBAL RD
5 HEMBAL CL
6 THE GREEN
7 SOCOTRA DR
8 COOPERAGE GDNS

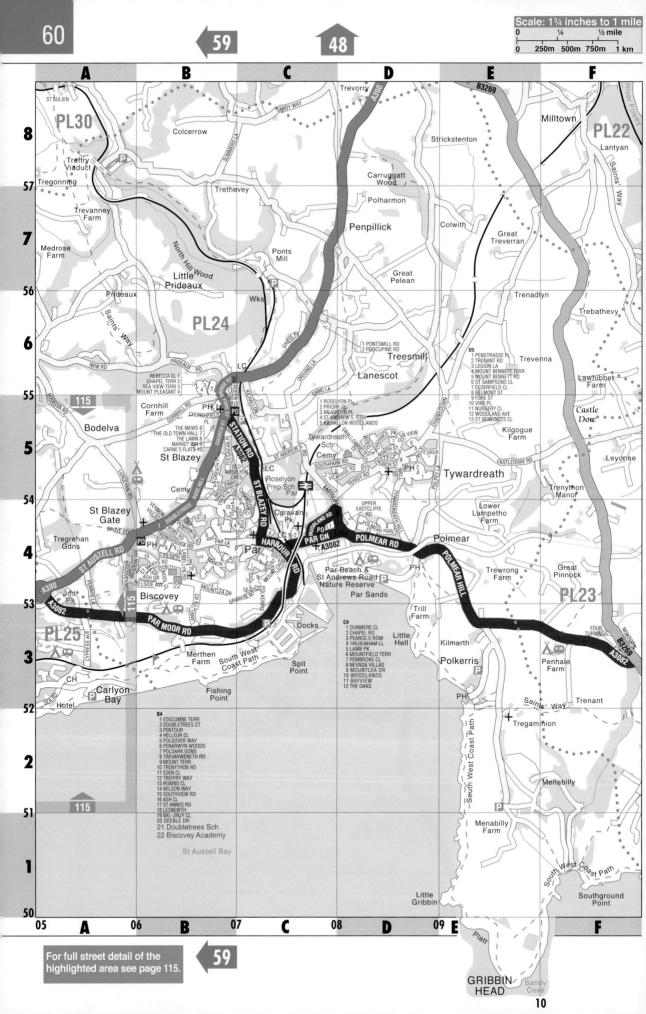

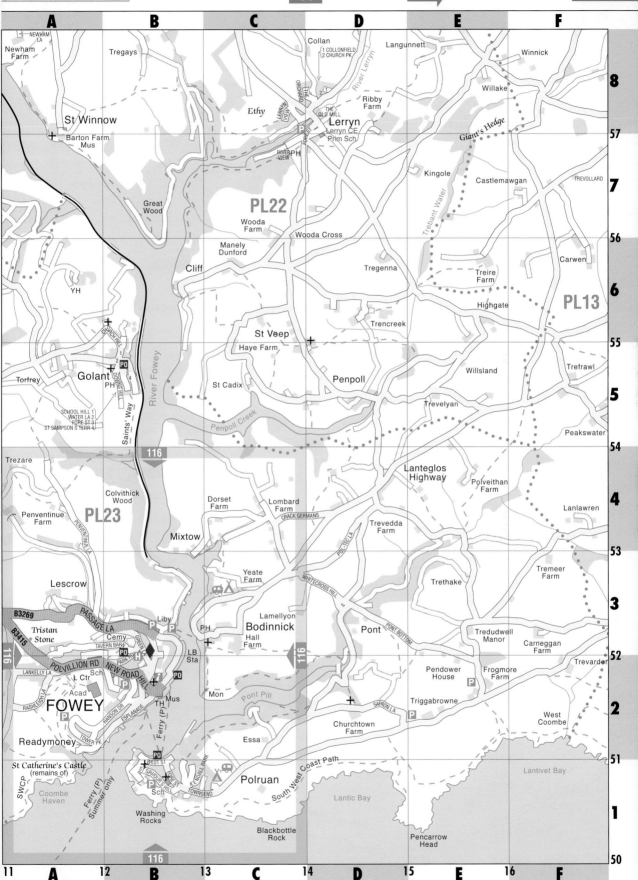

Scale: 1¾ inches to 1 mile

0 ¼ ½ mile
0 250m 500m 750m 1 km

49
62

A **B** **C** **D** **E** **F**

NEWHAM LA
Newham Farm
Tregays
Collan
1 COLLONFIELD
2 CHURCH PK
Langunnett
Winnick
8

St Winnow
Barton Farm Mus
Ethy
THE ORCHARD
LERRYN VIEW
THE OLD MILL
Lerryn
Lerryn CE Prim Sch
Ribby Farm
Willake
Giant's Hedge
57

RIVER VIEW PH
FORE ST
Kingole
Castlemawgan
TREVOLLARD
7

PL22
Great Wood
Wooda Farm
Wooda Cross
Trebant Water
PL13
56

Cliff
Manely Dunford
Tregenna
Treire Farm
Carwen
6

YH
St Veep
Haye Farm
Trencreek
Highgate
55

Torfrey
Golant
PO
PH
DOWN HILL
SCHOOL HILL 1
WATER LA 2
FORE ST 3
ST SAMPSON S TERR 4
St Cadix
Penpoll
Willsland
Trevelyan
Trefrawl
5

River Fowey
Penpoll Creek
Peakswater
54

Trezare
116
Lanteglos Highway
Polveithan Farm
Lanlawren
4

Penventinue Farm
PL23
Colvithick Wood
Dorset Farm
Lombard Farm
CRACK GERMANS
POLTELA
Trevedda Farm
Tremeer Farm
53

Lescrow
Mixtow
Yeate Farm
WHITECROSS HILL
Trethake
3

B3269
PASSAGE LA
Liby
PH
Lamellyon
Hall Farm
Bodinnick
Pont
PONT BOTTOM
Tredudwell Manor
Carneggan Farm
Trevarder
52

B3415
Tristan Stone
116
Cemy
TAVERN BARN
PO
PARK
GREEN ST
LB Sta
Mon
Pendower House
Frogmore Farm
West Coombe
2

POLVILLION RD
NEW ROAD HILL
Sch
PO
TH Mus
Ferry (P)
SAFRON LA
Triggabrowne
RASHLEIGH LA
LANKELLY LA
L Ctr
Acad
FOWEY
HANSON DR
ESPLANADE
Essa
Churchtown Farm

Readymoney
TOWER PK
Pont Pill
South West Coast Path
51

St Catherine's Castle (remains of)
SWCP
Coombe Haven
Ferry (P) Summer only
PO
BEST ST
ST SAVIOUR'S HILL
FORE ST
KENDALL PARK
TOWNSEND
Polruan
Lantic Bay
Lantivet Bay
1

Washing Rocks
Blackbottle Rock
Pencarrow Head
50

A 11 **B** 12 **C** 13 **D** 14 **E** 15 **F** 16

116

62

For full street detail of the highlighted area see page116.

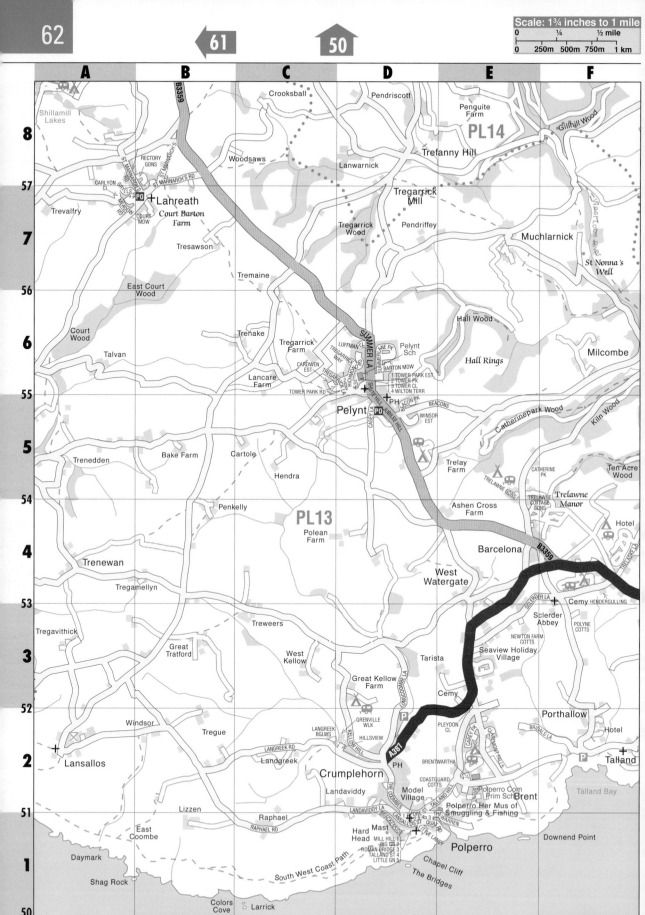

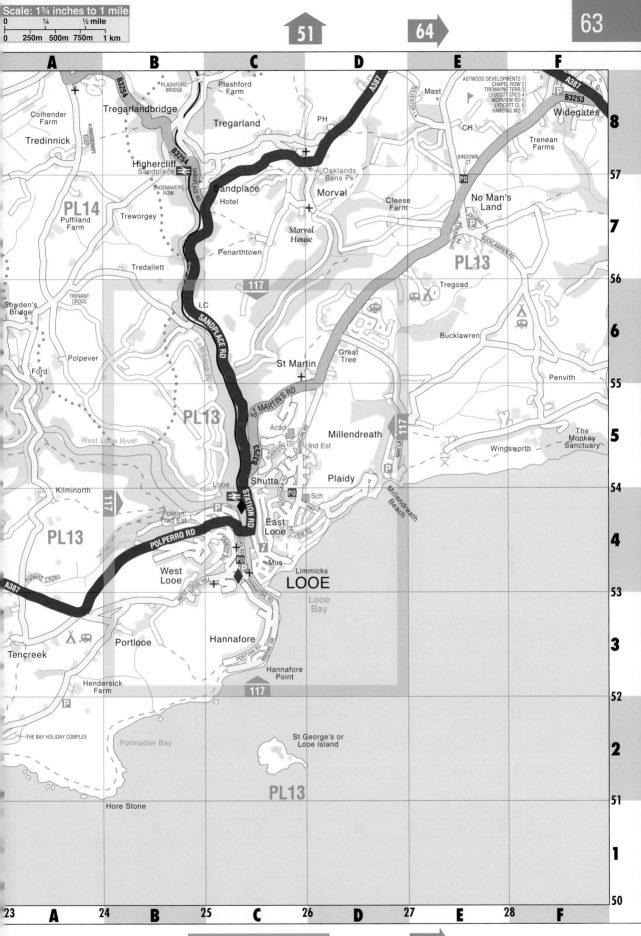

Scale: 1¾ inches to 1 mile

0   ¼   ½ mile
0 250m 500m 750m 1 km

A B C D E F

Colhender Farm

Tredinnick

Tregarlandbridge

Plashford Bridge

Plashford Farm

Tregarland

B3254

PH

Mast

ASTWOOD DEVELOPMENTS 1
CHAPEL ROW 2
TREMAYNE TERR 3
LYDCOTT CRES 4
MORVIEW RD 5
LYDCOTT CL 6
HARDING MD 7

A387

B3253

Widegates

8

Highercliff
Sandplace

B3254

Sandplace

Hotel

Oaklands Bsns Pk

Morval

CH

BINDOWN CT

PO

Trenean Farms

57

PL14

Puffiland Farm

SHOEMAKERS ROW

Treworgey

No Man's Land

HOLLAND PK

P

7

Tredallett

Penarthtown

Morval House

Cleese Farm

SPRINGFIELD PK

BUCKLAWREN RD

PL13

56

SANDPLACE RD

LC

117

BOLVENTOR LA

Tregoad

7

Sowden's Bridge

TRENANT CROSS

Polpever

East Looe River

St Martin

Great Tree

Bucklawren

Penvith

6

Ford

Kilminorth

West Looe River

ST MARTIN'S RD

Acad

Millendreath

117

MAY LA

Windsworth

The Monkey Sanctuary

55

117

PL13

Looe

B3253

SUNRISING EST

BARBICAN RD

Ind Est

P

Plaidy

Millendreath Beach

5

PL13

STATION RD

P

Shutta

BODIGGA RD

PO

Sch

BAY VIEW RD

MAY LA

54

POLPERRO RD

Polean Trad Est

QUAY RD

THE DOWNS

East Looe

i

Mus

Limmicks

LOOE

4

A387

PARKERS CROSS

West Looe

WEST LOOE HILL

PO

P

HANNAFORE RD

Looe Bay

53

Tencreek

Portlooe

Hannafore

PORTVAN RD

MARINE DR

Hannafore Point

3

Hendersick Farm

P

117

52

THE BAY HOLIDAY COMPLEX

Portnadler Bay

St George's or Looe Island

2

PL13

51

Hore Stone

50

23 A 24 B 25 C 26 D 27 E 28 F

For full street detail of the highlighted area see page 117.

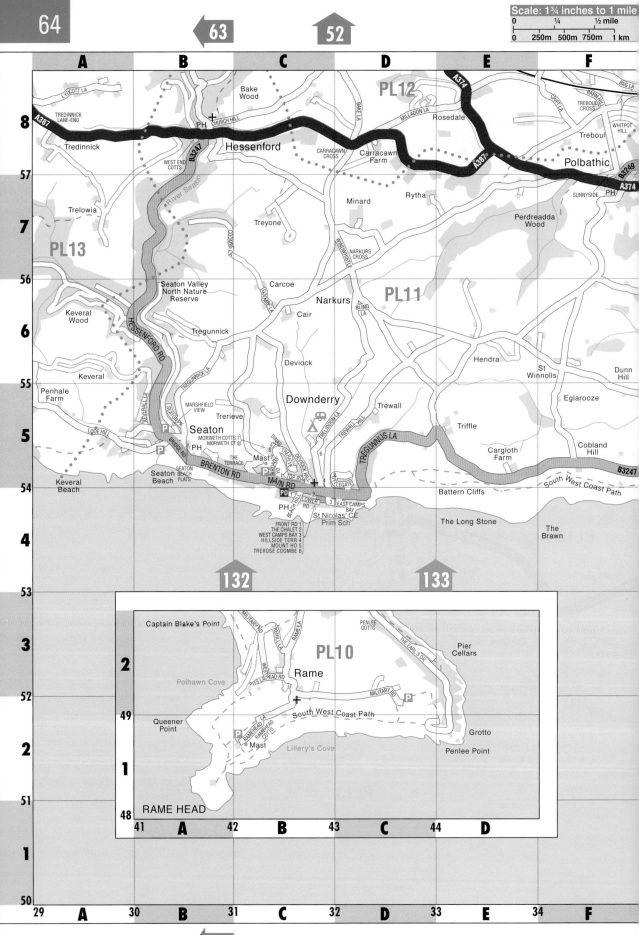

Scale: 1¾ inches to 1 mile

0   ¼   ½ mile
0   250m 500m 750m 1 km

A   B   C   D   E   F

LYDCOTT LA

BAG LA

BARN HILL

TREBOUL CROSS

WHITPOT HILL

A374

PL 12

A387

TREDINNICK LANE-END

8

Tredinnick

PH   CHURCH HILL

Bake Wood

BAKE LA

MILLADON LA

Rosedale

Treboul

57

B3247

WEST END COTTS

Hessenford

CARRACAWN CROSS

Carracawn Farm

A387

A374

CRIFT LA

Polbathic

B3249

B3247

River Seaton

SUNNYSIDE   PH   A374

Trelowia

Minard

Rytha

7

PL13

Treyone

Perdreadda Wood

56

COOMBE LA

Seaton Valley North Nature Reserve

Carcoe

Narkurs

NARKURS CROSS

WINDWHISTLE

Keveral Wood

COOMBE LA

Cair

BLIND LA

PL11

6

HESSENFORD RD

Tregunnick

Deviock

55

TREGUNNICK LA

Keveral

Downderry

Trewall

Hendra

St Winnolls

Dunn Hill

Penhale Farm

MARSHFIELD VIEW

Trerieve

TRELOONIN LA

TREWALL HILL

Eglarooze

Triffle

Cobland Hill

LOOE HILL

KEVERAL LA

SEATON PK

P   Seaton

MORWETH COTTS 7
MORWETH CT 8

TREFIEVE

DEVIOCK RD

TREGUNNUS LA

Cargloth Farm

B3247

5

BRIDGE RD

P   PH

THE TERRACE

Mast

DIMA CT

TOP RD

LEGATE

Battern Cliffs

South West Coast Path

Keveral Beach

Seaton Beach

SEATON BEACH FLATS

BRENTON RD

P

MAIN RD

54

PO

BEACH HILL

PH

LOWER RD

3

East Camps Bay

St Nicolas' CE Prim Sch

The Long Stone

The Brawn

FRONT RD 1
THE CHALET 2
WEST CAMPS BAY 3
HILLSIDE TERR 4
MOUNT HO 5
TREROSE COOMBE 6

4

53

132

133

Captain Blake's Point

MILITARY RD

RAME LA

PENLEE COTTG

THE EARL'S DR

Pier Cellars

2

PL10

PREHILL LA

Rame

WEST HEAD RD

Polhawn Cove

PITS LA

MILITARY RD

P

49

South West Coast Path

Queener Point

RAMEHEAD LA

P

Mast

RAMEHEAD COTTS

Lillery's Cove

Grotto

Penlee Point

2

1

51

48

RAME HEAD

41   A   42   B   43   C   44   D

1

50

29   A   30   B   31   C   32   D   33   E   34   F

Scale: 1¾ inches to 1 mile
0   ¼   ½ mile
0   250m 500m 750m 1 km

B3249
GALLERY LA
BAG LA
NEWPORT
FORE ST
TIDEFORD
CHURCH ST
St Germans
DOCTORS LA
LOVELY LA
Port Eliot House
OLD QUAY LA
QUARRY ST 1
QUARRY ST 2
MILL LA 4
THE SIR WILLIAMS 5
MOYLES ALMSHOUSES
St Germans
St Germans Prim Sch
FAIRFIELD
LOWER
FAIRFIELD
St Germans Quay
THE QUAY
QUAY RD

1 TIDDY CL
2 TREBOUL WAY
3 ELIOT DR
4 TREGALISTER GDNS
5 DUDDENBEAKE TERR
6 NUT TREE HILL

Grove

PL12

ELMGATE CROSSWAYS
Elm Gate
Mon
Wivelscombe

Trehan

Shillingham Manor

Ince Castle

KELLOW PK
Trewin House
Tredis
Dunn Hill
Tredrossel
PL11
Haye
HAY LA
Sheviock
B3247
HORSEPOOL LA
HORSEPOOL RD
GEORGES LA
CHURCH ROW
Sheviock Wood
Erth Barton
Erth Hill
Berry Down
St Germans or Lynher River
Black Rock

126

Bulland Quay
Clift Quay
West Clift

A374

Trewrickle Farm
The Beacon
TREWRICKLE LA
SAUNDERS LA
KIMBERLEY FOSTER CL 1
WEST LA 2
DAWNEY TERR 3
THE TERRACE 4
TREDIS VW 5
CROSS PK
SHEVIOCK LA
Crafthole
B3247
CAREW LA
COOMBE LA
PH
Cross
Hotel
TRETHILL LA
Trethill
CROOKEDOR LA
Screesdon Fort
ANTONY HILL
HOLLONG PK
PH
Antony
Antony CE VA Sch
ABBOTS RD
Cemy
Wolsdon House

Old Coastguard Cotts
VIEW LA
WHITSAND BAY VIEW
BURNS VIEW
FINNYGOOK LA
PH
Portwrinkle
CH
THE TERRACE
PO
Hotel
Trethill Cliffs
Blerrick
B3247
DANGER AREA
Tregantle Fort
DANGER AREA
Mast Ranges
Lower Tregantle
CLAMPIT LA
P

St Johns LA
JACK'S LA
PH
St John
B3247

Tregantle Cliff
P
Higher Tregantle Farm
Freathy
PL10
WITHNOE LA
BRAKE LA
Withnoe

132

Sharrow Point
WITHNOE TERR
CLIFF
Tregonhawke
MILITARY RD
Mon

Whitsand Bay

For full street detail of the highlighted area see pages 126 and 132.

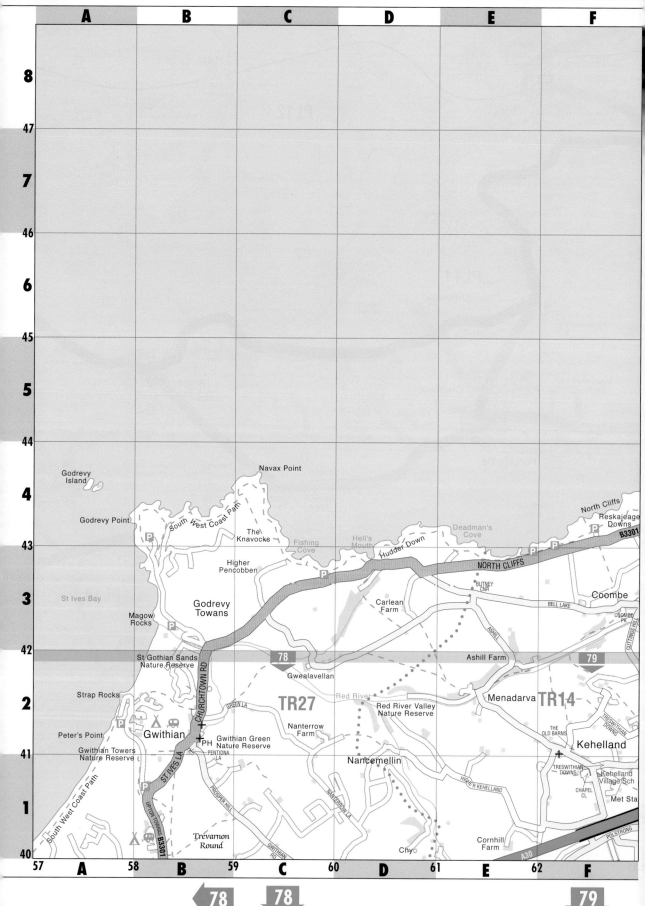

Scale: 1¾ inches to 1 mile

0   ¼   ½ mile

0 250m 500m 750m 1 km

A   **B**   **C**   **D**   **E**   **F**

48

47

7

46

6

45

5

44

4   Godrevy Island

Navax Point

North Cliffs
Reskajeage Downs

Godrevy Point

South West Coast Path

The Knavocks

Fishing Cove

Hell's Mouth

Deadman's Cove

B3301

43

St Ives Bay

Higher Pencobben

Hudder Down

NORTH CLIFFS

Coombe

3   Magow Rocks

Godrevy Towans

Carlean Farm

BUTNEY CNR

BELL LAKE

COOMBE PK

CUTTINGS HILL

42   St Gothian Sands Nature Reserve

78

Gwealavellan

Ashill Farm

ASHILL

79

Strap Rocks

CHURCHTOWN RD

GREEN LA

TR27

Red River

Red River Valley Nature Reserve

Menadarva   TR14

TRESWITHIAN DOWNS

2

Peter's Point

Gwithian

ST IVES LA

PH

Gwithian Green Nature Reserve

Nanterrow Farm

THE OLD BARNS

Kehelland

TRESWITHIAN DOWNS

41

Gwithian Towers Nature Reserve

PENTIDNA LA

PROSPER HILL

NANTERROW LA

Nancemellin

HIGHER KEHELLAND

CHAPEL CL

Kehelland Village Sch

Met Sta

1

South West Coast Path

UPTON TOWANS B3301

GWITHIAN RD

Trevarnon Round

Chyo

Cornhill Farm

A30

POLSTRONG

40

57   **A**   58   **B**   59   **C**   60   **D**   61   **E**   62   **F**

78   78   79

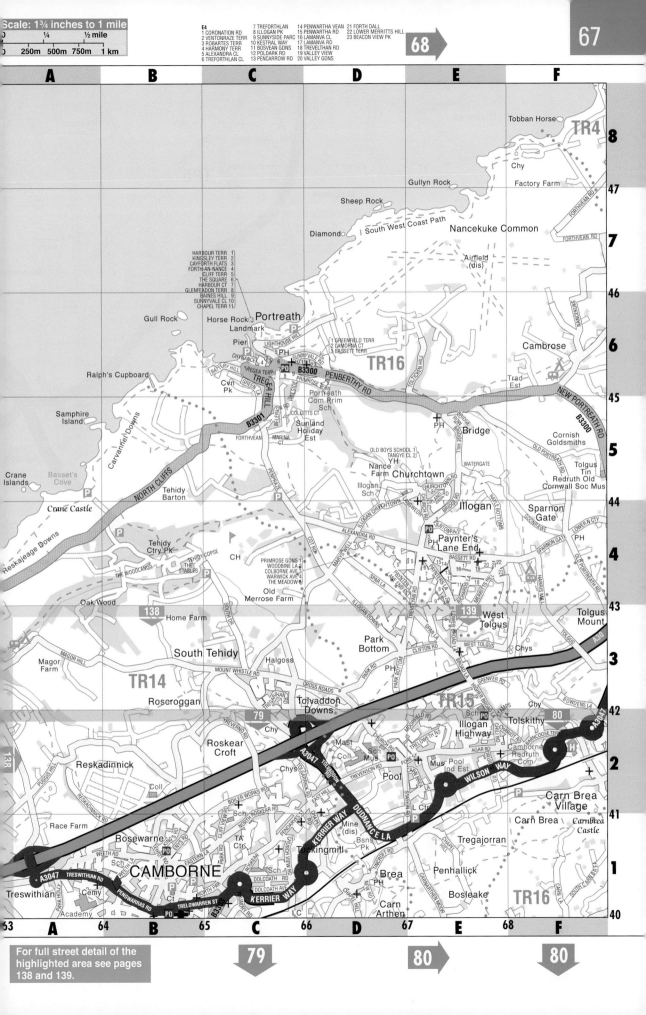

E4
1 CORONATION RD
2 VENTONRAZE TERR
3 ROBARTES TERR
4 HARMONY TERR
5 ALEXANDRA CL
6 TREFORTHLAN CL
7 TREFORTHLAN
8 ILLOGAN PK
9 SUNNYSIDE PARC
10 KESTRAL WAY
11 BOSVEAN GDNS
12 POLDARK RD
13 PENCARROW RD
14 PENWARTHA VEAN
15 PENWARTHA RD
16 LAMANVA CL
17 LAMANVA RD
18 TREVELTHAN RD
19 VALLEY VIEW
20 VALLEY GDNS
21 FORTH DALL
22 LOWER MERRITTS HILL
23 BEACON VIEW PK

A **B** **C** **D** **E** **F**

Tobban Horse

TR4

8

Chy

Factory Farm

Gullyn Rock

47

Sheep Rock

7

Diamond

South West Coast Path

Nancekuke Common

Airfield
(dis)

46

HARBOUR TERR 1
KINGSLEY TERR 2
CAYFORTH FLATS 3
FORTH-AN-NANCE 4
CLIFF TERR 5
THE SQUARE 6
HARBOUR CT 7
GLENFEADON TERR 8
BAINES HILL 9
SUNNYVALE CL 10
CHAPEL TERR 11

Gull Rock

Horse Rock
Landmark

Portreath

Cambrose

6

Pier

1 GREENFIELD TERR
2 LAMORNA CT
3 BASSETT TERR

TR16

Ralph's Cupboard

PO
B3300

PENBERTHY RD

Trad
Est

45

Samphire
Island

B3301

FORTHVEAN

Portreath
Com Prim
Sch

PH

Bridge

Cornish
Goldsmiths

NEW PORTREATH RD
B3300

Crane
Islands

Basset's
Cove

NORTH CLIFFS

Tehidy
Barton

Colletts Ct

Sunland Holiday
Est

OLD BOYS SCHOOL 1
TANGYE CL 2
YH
Nance
Farm

Churchtown

Illogan
Sch

Redruth Old
Cornwall Soc Mus

Tolgus
Tin

5

Crane Castle

Tehidy
Ctry Pk

CH

Old
Merrose Farm

Illogan Churchtown

PH

Illogan

Sparnon
Gate

44

Oak Wood

Tehidy
Copse
THE
STABLES
THE WOODLANDS

PRIMROSE GDNS 1
WOODBINE LA 2
COLBORNE AVE 3
WARWICK AVE 4
THE MEADOW 5

ALEXANDRA RD

Paynter's
Lane End

PH

4

138

Home Farm

South Tehidy

TR14

Magor
Farm

Roscroggan

Halgoss

Park
Bottom

West
Tolgus

139

West Tolgus

PH

Tolgus
Mount

43

MOUNT WHISTLE RD

CROSS ROADS

PH

A30

3

79

Tolvaddon
Downs

TR15

Illogan
Highway

Tolskithy

80

A3047

42

Reskadinnick

Roskear
Croft

A3047

Mast
Coll

Pool

Camborne
Redruth
Com

2

WILSON WAY

Carn Brea
Village

41

Race Farm

Rosewarne

KERRIER WAY

DUDNANCE LA

Mine
(dis)

Tregajorran

Carn Brea

Carnbrea
Castle

1

Treswithian

A3047 TRESWITHIAN RD

CAMBORNE

Cemy

Academy

TRELOWARREN ST

KERRIER WAY

DOLCOATH RD

Tuckingmill

Penhallick

Bosleake

TR16

Brea
PH

Carn
Arthen

A 63 **B** 64 **C** 65 **D** 66 **E** 67 **F** 68

40

For full street detail of the
highlighted area see pages
138 and 139.

79

80

80

67 54

Scale: 1¾ inches to 1 mile

0 ¼ ½ mile
0 250m 500m 750m 1 km

8
Chapel Porth
Goonvrea
B3277
ALBANY CL
GOONOWN RD
KERENSA GDNS
CHIVERTON GREENACRES
ALMA CL
1 BUTSON PK
2 HEAD LA
Goonbell
Mithian Downs

49
Shaft (dis)
Chy
Mingoose
Hurlingbarrow Ind Est
WHEAL BUTSON RD
PENWINNICK RD
TR5
Whitestreet

7
South West Coast Path
1 EASTCLIFF AVE NO 1
2 EASTCLIFF AVENUE NO 2
3 EASTCLIFF AVE NO 3
4 LOWER EASTCLIFF
5 GOYNE S FIELD
6 SEASPRAY LEISURE FLATS
7 KINGSLEY COVE
8 OCEAN CT
9 SANDY COVE TRAVEL LODGE
TOWAN RD
Towan Cross
PH
Silverwell Farm
Silverwel

48
Porth Towan
West WEST BEACH RD
WEST CLIFF
BEACH RD
SANDY RD
COAST RD
SOUTH TOWAN
ATLANTIC WAY
Trevissick Farm
Banns
BANNS RD
PENHALL
GOVER HILL
Gover Farm
PH
Works

PO
Porthtowan
Chy
Chys
Mount Hawke
ROPE WLK
CORE
SHORT CROSS RD
PODDAS RD
1 HENLEY CRES
2 HENLEY DR
3 HENLEY CL
4 SHORT CROSS MEWS
5 ALEXANDRA TERR
6 PENHALLOW CL
7 TRENITHICK MDW
8 GOVER CL
9 HIGH FIELD RD
10 MARSHALLEN RD
11 CHURCH RD
12 CHARLOTTE CL
13 ELLEN CL
Penhallow Farm
TR4

6
1 BEACHSIDE CT
2 BEACHVIEW FLATS
3 TYWARBHALE WAY
4 SOUTH VIEW PARC
ROSE HILL
PORTHVEAN
FORTHVEAN CRES
CHAPEL HILL
Chy
Mount Hawke Academy
GLENDA
Chy
Cemy
Goosewartha Farm
Two Burrows
CHIVERTON CROSS
THE OLD CHAPEL
B3277
A3075
A30
A390
Three Burrows

47
Wheal Bassett Farm
NANGE KUKE
Manor Parsley
Menagissey
1 HIGHVIEW CRES
2 HIGHVIEW
3 SYMONDS CL
4 PASSMORE CL
Blackwater
PO

5
MILE HILL
Laity Moor
Mawla
Skinners Bottom
Blackwater Prim Sch
PH
NORTH HILL
WHEAL BUSY LA
THE TERRACE

46
CHAPEL HILL
Stencoose
1 GWEL GWARTHE
2 PARK LEDER
3 TREVEN NOWETH
4 PRAS COTH
Boscawen Farm
STATION RD
Carnhot

4
Forge
LAITY MOOR
OLD TRAM RD
Wheal Plenty
Chy
Wheal Busy
BUCKINGHAM NIP 1
SERGEANTS HILL 2
Chacewater
WHEAL BUSY LA
HIGH ST

45
Sinns Barton
LITTLE SINNS
SINNS COMMON
GREEN LA
Chy
WHITE CROSS
Chys
Hallenbeagle
1 SCORIA CL
2 RADNOR RD
Salem
Cox Hill
CHURCH HILL

3
Parc Erissey
Parc Erissey Ind Est
TR16
North Downs
Wheal Rose
PH
Motel
Scorrier
Chys
Creegbrawse

44
B3300
NEW PORTREATH RD
North Country
RADNOR RD
140
B3298
SCORRIER RD
A3047
Scorrier House
Killifreth Farm
Todpool
BORLASE A N

2
BASSETT RD
Treleigh
LC
Sch
A3047
Highway
TRESKERBY
SCORRIER HOUSE WORKSHOPS
Tregullow
WHEAL GORLAND RD 1
CHYROSE RD 2
FORTH-AN-PRAZE 3
TRENANT 5
BALCOATH 4
CHAPEL ST 6
BUCKINGHAM TERR 7
TELEGRAPH ST 8
MARKET SQ 9
FORE ST 10
WEST END 11
CAREW RD 12
FORTH-AN-EGLOS 13
BURNWITHIAN TERR 14
1 TELEGRAPH HILL
2 NORTHFIELD CL
3 MILLS ST
4 SCORRIER ST
5 CHURCH ST
6 CAREW CL
7 BOSAWNA EL
8 MILLS GDNS

43
TR15
SANDY LA
Mount Ambrose
Treskerby
Tolgullow
POLDICE TERR
Goon Gumpas
HIGHER GOONGUMPAS LA
LOWER GOONGUMPAS LA

1
TRELEIGH
PO
STRAWBERRY
Mast
REDRUTH
Trefula
Vogue
PH
St Day
VICARAGE HILL
Crofthandy
Chy

42
Coll
TOLGUS HILL
FORDS ROW
Sch
Cemy
Chy
Ninnis
St Day
Carharrack Com Sch
Ghys

Redruth

For full street detail of the highlighted area see page 140.

67 80 81

TR5

TR4

TR1

TR3

TR16

A3
1 JAKE'S LA
2 THE SQUARE
3 RIVERSIDE
4 EAST BRIDGE
5 LOWER MDW
6 ROSELAND CRES
7 BOSCAWEN RD
8 THE RETREAT

Park Hoskyn
Penwartha House
Higher Penwartha
Silverwell
Higher Callestick Farm
Callestick Vean
Chynhale
Tresawsen
Killivose
Ninnes
Nanteague Farm
Allet
Trevellan Farm
Pendale
Pendown
Wind Farm
Chybucca
Four Burrows
Wind Farm
Garvinack
Choon
Roseworthy
Shortlanesend Com Prim Sch
Shortlanesend
Bussavean
Roscarnick Farm
Silver Valley
Causilgey
Nancewrath
Tregavethan Manor
Trevaskis
Little Croft West
Treworder
Airfield
Croft West
Three Burrows
Penstraze Bsns Ctr
River Kenwyn
Boscolla
New Mills
New Mills
West Langarth
Governs
Penstraze
Threemilestone Ret Pk
Langarth
Wren Ind Est
Duchy
Truro
Royal Cornwall
Jolly's Bottom
Green Bottom
Threemilestone Ind Est
Threemilestone
Treliske Ind Est
Highertown
Saveock
Truro Bsns Pk
Truro L Ctr
Besore
Gloweth
Highertown
Newbridge
Kerley Downs
Temperrow
Penweathers
Hugus
Hugus Farm
Goodern Manor Farm
Carrine Common
Cusveorth Coombes
Rossventon
Baldhu
Mine (dis)
Sparnock Farm
Kea
Poldice Valley
Hale Mills
Twelveheads
Wheal Baddon
Killiow
THE CARRIAGE HO

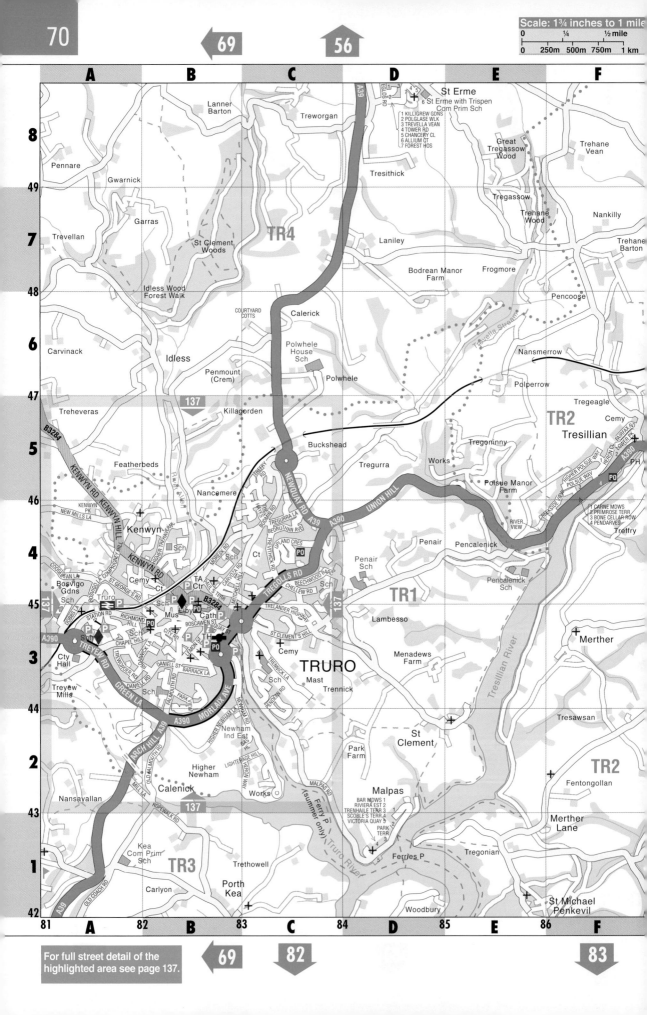

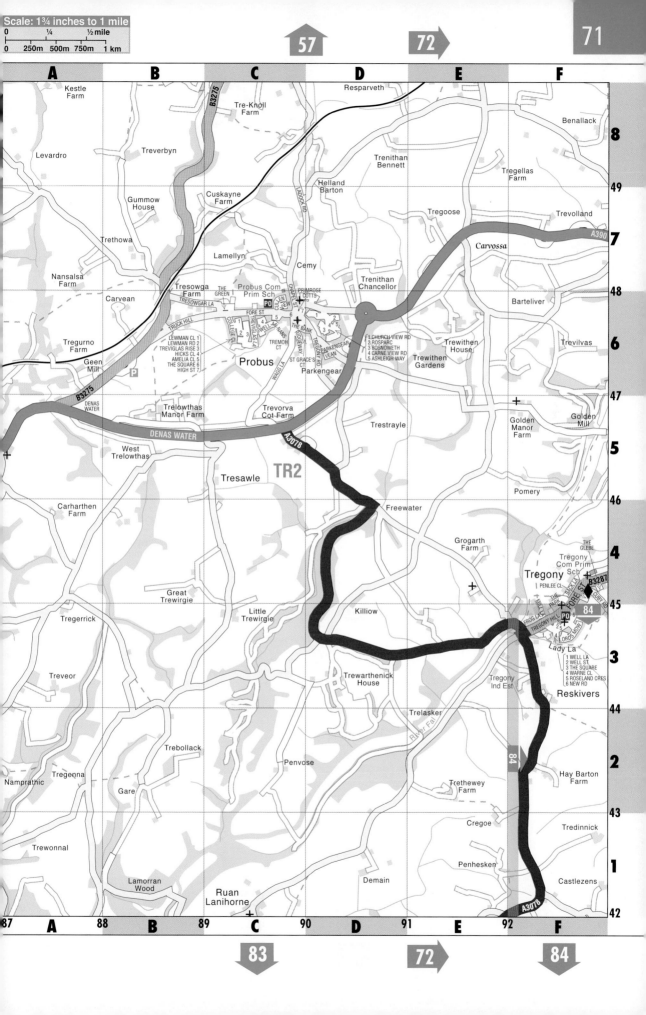

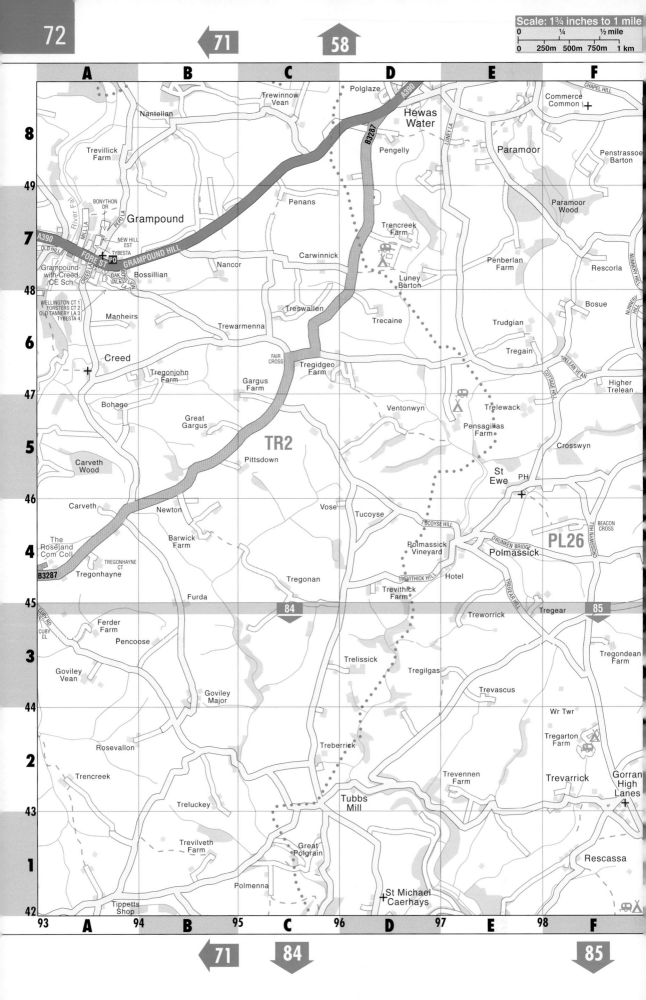

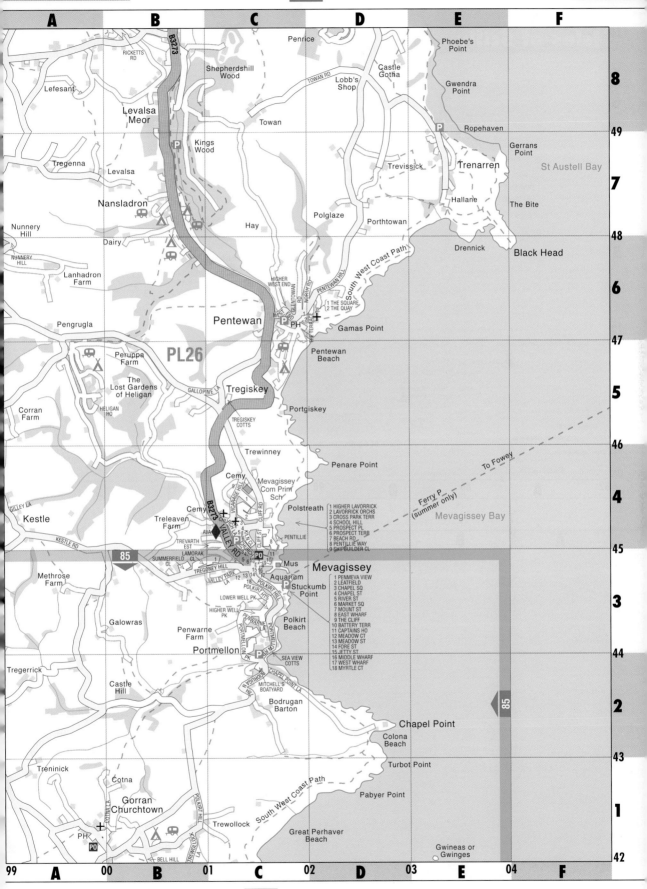

Scale: 1¾ inches to 1 mile
0   ¼   ½ mile
0 250m 500m 750m 1 km

A   **B**   **C**   **D**   **E**   **F**

Penrice
Lefesant
RICKETTS RD
Levalsa Meor
Shepherdshill Wood
Castle Gotha
Phoebe's Point
Towan
Tregenna
Kings Wood
Lobb's Shop
TOWAN RD
Gwendra Point
Ropehaven
Levalsa
Trevissick
Trenarren
Gerrans Point
St Austell Bay
Nansladron
Hay
Polglaze
Hallane
The Bite
Nunnery Hill
Dairy
Porthtowan
Drennick
Black Head
NUNNERY HILL
Lanhadron Farm
HIGHER WEST END
South West Coast Path
Pengrugla
Pentewan
PH
Gamas Point
1 THE SQUARE
2 THE QUAY
PL26
Peruppa Farm
The Lost Gardens of Heligan
Pentewan Beach
GALLOPINE
Tregiskey
HELIGAN HO
Corran Farm
Portgiskey
TREGISKEY COTTS
Trewinney
Penare Point
To Fowey
Kestle
Cemy
Mevagissey Com Prim Sch
Polstreath
1 HIGHER LAVORRICK
2 LAVORRICK ORCHS
3 CROSS PARK TERR
4 SCHOOL HILL
5 PROSPECT PL
6 PROSPECT TERR
7 BEACH RD
8 PENTILLIE WAY
9 SHIPBUILDER CL
Ferry P (summer only)
Mevagissey Bay
GILLEY LA
Cemy
Treleaven Farm
Pentillie
B3273
VALLEY RD
VICARAGE HILL
CLIFF RD
KESTLE RD
TREVARTH EST
LAMORAK CL
85
SUMMERFIELD CL
TREGONEY HILL
VALLEY PARK LA
Mevagissey
1 PENMEVA VIEW
2 LEATFIELD
3 CHAPEL SQ
4 CHAPEL ST
5 RIVER ST
6 MARKET SQ
7 MOUNT ST
8 EAST WHARF
9 THE CLIFF
10 BATTERY TERR
11 CAPTAINS HO
12 MEADOW CT
13 MEADOW ST
14 FORE ST
15 JETTY ST
16 MIDDLE WHARF
17 WEST WHARF
18 MYRTLE CT
Mus
Aquarium
Stuckumb Point
Methrose Farm
Galowras
LOWER WELL PK
HIGHER WELL PK
Penwarne Farm
PENWARNE LA
Polkirt Beach
PORTMELLON PK
Portmellon
SEA VIEW COTTS
85
POLKIRT HTS
Tregerrick
Castle Hill
BODRUGAN HILL
CHAPEL POINT LA
MITCHELL'S BOATYARD
Bodrugan Barton
Chapel Point
Colona Beach
Treninick
Cotna
Turbot Point
Gorran Churchtown
POLKIRT HILL
COTNA LA
PH
PO
Trewollock
South West Coast Path
Pabyer Point
BELL HILL
Great Perhaver Beach
Gwineas or Gwinges

49
8
7
48
6
47
5
46
4
45
3
44
2
43
1
42

99   A   00   B   01   C   02   D   03   E   04   F

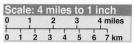

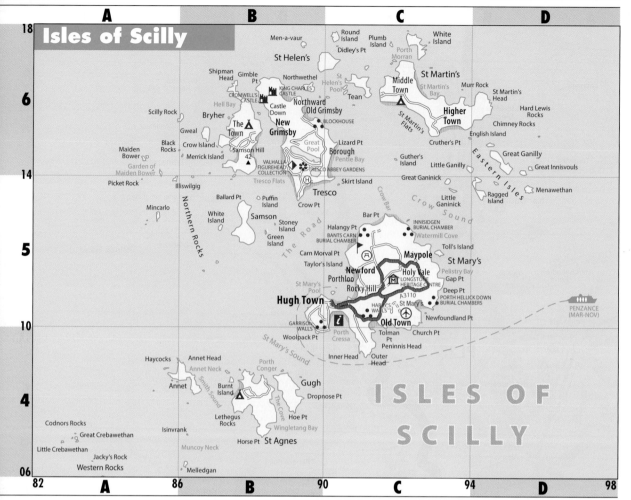

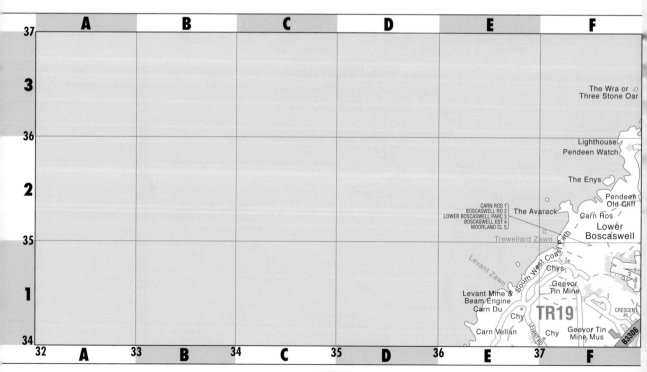

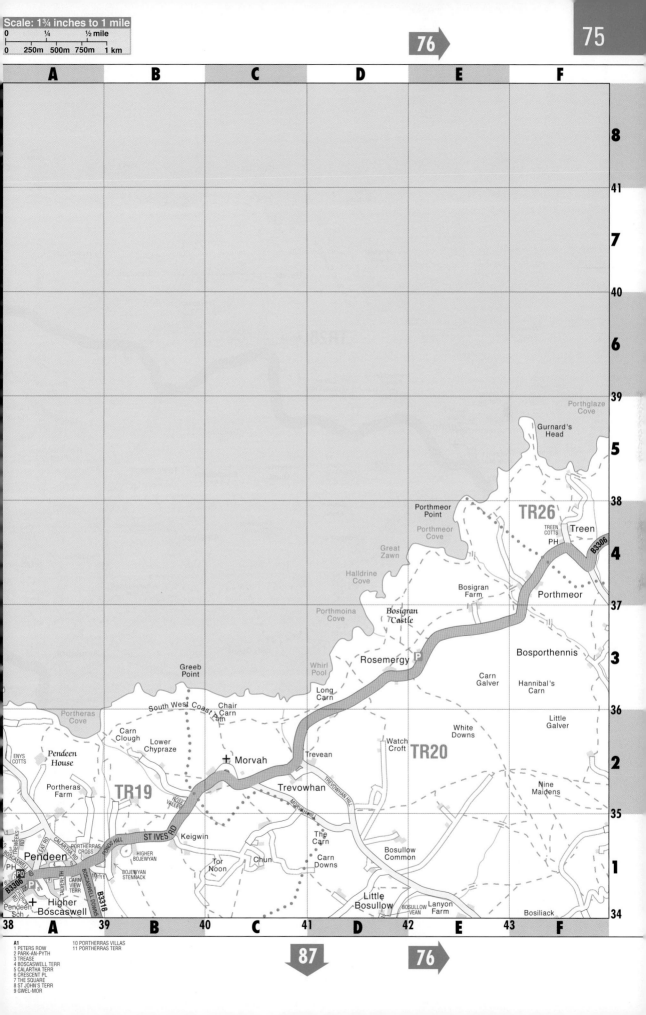

A   B   C   D   E   F

8

41

7

40

6

39

Porthglaze
Cove

Gurnard's
Head

5

Porthmeor
Point

TR26

38

Porthmeor
Cove

TREEN
COTTS   Treen

PH   B3306   4

Great
Zawn

Halldrine
Cove

Bosigran
Farm

Porthmeor

37

Porthmoina
Cove

Bosigran
Castle

Bosporthennis

3

Whirl
Pool

Rosemergy   P

Carn
Galver

Hannibal's
Carn

Greeb
Point

Long Carn

Little
Galver

36

South West Coast Path

Chair
Carn

Carn
Clough

White
Downs

2

Porthmeras
Cove

Lower
Chypraze

Watch
Croft

TR20

ENYS
COTTS

Pendeen
House

Morvah

Trevean

Nine
Maidens

TR19

Porthmeras
Farm

Trevowhan

35

St IVES RD

ROSE
VALLEY

MORVAH HILL

TREVOWHAN HILL

Keigwin

The
Carn

Bosullow
Common

PENDEEN CROSS
PONDS HILL

HIGHER
BOJEWYAN

Tor
Noon

Chun

Carn
Downs

Pendeen

PO

Bosullow
Vean   Lanyon
Farm

1

PH

BOJEWYAN
STENNACK

Little
Bosullow

Bosiliack

B3306
P

Higher
Boscaswell

B3318

Pendeen
Sch

34

38   A   39   B   40   C   41   D   42   E   43   F

A1
1 PETERS ROW
2 PARK-AN-PYTH
3 TREASE
4 BOSCASWELL TERR
5 CALARTHA TERR
6 CRESCENT PL
7 THE SQUARE
8 ST JOHN'S TERR
9 GWEL-MOR
10 PORTHERRAS VILLAS
11 PORTHERRAS TERR

Scale: 1¾ inches to 1 mile

0   ¼   ½ mile
0 250m 500m 750m 1 km

A **B** **C** **D** **E** **F**

8

41

Hor Point

Carn Naun Point

Pen Enys Point

7

The Carracks

Trowan

Mussel Point

Treval gan

TROWAN LA

Wicca Pool

Treveal

Chy

South West Coast Path

40

6

Zennor Head

Porthzennor Cove

TR26

Wicca

Trevessa Farm

Trendrine Farm

B3306

Chys

Pendour Cove

Tremedda Farm

Lower Tregerthen

Rosewall Hill

39

Portglaze Cove

Carn Cobba

Giant's Rock

Zennor

Trendrine Hill

TOWEDNACK RD

Culver House

5

Carnelloe Farm

PH

Wayside Folk Mus.

Logan Stone

Sperris Quoit

Beagletodn Downs

Towednack

THE OLD VICARAGE

Breja Farm

High Bussow Farm

Trewey

38

Poniou

Kerrowe Farm

Zennor Quoit

Amalveor Downs

Amalveor

Chy

HOLMANS MOOR RD

4

B3306

Boswednack

Pennance

TREWEY HILL

Foage Farm

Penderleath

Chy

37

Embla

Amalwhidden Farm

Trewey Common

Mill Downs

Nancledra Prim Sch

3

Higher Kerrowe

Lady Downs

Georgia Hill

Amalebra

B3311

Georgia

CHYPONS EST

36

Try Valley

Conquer Downs

Chy

Nancledra

BALDHU ROW

THE FIELD

2

Mulfra Hill

Carnaquidden Downs

TR20

Borea

NEW ROW

NANCLEDRA HILL

NANCLEDRA BOTTOMS

Bodrifty

Mulfra Quoit

Trye Farm

Trenowin Downs

Castle-an-Dinas

35

Tredinnick

Mulfra

Carnaquidden Farm

Chysauster Ancient Village

Settlement

Roger's Tower

Trenowin Farm

1

TREDINNICK COTTS

Boskednan

Bosulval

Chysauster

Gulval Downs

B3311

Castle Gate

Lower Ninnes

CHYSAUSTER RD

Carfury

Trythall Prim Sch

Newmill

Boscreege Farm

Hellangove Farm

34

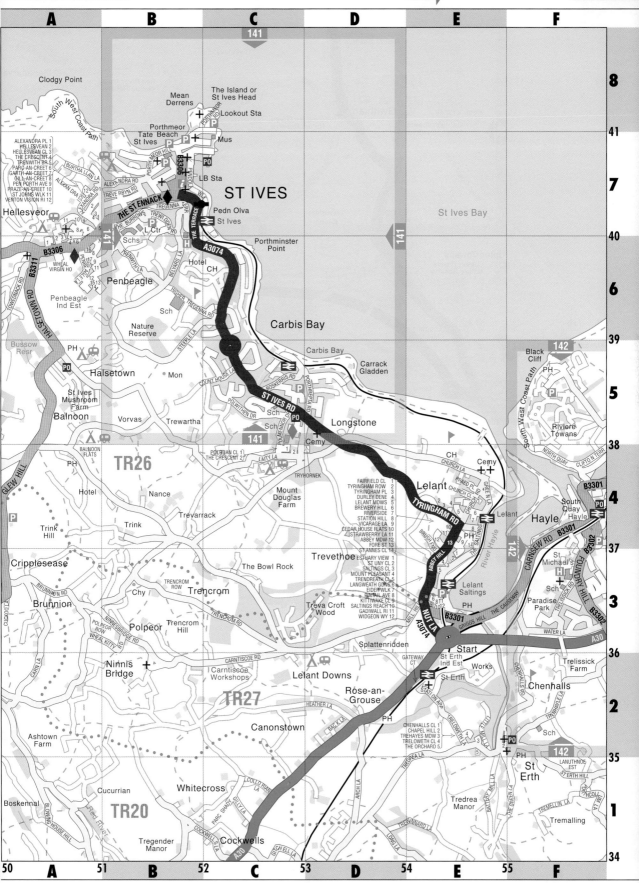

A   B   C   D   E   F

8
41
7
40
6
39
5
38
4
37
3
36
2
35
1
34

ALEXANDRA PL 1
HELLESVEAN 2
HELLESVEAN CL 3
THE CRESCENT 4
TRENWITH BR 5
PARC-AN-CREET 6
GARTH-AN-CREET 7
GILL-AN-CREET 8
PEN PORTH AVE 9
PRAZE-AN-CREET 10
ST JOHNS WLK 11
VENTON VISION RI 12

Clodgy Point
South West Coast Path
Hellesveor

The Island or
St Ives Head
Mean
Derrens
Lookout Sta
Porthmeor
Tate Beach
St Ives
Mus
LB Sta

ST IVES

St Ives Bay

Pedn Olva
St Ives
Porthminster
Point

Wheal
Virgin Ho
Penbeagle
Hotel
CH
Penbeagle
Ind Est

Carbis Bay

Carbis Bay
Carrack
Gladden

Black
Cliff
Riviere
Towans
South West Coast Path

Bussow
Resr
Halsetown
St Ives
Mushroom
Farm
Balnoon
Vorvas
Trewartha
Mon
Nature
Reserve
Sch
St IVES RD
Longstone
Cemy

142
North Quay
South
Quay Hayle
Hayle

FAIRFIELD CL 1
TYRINGHAM ROW 2
TYRINGHAM PL 3
DURLEY DENE 4
LELANT MDWS 5
BREWERY HILL 6
RIVERSIDE 7
STATION HILL 8
VICARAGE LA 9
CEDAR HOUSE FLATS 10
STRAWBERRY LA 11
ABBEY MDW 12
FORE ST 13
ST ANNES CL 14

Lelant
Church La
Cemy
CH
TYRINGHAM RD
St
Michael's
Sch
Paradise
Park

Trink
Hill
Balnoon
Flats
TR26
Hotel
Nance
Trevarrack
Trink
Mount
Douglas
Farm
Tryhornek
Trevethoe

ESTUARY VIEW 1
ST UNY CL 2
SALTINGS CL 3
MOUNT PLEASANT 4
TRENDREATH CL 5
LANGWEATH GDNS 6
EIDER WLK 7
PINTAIL AVE 8
KITTIWAKE CL 9
SALTINGS REACH 10
GADIWALL RI 11
WIDGEON WY 12

Lelant
Saltings
Cripplesease
Brunnion
Chy
Trencrom
Row
Trencrom
Polpeor
Trencrom
Hill
The Bowl Rock
Treva Croft
Wood
Splattenridden
Start
St Erth
Ind Est
Works
Chenhalls
Trelissick
Farm

Ninnis
Bridge
Carntiscoe
Workshops
Lelant Downs
Gateway
Ct
St Erth
Rose-an-
Grouse
TR27
Heather La
Back La
PH

CHENHALLS CL 1
CHAPEL HILL 2
TREHAYES MDW 3
TRELOWETH CL 4
THE ORCHARD 5

St
Erth

Ashtown
Farm
Canonstown
Tredrea
Manor
Tremalling

Boskennal
Cucurrian
Whitecross
TR20
Tregender
Manor
Cockwells

89 ↓

78 →

For full street detail of the
highlighted area see pages
141 and 142.

A6
1 CHYANDOUR CL
2 HELLESVEAN
3 HELLESVEAN CL
4 PARC-AN-STAMPS
5 CROWS-AN-EGLOS
6 PARC-AN-FORTH
7 PENBEAGLE TERR
8 PENBEAGLE CRES
9 CORVA RD
10 PRIORS CL
11 CORVA CL
12 PORTHIA RD
13 CARNSTABBA RD
14 ALAN HARVEY CL
15 JUBILEE CT
16 TINNERS WAY
17 PENBEAGLE CL

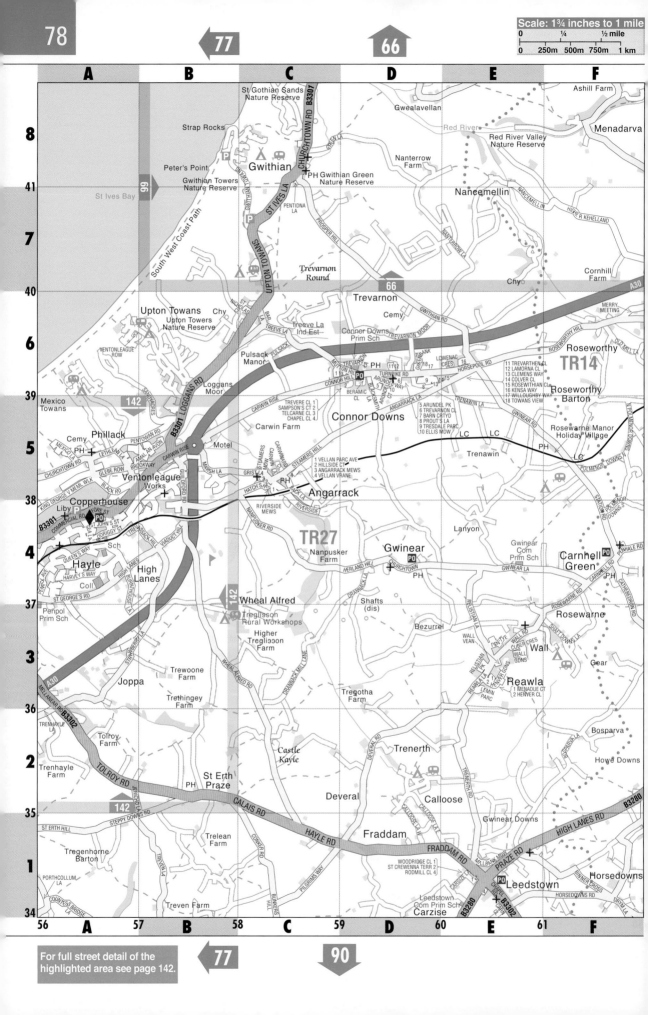

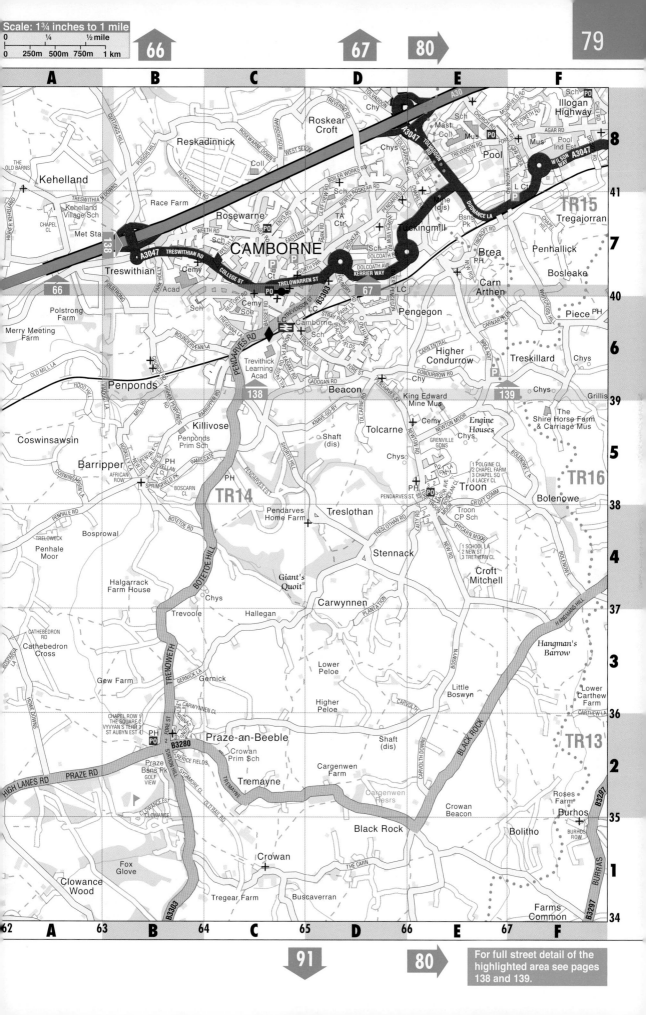

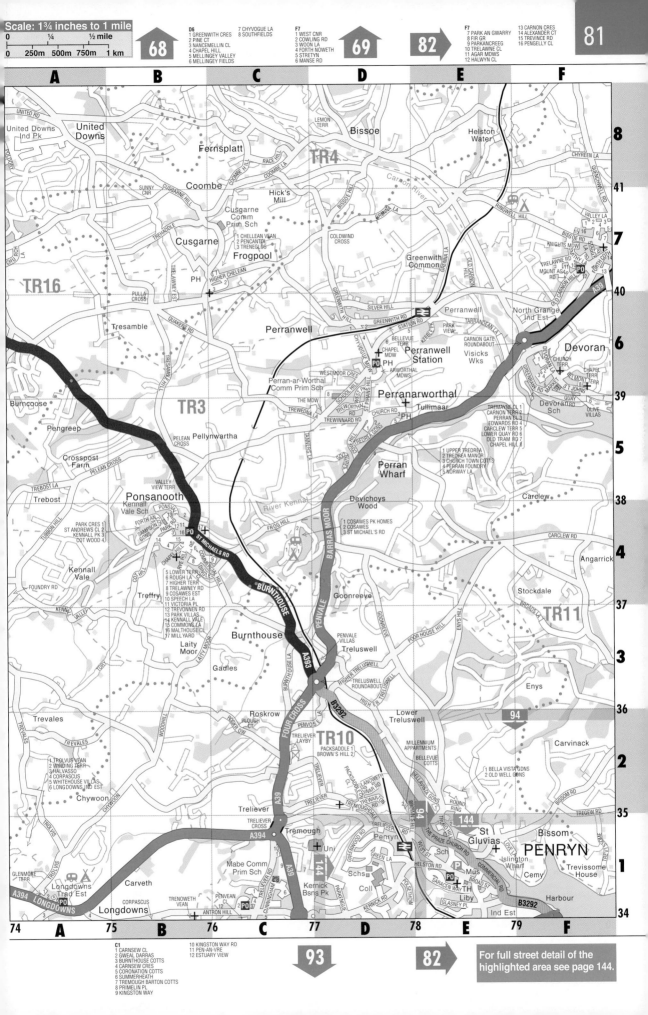

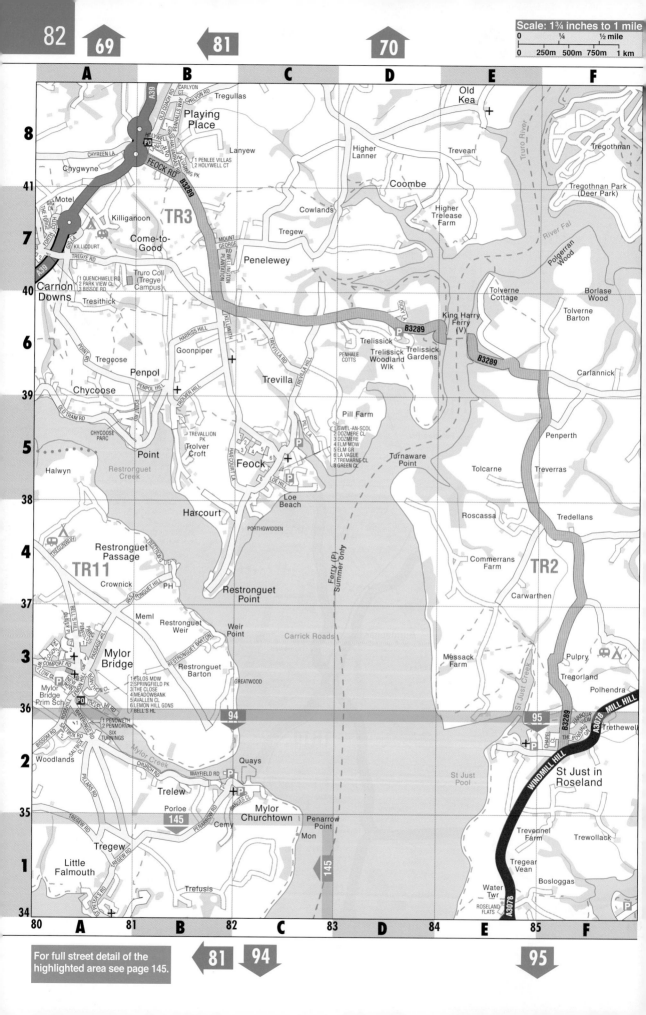

A B C D E F

Lamorran

Ruan
Lanihorne

PH

Tregongon

Treswithian

A3078

Nancarrow

Trethella

Tregisswyn

Penkevel

Chy

Trelonk

Trolonk

Treviles

Ardevora
Veor

Treworga

Hotel

Treburthes

River Fal

Ardevora

Veryan
Green

Coronation
Terr

THE SQUARE 1
BACK LA 2
THE HOMEYARD HOMES 3
PARK AN DREAS 4

Parc Behan

Polmesk

Trenstrall

Ruan High
Lanes

Veryan CE
Prim Sch

Parc
Behan

Philleigh

PH

Polsue Manor
Hotel

Veryan

ROSELAND
GDNS

ELERKEY LA

GREEN LA

CENTURY LA

FOUR
RD

PO

Polmenna

WHITE LA

Penhallow

Crugsillick
Manor

Melinsey

PENDOWER RD TO LIVERUIK TO CHESTER

Treworthal

PENHALLOW CL

TR2

Lower
Mill

Tregamenna
Manor

Trelissa

Treworlas

Gwendra

Hotel

Carne

Tregairewoon
Farm

Treluggan

Hotel

ROCKY LA

PENDOWER
CT

Pendower
Beach

Carne
Beach

Polcreek

Lanhoose

Merrose
Cvn Site

Curgurrell

Gerrans
Bay

Shannick
Point

Trewithian

Dingerein
Castle

Creek Stephen
Point

Nare
Head

MILL HILL

Pollaughan

Hotel

Porthbean
Beach

Trethem
Mill

MERTHER COLLYN

Rosevine

Hotel

Lanhay

Tregassa

Pednvaden
Porthcurnick
Beach

95

1 ADMIRALTY TERR
2 SPRINGFIELD
3 PARC MERYS
4 SUNNYSIDE
5 RIVER ST
6 THE SQUARE
7 VICTORIA TERR
8 HIGHERTOWN
9 GWARAK GWEL AN MOR
10 TREVENTON CL
11 CALIFORNIA GDNS
12 GERRANS SQUARE
13 THE QUARRY
14 WELLINGTON TERR
15 MOUNT VIEW CL
16 WELL LA

PARC-AN-DILLON
RD

NORTH PAR

Portscatho

THE QUAY

Percuil River

Gerrans

Gerrans Parish
Her Ctr

Hotel

Gerrans
Sch

CHURCHTOWN RD

GERRANS HILL

NEW RD

TREVARTON RD

TRELOAN LA

THE
LUGGER

PO

Pencabe

PORTH
SAWLE
FLATS

95

Tregassick

Treloan LA

South West Coast Path

Percuil

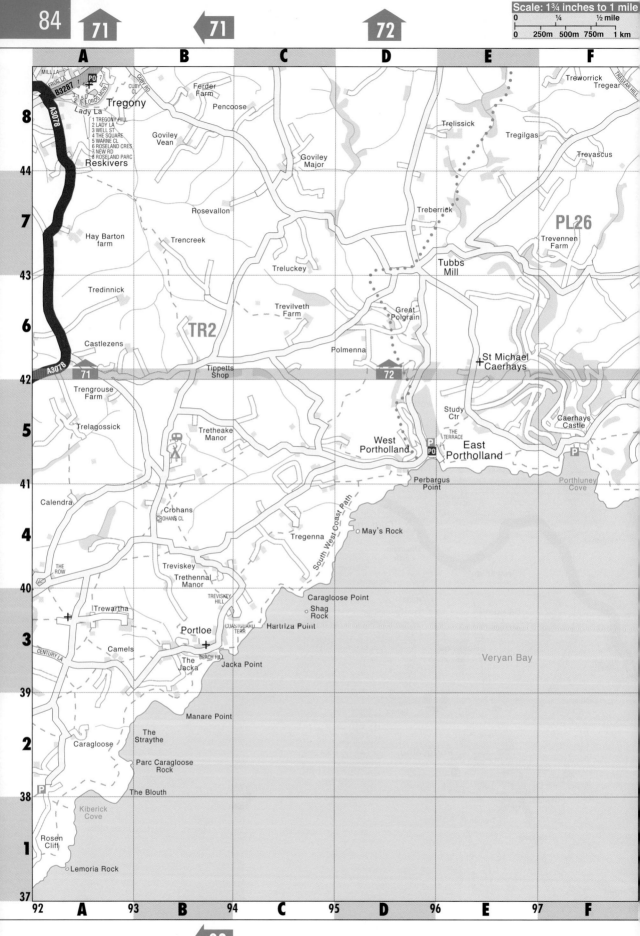

Tregony

MILL LA
HIGGE CL
PO
B3287
Lady La
LORDS MDW

CUBY RD
CUBY CL

Ferder Farm
Pencoose

1 TREGONY HILL
2 LADY LA
3 WELL ST
4 THE SQUARE
5 WARNE CL
6 ROSELAND CRES
7 NEW RD
8 ROSELAND PARC

Reskivers

Goviley Vean

Goviley Major

Trelissick

Tregilgas

Treworrick
Tregear

Trevascus

PL26

Trevennen Farm

Rosevallon

Treberrick

Trencreek

Hay Barton farm

Treluckey

Tubbs Mill

Tredinnick

TR2

Trevilveth Farm

Great Polgrain

Polmenna

St Michael Caerhays

Castlezens

Tippetts Shop

71

72

Caerhays Castle

Trengrouse Farm

Trelagossick

Tretheake Manor

West Portholland

Study Ctr
THE TERRACE

East Portholland

Perbargus Point

Porthluney Cove

Calendra

Crohans
CROHANS CL

Tregenna

May's Rock

South West Coast Path

THE ROW

Treviskey

Trethennal Manor

TREVISKEY HILL

Caragloose Point

Shag Rock

Trewartha

Portloe
COASTGUARD TERR

Hartriza Point

Veryan Bay

Camels
BEACH HILL

The Jacka

Jacka Point

CENTURY LA

Manare Point

The Straythe

Caragloose

Parc Caragloose Rock

The Blouth

Kiberick Cove

Rosen Cliff

Lemoria Rock

A   B   C   D   E   F

Mevagissey

1 PENMEVA VIEW
2 LEATFIELD
3 CHAPEL SQ
4 CHAPEL ST
5 RIVER ST
6 MARKET SQ
7 MOUNT ST
8 EAST WHARF
9 THE CLIFF
10 BATTERY TERR
11 CAPTAINS HO
12 MEADOW CT
13 TREGONEY CT
14 FORE ST
15 JETTY ST
16 MIDDLE WHARF
17 WEST WHARF
18 WESLEY CT

Mevagissey Bay

Summerfield Cl
Lamorak Cl
Kestle Rd
Tregoney Hill

Valley Pk La 19
Valley Pk 20
Elm Terrace 21
Trevarth 22

Higher Well Pk
Lower Well Pk
Polkirt Hill

Mus
Aquarium
Stuckumb Point
Polkirt Beach
Polkirt

Penwarne La
Portmellon Pk

Sea View Cotts
The Boatyard
Bodrugan La
Chapel Point La

Methrose Farm

Tregondean Farm

Galowras

Penwarne Farm

Portmellon

Bodrugan Barton

Chapel Point

Wr Twr

Tregerrick

Castle Hill

Colona Beach

Tregarton Farm

Trevarrick

Gorran High Lanes

Treninick

Cotna

PL26

Gorran Churchtown

Trewollock

South West Coast Path

Turbot Point

Pabyer Point

Great Perhaver Beach

Rescassa

PH
PO

Polkirt Hill
Trewollock La

Gwineas or Gwinges

72   73

Treveor

Gorran Sch

Trelispen Park Dr
Bell Hill
Trelispen Pk
Watsford Rd
Portheast Way 4
Perhaver Way
Perhaver Pk
Rice La
Chute La
Cliff Rd
Canton
Rattle La
Lample Dr
Boswinger La

Gorran Haven

Tregavarras Row
Tregavarras

Trevesson Farm

Derby's La 1
Wills Moor 2
Cook's Level 3
Trewollock Cl 4
Portheast Cl 5
Lighthouse La 6

Mowhay Cotts

Tréveague Farm

1 QUILVER CL
2 RATTLE ST
3 CHURCH ST

Boswinger
YH

Lamledra

Pen-a-maen or Maenease Point

Cadythew Rock

Penare

Hemmick Beach

Bow or Vault Beach

Gell Point

Penveor Point

High Point

Dodman Horse

Lizard Pool

Dodman Point

8 44 7 43 6 42 5 41 4 40 3 39 2 38 1 37

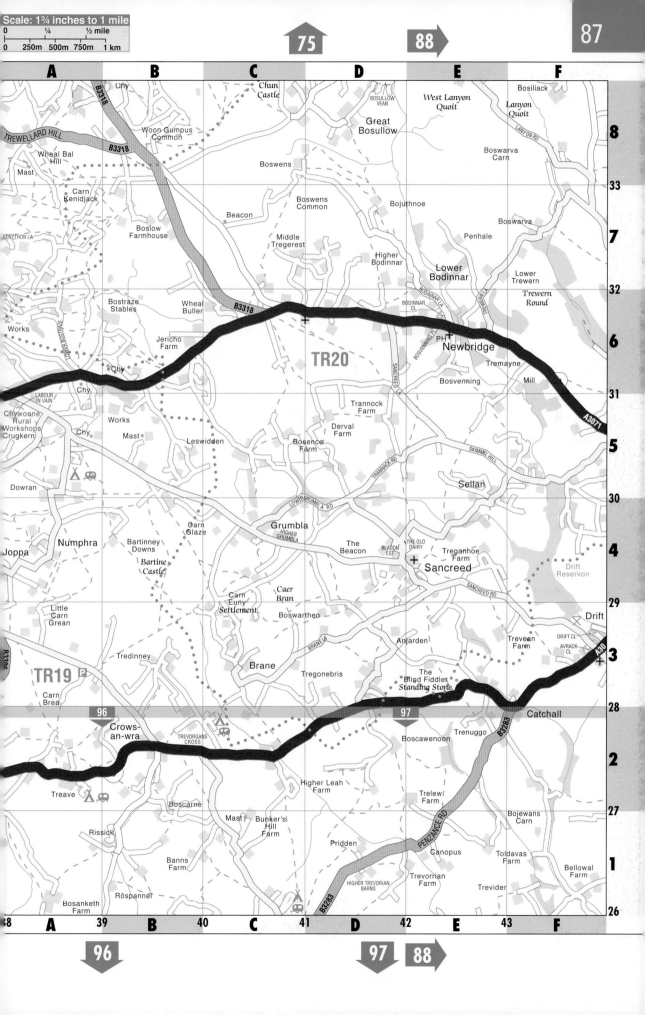

A B C D E F

8

Trythall Farm

Crankan

Noongallas

Trezelah

Garris Cotts

CHYSAUSTER RD

B3311 B3309

CASTLE RD

Treassowe Riding Treassowe Manor

TREASSOWE MEWS

B3309

THE GARTHEN

33

Boswarthen

Bosoljack

Gear Farm

Badger's Cross

7

Chapel (rems of)

Madron Well Cross

WISHING WELL LA

MOUNT VIEW

PARCANBRIAC

Kennels

Trevaylor

TR20

Bone

Tremearne

Rosemorran Farm

Kenegie Manor

Tolver
1 TRENEGLOS TERR
2 TREVARRACK ROW
3 BARNFIELD GDNS
4 VELLANHOGGAN MEWS
5 MILLFIELD
6 BRANWELL LA
7 FOXES FIELD
8 EASTERN GREEN PK
9 FRESHBROOK CL
10 GWEL LEWERN
11 MOUNT'S BAY HOL ETS
12 THE CHALETS

Pleming

Tregarthen

32

1 ALDREATH CL
2 TREGODDICK CL
3 VINGOE'S LA
4 HILLSIDE PARC
5 TRAFALGAR FIELDS
6 TALLY HO
7 ENSIGN WAY
8 VICTORY CL

143

Gulval

Longrock

FORE ST

Madron

Sch

PO

ALDREATH RD

MANSEGLOS HILL

B3312

MADRON RD

PO

Academy

Trythogga

TR18

SCHOOL LA

Gulval Comm Prim Sch Trevarrack

POSES LA

QUARRY HILL

PONKEY LA

GOOD PL

A30

6

Trengwainton House

Trengwainton Gdns

Heamoor

BOSCATHNOE LA

BOSCATHNOE WAY

ROSCADGHILL RD

COOMBE RD

CHYANDOUR LA

JELBERT WAY

EASTERN GN

LC

2 PONIOU

PONIOU LA

RODNEY LA

PORONA

P

31

ROSEHILL

Boscathnoe Resr

Heamoor Com Prim Sch

Coll

Sch

CHYANDOUR CLIFF

Chyandour

Superstore

CHY-AN-MOR 1
Penwith Bsns Ctr 2
Long Rock Bsns Pk 3
Long Rock Ind Est 4
CUXHAVEN WAY 5
PONIOU WAY 6
BAY VILLAS 7
GLADSTONE TERR 8
CASTLE VIEW 9
TOLVERTH TERR 10
TRESCOE RD 11
DARLINGTON TERR 12

Long Rock

5

Tremethick Cross

A3071

Tremethick Farm

LESINGEY LA

Cemy

L Ctr

West Cornwall

Sch

PO

P

H

Penzance

PENZANCE

Cressars

Western Cressar

Ryeman

30

Tregavarah

STRINGERS HILL

143

B3315

Trereife

Lesingey Round

Castle Horneck

YH

Rosehill

Sch

Ct

ALVERTON RD

ALEXANDRA RD

Gall & Mus

Liby

MURRAB RD

MARKET JEW ST

THE QUAY

Piers

143

4

Trewidden

Trewidden Gdn

Ind Est

Tolcarne

Sch

NEW RD

LOVE LA

CREEPING LA

Wherry Town

WESTERN PROMENADE RD

St Mary's CE Prim Sch

The Gear

29

Buryas Bridge

THE COOMBE

The Pilchard Wks

Newlyn Art Gall

PO

P

NEWLYN

A30

3

PUMP LA

TRESVENNACK

Tredavoe

CHYWOONE HILL

BURNOW LA

FORBES RD

STRAND

FORE ST

LB Sta

Pier

Tidal Observatory

GWAVAS RD

Ferry (P) Isles of Scilly

Gwavas Lake

28

Tresvennack

97

Tresvennack Pillar

Chyenhal Hotel

143

TREWARVENETH FARM COTTS

Skilly

2

TR19

Kerris

CHYWOONE GROVE

GURNICK RD

Roskilly Cotts

Paul

CLIFF RD

MOUSEHOLE LA

1 ST POL DE LEON VIEW
2 TRUNGLE TERR
3 TRUNGLE PARC
4 BOSLANDEW HILL

Roskilly Meml

Penlee Point

27

Rosevale Farm Penaluna

QUARRY LA

LONG ROW

97

Cemy

PH

PARC AN GATE

1

Redhouse

Sheffield

B3315

FOUR LANES END

LOWER SHEFFIELD

HALWYN FARM

Mousehole Com Prim Sch Trevithal

LOW LEE RD

THE PRAZE

CHYFIELD

PH

P

1 PARADE HILL
2 CARN TODDEN

Mousehole

St Clements Isle

MOUNT PLEASANT TERR

PO

KEIGWEN PL

MERLIN PL

26

44 A 45 B 46 C 47 D 48 E 49 F

C1
1 LYNWOOD COTTS
2 PREVENNA RD
3 GWELENYS RD
4 PARKRYN RD
5 FOXES LA
6 MARCWHEAL
7 DUMBARTON TERR
8 SOUTHVIEW TERR
9 DUCK ST

10 COMMERCIAL RD
11 QUAY ST
12 NORTH CLIFF
13 FORE ST
14 NORTH ST
15 CHERRY GDN ST
16 VIRGIN PL
17 BROOK ST
18 SOUTH CLIFF
19 GRENFELL ST

20 MILL LA
21 CHAPEL ST
22 THE WHARF
23 PORTLAND PL
24 GURNICK ST
25 RAGINNIS HILL
26 MERLIN PL
27 SALTPONDS

For full street detail of the highlighted area see page 143.

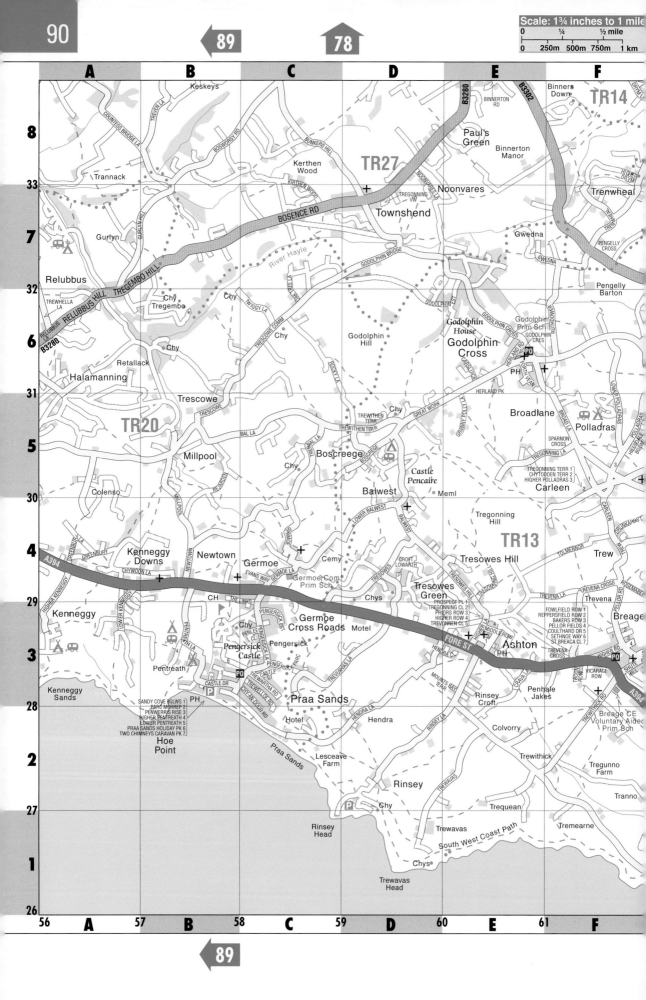

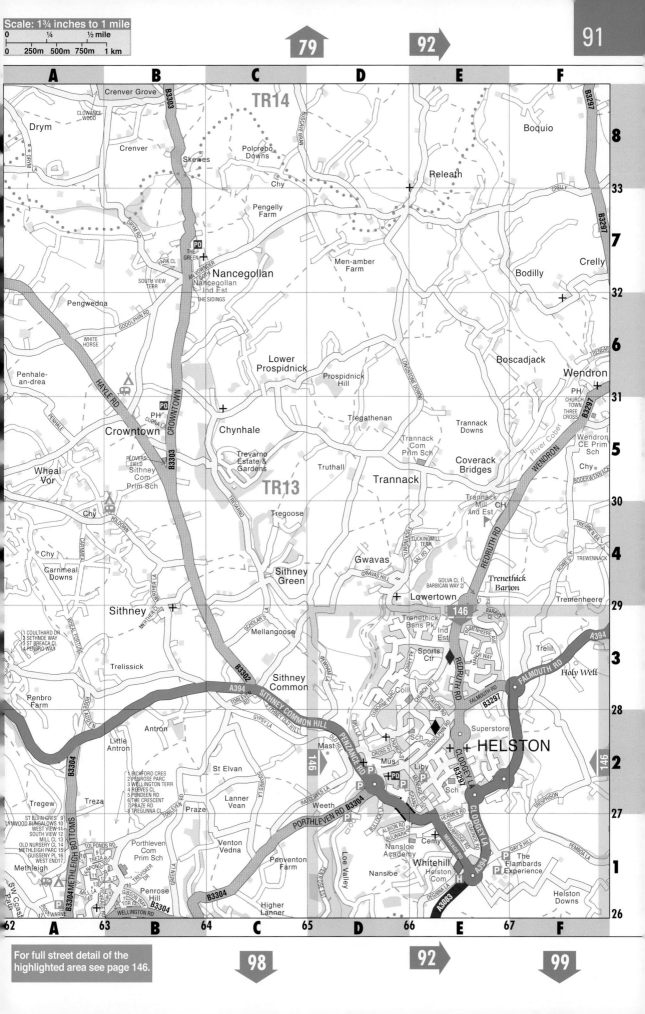

Scale: 1¾ inches to 1 mile

0   ¼   ½ mile
0 250m 500m 750m 1 km

79
92

TR14

Drym

Crenver Grove

CLOWANCE WOOD

Crenver

Skewes

Polcrebo Downs

Chy

Boquio

Releath

CRELLY

Crelly

Pengelly Farm

Men-amber Farm

THE GREEN

PARK CL

SOUTH VIEW TERR

Nancegollan

AN VOWNDER GOTH

Nancegollan Ind Est

THE SIDINGS

Bodilly

B3297

Pengwedna

WHITE HORSE

GODOLPHIN RD

Penhale-an-drea

Boscadjack

Wendron

PH

CHURCH TOWN THREE CROSS

Lower Prospidnick

Prospidnick Hill

Tregathenan

Trannack Downs

Wendron CE Prim Sch

PENTHALE

HAYLE RD

Crowntown

PH CUDNA LA

P.O.

CROWNTOWN

Chynhale

Trevarno Estate & Gardens

Truthall

Trannack Com Prim Sch

Trannack

Coverack Bridges

River Cober

WENDRON

Chy

BODERWENNACK

Wheal Vor

PLOVERS FIELD

Sithney Com Prim Sch

B3303

TR13

Tregoose

Trannack Mill Ind Est

TREVARNO

Chy

CARNMEAL

Chy

Carnmeal Downs

Sithney Green

Gwavas

GWAVAS HILL

TUCKINGMILL TERR

BAL RD

Trenethick Barton

Tremenheere

REDRUTH RD

TREVERVA BK

ROWE'S A

TREWENNACK

WHEAL FORTUNE

METHER CL

Sithney

Mellangoose

SCHOLAR'S LA

GOLVA CL 1
BARBICAN WAY 2

Lowertown

146

ROSE A DDL LA

Trelissick

Sithney Common

B3302

A394

Trenethick Bsns Pk

Ind Est

Sports Ctr

TREMENHEERE AVE

DOR WAY

Trelil

A394

Holy Well

1 COULTHARD DR
2 SETHNOE WAY
3 ST BREACA CL
4 PENBRO WAY

Penbro Farm

Antron

Little Antron

SITHNEY COMMON HILL

TORLEVEN RD

SITHNEY COLFHILL

GYPSY LA

NEWHALL LA

CARFORY

CHURCH HILL

OSBORNE PARK COLL

Trenethick Bsns Pk

Sch

Superstore

HELSTON

FALMOUTH RD

B3297

B3304

Tregew

Treza

St Elvan

Lanner Vean

1 BICKFORD CRES
2 PENROSE PARC
3 WELLINGTON TERR
4 REEVES CL
5 PENDEEN RD
6 THE CRESCENT
7 PRAZE RD
8 TREGUNNA CL

Praze

RATCLIFF'S LA

PORTHLEVEN RD

Weeth

Mast

OLD HELST

PENZANCE RD

146

MILLS A

P

Mus

P.O.

P

Liby

Sch

CLODGEY LA

HERMES RD

TRESPRISON

St Elvin Cres 9
Lynwood Bungalows 10
West View 11
South View 12
Mill Cl 13
Old Nursery Cl 14
Methleigh Parc 15
Guisseny Pl 16
West End 17

METHLEIGH BOTTOMS

Methleigh

B3304

TOLPONDS RD

TREZA RD

TREVISKER DR

GREEN LA

Venton Vedna

Penventon Farm

Loe Valley

Nansloe Academy

ALBION RD

BULWARK

Cemy

Whitehill

Helston Com

The Flambards Experience

Helston Downs

SW COAST PATH

ROSEWARNE

B3304

MILL LA

GIBSON WAY

TOR OR

WELLINGTON RD

Penrose Hill

B3304

Higher Lanner

Nansloe

HERRIDGE RD

ESTUARY RD

MINERAGE RD

DEGIBNA LA

A3083

A394

H

GAY'S HILL

PEMBOA LA

146

For full street detail of the highlighted area see page 146.

98
92
99

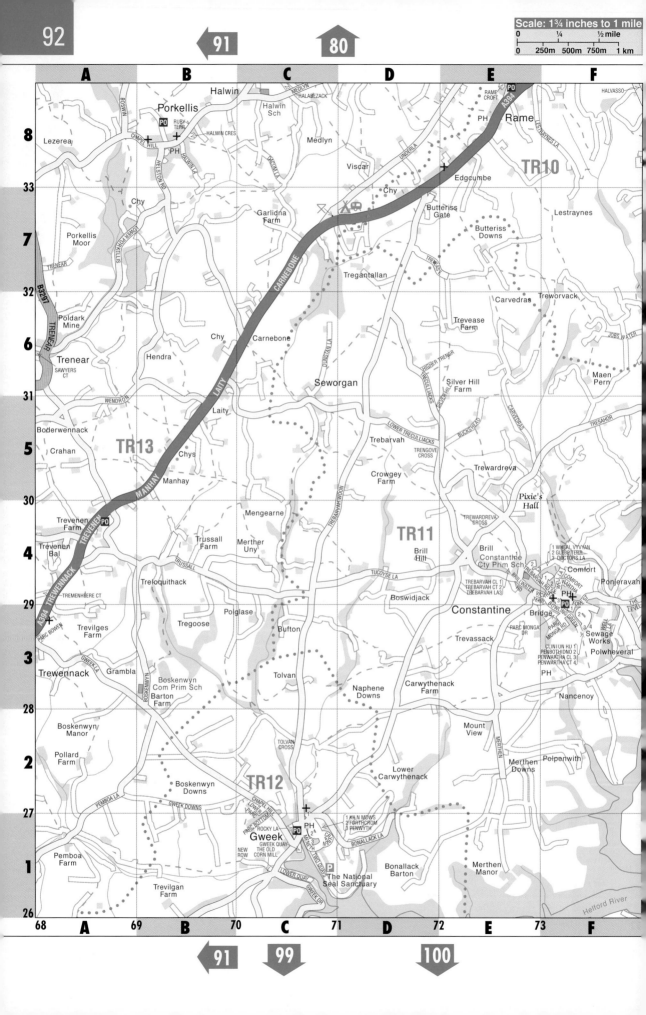

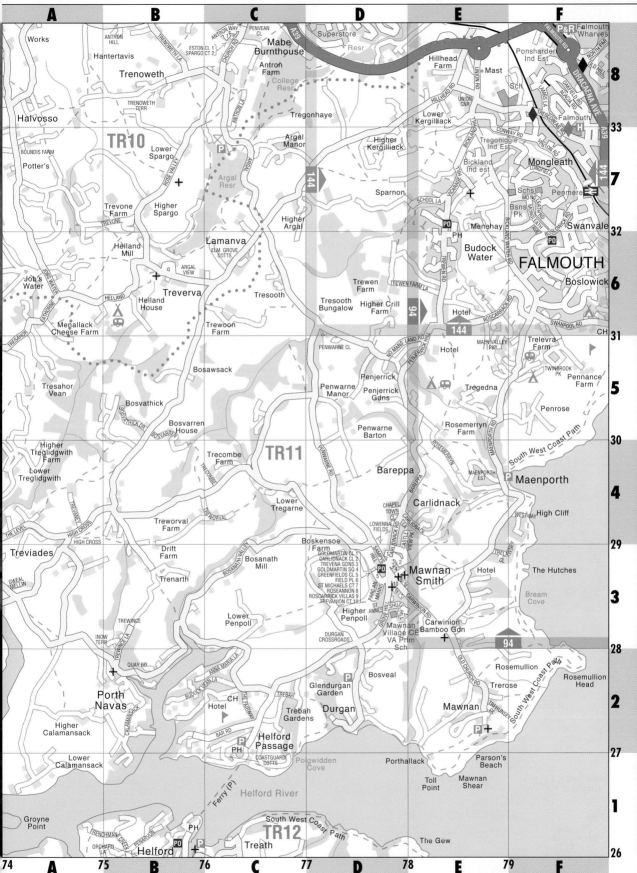

Works

ANTRON HILL

Hantertavis

TRENOWETH LA

Trenoweth

PENVEAN CL

ANTRON WAY

CHURCH RD

ESTON CL 1
SPARGO CT 2

Mabe
Burnthouse

A39

Superstore

Resr

Antron
Farm

College
Resr

Tregonhaye

Hillhead
Farm

HILLHEAD RD

UNION RD

Mast

Sch

Ponsharden
Ind Est

P&R

FALMOUTH RD

BRACKEN AVE

Falmouth
Wharves

NORTH PAR

OLD HILL

8

Halvosso

BOUNDIS FARM

Potter's

TRENOWETH
TERR

TR10

Lower
Spargo

RISE VALLEY

ANTRON LA

ARGAL

Argal
Manor

Argal
Resr

P

Higher
Argal

Higher
Kergilliack

Lower
Kergilliack

UNION
CNR

SCHOOL LA

VICARAGE RD

CONWAY RD

Tregoniggie
Ind Est

Bickland
Ind est

LONGFIELD

OAKFIELD RD

ACACIA RD

TRESCOBEAS RD

A39

Falmouth

H

Mongleath

MONGLEATH RD

Penmere

33

144

7

Trevone
Farm

Higher
Spargo

TREVONE

144

Sparnon

PH

PO

Schs

MONG
LEATH AVE

Bsns
Pk

Menehay

BICKLAND WATER RD

BOSCAWEN RD

PO

Swanvale

FALMOUTH

Boslowick

32

Job's
Water

EATHORNE

Helland
Mill

ELM GROVE
COTTS

Lamanva

ARGAL
VIEW

Helland
House

Treverva

TRESAHOR

Megallack
Cheese Farm

HELLAND

Tresooth

Trewoon
Farm

Trewen
Farm

TREWEN FARM LA

Tresooth
Bungalow

Higher Crill
Farm

94

TREWEN RD

Budock
Water

Hotel

ROSCARRACK RD

144

SWANPOOL RD

CH

6

31

BOSVATHICK DR

BOSVARROW

Tresahor
Vean

Bosvathick

Bosawsack

Bosvarren
House

PENWARNE CL

NO MANS LAND RD

PENJERRICK HILL

Penwarne
Manor

Penjerrick

Penjerrick
Gdns

Penwarne
Barton

Hotel

MAEN VALLEY
PK

Tregedna

Rosemerryn
Farm

ROSEMERRYN RD

MAENPORTH RD

South West Coast Path

Trelevra
Farm

TWINBROOK
PK

Pennance
Farm

Penrose

5

30

Higher
Treglidgwith
Farm

Lower
Treglidgwith

Trecombe
Farm

TRECOMBE

PENWARNE RD

TR11

Bareppa

BAREPPA

Carlidnack

MAENPORTH
EST

P

Maenporth

4

Treviades

GWEAL
MELLIN

THE LEVEL

TRETANKY

HIGH CROSS

HIGH CROSS

Treworval
Farm

TREWORVAL

Drift
Farm

Lower
Tregarne

BOSANATH VALLEY

Bosanath
Mill

Trenarth

Boskensoe
Farm

CHAPEL
TOWN

LOWENNA
FIELDS

CASTLE DR

CARLIDNACK RD

CASTLE
VIEW PK

ROSEMERRYN

CARLIDNACK LA

High Cliff

WEST BAY

The Hutches

Bream
Cove

29

TREWINCE LA

INOW
TERR

Trewince

Lower
Penpoll

DURGAN
CROSSROADS

GOLDMARTIN CL 1
CARLIDNACK CL 2
TREVENA GDNS 3
GOLDMARTIN SQ 4
GREENFIELDS CL 5
FIELD PL 6
ST MICHAELS CT 7
ROSEANNON 8
ROSCARRICK VILLAS 9
TREVANION CT 10

PARC AN
MAINS

ST ANNES HILL

GROVE HILL

CARWINION RD

Mawnan
Smith

Higher
Penpoll

Mawnan
Village CE
VA Prim
Sch

Carwinion
Bamboo Gdn

Hotel

TREGELL CL

Hotel

94

3

28

Porth
Navas

Higher
Calamansack

CALAMANSACK

QUAY RD

BUDOCK VEAN LA

ANNA MARIA LA

P

CH

THE FAIRWAY

Hotel

BAR RD

P

PH

Glendurgan
Garden

Trebah
Gardens

TREBAH

Durgan

Bosveal

OLD CHURCH RD

TREROSE

Trerose

Mawnan

TREHUNSEY CL

P

Rosemullion

South West Coast Path

Rosemullion
Head

2

Lower
Calamansack

Groyne
Point

FRENCHMAN'S CREEK

PENARVON

ORCHARD

Helford

PH

PO

P

Helford
Passage

COASTGUARD
COTTS

Polgwidden
Cove

Ferry (P)

Helford River

South West Coast Path

TR12

Treath

Porthallack

Toll
Point

Mawnan
Shear

Parson's
Beach

The Gew

27

1

26

74 A 75 B 76 C 77 D 78 E 79 F

100 101

For full street detail of the
highlighted area see page 144.

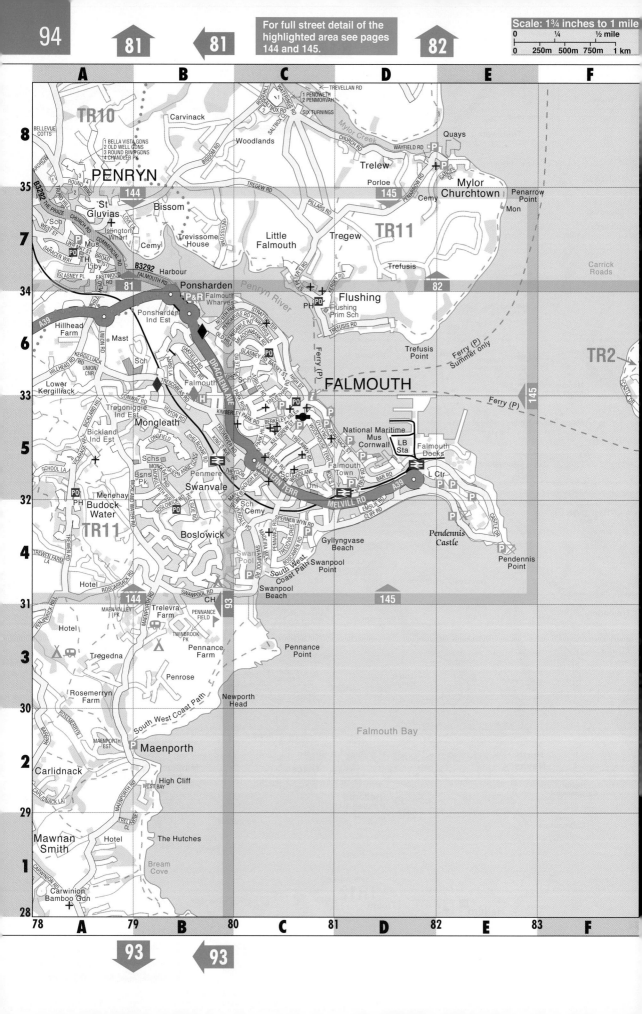

For full street detail of the
highlighted area see pages
144 and 145.

Scale: 1¾ inches to 1 mile
0   ¼   ½ mile
0   250m 500m 750m 1 km

Scale: 1¾ inches to 1 mile

| 0 | ¼ | ½ mile |
| 0 | 250m | 500m 750m 1 km |

82

83

A B C D E F

Messack
Point

St Just
Pool

Trethewell

Lanhay

Tregassa

Porthcurnick
Beach

Pednvadan

B3289
B3078
A3078

WINDMILL HILL

TREVENNEL
CL

St Just in
Roseland

Trevennel
Farm

Trewollack

PARC-AN-DILLON
RD

Portscatho

1 ADMIRALTY TERR
2 SPRINGFIELD
3 PARC MERYS
4 HARBOUR CT FLATS
5 RIVER ST
6 THE SQUARE
7 VICTORIA TERR
8 HIGHERTOWN
9 GWARAK GWEL AN MOR
10 TREVENTON CL
11 CALIFORNIA GDNS
12 GERRANS SQUARE

Gerrans

Gerrans Parish
Her Ctr
Hotel

Gerrans
Sch

Pencabe

NORTH PK

THE QUAY
THE LUGGER

PORTH
SAWLE
FLATS

Tregear
Vean

Bosloggas

Tregassick

Treloan

TR2

Water
Twr

ROSELAND
FLATS

Percuil

South West Coast Path

82 St
Mawes

POLVARTH RD

UPPER CASTLE RD

1 PORTH VIEW
2 PEN BREA CL
3 POLVARTH E6
4 POLVARTH LA

Trewince

Greeb
Point

83

PERCUIL VIEW

FRESHWATER LA

TREWINCE
MANOR

Rosteague

Percuil River

Quay

Froe

St Mawes
Prim Sch

A3078

MARINE PAR

THE QUAY

TREDENHAM RD

Porth
Farm

Towan
Beach

St Mawes
Castle

St Mawes
Harbour

Ferry P
(summer only)

Castle
Point

Bohortha

Killigerran
Head

St Anthony

146
1 MANOR CT
2 ST AUSTELL ROW
3 THE SQUARE
4 KINGS RD
5 COMMERCIAL RD
6 GIBRALTAR TERR
7 CHURCH HILL
8 PEN-EGLOS
9 ROPEWLK
10 CHAPEL TERR
11 SEA VIEW CRES
12 NEWTON PK
13 LARKFIELD RISE
14 HANCOCK LA
15 PLACE VIEW RD
16 KENNERLEY TERR
17 BROOKLYN FLATS
18 BEECH HALL FLATS
20 BOHELLA RD
21 SEA VIEW RD
22 SPINNAKER DR

St Anthony
Head

Carricknath
Point

Place
House

Place
Barton

MILITARY RD

Porthbeor
Beach

Porthmellin
Head

Zone
Point

8
35
7
34
6
33
5
32
4
31
3
30
2
29
1
28

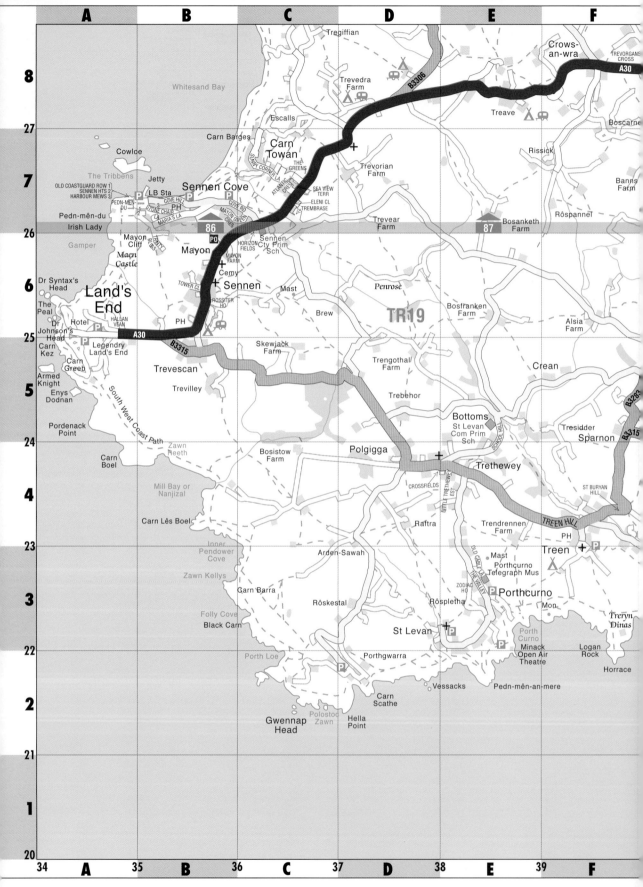

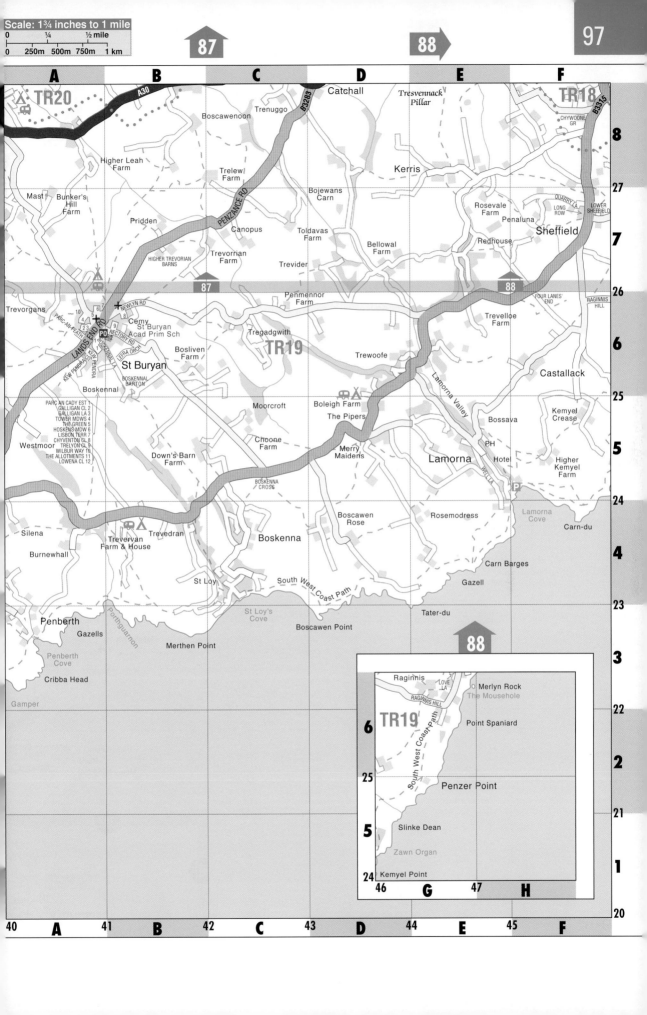

98

90

91

For full street detail of the
highlighted area see page 146.

B8
1 METHLEIGH BOTTOMS
2 METHLEIGH PARC
3 THE MOORS
4 FORE ST
5 HARBOUR VIEW
6 SHUTE LA
7 KESTREL CL
8 PROSPECT PL
9 CHAPEL TERR
10 SALT CELLAR HILL
11 MOUNT PLEASANT RD
12 HARBOURSIDE
13 BAY VIEW TERR
14 INSTITUTE HILL
15 WEST END
16 CLAREMONT TERR
17 WEST END

C8
1 HOLMAN'S PL
2 THE GUE
3 ELLISTON GDNS
4 THOMAS ST
5 THOMAS TERR
6 FORTH SCOL
7 PEVERELL RD
8 SUNSET DR
9 SUNSET GDNS
10 MATELA CL
11 PARC-AN-MAEN
12 HAMMILLS DR
13 HAMMILL'S CL
14 ST PIRANS PARC
15 BALFIELD RD
16 TREMEARNE RD
17 TREGONNING VIEW
18 CLAREMON RD
19 WHEAL ROSE
20 MOUNTS RD
21 MOUNT'S BAY TERR
22 OCEAN CRES
23 SUNNYBANK
24 HIGHBURROW
25 WESLEY CT
26 THE SHRUBBERIES

Mon
Mast

B3304

PO

B3304

Pier
Porthleven

Tye Rocks

Penrose

TR13

Nancewidden

Degibna

Goonhusband

Penrose Walks

Higher
Pentire

Tangies

Burnwick
Farm

Carminowe

Porthleven Sands

Carminowe Creek

The Loe

Low
Bar

Clies
Farm

Burnow

Chyvarloe

Berepper
Cross

Berepper

TR12

Gunwalloe

PH
Chyanvounder

Gunwalloe
Fishing Cove

Trenoweth
Farm

Baulk Head

Halzephron
Cove

Hingey
Farm

Green
Rock

Halzephron
Cliff

Pedngwinian

Winnianton
Farm

CH

Jangye-ryn

The
Towans

Church Cove

Poldhu Cove

Poldhu Point

Marconi Centre
(Mus)

Masts

Mên-y-grib Point
Mon

ANGROUSE LA

102

LAFLOUDER LA

Polurrian Cove

COASTGUARD COTTS 1
MULLION COVE 2
POLURRIAN CLIFFS 3

Hotel

Henscath

South West Coast Path

102

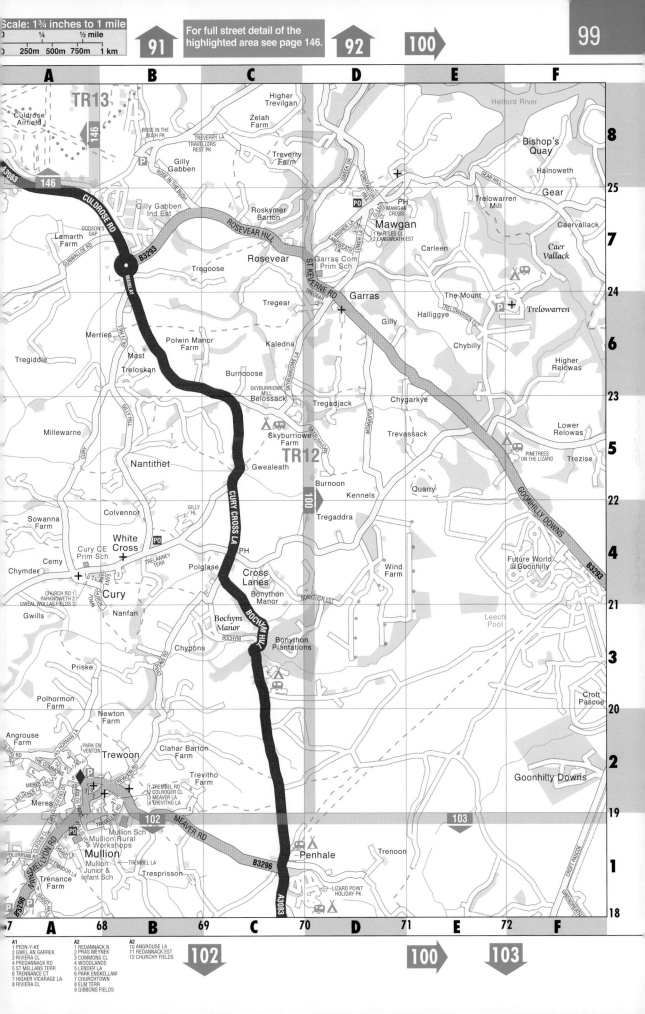

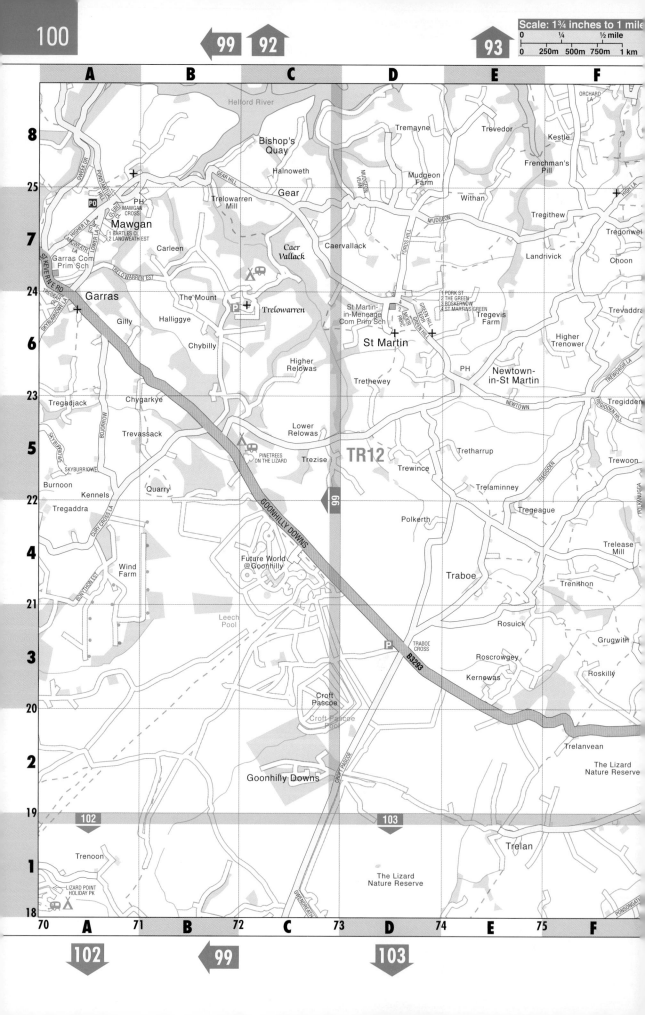

Scale: 1¾ inches to 1 mile
0   ¼   ½ mile
0   250m   500m   750m   1 km

A   B   C   D   E   F

Helford River

8

Bishop's
Quay

Tremayne
Trevedor
Kestle

25
Halnoweth
Frenchman's
Pill

GEAR HILL
Gear
Mudgeon
Farm
Tregithew

PO
Trelowarren
Mill
Withan
Landrivick

PH
MAWGAN
CROSS
Caervallack
Tregonwel

7
Mawgan
1 BARTLES CL
2 LANGWEATH EST
Carleen
Caer
Vallack
Choon

Garras Com
Prim Sch
TRELOWARREN EST
1 PORK ST
2 THE GREEN
3 BOSKERNOW
4 ST MARTINS GREEN

24
Garras
The Mount
St Martin-
in-Meneage
Com Prim Sch
Tregevis
Farm
Trevaddra

Gilly
Halliggye
P
Trelowarren
St Martin
Higher
Trenower

6
Chybilly
PH
Newtown-
in-St Martin

Higher
Relowas
Trethewey
NEWTOWN
Tregidden

23
Tregadjack
Chygarkye
Lower
Relowas
Tretharrup
Trewoon

Trevassack
Trezise
TR12
Trewince
Trelaminney

5
Burnoon
Kennels
Quarry
PINETREES
ON THE LIZARD
Polkerth
Tregeague

22
Tregaddra
GOONHILLY DOWNS
66
Trelease
Mill

SKYBURRIOWE
Traboe
Trenithon

4
Wind
Farm
Future World
@Goonhilly

21
Leech
Pool
Rosuick
Grugwith

3
P
TRADOE
CROSS
B3293
Roscrowgey
Roskilly
Kernewas

20
Croft
Pascoe
Croft Pascoe
Pool
Trelanvean

2
Goonhilly Downs
The Lizard
Nature Reserve

19
102
103
Trelan

1
Trenoon

LIZARD POINT
HOLIDAY PK
The Lizard
Nature Reserve

18
70   A   71   B   72   C   73   D   74   E   75   F

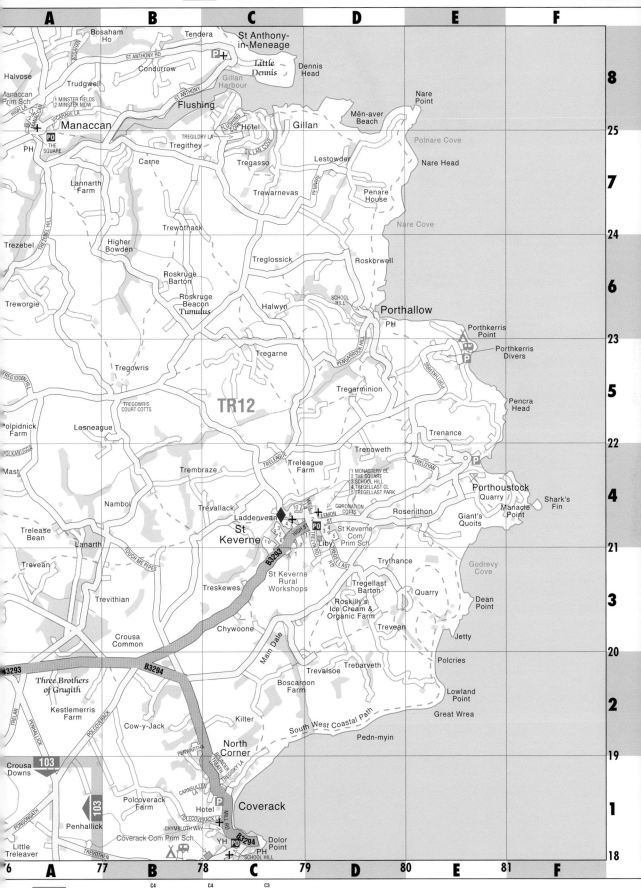

C4
1 TRESKEWES EST
2 TREVALLACK VIEW
3 TREVALLACK PARC
4 LANHEVERNE PARC
5 DOCTORS HILL
6 POLVENTON PARC
7 PENMENNER EST
8 COMMERCIAL RD
9 TREVALLACK CL

C4
10 TREGONNING PARC

C3
1 TRESKEWES IND EST

Scale: 1¾ inches to 1 mile

0	¼	½ mile
0	250m 500m 750m	1 km

A **B** **C** **D** **E** **F**

Laflouder La

LAFLOUDER
FIELDS

Polurrian Cove

POLURRIAN RD

Mullion Rural
Workshops

Mullion Sch

MEAVER RD

Trenoo

Penhale

A3083

B3296

PEDN-Y-KE 1
GWEL AN GARREK 2
TRENANCE LA 3
PREDANNACK RD 4
ST MELLANS TERR 5
TRENANCE COURT BGLWS 6
HIGHER VICARAGE LA 7
RIVIERA CL 8
MULLION COVE BGLWS 1
COASTGUARD COTTS 2

Trenance
Farm

Mullion

Mullion
Junior &
Infant Sch

Trembel
La

Tresprisson

LIZARD POINT
HOLIDAY PARK

8

Hotel

Henscath **98**

99

Hendra

18

Mullion
Cove

B3296

Trelease

NANSMELLYON RD

Mullion
Island

Mullion
Cliff

Trelugga

7

Toldhu

FRIARS LA

The Chair

17

Hayle Kimbro
Pool

Eglos
Farm

Mên-te-heul

PREDANNACK RD

TR12

Ruan
Major

Predannack
Manor Farm

Pedn Crifton

Predannack
Wollas

Predannack
Airfield

Church
(remains of)

6

PREDANNACK HOLIDAY
VILLAGE

Predannack
Head

TREVELYAN HOLIDAY
HOMES

EBENEZER RD

Mount
Hermon

16

Ruan
Pool

Ogo-dour Cove

St Helena

WORVAS LA

Pol Cornick

5

Windmill
(remains of)

Worvas
Farm

South West Coast Path

Windmill
Farm

Vellan
Head

15

GRADE RD

Gew-graze

Grochall

MILE END

MILE
END

Trethvas
Farm

4

Pigeon Ogo

Soap
Rock

The Horse

14

Kynance Cliff

Lizard
Downs

The Pound

The
Rill

Tor
Balk

3

Rill
Ledges

KYNANCE COVE

CHAPEL
LA

CROSS COMM

Landewednac
Com Prim Sch

THE LIZARD

The Bellows

Asparagus Island

Gull Rock

Lion
Rock

Holestrow

A3083

CHURC

13

Kynance Cove

Pentreath
Beach

BEACON TERR

LOVDS C

PER KITHEN 1
LUSART DR 2
MITCHELL CL 3
GREEN FIELD CL 4
BOS VEAN 5
CROFT PARC 6
PARC-AN-ITHAN 7
THE SQUARE 8
KYNANCE TERR 9
TRENOWETH CT 10
TRENOWETH MDW 11
PARC BRAWSE 12
MAN OF WAR VIEW 13
PENMENNER GDNS 14
PARC GARLAND 15
THE TRIANGLE 16
HIGHER CROFT PARC 17
HENRYS CROFT 18
LIGHTHOUSE RD 19
CLOUDS HILL 20

PENTREATH LA

PH

PO

Lizard

Hotel

2

Crane Ledges

Venton Hill
Point

House
Bay

LIZARD POINT

Quadrant

LIZARD
LIGHTHOUSE
COTTS

Lion's
Den

Lighthouse
Her Ctr

Bumble
Rock

1

Polpeor Cove

Polbream Cove

YH

Tizard
Den

Vellan
Drang

11

65 **A** **66** **B** **67** **C** **68** **D** **69** **E** **70** **F**

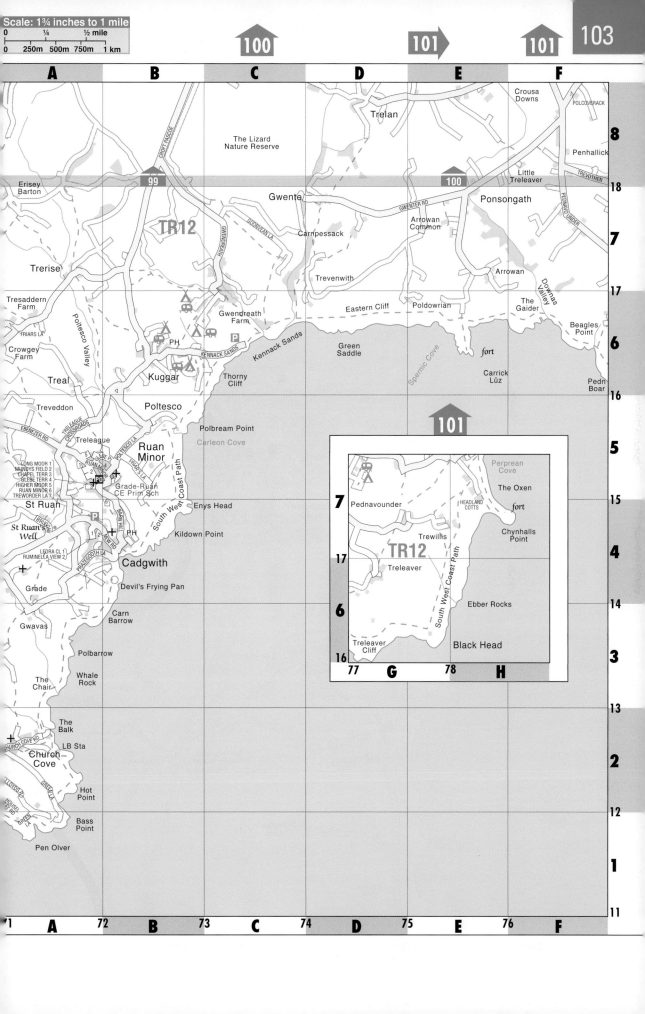

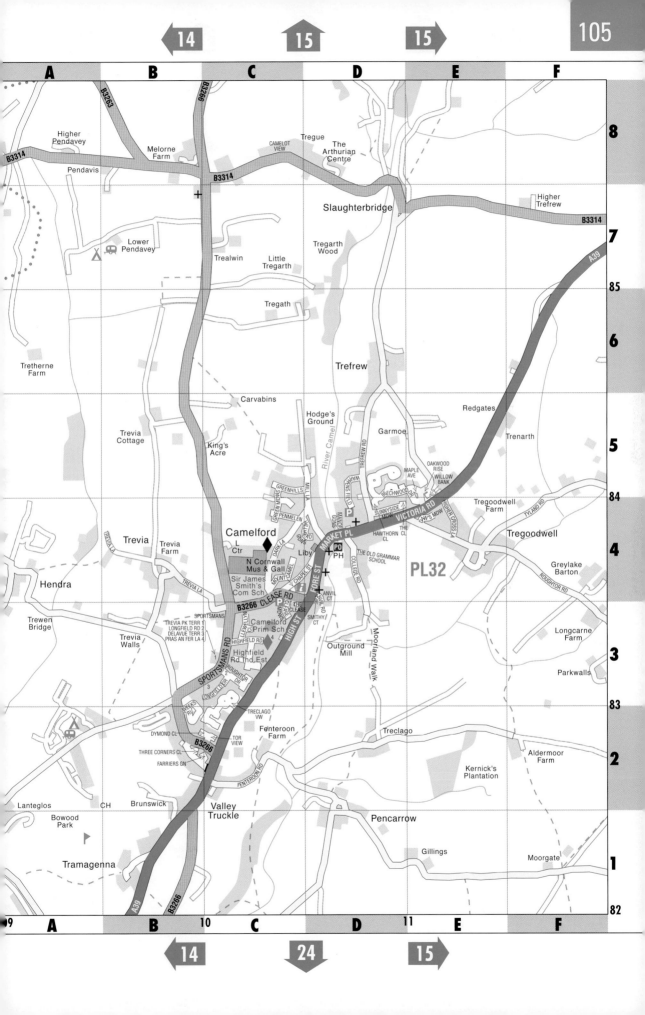

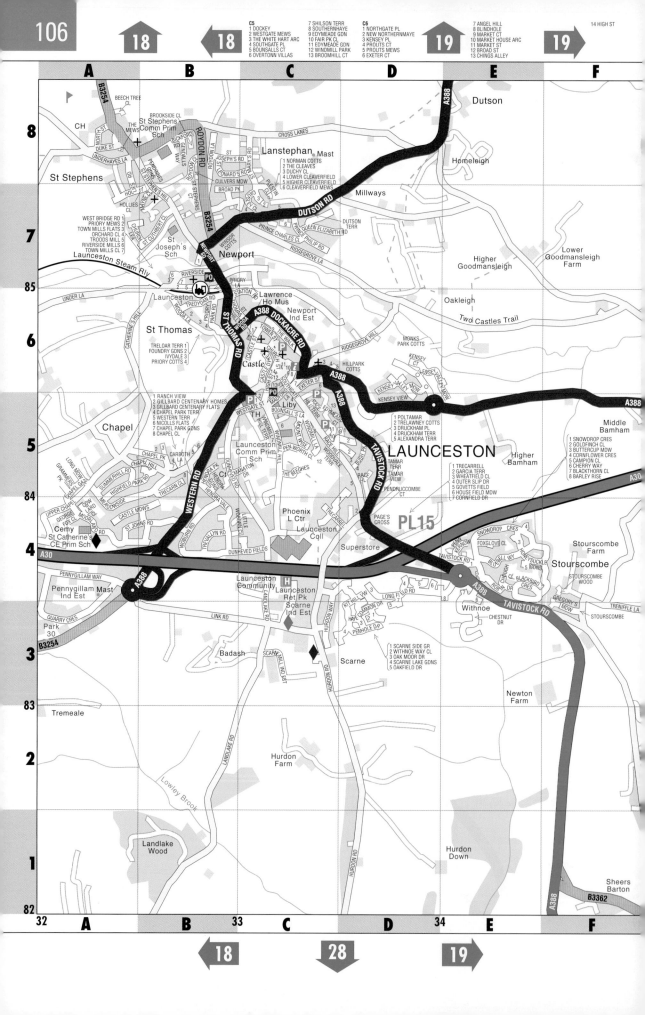

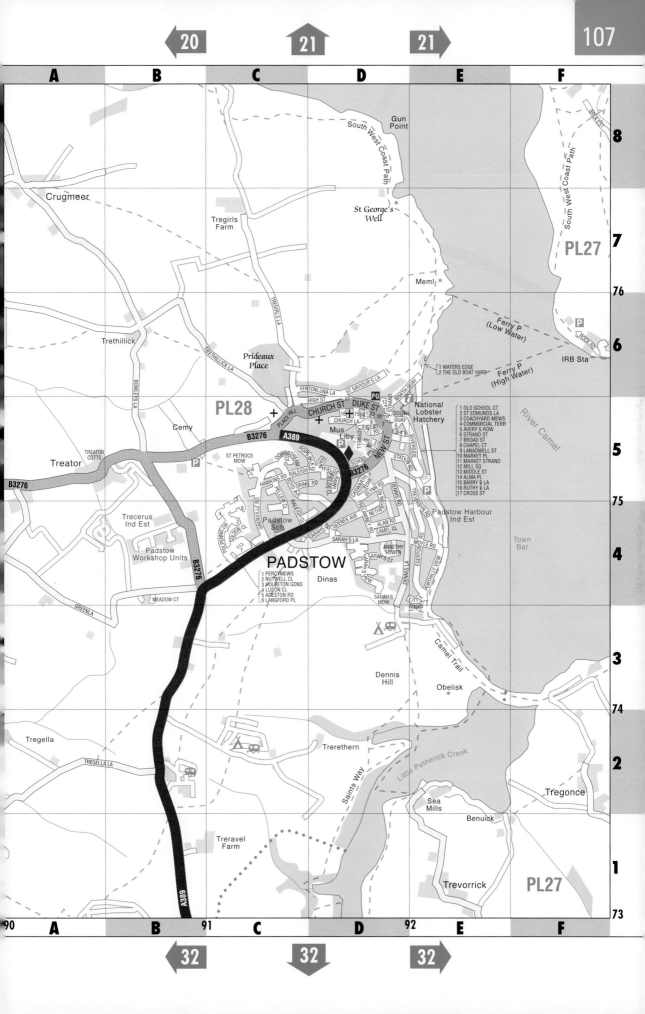

A　B　C　D　E　F

8

Crugmeer

South West Coast Path

Gun Point

Tregirls Farm

St George's Well

PL27

7

TREGIRLS LA

Trethillick

TRETHILLICK LA

Prideaux Place

Meml

76

Ferry P (Low Water)

BOWLEYS LA

6

Trerethern

IRB Sta

ROCK RD

P

Ferry P (High Water)

PL28

Cemy

FENTONLUNA LA
HIGH ST
ST SAVIOUR'S LA

PO

NORTH QUAY
SOUTH QUAY

1 WATERS EDGE
2 THE OLD BOAT YARD

River Camel

CHURCH ST
DUKE ST

National Lobster Hatchery

1 OLD SCHOOL CT
2 ST EDMUNDS LA
3 COACHYARD MEWS
4 COMMERCIAL TERR
5 AVERY S ROW
6 STRAND ST
7 BROAD ST
8 CHAPEL CT
9 LANADWELL ST
10 MARKET PL
11 MARKET STRAND
12 MILL SQ
13 MIDDLE ST
14 ALMA PL
15 BARRY S LA
16 RUTHY S LA
17 CROSS ST

B3276
A389
Mus
Liby
CHURCH LA

PLACE HILL

Treator

TREATOR COTTS

B3276

ST PETROCS MDW
P

DOWNSTREAM CL
ROPE WALK
HAWKINS RD
RALEIGH RD
BOYD DR
DRAKE RD
RALEIGH RD

HILL ST
STRAND
NEW ST
RIVERSIDE

STATION RD

5

Padstow Harbour Ind Est

75

GRENVILLE RD
PELLEW CL

Padstow Sch

CASWARTH
SCHOOL HILL
KEVERAL
FREEMANTLE RD
GLYNN RD
DENNIS RD

P

TREVATHAN RD

B3276

PENNINGTON
SEXTON CL

PADSTOW

Trecerus Ind Est

PYFIELDS
RALEIGH CL

SARAH'S LA
LODENEK AVE
NETHERTON
ALAN RD
CAMEL CL

ANNETHY LOWEN

Town Bar

4

Padstow Workshop Units

1 PERCY MEWS
2 NUTWELL CL
3 HOLBETON GDNS
4 LUSON CL
5 ADESTON RD
6 LANGFORD PL

Dinas

SARAH'S CT
SARAH'S VIEW

MOYLE RD
EGERTON RD
PORTHILLY VIEW

GREENLA

MEADOW CT

SARAH'S MDW

DINAS
LITT

Camel Trail

3

Dennis Hill

Obelisk

74

A389

Tregella

TREGELLA LA

Trerethern

Saints Way

Little Petherick Creek

2

Tregonce

Treravel Farm

Sea Mills

Benuick

PL27

1

Trevorrick

73

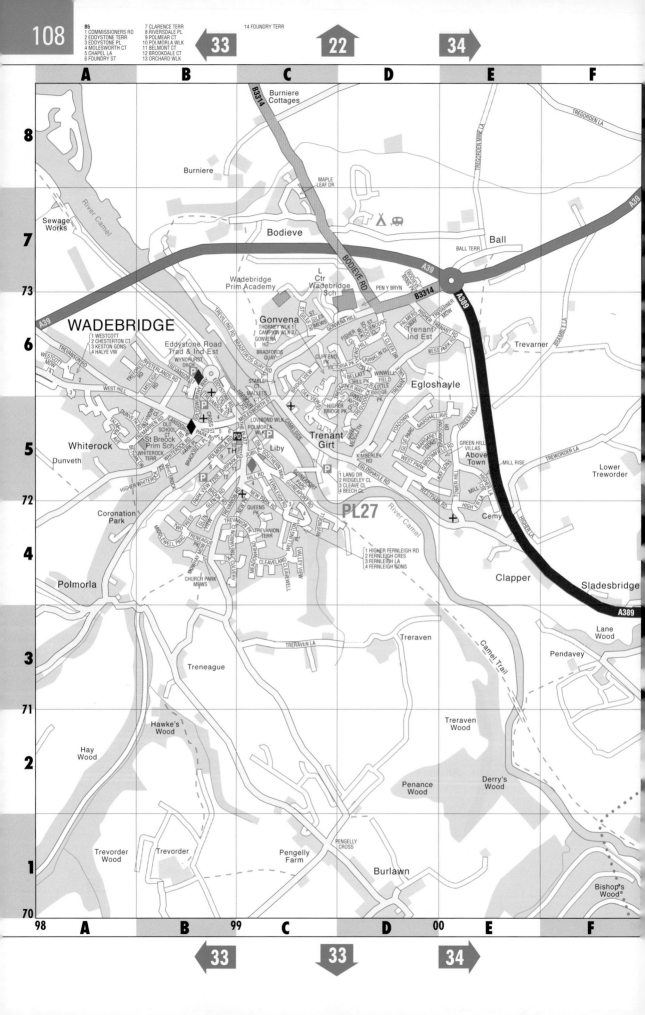

A   B   C   D   E   F

Clerkenwater

Outlands Wood

8

Copshorn

Whitley Wood

Clerkenwater House
PL30

Penquite

Outlands

Crabb's Pool

East Wood

7

Camel Trail

Whitley

Penbugle

River Camel

Middle Bodiniel

HIGHER BODINIEL RD

Penbugle La

68

Bodiniel

PL31

BODINIEL RD

D5
1 WALLACE MEWS
2 MARTIN'S CT
3 BERATON CT
4 STANLEY CT
5 BROWNLOW PL
6 Station Yd
7 BURNARDS CT
8 RINGWAY FLATS
9 BEACON HILL MEWS
10 GREGORY'S CT
11 BARTON CL
12 AGAR TERR
13 CRIBBAGE TERR
14 CLIFDEN TERR
15 BERRYCOMBE VIEW
16 KESTENENN
17 FLAXMOOR TERR
18 FINN VC EST

Cemy

Cemy
Berry
Tower

E5
1 BELL YD
2 NORTON CT
3 MARKET HOUSE ARC
4 BREE SHUTE LA
5 THE PIAZZA
6 GUARDIAN CT
7 CARLTON HO
8 CHURCH SQ
9 WINDSOR HO
10 BREE SHUTE LA
11 KEW KLAVJI
12 TOWER HILL GDNS

6

Factory

Works

BODMIN

A389

Berrycoombe Prim Sch

Bodmin Jail Superstore

WALLACE RD

5

MIDWAY RD

Works

DUNMERE RD

DENNISON RD

Shire Hall

67

St LEONARDS HIGHER BORE ST

B3268

Lib

Co Off
Bodmin Town Mus

Bodmin Town FC

PRIORY RD

LAUNCESTON RD

A389

Mag Ct
Super-store

Bodmin Com

St Mary's RC Prim Sch

The Beacon Inf & Nur Sch

B3268

Bodmin Town War Memorial

St Petrocs CE VA Prim Sch

4

WESTHEATH AVE

Robartes Ace Acad

1 WESTERN TERR
2 ST MARY'S GDNS
3 CONVENT OF MERCY
4 QUARRY PARK TERR
5 KESTLE CT

Bodmin Beacon Nature Reserve

Bodmin General

Cornwall's Regimental Mus

Coldharbour Farm

3

Laveddon House

Bodmin Bsns Ctr

LOSTWITHIEL RD

Gilbert's Mon

Beacon Lanes

Walker Lines Ind Est

66

A389

Laveddon Mill Nursery

Bodmin & Wenford Rly

Bodmin Coll Playing Fields

Mast

Woods-Browning Ind Est

2

Kymsland

Blowinghouse

Kirland Manor

Kirland

Hawke's Bridge

Halgavor Farm

PL30

Little Kirland

The Dragon L Ctr

1

Stephen Gelly

Trekillick Farm

Sunny Corner

Lidcutt Farm

B3268

65

F3
1 CANYKE FIELDS
2 CORNWALL RISE
3 BRAY CL
4 HOLMES WAY
5 RALEIGH GDNS
6 BATTALION CL

A5
1 BOYER SQ
2 TREWIN RD
3 GARTLAND DR
4 GILLIFLOWER CRES
5 NEGUS GDNS
6 NANTERROW DR
7 OUTTA SIGHT CT
8 SAWMILLS CL
9 BADGERS WOOD

A5
10 TRADEWINDS CL
11 MEAD GDNS
12 FAIRING CL
13 SILVER BIRCH CRES
14 JUNIPER CL
15 FOXGLOVE RD
16 HEATHER GDNS
17 DARLEY OAK CL

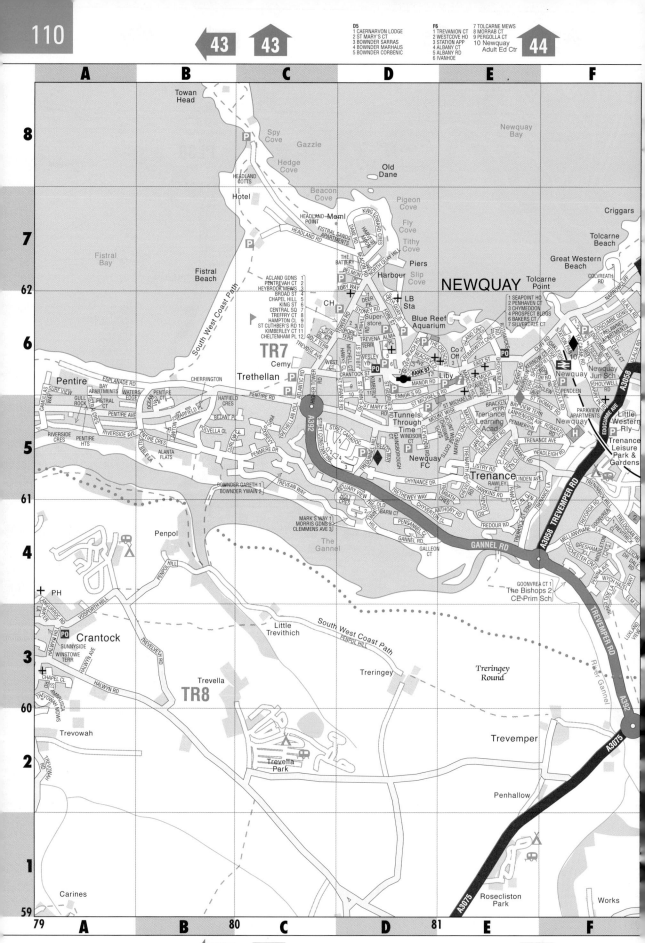

D5
1 CAERNARVON LODGE
2 ST MARY'S CT
3 BOWNDER SARRAS
4 BOWNDER MARHAUS
5 BOWNDER CORBENIC

F6
1 TREVANION CT
2 WESTCOVE HO
3 STATION APP
4 ALBANY CT
5 ALBANY RD
6 IVANHOE

7 TOLCARNE MEWS
8 MORRAB CT
9 PERGOLLA CT
10 Newquay
Adult Ed Ctr

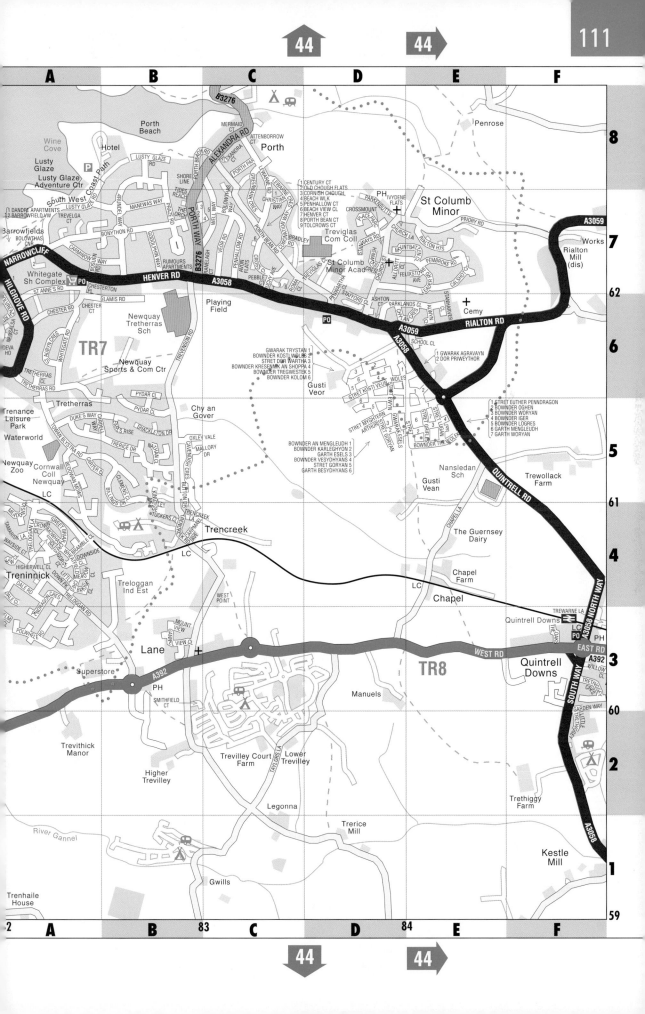

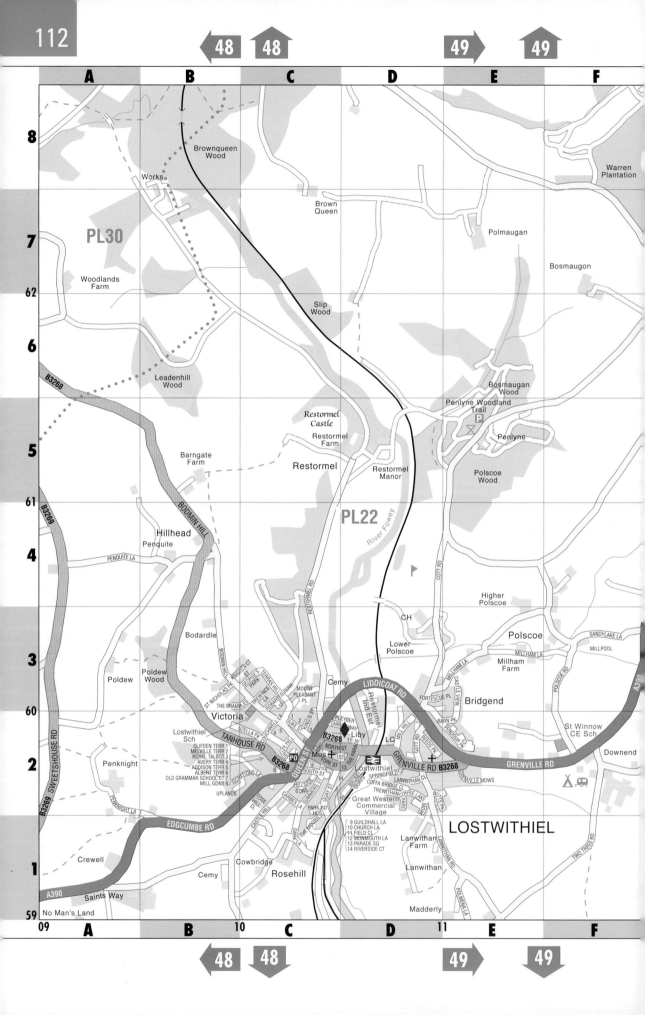

A B C D E F

8
Brownqueen Wood
Works
Warren Plantation

PL30
Brown Queen
Polmaugan

7
Woodlands Farm
Slip Wood
Bosmaugon

62

6
Leadenhill Wood
Bosmaugan Wood
Penlyne Woodland Trail

B3268

Restormel Castle
Penlyne

5
Barngate Farm
Restormel Farm
Polscoe Wood

Restormel
Restormel Manor

61
B3269
PL22
River Fowey

BODMIN HILL

4
Hillhead
Penquite
PENQUITE LA
Higher Polscoe

CH

3
Bodardle
Lower Polscoe
Polscoe
SANDYLAKE LA
MILLHAM LA
MILLPOOL

Poldew
Poldew Wood
Cemy
LIDDICOAT RD
Millham Farm

SWEETSHOUSE RD
KNIGHTS CT
ST NICHOLAS PK
GEORGE'S PARK
TREWINCE
TERRAS HILL
ROBARTS TERR
MOUNT PLEASANT PL
Restormel Ind Est
FORTESCUE PL
Bridgend

60
Victoria
THE BRAMBLES
B3268
Liby
CASTLE VIEW
BARN PK
PENDOUR PK
St Winnow CE Sch

Lostwithiel Sch
CLIFDEN TERR 1
MELVILLE TERR 2
ROYAL TALBOT 3
AVERY TERR 4
ADDISON TERR 5
ALBERT TERR 6
OLD GRAMMAR SCHOOL CT 7
MILL GDNS 8
TANHOUSE RD
UZELLA PK
DUKE ST
KING'S ST
Mus
FORE ST
Lostwithiel
GRENVILLE RD
MILL HILL
COTT RD
REEDS PK
B3268
GRENVILLE RD
Downend

2
PO
B3268
QUEEN ST
SOUTH ST
HILLSIDE GDNS
Lanwithan CL
SPRINGFIELD
COFFA BRIDGE CL
TREWITHAN CL
COFFA LAKE
GRENVILLE MDWS

PENKNIGHT LA
Penknight
UPLANDS
ROSE HILL
CASTLE HILL
THE MOORS
CARBES LA
SUMMERS ST
QUAY ST
PARK RD
HOS
Great Western Commercial Village
BUTTS PK

EDGCUMBE RD
DARK LA
9 GUILDHALL LA
10 CHURCH LA
11 FIELD CL
12 MONMOUTH LA
13 PARADE SQ
14 RIVERSIDE CT
LOSTWITHIEL

1
Crewell
Cemy
Cowbridge
Rosehill
Lanwithan Farm
Lanwithan
TWO TREES RD

A390
Saints Way
Maddderly
POLMENA LA

59
No Man's Land

09 A 10 B C 11 D E F

						113

37
B5
1 VARLEY TERR
2 GWEL-AN-NANS CL
3 CRABBTREE CL
4 VICTORIA TERR
5 MANLEY TERR
6 LAWRY CL
7 MEADOW PK
8 OAK DR
9 JEANNE REES CT
10 KENNETH
LAUNDER CT
11 DONIERT'S CL
12 FOWENN CT

51
C5
1 PONDBRIDGE HILL
2 CANNON TERR
3 CHURCH GATE
4 WADHAM CL
5 WADHAM HO
6 PAVLOVA CT
7 RUSSELL ST
8 CARADON BSNS CTR
9 HEATHLANDS IND EST
10 MARTHUS CT
11 HURLERS CT

38

51
C6
1 LUXSTOWE DR
2 TREMEDDAN CT
3 GLENCROSS CT
4 TREWARTHA CT
5 LOWER LUX ST
6 CASTLE HILL
7 CASTLE HILL CT
8 THE WELLHOUSE
9 WEBBS CT
10 CASTLE VW

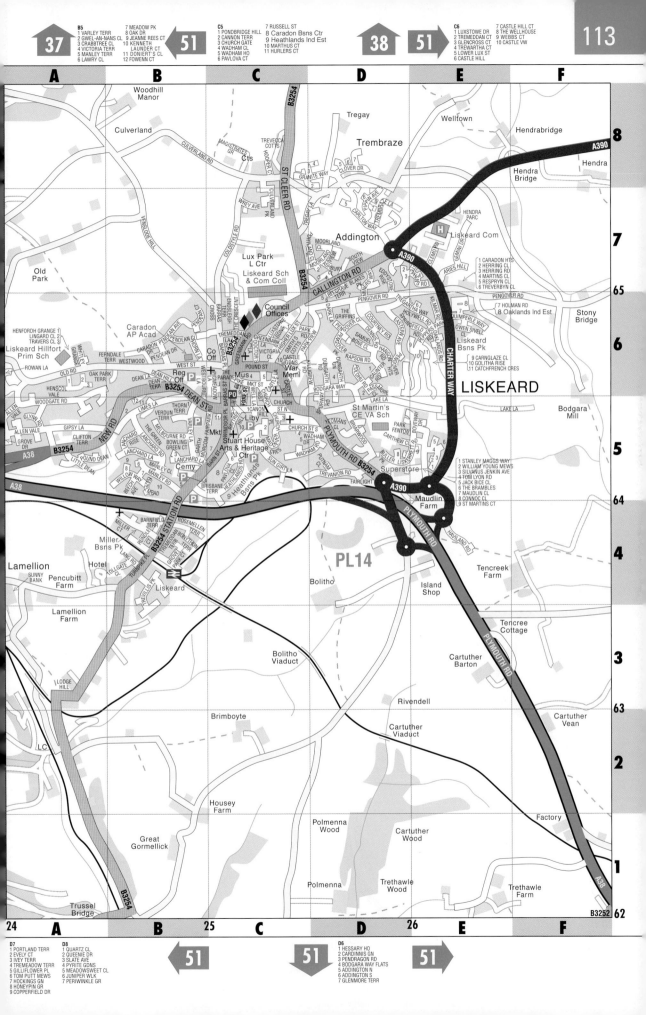

51
D7
1 PORTLAND TERR
2 EVELY CT
3 IVEY TERR
4 TREMEADOW TERR
5 GILLIFLOWER PL
6 TOM PUTT MEWS
7 HOCKINGS GN
8 HONEYPIN GR
9 COPPERFIELD DR

D8
1 QUARTZ CL
2 QUEENIE CT
3 SLATE AVE
4 PYRITE GDNS
5 MEADOWSWEET CL
6 JUNIPER WLK
7 PERIWINKLE GR

51

51
D6
1 HESSARY HO
2 CARDINNIS GN
3 PENDRAGON RD
4 BODGARA WAY FLATS
5 ADDINGTON N
6 ADDINGTON S
7 GLENMORE TERR

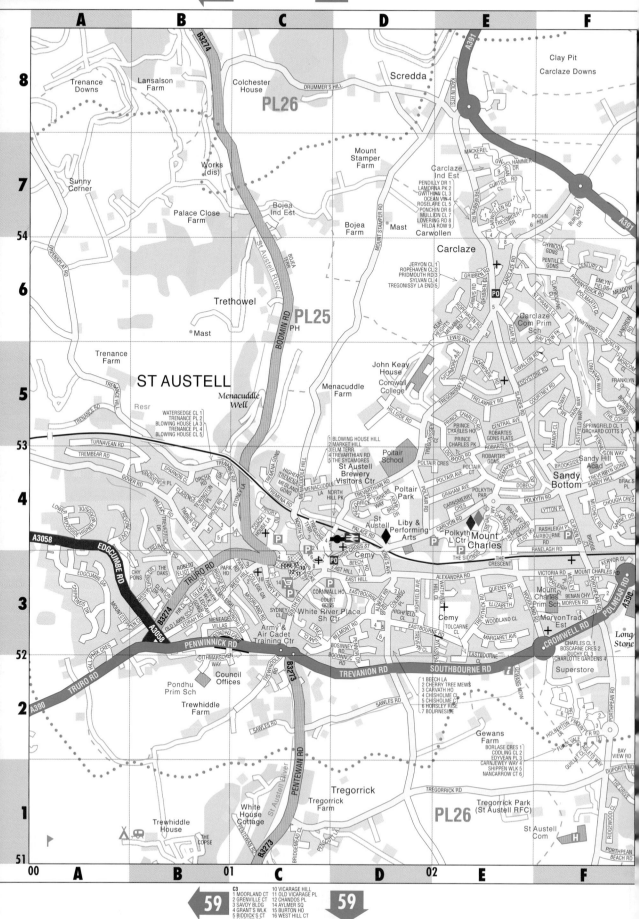

A B C D E F

8
7
54
6
5
53
4
3
52
2
1
51

00 A B 01 C D 02 E F

Trenance Downs
Lansalson Farm
Colchester House
PL26
Scredda
Clay Pit
Carlaze Downs
DRUMMER'S HILL
B3274
A391
KAOLIN HTS
Sunny Corner
Works (dis)
Mount Stamper Farm
Carclaze Ind Est
MACKEREL CL
HAMMER DR
Palace Close Farm
Bojea Ind Est
Bojea Farm
Mast
Carclaze Ind Est
PENDILLY DR 1
LAMORNA PK 2
GWITHIAN CL 3
OCEAN VW 4
ROSELARE CL 5
PONCHIN DR 6
MULLION CL 7
LOVERING RD 8
HILDA ROW 9
Carwollen
Carclaze
CURTICE RD
TREVERBYN RD
POCHIN HO
BURN LAWN DR
Trethowel
PL25
PH
Mast
ST AUSTELL
Menacuddle Well
Resr
Menacuddle Farm
JERYON CL 1
ROPEHAVEN CL 2
PRIDMOUTH RD 3
SYLVAN CL 4
TREGONISSY LA END 5
GRIBBEN RD
Carclaze Com Prim Sch
CHYNOON GDNS
PENTILLIE GDNS
EMLYN FIELDS
CENTURY CL
PO
Trenance Farm
John Keay House
Cornwall College
HILLSIDE RD
LEWIS WAY
KEAY HEIGHTS
THORPARK RD
GWALLON RD
EDGCOMBE AVE
TRELAWNEY RD
PRINCE CHARLES HO
PRINCE CHARLES PK
CENTRAL AVE
ROBARTES GDNS FLATS
ROBARTES PL
SPRINGFIELD CL 1
ORCHARD COTTS 2
Sandy Hill Acad
GON WAY
TRENANCE RD
TREMBEAR RD
TURNAVEAN RD
TRENANCE HILL
WATERSEDGE CL 1
TRENANCE PL 2
BLOWING HOUSE LA 3
TRENANCE PL 4
BLOWING HOUSE CL 5
1 BLOWING HOUSE HILL
2 MARKET HILL
3 ELM TERR
4 TREVARTHIAN RD
5 THE SYCAMORES
St Austell Brewery Visitors Ctr
Poltair School
POLTAIR CRES
POLTAIR
GRAHAM AVE
CARNSMERRY CRES
TRENANCE RD
SPARNON CL
ORCHA
CLARENCE EWINSTON
STONE LA
TREMENA GDNS
HIGHER TREMENA
MEDLAND GDNS
TREMENA RD
NORTH HILL PK
DARICK TINNERS WAY
TREVARTHIAN RD
ASHAM RD
Poltair Park
POLKYTH PAR
POLKYTH RD
LYTTON PL
CHOUGH CRES
A3058
EDGCUMBE RD
LOWER WOODSIDE
HIGHER WOODSIDE
EDGCUMBE GDNS
CHIPPONDS DR
TREVORRICK RD
TRELANCE CRES
TREVONE
CLINTON CL
OLD LAWN
ROBERT ELIOT CL
THE OAKS
CHY PONS
PRIORY RD
PALACE RD
PENTEWAN
St Austell
Liby & Performing Arts
Polkyth L Ctr
Mount Charles
RASHLEIGH CL
FAIRBOURNE RD
RANELAGH RD
KERVOR CL
A390
TRURO RD
PENWINNICK RD
B3274
A3058
Council Offices
DITHMARSCHEN WAY
Pondhu Prim Sch
Trewhiddle Farm
TREVANION RD
SOUTHBOURNE RD
B3273
CROMWELL RD
POLMEAR RD
A390
Superstore
Long Stone
Army & Air Cadet Training Ctr
SYDNEY CL
FORE ST
FRIARS
Cornwall Ho
Court Gdns
White River Place Sh Ctr
EAST HILL
BEECH
EAST HILL
Cemy
Alexandra Rd
HIGHFIELD AVE
Cemy
Mount Charles Prim Sch
MORVEN RD
ELIZABETH
MARGARET AVE
Morvon Trad Est
Gewans Farm
BORLASE CRES 1
CODLING CL 2
EDYVEAN PL 3
CARNJEWEY WAY 4
SHIPPEN WLK 5
NANCARROW CT 6
1 BEECH LA
2 CHERRY TREE MEWS
3 CARVATH HO
4 CHISHOLME CL
5 CHISHOLME CL
6 HORSLEY RISE
7 BOURNESIDE
CHARLES CL 1
BOSCARNE CRES 2
DUCHY CL
CHARLOTTE GARDENS 4
i
Gewans
FURZE VALE
BAY VIEW RD
SAWLES RD
SAWLES RD
White House Cottage
Tregorrick Farm
Tregorrick
TREGORRICK RD
Tregorrick Park (St Austell RFC)
PL26
St Austell Com
H
B3273
PENTEWAN RD
BRIDGEMEAD CL
PENSCOL LA
RIDGEWOOD CL
PORTHPEAN BEACH RD
THE DRIVE
Trewhiddle House
THE COPSE

C3
1 MOORLAND CT
2 GRENVILLE CT
3 SAVOY BLDG
4 GRANT'S WLK
5 BIDDICK'S CT
6 MARKET ST
7 CROSS LA
8 CHURCH ST
9 VICTORIA PL
10 VICARAGE HILL
11 OLD VICARAGE PL
12 CHANDOS PL
14 AYLMER SQ
15 BURTON HO
16 WEST HILL CT

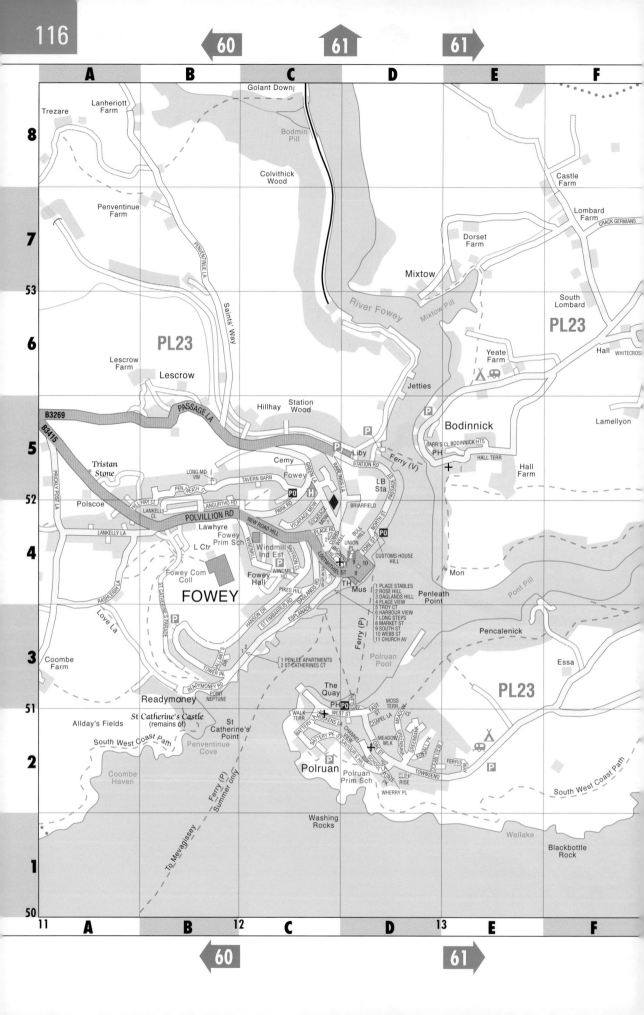

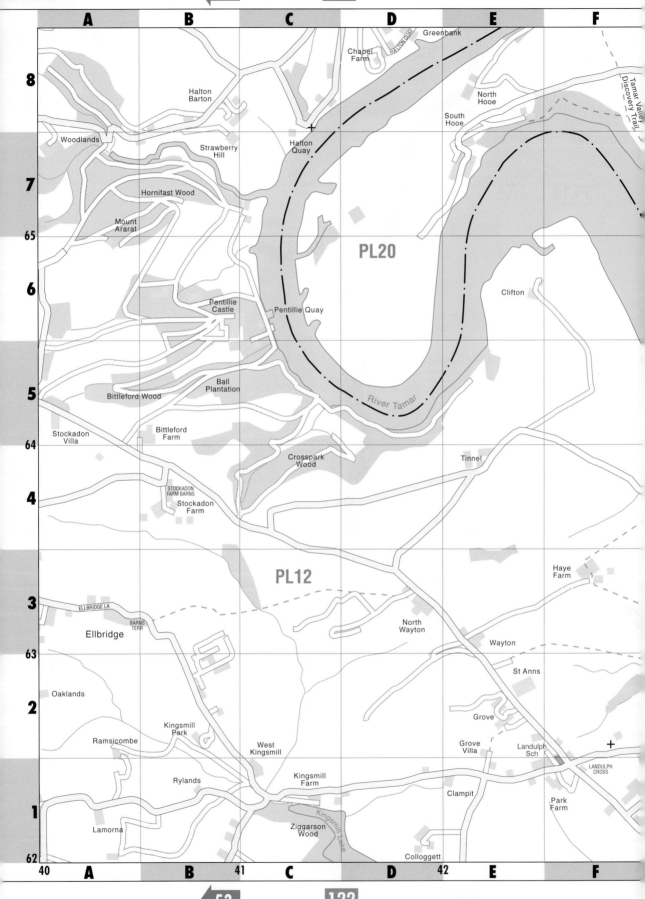

A B C D E F

8

Wottons Farm

Well Farm

Hewton

COTTS

Down Farm

HOLE CROSS

7

Down Wood

Hole's Hole

Leeches

65

Quay

Weir Quay

Shangri-La

Hole Farm

HOLE RD

6

Cleave Farm

Clamoak Poll Wood

LEY LA

Ley Farm

Clamoak

Tuckham Bridge

5

Clamoak Quay

Fairway

64

Shutecombe

Ormonde House

Parsonage Farm

HENSBURY LA

4

Liphil Quay

New Park Farm

PL20

PH

TREVETHANICK

Greystone

STATION RD

PO

FORE ST

PH

SILVER ST

Tamar Valley Discovery Trail

Bere Ferrers

DREAMLAND WAY

Bere Ferrers

Bere Barton

3

River Tamar

63

Thorn Point

Cargreen

COOMBE LA

COOMBE DR

2

Hall

HODDERS WAY

PH

CLOAKE PL

FORE ST

SLIPWAY QUAY

New Barn Farm

PENWIKE LA

Quays

HILL GDNS

CHURCH LA

Pennard's Point

River Tavy

1

PL12

62

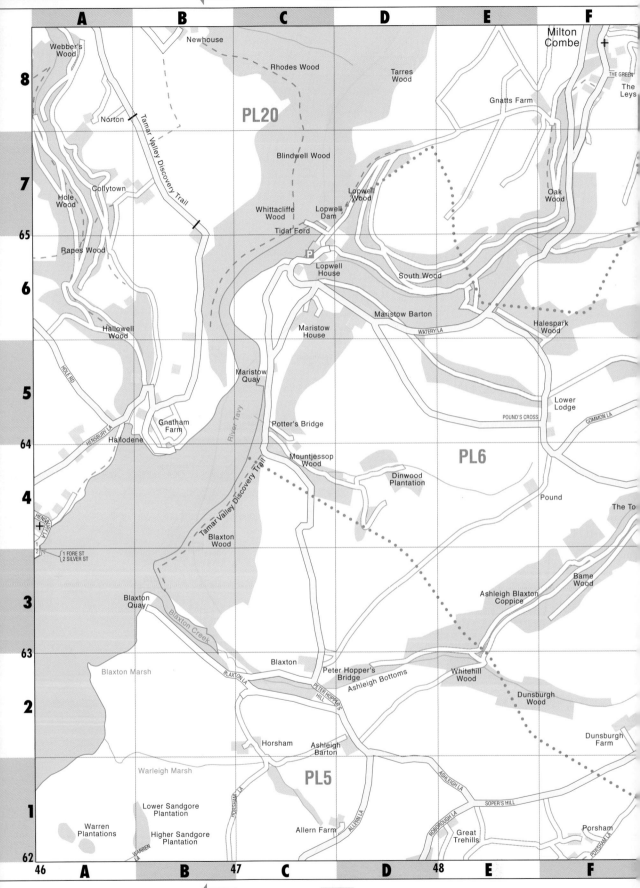

A B C D E F

8
7
65
6
5
64
4
3
63
2
1
62

Devon STREET ATLAS

Uphill
Morey House
Dashel
Bickham
Bickham
Upper Road Plantation
Charity Bickham
Bulteel Bickham
Middlelodge Plantation
The Wilderness
Higher Park
Middle Lodge
Henshears
Welltown Bridge
North Broadley
Coppers
Broadley
Haxter Lodge
Roborough Farm
Roborough House
Roborough Plantation
Broadley Ind Pk
Haxter Wood
Porsham Plantation
Ten Acre Brake
Belliver Ind Est

PL20
PL6

Hotel
Webbers
Commonlane Plantation
Higher Lodge
Combe Park Farm
Lower Upperton
Little Down
Marrowpark Plantation
Leigh
Leigh
Vicarage
Roborough
Coombe Barton
Coombe Wood
Hursley Bsns Pk

COMMON LA
DEVONPORT LEAT
A386
SOWTON RD
MOORLAND CL
TECSADE DOWN
ROBOROUGH DOWN LA
UPPERTON LA
LITTLE DOWN LA
HELE LA
NEW RD
LEIGH LA
TAMERTON RD
SOPERS HILL
PARKWOOD RD
BROADLEY PARK RD
BROADLEY CL
HAXTER CL
BELLIVER WAY
PORSHAM CL
TAVISTOCK RD
CARSON LA
BLACKVEN HILL
BICKLEIGH DOWN RD
JUMP CL
LEAT SIDE
LEAT WLK
PICKLEVEN CL
INGRA WLK
HESSARY DR

LOPES DR 1
VILLAGE DR 2
CRAMBER CL 3
STAPLE CL 4
LADY CL
RIDGE CL

PH

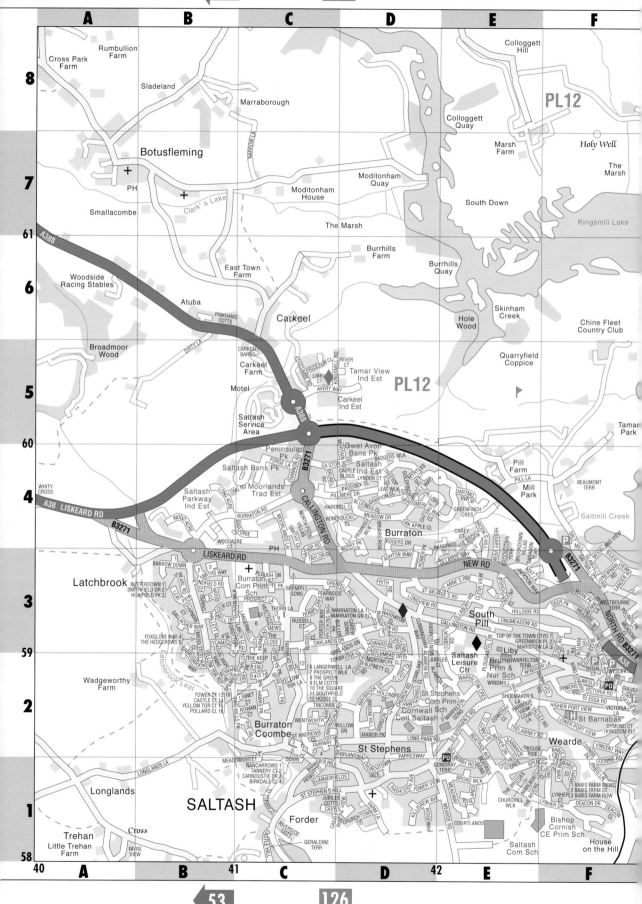

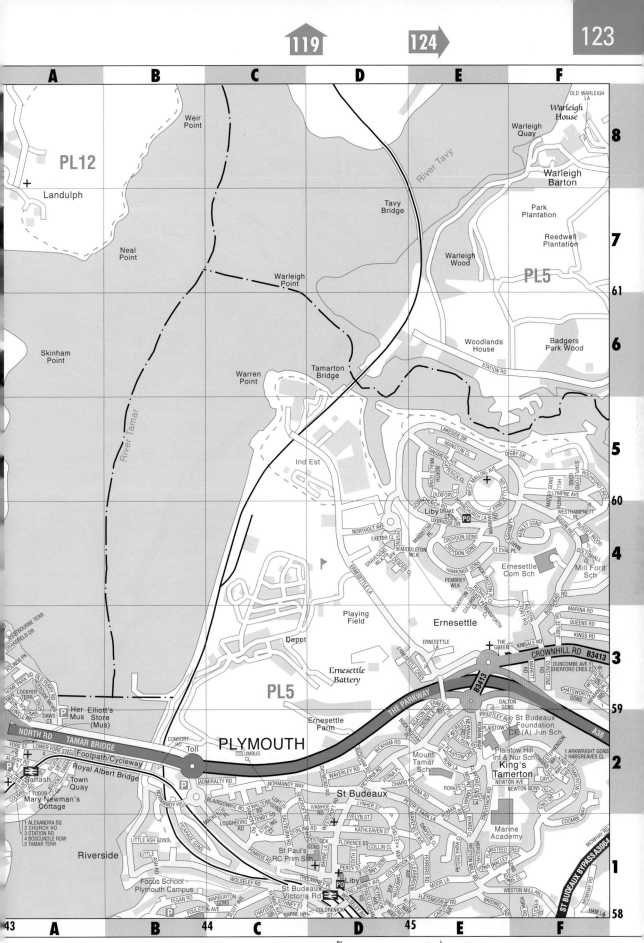

PL12

Landulph

Weir Point

Neal Point

Skinham Point

River Tamar

Warleigh Point

Warren Point

Tamarton Bridge

Tavy Bridge

River Tavy

OLD WARLEIGH LA

Warleigh House

Warleigh Quay

Warleigh Barton

Park Plantation

Reedwell Plantation

PL5

Warleigh Wood

STATION RD

Woodlands House

Badgers Park Wood

Ind Est

LAKESIDE DR

MANSTON CL

TANGMERE AVE

WEALD GDNS

DUXFORD

NORTH CL

MAVERICK CL

WEST MALLING AVE

DIGBY GR

STAPLEFORD GDNS

ROCHFORD CRES

HILL

SNGD ASHWY

LYMPNE AVE

WESTHAMPNETT PL

RUSSEL WOOD

BIGGIN HILL

KENLEY GDNS

Liby Drake

PO

HORNCHURCH LA

HOPE CHURCH RD

CHIVENOR AVE

UXBRIDGE DR

MAIDSTONE

CROYDON GDNS

CROYDON GDNS

ST EVAL PL

HAWKINGE GDNS

MACKINGTON CL

ERNESETTLE LA

HACKINGTON CL

KENWAY

MANSHAW

COLTISHALL CL

Mill Ford Sch

Ernesettle Com Sch

PEMBREY WLK

PERNANPORTH

EXETER CL

MIDDLETON WLK

ABERDEEN CL

GRAVESEND WLK

NORTHOLT AVE

YELVERTON CL

TAGATON RD

BUDSHEAD RD

MARINA RD

QUEENS RD

KINGS RD

Playing Field

Ernesettle

ERNESETTLE CRES

ERNESETTLE LA

JUBILEE PL

THE GREEN

KINSALE RD

CROWNHILL RD B3413

DUNCOMBE AVE 1

SHERFORD CRES 2/2

MARTI

DUNSTONE

CHATSWORTH GDNS

POLLARD

Depot

Ernesettle Battery

PL5

Ernesettle Farm

THE PARKWAY

B3413

A38

59

DALTON GDNS

PRIESTLEY AVE

St Budeaux Foundation CE(A) Jun Sch

Plaistow Hill Inf & Nur Sch

ARKWRIGHT GDNS 1

HARGREAVES 2

King's Tamerton

STEPHENSON

WESTBOURNE TERR

DRAKEFIELD DR

HOME PARK AV

POUNDS PK

LOCKYER TERR

OLD FERRY RD

TAVY RD

BIGG RD

BGMORE

CHURCH RD

BEWELL RD

Her Mus

Elliott's Store (Mus)

P

DAWS CT

NORTH RD TAMAR BRIDGE

TAMAR BRIDGE

Footpath/Cycleway

CONSORT HO

Toll

PLYMOUTH

COLUMBUS CL

FORE ST

LOWER FORE ST

ALBERT RD

CULVER

Saltash

Town Quay

P

Mary Newman's Cottage

1 TUDOR CT

1 ALEXANDRA SQ

2 CHURCH HO

3 STATION RD

4 BOSCUNDLE ROW

5 TAMAR TERR

Riverside

Royal Albert Bridge

NORMANDY HILL

ADMIRALTY RD

NORMANDY WAY

BLAIRGOWRIE GDNS

MACKETTLE

WALTERS

STANBOROUGH

DENBY WY

STIRLING RD

LOUGHBORO RD

LITTLE ASH GDNS

LITTLE ASH RD

VICARAGE GDNS

IVANHOE RD

WESTCROFT RD

LOFTUS GDNS

SALTBURN RD

CODSTOCK GDNS

BARNE LA

Focus School - Plymouth Campus

P

FEGAN RD

FOULSTON AVE

WARBURTON GDNS

SCOTT AVE

HAYDON GR

PENROS RD

SITHNEY ST

BARNE RD

St Paul's RC Prim Sch

St Budeaux Victoria Rd

WOLSELEY RD

TRELAWNEY PL

PERCY ST

COLDRENICK ST

Liby

PO

TRELAWNEY AVE

FRESHFORD

BICKHAM RD

WAVERLEY RD

DAIMOND RD

BUCKINGHAM

Mount Tamar Sch

VERNA PL

CHARD RD

VERNA RD

St Budeaux

PETER'S PARK LA

ROMAN WAY

ROW LA

EVELYN ST

LYNHER ST

KATHLEAVEN ST

FLORENCE ST

COLLIN CL

PLAISTOW CRES

SHELLEY WAY

WAKEFIELD CL

DAWSON ST

ROMAN RD

TREVITHICK RD

KNGS TAMERTON RD

NEWTON AVE

NEWTON GDNS

CAYLEY WAY

Marine Academy

KEAST MEAD

COOMBE WAY

SNGD CL

HERSCHEL RD

WESTON MILL RD

FERRERS RD

MOOR LA

PETERS PARK LA

CLEARBROOK AVE

HALLEY GDNS

HALSTEAD CRES

TAMERTON

VINGOLE RD

CARDINAL

FLETEMOOR RD

BRIDWELL RD

WESTON MILL HILL

TUCKER CL

YORK RD

MOWHAY RD

ST BUDEAUX BYPASS A3064

HAM LA

58

A B C D E F

8

WARREN LA

OLD WARLEIGH LA

Warleigh Lodge

West Trehills

North Coombe Farm

Porsham Wood

Tamar Valley Discovery Trail

FRASER SQ

LINTON SQ

LINTON RD

CUNNINGHAM RD

ALLERN LA

ROROROUGH LA

SADDLERS WAY

WHITSON CROSS

1 HARVEST CL
2 HALTER CL
3 HIGHFIELD VIEW

Yappers Wood

PORSHAM LA

Coombe Farm

LIZARD CL

7

Tamerton Foliot

Frenoes Farm

Mary Dean's CE Prim Sch

FRASER RD

MARY DEAN AVE

HILL DEAN CL

WHITSWOOD LA

WHITSWOOD CL

HARWOOD AVE

ROCK HILL

GRASHAM AVE

HENLEY RD

Hayesend Farm

WARING RD

Clittaford Cottage

CLITTAFORD VIEW

BILTERN CL

WINNICOTT CL

Langley Plantation

KINNARD CRES

STROMA

Tor Plantation

OLD WARLEIGH LA

NURSERY RD

FORE ST

LAMBERT RD

SEVEN STARS LA

CHURCH HILL

PO

PH

LA

RIVERSIDE WLK

TAMERTON FOLIOT RD

B3313

Cann House

Cann Woods Nature Reserve

AMBER CL 1
GROVE CL 2
BUCKTHORN CL 3
GUELDER WAY 4

DUNNET RD

HANGER CL

PETHICK RD

BILLINGS CL

BEATTY WLK

SAUNDERS WLK

ROLSTON CL

BLACKMORE CL

WAYCOTT WLK

CHESHIRE DR

WILLIAM EVANS CL

SOUTHWAY DR

LATIMER WLK

GODDWIG GDNS

RADCLIFFE CL

LAW WLK

Southway La

PILLAR WLK 1
MOSES CT 2

ALGER WLK

SEC PELL

POND CT

BONVILLE RD

BAMPFYLDE WAY

Beechwood Prim Sch

BAMPFYLDE WAY

BURNARD CL

CLITTAFORD RD

ALDERNEY RD

INCHKEITH RD

ROCKFIELD AVE

Southway

PL6

61

Tor Rock

STATION RD

LAKE RD TO MASH

HOLLY PARK CL

HOLLY PARK DR

CAMBORNE CL

REDRUTH CL

TRURO DR

LAKEVIEW DR

MILFORD LA

NORTHAMPTON CL

TAUNTON PL

TAUNTON AVE

THERFORD RD

AYLESBURY CRES

Playing Fields

St Peter's RC Prim Sch

Whitleigh

Woodfield Prim Sch

Whitleigh Wood

FRONTFIELD CRES

COPLESTON RD

GRASMERE CL

TOXWOOD GDNS

The ARBOUR

LOOSELEIGH CL

MARSDON CL

WARLEIGH LA

LOPWELL

TRETOWER CL

ULLSWATER CRES

Notre Dame RC Sch

6

Budshead Creek

Budshead Wood

PL5

CANTERBURY DR

NEWCASTLE GDNS

NORWICH GDNS

OAKHAM RD

WINCHESTER GDNS

St HELENS

BRENTFORD AVE

SHREWSBURY RD

MONMOUTH GDNS

BUDSHEAD RD

WHITLEIGH GN

Sir John Hunt Com Sports Coll

READING WLK

HUNTINGDON GDNS

Woodlands Sch

Whitleigh Com Prim Sch

PICKLECOMBE DR

KENDAL PL

Christian Mill Bsns Pk

Water Works

WINDERMERE CRES

CONISTON CL

NOTRE DAME CL

DRAKES

LEATFIELD DR

5

60

Plymouth Knowle Prim Sch

Woodland Wood

ANZAC AVE

INST AVE RA

MARINA RD

PARADE PL

RINGMORE WAY

PENGELLY WAY

CANTERBURY DR

HONITON WLK

INSTOW WLK

TAMERTON

LAMBOURNE

HAYTOR CL

KEYHAM CL

CHERITON CL

BELCTONE

MERIVALE RD

1 FOXTOR CL
2 MODBURY CL
3 MARLDON CL
4 BLACKTHORN CL
5 GUY MILES WAY
6 BOXHILL CL

1 BRANSCOMBE GDNS
2 QUEENS RD
3 KINGS RD
4 HIRMANDALE RD
5 HALDON PL
6 WOODLANDS CT

Brook Green Ctr for Learning

Woodland Fort

Liby

LEWES GDNS

WHITLEIGH AVE

CHELMSFORD GDNS

Budshead Gn

IPSWICH CT

DERBY RD

Trowbridge CL

PO

P

BLAKE GDNS 1
CHESTERTON CL 2
BETJEMAN WLK 3
CRASHAM CL 4
HOUSMAN CL 5
CONSTABLE CL 6
GOLDSMITH GDNS 7
WILMOT GDNS 8
SEDLEY WAY 9

APPLEBY WLK

DORCHESTER AVE

WARWICK AVE

CARLISLE RD

BODMIN RD

LANCASTER GDNS

WHITLEIGH CT

GUILDFORD CL

Brooklands CT

OAK DR

LODGE GDNS

Crownhill Fort

SMALLACK CL 1
CHARLTON CL 2
LANSDOWNE RD 3

B3313

A386

4

3

59

West Park

B3413

P

Liby

ASHBURNHAM RD

COOMBE PARK LA

SHERFORD RD

REDLESTONE RD

WANSTEAD GR

LITTLE DOCK LA

ST FRANCIS CT

CHARD BARTON

CAREW GDNS

CAREW

BUSY DEAN

WAVENEY

HORSHAM

BICKERMOOR

OLD WOODLANDS RD

CROWNHILL RD

YEARS WAY

CARROLL RD

CONLEY RD

RUSWAY CRES

DRY CL

ELGIN CRES

KIRKWALL RD

DIGSWELL

DRAWBRIDGE

ROTHESAY GDNS

DUMFRIES AVE

BERWICK AVE

SELKIRK PL

Budshead Way

TAVISTOCK RD

SMALLACK DR

HUNTER CL

The LIMES

Crownhill

2

Drake's Hill

PL2

A38

NEW WAY RD

DUNCOMBE AVE

EASTBURY AVE

Burrington Ind Est

BURRINGTON RD

WESTON MILL LA

Walkham Bsns Pk

BURRINGTON WAY

MANSFIELD GDNS

THE PARKWAY

HONICKNOWLE LA

ASHRIDGE WAY

COURTNEY RD

MONTGOMERY CL

STOWE GDNS

MONTAGUE AVE

HAREWOOD CL

BOSWELL CL 1
DEFOE CL 2
TENNYSON GDNS

DICKENS RD

BEDE GDNS 1

THACKERAY GDNS

TYNDALE CL

SWINBURNE GDNS

COVERDALE WAY

SHIRLEY GDNS

Shakespeare Prim Sch

Honicknowle

Hypermarket

MOUNT PLEASANT

CORBETT RD

BYRON AVE

BUNYAN AVE

BURNS AVE

SHAKESPEARE RD

SWIFT GDNS

SONNET

BALLAD

WALTON CRES

DRAYTON RD

MACAULAY CRES

CONRAD RD

SHERIDAN RD

CHAUCER WAY

CONGREVE GDNS

HILTON AVE

PO

Manadon Football Ctr

ENTERPRISE DR

TEMERAIRE RD

RAMSEY GDNS

VANGUARD WAY

LEANDER WAY

CAPTAINS GDNS

Whitleigh Cotts

BLADDER LA

St Boniface RC Coll

PL2

Manadon

SHACKLETON CT

BARRIE GDNS

DARWIN CRES

HARDY GDNS

NEAVY WAY

MORADON HILL

MORADON HILL

A386

COLERIDGE RD

PO

P

Liby

CROSS PARK AVE

CROSS PARK WAY

GREAT BERRY RD

STANBURY AVE

BERRY HEAD

CROSS PARK

B3413

FORT AUSTIN AVE

Alexandra RD

CROWNHILL CT

TREVITHICK

WIDEY

Widey Court Prim Sch

Courtlands Sch

1

The All Saints CE Academy

Kestral Units

ST PANCRAS AVE

A38

C1
1 POETS CORNER
2 CAXTON GDNS
D2
1 PROTECTOR RD
2 MONTROSE WAY
D1
1 GLEANER CL
2 BULWARK CL

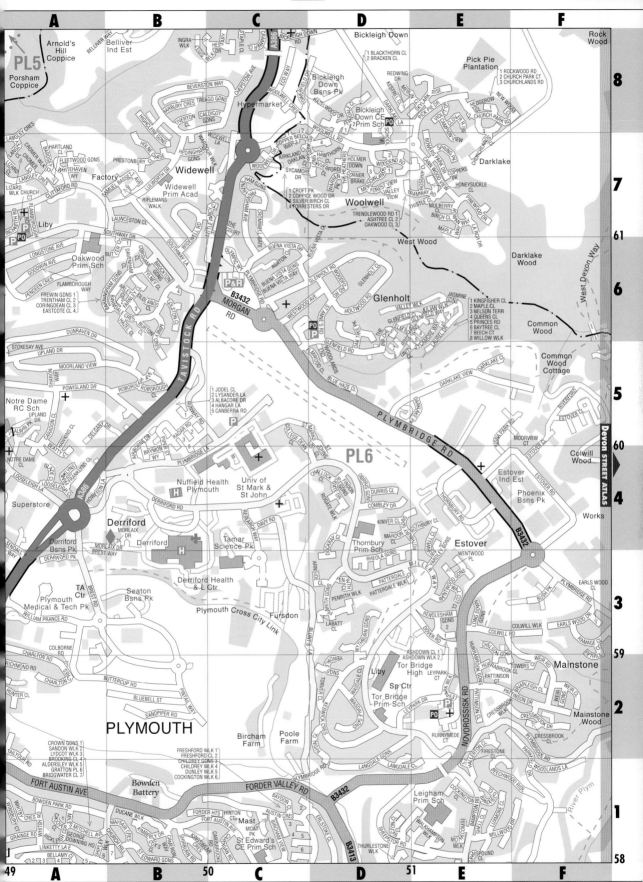

123
128
F5
1 NEPEAN ST
2 ADELAIDE ST
3 BRUNEL TERR
4 EPWORTH TERR
5 SUSSEX TERR
6 RAILWAY COTTS
7 YORK TERR
8 ST MAWES TERR

133
128
F3
1 CLARENDON HO
2 GARFIELD TERR
3 TRAFALGAR PL
4 THE MEWS
5 NELSON GDNS
6 BEYROUT PL
7 ST MICHAEL'S CT
8 ST MICHAEL'S TERR
9 PORTLAND CT
10 MOLYNEAUX PL
11 CLARENDON LA
F4
1 ST GEORGES CT
2 HORNBY ST
3 PHILLIMORE ST
4 FREMANTLE GDNS
5 FAIRFAX TERR
6 HARGOOD TERR
7 HARRISON ST
8 KEPPEL TERR
9 HEALY CT
10 BRUNSWICK PL

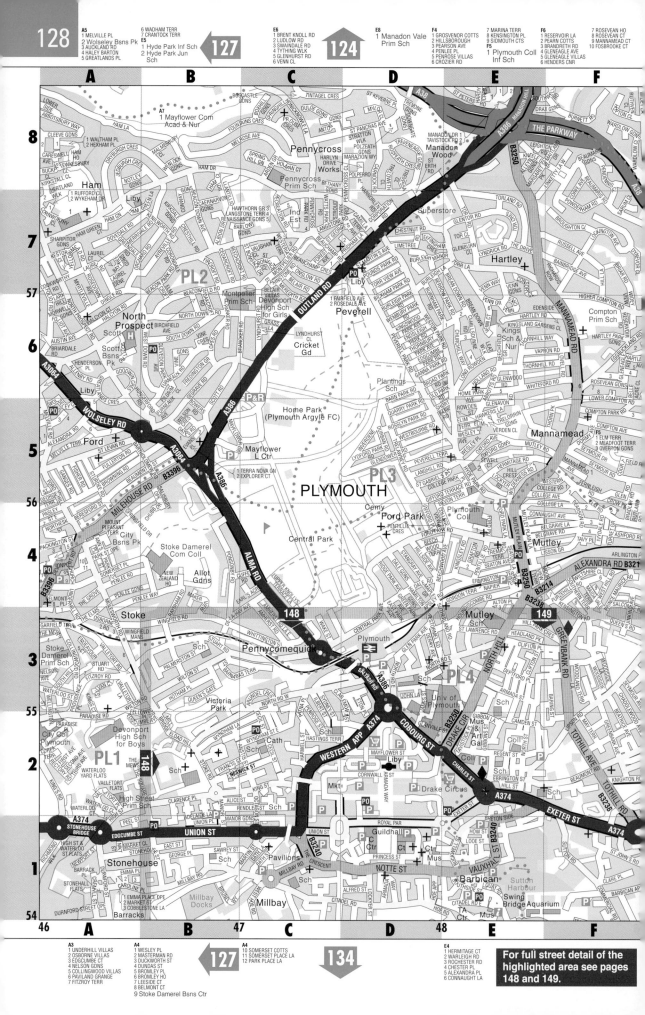

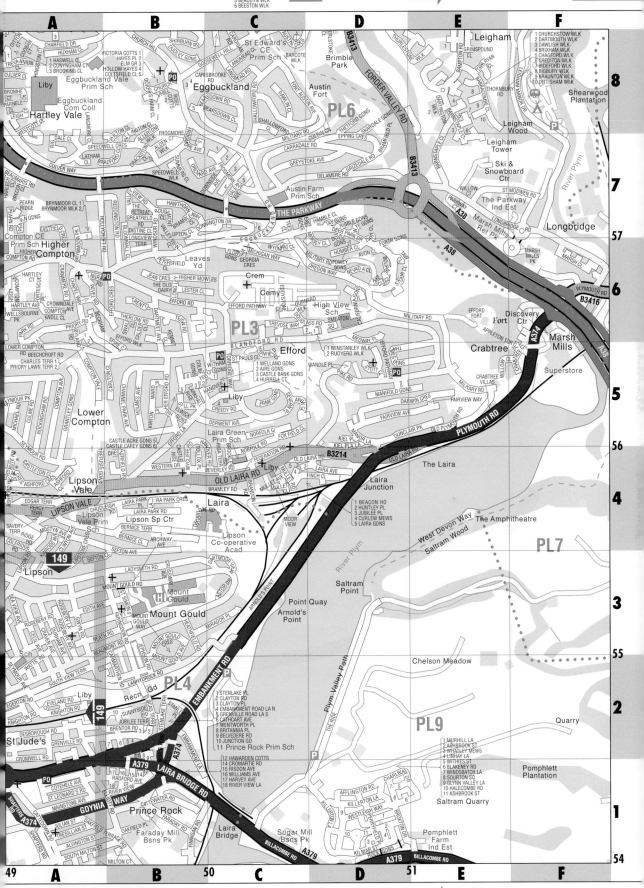

C7
1 BRAMBLE WLK
2 BOWHAYS WLK
3 BRISMAR WLK
4 MOORFIELD AVE
5 BEAUDYN WLK
6 BEESTON WLK

▲ 125

130 ▶

129

F
1 CHURCHSTOW WLK
2 DARTMOUTH WLK
3 DAWLISH WLK
4 BRIXHAM WLK
5 CHAGFORD WLK
6 CREDITON WLK
7 BIDEFORD WLK
8 BIGBURY WLK
9 BRAUNTON WLK
10 DITTISHAM WLK

Leigham

Shearwood
Plantation

Leigham
Wood

Leigham
Tower

Ski &
Snowboard
Ctr

The Parkway
Ind Est

Longbridge

Marsh
Mills

Crabtree

Discovery
Ctr

Marsh
Mills

Superstore

Brimble
Park

Austin
Fort

PL6

Austin Farm
Prim Sch

THE PARKWAY

Higher
Compton

Leaves
Yd

Crem

Cemy

High View
Sch

PL3

Efford

Lower
Compton

Laira Green
Prim Sch

Liby

OLD LAIRA RD

Laira
Junction

The Laira

Lipson
Vale

Laira

Lipson
Co-operative
Acad

West Devon Way

Saltram Wood

The Amphitheatre

PL7

Lipson

Mount
Gould

Mount Gould

Point Quay

Arnold's
Point

River Plym

Saltram
Point

Chelson Meadow

PL4

Recn
Gd

EMBANKMENT RD

PL9

Quarry

St Jude's

LAIRA BRIDGE RD

GDYNIA WAY

Prince Rock

Laira
Bridge

Sugar Mill
Bsns Pk

Faraday Mill
Bsns Pk

BILLACOMBE RD

A379

Pomphlett
Plantation

Saltram Quarry

Pomphlett
Farm
Ind Est

BILLACOMBE RD

For full street detail of the
highlighted area see page 149.

E7
1 PERSEVERANCE COTTS
2 BLANCHARD PL

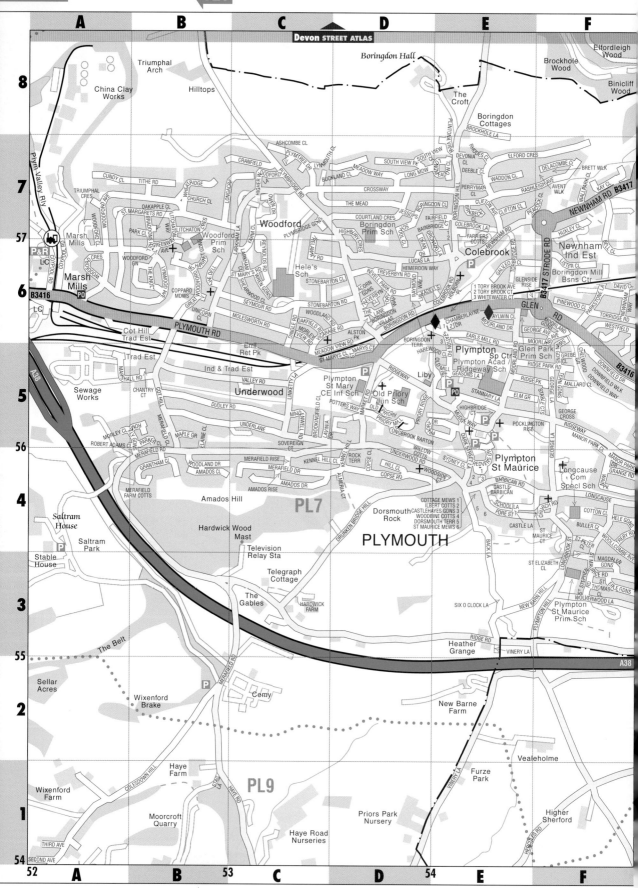

B5
1 CALEDONIA CL
2 ELDER CL
3 MAGNOLIA CL
4 TURBILL GDNS
5 PAYNTER WLK
6 Glen Park Prim Sch

C5
1 EIGHT ACRE CL
2 LAWN CL
3 ORCHARD CL
4 GREAT PARK CL
5 LONG TERRACE CL
6 CYPRESS CL

7 CAMPION CL
8 RODDICK WAY
9 BRANSON CT

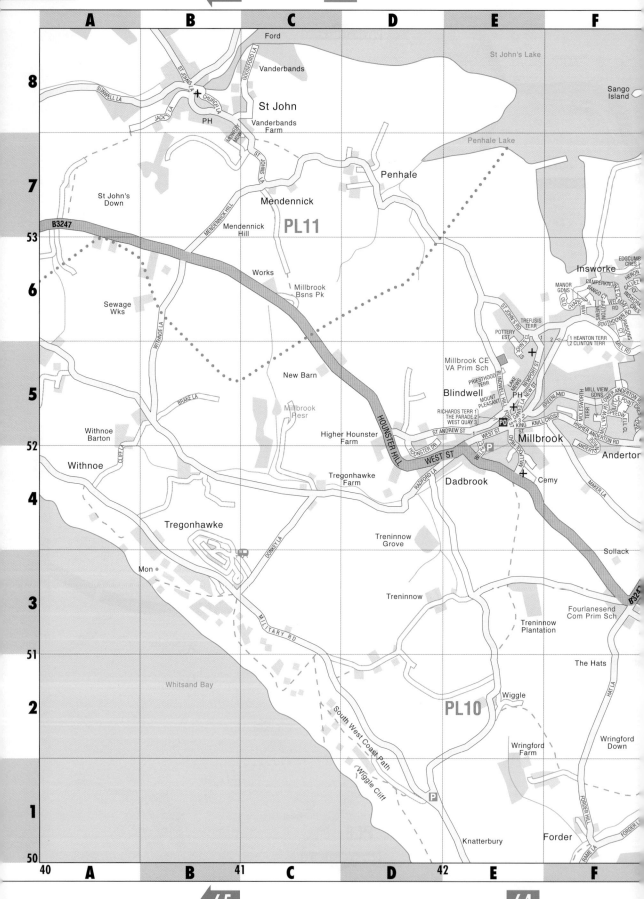

A B C D E F

8

Ford
Vanderbands
SURWELL LA
St John
PH
Vanderbands
Farm

7

St John's
Down
Penhale
Mendennick
Mendennick
Hill
PL11

B3247

6

Sewage
Wks
Works
Millbrook
Bsns Pk
Insworke
MANOR
GDNS
CAMPERKNOWLE
EDGCUMB
CRES
HERON
CALVEZ
CL
SANGO CT
CHAPEL
INSWORKE
CRES
PARSONS
CL
TREFUSIS
TERR
POTTERY
EST
1 HEANTON TERR
2 CLINTON TERR
SOUTHDOWN RD
MILL RD

5

Withnoe
Barton
BRAKE LA
New Barn
Millbrook
Resr
WITHNOE LA
Millbrook CE
VA Prim Sch
Blindwell
PRIESTHOOD
TERR
MOUNT
PLEASANT
PH
RICHARDS TERR 1
THE PARADE 2
WEST QUAY 3
BLINDWELL HILL
LAKE
MEWS
NEW ST
KING ST
KNILL CROSS
GREENLAND
MILL VIEW
GDNS
MOLESWORTH
LOWER ANDERTON RD
THE POINT RD
SPEEDWELL CL
CORN CL
HIGHER ANDERTON RD

52

Withnoe
CLIFF LA
Higher Hounster
Farm
HOUNSTER HILL
ST ANDREW ST
WEST ST
WEST ST
PO
P
Millbrook
ANDERTON
Anderton

4

Tregonhawke
DONKEY LA
Tregonhawke
Farm
RADFORD LA
Dadbrook
Cemy
MAKER LA
Sollack

Mon
MILITARY RD
Treninnow
Grove
Treninnow
Treninnow
Plantation
Fourlanesend
Com Prim Sch
B3247

3

51

Whitsand Bay
The Hats
HAT LA

2

South West Coast Path
PL10
Wiggle
Wringford
Farm
Wringford
Down

Wiggle Cliff
P

1

Knatterbury
FORDER HILL
BRAKE LA
Forder
FORDER LA

50

40 A 41 B C 42 D E F

65
64

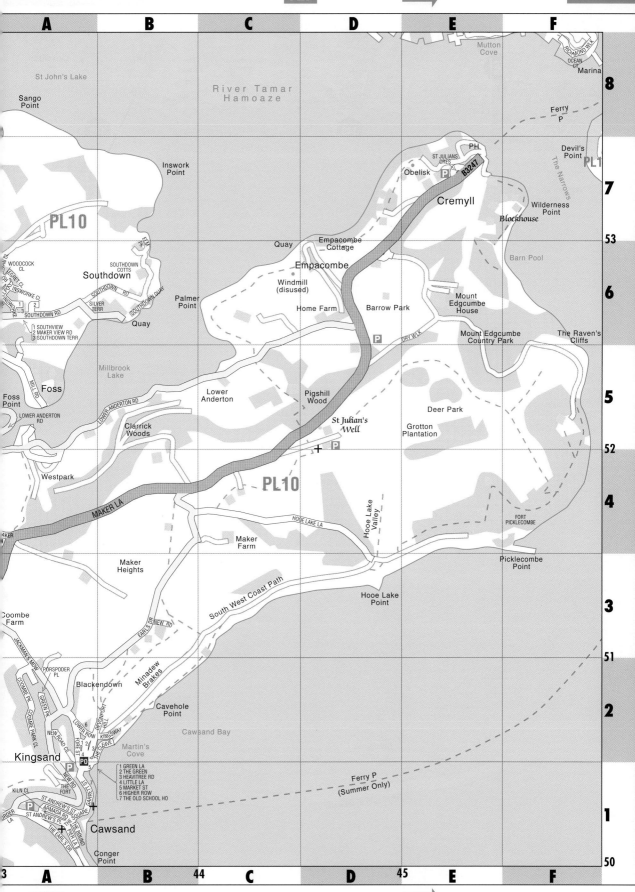

A **B** **C** **D** **E** **F**

8

St John's Lake

Sango
Point

River Tamar
Hamoaze

Mutton
Cove

OCEAN
CT
Marina

Ferry
P

Devil's
Point
PL1

St Julians
Cres
Obelisk

PH
P
B3247

The Narrows

7

Cremyll

Wilderness
Point

Blockhouse

53

PL10

Inswork
Point

Barn Pool

WOODCOCK
CL
EGRET CL
INSWORKE CL
INSWORKE
Southdown
SOUTHDOWN
COTTS
SOUTHDOWN RD
SILVER
TERR
SOUTHDOWN QUAY
SOUTHDOWN RD

Quay

Empacombe
Cottage

Empacombe

Windmill
(disused)

Palmer
Point
Home Farm

Barrow Park

Mount
Edgcumbe
House

6

Quay

1 SOUTHVIEW
2 MAKER VIEW RD
3 SOUTHDOWN TERR

P
DRY WLK

Mount Edgcumbe
Country Park

The Raven's
Cliffs

Millbrook
Lake

MILL RD
Foss

Foss
Point

LOWER ANDERTON
RD

LOWER ANDERTON RD

Lower
Anderton

Pigshill
Wood

St Julian's
Well

Deer Park

Grotton
Plantation

5

52

Westpark

Clarrick
Woods

+
P

PL10

Hooe Lake
Valley

FORT
PICKLECOMBE

4

MAKER LA

Maker
Farm

HOOE LAKE LA

Picklecombe
Point

Maker
Heights

Coombe
Farm

EARLS DR NEW RD

South West Coast Path

Hooe Lake
Point

3

51

PORSPODER
PL
JACKMAN'S MDW
COOMBE PK
GREEN PK
COOMBE PARK CL

Blackendown

Minadew
Brakes

REDINGPORT
HILL
GREEN HILL

Cavehole
Point

Cawsand Bay

2

NEW RD
LOWER ROW
FORE ST
6
2
CAVE
KINGSWAY

Kingsand

PO

1 GREEN LA
2 THE GREEN
3 HEAVITREE RD
4 LITTLE LA
5 MARKET ST
6 HIGHER ROW
7 THE OLD SCHOOL HO

Martin's
Cove

Ferry P
(Summer Only)

KILN CL
THE
FORT

P
ST ANDREW'S ST
ARMADA RD
THE SQUARE
ST ANDREW'S PL
THE ROUND
PIER LA
THE EARL'S DR
+
+
Cawsand

Conger
Point

1

50

3 **A** **B** 44 **C** **D** 45 **E** **F**

133
128

For full street detail of the highlighted area see pages 148 and 149.

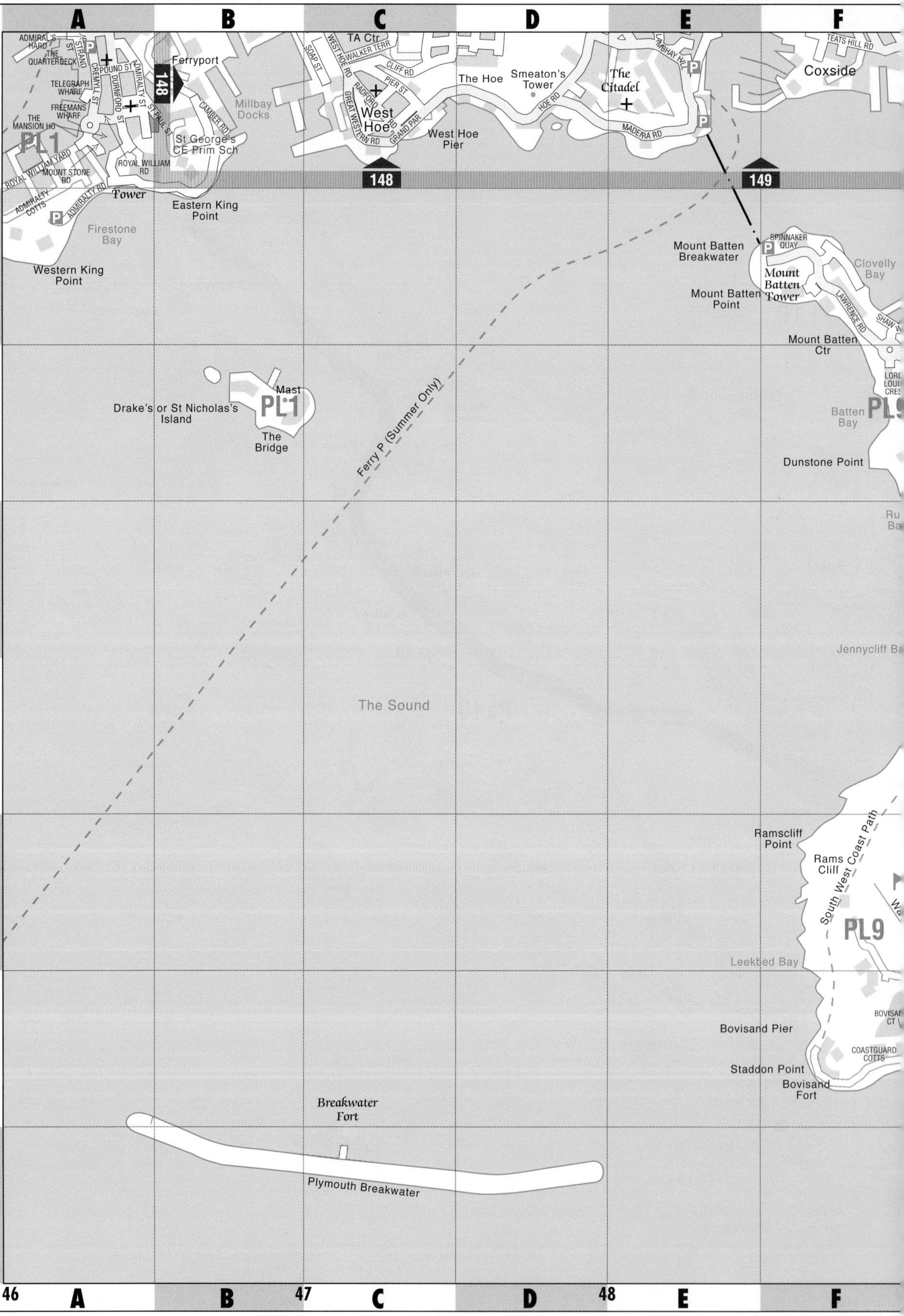

A B C D E F

ADMIRAL'S HARD
THE QUARTERDECK
ROUND ST
Ferryport
TA Ctr
WEST HOE RD
WALKER TERR
CLIFF RD
PIER ST
Coside
TEATS HILL RD
LAMBHAY HILL

TELEGRAPH WHARF
FREEMANS WHARF
CRANMIL ST
DURNFORD ST
STONEHOUSE
ADMIRALTY ST
STONE ST
CAMBER RD
Millbay Docks
SOAP ST
RADFORD
GREAT WESTERN RD
GRAND PAR
The Hoe
Smeaton's Tower
HOE RD
The Citadel
MADEIRA RD
Coxside

8

THE MANSION HO
PL1
ROYAL WILLIAM YARD
MOUNT STONE
Tower
ADMIRALTY COTTS
ADMIRALTY RD
MOUNT STONE RD
ROYAL WILLIAM RD
St George's CE Prim Sch
West Hoe
West Hoe Pier

148
148
149

Eastern King Point

Firestone Bay

7

Western King Point

Mount Batten Breakwater

Mount Batten Point

Spinnaker Quay
Mount Batten Tower
Clovelly Bay
LAWRENCE RD
SHAW

Mount Batten Ctr
LORE LOUI CRES

53

Drake's or St Nicholas's Island
Mast
PL1

The Bridge

6

Batten Bay
PL9

Dunstone Point

Ferry P (Summer Only)

Ru Ba

5

Jennycliff Ba

52

The Sound

4

South West Coast Path
Ramscliff Point
Rams Cliff

3

PL9

Leekbed Bay

51

Bovisand Pier

BOVISAN CT

2

Staddon Point
Bovisand Fort
COASTGUARD COTTS

Breakwater Fort

Plymouth Breakwater

1

50

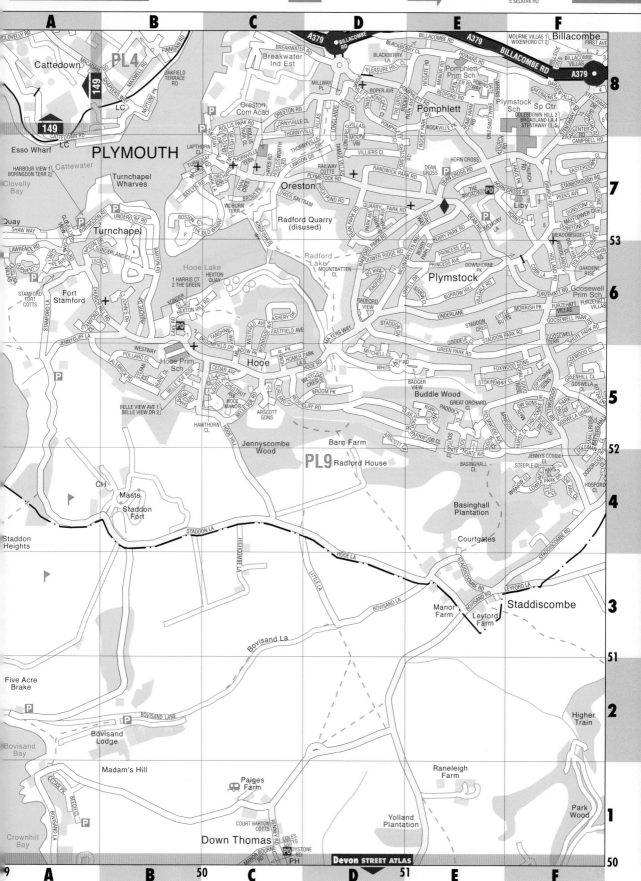

For full street detail of the highlighted area see page 149.

129

136

F5
1 CHALLGOOD CL
2 ORCHARDTON TERR

F7
1 THE DUKES RYDE
2 MAPLE CT
3 MAGNOLIA CT
4 HORN LANE FLATS
5 SELKIRK HO

135

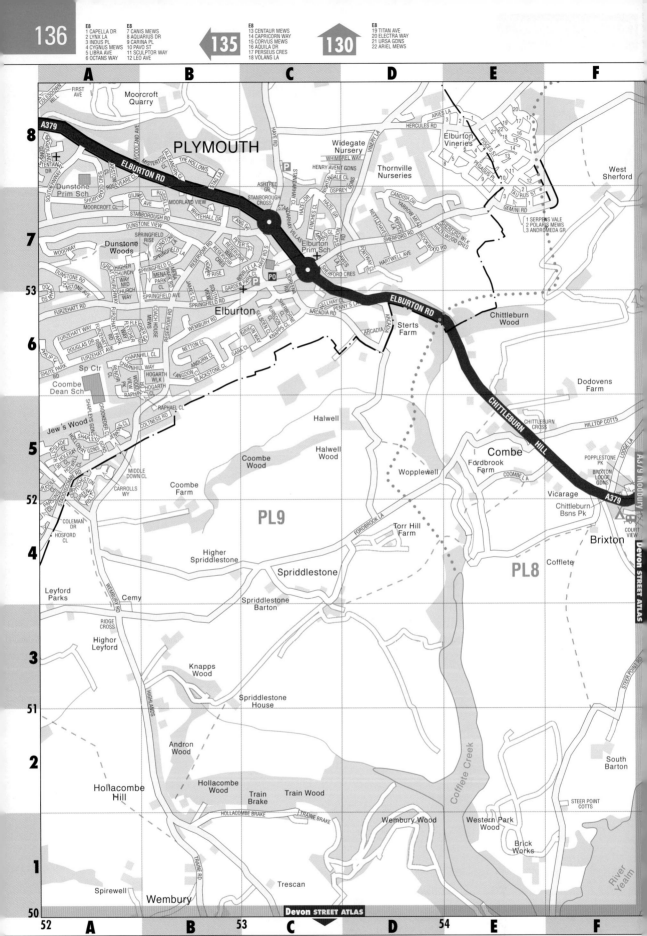

E8
1 CAPELLA DR
2 LYNX LA
3 INDUS PL
4 CYGNUS MEWS
5 LIBRA AVE
6 OCTANS WAY

E8
7 CANIS MEWS
8 AQUARIUS DR
9 CARINA PL
10 PAVO ST
11 SCULPTOR WAY
12 LEO AVE

E8
13 CENTAUR MEWS
14 CAPRICORN WAY
15 CORVUS MEWS
16 AQUILA DR
17 PERSEUS CRES
18 VOLANS LA

E8
19 TITAN AVE
20 ELECTRA WAY
21 URSA GDNS
22 ARIEL MEWS

135

130

1 SERPENS VALE
2 POLARIS MEWS
3 ANDROMEDA GR

PLYMOUTH

West Sherford

Elburton Vineries

PL9

PL8

Brixton

Combe

Elburton

135

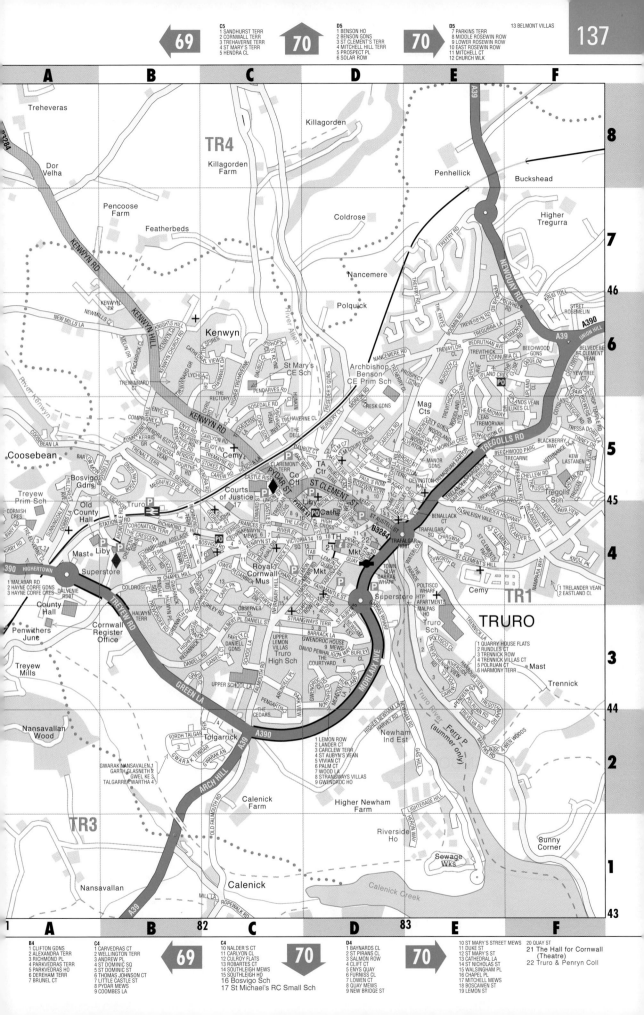

C5
1 SANDHURST TERR
2 CORNWALL TERR
3 TREHAVERNE TERR
4 ST MARY'S TERR
5 HENDRA CL

D5
1 BENSON HO
2 BENSON RD
3 ST CLEMENT S TERR
4 MITCHELL HILL TERR
5 PROSPECT PL
6 SOLAR ROW

D5
7 PARKINS TERR
8 MIDDLE ROSEWIN ROW
9 LOWER ROSEWIN ROW
10 EAST ROSEWIN ROW
11 MITCHELL CT
12 CHURCH WLK

69 70 70

B4
1 CLIFTON GDNS
2 ALEXANDRA TERR
3 RICHMOND PL
4 PARKVEDRAS TERR
5 PARKVEDRAS HO
6 DEREHAM TERR
7 BRUNEL CT

C4
1 CARVEDRAS CT
2 WELLINGTON TERR
3 ANDREW PL
4 ST DOMINIC SQ
5 ST DOMINIC ST
6 THOMAS JOHNSON CT
7 LITTLE CASTLE ST
8 PYDAR MEWS
9 COOMBES LA

C4
10 NALDER'S CT
11 CARLYON CL
12 CULROY FLATS
13 ROBARTES CT
14 SOUTHLEIGH MEWS
15 SOUTHLEIGH HO
16 BOSVIGO SCH
17 ST MICHAEL'S RC SMALL SCH

D4
1 BAYNARDS CL
2 ST PIRANS CL
3 SALMON ROW
4 CLIFT CT
5 ENYS QUAY
6 FURNISS CL
7 LOWEN CT
8 QUAY MEWS
9 NEW BRIDGE ST

10 ST MARY'S STREET MEWS
11 DUKE ST
12 ST MARY'S ST
13 CATHEDRAL LA
14 ST NICHOLAS ST
15 WALSINGHAM PL
16 CHAPEL PL
17 MITCHELL MEWS
18 BOSCAWEN ST
19 LEMON ST

20 QUAY ST
21 The Hall for Cornwall
(Theatre)
22 Truro & Penryn Coll

69 70 70

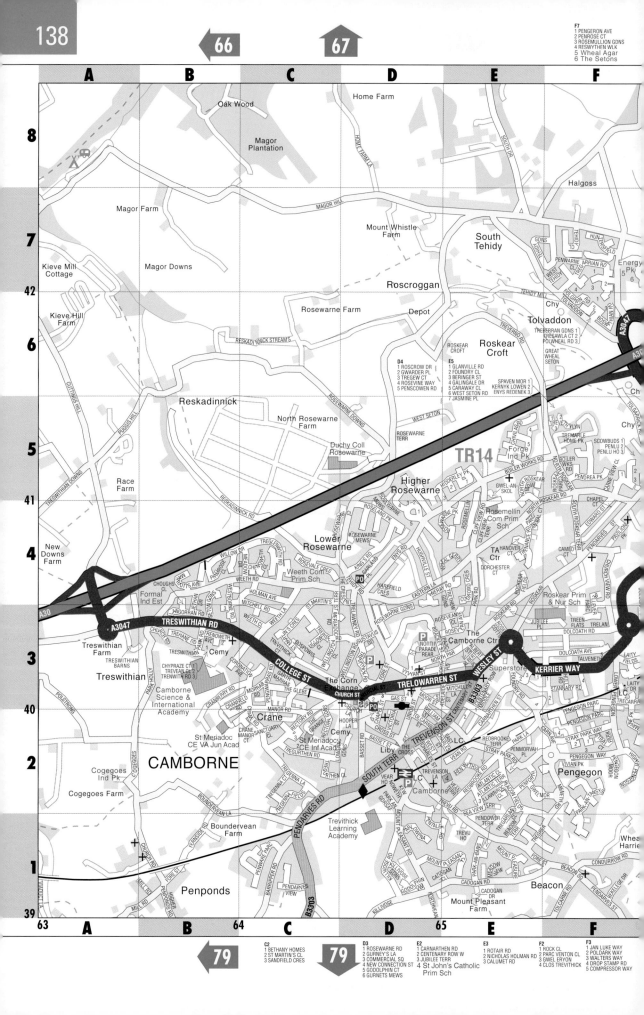

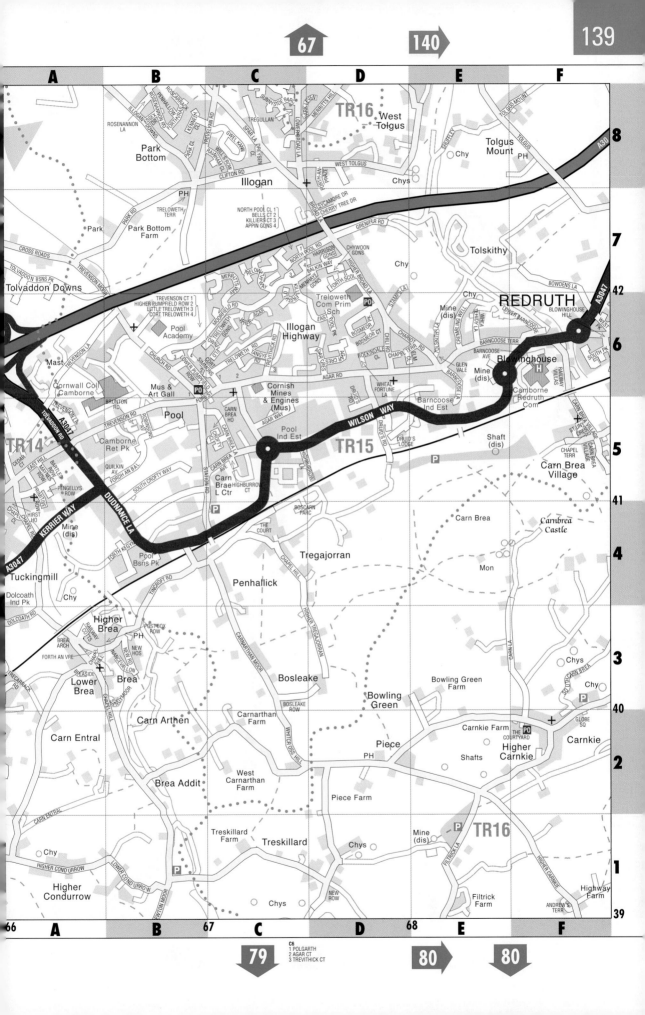

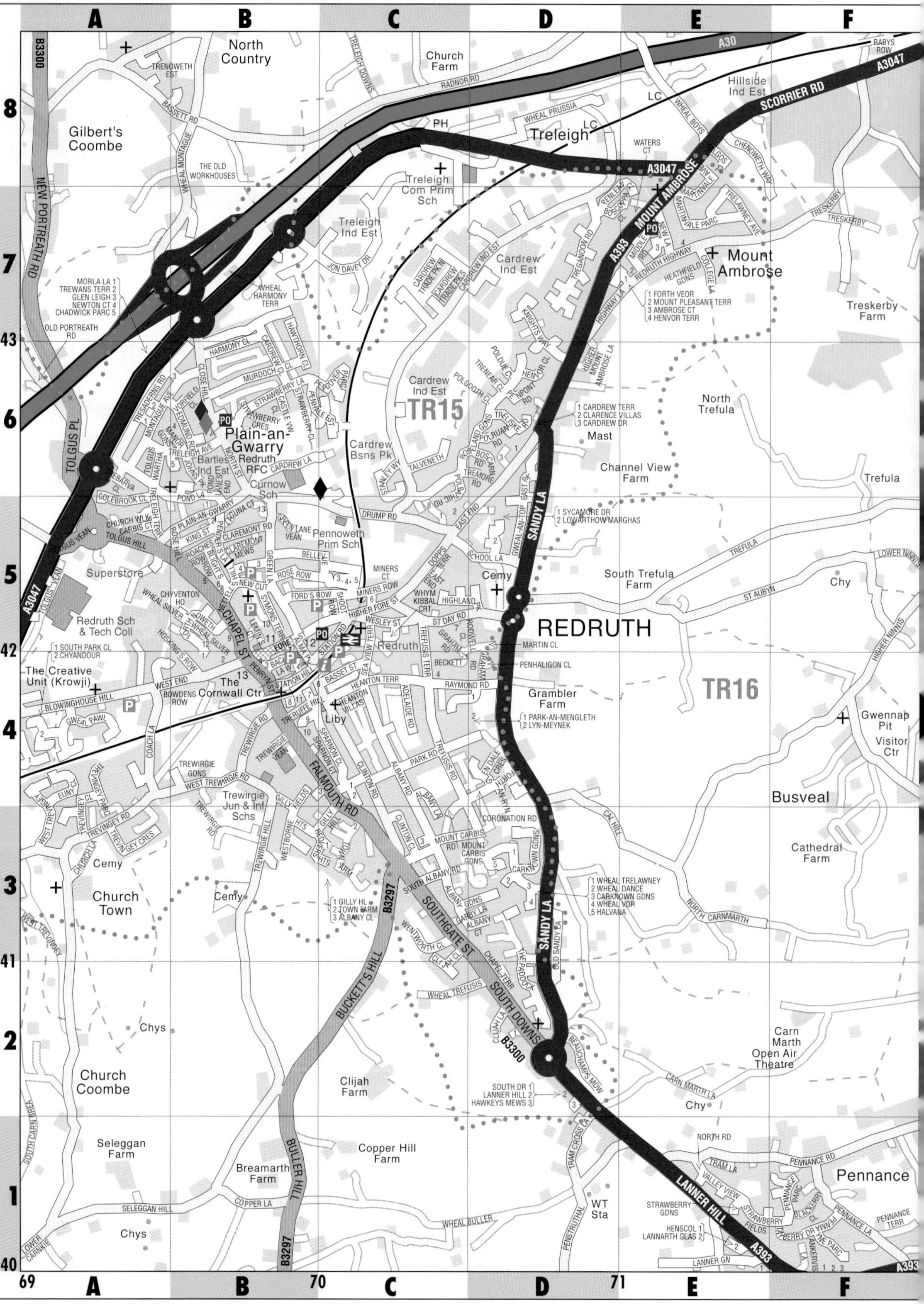

B5
1 STANLEY TERR
2 CHAPEL ROW
3 BALMORAL PL
4 BALMORAL TERR
5 FOUNDRY ROW
6 TREVENNER MEWS

7 MARKET STRAND
8 TREVENNER HO
9 CHAPEL CT
10 LEGGOS CT
11 Regal Cinema & Theatre

12 The Murdoch Flyer & The Tregellas Tapestry
13 LOWARTH ELMS

C5
1 CARDREW LA
2 HILLSIDE TERR
3 GLADSTONE TERR
4 PAULLS ROW
5 JENKINS TERR
6 MIDDLETONS ROW

7 SIDNEY TERR
8 ROSE ACRE DR

67   68   68

A B C D E F

North Country
Gilbert's Coombe
Church Farm
Treleigh
Mount Ambrose
Treskerby Farm
North Trefula
Trefula
Plain-an-Gwarry
Cardrew Ind Est
TR15
Channel View Farm
South Trefula Farm
Chy
REDRUTH
TR16
Busveal
Cathedral Farm
Church Town
Grambler Farm
Gwennap Pit Visitor Ctr
Church Coombe
Carn Marth Open Air Theatre
Seleggan Farm
Clijah Farm
Copper Hill Farm
Breamarth Farm
Pennance
Lanner Hill

B4
1 SILVER CT
2 WEST END CT
3 CROSS ST
4 CLINTON PAS
5 MARKET WAY
6 BOND ST
7 SUNNYSIDE
8 GAS LA
9 TRERUFFE TERR

10 NANSCOTHAN
11 MARTIN HO
12 CAPTAINS CT
13 Murdoch House & St Rumon's Gdn

C4
1 SPARNON HILL
2 SPARNON TERR
3 LITTLE GILLY HILL
4 CHANNEL VIEW TERR

F1
1 GREYS TERR
2 BRAYS TERR
3 WOODLANDS TERR

139   80   80

69 A B 70 C D 71 E F

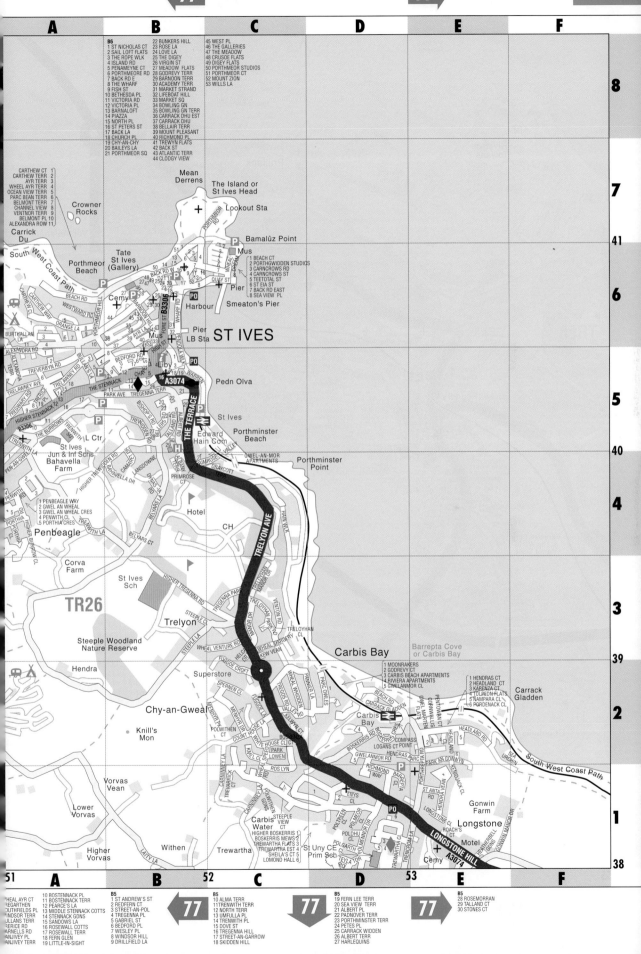

B6
1 ST NICHOLAS CT
2 SAIL LOFT FLATS
3 THE ROPE WLK
4 ISLAND RD
5 PENAMEYNE ST
6 PORTHMEOR RD
7 BACK RD E
8 THE WHARF
9 FISH ST
10 BETHESDA PL
11 VICTORIA RD
12 VICTORIA PL
13 BARNALOFT
14 PIAZZA
15 NORTH PL
16 ST PETERS ST
17 BACK LA
18 CHURCH PL
19 CHY-AN-CHY
20 BAILEYS LA
21 PORTHMEOR SQ

22 BUNKERS HILL
23 ROSE LA
24 LOVE LA
25 THE DIGEY
26 VIRGIN ST
27 MEADOW FLATS
28 GODREVY TERR
29 BARNOON TERR
30 ACADEMY TERR
31 MARKET STRAND
32 LIFEBOAT HILL
33 MARKET SQ
34 BOWLING GN
35 BOWLING GN TERR
36 CARRACK DHU EST
37 CARRACK DHU
38 BELLAIR TERR
39 MOUNT PLEASANT
40 RICHMOND PL
41 TREWYN FLATS
42 BACK ST
43 ATLANTIC TERR
44 CLODGY VIEW

45 WEST PL
46 THE GALLERIES
47 THE MEADOW
48 CRUSOE FLATS
49 DIGEY FLATS
50 PORTHMEOR STUDIOS
51 PORTHMEOR CT
52 MOUNT ZION
53 WILLS LA

CARTHEW CT 1
CARTHEW TERR 2
AYR TERR 3
WHEEL AYR TERR 4
OCEAN VIEW TERR 5
PARC BEAN TERR 6
BELMONT TERR 7
CHANNEL VIEW 8
VENTNOR TERR 9
BELMONT PL 10
ALEXANDRA ROW 11

1 BEACH CT
2 PORTHGWIDDEN STUDIOS
3 CARNCROWS RD
4 CARNCROWS ST
5 TEETOTAL ST
6 ST EIA ST
7 BACK RD EAST
8 SEA VIEW PL

1 PENBEAGLE WAY
2 GWEL AN WHEAL
3 GWEL AN WHEAL CRES
4 PENWITH CL
5 PORTHIA CRES

1 MOONRAKERS
2 GODREVY CT
3 CARBIS BEACH APARTMENTS
4 RIVIERA APARTMENTS
5 GWELANMOR CL

1 HENDRAS CT
2 HEADLAND CT
3 KARENZA CT
4 TOLROON FLATS
5 NAMPARA CL
6 PORDENACK CL

10 BOSTENNACK PL
11 BOSTENNACK TERR
12 PEARCE'S LA
13 MIDDLE STENNACK COTTS
14 STENNACK GDNS
15 SANDOWS LA
16 ROSEWALL COTTS
17 ROSEWALL TERR
18 FERN GLEN
19 LITTLE-IN-SIGHT

B5
1 ST ANDREW'S ST
2 REDFERN CT
3 STREET-AN-POL
4 TREGENNA LA
5 GABRIEL ST
6 BEDFORD PL
7 WESLEY PL
8 WINDSOR HILL
9 DRILLFIELD LA

B5
10 ALMA TERR
11 TRENWITH TERR
12 NORTH TERR
13 UMFULLA PL
14 TRENWITH PL
15 DOVE ST
16 TREGENNA HILL
17 STREET-AN-GARROW
18 SKIDDEN HILL

B5
19 FERN LEE TERR
20 SEA VIEW TERR
21 ALBERT PL
22 PADNOVER TERR
23 PORTHMINSTER TERR
24 PETES PL
25 CARRACK WIDDEN
26 ALBERT TERR
27 HARLEQUINS

B5
28 ROSEMORRAN
29 TALLAND CT
30 STONES CT

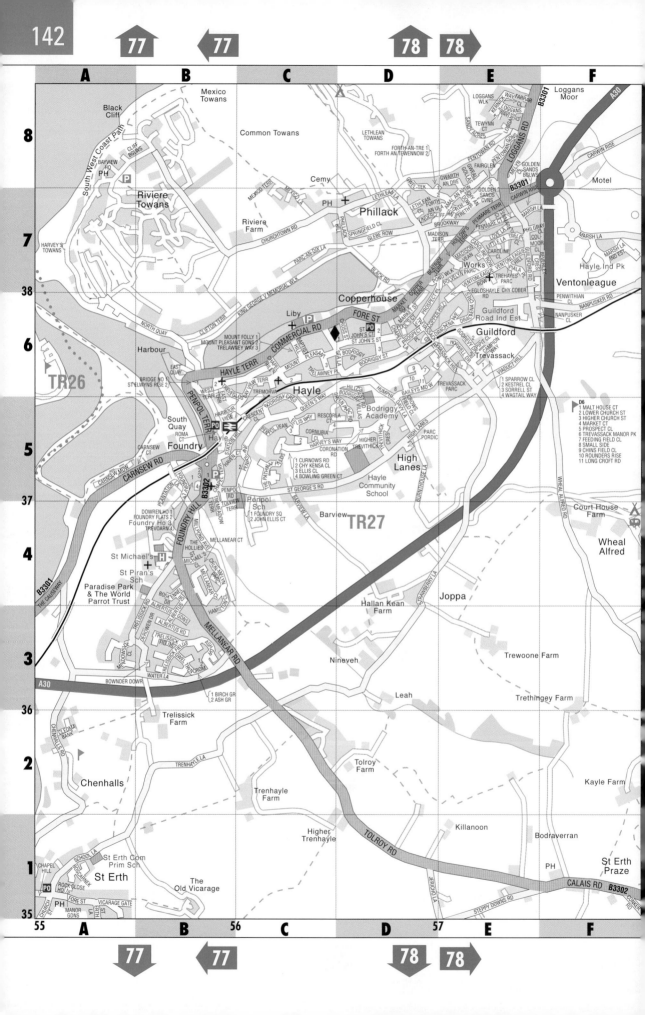

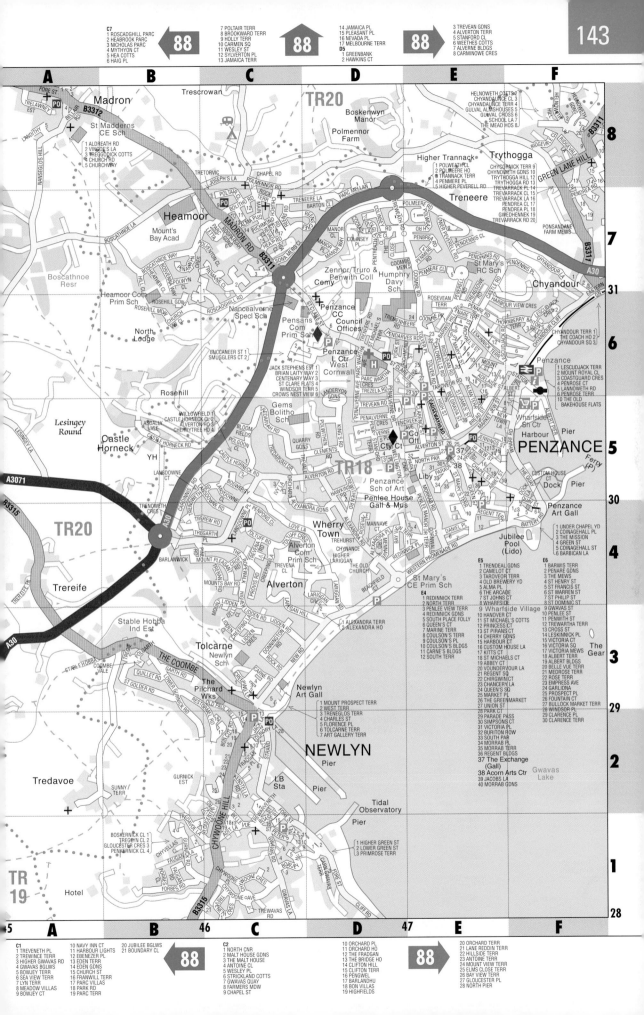

A8
1 GWITHIAN LA
2 GLASNEY VIEW
3 PERRANPORTH CL

◀ **81**

C7
1 HARRIS CT
2 SLADES LA
3 BENNETTS COTTS
4 RUSSELL WAY
5 SARACEN HO
6 BANK COTTS

▲ **81**

C8
1 Three Bridges
Specl Sch

8

Falmouth University (Penryn Campus)

Penryn Campus

Beehive Workshops

Penryn Com Inf Sch

Kernick Bsns Pk

Penryn Jun Sch

Penryn Coll

PENRYN

TR10

Penryn

TH Mus

St Gluvias

Islington Wharf

Cemy

1 ST GLUVIAS PARC
2 BOHELLAND RISE

Bissom
Bissom Farm

Gorran Gorras

TR11

Trevissome Farm

Trevissome House

1 CHARTER CT
2 BOHILL CT
3 SUMMERCOURT
4 SOUTH HARBOUR
5 DANIELS SAIL LOFT
6 FOXS YD
7 FOXSTANTON DR
8 CARN ROCK
9 TRESOETH TERR
10 TRESOETH CT
11 THE BAKEHOUSE
12 ANCHOR QUAY
13 HILL HOUSE
14 THE COACH HO

Quay Harbour

Penryn River

7

Kernick Ind Est

Superstore

Kernick House

Kernick Pk

Kernick Gdns

34

Falmouth Rd **B3292**

Ponsharden

P&R

Ponsharden Cotts

Ponsharden Ind Est

Homestead Ct

Falmouth Wharves

6

College Resr

Resr

Hillhead Farm

Eastwood Park Ind Est

Mast

Falmouth Sch

Ashfield Gdns

Porhan Gdns

Arundell Gdns

Penwerris Farm

Dracaena View

DRACAENA AVE

Grenville Rd

LONG MDW LA 1
BUDOCK RD 2
BISHOPS WAY 3
TRESCOBEAS RD 4

Kergilliack Rd

Union Rd

Union Cnr

Pengelly

Lowenek

Kitchen Gdns

Hayman Way

5

Tregonhaye

Oakland Pk

Lower Kergilliack

The Nurseries

Frost Ct

Trescobeas Rd

33

Higher Kergilliack

Hillhead Rise

Manor Cres

Fremando Way

Manor

Highfield Rd

Falmouth **H**

4

Kergillack View

Kergillack Cl

Bickland Water Cotts

Bickland Water

Conway Gdns

Conway Rd

Tregoniggie Ind Est

Mongleath

MOUNT STEPHENS LA 1
MEARWOOD LA 2
TRESCOBEAS RD 3
TREGENVER LA 4
TRESIDDER CL

TR11

Nangitha Farm

Bickland Ind Est

Empire Way

Longfield

Crouch Ct

Faulkner Cl

3

Sparnon

Coronation Cotts

Nangitha Cl

Nangitha Terr

School La

Victoria Cotts

Vicarage Rd

Eglos Farm

Budock Cl

St Francis CE Sch

Church Way

St Mary's RC Prim Sch

Falmouth Bsns Pk

Penmere

32

Merry Mt

Merry Meet La

Menehay View

Menehay Farm

PO

PH

Menehay

Bosmeor Rd

Bickland Water Rd

PO

Swanvale

Marlborough Ave

1 PICKLE CL
2 TALL SHIPS QL
3 MENA CHINOWYTH
4 CHI AN DOWR
5 CROSSWAYS

2

Budock Water

Watershed Parc

Trewen Parc

Stepheny Cl

Rose Eglos

Trewen House

Condor Cotts

Roscarrack House

Roscarrack

Beagle Ct

Darwin Dr

Boslowick

1

Tresooth Bungalow

Higher Crill Farm

Higher Crill

Trewen Farm

Bay View Terr

Trewen Farm La

Higher Roscarrack Farm

Elm Villas

Hotel

Maen Valley Pk

Golden Bank Pk

Spear's Terr

Tremorvah Ct

Tremorvah Pk

31

Penwarne Rd

Penwarne Cl

Crill Cnr

Kargel Gdns

Trelevra Farm

CH

1 SWANS REACH
2 STEWART CT
3 ST NAZAIRE CT
4 TREMORVAH WA

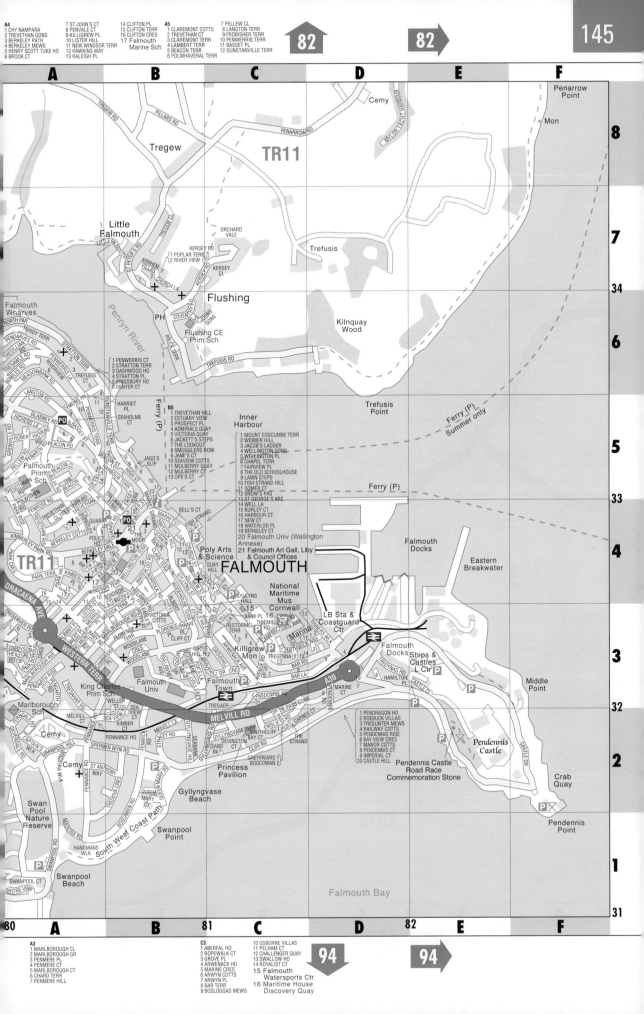

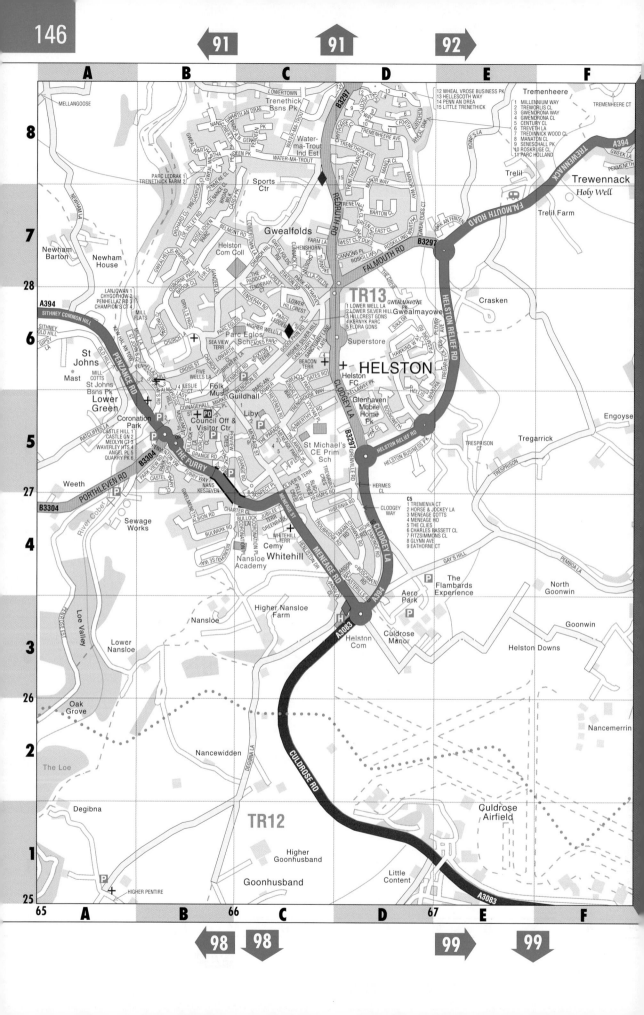

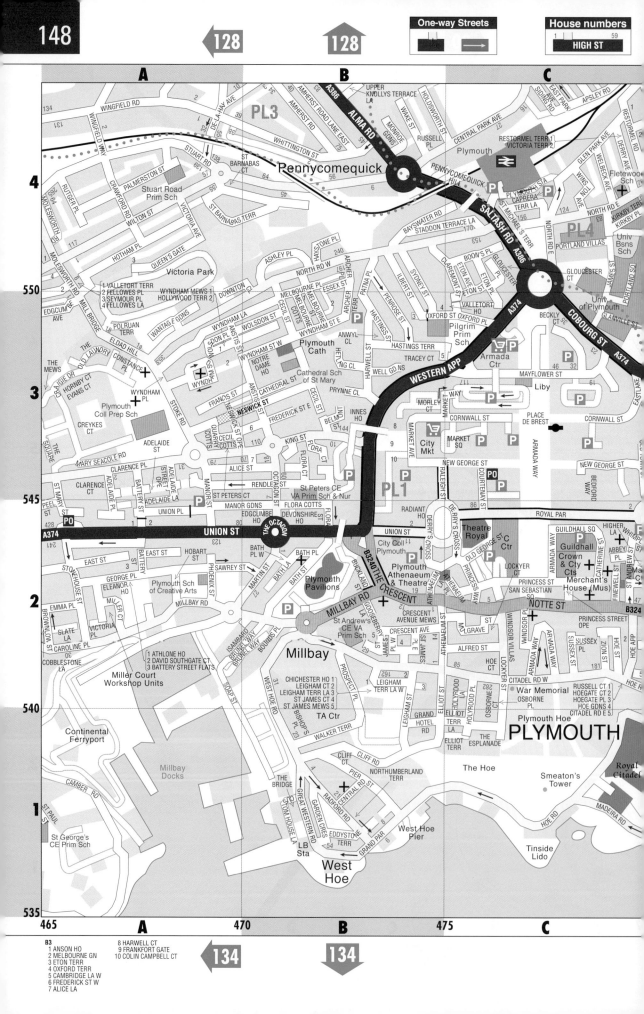

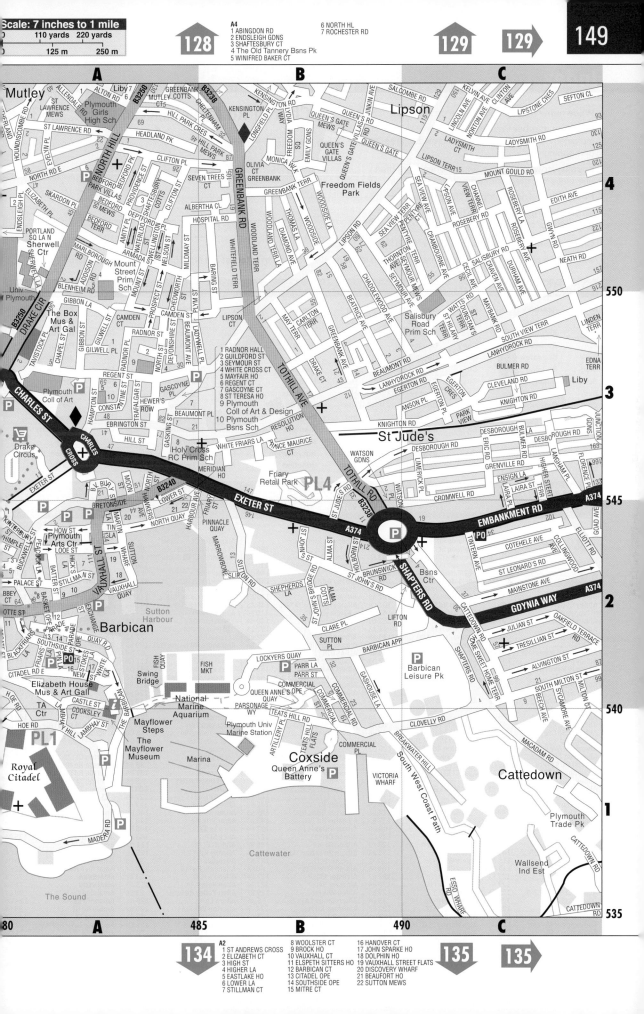

Index

Place name May be abbreviated on the map

Location number Present when a number indicates the place's position in a crowded area of mapping

Locality, town or village Shown when more than one place has the same name

Postcode district District for the indexed place

Page and grid square Page number and grid reference for the standard mapping

Church Rd 6 Beckenham BR2..........**53** C6

Cities, towns and villages are listed in CAPITAL LETTERS

Public and commercial buildings are highlighted in **magenta** **Places of interest** are highlighted in **blue** with a star★

Abbreviations used in the index

Acad	**Academy**	Comm	**Common**	Gd	**Ground**	L	**Leisure**	Prom	**Promenade**
App	**Approach**	Cott	**Cottage**	Gdn	**Garden**	La	**Lane**	Rd	**Road**
Arc	**Arcade**	Cres	**Crescent**	Gn	**Green**	Liby	**Library**	Recn	**Recreation**
Ave	**Avenue**	Cswy	**Causeway**	Gr	**Grove**	Mdw	**Meadow**	Ret	**Retail**
Bglw	**Bungalow**	Ct	**Court**	H	**Hall**	Meml	**Memorial**	Sh	**Shopping**
Bldg	**Building**	Ctr	**Centre**	Ho	**House**	Mkt	**Market**	Sq	**Square**
Bsns, Bus	**Business**	Ctry	**Country**	Hospl	**Hospital**	Mus	**Museum**	St	**Street**
Bvd	**Boulevard**	Cty	**County**	HQ	**Headquarters**	Orch	**Orchard**	Sta	**Station**
Cath	**Cathedral**	Dr	**Drive**	Hts	**Heights**	Pal	**Palace**	Terr	**Terrace**
Cir	**Circus**	Dro	**Drove**	Ind	**Industrial**	Par	**Parade**	TH	**Town Hall**
Cl	**Close**	Ed	**Education**	Inst	**Institute**	Pas	**Passage**	Univ	**University**
Cnr	**Corner**	Emb	**Embankment**	Int	**International**	Pk	**Park**	Wk, Wlk	**Walk**
Coll	**College**	Est	**Estate**	Intc	**Interchange**	Pl	**Place**	Wr	**Water**
Com	**Community**	Ex	**Exhibition**	Junc	**Junction**	Prec	**Precinct**	Yd	**Yard**

Index of towns, villages, streets, hospitals, industrial estates, railway stations, schools, shopping centres, universities and places of interest

Abb–Amh

A

Abbey Cl PL20 .... 42 B2
Abbey Ct 19 Penzance TR18 143 E5
Plymouth PL1 .... 149 A2
Abbey Hill TR26 .... 77 E3
Abbey Mdw
5 Crapstone PL20 .... 42 A2
Lelant TR26 .... 77 E4
Abbeymead Mews PL19 .... 147 C5
Abbey Mews PL31 .... 109 C4
Abbey Pl Plymouth PL1 .... 148 C2
Tavistock PL19 .... 147 C5
Abbey Rise PL19 .... 147 C5
Abbey St TR18 .... 143 E5
Abbotsbury Way PL2 .... 127 F8
Abbots Cl PL31 .... 109 F4
Abbotscourt La PL11 .... 126 A2
Abbotsfield Cl PL19 .... 41 D8
Abbotsfield Cres PL19 .... 41 D8
Abbotts Rd PL3 .... 128 E6
Aberdeen Ave PL5 .... 124 D1
Aberdeen Cl PL24 .... 60 B6
Aberfal Ho 1 TR11 .... 145 C3
Abingdon Rd 1 PL4 .... 149 A4
Abney Cres PL6 .... 125 B6
Above La PL15 .... 16 F3
Above Town Cl PL27 .... 21 F3
Abscott La PL9 .... 135 C5
Acacia Rd TR11 .... 144 F5
Academy Terr 30 TR26 .... 141 B6
Acklington Pl PL5 .... 123 E4
Acland Cl EX23 .... 104 E7
Acland Gdns TR7 .... 110 D6
Acorn Arts Ctr★ 38 TR18 .... 143 E5
Acorn Dr PL25 .... 115 A3
Acorn Gdns PL7 .... 130 D6
Acre Cotts PL1 .... 127 F3
Acre Pl PL1 .... 127 F3
Adams Cl Plymouth PL5 .... 123 F1
Torpoint PL11 .... 126 F3
Adams Cres PL11 .... 126 E3
ADDINGTON 113 D7
Addington N 5 PL14 .... 113 D6
Addington S 6 PL14 .... 113 D6
Addison Rd PL4 .... 149 A4
Addison Terr PL22 .... 112 C2
Adelaide La PL1 .... 148 A2
Adelaide Pl PL1 .... 148 A3
Adelaide Rd TR15 .... 140 C4
Adelaide St Camborne TR14 138 E3
Penzance TR18 .... 143 E6
Plymouth PL1 .... 148 A3
2 Plymouth, Ford PL2 .... 127 F5
Adelaide Street Ope PL1 .... 148 A3
Adelaide Terr TR1 .... 137 B4
Adela Rd PL11 .... 127 A3
Adeston Rd 5 PL28 .... 107 C4
Adit La Newlyn TR18 .... 143 C1
Saltash PL12 .... 122 E3
Adits The PL18 .... 41 A3
Admiral's Hard PL1 .... 134 A8
Admirals Quay 4 TR11 .... 145 B5
Admiralty Cotts PL1 .... 134 A7
Admiralty Ct PL13 .... 117 D3
Admiralty Ope S PL2 .... 127 F6
Admiralty Rd
Plymouth, Millbay PL1 .... 134 A8
Plymouth, St Budeaux PL5 .... 123 C2
Admiralty St
Plymouth, Keyham PL2 .... 127 E6
Plymouth, Millbay PL1 .... 134 A8
Admiralty Terr TR2 .... 83 B2
Aerohub Business Park TR8 44 F6
Affaland Moor Rd EX22 .... 8 E3
Afflington Rd PL9 .... 129 D1
African Row TR14 .... 79 B5
Agar Cres TR15 .... 139 D6
Agar Ct 2 Camborne TR15 .... 139 C6
Truro TR1 .... 137 D5
Agar Mdws 11 TR3 .... 81 F7
Agar Rd Camborne TR15 .... 139 D6
Newquay TR7 .... 110 E5
St Austell PL25 .... 114 E6
Truro TR1 .... 137 E5
Agar Terr 12 PL31 .... 109 D5
Agar Way TR15 .... 139 C5
Agaton Fort Rd PL5 .... 123 F3
Agaton Rd PL5 .... 123 E3
Aglets Way PL26 .... 114 F2
Agnes Cl EX23 .... 104 F4
Ainslie Terr PL2 .... 127 E7
Airborne Dr PL6 .... 125 B4
Aire Gdns PL3 .... 129 B5
Airfield Rd PL30 .... 35 E4
Alamein Ct PL12 .... 122 E2
Alamein Rd PL12 .... 122 D2
Alan Harvey Cl 14 TR26 .... 77 A6
Alan Rd PL28 .... 107 D4
Alansmere Ct TR2 .... 57 A1
Alanta Flats TR7 .... 110 B5
Albacore Dr 3 PL6 .... 125 B5
Albany Cl Redruth TR15 .... 140 C3
Albany Cl *continued*
Redruth TR15 .... 140 C3
St Agnes TR5 .... 68 D8
Albany Ct 4 Newquay TR7 .... 110 F6
Redruth TR15 .... 140 D3
Albany Gdns TR15 .... 140 C3
Albany La TR15 .... 140 C4
Albany Pl TR11 .... 145 A3
Albany Rd Falmouth TR11 .... 145 A3
5 Newquay TR7 .... 110 F6
Redruth TR15 .... 140 C4
Truro TR1 .... 137 A4
Albany St PL1 .... 127 F2
Albany Terr TR26 .... 141 B4
ALBASTON 40 E5
Albemarle Villas PL1 .... 127 F3
Albert Bldgs 19 TR18 .... 143 E6
Albert Cotts TR11 .... 145 B4
Albertha Cl PL4 .... 149 B4
Albert Pier TR18 .... 143 F5
Albert Pl Camborne TR14 .... 138 E3
21 St Ives TR26 .... 141 B5
Truro TR1 .... 137 C3
Albert Rd Plymouth PL2 .... 127 F3
St Austell PL25 .... 114 D3
St Ives TR26 .... 141 B5
Saltash PL12 .... 123 A2
Albert St Camborne TR14 .... 138 E3
Penzance TR18 .... 143 F6
Albert Terr Gunnislake PL18 .... 40 F5
Lostwithiel PL22 .... 112 C2
18 Penzance TR18 .... 143 E6
26 St Ives TR26 .... 141 B5
Albertus Dr TR27 .... 142 B3
Albertus Gdns TR27 .... 142 B3
Albertus Rd TR27 .... 142 B3
Albert Villas PL2 .... 127 E4
Albion Ct PL11 .... 127 B3
Albion Dr PL2 .... 128 B7
Albion Rd Helston TR13 .... 146 B4
Torpoint PL11 .... 127 B3
Albion Row TR16 .... 80 F8
Alcester Cl PL2 .... 127 E4
Alcester St PL2 .... 127 F4
Alden Wlk PL6 .... 129 B7
Aldercombe La EX23 .... 5 A6
Alderney Rd PL6 .... 124 F7
Alder Rd PL19 .... 147 C3
Aldersley Wlk PL6 .... 125 A1
Alderwood Parc TR10 .... 144 B8
Aldreath Cl TR20 .... 88 B7
Aldreath Rd TR20 .... 88 B7
Alexander Ct
14 Carnon Downs TR3 .... 81 F7
Alexander Ct *continued*
Gorran Haven PL26 .... 85 D5
Alexandra Cl 5 Illogan TR16 67 E4
Plymouth PL9 .... 136 B8
St Ives TR26 .... 77 A7
Alexandra Ct TR7 .... 111 C8
Alexandra Dr PL20 .... 41 C1
Alexandra Gdns TR18 .... 143 D4
Alexandra Ho TR18 .... 143 D3
Alexandra Pl
Penzance TR18 .... 143 D4
5 Plymouth PL4 .... 128 E4
St Ives TR26 .... 77 A7
Alexandra Rd Bodmin PL31 109 B5
Illogan TR16 .... 67 D4
Newquay TR7 .... 111 C8
Penzance TR18 .... 143 D4
Plymouth, Crownhill PL6 .... 124 F2
Plymouth, Ford PL2 .... 127 F5
Plymouth, Mutley PL4 .... 128 F4
St Austell PL25 .... 114 E3
St Ives TR26 .... 77 A7
Alexandra Sq PL12 .... 123 A2
Alexandra Terr
Mount Hawke TR4 .... 68 C6
Penzance TR18 .... 143 D3
Plymouth PL2 .... 127 F5
St Ives TR26 .... 141 A5
Tremar PL14 .... 38 A4
2 Truro TR1 .... 137 B4
ALFARDISWORTHY 5 E6
Alford Cl EX23 .... 104 F5
Alfred Pl PL2 .... 127 F5
Alfred Rd PL2 .... 127 F5
Alfred St PL1 .... 148 C2
Alger Wlk PL6 .... 124 E6
Alice La 7 PL1 .... 148 B3
Alice St PL1 .... 148 A3
Alldritt Cl TR7 .... 111 D7
Allenby Rd PL2 .... 128 A6
Allendale PL26 .... 58 E8
Allendale Rd PL4 .... 149 A4
Allen Pk PL30 .... 23 B2
Allen Vale PL14 .... 113 A5
Allen Valley Rd PL30 .... 23 E6
Allern La PL5 .... 120 D1
Allerton Wlk PL6 .... 129 B7
Alley Hill PL20 .... 42 A1
Alleyn Gdns PL3 .... 128 E8
Allium Ct TR4 .... 70 D8
All Saints Pk PL18 .... 40 E5
Alma Cl TR5 .... 68 D8
Alma Cotts PL4 .... 149 B2
Alma Pl Heamoor TR18 .... 143 C7
Alma Pl *continued*
Newquay TR7 .... 110 D6
Padstow PL28 .... 107 D5
5 Penzance TR18 .... 143 E5
Redruth TR15 .... 140 B5
Alma Rd Plymouth PL3 .... 128 C4
Truro TR1 .... 69 F3
Alma St PL4 .... 149 B2
Alma Terr Carharrack TR16 .... 80 F8
Gunnislake PL18 .... 41 A6
Penzance TR18 .... 143 E5
10 St Ives TR26 .... 141 B5
Almeria Ct PL7 .... 130 D4
Almond Dr PL7 .... 131 B6
Almshouse Hill TR13 .... 146 B5
Alouts PL32 .... 15 D7
Alston Pk PL7 .... 130 D6
ALTARNUN 26 C8
Altarnun Com Prim Sch
PL15 .... 26 C7
Altarnun Rd PL15 .... 16 E2
Alton Pl PL4 .... 128 E4
Alton Rd PL4 .... 149 A4
Alverne Bldgs 7 TR18 .... 143 D5
ALVERTON 143 C4
Alverton Com Prim Sch
TR18 .... 143 C4
Alverton Ct TR1 .... 137 E5
Alverton Ho TR18 .... 143 C5
Alverton Rd TR18 .... 143 D5
Alverton St TR18 .... 143 E5
Alverton Terr
4 Penzance TR18 .... 143 D5
Truro TR1 .... 137 D5
Alvington St PL4 .... 149 C2
Alwin Pk PL6 .... 125 A5
Alwyn Cl TR7 .... 111 E6
Amacre Dr PL9 .... 135 B6
Amados Cl PL7 .... 130 B4
Amados Dr PL7 .... 130 C4
Amados Rise PL7 .... 130 C4
Amal An Avon TR27 .... 142 E7
AMALEBRA 76 F3
AMALVEOR 76 E4
Amanda Way PL14 .... 38 E4
Amber Cl 1 PL6 .... 124 C6
Amble Rd 26 PL17 .... 39 F4
Ambrose Ct TR15 .... 140 E7
Ambrose Lake Hill PL14 .... 37 A2
Amelia Cl TR2 .... 71 C6
Amherst Rd PL3 .... 148 B4
Amherst Rd La E PL3 .... 128 C4
Amherst Road Lane East
PL3 .... 148 B4

Amity Pl PL4	149 A4	
Anchor Quay **12** TR10	144 D7	
ANDERTON	132 F4	
Anderton Ct PL19	147 E2	
Anderton La PL19	147 D2	
Anderton Rise PL10	132 F4	
Andrewartha Rd TR10	144 B8	
Andrew Pl **3** TR1	137 C4	
Andrew's Terr TR16	139 F1	
Andrews Way PL12	53 E5	
Andromeda Gr **3** PL9	136 E7	
Andurn Cl PL9	136 B6	
Aneray Rd TR14	138 D3	
ANGARRACK	78 C5	
Angarrack Ct PL26	46 F2	
Angarrack La TR27	78 D5	
Angarrack Mews TR27	78 C5	
Angavran Mdw TR8	55 D8	
Angel Hill **7** PL15	106 C6	
Angel Pl **5** TR13	146 B5	
An Gof Gdns PL31	109 C4	
Angrouse La		
Poldhu Cove TR12	98 F2	
10 Trewoon TR12	99 A2	
Angwin Ave **4** TR5	54 C1	
Anjardyn Pl PL24	60 C5	
Ankervis La TR16	140 F1	
Anna Maria La TR11	93 C2	
Annear Rd TR10	144 A6	
Ann's Pl PL3	128 A4	
Anson Ho **1** PL1	148 B3	
Anson Pl		
Plymouth, Devonport PL2	127 F4	
Plymouth, St Jude's PL4	149 C4	
Anson Rd PL27	31 F3	
Anson Way TR13	146 D4	
Anstis St PL1	148 A3	
Anthony Cl EX23	4 C3	
Anthony Lowen PL28	107 D4	
Anthony Rd TR7	110 E4	
Antoine Cl **4** TR18	143 C2	
Antoine Terr **23** TR18	143 C2	
ANTONY	65 E5	
Antony CE VA Sch PL11	65 E5	
Antony Gdns PL2	128 C8	
Antony Hill PL11	65 E5	
Antony House ★ PL11	126 D5	
Antony Rd PL11	127 B3	
Antony Woodland Gdn★		
PL11	126 D6	
Antron Hill PL10	81 B1	
Antron La		
Mabe Burnthouse TR10	93 C8	
Trenoweth TR10	93 C8	
Antron Way TR10	93 C8	
Anvil Ct Camelford PL32	105 D3	
Venterdon PL17	28 D1	
Anvil Rd PL32	105 D4	
An Vownder Goth TR13	91 B7	
Anwyl Cl PL3	148 B3	
Anzac Ave PL5	124 A4	
Appin Gdns TR15	139 C7	
Appleby Wlk PL5	124 D4	
Appledore La PL14	39 B3	
Appleton Tor Cl PL3	129 F5	
Appletree La PL25	115 D3	
Apsley Rd PL4	128 D4	
Aquarius Dr **8** PL9	136 E8	
Aquila Dr **16** PL9	136 E8	
Arbour The PL6	124 E5	
Arcade The **6** TR18	143 E5	
Arcadia PL9	136 B6	
Arcadia Rd PL9	136 B6	
Archbishop Benson CE Prim		
Sch TR1	137 D6	
Archer Pl PL1	148 B4	
Archer Terr PL1	148 B3	
Arch Hill TR1	137 C2	
Architects Way PL5	127 B8	
Arch La TR27	77 D1	
Archway Ave PL4	129 B3	
Arden Gr PL2	128 C8	
Ardhow TR10	94 A8	
Arena Cres PL25	115 B4	
Argal TR11	93 C7	
Argal View TR10	93 B6	
Ariel Mews **22** PL9	136 E8	
Aries Hill PL14	113 E7	
Aries La PL9	136 D8	
Ark Royal Cl PL5	127 D8	
Arkwright Gdns PL5	123 F2	
Arley Cl PL6	125 B6	
Arlington Rd PL4	128 F4	
Armada Ct PL19	147 B4	
Armada Rd PL10	133 A1	
Armada St PL4	149 A4	
Armada Way PL1	148 C3	
Armchair Cnr PL31	109 C5	
Arnheim Terr TR11	145 B7	
Arnhem Villas TR11	145 B7	
Arnison Cl PL9	135 F5	
Arnold's Point PL4	129 C3	
Arnside Cl PL6	125 D3	
Arrallas Barns TR2	57 B4	
Arrallas Rd TR8	57 A6	
Arscott Gdns PL9	135 C5	
Arscott La PL9	135 D5	
Art Gallery Terr TR18	143 C3	
Arthurian Ctr The★ PL32	105 E8	
Arthur Terr PL11	127 B2	
Artillery Pl PL4	149 B1	
Arun Cl PL3	129 C5	
Arundel Ct TR27	78 C6	
Arundell Cl PL6	19 F4	
Arundell Gdns		
Falmouth TR11	144 E6	
Lifton PL16	19 F4	
Arundel Pl TR1	137 C3	
Arundel Pk TR27	78 D6	
Arundel Terr Bude EX23	104 D4	
Plymouth PL2	127 F4	
Arundel Way		
Connor Downs TR27	78 D6	
Newquay TR7	111 B7	
Arundle Cl PL26	58 C8	
Arwenack Ave TR11	145 C3	
Arwenack Ho **4** TR11	145 C3	
Arwenack St TR11	145 C4	
Arworthal Mdws TR3	81 D6	
Arwyn Cotts **6** TR11	145 C3	
Asdally Vale TR18	143 B5	
Ashbrook St		
11 Prince Rock PL9	129 D1	
2 Prince Rock PL9	129 D1	
Ashburgh Parc PL12	122 B3	
Ashburnham Rd PL5	124 A3	
Ashbury Cl PL14	113 D7	
Ash Cl **16** Par PL24	60 B4	
7 Yelverton PL20	42 C3	
Ashcombe Cl PL7	130 C7	
Ashdown Cl Plymouth PL6	125 E3	
Sticker PL26	58 E1	
Ashdown Wlk PL6	125 E3	
Ash Dr TR27	142 B3	
Ashery Dr PL9	135 C6	
Ashfield Gdns TR11	144 E6	
Ashfield Rd TR11	144 F6	
Ashfield Villas TR11	144 F6	
Ashford Cl PL3	129 A4	
Ashford Cres PL3	129 A4	
Ashford Hill PL4	129 A4	
Ashford Rd PL4	128 F4	
Ash Gr Hayle TR27	142 B3	
Par PL24	60 B4	
Plymouth PL2	127 F7	
Ashill TR14	66 E3	
Ashleigh Cl PL5	124 C7	
Ashleigh La PL5	120 D1	
Ashleigh Way Plymouth PL7	131 C4	
Probus TR2	71 D6	
Ashley Cl **9** PL26	59 D7	
Ashley Pl PL1	148 B4	
Ashley Rd Shortlanesend TR4	69 F6	
Truro TR1	137 D6	
Ashmead TR2	57 E1	
Ash Park Cl TR15	38 A4	
Ashridge Gdns PL5	124 B2	
ASHTON	90 E3	
Ashton Cl PL6	125 C6	
Ashton Ct TR7	111 D6	
Ashton Way PL12	122 D3	
Ashton Wlk EX23	6 F5	
Ashtree Cl PL6	125 D7	
Ashtree Gr PL9	136 C8	
Ash Vale PL16	19 F4	
Ashwood Cl PL7	131 B5	
Ashwood Park Rd PL7	131 C6	
Aspen Cl PL19	147 C3	
Aspen Gdns PL7	131 B5	
Astor Dr PL4	129 C3	
Astwood Developments		
PL13	63 F8	
Athelstan Pk PL31	109 C4	
Athenaeum Gdns PL1	148 B2	
Athenaeum Pl PL1	148 C2	
Athenaeum St PL1	148 B2	
Atherton Pl PL2	127 E4	
Athlone Ho PL1	148 A2	
Atlanta PL28	20 E2	
Atlantic Bays Holiday Pk		
PL28	31 F6	
Atlantic Cl Camborne TR14	138 C2	
Treknow PL34	14 C5	
Widemouth Bay EX23	6 F5	
Atlantic Cres TR19	96 C7	
Atlantic Highway PL32	10 D2	
Atlantic Mews		
New Polzeath PL27	21 D6	
8 St Agnes TR5	54 D1	
Atlantic Rd Delabole PL33	14 D2	
Newquay TR7	110 C6	
Tintagel PL34	14 C7	
Atlantic Reach TR8	45 D3	
Atlantic Terr		
Camborne TR14	138 C2	
New Polzeath PL27	21 D6	
43 St Ives TR26	141 B6	
Trevone PL28	20 E2	
Atlantic View Rd EX23	5 A6	
Atlantic Way Porthtowan TR4	68 A6	
4 Tintagel PL34	14 C7	
Attenborrow Ct TR7	111 C8	
Attery View PL15	18 E6	
Attwood La PL14	38 D3	
Auckland Rd **3** PL2	128 A5	
Audierne Rd TR10	144 C7	
Austin Ave PL2	128 A6	
Austin Cres PL6	125 C1	
Austin Farm Prim Sch PL6	129 C7	
Ava PL26	73 C4	
Avallen Cl TR11	82 A3	
Avent Wlk PL7	130 F7	
Avenue Rd TR11	145 C3	
Avenue The St Hilary TR20	89 F6	
Truro TR1	137 D5	
Averys Gn PL30	35 F3	
Avery's Row PL28	107 D5	
Avery Terr PL22	112 C2	
Avery Way PL12	122 D3	
Avon Cl Plymouth PL3	129 D6	
St Austell PL25	115 A5	
Avondale Rd TR1	137 B4	
Avon Flats TR7	111 C7	
Avrack TR19	87 F3	
Axe Cl PL3	129 D6	
Axford Hill PL17	39 F2	
Axtown La PL20	42 C2	
Aycliffe Gdns PL7	131 A3	
Aylesbury Cres PL5	124 B5	
Aylmer Sq **14** PL25	114 C3	
Aylwin Cl PL7	130 E6	
Ayreville Rd PL2	128 B7	
Ayr La TR26	141 B6	
Ayr Terr TR26	141 B6	
Ayshton Gdns **15** PL17	39 F4	
Azenor Ave TR11	144 D3	

B

Babbacombe Cl PL6	129 E8	
Baber Cl PL12	40 C2	
Baber Ct PL12	40 D2	
Babis Farm Cl PL12	122 F1	
Babis Farm Ct PL12	122 F1	
Babis Farm Mews PL12	122 F2	
Babis Farm Row PL12	122 F1	
Babis Farm Way PL12	122 F2	
Babis La PL12	122 F1	
Baby Beach La PL27	21 D6	
Backen La PL32	10 D2	
Back Hill Port Isaac PL29	22 D7	
Saltash PL12	122 D2	
Back La Angarrack TR27	78 C5	
Callington PL17	39 F4	
Crowlas TR20	89 B8	
Marazion TR17	89 B5	
Plymouth PL7	130 E4	
St Erth TR27	77 D2	
17 St Ives TR26	141 B6	
St Neot PL14	36 F2	
Tintagel PL34	14 D7	
Tregony TR2	71 F4	
Veryan TR2	83 F6	
Back Lane W TR15	140 B4	
Back Rd PL18	41 A3	
Back Quay TR1	137 D4	
Back Road E **7** TR26	141 B6	
Back Road W TR26	141 B6	
BADGALL	17 C5	
Badgall Rd PL15	17 C5	
Badger's Cross TR20	88 E8	
Badgers Wlk PL12	122 D4	
Badgers Wood **9** PL31	109 A5	
Badger Way PL9	135 C5	
BADHARLICK	17 E5	
Bagbury Rd EX23	104 E3	
Bag La Lanjore PL12	52 F1	
Polbathic PL12	64 F8	
St Germans PL12	65 A8	
Bahavella Dr TR26	141 B4	
Bailey Gdns PL25	8 A5	
Baileys Field **7** EX23	5 A6	
Baileys La TR26	141 B6	
Bailey Terr EX22	8 A5	
Bainbridge Ave PL3	128 F7	
Bainbridge Ct PL7	130 E7	
Baines Hill TR16	67 C6	
Bakehouse La **12** PL17	39 E4	
Bakehouse The TR10	144 D7	
Bake La Bake PL12	52 D1	
Rosedale PL12	64 D8	
Bake Lane End PL12	52 D1	
Bakers Cl PL7	131 C5	
Bakers Ct TR7	110 E6	
Bakers Gn PL25	115 B4	
Bakers Pl PL1	127 F1	
Bakers Row TR13	90 F3	
BAKESDOWN	7 D3	
Balcoath TR16	68 D1	
BALDHU	69 C1	
Baldu Row TR20	76 F2	
Bal East La PL26	59 A1	
Balfield Rd **15** TR13	98 C8	
Balfour Terr PL2	127 E4	
Bal-Jinjy Cl **19** PL24	60 B4	
Balkin Way PL15	139 D7	
BALL	108 E7	
Bal La TR27	90 C5	
Ballad Gdns PL14	122 D4	
Ballaminers La PL27	32 C6	
Ballard Cl TR16	80 B5	
Ballard Est TR16	80 B5	
Ball La TR8	45 A8	
Ball Terr PL27	108 E7	
Balmoral Ave PL2	127 C8	
Balmoral Pl **3** TR15	140 B5	
Balmoral Terr **4** TR15	140 B5	
BALNOON	77 A5	
Balnoon Flats TR26	77 A4	
Bal Rd TR13	91 E4	
BALWEST	90 D5	
Bambry Cl TR20	89 E5	
Bampflyde Way		
Goldsithney TR20	89 F5	
Plymouth PL6	124 D6	
Bampton Rd PL6	125 E1	
Band House La PL26	59 C7	
BANGORS	6 F2	
Bangors Est EX23	6 F2	
Bangors Rd PL15	18 E2	
Banjo La PL27	32 D6	
Bank Cotts **6** TR10	144 C7	
Bank Sq TR19	86 F6	
Bank St Newquay TR7	110 C6	
St Columb Major TR9	45 E6	
Bank Terr TR4	56 A2	
Bannawell Ct **1** PL19	147 B6	
Bannawell St PL19	147 B6	
Banns Rd TR4	68 C6	
Baptist Hill TR27	142 C6	
Baptist St PL17	41 A3	
Bara Pl PL17	39 F6	
Barbara Hepworth Mus &		
Sculpture Gdn★ TR26	141 B6	
BARBICAN	149 A2	
Barbican App PL4	149 B2	
Barbican Cl PL13	117 D4	
Barbican Ct Looe PL13	117 D5	
12 Plymouth PL4	149 A2	
Barbican Farm La PL13	117 E5	
Barbican Hill PL13	117 D4	
Barbican La PL18	117 E5	
Barbican Leisure Pk PL4	149 C2	
Barbican Rd Looe PL13	117 E6	
Plymouth PL7	130 E4	
Barbican Rise Ind Est		
PL13	117 E5	
Barbican The PL1	149 A2	
Barbican Theatre PL1	149 A1	
Barbican Way TR13	91 E4	
Barbury Cres PL6	125 B8	
BARCELONA	62 E4	
Barcote Wlk PL6	129 C8	
Bardsey Cl PL6	125 A7	
BAREPPA	93 D4	
Bareppa Bareppa TR11	93 E4	
Carlidnack TR11	94 A2	
Baring St PL4	149 B4	
Barker's Hill PL12	122 F1	
Barkhouse La PL25	115 B2	
BARKLA SHOP	54 E1	
Bar La Connor Downs TR27	78 C6	
Falmouth TR11	145 C3	
Barlandhu **17** TR18	143 C2	
Barlanwick TR18	143 B4	
Barley Market St PL19	147 C6	
Barlowena TR14	138 D1	
Barlow Gdns PL2	128 B7	
Bar Mdws TR1	70 D2	
Barnaloft **13** TR26	141 B6	
Barn Cl Plymouth PL7	131 D4	
Wainhouse Corner EX23	10 F6	
Barncoose Ave TR15	139 F6	
Barncoose Ind Est TR15	139 E5	
Barncoose La TR15	139 E6	
Barncoose Terr TR15	139 E6	
Barn Courtyard TR27	78 D6	
Barndale Cres PL6	125 B6	
BARNE BARTON	127 C8	
Barne Cl PL5	127 C8	
Barnecut Cl **6** PL14	38 A3	
Barne La PL5	123 D1	
Barne Rd PL5	127 C8	
Barnfield Dr PL7	131 C5	
Barnfield Gdns TR18	88 E6	
Barnfield Pk EX23	4 E1	
Barnfield Terr		
3 Indian Queens TR9	45 E1	
Liskeard PL14	113 B4	
Barn Hill Cadgwith TR12	103 B4	
Polbathic PL12	64 F8	
Tideford PL12	52 F1	
Barnicott Cl PL14	38 A8	
Barn La Bodmin PL31	109 C4	
Bokelly PL30	23 C3	
18 St Columb Major TR9	45 E6	
Barn Meadow Pk PL13	117 B2	
Barnoon Hill TR26	141 B6	
Barnoon Terr **29** TR26	141 B6	
Barn Park La PL31	35 B2	
Barnpark Rd PL35	9 C1	
Barn Park Rd PL3	128 D6	
Barn Pk Lostwithiel PL22	112 C2	
Saltash PL12	122 F3	
Barn St PL14	113 C5	
Barns Terr PL12	118 A3	
Barnstaple Cl PL6	129 E7	
Barnwood Cl PL9	135 E5	
Baron Ct PL15	17 D5	
Barons Mdw PL31	109 F5	
Barons Rd PL20	42 E3	
Barossa Rd PL11	127 B3	
Barracades PL15	18 E5	
Barrack La TR1	137 D3	
Barrack Pl PL1	128 A1	
Barrack's La TR16	68 E1	
Barrack St PL1	127 E2	
Barras Cross PL14	113 C6	
Barras Moor TR10	81 D4	
Barras Pl PL14	113 C6	
Barras St PL14	113 C6	
Bar Rd Falmouth TR11	145 C3	
Mawnan Smith TR11	93 C2	
Barrepta St TR26	141 D1	
Barrie Cres PL31	109 C2	
BARRIPPER	79 B5	
Barripper Rd		
Camborne TR14	138 C1	
Penponds TR14	79 C5	
Barrow Down PL12	122 B3	
Barrowfield View TR7	111 A7	
Barr's Cl PL23	116 D5	
Barry's La PL28	107 D5	
Bar Terr **8** TR11	145 C3	
Bartholomew Rd PL2	128 B5	
Bartles Cl TR12	99 D7	
Bartles Ind Est TR15	140 B6	
Bartles Row TR14	139 C5	
Bartlett Ave EX23	104 F5	
Barton Ave PL2	127 C5	
Barton Cl **11** Bodmin PL31	109 D5	
Heamoor TR18	143 D7	
Helston TR13	146 D4	
Landrake PL12	53 C3	
Plymouth PL7	131 C5	

Ami – Bea 151

Barton Ct PL26	58 A7	
Barton La TR9	45 E1	
Barton Mdws PL26	53 B7	
Barton Mdw Pelynt PL13	62 D6	
Truro TR1	137 A5	
Barton Mews Landrake PL12	53 C3	
Millbrook PL10	132 F6	
Barton Rd Helland PL30	35 A5	
Plymouth PL9	135 B6	
St Dennis PL26	58 A7	
Barton Row PL30	23 A3	
Barton The PL29	22 D6	
Barview La TR27	142 C6	
Barwis Hill TR18	143 E6	
Barwis Terr **1** TR18	143 E6	
Basil Rd PL15	16 F3	
Basinghall Cl PL9	135 E5	
Basket Ope PL4	149 A2	
Basset Rd TR14	138 D2	
Basset St Camborne TR14	138 C2	
Falmouth TR11	145 A5	
Redruth TR15	140 C4	
Bassett Cl PL26	47 A1	
Bassett Pl **11** TR11	145 A5	
Bassett Rd Illogan TR16	67 E4	
Redruth TR15	140 B8	
Bassett Terr TR16	67 D6	
Bastville EX22	11 E8	
Bath La PL1	148 B2	
Bath Pl PL1	148 B2	
Bath Place W PL1	148 B2	
BATHPOOL	27 C1	
Bath St PL1	148 B2	
Battalion Cl **6** PL31	109 F3	
Battershall Cl PL9	135 F5	
Batter St PL4	149 A2	
Battery Hill TR16	67 C6	
Battery La Polruan PL23	116 C2	
Tavistock PL19	147 C4	
Battery Mill La TR27	77 E1	
Battery Park Rd PL13	116 C2	
Battery Rd TR18	143 F4	
Battery St PL1	148 A2	
Battery Street Flats PL1	148 A2	
Battery Terr	73 C3	
Battery The TR7	110 D7	
Battisford Pk PL7	131 E3	
Bawden Rd PL31	109 B3	
Bay Apartments TR7	110 A6	
Bay Ct TR11	145 C3	
Baydon Cl PL6	125 C1	
Bay Down PL13	117 D5	
Bayly's Rd PL9	135 B7	
Baynards Cl **1** TR1	137 D4	
Baynes Ct **3** PL14	38 A3	
Bay Rd PL28	20 F2	
Bay Retreat Padstow PL28	31 F7	
19 Tregolds PL28	31 F7	
Bay St PL13	117 D3	
Bayswater Rd PL1	148 B4	
Bay The PL13	117 D3	
Baytree Cl PL6	125 D6	
Bay Tree Cotts **3** EX23	4 D1	
Baytree Gdns PL2	128 C3	
Baytree Hill PL13	113 C5	
Bay Tree Orch EX23	4 D2	
Bayview **11** PL24	60 C4	
Bay View Cres TR11	145 D3	
Bayview Dr PL13	117 E4	
Bayview Ho TR27	142 A8	
Bay View PL25	114 F6	
Bay View Rd Looe PL13	117 D4	
St Austell PL26	115 A1	
Bay View Terr		
Budock Water TR11	144 C1	
Hayle TR27	142 C6	
26 Newlyn TR18	143 C2	
Newquay TR7	110 E5	
Penzance TR18	143 D4	
13 Porthleven TR13	98 B8	
Bay Villas TR20	88 F6	
Beach Ct TR26	141 C6	
Beachfield Ave TR7	110 E6	
Beachfield Ct TR18	143 D4	
Beach Hill Downderry PL11	64 C4	
Portloe TR2	84 B3	
Beach La **12** TR6	55 A5	
Beach Rd Carbis Bay TR26	141 D2	
Crantock TR8	43 D3	
Marazion TR17	89 B6	
Mevagissey PL26	73 C4	
Newquay TR7	110 D6	
Perranporth TR6	55 A5	
Porthtowan TR4	68 A6	
St Austell PL25	115 D3	
St Ives TR26	141 A6	
Trevone PL28	20 F2	
Beachside TR4	68 A6	
Beach View Cl TR7	111 C7	
Beachview Flats TR4	68 A6	
Beach Way PL15	27 C1	
Beach Wlk TR7	111 C7	
BEACON	138 F1	
Beacon Cl Falmouth TR11	145 A5	
St Austell PL25	115 A5	
Beacon Cross PL26	72 F4	
Beacon Down Ave PL2	128 B7	
Beacon Dr TR5	54 B1	
Beacon Est TR20	87 D4	
Beacon Farm TR5	54 C1	
Beaconfield Rd PL2	128 B7	
Beacon Fields TR14	138 F1	
Beacon Hill Bodmin PL31	109 D4	
Withielgoose Mills PL30	47 B8	
Beacon Hill Mews **9** PL31	109 D5	

Beacon Ho PL3 . . . . .129 D4
Beacon Inf & Nur Sch The
PL31 . . . . .109 D4
Beacon La Henon PL30 . . . . . 24 A6
Treveighan PL30 . . . . 23 F6
Beacon Lanes PL31 . . . . . . .109 D3
Beacon Parc TR13 . . . . .146 C6
Beacon Park Rd PL2 . . . . . .128 B7
Beacon Pk Boyton PL15 . . . . 13 A2
Pelynt PL13 . . . . 62 D5
Beacon Rd Belowda PL26 . . 46 E4
Bodmin PL31 . . . . .109 D4
Bodmin PL31 . . . . .109 E3
Falmouth TR11 . . . . .145 A5
Foxhole PL26 . . . . 58 D5
Marazion TR17 . . . . 89 B5
Newquay TR7 . . . . .110 D7
Porthleven TR13 . . . . 98 B8
St Agnes TR5 . . . . 54 C1
Summercourt TR8 . . . . 57 B7
Beacons PL13 . . . . 62 E5
Beaconsfield Pl **2** TR5 . . 54 C1
Beaconsfield Terr PL31 . . .109 C5
Beaconside Foxhole PL26 . . 58 D5
Summercourt TR8 . . . . 57 B7
Beacon Sq TR14 . . . . .138 F1
Beacon St TR11 . . . . .145 B5
Beacon Technology Pk
PL31 . . . . .109 B4
Beacon Terr
Camborne TR14 . . . . .138 E1
5 Falmouth TR11 . . . . . .145 A5
Foxhole PL26 . . . . 58 D5
Helston TR13 . . . . .146 C6
Lizard TR12 . . . . .102 F2
BEACON THE 10 F6
Beacon The TR11 . . . . .145 A5
Beacon View TR4 . . . . 55 B2
Beacon View Pk **23** TR16 . . 67 E4
Beacon Vw PL15 . . . . 27 B7
Beadle Ct **6** PL19 . . . . . . .147 B4
Beagle Ct TR11 . . . . .144 F2
BEALSMILL 28 E3
Bealswood Cl PL18 . . . . 41 A6
Bealswood Rd PL18 . . . . . . 41 A6
Beam Rd PL26 . . . . 47 C1
Beam Terr PL26 . . . . 47 B1
Beam Villas PL30 . . . . 47 D5
Beare Cl PL9 . . . . .135 B5
Bearsdown Cl PL6 . . . . . . .129 C8
Bearsdown Rd PL6 . . . . . . .129 C8
Bears Terr TR16 . . . . 80 E7
Beatrice Ave
Plymouth, Keyham PL2 . . . .127 E5
Plymouth, St Jude's PL4 . . .149 B3
Saltash PL12 . . . . .122 E2
Beatrice Gdns PL12 . . . . . .122 E1
Beatrice Rd PL31 . . . . 48 D8
Beatrice Terr TR27 . . . . . . .142 D7
Beattie Rd PL5 . . . . .127 B8
Beatty Cl PL6 . . . . .125 A4
Beauchamp Cres PL2 . . . . .128 C7
Beauchamp Rd PL2 . . . . . .128 C7
Beauchamps Mdw TR15 . .140 D2
Beaudyn Wlk **5** PL6 . . . . . .129 C7
Beaufighter Ave PL27 . . . . 31 F3
Beaufort Ave **8** PL27 . . . . 31 F3
Beaufort Ho **21** PL4 . . . . .149 A2
Beauly Cl PL7 . . . . .131 A5
Beaumaris Gdns PL3 . . . . .128 F8
Beaumaris Rd PL3 . . . . . . .128 F7
Beaumont Ave PL4 . . . . . . .149 A3
Beaumont Pl PL4 . . . . .149 A3
Beaumont Rd PL4 . . . . .149 B3
Beaumont St PL2 . . . . .128 A5
Beaumont Terr PL12 . . . . . .122 F4
Beck Adams PL12 . . . . 53 C3
Beckett Cl TR15 . . . . .140 C4
Beckford Cl PL7 . . . . .131 A5
Beckham Pl PL3 . . . . .129 A6
Beckly Ct PL1 . . . . .148 C3
Beckys La PL27 . . . . 31 E6
Bede Gdns PL5 . . . . .124 C1
Bede Haven Cl EX23 . . . . . .104 E4
Bederkesa Ct PL31 . . . . . . .109 D4
Bedford Cl PL18 . . . . 40 F6
Bedford Mews PL4 . . . . . . .149 A4
Bedford Park Villas PL4 . . .149 A4
Bedford Pk
10 Bere Alston PL20 . . . . . 41 B1
Plymouth PL4 . . . . .149 A4
Bedford Pl
6 Bere Alston PL20 . . . . . 41 B1
6 St Ives TR26 . . . . .141 B5
Bedford Rd Horrabridge PL20 42 C4
Plymouth PL9 . . . . .135 E8
St Ives TR26 . . . . .141 B5
Bedford Sq PL19 . . . . .147 C5
Bedford St Bere Alston PL20 . 41 B1
Plymouth PL2 . . . . .127 F5
Bedford Terr PL4 . . . . .149 A4
Bedford Units PL18 . . . . . . 40 F5
Bedford Villas **7** PL20 . . . 41 B1
Bedford Way PL1 . . . . .148 C3
Bedowan Mdws TR7 . . . . . .111 A4
Bedruthan Ave TR1 . . . . . . .137 E6
Bedruthan Steps ★ PL31 . . 31 B4
Beech Ave Liskeard PL14 . . .113 B5
Plymouth PL4 . . . . .149 C2
Beech Cl Down Thomas PL9 .135 A1
Falmouth TR11 . . . . .144 F5
Tavistock PL19 . . . . .147 C2
Torpoint PL11 . . . . .127 A3
4 Whiterock PL27 . . . . . .108 C5
Beechcombers TR8 . . . . . . 44 D7

Beechcroft Rd
Plymouth, Lower Compton
PL3 . . . . .129 A6
Plymouth, North Prospect
PL2 . . . . .128 B7
Beech Ct PL6 . . . . .125 D5
Beech Dr Bodmin PL31 . . . .109 B4
4 St Columb Major TR9 . . 45 C6
Beeches The
Launceston PL15 . . . . .106 C5
8 Pensilva PL14 . . . . 38 E4
Beechfield Ave PL20 . . . . . . 42 D3
Beechfield Gr PL3 . . . . .128 E6
Beeching Pk PL17 . . . . 39 F6
Beech La PL25 . . . . .114 D3
Beech Rd **17** Callington PL17 . 39 F4
Falmouth TR11 . . . . .144 F5
St Austell PL25 . . . . .114 D3
Beech Terr PL13 . . . . .117 C4
Beech Tree Cl PL15 . . . . . .106 A8
Beechwood Ave PL4 . . . . . .128 D4
Beechwood Cross PL7 . . . .131 F7
Beechwood Dr PL32 . . . . . .105 D5
Beechwood Gdns TR1 . . . .137 E6
Beechwood Parc TR1 . . . . .137 F5
Beechwood Prim Sch PL6 .124 E6
Beechwood Rise PL6 . . . . .125 E1
Beechwood Terr PL4 . . . . . .128 D4
Beechwood Way PL7 . . . . . .131 D5
Beehive Workshops TR10 .144 A7
BEENY 9 E3
Beeston Wlk **6** PL6 . . . . . .129 C7
Behenna Dr TR1 . . . . 69 F3
Bekelege Dr TR14 . . . . .138 F1
Belah Mdws PL15 . . . . 16 A8
Belair Rd PL2 . . . . .128 C7
Belair Villas PL2 . . . . .128 C7
Belerion Rd TR16 . . . . 67 C5
Belgrave La PL4 . . . . .128 F4
Belgrave Rd PL4 . . . . .128 F4
Belgrave Terr PL14 . . . . . . .113 D6
Belgravia St TR18 . . . . .143 E5
Belhay TR10 . . . . .144 C8
Bellair Rd PL20 . . . . .143 A8
Bellair Terr **38** TR26 . . . . .141 B6
Bellamy Cl PL6 . . . . .125 A1
Bellatt PL27 . . . . .108 D6
Bella Vista Gdns TR10 . . . . 81 E2
Bell Cl PL7 . . . . .130 F6
Belle Acre Cl PL3 . . . . .128 F6
Bellever Barc TR14 . . . . . . .138 F4
Bellevue TR15 . . . . .140 C5
Belle Vue Bude EX23 . . . . . .104 D6
Newlyn TR18 . . . . .143 C1
Belle Vue Ave Bude EX23 . .104 D6
Plymouth PL9 . . . . .135 B5
Belle Vue Cotts TR10 . . . . . 81 E2
Belle Vue Dr PL9 . . . . .135 B5
Belle Vue La EX23 . . . . .104 D6
Belle Vue Rd Plymouth PL9 .135 C5
Saltash PL12 . . . . .122 F2
Belle Vue Rise PL9 . . . . . . .135 B5
Bellevue Sq PL11 . . . . .127 B2
Bellevue Terr TR3 . . . . 81 D6
Belle Vue Terr **20** TR18 . . .143 E6
Bellflower Cl PL6 . . . . .121 C1
Bell Hill PL26 . . . . 85 C5
Belliers La TR26 . . . . .141 B5
Bellingham Cres PL7 . . . . .131 C4
Belliver Ind Est PL6 . . . . . .121 B1
Belliver Way PL6 . . . . .121 B1
Bell La TR16 . . . . 80 D6
Bell Lake TR14 . . . . 66 F3
Bells Ct TR15 . . . . .139 C2
Bell's Ct TR11 . . . . .145 B4
Bell's Hill Falmouth TR11 . . 82 A3
Mylor Bridge TR11 . . . . 82 A3
Bell Veor TR16 . . . . 80 E6
Bell Yd **1** PL31 . . . . .109 E5
Belmont PL13 . . . . .117 C4
Belmont Cl PL33 . . . . 14 D2
Belmont Ct
8 Plymouth PL3 . . . . . . .128 A4
11 Wadebridge PL27 . . . .108 B5
Belmont Mews PL14 . . . . . . 38 D4
Belmont Pk PL14 . . . . 38 D4
Belmont Pl Newquay TR7 . .110 D7
Plymouth PL3 . . . . .128 A4
St Ives TR26 . . . . .141 A6
Belmont Rd Falmouth TR11 .145 A3
Helston TR13 . . . . .146 B7
St Austell PL25 . . . . .114 D3
Belmont St Plymouth PL1 . .148 B3
8 Tywardreath PL24 . . . . 60 D5
Belmont Terr Devoran TR3 . . 81 F6
St Ives TR26 . . . . .141 A6
Belmont Villas **13** TR1 . . .137 D5
BELOWDA 46 D4
Belstone Cl PL5 . . . . .124 A3
Belvedere TR1 . . . . .137 F6
Belvedere La TR20 . . . . 89 F5
Belvedere Rd PL4 . . . . .129 B2
Belyars Ct TR26 . . . . .141 B4
Belyars La TR26 . . . . .141 B4
Benallack Ct TR1 . . . . .137 E4
Benan Chy PL25 . . . . .114 F3
Benbow St PL2 . . . . .127 F4
Bencoolen Rd EX23 . . . . . . .104 D5
Beneathway PL14 . . . . 50 E7
BENNACOTT 12 E2
Bennets La PL12 . . . . .122 F3
Bennetts Cotts **3** TR10 . .144 C7
Bennett St PL1 . . . . .127 E1
Benny Halt Sta ★ TR8 . . . . 56 C8
Benson Gdns **2** TR1 . . . . .137 D5
Benson Ho **1** TR1 . . . . . . .137 D5
Benson Rd TR1 . . . . .137 B5

Bentley Dr **5** EX23 . . . . 4 D1
Beramic Cl TR27 . . . . 78 D6
Beraton Ct **3** PL31 . . . . . .109 D5
BERE ALSTON 41 B1
Bere Alston Prim Sch PL20 . 41 B1
Bere Alston Sta PL20 . . . . . 41 B2
BERE FERRERS 119 E3
Bere Ferrers Sta PL20 . . . . .119 E3
BEREPPER 98 F5
Berepper Cross TR12 . . . . . 98 E5
Beresford St PL2 . . . . .128 A4
Beringer St **3** TR14 . . . . . .138 E5
Berkeley Cl EX23 . . . . 4 D1
Berkeley Cotts TR11 . . . . . .145 A4
Berkeley Ct Falmouth TR11 .145 A4
Looe PL13 . . . . .117 C5
Berkeley Hill TR11 . . . . .145 A4
Berkeley Mews **4** TR11 . . .145 A4
Berkeley Path **3** TR11 . . . .145 A4
Berkeley Vale TR11 . . . . . . .145 A4
Berkshire Dr PL2 . . . . .127 F5
Bernice Cl PL4 . . . . .129 A4
Bernice Terr PL4 . . . . .129 A4
Berries Ave EX23 . . . . .104 E4
Berries Mount EX23 . . . . . .104 F4
Berriowbridge 27 B2
Berrow Park Rd PL3 . . . . . .128 E6
Berrycombe View **15** PL31 109 D5
Berrycoombe Hill PL31 . . . .109 C5
Berrycoombe Prim Sch
PL31 . . . . .109 B5
Berrycoombe Rd PL31 . . . .109 C5
Berrycoombe Vale PL31 . . .109 C5
Berryfields Ho PL31 . . . . . .109 E5
Berry Head Gdns PL6 . . . . .124 E1
Berryhill PL30 . . . . 47 C6
Berry La PL31 . . . . .109 E5
Berryman Cres TR11 . . . . . .144 F3
Berry Park Cl PL9 . . . . .135 E6
Berry Park Rd PL9 . . . . .135 E7
Berry Pk PL12 . . . . .122 D4
Berry Rd TR7 . . . . .110 E6
Berwether Cl PL5 . . . . .124 E3
Berveth Cl TR3 . . . . 69 D3
Berwick Ave PL5 . . . . .124 E3
BESOUGHAN 45 A3
Bess Park Rd PL27 . . . . . . .108 E6
Beswetherick Field PL30 . . 47 F1
Bethan Dr PL27 . . . . .108 B5
Bethan View **20** TR6 . . . . . 55 A4
Bethany Homes **1** TR14 . .138 C2
Bethany Pl TR19 . . . . 86 F6
BETHEL 115 A5
Bethel Rd PL25 . . . . .115 A4
Bethesda Pl **10** TR26 . . . . .141 B6
Betjeman Wlk PL5 . . . . .124 C3
Beverley Cres TR27 . . . . . . .142 E7
Beverley Rd PL3 . . . . .129 C4
Beverston Way PL6 . . . . . . .125 B8
Beweys Pk PL12 . . . . .122 C2
Beyrout Pl **2** PL1 . . . . . . .127 F3
Bezant Pl TR7 . . . . .110 B5
Bickern Rd PL11 . . . . .127 B3
Bickford Cres TR13 . . . . 91 B1
Bickford Rd PL15 . . . . .106 B8
BICKHAM 121 A7
Bickham Park Rd PL3 . . . . .128 D7
Bickham Rd PL5 . . . . .123 D2
Bickland Hill TR11 . . . . . . .144 D4
Bickland Ind Est TR11 . . . .144 D4
Bickland View TR11 . . . . . .144 C4
Bickland Water Cotts
TR11 . . . . .144 D4
Bickland Water Rd TR11 . . .144 D2
Bickleigh Cl PL6 . . . . .125 A1
Bickleigh Down Bsns Pk
PL6 . . . . .125 D8
Bickleigh Down CE Prim Sch
PL6 . . . . .125 D7
Bickleigh Down Rd PL6 . . .121 D1
Bicton Cl PL6 . . . . .125 D1
Bicton Rd Gang PL14 . . . . . 38 F3
Penwarden PL14 . . . . 39 A4
Biddick Dr PL2 . . . . .127 F6
Biddick's Ct **5** PL25 . . . . .114 C3
Bideford Mews **13** EX23 . . 4 E1
Bideford Wlk PL6 . . . . .129 E8
Bigbury Wlk PL6 . . . . .129 E8
Biggin Hill PL5 . . . . .123 F4
Big On PL13 . . . . 62 D1
Big Treslea Hill PL30 . . . . . 36 A3
Bilbury St PL4 . . . . .149 A3
BILLACOMBE 135 F8
Billacombe Rd PL9 . . . . . . .129 E1
Billacombe Villas PL9 . . . . .135 F8
BILLACOTT 12 B1
Billacott Rd PL15 . . . . 12 A1
Billings Cl PL6 . . . . .124 D6
Billings Dr TR7 . . . . .111 B5
Billington Cl PL6 . . . . .129 B7
Bindown Ct PL13 . . . . 63 E8
Binhamy Cl EX23 . . . . .104 F4
Binhamy Rd EX23 . . . . 7 B8
Binkham Hill PL20 . . . . 42 D3
Binner Cross TR27 . . . . 78 F1
Bircham View PL6 . . . . .125 C1
Birch Cl PL6 . . . . .125 E7
Birches The PL6 . . . . .125 D6
Birchfield Ave PL2 . . . . . . .128 B6
Birch Gr TR27 . . . . .142 B3
Birchill PL30 . . . . 47 C6
Birch Pond Rd PL9 . . . . . . .135 D2
Birchwood Cl PL19 . . . . . . .147 C3
Birchwood Gdns PL7 . . . . .131 A2
Birkbeck Cl PL7 . . . . .130 E7
Birkdale Cl PL12 . . . . .122 C2

Birlea Business Pk EX23 . . . 7 C8
Biscombe Gdns PL12 . . . . .123 A2
Biscombes La **8** PL17 . . . . 39 E4
BISCOVEY 60 B4
Biscovey Academy **22** PL24 . 60 B4
Biscovey Rd PL24 . . . . .115 F5
Bishop Bronescombe CE Prim
Sch PL25 . . . . .115 B5
Bishop Cornish CE Prim Sch
PL12 . . . . .122 F1
Bishops Cl Saltash PL12 . . .122 E3
Truro TR1 . . . . .137 C6
Bishops Ct TR9 . . . . 45 E6
Bishop's Hill Rd PL27 . . . . . 21 D6
Bishop's Pl PL1 . . . . .148 B1
Bishops Way **3** TR11 . . . . .144 D5
Bishop Temple Rd TR1 . . . .137 C6
BISSOE 81 D8
Bissoe Hill TR4 . . . . 81 D7
Bissoe Rd TR3 . . . . 81 F7
BISSOM 144 E8
Bissom Rd Carvinack TR11 . . 81 F2
Penryn TR10 . . . . 81 F2
Bittern Cl **3** EX23 . . . . 7 B8
Bitthams La PL18 . . . . 40 E7
Blable La PL27 . . . . 32 F5
Blackberry Cl PL9 . . . . .135 E8
Blackberry La PL9 . . . . .135 E8
Blackberry Way TR1 . . . . . .137 F5
Blackbird Cres PL15 . . . . . .106 E4
Blackbrook Cl PL20 . . . . . . 42 E4
BLACK CROSS 45 E3
Blackerry Cl TR16 . . . . .140 F1
Blackeven Cl PL6 . . . . .121 D1
Blackeven Hill PL6 . . . . . . .121 D1
Blackfriars La PL1 . . . . .149 A2
Blackhall Gdns PL6 . . . . . .124 D6
Black La PL15 . . . . 18 A8
Blackmore Cres PL6 . . . . . .124 D6
Black Rd TR27 . . . . .142 D7
BLACK ROCK 79 D1
Blacksmith La TR27 . . . . . . 78 D6
Blacksmiths Mdw **5** PL15 . 27 D7
Blackstone Cl PL9 . . . . .136 B6
Blackthorn Cl
Plymouth, Honicknowle
PL5 . . . . .124 B3
Plymouth, Woolwell PL6 . . .125 D8
Withnoe PL15 . . . . .106 E4
BLACKWATER 68 E5
Blackwater Prim Sch TR4 . . 68 E5
Bladder La PL5 . . . . .124 E2
Blagdon Cross EX21 . . . . . . 13 F7
Blagdon Lodge Cross EX21 . 13 F8
Blairgowrie Rd PL5 . . . . . . .123 C2
Blake Gdns PL5 . . . . .124 C3
Blakeney Rd **6** PL9 . . . . . .129 D1
Blakes Pk PL14 . . . . .113 D7
Blanchard Pl **2** PL7 . . . . . .130 E7
Blanchdown Dr
Gunnislake PL18 . . . . 40 F7
Horsebridge PL19 . . . . 29 D1
Saw Mill PL19 . . . . 41 A7
Blanchminster Rd EX23 . . .104 E5
Blandford Rd PL3 . . . . .129 C6
Blatchborough Cross EX22 . 3 E1
Blaxton La PL5 . . . . .120 C2
Blenheim Rd PL4 . . . . .149 A4
Bligh Cres TR13 . . . . .146 C5
Blight's Row TR15 . . . . .140 B5
Blindhole **8** PL15 . . . . . . .106 C6
Blind La PL11 . . . . 64 D6
BLINDWELL 132 E5
Blindwell Hill PL10 . . . . . . .132 E5
BLISLAND 35 D8
Blisland Com Prim Sch
PL30 . . . . 35 D7
Bloomball Cl PL13 . . . . . . .129 B6
Bloom Fields TR18 . . . . . . .143 C5
BLOWINGHOUSE Bodmin . .109 B2
Redruth 139 F6
Blowing House Cl PL25 . . . .114 B4
Blowinghouse Hill TR15 . . .140 A4
Blowing House Hill
Crowlas TR20 . . . . 89 B8
Hayle TR20 . . . . 77 A1
St Austell PL25 . . . . .114 C4
Blowinghouse La PL30 . . . .109 B2
Blowing House La PL25 . . . .114 B4
BLUE ANCHOR 57 D8
Bluebell Cl PL12 . . . . .122 D4
Bluebell La PL14 . . . . 38 F6
Bluebell St PL6 . . . . .125 B2
Bluebell Way
Launceston PL15 . . . . .106 E4
Tavistock PL19 . . . . .147 E4
Blue Haze Cl PL6 . . . . .125 D5
Blue Reef Aquarium ★
TR7 . . . . .110 D6
Blunt's La PL6 . . . . .125 C3
Boaden Cl PL12 . . . . 53 E5
Boase St TR18 . . . . .143 C1
Boatyard, The PL26 . . . . . . 85 D7
Bobs Rd PL24 . . . . 60 B4
Bochym TR12 . . . . 99 C3
Bochym Hill TR12 . . . . 99 C3
Boconnic La PL20 . . . . 42 D3
Boconnoc Ave PL11 . . . . 39 F3
Boconnoc Rd PL25 . . . . . . .114 D2
BODELVA 115 F8
Bodelva Rd PL24 . . . . .115 E8
Bodgara Way Flats **4**
PL14 . . . . .113 D6
Bodgate Rd PL15 . . . . 12 C1

BODIEVE 108 C7
Bodieve Bsns Pk PL27 . . . .108 D7
Bodieve Rd PL27 . . . . .108 D7
BODILLY 91 F7
Bodinar Rd TR10 . . . . 81 D2
Bodiniel Rd PL31 . . . . .109 C6
Bodiniel View PL31 . . . . . . .109 B5
Bodinnar Cl TR20 . . . . 87 E6
Bodinnar La TR20 . . . . 87 E6
BODINNICK 116 E5
Bodinnick Hts PL23 . . . . . .116 E5
Bodinnick Parc PL30 . . . . . 23 E3
Bodinnick Rd PL30 . . . . 23 E3
BODMIN 109 B5
Bodmin Beacon Nature
Reserve ★ PL31 . . . . .109 D4
Bodmin Bsns Ctr PL31 . . . .109 E3
Bodmin Bsns Pk PL31 . . . . 35 B2
Bodmin Coll PL31 . . . . .109 F2
Bodmin Community Hospital
PL31 . . . . .109 B4
Bodmin General Sta ★
PL31 . . . . .109 E3
Bodmin Hill PL22 . . . . .112 B4
Bodmin Jail ★ PL31 . . . . . .109 D5
Bodmin Parkway PL22 . . . . 48 E6
Bodmin Parkway Sta PL30 . 49 A7
Bodmin Rd Plymouth PL5 . .124 D3
St Austell PL25 . . . . .114 C6
Trebyan PL30 . . . . 48 D5
Trenhorne PL15 . . . . 27 C5
Truro TR1 . . . . .137 E6
Bodmin Ret Pk PL31 . . . . . . 35 B1
Bodmin Road TR4 . . . . 55 E4
Bodmin Town Mus ★ PL31 109 E4
Bodmin & Wenford Rly ★
PL30 . . . . .109 D2
Bodrigan Rd PL13 . . . . .117 D5
Bodriggy Academy TR27 . .145 D5
Bodriggy Cres TR27 . . . . . .142 C5
Bodriggy St TR27 . . . . .142 C5
Bodriggy Villas TR27 . . . . .142 C6
Bodrugan Hill
Portmellon PL26 . . . . 73 C2
Portmellon PL26 . . . . 85 D8
Tregony PL26 . . . . 85 D7
BODWEN 47 E3
Bodwen La PL30 . . . . 35 A6
Body's Ct PL18 . . . . 40 F6
Bohelland Rd TR10 . . . . . . .144 D8
Bohelland Rise TR10 . . . . . .144 D8
Bohelland Way TR10 . . . . . .144 D8
Bohella Rd **20** TR2 . . . . 95 A6
BOHETHERICK 40 F2
Bohill TR10 . . . . .144 D7
Bohill Ct TR10 . . . . .144 D7
BOHORTHA 95 C5
Boiler Works Rd TR14 . . . . .138 E5
Bojea Ind Est PL25 . . . . . . .114 C7
Bojea Terr PL25 . . . . .114 C6
Bojewyan Stennack TR19 . . 75 B1
Bojorrow Trevassack TR12 . . . 99 D5
Trevassack TR12 . . . . .100 A5
Bokelly La PL30 . . . . 23 B3
Bokenna Cl **12** PL14 . . . . . 50 E7
Bokenna Cross PL14 . . . . . . 37 C1
Boldventure Ave PL25 . . . .115 B5
Boldventure Cl PL25 . . . . . .115 B5
Boldventure Rd PL25 . . . . .115 B5
Bolenna La TR6 . . . . 55 A4
BOLENOWE 79 F4
Bolenowe TR14 . . . . 79 F4
Bolenowe La TR14 . . . . 79 F5
BOLINGEY 55 A4
Bolingey Chapel Flats TR6 . 55 A4
Bolingey Rd TR6 . . . . 55 A4
BOLITHO 79 F1
Bolitho Rd TR18 . . . . .143 D5
Bollowal Pl TR19 . . . . 86 E6
Bolowths Cnr TR7 . . . . .111 A7
Bolowths Way TR7 . . . . . . .111 C7
Bolster Cl **8** TR5 . . . . 54 C1
Boltern Rd TR17 . . . . 89 C5
Bolt House Cl PL19 . . . . . . .147 A5
BOLVENTOR 25 E3
Bolventor La PL13 . . . . 63 E8
Bonallack La TR12 . . . . 92 D1
Bon Cot Rd TR18 . . . . .143 C2
Bond St Plymouth PL6 . . . .124 E6
6 Redruth TR15 . . . . .140 B4
Bone Cellar Row TR2 . . . . . 70 F5
Bone Mill Rd TR6 . . . . 55 B4
Bones La Padderbury PL14 . . 52 D4
Tideford PL12 . . . . 52 E4
Bonson Cl PL13 . . . . .117 C4
Bon Villas **18** TR18 . . . . . .143 C2
Bonville Rd PL6 . . . . .124 E6
Bonython Cl TR11 . . . . 82 A3
Bonython Dr TR2 . . . . 72 A7
Bonython Est
Tregaddra TR12 . . . . 99 D4
Tregaddra TR12 . . . . .100 A4
Bonython Rd TR7 . . . . .111 B7
Bonython Terr PL14 . . . . . . .113 B4
Boon's Pl PL1 . . . . .148 C4
BOQUIO 91 F8
BOREA 76 F2
Borgwitha TR16 . . . . 80 B5
Boringdon Ave PL5 . . . . . . .127 D8
Boringdon Cl PL7 . . . . .130 D7
Boringdon Hill PL7 . . . . . . .130 E7
Boringdon Mill Bsns Ctr
PL7 . . . . .130 E7
Boringdon Prim Sch PL7 . .130 D7
Boringdon Rd
Plymouth, Plympton PL7 . . .130 D6
Plymouth, Turnchapel PL9 . .135 A7

Boringdon Terr
Plymouth, Plympton PL7 . . . .130 D6
Plymouth, Turnchapel PL9 . . . .135 A7
Borlase Cl TR13 . . . . .146 B5
Borlase Cres 1 PL25 . . . . . .114 F2
Borough Cross EX22 . . . . .7 F5
Borough Ct PL11 . . . . .126 C4
Borough Pk PL11 . . . . .126 C4
Borrowdale Cl PL6 . . . . .124 D5
Bosahan TR12 . . . . .101 A8
Bosanath Valley TR11 . . . . . .93 C3
BOSCADJACK 91 F6
Boscarn Ct TR14 . . . . .79 B5
BOSCARNE 34 C2
Boscarne Cres PL25 . . . . . . .114 F3
Boscarne Junction Sta★
PL30 . . . . .34 D2
Boscarne View PL30 . . . . . . .34 D2
Boscarn Parc TR15 . . . . .139 C4
Boscarn Rd TR15 . . . . .140 D6
BOSCASTLE 9 C1
Boscastle Com Prim Sch
PL35 . . . . .9 C1
Boscastle Gdns PL2 . . . . . . .128 C8
Boscastle Visitor Ctr★ PL35 . .9 D2
Boscaswell Downs TR19 . . . . .75 A1
Boscaswell Est TR19 . . . . . . .74 F1
Boscaswell Rd TR19 . . . . . . .75 A1
Boscaswell Terr 4 TR19 . . . . .75 A1
Boscathnoe La TR18 . . . . . . .143 B7
Boscathnoe Way TR18 . . . . .143 B7
Boscawen Ct 17 TR6 . . . . . . .55 A4
Boscawen Gdns 11 TR6 . . . . .55 A4
Boscawen Pk PL26 . . . . .58 B8
Boscawen Pl PL2 . . . . .127 E4
Boscawen Rd
7 Chacewater TR4 . . . . . . .69 A3
Falmouth TR11 . . . . .145 B4
Helston TR13 . . . . .146 D4
Perranporth TR6 . . . . .55 A4
St Dennis PL26 . . . . .58 C8
Boscawen St 18 TR1 . . . . . . .137 D4
Boscawen Woods TR1 . . . . . .137 F2
Boscean Ct TR14 . . . . .79 E4
BOSCOPPA 115 A6
Boscoppa Cl TR15 . . . . .140 D7
Boscoppa Rd
St Austell, Bethel PL25 . . . . .115 A5
St Austell, Boscoppa PL25 . . .115 B5
Boscowan TR11 . . . . .145 C2
BOSCREEGE 90 C5
Boscrege TR13 . . . . .90 C5
Boscundle Ave TR11 . . . . . . .144 F1
Boscundle Cl PL25 . . . . .115 D5
Boscundle Row PL12 . . . . . . .123 A2
Bosence Rd TR27 . . . . .90 C7
Bosillion La TR2 . . . . .72 A7
Bosil Rd PL15 . . . . .16 E3
Bosinney Rd PL25 . . . . .114 D3
Bosinver La PL26 . . . . .59 A1
Boskear La PL31 . . . . .109 A4
BOSKEDNAN 76 A1
BOSKENNA 97 C4
Boskenna Cross TR19 . . . . . .97 C5
Boskennal Barton TR19 . . . . .97 B6
Boskennal La TR19 . . . . .97 B6
Boskenna Rd TR16 . . . . .80 A5
Boskennel Dr TR27 . . . . .142 B4
Boskenwyn TR13 . . . . .92 B3
Boskenwyn Com Prim Sch
TR13 . . . . .92 B3
Boskenza Ct TR26 . . . . .141 C2
Boskernick Cl TR18 . . . . .143 B1
Boskernow TR12 . . . . .100 D6
Boskerris Cres TR26 . . . . . . .141 D2
Boskerris Mews TR26 . . . . . .141 D1
Boskerris Rd TR26 . . . . .141 D2
Boslandew Hill 4 TR19 . . . . . .88 C2
BOSLEAKE 139 C3
Bosleake Row TR15 . . . . . . .139 C3
Bosloggas Mews 9 TR11 . . . .145 C3
BOSLOWICK 144 F3
Boslowick Cl TR11 . . . . .144 F3
Boslowick Ct TR11 . . . . .144 E2
Boslowick Rd TR11 . . . . .144 E2
Boslymon Hill PL30 . . . . .48 D4
Bosmeor Cl TR11 . . . . .144 E2
Bosmeor Ct TR15 . . . . .139 D6
Bosmeor Pk TR15 . . . . .139 D6
Bosmeor Rd TR11 . . . . .144 E2
Bosneives Hill PL30 . . . . .33 D2
Bosneives Rd PL30 . . . . .33 E1
Bosnoweth Helston TR13 . . . .146 D5
Probus TR2 . . . . .71 D7
Bosorne Cl TR19 . . . . .86 E6
Bosorne Rd TR19 . . . . .86 E6
Bosorne St TR19 . . . . .86 E6
Bosorne Terr TR19 . . . . .86 E6
Bosparva La
Leedstown TR27 . . . . .78 F2
Praze-an-Beeble TR14 . . . . . .79 A3
Bospolvans Rd 2 TR9 . . . . . . .45 D6
BOSPORTHENNIS 75 F3
Bospowis TR14 . . . . .138 C3
BOSSINEY 14 D8
Bossiney Rd PL34 . . . . .14 D7
Bostennack Pl 10 TR26 . . . . .141 A5
Bostennack Terr 11 TR26 . . . .141 A5
Boston Cl PL9 . . . . .135 B7
Bosuen Rd TR7 . . . . .111 A7
Bosullow Vean TR20 . . . . .87 D8
Bosvargus Hill 3 TR19 . . . . . .93 B5
Bosvarren TR11 . . . . .93 B5
Bosvathick Dr TR11 . . . . .93 B5
Bos Vean TR12 . . . . .102 F2

Bosvean Gdns
11 Illogan TR16 . . . . .67 E4
Truro TR1 . . . . .137 B5
Bosvean Rd TR4 . . . . .69 E4
Bosvenna View PL31 . . . . . . .109 E4
Bosvenna Way TR18 . . . . . . .143 B3
Bosvenning Pl TR20 . . . . .87 E6
Bosvigo Gdns★ TR1 . . . . . . .137 A5
Bosvigo La TR1 . . . . .137 B5
Bosvigo Rd TR1 . . . . .137 C4
Bosvigo Sch 16 TR1 . . . . . . .137 C4
Boswedden Rd TR19 . . . . .86 D6
Boswedden Pl TR19 . . . . .86 E6
Boswedden Rd TR19 . . . . .86 E6
BOSWEDNACK 76 A4
Boswell Cl PL5 . . . . .124 B2
Boswergy TR18 . . . . .143 C5
Boswin TR13 . . . . .92 A8
BOSWINGER 85 B5
Boswithian Rd TR14 . . . . . . .138 F6
Bosworgey Cl 3 TR9 . . . . . . .45 D6
Bosworgy Rd TR20, TR27 . . . .90 B8
Boswyn TR14 . . . . .79 E3
BOTALLACK 86 E7
Botallack La TR19 . . . . .86 E7
Botetoe Hill TR14 . . . . .79 C4
Botetoe Rd TR14 . . . . .79 B4
Botha Rd 1 PL27 . . . . .31 F3
Bothwicks Rd TR7 . . . . .110 E6
BOTTOMS 96 E5
BOTUSFLEMING 122 B7
Boughthayes Est PL19 . . . . . .147 A5
Boulden Cl PL7 . . . . .131 C5
Boulter Cl PL6 . . . . .121 C1
Boundary Cl 21 TR18 . . . . . . .143 C1
Boundary Dr EX23 . . . . .7 B6
Boundary Rd Bodmin PL31 . . .109 A4
Bodmin PL31 . . . . .109 A5
Dousland PL20 . . . . .42 E3
Bounders La TR6 . . . . .55 B4
Bounder Treath TR12 . . . . . . .101 C1
Boundervean La TR14 . . . . . .138 B2
Boundis Farm TR10 . . . . .93 A7
Bounds Cross EX22 . . . . .8 B4
Bounds Pl 1 . . . . .148 B2
Bounsalls Ct 5 PL15 . . . . . . .106 C5
Bounsall's La PL15 . . . . .106 C5
Bourne Cl PL3 . . . . .129 D6
Bourneside PL25 . . . . .114 D3
Boveway Dr PL14 . . . . .113 E5
Boville La PL9 . . . . .136 C7
Bovisand Ct PL9 . . . . .134 F2
Bovisand La
Down Thomas PL9 . . . . .135 B2
Staddiscombe PL9 . . . . .135 D3
Bovisand Pk PL9 . . . . .135 A1
Bovisand Rd PL9 . . . . .135 E3
Bowden 14 EX23 . . . . .4 D1
Bowden Park Rd PL6 . . . . . . .125 A1
Bowdens La Redruth TR15 . . .139 F7
Tolskithy TR15 . . . . .67 F2
Bowdens Row TR15 . . . . . . .140 A4
Bowers Park Dr PL6 . . . . . . .125 E2
Bowers Rd PL2 . . . . .128 B5
Bowglas Ct TR20 . . . . .89 A8
Bowhays Wlk 2 PL6 . . . . . . .129 C7
Bowithick Rd PL15 . . . . .16 C2
Bowjey Ct 9 TR18 . . . . .143 C1
Bowjey Hill TR18 . . . . .143 C1
Bowjey Terr 6 TR18 . . . . . . .143 C1
Bow La EX23 . . . . .4 D2
Bowles Rd TR11 . . . . .145 B4
Bowleys La Trethellick PL28 . . .21 A2
Trethillick PL28 . . . . .21 A2
Bowling Gn Menheniot PL14 . . .51 F5
34 St Ives TR26 . . . . .141 B6
Bowling Gn The TR2 . . . . .82 F2
BOWLING GREEN Bugle 47 E1
Redruth 139 D3
Bowling Green TR11 . . . . .92 F3
Bowling Green Ct
Hayle TR27 . . . . .142 D5
Liskeard PL14 . . . . .113 D5
Bowling Green Rd TR11 . . . . .92 F3
Bowling Green Terr 35
TR26 . . . . .141 B6
Bownder An Mengleudh 1
TR8 . . . . .111 D6
Bownder An Sycamor TR16 68 F2
Bownder Corbenic 5 TR7 110 D5
Bownder Dowr TR27 . . . . . . .142 B3
Bownder Gareth TR7 . . . . . . .110 C5
Bownder Iger 4 TR7 . . . . . . .111 E5
Bownder Karleghyon 2
TR8 . . . . .111 D5
Bownder Kolom 6 TR7 . . . . . .111 D6
Bownder Kosti Woles 2
TR7 . . . . .111 D6
Bownder Kresennik An Shoppa
4 TR8 . . . . .111 D6
Bownder Logres 5 TR7 . . . . .111 D5
Bownder Marhaus 4 TR7 110 D5
Bownder Oghen 2 TR7 . . . . .111 E5
Bownder Sarras 3 TR7 . . . . .110 D5
Bownder Tregwestek 5
TR7 . . . . .111 D6
Bownder Trewolek TR8 . . . . .111 E5
Bownder Vean PL25 . . . . .115 A5
Bownder Vesydhyans 4
TR8 . . . . .111 D5
Bownder Woryan 3 TR7 . . . . .111 E5
Bownder Ywain 7 TR7 . . . . . .110 C5
Bowood Pk Delabole PL33 . . . .14 F1
Bos Vean TR12 . . . . .102 F2
Box Heater PL28 . . . . .31 F7
Boxhill Cl PL5 . . . . .124 B3
Boxhill Gdns PL2 . . . . .128 C8

Box's Shop EX23 . . . . .7 A4
Boxwell Pk PL31 . . . . .109 F4
Boyd Ave PL28 . . . . .107 C5
Boyer Sq 1 PL31 . . . . .109 A5
BOYTON 13 B2
Boyton Com Prim Sch PL15 13 A3
Bracken Cl Bodmin PL31 . . . .109 E5
Plymouth PL6 . . . . .125 D8
Brackenside PL13 . . . . .62 D1
Bracken Terr TR7 . . . . .110 E5
Brackwell Pl TR27 . . . . .108 B5
BRADDOCK 49 F5
Braddock CE Prim Sch
PL14 . . . . .50 B6
Braddock Cl PL26 . . . . .58 D6
Braddons Hill PL7 . . . . .130 B7
Braddon Cl PL6 . . . . .125 E1
BRADFORD 24 D2
Bradford Cl PL6 . . . . .129 B7
Bradfords Quay PL27 . . . . . .108 C6
Bradfords Quay Rd PL27 . . . .108 C6
Bradley Rd Newquay TR7 . . . .111 C7
Plymouth PL4 . . . . .128 F4
Bradridge Ct PL15 . . . . .13 A4
Braemar Cl PL7 . . . . .131 C4
Braeside Pk PL14 . . . . .50 E8
Braggs Hill PL15 . . . . .13 B3
Brake La PL10 . . . . .132 B5
Brake Rd PL5 . . . . .124 E2
Brake The PL14 . . . . .37 F4
Bramble Cl Newquay TR7 . . . .111 A4
Plymouth PL3 . . . . .129 B7
Widemouth Bay EX23 . . . . . . .6 F5
Bramble Hill EX23 . . . . .104 E5
Bramble La Egloshayle PL27 . . .33 F7
Trevarner PL27 . . . . .108 F6
Brambleside 1 PL30 . . . . .23 E7
Brambles The
Liskeard PL14 . . . . .113 E5
Lostwithiel PL22 . . . . .112 C3
Bramble Wlk 1 PL6 . . . . .129 C7
Bramfield Pl PL6 . . . . .129 D7
Bramley Cl PL25 . . . . .114 E4
Bramley Pk PL31 . . . . .109 F5
Bramley Rd PL3 . . . . .129 C4
Brancker Rd PL2 . . . . .128 C6
Brandon Rd PL25 . . . . .114 D3
Brandon Wlk EX23 . . . . .6 F5
Brandreth Rd 3 PL3 . . . . . . .128 F6
Brandy La PL20 . . . . .89 F4
BRANE 87 C3
Brane La TR20 . . . . .87 D3
Branksome Dr PL27 . . . . .108 E5
Brannel Rd PL26 . . . . .58 C2
Brannel Sch The PL26 . . . . . . .58 B3
Branscombe Gdns PL5 . . . . .124 A3
Branson Ct 9 PL7 . . . . .131 C5
Branson Pk PL19 . . . . .42 A6
Branwell La TR18 . . . . .88 E6
Braunton Wlk PL6 . . . . .129 E8
Bray Cl 3 Kirland PL31 . . . . . .109 F3
Tavistock PL19 . . . . .147 A5
Brayford Cl PL5 . . . . .124 B3
Bray Rise TR16 . . . . .80 A5
BRAY SHOP 28 B1
Bray's Pl PL25 . . . . .114 F4
Brays Terr 2 TR16 . . . . .140 F1
BRAZACOTT 12 B2
Brazacott Cross PL15 . . . . . . .12 B2
BREA 139 B3
BREA ADDIT 139 B2
Brea Arch TR14 . . . . .139 A3
Bread St TR18 . . . . .143 E5
Brea Est Crugmeer PL27 . . . .107 F8
Rock PL27 . . . . .21 D3
BREAGE 90 F3
Breage CE Voluntary Aided
Prim Sch TR13 . . . . .90 F3
Break My Neck La TR20 . . . . . .88 B8
Breakwater Hill PL4 . . . . .149 C3
Breakwater Ind Est PL9 . . . . .135 C8
Breakwater Rd Bude EX23 . . .104 D5
Plymouth PL9 . . . . .135 C8
Brean Down Cl PL3 . . . . .128 E6
Brean Down Rd PL3 . . . . .128 E7
Brea Rd Rock PL27 . . . . .21 D2
Rock PL27 . . . . .21 D3
Breaside TR14 . . . . .139 A3
Brecon Cl Plymouth PL3 . . . . .129 B7
1 St Agnes TR5 . . . . .54 C1
Bredon Ct TR7 . . . . .110 C6
Bree Shute La 10 PL31 . . . . .109 E5
4 Bodmin PL31 . . . . .109 E5
BRENT 62 E2
Brentford Ave PL5 . . . . .124 B5
Brent Knoll Rd 1 PL3 . . . . . .128 E6
Brenton Rd PL11 . . . . .64 B5
Brentons Pk PL29 . . . . .22 D6
Brentor Rd Mary Tavy PL19 . . .30 F6
Plymouth PL4 . . . . .129 B2
Brent Tor★ PL20 . . . . .30 D7
Brentwartha PL13 . . . . .62 E2
Brest Rd PL6 . . . . .125 A3
Brest Way PL6 . . . . .125 A3
Bretonside PL4 . . . . .149 A2
Brett Wlk PL7 . . . . .130 F7
Brewartha TR2 . . . . .57 E1
Brewers Cl PL30 . . . . .47 F6
Brewers Hill PL26 . . . . .58 C8
Brewers Rd TR1 . . . . .137 F5
Brewery Hill TR26 . . . . .77 E4
Brewery La TR13 . . . . .146 B8
Brian Laity Way 2 TR18 . . . . .143 D6
Briansway PL12 . . . . .122 D2
Briardale Rd PL2 . . . . .127 F5
Briarfield PL23 . . . . .116 D4
Briarleigh Cl PL6 . . . . .125 E1
Briar Rd Bude EX23 . . . . .104 E4

Briar Rd continued
Plymouth PL3 . . . . .128 F7
Briars Row PL12 . . . . .122 D4
Briars Ryn PL12 . . . . .53 B7
Briar Tor PL20 . . . . .42 D3
Briarwood PL14 . . . . .113 D5
Brickfields Sp Ctr PL1 . . . . . .127 F2
Brickworks Hill TR16 . . . . .68 D1
Bridals La PL13 . . . . .62 E2
BRIDGE 67 E5
Bridge TR9 . . . . .45 E7
Bridge Cl TR7 . . . . .111 A4
Bridge Ct PL25 . . . . .114 F4
Bridge Hill Illogan TR16 . . . . . .67 E5
St Columb Major TR9 . . . . . .45 E6
Trebyan PL30 . . . . .48 C5
Bridge Ho Delabole PL33 . . . . .14 E2
Hayle TR27 . . . . .142 B6
Bridge Ho The 13 TR18 . . . . .143 C2
Bridge La PL12 . . . . .53 A3
Bridgemead PL26 . . . . .114 C1
Bridgemoor Cross EX22 . . . . . .8 C6
BRIDGEND 112 E3
Bridge Pk PL23 . . . . .116 D4
Bridge Rd Goonhavern TR4 . . . .55 D4
Illogan TR16 . . . . .67 E4
St Austell PL25 . . . . .114 B3
Seaton PL11 . . . . .64 B5
Tideford PL12 . . . . .52 F2
Bridge Row TR16 . . . . .67 E5
BRIDGERULE 8 A6
Bridgerule CE Prim Sch
EX22 . . . . .8 A6
Bridgerule Ind Est EX22 . . . . . .7 F4
BRIDGES 59 F8
Bridge St Par PL24 . . . . .60 B6
7 Stratton EX23 . . . . .4 D1
Bridges The PL12 . . . . .122 E1
BRIDGETOWN 19 B8
Bridge View PL5 . . . . .127 D8
Wadebridge PL27 . . . . .108 C6
Bridge Wlk 2 PL35 . . . . .9 C2
Bridgwater Cl PL6 . . . . .125 B1
Bridle Cl PL7 . . . . .131 B7
Bridle Way
Quintrell Downs TR8 . . . . . . .44 E3
Saltash PL12 . . . . .122 D4
Bridwell Cl PL5 . . . . .127 E8
Bridwell Lane N PL5 . . . . . . .127 E8
Bridwell Rd PL5 . . . . .127 E8
Brighter La PL30 . . . . .23 C3
BRIGHTON 57 D5
Brighton Water Hill
Cardinham PL30 . . . . .35 F3
Welltown PL30 . . . . .36 A3
Brighton Water La PL30 . . . . . .36 A3
Brillwater Rd TR11 . . . . .92 E4
Brimford Cross EX22 . . . . .3 D4
Brimhill Cl PL7 . . . . .131 B3
Brimstone Hill PL30 . . . . .35 E3
Brinky Well Rd PL30 . . . . .34 E6
Brisbane Terr PL14 . . . . .113 C5
Brismar Wlk 3 PL6 . . . . .129 C7
Briston Orch PL12 . . . . .53 E7
Britannia Pl PL4 . . . . .129 B2
Briticheston Cl PL9 . . . . .136 A5
British Rd TR5 . . . . .54 D1
Briton's Hill TR18 . . . . .143 F6
Brixham Wlk PL6 . . . . .129 E8
BRIXTON 136 F4
Brixton Lodge Gdns PL8 . . . .136 F4
Brixton Terr TR13 . . . . .146 C6
Broad Cl EX22 . . . . .11 E7
Broadclose Hill EX23 . . . . . . .104 E5
Broad La Broadlane TR13 . . . . .90 F5
Illogan TR16 . . . . .139 D7
Trematon PL12 . . . . .53 E2
Welltown PL30 . . . . .36 A2
Broadland Gdns PL9 . . . . . . .136 A8
Broadland La PL9 . . . . .135 F8
Broadlands Cl PL7 . . . . .131 A3
BROADLANE 90 E5
Broadley Cl PL6 . . . . .121 B2
Broadley Ind Pk PL6 . . . . . . .121 B2
Broadley Park Rd PL6 . . . . . .121 B2
Broad Mead PL17 . . . . .39 E5
Broad Park Rd
Bere Alston PL20 . . . . .41 B2
Plymouth PL3 . . . . .128 D6
Broad Pk Launceston PL15 . . .106 B7
St Keyne PL14 . . . . .51 B3
Broadshell Cross EX22 . . . . . . .5 F4
Broads La TR11 . . . . .81 F3
Broad St
12 Launceston PL15 . . . . . .106 C6
Lifton PL16 . . . . .19 F4
Newquay TR7 . . . . .110 D6
Padstow PL28 . . . . .107 D5
Penryn TR10 . . . . .144 D7
7 St Columb Major TR9 . . . . .45 E6
Truro TR1 . . . . .137 E5
Broads Yd PL11 . . . . .64 C5
Broadview PL19 . . . . .30 A6
Broad View TR4 . . . . .56 D1
Broadway The PL9 . . . . .135 F7
Broad Wlk Helston TR13 . . . . .146 B7
Saltash PL12 . . . . .122 E1
Brock Ho 9 PL4 . . . . .149 A2
Brockhole La PL7 . . . . .130 E8
Brockley Rd PL3 . . . . .129 C4
Brocks La PL10 . . . . .132 F5
Brockstone Rd PL25 . . . . . . .115 D4
Brockton Gdns PL6 . . . . .125 B6
BROCTON 34 D4
Bromfield Cres TR2 . . . . .57 E1
Bromhead Ct PL6 . . . . .129 A8

Bromley Ho 6 PL2 . . . . .128 A4
Bromley Pl 5 PL2 . . . . .128 A4
Bronescombe Cl TR10 . . . . . .144 D7
Bronte Pl PL5 . . . . .124 D1
BROOK 147 B2
Brook Cl Helston TR13 . . . . . .146 B4
Plymouth PL7 . . . . .131 A3
Brook Ct 6 TR11 . . . . .145 A4
Brookdale Ct 12 PL27 . . . . . .108 B5
Brookdown Terr PL12 . . . . . . .122 E3
Brookdown Villas PL12 . . . . . .122 E3
Brook Dr EX23 . . . . .104 E3
Brooke Cl PL12 . . . . .123 A2
Brookfield Cl Lanjeth PL26 . . . .58 E3
Plymouth PL7 . . . . .131 B5
Brookfields PL1 . . . . .127 F1
Brook Green Ctr for Learning
PL5 . . . . .124 B4
Brooking Cl PL6 . . . . .129 A8
Brookingfield Cl PL7 . . . . . . .130 C5
Brooking Way PL12 . . . . .122 C3
Brook La PL19 . . . . .147 B2
Brooklands Cl PL6 . . . . .124 E3
Brooklands View PL29 . . . . . . .22 E7
Brooklyn Flats 18 TR2 . . . . . . .95 A6
Brooklyn Terr 17 TR2 . . . . . . .95 A6
Penryn TR10 . . . . .144 C7
Brook Pl Falmouth TR11 . . . . .145 A4
Wadebridge PL27 . . . . .108 B5
Brooks PL22 . . . . .49 E3
Brookside PL25 . . . . .114 F4
Brookside Cl PL15 . . . . .106 B8
Brook St Falmouth TR11 . . . . .145 A4
17 Mousehole TR19 . . . . . . .88 C1
Tavistock PL19 . . . . .147 C6
Brook The PL12 . . . . .122 E4
Brookward Terr 8 TR18 . . . . .143 C7
Brookway TR27 . . . . .142 E7
Brookwood Rd PL9 . . . . .136 D7
Broomfield Dr Bodmin PL31 109 B3
Plymouth PL9 . . . . .135 C5
Broomfield Rd PL27 . . . . .108 D5
Broom Hill PL12 . . . . .122 D2
Broomhill Cross EX22 . . . . .5 E3
Broomhill La EX23 . . . . .4 D5
Broom Pk PL9 . . . . .135 D5
Broughton Cl PL3 . . . . .128 F7
Browne Memorial Almshouses
PL19 . . . . .147 A5
Browning 14 TR9 . . . . .45 D6
Browning Dr PL31 . . . . .109 C3
Browning Rd PL2 . . . . .128 A5
Brownlow Pl 5 PL31 . . . . .109 D5
Brownlow St PL1 . . . . .148 A2
Browns Hill PL23 . . . . .116 C4
Brown's Hill Penryn TR10 . . . .144 C8
2 Treliever TR10 . . . . .81 D2
Broxton Dr PL9 . . . . .129 E1
Bruallen Cl PL30 . . . . .23 E7
Bruggan TR12 . . . . .103 A4
Brunel Ave PL2 . . . . .127 F5
Brunel Ct 7 TR1 . . . . .137 B4
Brunel Prim & Nur Sch
PL12 . . . . .122 E2
Brunel Quays PL22 . . . . .112 D2
Brunel Rd PL12 . . . . .122 C4
Brunel Terr 3 PL2 . . . . .127 E5
Brunel Way PL1 . . . . .148 A2
BRUNNION 77 A3
Brunnion Rd TR27 . . . . .77 A3
Brunswick Pl 10 PL2 . . . . . . .127 F4
Brunswick Rd PL4 . . . . .149 B2
Brunton Rd TR15 . . . . .23 B5
Brush End TR26 . . . . .77 E4
Bryher Cl PL17 . . . . .39 E6
Brymon Way PL6 . . . . .125 B4
Brynmoor Cl PL3 . . . . .129 A6
Brynmoor Rd PL3 . . . . .129 A6
Brynmoor Wlk PL3 . . . . .129 A6
Bryny Cl PL30 . . . . .23 E7
Buccaneer St 1 TR18 . . . . . . .143 D6
Buckett's Hill TR15 . . . . .140 C2
Buckeys La TR2 . . . . .95 B6
Buckfast Cl PL2 . . . . .128 A6
Buckingham Nip TR4 . . . . .68 F3
Buckingham Pl PL5 . . . . .123 E2
Buckingham's Ctr TR18 . . . . . .56 B7
Buckingham Terr TR16 . . . . . .68 D1
Buckland Abbey★ PL20 . . . . . .41 F1
Buckland Cl PL7 . . . . .130 D7
BUCKLAND
MONACHORUM 42 A3
Buckland St PL1 . . . . .148 B2
Buckland Terr PL20 . . . . .42 C2
Bucklawren Rd PL13 . . . . .63 E7
Bucklers Ho PL25 . . . . .115 B4
Bucklers La PL25 . . . . .115 B4
Buckler Village (Mobile Homes
Pk) PL25 . . . . .115 B4
Buckles Hill PL15 . . . . .10 E1
Buckthorn Ct 3 PL6 . . . . . . .124 C6
Buckwell St PL1, PL4 . . . . . . .149 A2
Buctor Pk PL19 . . . . .41 D8
Buddle Cl Plymouth PL9 . . . . .136 A5
Tavistock PL19 . . . . .147 B6
BUDE 104 E6
Budehaven Com Sch EX23 . . .104 F4
Budehaven L Ctr EX23 . . . . . .104 F5
Bude Marshes Nature
Reserve★ EX23 . . . . .104 D4
Bude Primary Academy Junior
& Infants School EX23 . . . .104 E5
Bude Ind Est EX23 . . . . .104 F4
Bude-Stratton Bsns Pk EX23 7 B8

Bude-Stratton Mus★
EX23..........104 D5
Budge Mdws PL15.........28 C4
Budleigh Cl PL9.........135 F5
Budnic Est TR6.........55 B5
Budnic Hill TR6.........55 B5
Budock Cl TR11.........144 D3
Budock Pl TR11.........145 B4
Budock Rd 2 TR11.........144 D5
Budock Terr TR11.........145 B3
Budock Vean La TR11...93 B2
BUDOCK WATER.........144 C2
Budshead Gn PL5.........124 C4
Budshead Rd PL5.........124 C4
Budshead Way PL5.........124 E2
Buena Vista Cl PL6.........125 D6
Buena Vista Dr PL6.........125 C6
Buena Vista Gdns PL6...125 C6
Buena Vista Way PL6.........125 C6
BUGLE..........47 D1
Bugle Rural Workshops
  PL26..........47 C1
Bugle Sch PL26..........47 C1
Bugle Sta PL26.........47 C2
Bugle Way PL31.........109 F3
Buildings The TR20.........89 A6
Bullan's La TR26.........141 A5
Bullans Terr 5 TR26...141 A5
Bulleid Cl PL2.........127 F7
Bulleid Way EX23.........104 E4
Buller Cl Plymouth PL7...130 F4
  Torpoint PL11.........127 A3
Buller Hill TR16.........80 B6
Buller Ho PL13.........117 D3
Buller Pk Liskeard PL14...113 D5
  Saltash PL12.........122 D3
Buller Rd PL11.........127 B3
Buller St PL13.........117 C3
Bull Hill PL23.........116 D4
Bullock La
  Helston, Lower Green
    TR13.........146 B5
  Helston, Whitehill TR13...146 C4
  Whitehill TR13.........146 B4
Bullock Market Terr 27
  TR18.........143 E6
Bulmer Rd PL4.........149 C3
Bulsworthy La PL15.........19 C2
Bulteel Gdns PL6.........124 E7
Bulwark Cl 2 PL5.........124 D1
Bulwark Rd TR13.........146 B4
Bungalows The Looe PL13..117 D6
  Tintagel PL34.........14 D7
Bunkers Hill
  22 St Ives TR26.........141 B6
  Townshend TR27.........90 C8
Bunneys Side PL14.........36 E1
Bunnys Hill PL30.........35 E2
Bunyan Cl PL5.........124 C2
Burden Cl PL31.........109 C4
Burgess Cl EX23.........4 D2
Burgois Rd PL27.........32 D7
BURHOS.........79 F2
Burhos Row TR13.........79 F1
Buriton Row 32 TR18...143 E5
BURLAWN.........108 D1
Burlawn Dr PL25.........114 F7
Burleigh La PL3.........128 D7
Burleigh Manor PL3.........128 D7
Burleigh Park Rd PL3...128 D6
Burley Cl TR1.........137 D3
Burley Ct TR11.........145 B4
Burnard Cl PL6.........124 E7
Burnards Ct 7 PL31...109 C5
Burnett Cl PL12.........122 D2
Burnett Rd PL6.........128 F8
Burngullow Rd PL26.........58 F3
Burnham Park Rd PL3...128 D6
Burniston Cl PL7.........131 A3
Burnistone Cl PL7.........131 A3
Burn La PL19.........30 E8
Burns Ave PL5.........124 C2
Burns View PL11.........65 B5
Burnthouse Burnthouse TR10 81 C4
  Dobwalls PL14.........37 C1
Burnthouse Cotts TR10...81 C4
Burnthouse La Hayle TR27 142 D5
  Roskrow TR10.........81 C3
Burn View EX23.........104 D6
Burnwithian Terr TR16...68 D1
Burras Bolitho TR14.........79 F1
  Tolcarne TR13.........80 A2
BURRATON.........122 C4
Burraton Com Prim Sch
  PL12.........122 C3
BURRATON COOMBE.........122 C2
Burraton Rd PL12.........122 C4
Burrator Rd PL20.........42 E3
Burrington Ind Est PL5...124 A1
Burrington Rd PL5.........124 A1
Burrington Way PL5.........124 B1
Burrow Hill PL9.........135 E6
Burrows The TR26.........141 A5
BURSDON.........3 B6
Bursdon Moor Cross EX39..3 B7
Burthallan La TR26.........77 A7
Burton Cl PL6.........125 B6
Burton Ho 18 PL25.........114 C3
Burwell Cl PL6.........125 E4
Bury Cl PL15.........11 B1
Buscaverran TR14.........91 C8
Bush Hill TR4.........36 A1
Bush Pk Launceston PL15...106 D5
  Plymouth PL6.........125 F3
BUSVEAL.........140 F4

Butcher Park Hill PL19...147 B7
Bute Rd PL4.........129 A4
Butler Cl PL6.........125 B6
Butney Cnr TR14.........66 E3
Butson Pk TR5.........68 D8
Buttercup Field EX23.........6 F2
Buttercup Mdw PL15...106 E4
Buttercup Rd PL6.........125 B2
Butterdown PL12.........122 B3
Buttlegate PL11.........64 D5
Button Dr TR8.........111 B5
Butt Park Rd PL5.........124 B3
BUTTSBEAR CROSS.........7 F7
Butts La PL35.........9 D1
Butts Pk PL22.........112 D2
Butts The St Newlyn East TR8.. 56 B7
  Tintagel PL34.........14 D7
Buzzard Rd PL19.........147 D2
Buzzard Rise 8 PL18...40 F5
Byard Cl PL5.........123 E1
Byland Rd PL3.........129 A6
Byron Ave PL5.........124 C2

C

Cabot Cl PL12.........122 E3
Cades Parc TR13.........146 C6
CADGWITH.........103 B4
Cadoc Cl PL28.........20 E1
Cadogan Cl TR14.........138 E1
Cadogan Dr TR14.........138 E1
Cadogan Rd TR14.........138 E1
Cadover Cl PL6.........125 A1
Caernarvon Gdns PL2...128 B7
Caernarvon Lodge 1 TR7 110 D5
Calais Rd TR27.........78 C2
Calamansack TR11.........93 B2
Calartha Rd TR19.........75 A1
Calartha Terr 5 TR19...75 A1
Calder Cl PL3.........129 B6
Caldicot Gdns PL6.........125 C8
Caldwells Rd PL18.........143 E6
Caledonia Cl 1 PL7...131 B5
CALENICK.........137 C1
Calenick St TR1.........137 C4
Cal Hill TR16.........140 D3
California Gdns
  Plymouth PL3.........129 D6
  Portscatho TR2.........83 B2
CALLESTICK.........55 C1
CALLINGTON.........39 F5
Callington Com Coll PL17.. 39 F5
Callington Her Ctr★ PL17.. 39 E4
Callington Prim Sch 20
  PL17.........39 E4
Callington Rd
  Harrowbarrow PL17.........40 C4
  Lewannick PL15.........27 B7
  Liskeard PL14.........113 D7
  Saltash PL12.........122 E3
  Tavistock PL19.........147 A4
CALLOOSE.........78 D2
Calloose Lane E TR27...78 D1
Calloose Lane W TR27...78 D1
Callybarrett Rd
  Callywith PL31.........35 B2
  Milltown PL30.........35 B2
Callywith Gate Ind Est PL31 35 B2
Calshot Cl TR7.........111 E7
CALSTOCK.........41 A3
Calstock Com Prim Sch
  PL18.........41 A3
Calstock Rd PL18.........41 A6
Calstock Sta PL17.........41 A3
Calumet Rd 3 TR14...138 E3
Calver Cl TR10.........144 C8
Calvez Cl PL10.........132 F6
Camaret Dr TR26.........141 B4
Cambeak PL35.........9 C1
Cambeak Cl EX23.........10 C6
Camber Rd PL1.........148 A1
CAMBORNE.........138 B2
Camborne Cl PL5.........124 C2
Camborne Ctr The★ TR14.. 138 E3
Camborne Geological Mus &
  Art Gal★ TR15.........139 C7
Camborne Redruth Com Hospl
  TR15.........139 F6
Camborne Ret Pk TR15...139 E6
Camborne Science &
  International Academy
  TR14.........138 B3
Camborne Sta TR14...138 D2
Cambridge La W 5 PL1.. 148 B3
Cambridge Pl TR11.........145 A3
Cambridge Rd PL2.........127 F5
CAMBROSE.........67 F6
Camden Ct PL4.........149 A3
Camden St PL4.........149 A3
Camel Cl PL28.........107 D4
Camel Ct PL30.........109 C6
CAMELFORD.........105 C4
Camelford L Ctr PL32...105 C4
Camelford Prim Sch PL32 105 C3
Camelot Ct 2 TR18...143 E5
Camelot View PL32.........105 C4
Camel Rd Carlyon PL27...21 F2
  Dinham PL27.........22 A1
CAMELS HEAD.........127 E7
Camelside PL27.........108 C5
Camel Valley Vineyard★
  PL30.........34 B2
Cameo Ct TR14.........138 E4
Cameron Cl EX23.........104 D7
Cameron Way PL6.........125 B1
Camilla Terr PL2.........128 D7
Campbell Rd PL9.........135 F7

Campbeltown Way TR11..145 C3
Camp Cross PL15.........19 F7
Camperdown St La N 4
  PL2.........127 F4
Camperdown St PL2.........127 F4
Camperknowle Cl PL10...132 F6
Campfield Hill TR1.........137 D5
Camp Hall Rd TR8.........43 B1
Campion Cl PL15.........106 E4
  7 Plymouth PL7.........131 C5
  Saltash PL12.........122 D4
Campion Rise PL19.........147 D6
Campion View PL6.........125 E8
Campion Way TR7.........142 E6
Campion Wlk 2 PL27...108 C6
Camp Rd TR8.........43 B1
Camullas Way TR7.........110 A5
Canal Rd PL19.........147 B5
Canberra Rd 5 PL6...125 B5
Candish Dr PL6.........136 D7
Canefields Ave PL7.........131 B3
Canhaye Cl PL7.........131 A3
Canis Mews 7 PL9...136 E8
CANNALIDGEY.........32 E4
Cannalidgey Rd PL27...32 E4
Cannamanning Rd 3 PL26 59 D7
Cann Gdns PL6.........124 D6
Cannis Rd PL25.........114 E6
Cannon Hill PL14.........113 C5
Cannons Pl TR13.........146 D7
Cannon St PL1.........127 D2
Cannon Terr 2 PL6...125 C1
Cann Woods Nature Reserve★
  PL5.........124 C6
Cann Wood View PL6...125 E7
CANONSTOWN.........77 C2
Canons Way PL19.........147 A3
Cansford Dip EX23.........10 E5
Canterbury Dr PL5.........124 B4
Cantillion Cl PL27.........21 E3
Cant La PL27.........21 F3
Canton PL26.........85 D5
CANWORTHY WATER.........11 D2
Canyke Fields 1 PL31...109 F3
Canyke Rd PL31.........48 D8
Cape Cl TR19.........86 E6
Cape Cornwall Rd TR19...86 E6
Cape Cornwall Sch TR19...86 E6
Cape Cornwall St TR19...86 E6
Capella Dr 1 PL9...136 E8
Cape Terr TR19.........86 E6
Cape Trelew TR19.........86 E6
Caprera Terr La PL4...148 C4
Capricorn Way 14 PL9...136 E8
Captains Gdns PL5.........124 E1
Captains Ho PL26.........73 C3
Captain's Wlk TR11...145 A2
Caradon Bsns Ctr 8 PL14 113 C5
Caradon Cl
  9 Callington PL17.........39 E4
  1 Pensilva PL14.........38 E4
  Plymouth PL6.........125 A5
Caradon Ct 2 PL20...42 C4
Caradon Dr PL14.........113 B6
Caradon Hts Liskeard PL14 .113 D7
  Tremar PL14.........38 B4
Caradon Terr PL12.........122 E3
CARADON TOWN.........38 E6
Caradon View TR14.........37 F3
Caravan Pk TR20.........89 C6
Caraway Cl 5 TR14...138 E5
Carbeile Jun Sch PL11...127 A2
Carbeile Rd PL11.........127 A2
Carbes La PL22.........112 C2
CARBIS.........47 A2
CARBIS BAY.........141 B3
Carbis Bay Sta TR26...141 D2
Carbis Cl TR15.........140 A5
Carbis Rd PL26.........59 D6
Carboth La PL15.........106 B5
CARCLAZE.........114 E6
Carclaze Com Prim Sch
  PL25.........114 E6
Carclaze Ind Est PL25...114 E7
Carclaze La PL27.........22 E2
Carclaze Rd PL25.........114 E6
Carclew Ave TR7.........110 E6
Carclew Rd TR11.........81 F4
Carclew St TR1.........137 D3
Carclew Terr Devoran TR3 .. 81 F6
  Truro TR1.........137 D3
Cardeast La PL30.........35 E4
Cardell Rd PL31.........109 D5
Cardell Way TR11.........111 A5
Cardiff Cl PL7.........131 B4
Cardigan Rd PL6.........125 C1
Cardinal Ave PL5.........127 D8
CARDINHAM.........35 E3
Cardinham Prim Sch PL30 35 F3
Cardinham Woods Forest
  Walks★ PL30.........35 C1
Cardinnis Gn 2 PL14...113 D6
Cardinnis Rd TR18.........143 B5
Cardrew Bsns Pk TR15...140 C6
Cardrew Cl TR15.........140 B6
Cardrew Dr TR15.........140 D6
Cardrew Ind Est
  Redruth TR15.........140 D7
  Redruth TR16.........68 B2
  Treleigh TR15.........140 C7
Cardrew La 1 TR15...140 C5
Cardrew Terr TR15.........140 C5
Cardrew Trade Park N
  TR15.........140 C7
Cardrew Trade Park S
  TR15.........140 C7
Cardwen Est PL13.........62 C6

Careswell Ave PL2.........127 F8
Carew Ave PL5.........124 B3
Carew Cl Crafthole PL11...65 B5
  St Day TR16.........68 E1
Carew Gdns Plymouth PL5.. 124 B3
  Saltash PL12.........122 D3
Carew Gr PL5.........124 B3
Carew-Pole Cl TR1.........137 E3
Carew Rd St Day TR16...68 D1
  Truro TR1.........137 C5
Carew Terr PL11.........127 B2
Carew Wharf PL11.........127 C2
Carew Wharf Bsns Ctr
  PL11.........127 C2
Carey Ct PL12.........122 E3
Carey Pk Helston TR13...146 B7
  Polperro PL13.........62 E2
  Truro TR1.........137 C4
CARFURY.........76 A1
Cargoll Rd TR8.........56 B7
CARGREEN.........119 A2
Cargwyn PL26.........59 D6
Cargy Cl TR8.........55 D8
CARHARRACK.........80 F8
Carina Pl 9 PL9...136 E8
Carisbrooke Rd PL6.........125 C1
Carkeek's Cl PL26.........58 B3
CARKEEL.........122 C6
Carkeel Barns PL12.........122 C5
Carkeel Ind Est PL12...122 D5
Carknown Gdns TR15...140 D3
Carland Cross TR8.........56 D4
Carland View TR8.........56 B7
CARLEEN.........90 F5
Carleon TR13.........90 F4
CARLIDNACK.........93 E4
Carlidnack Cl TR11.........93 D3
Carlidnack La TR11.........93 D4
Carlidnack Rd TR11.........93 E4
Carlisle Rd PL5.........124 D3
CARLOGGAS Foxhole.........58 C5
  Penwithick.........59 D7
  St Mawgan.........45 A8
Carloggas Cl TR8.........45 A8
Carloggas Farm TR8.........45 A8
Carloggas Gr 6 TR9...45 D6
Carloggas La PL26.........58 C4
Carloggas Way 10 TR9...45 D6
Carlton Cl PL3.........129 B5
Carlton Ho 7 PL31...109 E5
Carlton Terr
  Plymouth, Lipson PL4.........149 B3
  Plymouth, Weston Mill PL5.. 127 E8
Carlton Vills PL12.........53 E4
Carlton Way PL14.........113 D7
CARLUDDON.........59 D6
Carluddon Technology Park
  PL26.........59 D6
CARLYON BAY.........115 E3
Carlyon Cl Looe PL13...62 A7
  Threemilestone TR3.........69 D3
  Torpoint PL11.........126 F4
  11 Truro TR1.........137 C4
Carlyon Ho PL1.........69 E4
Carlyon Rd Playing Place TR3.. 82 B8
  St Austell PL25.........114 C4
  Truro TR1.........137 C5
Carmarthen Rd PL4.........129 B2
Carmel Gdns PL19.........147 A5
Carmen Sq 10 TR18...143 C7
Carminow Cross PL30...48 D8
Carminowe Cres 18 TR18 .143 D5
Carminow Rd PL31.........48 D8
Carminow Road Ind Est 4
  PL31.........48 D8
Carminow Way TR7.........111 A4
Carn TR3.........80 E3
Carnanton Rd TR8.........45 C6
Carnarthen Moor TR15...139 C3
Carnarthen TR14.........79 E6
CARN ARTHEN.........139 B2
Carnarthen Moor TR15...67 E1
Carnarthen Rd 1 TR14...138 E2
Carnarthen TR14.........138 E2
Carn Ave TR14.........138 F2
Carn Bargus PL26.........58 E8
Carn Bosavern TR19.........86 F6
Carn Bosavern Cl TR19...86 F6
Carn Brae Cl Ctr TR15...139 C5
Carn Brea Ave TR15...139 C5
Carn Brea Ho TR15.........139 C5
Carn Brea La TR15.........139 C5
Carn Brea Village TR15...139 F5
Carn Cl TR27.........78 E1
Carncrows Rd TR26.........141 C6
Carncrows St TR26.........141 C6
CARNE St Dennis.........46 C1
  Veryan.........83 F5
Carnebo Hill TR4.........55 E5
Carne Cross PL24.........59 F7
Carne Ct PL26.........58 C8
Carnedon PL14.........38 C7
Carne Hill St Dennis PL26...46 C1
  Trewoon PL25.........58 F4
Carnellis Rd 7 TR26...141 A5
Carne Mdws TR2.........70 F5
CARN ENTRAL.........139 A2
Carn Entral Brea Addit TR14 139 A1
  Pengegon TR14.........79 E6
Carne Quarry TR12.........102 D8
Carne Rd TR18.........143 C3
Carne's Bldgs 11 TR18...143 E4
Carnes Ct TR11.........145 C2
Carne's Flats PL24.........60 B5

Carneton Cl TR8.........43 D3
Carn Euny Settlement★
  TR20.........87 C3
Carne View Cl TR14...138 F5
Carne View Rd TR2...71 D6
Carnglaze Caverns★ PL14.. 36 F1
Carnglaze Cl PL14.........113 E6
Carn Gloose Rd TR19...86 D6
Carn Gwavas Terr TR18 ..143 D1
CARNHELL GREEN.........78 F4
Carnhell Rd TR14, TR27...78 F4
CARNHOT.........68 F4
Carninney La TR26.........141 C1
Carnjewey Way 4 PL25...114 F2
CARNKIE.........139 F2
CARNKIEF.........55 D3
Carnkief Cnr TR4.........55 D4
Carn La Bosleake TR16...67 F1
  Brunnion TR20.........77 A2
  Carnkie TR16.........139 F3
Carn Marth La TR16...140 E2
Carnmeal TR13.........91 A4
Carnock Rd PL2.........128 C8
Carnon Cres 13 TR3...81 F7
CARNON DOWNS.........82 A7
Carnon Gate Roundabout
  TR3.........81 E6
Carnon Terr TR3.........81 F6
Carnoustie Dr PL12...122 C2
Carn Ros TR10.........144 D7
Carn Ros TR10.........74 F1
Carnsew Cl TR10.........81 C1
Carnsew Cres TR10.........81 C1
Carnsew Ct TR27.........142 B5
Carnsew Mdw TR27.........142 A5
Carnsew Rd TR27.........142 A5
Carnsmerry PL26.........47 C1
Carnsmerry Cres PL25...114 E4
Carnstabba Rd 13 TR26...77 A6
Carnsullen La TR12.........101 B1
Carntiscoe Rd TR27.........77 C2
Carntiscoe Workshops
  TR27.........77 C2
Carn Todden TR19.........88 D1
CARN TOWAN.........96 C7
Carn View TR16.........80 F6
Carn View Terr TR19...75 A1
CARNYORTH.........86 F8
Carnyorth Hill TR19.........86 F8
Carnyorth Terr
  Carnyorth TR19.........86 F8
  Trewellard TR19.........86 F8
Caroe Rd PL32.........10 D3
Carolina Gdns PL2.........127 F7
Caroline Cl TR27.........142 E7
Caroline Row TR27.........142 E7
CARPALLA.........58 C5
Carpalla Rd PL26.........58 C5
Carpalla Terr PL26.........58 D5
Carpenter Ct PL31.........109 E5
Carpenter Rd PL9.........135 F8
Carpenter Way PL19...147 B4
Carpmael Ave TR8.........111 B4
Carracawn Cross PL12...64 D3
Carrack Dhu 37 TR26...141 B6
Carrack Dhu Est 36 TR26.. 141 B6
Carrack Gladden TR26...141 D2
Carrack Widden 25 TR26.. 141 B5
Carradale Rd PL6.........129 C4
Carrallack La TR19.........86 E5
Carrallack Mews TR19...86 E6
Carrallack Terr TR19...86 E6
Carriage Ho The TR3...69 F1
Carriage Parc TR4.........55 D4
Carrickowel Cres 1 PL25 115 A5
Carrick Rd TR11.........144 E2
Carrick Way TR2.........95 A6
Carrine Rd TR1.........69 F3
Carrisbrooke Way PL12...122 B3
Carrnown Gdns TR15...140 D3
Carroll Rd PL5.........124 C2
Carrolls Way PL9.........136 A5
Carron La PL6.........121 C1
Carsize La TR27.........78 E1
Carter Cl TR7.........111 A4
Carteret Rd EX23.........104 E5
CARTHEW.........59 B6
Carthew Cl Liskeard PL14...113 D6
  St Ives TR26.........141 A6
Carthew Ct TR26.........141 A6
Carthew La Four Lanes TR13 .80 A3
  Praze-an-Beeble TR13...79 F2
Carthew Terr TR26.........141 A6
Carthew Way TR26.........141 A6
Carvath Ho PL25.........114 D3
Carvedras TR11.........92 E5
Carvedras Ct 1 TR1...137 C4
Carvolth TR14.........79 D3
Carvolth Downs TR14...79 E2
Carvossa Est TR20.........89 B8
Carvoza Rd TR1.........137 D5
Carvynick Cotts TR8.........57 A7
Carwen Rd PL30.........35 D8
Carwinard Cl TR27.........78 C5
Carwinion Bamboo Gdn★
  TR11.........93 E3
Carwinion Rd TR11.........93 E3
Carwin La TR27.........78 E2
Carwin Rise Angarrack TR27.78 C5
  Hayle TR27.........142 E7
Carwollen Rd PL25.........114 E7
Carworgie Cl 10 TR9...45 E2
Carworgie Manor TR9...45 D3
Carworgie Way 7 TR9...45 D2
CARWYNNEN.........79 D4
Carwynnen Cl TR14.........79 B3
CARZISE.........78 D1
Casey La PL13.........62 D5

Cassacawn Hill PL30......35 D8
CASTALLACK............97 F6
Castel Wary Cl TR13....146 B5
Casterills Rd TR13.......146 D4
Castings Dr 2 PL25.....115 A3
Castle Acre Gdns PL3...129 B5
Castle Bank Gdns PL3...129 B5
Castle Barbican PL7.....130 E4
Castle Bldgs PL12.......122 D4
Castle Canyke Rd
　Bodmin PL31...........109 F3
　Bodmin PL31...........109 F3
Castle Carey Gdns PL3..129 B5
Castle Cl TR11...........146 C5
Castle Ct Praa Sands TR20..90 C3
　Saltash PL12...........122 C2
Castledore Rd PL24......60 E5
Castle Dr Bodmin PL31...109 F5
　Falmouth TR11.........145 F2
　Praa Sands TR20.......90 B3
　St Mawes TR2..........94 F5
Castle Dyke PL15........106 C6
CASTLE GATE............76 F1
Castle Gdns PL14........113 C6
Castle Gn 2 TR13.......146 B5
Castlehayes Gdns PL7...138 B4
Castle Hill Falmouth TR11..145 D3
　1 Helston TR13........146 B5
　6 Liskeard PL14.......113 C6
　Lostwithiel PL22.......112 C2
　Saltash PL12...........122 C1
Castle Hill Ct Bodmin PL31..109 E5
　7 Liskeard PL14.......113 C6
Castle Hill Gdns PL31...109 F5
CASTLE HORNECK.......97 C4
Castle Horneck Cl PL18..143 C5
Castle Horneck Rd TR18..143 C5
Castle Hts 3 PL34......14 C7
Castlek La PL15..........27 A4
Castle La Liskeard PL14..113 C6
　Plymouth PL7..........130 E4
Castle Mdws
　Launceston PL15.......106 A4
　2 St Agnes TR5.......54 D1
Castlemead Cl PL12......122 D1
Castlemead Dr PL12.....122 D1
Castle Rd Castle Down TR9..46 B4
　Longrock TR20.........88 F8
　Ludgvan TR20..........89 A8
　Penzance TR18.........143 E7
　Tintagel PL34..........14 C7
Castle Rise Plymouth PL3..129 B4
　Saltash PL12...........122 D1
　Truro TR1.............137 C5
Castle Rock PL29........22 D8
Castle St Bodmin PL31...109 F5
　Launceston PL15.......106 C6
　Liskeard PL14.........113 C6
　Looe PL13.............117 D3
　Plymouth PL1..........149 A2
　Truro TR1.............137 C4
Castleton Cl PL3.........129 A4
Castle View
　10 Liskeard PL14......113 C6
　Longrock TR20.........88 F6
　Lostwithiel PL22.......112 E3
　Saltash PL12...........122 D1
　Tintagel PL34..........14 C7
Castle View Cl TR15.....140 B6
Castle View Pk TR11.....93 D3
Caswarth Terr PL28......107 D5
Catalina Row PL27.......31 F3
Catalina Villas PL9......135 A6
CATCHALL..............97 D8
Catchfrench Cres PL14...113 C6
Cathcart Ave PL4.......129 B2
Cathebedron Rd
　Carnhell Green TR14...78 F4
　Praze-an-Beeble TR14..79 A3
Cathedral Church of the
　Blessed Virgin Mary ★
　TR1..................137 D4
Cathedral La 13 TR1....137 D4
Cathedral of St Mary &St
　Boniface PL1..........148 B3
Cathedral School of St Mary
　PL1..................148 B3
Cathedral St PL1........148 B3
Cathedral View TR1......137 C6
Catherine Cl EX23.......104 F4
Catherine Pk PL15.......62 E5
Catherine's Hill PL15....106 A6
Catherine St PL1........148 C2
CATTEDOWN............149 C1
Catterick Cl PL5........123 E5
Cattewater Rd PL4......129 B1
Caudledown La PL26.....59 C8
Caunter Rd PL14........113 D6
Causeland Sta PL14......51 B2
Causewayhead TR18.....143 E5
Causeway The
　Falmouth TR11........144 F4
　Hayle TR27............142 A4
Causley Cl PL15.........106 C7
Cavendish Cres TR7.....111 B5
CAWSAND..............133 B1
Caxton Gdns
　2 Manadon PL5.......124 C1
　Plymouth PL5..........124 C1
Cayforth Flats TR16.....67 C6
Cayley Way PL5.........123 F2
Cecil Ave PL4..........149 C4
Cecil Cotts PL1.........148 A3
Cecil St PL1............148 B3
Cedar Ave PL9..........135 C5
Cedar Cl 21 Callington PL17..39 F4
　Torpoint PL11.........126 F2
Cedarcroft Rd PL2......128 B7

Cedar Ct Camborne TR14..139 A5
　Saltash PL12...........122 F2
Cedar Dr PL11...........126 F2
Cedar Gr EX23...........104 E7
Cedar House Flats TR26..77 E4
Cedar Pk PL9............135 A1
Cedars The TR1..........137 C2
Celandine Gdns PL7......131 C5
Celia Hts PL31..........109 F2
Celtic Rd PL17..........39 F4
Cemetery Rd PL18.......40 F5
Centaur Mews 13 PL9...136 A6
Centenary Row Middle
　TR14.................138 E3
Centenary Row W 2 TR14..138 E2
Centenary St TR14.......138 E3
Centenary Way 3 TR18..143 D6
Central Ave PL25........114 E5
Central Cl PL26.........58 B4
Central Park Ave PL4....148 C4
Central Rd Holywell TR8..43 B1
　Plymouth PL1..........148 B1
Central Sq 7 PL7........110 D6
Central Treviscoe
　St Dennis PL26.........58 A7
　Treviscoe PL26.........58 B7
Century Cl Helston TR13..146 D8
　St Austell PL25........114 F6
Century Ct TR7..........111 C7
Century La TR7..........83 F6
Century Sq 6 PL14......38 E4
CHACEWATER...........68 F3
Chacewater Hill TR4....69 A3
Chacewater Prim Sch TR4..69 A3
CHADDLEWOOD..........131 B6
Chaddlewood Ave PL4...149 B3
Chaddlewood Cl PL7.....131 A4
Chaddlewood Ho PL7....131 B5
Chaddlewood Prim Sch
　PL7.................131 A5
Chadwick Parc TR15....140 B6
Chagford Wlk PL6.......129 E8
Chainwalk Dr TR1.......137 C6
Chalets The TR18.......88 E6
Chalet The PL11........64 C4
Challacombe Gdns TR10..144 C8
Challenger Quay 7 TR11..145 C3
Challgood Cl 1 PL9.....135 F5
Challgood Rise PL9......135 F5
Challis Ave PL8.........45 A8
Challock Cl PL26........125 D4
Chamberlayne Dr PL7....130 E6
Champion's Ct TR13.....146 B6
Chancery Ct TR4........70 D8
Chancery La 23 TR18....143 E5
Chandler Pk 4 TR10....94 A8
Chandlers Wlk PL15.....115 A3
Chandos Pl 12 PL25....114 C3
Channel Park Ave PL3...129 B5
Channel View Polruan PL23..116 D2
　St Austell PL25........115 A6
　St Ives TR26...........141 A6
Channel View Terr
　Plymouth PL4..........149 A4
　4 Redruth TR15.......140 C4
Channon Rd PL12........122 C4
Chantry Ct PL7.........130 B5
Chantry La PL13........117 E4
CHAPEL Launceston.....106 A5
　Quintrell Downs.......111 E4
Chapel Cl
　Camborne, Kehelland TR14..66 F1
　Camborne, Tuckingmill TR14..139 A4
　8 Chapel PL25........106 B5
　Connor Downs TR27....78 D6
　Crantock TR8..........110 A3
　Gunnislake PL18.......40 E5
　4 Horrabridge PL20...42 C4
　Lanivet PL30..........47 E6
　St Just in Roseland TR2..82 F2
Chapel Cnr EX22........8 A5
Chapel Cotts EX23......4 C8
Chapel Cres TR4........56 A2
Chapel Ct Camborne TR14..138 F4
　Padstow PL28..........107 D5
　9 Redruth PL15.......140 B5
Chapeldown PL24........60 D5
Chapeldown Rd PL11....127 A2
Chapel Farm TR14.......79 E5
Chapel Field PL25.......115 B5
Chapel Gate PL15.......106 A5
Chapel Gn PL26.........59 A1
Chapel Ground PL13....117 C3
Chapel Hill
　Camborne, Brea TR14..139 A3
　Camborne, Tregajorran
　　TR15................139 C4
　Carwen PL30..........35 B8
　Devoran TR3..........81 F6
　Gweek TR12...........92 C2
　Hayle TR27............142 C6
　Kerrow PL30..........24 D1
　Lanner TR16...........80 D6
　Launceston PL15.......106 B5
　Newquay TR7..........110 D6
　Perranporth TR6.......55 B4
　Polgooth PL26.........59 A1
　Ponsanooth TR3.......81 B4
　Porkellis TR13.........92 B8
　Porthtowan TR4.......68 A5
　Redruth TR16..........68 A4
　St Erth TR27..........142 A1
　Sticker PL26..........58 F1
　Truro TR1.............137 B4
Chapel La
　Berriowbridge PL15....27 B3

Chapel La continued
　Bodmin PL31..........109 D5
　Goldsithney TR20......89 F5
　Hayle TR27............142 D6
　Horrabridge PL20......42 C4
　Lizard TR12...........102 F2
　Penryn TR10...........144 C7
　Polmenna PL14.........36 E1
　Polruan PL23..........116 D2
　St Austell PL25........115 C6
　St Mabyn PL30.........34 D8
　St Teath PL30..........23 F6
　Treswithick PL30.......35 E5
　Trevenna PL14.........36 E2
　5 Wadebridge PL27...108 B5
Chapel Mdw
　Buckland Monachorum PL20..41 F3
　21 Callington PL17....39 E4
　Perranarworthal TR3...81 D6
Chapel Park Gdns PL15..106 B5
Chapel Park Terr PL15...106 B5
Chapel Pk PL15.........106 B5
Chapel Pl Pillaton PL12..53 B7
　16 Truro TR1.........137 D4
Chapel Point La PL26....73 C2
Chapel Rd Camborne TR14..139 A4
　Foxhole PL26..........58 D5
　Heamoor TR18.........143 C8
　Indian Queens TR9.....45 E1
　Langore PL15..........18 D5
　Leedstown TR27.......78 E1
　Nanstallon PL30.......34 C1
　9 Par PL24...........60 C4
　Roche PL26............46 F3
　St Just TR19..........86 E6
　St Tudy PL30..........23 E3
　Saltash PL12...........122 B3
Chapel Row
　Praze-an-Beeble TR14..79 B2
　2 Redruth TR15......140 B5
　Tremar PL14..........38 A3
　Truro TR1.............137 D4
　Widegates PL13.......63 F8
Chapel Sq Crowlas TR20..89 B8
　Mevagissey PL26.......73 C3
　Troon TR14............79 E5
Chapel St
　4 Bere Alston PL20...41 B1
　4 Callington PL17....39 F4
　Camborne TR14........138 D2
　Camelford PL32........105 C4
　Grimscott EX23........5 B2
　Gunnislake PL18.......40 F6
　Lifton PL16...........19 F4
　Marazion TR17.........89 B5
　Mevagissey PL26.......73 C3
　21 Mousehole TR19...88 C1
　9 Newlyn TR18.......143 C2
　Penzance TR18.........143 E5
　Plymouth PL4..........149 A3
　Plymouth, Mount Wise PL1..127 E2
　Probus TR2...........71 C6
　Redruth TR15..........140 B5
　St Day TR16...........68 D1
　St Ives TR26...........141 B5
　St Just TR19..........86 E6
　Tavistock PL19.........147 B5
Chapel Terr
　Camborne TR15........139 D6
　Devoran TR3..........81 F6
　Falmouth TR11.........145 B4
　Hayle TR27............142 B5
　Par PL24.............60 B6
　9 Porthleven TR13....98 B8
　Portreath TR16........67 C6
　Redruth TR15..........140 D2
　Redruth, Carn Brea Village
　　TR15................139 F5
　Ruan Minor TR12......103 A5
　St Day TR16...........68 E1
　10 St Mawes TR2.....95 A6
　Trewellard TR19.......86 F8
CHAPEL TOWN..........57 B6
Chapel Town Bsns Pk TR8..57 B7
Chapel Town Cl TR11....93 D4
Chapel Way PL3.........129 A6
CHAPLE AMBLE.........22 D2
Chapman Ct PL12.......122 B3
Chapmans Ope PL1.....127 D2
CHAPMAN'S WELL......13 E4
Chapmans Wy PL25.....114 E4
Charaton Cross PL14....38 F4
Charaton Rd PL14.......38 F4
Chard Barton PL5.......124 B3
Chard Rd PL5...........123 D2
Chard Terr 6 TR11.....145 A3
Charfield Dr PL6........129 A8
Chariot Rd TR15........139 E6
Chark La PL30..........48 D4
Charlbury Dr PL9.......129 D1
Charles Ave TR11.......144 E2
Charles Bassett Cl 6
　TR13.................146 C5
Charles Cl PL25.........114 F3
Charles Cross PL4......149 A3
Charles St Bugle PL26...47 C1
　Newlyn TR18..........143 C3
　Plymouth PL4..........149 A3
　Truro TR1.............137 C4
Charles Terr PL3........129 A6
CHARLESTOWN..........115 B2
Charlestown Prim Sch
　PL25.................115 C3
Charlestown Rd PL25....115 B3
Charlestown Shipwreck &
　Heritage Ctr ★ PL25...115 B2
Charlotte Cl TR4.......68 C6
Charlotte Gardens PL25..114 F3

Charlotte St PL2........127 E4
Charlton Cres PL6.......125 A2
Charlton Rd PL6........125 A3
Charnhill Cl PL9........136 A6
Charnhill Way PL9......136 A6
Charter Cl TR13........146 C5
Charter Ct TR10........144 D7
Charter Way PL14......113 C6
Chateau Cl PL26........46 D1
Chatry Pk 23 PL17.....39 E4
Chatsworth Gdns PL5...123 F3
Chatsworth Way PL25..115 C2
Chaucer Rd PL19.......147 D5
Chaucer Way PL5.......124 C1
Chawleigh Cl PL18......40 F5
Chedworth St PL4.......149 A3
Chegwin Gdns PL7......110 E5
Chegwyn Gdns 6 TR5...54 C1
Chegwyns PL26.........58 D5
Chegwyns Hill PL26.....58 D5
Chelfham Senior Sch PL20..40 F3
Chellean Vean TR4......81 C7
Chellew Rd TR1........137 F5
Chelmer Cl PL7.........131 A5
Chelmsford Pl PL5......124 C4
Chelson Gdns PL6.......125 E3
Cheltenham Pl
　Newquay TR7..........110 D6
　Plymouth PL4..........149 B4
Chelwood Gr PL7.......130 F5
CHENHALLS............142 A2
Chenhalls Cl TR27......77 E2
Chenhalls Rd TR27......142 A2
Chenoweth Cl TR14.....138 C4
Chenoweth Way TR16...140 E8
Chepstow Ave PL26.....125 C8
Chequer Tree Ct PL18...40 F5
Chequetts Cl 10 PL17...39 E4
Cheriton Cl PL5.........124 A3
Cherrill Gdns EX23......104 E7
Cherrington TR7........110 B5
Cherry Cross EX22......12 B7
Cherry Ct 1 PL19......30 A4
Cherry Gdns TR18......143 E5
Cherry Gdn St 15 TR19..88 C1
Cherry Hill TR9........45 D7
Cherry Pk PL7..........131 A3
Cherry Tree Dr TR15....139 D7
Cherrytree Ho TR18.....143 C5
Cherry Tree La PL7......131 A4
Cherry Tree Mews PL25..141 A4
Cherry Way PL15.......106 E4
Cheshire Dr PL6........124 D6
Chesnut Cl PL12........122 D4
Chester Ct TR7.........111 A6
Chesterfield Rd PL3.....129 B4
Chester Pl 4 PL4.......128 E4
Chester Rd TR7.........111 A6
Chesterton Cl PL5.......124 C3
Chesterton Ct PL27.....108 A6
Chesterton Pl TR7......111 A7
Chestnut Ave PL9.......135 C5
Chestnut Cl Callington PL17..40 A4
　Falmouth TR11........144 F5
　Lamerton PL19........30 A4
　St Tudy PL30..........23 E3
　Tavistock PL19.........147 D2
　Torpoint PL11.........126 F3
　24 Yelverton PL20....41 B1
Chestnut Dr 1 PL14....50 D7
Chestnut Gr PL31.......109 B4
Chestnut Rd PL3........128 D7
Chestnut Terr PL19......30 A4
Cheviot Rd TR7.........110 E4
Chi An Dowr 4 TR11....144 F2
Chichester Cl PL26......58 E5
Chichester Cres
　Newquay TR7..........110 F4
　Saltash PL12...........122 E1
Chichester Ct PL20......42 C4
Chichester Ho PL1......148 B2
Childrey Gdns PL6......125 C1
Childrey Wlk PL6.......125 C1
Chili Rd TR15..........139 D6
CHILLATON............29 F8
CHILSWORTHY.........40 E7
Chilton Cl PL6.........129 B7
Chimney Tops 7 PL25..47 E4
China Clay Ctry Pk ★ PL26..59 A7
China Alley PL9........135 A6
China Downs PL30......23 C8
Chings Alley PL6.......106 C6
Chins Field Cl 9 TR27..142 D6
Chipponds Dr PL25.....114 A3
Chirgwin Ct 22 TR18...143 E5
Chirgwin Rd TR1.......137 E4
Chisholme Cl PL25......114 D3
Chisholme Ct PL25......114 D3
Chittenburn Bsns Pk PL8..136 F6
Chittleburn Cross PL8...136 E5
Chittleburn Hill PL8.....136 E5
Chivenor Ave PL5.......123 D4
Chiverton Cl TR20......89 F4
Chiverton Cross
　Blackwater TR4.......68 F5
　Rosudgeon TR20.......89 F4
Chiverton Greenacres TR5..68 D8
Chiverton Way TR20.....89 F4
Chivilas Rd TR14.......138 E5
Chollacott Cl PL19......147 C4
Chollacott La PL19......147 D3
Chough Cl 12 Binhamy EX23..7 B8
　Falmouth TR11........144 E4
　Launceston PL15.......106 E4
Chough Cres PL25.......114 E4
Choughs Cl TR14.......138 B3
Christa Ct PL14.........38 D7
Christian Mill Bsns PL6..124 E4
Christian Way TR7......111 C4

Chubb Dr PL3..........128 B4
Chudleigh Rd PL4......129 A4
Chun Castle ★ TR20....87 C8
Church Av PL23........116 D4
CHURCHBRIDGE........50 F1
Church Cl Blisland PL30..35 D8
　Lelant TR26...........77 E4
　Plymouth PL7..........130 B7
　Trispen TR4...........56 D1
CHURCH COMBE........140 A2
CHURCH COVE.........103 A2
Church Cove Rd TR12...103 A2
Church Ct PL6..........125 A7
Church End PL13.......117 D3
Churchfield Cl TR8......89 A8
Churchfield Pl PL24.....60 B5
Churchfields Rd TR18....55 D8
Church Gate 3 PL14....113 C5
Church Hill Calstock PL18..41 A3
　Chacewater TR4.......68 F2
　Golant PL23...........61 B6
　Helston TR13..........146 C7
　Herodsfoot PL14......50 E3
　Hessenford PL11, PL12..64 B8
　Ludgvan TR20.........89 A8
　Milton Combe PL20....41 F1
　Navarino PL15.........18 A8
　Penryn TR10..........144 D8
　4 Pensilva PL14......38 E4
　Plymouth PL6.........125 B1
　Port Isaac PL29.......22 D7
　St Day TR16...........68 E1
　7 St Mawes TR2.....95 A6
　Sticker PL26..........58 F1
　Tavistock PL19........147 E2
　Tintagel PL34.........14 C7
　Trefranck PL15........16 F3
Church Hill Rd PL9.....135 A6
Church Ho PL12........123 A2
Churchill Rd PL19......147 D2
Churchill Way
　10 Penwithick PL26...59 D7
　Plymouth PL3.........128 E6
Churchill Wlk PL12.....122 E1
Church La Bodmin PL31..109 E5
　Bude EX23............104 D5
　Calstock PL18.........41 A3
　Camborne TR14........138 D3
　Cargreen PL12.........119 A1
　Flushing TR11.........145 B7
　Helston TR13..........146 B6
　Lelant TR26...........77 E4
　Lostwithiel PL22......112 C2
　Mevagissey PL26......73 C4
　Padstow PL28.........107 D5
　St Columb Minor TR7..111 E7
　St John PL11..........132 B8
　Tamerton Town EX22..13 A8
　Tresamble TR16.......81 A7
　Zelah TR4............56 A2
Churchlands PL13.......117 C5
Churchlands Cl PL6.....125 E7
Churchlands Rd PL6.....125 E8
Church Lea
　Launceston PL15.......106 A7
　Tavistock PL19........147 E2
Church Mews Stithians TR3..80 F3
　Week St Mary EX22....11 E8
Church Park Ct PL6.....125 C5
Church Park Mews PL27..108 B4
Church Park Rd
　Crackington Haven EX23..10 C6
　Plymouth PL6.........125 E8
Church Path EX23......104 C5
Church Pk Bodmin PL31..109 F5
　Horrabridge PL20......42 C4
　Lerryn PL22...........61 D8
　St Mellion PL12.......53 D8
Church Pl Liskeard PL14..113 C5
　18 St Ives TR26......141 B6
Church Rd Camborne TR15..139 B6
　Cardinham PL30.......35 F3
　Cury TR12............99 A4
　Four Lanes TR16......80 A5
　Heamoor TR18........143 C7
　Illogan TR16..........67 E4
　Lanivet PL30..........47 E7
　Launceston PL15.......18 F6
　Lelant TR26...........77 E4
　Mabe Burnthouse TR10..93 C8
　Madron TR20..........143 A8
　Merrymeet PL14.......38 C1
　Mount Hawke TR4.....68 C6
　Mylor Bridge TR11....82 B2
　Pendeen TR19.........75 A1
　Penponds TR14........138 B1
　Penryn TR10..........144 C8
　Perranarworthal TR3...81 D5
　Plymouth, Plympton PL7..130 F4
　Plymouth, Plymstock PL9..135 F7
　St Austell PL25........115 B3
　St Dennis PL26........46 C1
　St Tudy PL30..........23 E3
　Saltash PL12...........122 D2
　Shortlanesend TR4....69 F6
　Stithians TR3.........80 F4
　Tideford PL12.........52 F2
Church Road EX23......10 C7
Church Row Carharrack TR16..80 F8
　Lanner TR16..........80 D6
　Sheviock PL11........65 C6
Church Row La PL5.....124 C5
Church Sq 8 Bodmin PL31..109 E5
　St Just TR19..........86 F6

Church Sq *continued*
4 Stratton EX23 . . . 4 E1
Church St Callington PL17 . . . 39 E4
Calstock PL18 . . . . . 41 A3
Camborne TR14 . . . . 138 D3
Carharrack TR16 . . . . 80 F8
Falmouth TR11 . . . . . 145 B4
Gorran Haven PL26 . . . . 85 D5
Helston TR13 . . . . . 146 B6
Landrake PL12 . . . . . 53 C3
Launceston PL15 . . . . 106 C6
Liskeard PL14 . . . . . 113 C5
Looe, East Looe PL13 . . . 117 D3
Looe, West Looe PL13 . . . 117 C3
Mevagissey PL26 . . . . 73 C3
15 Newlyn TR18 . . . . 143 C1
Padstow PL28 . . . . . 107 D5
Par PL24 . . . . . 60 B5
Plymouth PL3 . . . . . 128 A4
Poughill EX23 . . . . 4 D2
8 St Austell PL25 . . . . 114 C3
St Columb Minor TR7 . . . 111 D7
St Day TR16 . . . . . 68 E1
St Erth TR27 . . . . . 142 A1
St Germans PL12 . . . . 65 A8
St Just TR19 . . . . . 86 F6
5 Stratton EX23 . . . . 4 E1
Tywardreath PL24 . . . . 60 D5
Churchstow Wlk PL6 . . . 129 E8
Church Street N PL14 . . . 113 C5
Church Street S PL14 . . . 113 C5
Church Terr Devoran TR3 . . 81 F6
Grampound Road TR2 . . . 57 E1
St Kew PL30 . . . . . 23 A3
CHURCHTOWN Bridgerule . . 8 B6
Camborne 67 E5
Lanivet 47 E7
St Breward 24 B4
Churchtown Cardinham PL30 35 F3
Colvennor TR12 . . . . 99 A4
Gwinear TR27 . . . . . 78 D4
Mellingey PL27 . . . . 32 D6
7 Mullion TR12 . . . . 99 A2
5 St Agnes TR5 . . . . 54 C1
St Kew PL30 . . . . . 23 A3
St Minver PL27 . . . . 22 A4
St Newlyn East TR8 . . . 56 B7
CHURCH TOWN 140 A3
Church Town
Falmouth TR11 . . . . 144 D3
Wendron TR13 . . . . 91 F6
Church Town Cl PL26 . . . 46 F2
Church Town Cotts TR3 . . 81 D5
Churchtown Dr PL12 . . . 122 D1
Churchtown Mdws PL26 . . 58 B4
Churchtown Mews PL30 . . 35 C8
Church Town Rd
Gwithian TR27 . . . . 66 B2
Illogan TR16 . . . . . 67 E5
Phillack TR27 . . . . . 142 C7
Portscatho TR2 . . . . 83 B2
St Stephen PL26 . . . . 58 B4
Church Town Rd PL32 . . . 10 D2
Churchtown Terr PL27 . . . 32 D6
Churchtown Vale PL12 . . . 122 D1
Church View Navarino PL15 . 18 A8
St Cleer PL14 . . . . . 37 F3
St Dominick PL12 . . . . 40 D2
St Neot PL14 . . . . . 36 F2
Treburley PL15 . . . . 28 B5
Walkhampton PL20 . . . 42 E4
Church View Cl TR18 . . . 143 B6
Church View Rd
Camborne TR14 . . . . 138 F4
Probus TR2 . . . . . 71 D6
Churchway Madron TR20 . . 143 A8
11 Marazion TR17 . . . . 89 C5
Church Way Falmouth TR11 144 E3
Plymouth PL5 . . . . . 127 E8
St Clether PL15 . . . . 17 B2
Church Wlk Redruth TR15 . . 140 A5
South Petherwin PL15 . . . 27 E8
12 Truro TR1 . . . . 137 C4
Churchy Fields 12 TR12 . . 99 A2
Chute La PL26 . . . . . 85 D5
Chy-an-Chy 19 TR26 . . . 141 B6
Chyandaunce Cl TR18 . . . 143 F8
Chyandaunce Terr TR18 . . 143 F8
Chyandor Cl TR24 . . . . 60 C4
CHYANDOUR 143 F7
Chyandour TR15 . . . . 140 A4
Chyandour Cl 1 TR26 . . . 77 A6
Chyandour Cliff TR18 . . . 143 F6
Chyandour La TR18 . . . . 143 F7
Chy-an-Dour Rd TR20 . . . 90 C3
Chyandour Sq TR18 . . . . 143 F7
Chyandour Terr TR18 . . . 143 F7
Chy an Dowr TR27 . . . . 142 E7
CHY-AN-GWEAL 141 B2
Chy-an-Gweal Est TR20 . . 89 A7
Chy-an-Mor TR20 . . . . 88 F6
Chycarn Moor TR14 . . . . 79 E4
Chy Cober TR27 . . . . . 142 E7
CHYCOOSE 82 A6
Chycoose Parc TR3 . . . . 82 A5
Chycornick Terr TR18 . . . 143 F8
Chygothow TR13 . . . . 146 B6
Chy Hwel TR1 . . . . . 137 F6
Chy Kensa Cl TR27 . . . . 142 C5
Chylan Cres TR7 . . . . . 111 E6
Chymblloth Way TR12 . . . 101 C1
Chymeddon TR7 . . . . . 110 E6
Chy Nampara 1 TR11 . . . 145 A4
Chynance Penzance TR18 . . 143 E6
Portreath TR16 . . . . . 67 C6

Chynance Dr TR7 . . . . . 43 F4
Newquay TR7 . . . . . 110 C5
CHYNHALE 91 C5
Chynoon Gdns PL25 . . . 114 F6
Chynowen La TR8 . . . . 43 D1
Chynowen Parc TR8 . . . 43 D1
Chynoweth PL26 . . . . 59 C8
Chynoweth Gdns TR18 . . 143 F8
Chynoweth La TR20 . . . 89 F6
Chy Pons PL25 . . . . . 114 A4
Chypons Est TR20 . . . . 76 F3
Chypons Rd TR12 . . . . 99 B3
Chypraze Ct TR14 . . . . 138 B3
Chyreen La
Carnon Downs TR3 . . . 81 F8
Playing Place TR3 . . . 82 A8
Chyrn Dr PL30 . . . . . 24 B3
Chyrose Rd TR16 . . . . 68 D1
Chysauster Ancient Village ★
TR20 . . . . . . 76 D2
Chysauster Rd
Chysauster TR20 . . . . 76 D1
Trezelah TR20 . . . . . 88 E8
Chytodden Terr TR13 . . . 90 F5
Chyvelah Ope TR1 . . . . 69 E3
Chyvelah Rd TR3 . . . . 69 D4
Chyvelah Vale TR1 . . . . 69 E3
Chyvellas Cl TR18 . . . . 143 B1
Chyventon Cl TR19 . . . . 97 B6
Chyventon Ho TR15 . . . 140 B5
Chyverton Cl TR7 . . . . 110 D4
Chyvogue Mdw TR3 . . . 81 D6
Chywoon TR10 . . . . . 81 A2
Chywoone Ave TR18 . . . 143 C1
Chywoone Cres TR18 . . . 143 C1
Chywoone Gr TR19 . . . . 97 F8
Chywoone Hill TR18 . . . 143 C1
Chywoone Pl TR18 . . . . 143 C1
Chywoone Rural Workshops
TR19 . . . . . . 87 A5
Chywoon Gdns TR15 . . . 139 D7
Chywoon La TR20 . . . . 90 A4
Citadel Ope 18 PL1 . . . . 149 A2
Citadel Road E PL1 . . . . 149 A2
Citadel Road W PL1 . . . 148 C2
Citadel The ★ PL1 . . . . 149 A1
City Bsns Pk PL3 . . . . 128 A4
City Coll Plymouth (Kings
Road Ctr) PL1 . . . . 128 A2
City Coll Plymouth (Learning
Warehouse) PL1 . . . 148 B2
City Rd PL1 . . . . . 137 C4
Clairemont Pl 1 PL14 . . . 38 A3
Clampet La PL11 . . . . . 65 E4
Clann Hl PL30 . . . . . 47 E7
Clann La PL30 . . . . . 47 E7
Clann Mdws PL30 . . . . 47 E7
CLAPPER 108 E4
Claremont Cotts 1 TR11 . . 145 A5
Claremont Falls PL13 . . . 62 E2
Claremont Mews TR15 . . 140 B5
Claremont Rd PL15 . . . 140 B5
Claremont St PL1 . . . . 148 C4
Claremont Terr
3 Falmouth TR11 . . . 145 A5
18 Porthleven TR13 . . . 98 B8
Truro TR1 . . . . . 137 C5
Clarence Ct PL1 . . . . . 148 A3
Clarence Pl
29 Penzance TR18 . . . 143 E6
Plymouth, Morice Town PL2 . 127 E4
Plymouth, Stonehouse PL1 . 148 A3
Clarence Rd St Austell PL25 114 B4
Torpoint PL11 . . . . . 127 B3
Clarence St TR18 . . . . 143 E5
Clarence Terr
30 Penzance TR18 . . . 143 E6
7 Wadebridge PL27 . . . 108 B5
Clarence Villas TR15 . . . 140 D6
Clarendon Ho 1 PL1 . . . 127 F3
Clarendon La 11 PL3 . . . 127 F3
Clare Pl PL4 . . . . . 149 B2
Clare Terr TR11 . . . . . 145 B4
Claybourne Cl PL25 . . . 114 F6
Claylands PL30 . . . . . 24 A1
Claypit La PL15 . . . . . 12 B2
Clay Rd PL30 . . . . . 36 B4
Clays Walk PL30 . . . . 59 C8
Claytonia Cl PL6 . . . . 121 C1
Clayton Pl PL4 . . . . . 129 B2
Clayton Rd PL4 . . . . . 129 B2
Clearbrook Ave PL5 . . . 123 E1
Clear Space EX23 . . . . 104 F3
Clear View PL12 . . . . 122 E3
Clease Mdws PL32 . . . . 105 C3
Clease Rd PL32 . . . . . 105 C4
Clease The PL32 . . . . 105 C3
Cleave Cl 3 PL27 . . . . 108 C5
Cleave Cres EX23 . . . . 4 B8
Cleaveland PL27 . . . . 108 C4
Cleaverfield Mews PL15 . . 106 C7
Cleaves The PL15 . . . . 106 C7
Cleave The PL10 . . . . 133 B2
Cleavewell PL27 . . . . 108 C4
Cledma Bank TR27 . . . . 142 A2
CLEERS 46 E1
Cleers Hill St Dennis PL26 . 46 E1
Whitemoor PL26 . . . . 58 E8
Cleeve Gdns PL2 . . . . 128 A8
Clegg Ave PL15 . . . . . 126 E3
Clemens Cl TR7 . . . . . 111 B5
Clemens Rd PL14 . . . . 51 B3
Clemens Way TR27 . . . . 78 D6
Clement Rd PL7 . . . . . 131 B5
Clements Rd TR13 . . . . 143 D5
Clemmens Ave TR7 . . . . 110 D4

Clemo Rd PL14 . . . . . 113 E7
CLERKENWATER 109 D8
Clevedon Park Ave PL2 . . 128 B6
Clevedon Rd TR7 . . . . 110 D5
Cleveland Ave PL13 . . . 117 D4
Cleveland Rd PL4 . . . . 149 C3
Clies The 5 TR13 . . . . 146 C5
Clifden Cl Mullion TR12 . . 99 A1
Newquay TR7 . . . . . 110 E5
Clifden Dr PL27 . . . . . 21 D6
Clifden Rd PL25 . . . . . 114 F4
Clifden Terr
14 Bodmin PL31 . . . . 109 D5
Lostwithiel PL22 . . . . 112 C2
CLIFF 61 B6
Cliff Bglws TR27 . . . . 142 A8
Cliff Ct Falmouth TR11 . . . 145 B3
Plymouth PL1 . . . . . 148 B1
Cliff End Pk PL27 . . . . 108 D6
Cliff La Millbrook PL10 . . . 132 A4
Mousehole TR19 . . . . 88 C1
New Polzeath PL27 . . . 21 D6
CLIFFORD 3 F8
Clifford Cl PL5 . . . . . 123 E2
Cliff Rd Falmouth TR11 . . . 145 C2
Gorran Haven PL26 . . . 85 D5
Mevagissey PL26 . . . . 73 C4
Mousehole TR19 . . . . 88 D2
Newlyn TR18 . . . . . 143 D1
Newquay TR7 . . . . . 110 F6
Perranporth TR6 . . . . 55 A5
Plymouth PL1 . . . . . 148 B1
Porthleven TR13 . . . . 98 B8
Cliff Rise PL23 . . . . . 116 D2
Cliff St PL26 . . . . . 73 C4
Cliff Terr TR16 . . . . . 67 C6
Cliff The PL26 . . . . . 73 C3
Cliff View Rd TR14 . . . . 138 E4
Cliff View Terr TR14 . . . 138 E4
Cliff Ct 4 TR1 . . . . . 137 D4
Clifton Ave PL7 . . . . . 130 E7
Clifton Cl PL7 . . . . . 130 E7
Clifton Cres 16 PL13 . . . 145 A4
Clifton Gdns 1 TR1 . . . . 137 B4
Clifton Hill 14 TR18 . . . 143 C2
Clifton Pl 14 Falmouth TR11 145 A4
Plymouth PL4 . . . . . 149 A4
Clifton Rd TR15 . . . . . 139 C8
Clifton St PL4 . . . . . 149 A4
Clifton Terr
15 Falmouth TR11 . . . 145 A4
Hayle TR27 . . . . . 142 B6
Liskeard PL14 . . . . . 113 A5
16 Newlyn TR18 . . . . 143 C2
Cligga Head Ind Est 3 TR6 . 54 F4
Cligga Workshops TR6 . . . 54 F4
Clijah Ct TR15 . . . . . 140 C2
Clijah La TR15 . . . . . 140 C2
Clinton Ave PL4 . . . . . 129 A4
Clinton Cl Bude EX23 . . . 104 E4
Redruth TR15 . . . . . 140 C3
Clinton Dr PL25 . . . . . 114 B3
Clinton Pas 4 TR15 . . . . 140 B4
Clinton Rd Constantine TR11 . 92 F3
Redruth TR15 . . . . . 140 C4
Clinton Terr PL10 . . . . 132 F6
Clittaford Rd PL6 . . . . 124 F7
Clittaford View PL6 . . . . 124 E7
Cloake Pl PL12 . . . . . 119 A2
Clodgey La Helston TR13 . . 146 D5
Whitehill TR13 . . . . . 91 E1
Clodgey Way TR13 . . . . 146 D4
Clodgy View 44 TR26 . . . 141 B6
Clonway 1 PL20 . . . . 42 C3
Close Hill TR15 . . . . . 140 B6
Close The
17 Bere Alston PL20 . . . 41 B1
Lanner TR16 . . . . . 80 E6
Mylor Bridge TR11 . . . 82 A3
Penzance TR18 . . . . 143 D7
Saltash PL12 . . . . . 122 C3
Trevone PL28 . . . . . 20 F2
Truro TR1 . . . . . 137 F6
Clos Trevithick 4 TR14 . . 138 F2
Clouds Hill 20 TR12 . . . 102 F2
Clovelly Rd PL4 . . . . . 149 C1
Clovelly View PL9 . . . . 135 A7
Clover Lane Cl 6 PL35 . . . 9 C1
Clover Rise PL6 . . . . . 125 E8
Clover Wlk PL12 . . . . 122 C3
Clowance TR14 . . . . . 79 B2
Clowance Cl PL1 . . . . 127 F1
Clowance Est TR14 . . . . 79 B2
Clowance La PL1 . . . . 127 E1
Clowance St PL1 . . . . 127 F1
CLOWANCE WOOD . . . 79 A1
Clowance Wood TR14 . . . 91 A8
CLUBWORTHY 12 C3
Clyde St PL2 . . . . . 127 F5
Coach Ho The Penryn TR10 144 D7
Penzance TR18 . . . . 143 F7
Coach House La PL25 . . . 114 C4
Coach House Mews PL9 . . 136 B6
Coach La TR15 . . . . . 140 A4
Coachyard Mews PL28 . . 107 D5
COAD'S GREEN 27 D4
Coad's Green Prim Sch
PL15 . . . . . . 27 D3
Coastguard Cotts
Down Thomas PL9 . . . 134 F2
Mawnan Smith TR11 . . . 93 C1
Mullion TR12 . . . . . 98 F1
Polperro PL13 . . . . . 62 E2
Rosudgeon TR20 . . . . 89 F3
Coastguard Cres TR18 . . 143 F6
Coastguard Hill PL29 . . . 22 D8

Coastguard Hos PL28 . . . 21 B4
Coastguard Sta Flats PL13 117 C3
Coastguard Terr TR2 . . . 84 B2
Coastline Ct TR8 . . . . 44 C6
Coast Rd Millook Common EX23 6 C2
Newton farm PL35 . . . 10 A4
Porthtowan TR4 . . . . 68 A7
Cobbett Rd PL5 . . . . . 124 B2
Cobb La PL9 . . . . . 135 F6
Cobble La TR9 . . . . . 57 E8
Cobblestone La PL1 . . . 128 A1
Cobbs Well PL23 . . . . 116 C4
Cober Cres TR27 . . . . 78 E3
Cobourg St PL1 . . . . . 148 C3
Cockington Cl PL6 . . . . 125 E1
Cockington Wlk PL6 . . . 125 C1
Cocklawelva TR27 . . . . 21 D2
COCKS 55 B3
Cocks Hill TR6 . . . . . 55 B3
Cock's Lake La PL12 . . . 53 D4
Cocksport Rd PL32 . . . 10 D3
COCKWELLS 77 C1
Cockwells La TR26 . . . 77 C1
Coddles La PL30 . . . . 47 A8
Codford Cres TR14 . . . . 138 E4
Codling Cl 2 PL25 . . . . 114 F2
Coffa Bridge Cl PL22 . . . 112 D2
Coffee Lake Mdw PL22 . . 112 D2
Cogegoes TR14 . . . . . 138 B2
Cogegoes Ind Pk TR14 . . 138 A2
Cogos Pk TR11 . . . . . 82 A3
Co Hill PL15 . . . . . 27 B3
Coinagehall Pl TR18 . . . 143 F4
Coinagehall St
Helston TR13 . . . . . 146 B5
Penzance TR18 . . . . 143 F4
COLAN 44 F4
Colborne Ave TR16 . . . . 67 D4
Colborne Rd PL6 . . . . 125 A2
COLD NORTHCOOT . . . 16 F5
Coldrenick St PL5 . . . . 123 D1
Coldrose Ct TR1 . . . . . 137 B4
Coldstyle Rd PL14 . . . . 113 C7
COLDVREATH 46 F1
Coldvreath Rd PL26 . . . 46 F1
Coldwind Cross TR3 . . . 81 D7
COLEBROOK 130 E6
Colebrook Cl TR15 . . . . 140 A5
Colebrook La PL7 . . . . 130 E7
Colebrook Rd
Plymouth, Colebrook PL7 . . 130 E6
Plymouth, St Budeaux PL5 . 123 D1
Coleman Dr PL9 . . . . . 135 F4
Colemans Cross PL15 . . . 19 C5
Cole Moore Mdw PL19 . . 147 B6
Colenso Cross TR20 . . . 89 F5
Colenso Pl PL25 . . . . 114 D3
Coleridge Ave PL6 . . . . 124 F2
Coleridge Rd PL4 . . . . 129 A4
Coles Cotts PL9 . . . . . 135 C1
Colesloggett Halt Sta ★
PL30 . . . . . . 130 B1
Colin Campbell Ct 10 PL1 . 148 B3
Colinsey Pl TR18 . . . . 143 D7
Colinsey Rd TR18 . . . . 143 D7
Coliza Hill PL26 . . . . . 59 A2
Collacombe Cross PL19 . . 29 F4
Collaford Cl PL7 . . . . . 131 A4
Collan's Cross PL32 . . . 15 D1
College Ave Plymouth PL3 . 128 E5
Tavistock PL19 . . . . 147 D6
College Cl TR2 . . . . . 71 C6
College Dean Cl PL6 . . . 125 C5
College Gn Bodmin PL31 . 109 E2
Penryn TR10 . . . . . 144 C2
St Austell PL25 . . . . . 114 C3
College Green PL31 . . . 109 E2
College Hill TR10 . . . . 144 C7
College La Bodmin PL31 . . 109 F2
Plymouth PL4 . . . . . 128 F4
Redruth TR15 . . . . . 140 E7
College Ope TR10 . . . . 144 D7
College Park PL1 . . . . 127 E3
College Rd Camelford PL32 . 105 D4
Plymouth PL2 . . . . . 127 E5
College Road Prim Sch
PL2 . . . . . . 127 E5
College St TR14 . . . . . 138 C3
College View PL3 . . . . 128 E4
College Way TR1 . . . . 69 E3
College Wood TR10 . . . 144 B6
Colletts Ct TR16 . . . . . 67 C5
Colliford Lake Pk ★ PL14 . 36 E8
Collin Cl PL5 . . . . . 123 D1
Collingwood Ave PL4 . . . 149 C2
Collingwood Rd PL1 . . . 128 A3
Collingwood Villas 5 PL1 128 A3
Collins Parc TR3 . . . . 80 F3
Collon Field PL22 . . . . 61 D8
Collorian La TR26 . . . . 77 C1
Collygree Parc TR20 . . . 89 E5
Colmer Cl PL13 . . . . . 117 D6
Colmers La PL17 . . . . 39 E4
Colmers Row PL14 . . . . 51 F5
Col-Moor Cl TR27 . . . . 142 E7
Colne Gdns PL3 . . . . . 129 B5
Colroger Cl TR12 . . . . 99 B2
Colston Cl PL6 . . . . . 125 B6
Coltishall Cl PL5 . . . . 123 F4
Coltness Rd PL9 . . . . . 136 B5
Coltsfield Cl PL6 . . . . 129 B8
Columbus Cl PL5 . . . . 123 C2
Colver Cl TR7 . . . . . 78 D6
Colvreath Rd TR7 . . . . 110 F6
Colwill Rd PL6 . . . . . 125 E3
Colwill Wlk PL6 . . . . . 125 F3
Colworth Ave TR11 . . . 144 F3

Colwyn Rd PL11 . . . . . 127 A3
COMBE 136 E5
Combe La EX23 . . . . . 6 F4
Combley Dr PL6 . . . . . 125 D4
COME-TO-GOOD 82 B7
COMFORD 80 F6
Comfort Rd TR11 . . . . 82 A3
Comfort Wartha TR11 . . . 92 F4
Commercial Hill TR3 . . . 81 B4
Commercial Ope PL4 . . . 149 B2
Commercial Pl PL4 . . . . 149 B1
Commercial Rd
Calstock PL18 . . . . . 41 A3
Hayle TR27 . . . . . 142 C6
Horrabridge PL20 . . . 42 C4
10 Mousehole TR19 . . . 88 C1
Penryn TR10 . . . . . 144 D7
Plymouth PL4 . . . . . 149 B2
Porthleven TR13 . . . . 98 B8
8 St Keverne TR12 . . . 101 C4
5 St Mawes TR2 . . . . 95 A6
Commercial Sq 3 TR14 . . 138 D3
Commercial St
Camborne TR14 . . . . 138 D3
Gunnislake PL18 . . . . 41 A6
Plymouth PL4 . . . . . 149 B2
Commercial Terr PL28 . . 107 D5
Commissioners Rd 1
PL27 . . . . . . 108 B5
Common La PL6 . . . . . 121 B5
COMMON MOOR 37 F4
Commons Cl 3 TR12 . . . 99 A2
Commons Gate EX22 . . . 13 B8
Commons La 15 TR3 . . . 81 B4
Commons Rd TR3 . . . . 43 D1
Commons The TR12 . . . 99 A2
Compass Dr PL7 . . . . . 131 A7
Compass Point TR26 . . . 141 D2
Compass W PL15 . . . . 18 C2
Compressor Way 5 TR14 138 F3
Comprigney Cl TR1 . . . . 137 B5
Comprigney Hill TR1 . . . 137 B5
Compton Ave PL3 . . . . 129 A5
Compton CE Prim Sch
PL3 . . . . . . 129 A6
Compton Knoll Cl PL3 . . 129 A6
Compton Leigh PL3 . . . 129 A6
Compton Park Rd PL3 . . 128 F5
Compton Rd 2 PL17 . . . 39 E4
Compton Vale PL3 . . . . 129 A5
CONDON'S SHOP 27 B5
Condor Cotts TR11 . . . . 144 C2
Congreve Gdns PL5 . . . 124 C2
Coniston Gdns PL6 . . . . 124 F4
Conker Rd TR27 . . . . . 78 C5
Connaught Ave PL4 . . . 128 F4
Connaught La 6 PL4 . . . 128 E4
Connoc Cl PL14 . . . . . 113 D5
CONNOR DOWNS 78 D5
Connor Downs Prim Sch
TR27 . . . . . . 78 D6
Connor Hill TR27 . . . . 78 D6
Conqueror Dr PL5 . . . . 124 E1
Conrad Rd PL5 . . . . . 124 D1
Consols Rd TR16 . . . . 80 F8
Consort Cl PL3 . . . . . 128 E7
Consort Ho PL5 . . . . . 123 B2
Constable Cl PL5 . . . . 124 D3
Constance Pl PL1 . . . . 148 A3
CONSTANTINE 92 E3
CONSTANTINE BAY . . . 20 D1
Constantine Cty Prim Sch
TR11 . . . . . . 92 E4
Constantine St PL4 . . . 149 A2
Convent Cl PL12 . . . . . 122 C3
Convent of Mercy PL31 . . 109 C4
Conway Cl TR11 . . . . . 144 E4
Conway Gdns
Falmouth TR11 . . . . 144 D4
Plymouth PL2 . . . . . 128 B3
Conway Rd TR11 . . . . 144 D4
Conyngham Ct PL6 . . . . 129 A8
Cooban Ct PL6 . . . . . 129 A8
Cook Ct PL12 . . . . . 122 B3
COOKSLAND 35 B2
Cooksland Ind Est PL31 . . 35 B2
Cooksland La PL31 . . . . 35 B1
Cooksland Rd PL31 . . . 35 B1
Cook's Level PL26 . . . . 85 C5
Cooksley Ct PL1 . . . . 149 A1
Cookworthy Cl 14 PL26 . . 59 D7
Cookworthy Rd PL27 . . . 127 F6
COOMBE Camborne . . . 66 F3
Perranarworthal 81 B8
Playing Place 82 D8
St Stephen 58 B2
Coombe Dean Sch PL9 . . 136 A6
Coombe Dean Sp Ctr PL9 136 A6
Coombe Dr PL12 . . . . 119 A2
Coombe Hill Coombe PL26 . 58 C2
Coombe PL4 . . . . . 81 C8
Coombe Junction Halt
PL14 . . . . . . 51 A6
Coombe La Cargreen PL12 . 119 A2
Combe PL18 . . . . . 136 E5
Crafthole PL11 . . . . . 65 B5
Penzance TR18 . . . . 143 D7
Plymouth PL5 . . . . . 124 D7
Seaton PL11 . . . . . 64 B7
Trebyan PL30 . . . . . 48 D5
Trelill PL30 . . . . . 23 D5
Truro TR4 . . . . . 81 C8
Coombe Ln PL15 . . . . 17 E2
Coombe Mews TR18 . . . 143 E7
Coombe Park Cl PL10 . . . 133 A2
Coombe Park La PL5 . . . 124 D7
Coombe Pk Camborne TR14 . 66 F3
Kingsand PL10 . . . . . 133 A2

Coombe Pk *continued*
Penzance TR18 . . . . .143 E6
Saltash PL12 . . . . .123 F1
Coombe Rd Callington PL17. . 39 F4
Lanjeth PL26 . . . . .58 D3
Lanjeth PL26 . . . . .58 E3
Penzance TR18 . . . . .143 E7
St Breward PL30 . . . . .24 A3
Saltash PL12 . . . . .123 A2
Coombes La 9 TR1. . . . . . .137 C4
Coombe The
Crumplehorn PL13. . . . . .62 D2
Newlyn TR18 . . . . .143 B3
Coombe Vale TR18 . . . . . . .143 B3
Coombe View
15 Perranporth TR6. . . . . . . .55 A4
Plymouth PL2 . . . . .127 F7
Coombe Way PL5. . . . . .123 F1
Cooperage Gdns 8 PL25 . .59 A3
Cooperage Rd PL25. . . . . . . .59 A3
Cooper's La TR13. . . . . .98 C8
COOSEBEAN 137 A5
Coosebean La TR4. . . . . . . .137 A5
Copes Gdns TR1 . . . . .137 C5
Copleston Rd PL6 . . . . .124 E5
COPPATHORNE 7 A3
Copper Beech Way PL6. .125 C7
Copperfield Dr 9 PL14 . . .113 D7
Copperfields PL20. . . . . .42 B5
Copper Hill TR27 . . . . .142 D6
COPPERHOUSE 142 D6
Copper La TR16 . . . . .140 A1
Copper Pl PL1. . . . . .148 A3
Coppers Pk PL6 . . . . .125 E7
Copper Terr TR27 . . . . .142 D7
Coppice Gdns PL5 . . . . . . .124 E2
Coppice Wood Dr PL6 . . . .125 C7
Copse Cl PL7 . . . . .130 D4
Copse Rd PL7 . . . . .130 D4
Copse The
St Austell, Sandy Bottom
PL25 . . . . .114 F5
St Austell, Tregorrick PL26. .114 A5
Copshorn Rd PL31. . . . . . . .109 C7
COPTHORNE 12 B3
Copthorne Cross PL15 . . . .12 B2
Copthorne Gdns PL9. . . . . .135 F5
Copthorne Rd PL15. . . . . . . .12 B3
Corea Terr PL1. . . . . .128 A2
Corfe Ave PL3 . . . . .128 F8
Coringdean Cl PL6 . . . . . . .125 B6
Cormoran Ct TR17. . . . . .89 C5
Cormoran Cl 2 EX23 . . . . . . .7 B8
Cormorant Dr PL25. . . . . . .115 A4
Corner Brake PL6 . . . . .125 D7
Corner Gdns EX23 . . . . .4 D1
Corner Pk PL15. . . . . .26 C7
Cornerstone Ct PL11. . . . . .127 B3
Cornfield Dr 7 PL15. . . . . .106 D4
Cornfield Gdns PL7. . . . . . .131 B7
Cornflower Cres PL15 . . . .106 E4
Cornhill Rd PL24. . . . . .60 B5
Cornish Birds of Prey Ctr
The ★ TR9 . . . . .32 D1
Cornish Chough TR7. . . . . .111 B7
Cornish Cider Farm ★ TR4. .55 B1
Cornish Cres TR1. . . . . .69 F4
Cornish Goldsmiths ★ TR16. 67 F5
Cornish Mines & Engines
(Mus) ★ TR15 . . . . .139 C6
Cornubia Cl Hayle TR27. . . .142 C5
Truro TR1 . . . . .137 F6
Cornwall Beach PL1. . . . . . .127 D2
Cornwall Coll Camborne
TR15 . . . . .139 B6
Cornwall Coll Newquay
TR7. . . . . .111 A5
Cornwall Coll St Austell
PL25 . . . . .114 D5
Cornwall Coll Saltash
PL12 . . . . .122 D2
Cornwall Ctr ★ TR15. . . . . .140 B4
Cornwall Ho PL25 . . . . .114 C3
Cornwallis TR26 . . . . .141 E2
Cornwall Rise 2 PL31. . . . .109 F3
Cornwall's Regimental Mus
(Duke of Cornwall's Light
Infantry Mus) ★ PL31. . . . .109 F3
Cornwall St Bere Alston PL20 41 B1
Plymouth PL1. . . . . .148 A3
Plymouth, Morice Town PL1. .127 D2
Cornwall Terr
Penzance TR18 . . . . .143 E4
2 Truro TR1 . . . . .137 C5
Cornwood Rd PL7 . . . . .131 B4
Cornworthy Cl PL2 . . . . . . .128 A7
Coronation Ave TR14. . . . . .138 C3
Coronation Cl 2 PL17. . . . . .39 F4
Coronation Cotts
Budock Water TR11 . . . . .144 C3
Mabe Burnthouse TR10. . . . . .81 C1
St Keverne TR12. . . . . .101 D4
Coronation Pl Helston TR13 146 C4
Plymouth PL5. . . . . .127 E8
Coronation Rd
10 Callington PL17 . . . . .39 F4
Hayle TR27. . . . . .142 D5
1 Illogan TR16. . . . . .67 E4
Redruth TR15. . . . . .140 D4
Coronation Terr Truro TR1 137 B4
Veryan TR2. . . . . .83 D7
Corondale Rd PL2 . . . . .128 B7
Corpascus Carveth TR10 . . .81 B1
4 Longdowns TR10 . . . . .81 A1
Corporation Rd
Bodmin PL31 . . . . .109 B4

Corporation Rd *continued*
Plymouth PL2. . . . . .128 D7
Corsham Cl PL6 . . . . .125 B6
Cort Simmons TR15 . . . . . .139 C6
Cort Treloweth TR15. . . . . .139 B6
Corva Cl 11 TR26. . . . . .77 A6
Corva Rd 9 TR26 . . . . .77 A6
Corvus Mews 15 PL9 . . . . .136 E8
Cory Cl EX23 . . . . .10 F1
Cosawes 2 TR3 . . . . .81 C4
Cosawes Est TR3 . . . . .81 B4
Cosawes Pk Homes 1 TR3. 81 C4
Cosdon Pl PL6. . . . . .124 F1
COSWINSAWSIN 79 A5
Coswinsawsin La TR14. . . . .79 A5
Cotehele Ave
Plymouth, Keyham PL2 . . . . . .127 F5
Plymouth, Prince Rock PL4 . .149 C2
Cotehele Ho ★ PL12. . . . . . . .40 F3
Cotehele Quay Discovery Ctr ★
PL12. . . . . .40 F3
Cotehele View PL18 . . . . . . .41 A3
Cothele Cl PL17 . . . . .39 E3
Cot Hill Plymouth PL7 . . . . .130 B5
Ponsanooth TR3. . . . . .81 B4
2 Stratton EX23. . . . . .4 E1
Cot Hill Trad Est PL7 . . . . . .130 B6
Cotna La Cotna PL26. . . . . . . .73 A1
Cotna PL26 . . . . .85 C6
Cot Rd TR15, TR16. . . . . .67 D4
Cotsland Rd TR1. . . . . .137 F5
Cotswold Ave PL26 . . . . .58 E1
Cotswold Cl PL26 . . . . .58 E1
Cottage Gdns PL15 . . . . .27 B7
Cottage Hill PL26 . . . . .72 F6
Cottage Mews PL7. . . . . . . .130 E4
Cotton Cl PL7 . . . . .130 F4
Cott Rd Lostwithiel PL22 . . . .112 D2
Lostwithiel, Polscoe PL22 . . . .112 C1
Cotts PL20 . . . . .119 B7
Cot Wood TR3 . . . . .81 B4
Couchwell La PL22 . . . . .112 C2
Coulson's Bldgs 10 TR18 . .143 E4
Coulson's Pl 9 TR18 . . . . . .143 E4
Coulson's Terr 8 TR18 . . . . .143 E4
Coulthard Dr TR13. . . . . .91 A3
Countess Bridge La TR27 . .90 A8
Count House La TR26 . . . . . .141 C2
Count House Mews 3 TR5 .54 D1
County Cl PL7 . . . . .131 A5
County Rd EX23 . . . . .104 E2
Court Barton Cotts PL9 . . .135 C1
Court Barton Mews PL19. . .30 B4
Courtenay Rd PL19 . . . . .147 B6
Courtenay St PL1. . . . . .148 C3
Courtfield Rd PL3 . . . . .128 F5
Court Gdns PL25. . . . . .114 C3
Courtland Cres PL7. . . . . . . .130 D7
Courtlands PL22 . . . . .122 E1
Courtlands Cl PL19 . . . . .147 B6
Courtlands Cres 4 PL25. . .115 A5
Courtlands Rd PL19. . . . . . . .147 B6
Courtlands Sch PL6. . . . . . . .124 F1
Court Mdw PL13. . . . . .62 B7
Courtnay Cl PL13 . . . . .117 D4
Courtney Ho PL5 . . . . .124 B2
Courtney Rd Liskeard PL14 .113 D6
St Austell PL25. . . . . .114 F5
Truro TR1. . . . . .137 B5
Court The Camborne TR15 .139 C4
Plymouth PL6. . . . . .125 C7
Saltash PL12 . . . . .122 C2
Court View PL8. . . . . .136 F4
Courtyard Cotts TR4 . . . . . . .70 C6
Courtyard The
Redruth TR16. . . . . .139 F2
Truro TR1. . . . . .137 D3
Cove Hill
Perranarworthal TR3. . . . . . . .81 D5
Sennen Cove TR19. . . . . .96 B7
Cove Mdw PL11. . . . . .127 A6
Coventry Rd TR11 . . . . .145 B6
COVERACK 101 C1
Coverack Com Prim Sch
TR12. . . . . .101 C1
Cove Rd TR19 . . . . .96 C7
Coverdale Pl PL5 . . . . .124 C1
Cove The TR4 . . . . .68 A7
Cowdray Cl PL12 . . . . .122 E2
Cowdray Terr PL12 . . . . .122 E1
Cow Lard Cl PL15 . . . . .106 A4
Cowley Rd PL5 . . . . .124 D3
Cowling Gdns PL14. . . . . .51 F6
Cowling Rd 2 TR3. . . . . .81 F7
Cowslip Ave PL19 . . . . .147 A5
COXFORD 10 D7
COX HILL 68 F2
Cox Hill TR6 . . . . .55 B3
COXPARK 40 D7
Cox Park Terr PL18 . . . . .40 C6
Cox's Cl PL25 . . . . .125 B1
COXSIDE 149 B1
Coxs Mdw EX22. . . . . .13 C7
Cox Tor Cl 6 PL20 . . . . .42 C3
Cox Tor Rd PL19 . . . . .147 E5
Coypool Rd PL7 . . . . .130 A6
Crabbs Cl PL15 . . . . .13 F1
Crabbtree Cl 3 PL14 . . . . . .113 B5
CRABTREE 129 E5
Crabtree Cl 5 PL14 . . . . . . .129 F5
Crabtree La PL30, PL31 . . . .109 D2
Crabtree Villas PL3 . . . . . . .129 E5
Crack Germans Mixtow PL23 61 C4
Mixtow PL23 . . . . .116 F7
CRACKINGTON HAVEN 10 B7
Crackston Cl PL6. . . . . .129 B7
CRAFTHOLE 65 B5

Craigie Dr PL1. . . . . .148 A3
Craigmore Ave PL2. . . . . . . .127 F5
Craigside PL13 . . . . .117 D4
Cramber Cl Roborough PL6 .125 C8
5 Tavistock PL19 . . . . .147 B4
Cranberry Rd TR14 . . . . .138 B3
Cranbourne Ave PL4. . . . . . .149 C4
CRANE. 138 C2
Crane Manor Ct TR14. . . . . .138 C2
Crane Rd TR14 . . . . .138 C2
Cranfield PL7 . . . . .130 C7
Cranfield Rd TR14 . . . . .138 B3
Cranmere Rd PL3. . . . . .129 A6
CRANTOCK 43 D3
Crantock St TR7. . . . . .110 D6
Crantock Terr 7 PL2 . . . . . .128 A5
CRAPSTONE 42 B2
Crapstone Rd PL20. . . . . .42 C2
Crapstone Terr PL20. . . . . . . .42 B2
Crashaw Cl PL5. . . . . .124 D3
Crava La TR20 . . . . .90 E3
Craven Ave PL4. . . . . .149 C4
Crawford Rd PL1 . . . . .148 A4
Creakavose PL26 . . . . .58 B4
Creakavose Pk PL26 . . . . . . .58 A4
Crealy Adventure Park
(Cornwall) ★ PL27 . . . . .32 D4
CREAN 96 F5
Crease La Millhill PL19 . . . . . .30 B1
Tavistock PL19 . . . . .147 A4
Creathorne Rd EX23 . . . . . . .104 E7
Creative Unit (Krowji) ★
TR15 . . . . .140 A4
Creaz-an-Bre PL26 . . . . .58 D5
Crebor Rd PL19 . . . . .147 B7
Crediton Wlk PL6 . . . . .129 E8
CREED 72 A6
Creed La TR2 . . . . .72 A7
Creedy Rd PL3 . . . . .129 C5
CREEGBRAWSE 68 F2
Creekside View TR2 . . . . . . .70 F4
Creeping La Newlyn TR18 . .143 C3
Penzance TR18 . . . . .143 C4
Crelake Cl PL19 . . . . .147 C4
Crelake Ind Est 1 PL19 . . . .147 B4
Crelake Pk PL19. . . . . .147 C4
Crellow Fields TR3 . . . . .80 F3
Crellow Hill TR3. . . . . .80 F3
Crellow La TR3 . . . . .80 F3
Crellow Terr TR3 . . . . .80 F3
Crellow Vale TR3 . . . . .80 F3
CRELLY 91 F7
Crelly TR13. . . . . .91 F7
Crembling Well TR15 . . . . . .139 E6
CREMYLL 133 E7
Cremyll Rd PL11. . . . . .127 B2
Cremyll St PL1 . . . . .134 A8
Crescent Ave PL1. . . . . .148 B2
Crescent Avenue Mews
PL1 . . . . .148 B2
Crescent Cl Hayle TR27 . . . .142 C5
Widemouth Bay EX23 . . . . .6 F5
Crescent Gdns TR1 . . . . . . .137 B5
Crescent Pl 6 TR19 . . . . .74 F1
Crescent Rd Bugle PL26. . . . .47 C1
Truro TR1 . . . . .137 B4
Crescent Rise
Constantine Bay PL28 . . . . . . .20 C1
Newquay TR7 . . . . .110 D6
Crescent The Bude EX23 . . .104 D5
Camborne TR14 . . . . .138 D4
Carbis Bay TR26. . . . . .77 C4
Common Moor PL14 . . . . .37 F4
Crapstone PL20 . . . . .42 B3
Gunnislake PL18 . . . . .41 A6
Landrake PL12. . . . . .53 C3
Lifton PL16. . . . . .19 F4
Liskeard PL14 . . . . .113 C6
Looe PL13 . . . . .117 D1
Newquay TR7. . . . . .110 E6
Plymouth PL1. . . . . .148 B2
Porthleven TR13 . . . . .91 B1
St Austell PL25. . . . . .115 B5
St Ives TR26. . . . . .77 A7
St Mabyn PL30 . . . . .34 D8
Truro TR1. . . . . .137 B4
Widemouth Bay EX23 . . . . .6 F5
Cressbrook Cl PL6. . . . . .125 F2
Cressbrook Dr PL6. . . . . .125 F2
Cressbrook Wlk PL6. . . . . . . .125 E2
Cresthill Rd PL2 . . . . .128 B7
Creswell Terr TR19 . . . . .86 F7
Creykes Ct PL1 . . . . .148 A3
Cribbage Terr 11 PL31 . . . .109 D5
Cricketers Cl 3 PL27 . . . . . .21 E3
Cricketers Hollow PL27 . . . .21 E3
Cricket Pk EX23 . . . . .7 B6
Cricks PL30 . . . . .23 A3
Crift Cotts PL14. . . . . .51 F7
Crift La PL12 . . . . .64 F8
Criftoe Rd TR9 . . . . .46 B6
Crill Cnr TR11 . . . . .144 C1
CRIMP 3 A2
Crinnick's Hill PL31. . . . . . .109 E4
Crinnis Cl PL25 . . . . .115 E3
Crinnis Rd PL25 . . . . .115 B3
Crinnis Wood PL25 . . . . .115 E3
Crinnis Wood Ave PL25 . . . .115 E3
CRIPPLESEASE 77 A3
CROANFORD 34 C6
Crocker's Row PL18 . . . . . . .41 A6
Crockers Way PL15. . . . . .13 F1
Crockwell St PL31. . . . . . . .109 E5
Croft Comm TR14. . . . . .79 E5
Croft Farm Park ★ PL30 . . . .54 D7
CROFTHANDY 68 E1
Croftlands PL27 . . . . .21 E3
CROFT MITCHELL 79 E4

Croft Parc TR12 . . . . .102 F2
Croft Pascoe
Goonhilly Downs TR12. . . . . . .100 D3
Gwente TR12. . . . . .103 B8
Penhale TR12. . . . . .99 F1
Croft Pk PL6. . . . . .125 C7
Croft Rd PL18 . . . . .143 C4
Croft Row TR16. . . . . .80 F8
Crofty Cl TR15 . . . . .139 C5
Crohans Cl TR12 . . . . .84 B4
Cromartie Rd PL4 . . . . .129 B1
Cromer Cl PL6. . . . . .125 A7
Cromer Wlk PL6 . . . . .125 A7
Cromwell Gate PL6 . . . . .125 C7
Cromwell Rd Plymouth PL4 149 C3
St Austell PL25. . . . . .114 F3
Crookeder Cl PL9. . . . . .136 A5
Crookedor La PL11. . . . . .65 D5
Crooklets EX23 . . . . .104 C7
Crooklets Rd EX23. . . . . .104 D6
Cross PL30 . . . . .47 F1
Cross Cl TR7 . . . . .111 C7
Cross Comm TR12. . . . . .102 F2
Crossfields TR19 . . . . .96 E4
CROSSGATE 19 A7
Cross Gn PL15 . . . . .19 F7
Cross Hill PL2 . . . . .127 E4
Cross La Bodmin PL31. . . . . .109 E5
7 St Austell PL25 . . . . .114 C3
CROSS LANES 99 C4
Cross Lanes Chacewater TR4 69 B1
Launceston PL15 . . . . .106 C8
Stratton EX23 . . . . .4 F1
Crossmount TR7. . . . . .111 D7
Cross Park Ave PL6 . . . . .124 F1
Cross Park Rd PL6 . . . . .124 F1
Cross Park Terr PL26 . . . . . . .73 C4
Cross Park Way PL6 . . . . .124 F1
Cross Pk
Buckland Monachorum PL20. .42 A3
Crafthole PL11. . . . . .65 B5
Cross Roads Halgoss TR14 . .67 D3
Saveock TR4 . . . . .69 A3
Trevenson Moor TR14 . . . . . . .139 A7
Crossroads Cl PL28 . . . . .31 F8
Cross St Camborne TR14. . . .138 D2
Hayle TR27. . . . . .142 D6
Helston TR13 . . . . .146 B6
Padstow PL28 . . . . .107 D5
13 Penzance TR18 . . . . .143 E6
3 Redruth TR15 . . . . .140 B4
Wadebridge PL27 . . . . .108 B5
Cross Terr PL18 . . . . .40 F5
Cross The Camborne TR14 .138 D2
St Dominick PL12. . . . . .40 D2
St Newlyn East TR8 . . . . .56 B7
CROSSTOWN 2 B1
Crosswalla Fields TR13 . . . .146 C7
Crosswater EX23 . . . . .2 C1
Crossway PL7 . . . . .130 D7
Crossway Ave PL4 . . . . .129 B3
Crossways 5 TR11 . . . . .144 F2
Crosswyn Hill PL26 . . . . .72 F4
CROWAN 79 C1
Crowan Prim Sch TR14. . . . . .79 C2
Crow Hill PL26. . . . . .58 A2
CROWLAS 89 C4
Crowlas Ind Est TR20. . . . . . .89 B8
Crown Cl TR7 . . . . .111 A4
Crown Cres TR8 . . . . .56 B7
Crowndale Ave PL3. . . . . . . .129 A6
Crowndale Rd PL19. . . . . . . .147 A2
Crown Gdns PL6. . . . . .125 A1
CROWNHILL 124 F2
Crownhill Ct PL6 . . . . .124 F2
Crownhill Fort ★ PL6 . . . . . .124 F3
Crownhill Fort Rd PL6 . . . . .124 F3
Crownhill Rd PL5. . . . . .124 C3
Crown Rd PL26 . . . . .58 D8
Crown Terr PL26 . . . . .58 D8
Crows-an-Eglos 5 TR26 . . .77 A6
CROW'S NEST 38 B4
Crows Nest View 6 TR8 . . .143 D6
Croydon Gdns PL5. . . . . .123 E4
Crozier Rd 6 PL4. . . . . .128 F4
CRUGMEER 107 A7
CRUMPLEHORN 62 D2
Crun-Melyn Parc TR27 . . . .142 B4
Crusoe Flats 48 TR26 . . . . .141 B6
Cryben TR12 . . . . .92 C1
Cryon View TR1 . . . . .69 E3
CUBERT 55 D8
Cubert C P School TR8. . . . . .43 D1
Cuby Cl TR2 . . . . .72 A3
Cuby Rd TR2 . . . . .71 F4
Cuckoo La TR20 . . . . .77 A3
Cuddenbeake Terr PL12 . . . .65 B8
Cuddra Rd PL25 . . . . .115 C4
Cudna La TR13 . . . . .91 B5
Cuffe Rd PL3 . . . . .128 C4
Culbin Gn PL6 . . . . .129 D7
Culdrose Airfield TR12. . . . .146 E1
Culdrose Cl PL5 . . . . .123 E4
Culdrose Rd
Goonhusband TR12. . . . . .98 F8
Goonhusband TR12. . . . . .146 C2
Rosevear TR12 . . . . .99 A7
Cullen View TR2 . . . . .71 C6
Culme Rd PL3 . . . . .129 A5
Cul-Rian PL26. . . . . .58 D7
Culroy Flats 12 PL14. . . . . .137 C4
Culver Cl PL6. . . . . .129 A8
Culver Ct PL12. . . . . .122 F2

Culverland Pk PL14. . . . . . . .113 C7
Culverland Rd PL14. . . . . . . .113 B8
Culver Rd PL12 . . . . .122 F2
Culvers Mdw PL15 . . . . .106 B8
Culver Way PL6. . . . . .129 A7
Culverwood Cl PL7. . . . . . . .131 C6
Culvery The PL27 . . . . .108 B4
Cumberland Rd PL1 . . . . . . .127 F1
Cumberland St PL1. . . . . . . .127 E2
Cumble Tor La PL12 . . . . .53 D2
Cundy Cl PL7 . . . . .130 A7
Cundy's La PL26 . . . . .58 D4
Cunliffe Ave PL9. . . . . .135 A6
Cunnack Cl TR13 . . . . .146 C7
Cunningham Pk TR10. . . . . . .81 C1
Cunningham Rd PL5. . . . . . .124 C8
Cunningham Way PL12 . . . .122 D3
CURGURRELL 83 C4
Curlew Cl TR7 . . . . .110 B5
Curlew Mews PL3 . . . . .129 C4
Curlew Pk Ind Est TR4 . . . . .69 C3
Curlew Rd 4 EX23 . . . . .7 B8
Curlews TR8 . . . . .43 B1
Curnow Sch TR15. . . . . .140 B6
Curnows Rd TR27. . . . . .142 C5
Currian Hill PL26 . . . . .58 D8
Currian Rd PL26 . . . . .58 D8
CURRIAN VALE 58 D8
CURRY LANE 12 E4
Currys Hill PL15 . . . . .16 A6
Curtice Cl PL25. . . . . .114 E7
Curtis St PL1 . . . . .127 E1
Curtis VC Cl TR8. . . . . .56 B7
CURY .99 B4
Cury Colvennor TR12 . . . . . . .99 A5
Poldhu Cove TR12 . . . . .98 F3
Cury CE Prim Sch TR12 . . . .99 A4
Cury Cross La Nantithet TR12 99 C4
Tregaddra TR12. . . . . .100 A3
CUSGARNE 81 B7
Cusgarne Comm Prim Sch
TR4. . . . . .81 C7
Cusgarne Hill TR4, TR16 . . . .81 B8
Custom House Ct TR18. . . . .143 F5
Custom House La
16 Penzance TR18 . . . . .143 E5
Plymouth PL1. . . . . .148 B1
Customs House Hill PL23 .123 E4
CUSVEORTH COOMBES. 69 B2
Cutcrew La PL12 . . . . .52 E3
Cuth Avallon TR1 . . . . .137 C4
Cutmere Hill PL12 . . . . .52 D3
Cutmere La PL12. . . . . .52 D3
Cuttings Hill Coombe TR14 . .66 F3
Kehelland TR14 . . . . .79 B7
Reskadinnick TR14 . . . . .138 A6
CUTTIVETT 53 B5
Cuxhaven Way TR20 . . . . . . .88 F6
Cuxton Mews PL20. . . . . .41 F3
Cygnus Mews 4 PL9 . . . . . .136 E8
Cypress Ave PL25. . . . . .115 F4
Cypress Cl 6 PL7. . . . . .131 C5
Cyril Rd TR1. . . . . .137 C5

Dabryn Way PL26 . . . . .58 B4
Dacum La TR13 . . . . .92 C3
DADBROOK. 132 E4
Daglands Hill PL23. . . . . . . .116 C4
Daglands Rd PL23 . . . . .116 C4
DairyLand Farm World ★
TR8. . . . . .44 F1
Daisymount Dr PL28 . . . . . . .31 F7
Dale Ave PL6. . . . . .129 C7
Dale Cl TR7 . . . . .111 A4
Dale Gdns PL4. . . . . .128 D4
Plymouth PL4. . . . . .128 D4
Dale Rd Newquay TR7 . . . . . .111 A4
Plymouth PL4. . . . . .128 D4
Daleswood Rd PL19 . . . . . . .147 A4
Dallard PL27 . . . . .22 E3
Dalton Gdns PL5. . . . . .123 E3
Damerel Cl PL1. . . . . .127 F2
Dandre Apartments TR7 . . .111 A7
Dane Rd TR7 . . . . .110 D7
Daniel Cl PL25. . . . . .115 A4
Daniell Ct TR1. . . . . .137 C3
Daniell Gdns TR1 . . . . .137 C3
Daniell Rd TR1 . . . . .137 B3
Daniell St TR1 . . . . .137 C3
Daniel Pl TR18. . . . . .143 E5
Daniels La PL25 . . . . .115 B4
Daniels Sail Loft TR10 . . . .144 D7
Danmore Cl PL34. . . . . .14 C7
Danum Dr PL7. . . . . .131 B3
DARITE 38 B4
Darite Prim Sch PL14 . . . . . .38 A4
Darke La PL19 . . . . .30 E1
Darke Cl PL6 . . . . .125 E5
Darkey La PL16. . . . . .19 F4
Dark La Camelford PL32 . . . .105 C4
Liskeard PL14 . . . . .113 D6
Lostwithiel PL22 . . . . .112 C1
Trevillador PL27. . . . . .32 D5
Darklake Cl PL6 . . . . .125 E5
Darklake La PL6. . . . . .125 D8
Darklake Pk PL6. . . . . .125 E5
Darklake View PL6 . . . . .125 E5
Dark Street La PL7. . . . . . . .130 E4
Darley Oak ★ 17 PL31. . . . . .109 A5
Darlington Rd TR20. . . . . .88 F6
Darloe La PL13 . . . . .117 C3
DARRACOTT 2 D4
Darracott Hill EX39 . . . . .2 E3
Dart Cl Plymouth PL3 . . . . . .129 D7

Dart Cl continued
St Giles on the Heath PL15 . . . . 13 F1
Dartington Wlk PL6 . . . . . . 129 E8
Dartmeet Ave PL3 . . . . . . 129 B6
Dartmoor View
Plymouth PL4 . . . . 129 C3
Saltash PL12 . . . . 122 E4
Dartmouth Wlk PL6 . . . . . . 129 E8
Darwin Cres PL3 . . . . 129 D5
Darwin Dr TR1 . . . . 144 F2
Dashwood Ho TR11 . . . . . . 145 A6
Daubuz Cl TR1 . . . . 137 C6
Daubuz Ct TR1 . . . . 137 D5
Daucus Cl PL19 . . . . 147 B4
Davenham Ct PL6 . . . . 125 B6
Davey's Cl TR11 . . . . 144 E1
David Cl PL7 . . . . 130 F6
David Penhaligon Way
TR1 . . . . 137 D3
David Southgate Ct PL11 . . 148 A2
DAVIDSTOW 16 A6
Davidstow Aerodrome ★
PL32 . . . . 15 F4
Davidstow Airfield & Cornwall
at War Mus ★ PI32 . . . . . . 15 F5
Davy Cl Torpoint PL11 . . . . . 126 F3
Tremar PL14 . . . . 38 A3
Davy Rd PL6 . . . . 125 C4
Davys Row PL14 . . . . 37 E4
Dawe Cres PL31 . . . . 109 C3
Dawes Cl PL14 . . . . 50 E7
Dawes La Millbrook PL10 . . 132 E5
Plymouth PL9 . . . . 136 D7
Dawlish Wlk PL6 . . . . 129 E8
Dawney Terr PL11 . . . . 65 B5
Dawn Rd PL13 . . . . 117 D2
Daws Ct PL12 . . . . 123 A2
DAW'S HOUSE 18 E1
Daw's Mdw PL32 . . . . 105 E4
Dawson Cl PL1 . . . . 123 E1
Daymans Denzell Downs TR8 . 32 A2
Trevilledor TR8 . . . . 31 F2
Daymer La PL27 . . . . 21 D4
Daymond Rd PL5 . . . . 123 D2
Dayton Cl PL6 . . . . 124 E3
Deacon Dr PL12 . . . . 122 F1
Deacons Gn PL19 . . . . 147 A3
Dean Cross PL9 . . . . 135 E7
Dean Cross Rd PL9 . . . . . . 135 E7
Dean Hill Liskeard PL14 . . . 113 B6
Plymouth PL9 . . . . 135 E7
Dean La PL14 . . . . 113 B6
Dean Park Rd PL9 . . . . 135 D7
Dean Rd PL7 . . . . 130 D6
Dean St PL14 . . . . 113 B5
Dean Terr PL14 . . . . 113 B6
Debden Cl PL5 . . . . 123 D4
Deeble Cl Plymouth PL7 . . . 130 E7
Threemilestone TR3 . . . . . . 69 C3
Deeble Dr 20 PL24 . . . . . . 60 B4
Deep La PL7 . . . . 131 C3
Deer La EX22 . . . . 13 A8
Deer Leap PL19 . . . . 147 D4
Deer Park Cl PL19 . . . . 147 C5
Deer Park Cres PL19 . . . . . 147 C5
Deer Park Dr PL3 . . . . 129 D7
Deerpark Forest Trail ★
PL14 . . . . 50 C3
Deer Park La PL19 . . . . 147 C5
Deer Park Rd PL19 . . . . 147 C5
Deer Pk Newquay TR7 . . . . . 110 D6
Saltash PL12 . . . . 122 F3
Defoe Cl PL5 . . . . 124 C1
Degibna La TR12, TR13 . . . . 146 C2
DELABOLE 14 D3
Delabole Comm Prim Sch
PL33 . . . . 14 D2
Delacombe Cl PL7 . . . . 130 F7
De-la-Hay Ave PL3 . . . . . . 148 A4
Delamere Holiday Village
PL33 . . . . 14 D2
Delamere Rd PL6 . . . . 129 D7
Delavue Terr PL32 . . . . 105 C3
Delaware Com Prim Sch
PL18 . . . . 40 F5
Delaware Cotts PL18 . . . . . 40 F6
Delaware Ct PL18 . . . . 40 F6
Delaware Gdns PL2 . . . . . . 127 F7
Delaware Rd
11 Gunnislake PL18 . . . . . 40 F5
Gunnislake PL18 . . . . 40 F6
Delgany Dr PL6 . . . . 125 A5
Dell Cl TR18 . . . . 143 C3
Dell Mdw PL15 . . . . 18 B8
Dell The Plymouth PL7 . . . . 130 B6
Tavistock PL19 . . . . 147 B6
Truro TR1 . . . . 137 C5
DEMELZA 46 E6
Demelza Rd PL30 . . . . 46 E7
Denas Water TR2 . . . . 71 A5
Dengie Cl PL7 . . . . 131 B5
Denham Cl PL5 . . . . 124 C2
Dennis Cl PL5 . . . . 124 C2
Dennis Gdns PL15 . . . . 18 C2
Dennis La PL28 . . . . 107 D4
Dennison Ave PL25 . . . . . . 115 A4
Dennison Rd PL31 . . . . 109 D5
Dennis Rd Liskeard PL14 . . 113 D6
Padstow PL28 . . . . 107 D5
Dennybowl La PL12 . . . . . . 52 E3
Dens Meadow PL12 . . . . . . 52 F6
Denyer Ct TR11 . . . . 145 A6
Denys View TR9 . . . . 45 F2
De Pass Gdns TR11 . . . . . . 145 C3
De Pass Rd TR11 . . . . 145 C2

Deptford Pl PL4 . . . . 149 A4
Derby Rd PL5 . . . . 124 C4
Derby's La PL26 . . . . 85 C5
Dereham Terr TR1 . . . . 137 B4
Derowen Dr TR27 . . . . 142 B3
DERRIFORD 125 B4
Derriford Bsns Pk PL6 . . . . 125 A4
Derriford Health & L Ctr
PL6 . . . . 125 B3
Derriford Hospl PL6 . . . . . . 125 B4
Derriford Pk PL6 . . . . 125 A3
Derriford Rd PL6 . . . . 125 B4
DERRIL 8 D6
Derriton Rd EX22 . . . . 8 F6
Derry Ave PL4 . . . . 148 C4
Derry's Cross PL1 . . . . 148 B2
Derwent Ave PL3 . . . . 129 C5
Desborough La PL4 . . . . . . 149 C3
Desborough Rd PL4 . . . . . . 149 C3
Deva Ho TR7 . . . . 111 A6
DEVERAL 78 D2
Deveral Rd TR27 . . . . 78 D2
Deveron Cl PL7 . . . . 131 A5
Devington Ct TR11 . . . . 145 C2
Devington Hall TR1 . . . . . . 137 E5
Deviock Hill PL11 . . . . 64 C5
Devonia Cl PL7 . . . . 130 E7
Devon Oaks PL20 . . . . 42 B5
DEVONPORT 127 D4
Devonport High Sch for Boys
PL1 . . . . 128 A2
Devonport High Sch for Girls
PL2 . . . . 128 C6
Devonport Hill
Kingsand PL10 . . . . 133 A2
Plymouth PL1 . . . . 127 F1
Devonport Leat PL6 . . . . . . 121 B5
Devonport Rd PL3 . . . . 127 F3
Devonport Sta PL1 . . . . 127 F3
Devon Progressive Sch
PL19 . . . . 42 A5
Devonshire Ct PL11 . . . . . . 127 B3
Devonshire Ho
Plymouth PL1 . . . . 148 B1
2 Tavistock PL19 . . . . . . 147 B5
Devonshire St PL4 . . . . 149 A3
Devon Terr PL3 . . . . 128 E5
Devon Tors Rd 9 PL20 . . . . 42 C3
DEVORAN 81 F6
Devoran La TR3 . . . . 81 F6
Devoran Sch TR3 . . . . 81 F6
Diamond Ave PL4 . . . . 149 B4
Diana Cl TR11 . . . . 144 E2
Dickens Rd PL5 . . . . 124 B1
Dickiemoor La PL5 . . . . 124 C2
Dickna St PL15 . . . . 13 F1
Dicky La PL3 . . . . 82 D6
Diddies La EX23 . . . . 4 E1
Diddies Rd EX23 . . . . 4 E1
Dieppe Cl PL1 . . . . 127 F2
Digby Gr PL5 . . . . 123 F5
Digey Flats 49 TR26 . . . . . 141 B6
Digey The 25 TR26 . . . . . . 141 B6
Diggory's Field 4 PL14 . . . . 38 A3
Dinas Cl PL11 . . . . 64 C5
Dinas Rd 1 TR9 . . . . 45 D6
Dingle Cl PL11 . . . . 28 D1
Dingle Rd
Plymouth, North Prospect
PL2 . . . . 128 A6
Plymouth, Plympton PL7 . . 130 C6
Dingles Cl TR3 . . . . 81 B4
Dingle's Folly PL13 . . . . . . 117 C3
Dingles Way PL27 . . . . 21 E3
Dingwall Ave PL5 . . . . 124 E3
Dinham La Haywood PL30 . . 34 C8
Leeches PL30 . . . . 23 A1
DINWORTHY 3 F2
Dipper Cl EX23 . . . . 5 A6
Dipper Dr PL19 . . . . 147 D2
Dipper La EX23 . . . . 5 A7
Dirty La PL12 . . . . 122 B5
Discovery Wharf 20 PL4 . . 149 A2
Distine Cl PL3 . . . . 129 B7
Dithmarschen Way PL25 . . 114 B2
Dittisham Wlk PL6 . . . . 129 E8
Ditton Ct PL6 . . . . 129 A8
Dixon Pl PL2 . . . . 127 F4
Dobbin Cl PL28 . . . . 20 F2
Dobbin La PL28 . . . . 20 F2
Dobbin Rd PL28 . . . . 20 F2
Dobbs La TR1 . . . . 137 A4
Dobell Rd PL25 . . . . 114 E4
DOBWALLS 50 E8
Dobwalls Prim Sch PL14 . . . 50 E7
Dockacre Rd PL15 . . . . 106 C6
Dockey 1 PL15 . . . . 106 C5
Dock La TR18 . . . . 143 F5
Dockray Cl PL6 . . . . 125 D4
Dockyard Sta PL2 . . . . 127 E4
DOCTON 2 F8
Doctors Hill 8 Boscastle PL35 9 C1
5 St Keverne TR12 . . . . . 101 C4
Doctors La PL12 . . . . 65 A8
Doctor's La PL14 . . . . 113 C6
Doctors Lane TR11 . . . . 92 F4
Doddridge Cl PL9 . . . . 135 F4
Dodson's Gap PL12 . . . . . . 99 B7
Doidges Farm Cl PL6 . . . . . 129 B8
Dola La PL26 . . . . 89 E5
Dolcath Ave TR14 . . . . 138 F3
Dolcoath Cl TR14 . . . . 138 F3
Dolcoath Ind Pk TR14 . . . . 139 A4
Dolcoath Rd TR14 . . . . 138 F3
Dolgey Post PL27 . . . . 32 A4
Dolphin Cl PL9 . . . . 135 F6

Dolphin Court Rd PL9 . . . . 135 F6
Dolphin Ho 18 PL4 . . . . . . 149 A2
Dolphin Sq PL9 . . . . 135 F6
Dolphin St PL29 . . . . 22 D7
Dolphin St PL19 . . . . 147 C5
Dolvin Rd PL19 . . . . 147 C5
Domellick Cnr PL26 . . . . . . 46 B1
Domellick Hill PL26 . . . . . . 46 B1
Doneys Mdw PL15 . . . . 17 F1
Doniert's Cl 11 PL14 . . . . . 113 B5
Donkey La Millbrook PL10 . . 132 C4
Portwrinkle PL11 . . . . 65 A4
Donnington Dr PL3 . . . . . . 129 C7
Donnington Rd TR18 . . . . . 143 C3
Donovan Way PL31 . . . . . . 109 B4
Dopps Terr TR15 . . . . 140 C5
Dorchester Ave PL5 . . . . . . 124 D4
Dorchester Ct TR14 . . . . . . 138 E4
Doreena Rd PL9 . . . . 136 C7
Dormy Ave PL3 . . . . 128 F5
Dor Priweythor 2 TR7 . . . . 111 E6
Dorset Pk PL15 . . . . 13 A2
Dorsmouth Terr PL7 . . . . . 130 E4
DOUBLEBOIS 50 C8
Doublebois Ind Est PL14 . . 50 D7
Doubletrees PL24 . . . . 60 B4
Doubletrees Ct 2 PL24 . . . 60 B4
Doubletrees Sch 21 PL24 . . 60 B4
Double White Rise 1 PL18 . 40 E5
Douglas Rd PL25 . . . . 47 A3
Douglas Dr PL9 . . . . 136 A6
Douglass Rd PL3 . . . . 129 C6
Doulton Rd PL25 . . . . 115 A4
DOUSLAND 42 F3
Dousland Ho PL20 . . . . 42 E3
Dousland Rd PL20 . . . . 42 D3
Dousland Terr PL20 . . . . . . 42 E3
Dovedale Rd PL2 . . . . 128 A7
Dove Gdns PL3 . . . . 129 D7
Dover Rd PL6 . . . . 125 E3
Dove St 15 TR14 . . . . 141 B5
Dower's Terr TR16 . . . . 80 B5
Down Cl PL12 . . . . 122 C2
DOWNDERRY 64 C5
Downfield Dr PL7 . . . . 130 F5
Downfield Way PL7 . . . . . . 130 F5
Downfield Wlk PL7 . . . . . . 130 F5
DOWNGATE Kelly Bray 40 A7
Pensilva 38 D5
Downgate Gdns PL2 . . . . . 128 D8
Downham Gdns PL5 . . . . . 124 C7
Downhorne Pk PL9 . . . . . . 135 F6
DOWNINNEY 11 B1
Downlea PL19 . . . . 147 D4
Down Ln PL15 . . . . 17 E2
Down Park Dr PL19 . . . . . . 147 D4
Down Parks EX23 . . . . 5 B7
Down Rd Plymouth PL7 . . . 131 C5
Tavistock PL19 . . . . 147 D4
Downs Cl PL26 . . . . 58 C8
Downs Hill PL23 . . . . 61 B5
Downside Ave PL6 . . . . 129 C7
Downside Cl TR7 . . . . 111 A4
Downs La Looe PL13 . . . . . . 117 B3
Polmenna PL14 . . . . 36 E1
Downs Lane Pk PL13 . . . . . 117 B3
Downs Rd PL13 . . . . 117 C4
Downs The PL13 . . . . 117 C3
Downstream Ct PL28 . . . . . 107 C5
Downs View Bude EX23 . . . 104 D7
Looe PL13 . . . . 117 C3
Down The PL20 . . . . 41 C1
DOWN THOMAS 135 C1
Downton Cl PL1 . . . . 148 A4
Dowren Ho TR27 . . . . 142 B5
Dozmere TR3 . . . . 82 C5
Dozmere Cl TR3 . . . . 82 C5
Dracaena Ave
Falmouth TR11 . . . . 144 F5
Hayle TR27 . . . . 142 E6
Dracaena Cres TR27 . . . . . 142 E6
Dracaena Pl TR11 . . . . 144 F4
Dracaena View TR11 . . . . . 144 F5
Dragon L Ctr The PI31 . . . . 109 F1
Drake Cir PL1, PL4 . . . . 149 A3
Drakecircus Sh Ctr PL1 . . . 149 A3
Drake Ct
Plymouth, Ernesettle PL5 . . 123 C4
Plymouth, St Jude's PL4 . . 149 B3
Drakefield Dr PL12 . . . . . . 123 A3
Drake Gdns PL19 . . . . 147 C4
Drake Prim Sch PL2 . . . . . . 127 E6
Drake Rd Padstow PL28 . . . 107 C5
Tavistock PL19 . . . . 147 C6
Drakes Cl PL6 . . . . 124 F4
Drake's Pk 3 PL20 . . . . 41 B1
Drake Villas PL19 . . . . 147 A4
Drakewalls Gdns PL18 . . . . 40 F5
Drakewalls Pl PL18 . . . . . . 40 F5
Drake Way PL7 . . . . 135 E7
Drang The TR9 . . . . 45 E1
Drannack La TR27 . . . . 78 C4
Drannack Mill Lane TR27 . . 78 C3
Draper Terr 3 PL19 . . . . . . 147 B5
DRAWBRIDGE 49 F8
Drax Gdns PL2 . . . . 128 E8
Draycott Terr TR26 . . . . . . 141 C4
Drayton Rd PL5 . . . . 124 C1
Dreysen Cl TR15 . . . . 139 C8
DRIFT 87 F3
Drift Cl TR20 . . . . 87 F3
Drift La PL14 . . . . 49 C7
Drillfield La 9 TR26 . . . . . . 141 B5
Drina La PL5 . . . . 123 E2
Drinnick Hill PL15 . . . . 27 E6
Drinnick Rd PL26 . . . . 58 C6
Drinnick Terr PL26 . . . . 58 D6
Drive The Helston TR13 . . . 146 D7

Drive The continued
Plymouth PL3 . . . . 128 E7
Driving La PL24 . . . . 60 C6
Drogeada Cl
Coad's Green PL15 . . . . 27 D3
6 Landreyne PL15 . . . . . . 27 D3
Drop Stamp Rd 4 TR14 . . . 138 F3
Droskyn Castle 19 TR6 . . . . 55 A5
Droskyn Cl 22 TR6 . . . . 55 A5
Droskyn House Villas TR6 . . 55 A5
Droskyn Way TR6 . . . . 55 A5
Druckham Pl PL15 . . . . 106 D5
Druckham Terr PL15 . . . . . 106 D5
Druid Ave PL31 . . . . 109 B4
Druid's Lodge TR15 . . . . . . 139 D5
Druid's Rd Camborne TR15 . 139 D5
Redruth TR15 . . . . 139 D6
Drummer's Hill PL26 . . . . . 114 C8
Drummond Cl PL2 . . . . 127 F7
Drummond Pl PL1 . . . . 127 F3
Drummond Way PL20 . . . . 119 E4
Drump Rd TR15 . . . . 140 C5
Drunkards La TR13 . . . . 90 F4
Drunken Bridge PL26 . . . . . 72 E4
Drunken Bridge Hill PL7 . . 130 D4
Dryburgh Cres PL2 . . . . . . 128 A8
Dryden Ave PL5 . . . . 124 C1
Dry La PL30 . . . . 24 A4
DRYM 91 A8
Drym La Leedstown TR14 . . 78 F1
Nancegollan TR14 . . . . 91 A8
Drym Rd TR13 . . . . 91 B7
Dry Wlk PL10 . . . . 133 E6
Dualstone Cross EX22 . . . . . 8 D3
Ducane Wlk PL6 . . . . 125 B1
Duchy Ave TR7 . . . . 111 C7
Duchy Cl Launceston PL15 . 106 C7
St Austell PL25 . . . . 114 C7
Duchy Coll St Breock PL27 . . 33 C7
Stoke Climsland PL17 . . . . . 28 D1
Duchy Coll Rosewarne
TR14 . . . . 138 D5
Duchy Cotts PL17 . . . . 28 D1
Duchy Hospl TR1 . . . . 69 E4
Duchy Terr Minions PL14 . . 38 B6
Upton Cross PL14 . . . . 38 D7
Duck La PL12 . . . . 53 E2
Duck St 9 Mousehole TR19 . 88 C1
St Austell PL25 . . . . 115 B2
Duckworth St 8 PL2 . . . . . . 128 A4
Ducky La PL12 . . . . 53 C3
Ducky Row PL17 . . . . 40 D4
Dudley Gdns PL6 . . . . 129 B8
Dudley Rd PL7 . . . . 130 D5
Dudman Rd TR1 . . . . 69 F3
Dudnance La TR15 . . . . 139 B4
Duke's Ct PL26 . . . . 46 F3
Dukes Dr PL9 . . . . 41 B4
Duke's Dr PL17 . . . . 28 F4
Dukes Ryde The 1 PL9 . . . 135 F7
Duke St Launceston PL15 . . 106 A8
Lostwithiel PL22 . . . . 112 C2
Padstow PL28 . . . . 107 D5
Plymouth PL1 . . . . 127 E5
St Austell PL25 . . . . 114 C3
Tavistock PL19 . . . . 147 C6
11 Truro TR1 . . . . 137 D4
Duke's Way TR7 . . . . 111 A5
DULOE 51 A1
Duloe CE VA Jun & Inf Sch
PL14 . . . . 51 A1
Duloe Gdns PL2 . . . . 128 C8
Duloe Rd PL14 . . . . 50 E7
Dumbarton Terr 7 TR19 . . . 88 C1
Dumfries Ave PL5 . . . . 124 D3
Duncan St PL1 . . . . 127 E1
Dunclair Pk PL3 . . . . 129 D5
Duncombe Ave PL5 . . . . . . 124 A2
Dundas St 4 PL2 . . . . 128 A4
Dunders Hill PL27 . . . . 21 D5
Dundonald St PL2 . . . . 127 F4
Dungarth Gn PL14 . . . . 113 D6
Dungarth Rd PL14 . . . . 113 D6
Dunhead View PL15 . . . . . . 28 B6
Dunheved Fields PL15 . . . . 106 C4
Dunheved Rd
Launceston PL15 . . . . 106 C5
Saltash PL12 . . . . 122 F2
Dunkeswell Cl PL2 . . . . 127 F8
Dunley Wlk PL6 . . . . 125 C1
DUNMERE 34 D2
Dunmere Cl 1 PL24 . . . . . . 60 C4
Dunmere Rd PL31 . . . . 109 B5
Dunnet Rd PL6 . . . . 124 D7
Dunn St 10 PL35 . . . . 9 C1
Dunraven Dr PL6 . . . . 125 A6
Dunsdon Cross EX22 . . . . . . 5 F3
DUNSLEY 38 C6
Dunstable Cl PL26 . . . . 58 D6
Dunstan Cl TR10 . . . . 144 C8
Dunstan La St Mellion PL12 . 40 A1
Sewogran TR10 . . . . 92 C6
Dunstanville Terr
12 Falmouth TR11 . . . . . 145 A5
Falmouth TR11 . . . . 145 B5
Dunster Cl PL26 . . . . 58 C8
Dunstone Ave PL9 . . . . 136 A7
Dunstone Cl PL9 . . . . 135 F7
Dunstone Dr PL9 . . . . 135 F7
Dunstone La PL9 . . . . 136 A7
Dunstone Prim Sch PL9 . . . 136 A8
Dunstone Rd
Plymouth, Plymstock PL9 . . 135 F7
Plymouth, St Budeaux PL5 . 123 F3
Dunstone View PL9 . . . . . . 136 A7
DUNTERTON 28 F6
Duntz Hill PL16 . . . . 19 F4

Dunvegan Rd TR10 . . . . . . 144 B8
Dunveth Bsns Pk PL27 . . . . 33 C7
Dunveth Industrial Estate
PL27 . . . . 33 C7
Dunveth Rd PL27 . . . . 108 A5
Dupath La PL17 . . . . 40 A4
DUPORTH 115 A1
Duporth Bay PL26 . . . . 115 A1
Duporth Rd PL24, PL26 . . . 115 A2
Dural Cross EX22 . . . . 3 E3
Durban Rd PL3 . . . . 128 D5
DURGAN 93 D2
Durgan Crossroads TR11 . . 93 D3
Durgan La TR10 . . . . 144 C8
Durham Ave PL4 . . . . 149 C4
Durley Dene TR26 . . . . 77 E4
Durnford St PL1 . . . . 128 A1
Durnford Street Ope PL1 . . 128 A1
Durning Rd TR5 . . . . 54 C1
Durrant Cl PL1 . . . . 127 E3
Durris Cl PL6 . . . . 125 D4
Durris Gdns PL6 . . . . 125 D4
Durston Rd EX23 . . . . 104 E7
Durwent Cl PL9 . . . . 135 A6
DUTSON 106 E8
Dutson Rd PL15 . . . . 106 C7
Dutson Terr PL15 . . . . 106 C7
Dux Cross EX22 . . . . 8 C6
Duxford Cl PL5 . . . . 123 E5
Dye House Cotts PL14 . . . . 36 F2
Dymond Cl PL32 . . . . 105 B2
Dymond St PL31 . . . . 109 C6
Dymond Ct (Kingdom Pl)
PL12 . . . . 122 F2
Dynas-la Rd TR26 . . . . 141 B4
Dynevor Cl PL3 . . . . 128 F7

E

Eagle Cl PL7 . . . . 131 C4
Eagle Rd PL7 . . . . 131 C4
Earle's Retreat TR11 . . . . . 145 B3
Earl's Acre PL3 . . . . 128 C4
Earls Dr PL10 . . . . 133 B3
Earl's Dr The Cawsand PL10 133 A1
Kingsand PL10 . . . . 133 B3
Earls Mill Rd PL7 . . . . 130 E6
Earls Rise TR7 . . . . 111 B5
Earls Wood Cl PL6 . . . . 125 F3
Earls Wood Dr PL6 . . . . 125 F3
Eastbourne Rd PL25 . . . . . 114 E3
Eastbourne Rd PL25 . . . . . 114 E4
East Bridge 4 TR4 . . . . 69 A3
Eastbury Ave PL5 . . . . 124 A2
East Camps Bay PL11 . . . . . 64 D4
East Charles St TR14 . . . . . 138 E2
East Cl TR13 . . . . 146 D7
East Cliff PL13 . . . . 117 D3
Eastcliff Ave TR4 . . . . 68 A7
East Cliff Avenue No 2 TR4 . 68 A7
Eastcliffe Rd PL24 . . . . 60 C5
East Cliff La TR17 . . . . 89 C5
Eastcote Cl PL6 . . . . 125 B6
EASTCOTT 3 A3
Eastcott Cross EX23 . . . . . . 3 A2
East Dr Braddock PL22 . . . . 49 F5
Penhole PL14 . . . . 50 A5
Estella Rd PL20 . . . . 42 D2
East End TR15 . . . . 140 C5
Easterdown Cl PL9 . . . . . . 135 F7
Eastern Ave PL14 . . . . 113 D6
Eastern Gn Gulval TR18 . . . 88 E6
Penzance TR18 . . . . 143 F7
Eastern Green Pk TR18 . . . 88 E6
Eastern La TR14 . . . . 138 D4
Eastern Wood Rd PL7 . . . . 131 C4
East Fairholme Rd EX23 . . 104 F7
Eastfield Ave PL9 . . . . 135 C6
Eastfield Cres PL3 . . . . 129 A6
Eastfield Way PL25 . . . . . . 114 F5
East Hill Camborne TR14 . . 139 A5
St Austell PL25 . . . . 114 D3
Eastlake Ho 5 PL1 . . . . . . 149 A2
Eastlake St PL4 . . . . 148 C3
Eastland Cl TR1 . . . . 137 F4
EAST LOOE 117 D3
EAST PANSON 13 F3
East Park Ave PL4 . . . . 148 C4
East Park Cl EX23 . . . . 5 B2
East Pk Pensilva PL14 . . . . . 38 D4
Redruth TR15 . . . . 140 D6
Tregadillett PL15 . . . . 18 C2
East Pool Pk TR15 . . . . 139 D6
EAST PORTHOLLAND 84 E5
East Quay TR27 . . . . 142 B6
East Quay Ho PL13 . . . . . . 117 D3
East Rd Kilkhampton EX23 . . 5 A6
Menheniot PL14 . . . . 52 A5
Quintrell Downs TR8 . . . . . 44 E3
Stithians TR3 . . . . 80 F3
East Rise TR11 . . . . 144 F3
East Rosewin Row 10 TR1 . 137 D5
East St Newquay TR7 . . . . . 110 E6
Plymouth PL1 . . . . 148 A2
Polruan PL23 . . . . 116 D3
1 St Columb Major TR9 . . 45 E6
EAST TAPHOUSE 50 B6
East Terr TR26 . . . . 142 B6
East View PL14 . . . . 51 F5
East Wharf PL26 . . . . 84 E5
East Wheel Rose Sta ★ TR8 . 56 C6
Eastwood Park Ind Est
TR10 . . . . 144 F4
Eastwood Rd TR10 . . . . . . 144 D7
EAST YOULSTONE 3 C2
East Youlstone Cross EX23 . 3 C2
Eathorne TR11 . . . . 93 A6

Eathorne Ct **9** TR13 . . . . . .146 C5
Ebenezer PL26 . . . . .47 E3
Ebenezer Pl **12** TR18 . . . . .143 C1
Ebenezer Rd
  St Helena TR12 . . . . .102 F5
  Treveddon TR12 . . . . .103 A5
Ebrington St PL4 . . . . .149 A3
Echo Cres PL5 . . . . .124 D2
Eco Way PL6 . . . . .125 C8
Eddystone Ct PL13 . . . . .129 C6
Eddystone Ct PL13 . . . . .117 D2
Eddystone Pl **3** PL27 . . . . .108 B5
Eddystone Rd
  Down Thomas PL9 . . . . .135 C1
  St Austell PL25 . . . . .114 E5
  Wadebridge PL27 . . . . .108 B6
Eddystone Road Trad & Ind Est
  PL27 . . . . .108 B6
Eddystone Terr
  Plymouth PL1 . . . . .148 B1
  2 Wadebridge PL27 . . . . .108 B5
Eden Cl **11** PL24 . . . . .60 B4
Eden Gdns **14** TR18 . . . . . .143 C1
Eden Project★ PL24, PL26 . . .115 D8
Edenside PL3 . . . . .128 F6
Eden Terr **13** TR18 . . . . . . .143 C1
Eden Way **16** PL26 . . . . .59 D7
Edgar Rd Jacobstow Gn23 . . . .11 A2
  Wainhouse Corner EX23 . . . . .10 F6
Edgar Terr PL4 . . . . .129 A4
Edgcumbe Ave
  Newquay TR7 . . . . .110 F5
  Plymouth PL1 . . . . .148 A3
Edgcumbe Cl PL18 . . . . .41 A6
Edgcumbe Cres PL10 . . . . . . .132 F6
Edgcumbe Ct **3** PL3 . . . . .128 A3
Edgcumbe Dr PL19 . . . . .147 B6
Edgcumbe Gdns TR7 . . . . . . .110 F6
Edgcumbe Gn PL25 . . . . .114 A3
Edgcumbe Ho PL1 . . . . .148 B2
Edgcumbe Park Rd PL3 . . . . .128 D6
Edgcumbe Rd
  3 Edgcumbe PL19 . . . . . . .29 C6
  Lostwithiel PL22 . . . . .112 B1
  Roche PL26 . . . . .46 F3
  St Austell PL25 . . . . .114 A3
  St Dominick PL12 . . . . .40 D2
  Saltash PL12 . . . . .122 C5
Edgcumbe St PL1 . . . . .148 A2
Edgcumbe Terr **1** PL24 . . . . .60 B4
Edgecombe Way PL18 . . . . . . .40 E5
Edgecumbe Terr **14** PL20 . . .41 B1
Edgemoor Cl PL14 . . . . .38 A3
Edinburgh Cl PL25 . . . . .115 C3
Edinburgh St PL1 . . . . .127 E1
EDISTONE 2 F8
Edith Ave PL4 . . . . .149 C4
Edith St PL5 . . . . .123 D1
EDMONTON 33 B7
Edmund Rd TR15 . . . . .140 B6
Edna Terr PL4 . . . . .149 C3
Ednovean La TR20 . . . . .89 E4
Edward Hain Com Hospl
  . . . . .141 B5
Edwards Cl PL7 . . . . .131 B4
Edwards Cres PL12 . . . . .122 C2
Edwards Dr PL7 . . . . .131 B5
Edwards Rd Devoran TR3 . . . . .81 F6
  St Giles on the Heath PL15 . . .13 F1
Edward St Camborne TR14 . . .138 F4
  Truro TR1 . . . . .137 C4
Edymeade Ct PL15 . . . . .106 C5
Edymeade Gdn **11** PL15 . . .106 C5
  9 Launceston PL15 . . . . . .106 C5
Edyvean Pl **3** PL25 . . . . . .114 F2
Effingham Cres PL3 . . . . .128 D7
EFFORD 129 C5
Efford Cres PL3 . . . . .129 B6
Efford Down Pk EX23 . . . . . . .104 C4
Efford Farm Cotts EX23 . . . . .104 C4
Efford Fort PL3 . . . . .129 E6
Efford La PL3 . . . . .129 C6
Efford Pathway PL3 . . . . .129 C6
Efford Rd PL3 . . . . .129 B6
Efford Wlk PL3 . . . . .129 B6
Egerton Cres PL4 . . . . .149 C3
Egerton Pl PL4 . . . . .149 C3
Egerton Rd Padstow PL28 . . . .107 E4
  Plymouth PL4 . . . . .149 C3
EGGBEARE 19 A7
EGGBUCKLAND 129 C8
Eggbuckland Rd PL3 . . . . . . .129 C7
Eggbuckland Vale Prim Sch
  PL6 . . . . .129 A8
Eglos Ct PL30 . . . . .23 E7
Egloshayle Rd Hayle TR27 . . .142 E6
  Wadebridge PL27 . . . . .108 D5
EGLOSKERRY 18 A5
Egloskerry Sch PL15 . . . . .18 A5
Eglos Mdw TR11 . . . . .82 A3
Eglos Parc Mullion TR12 . . . . .99 A2
  Wadebridge PL27 . . . . .108 D5
Eglos Rd Ludgvan TR20 . . . . . .89 A7
  St Erme TR4 . . . . .70 D8
  Shortlanesend TR4 . . . . .69 F6
Eglos View **2** PL35 . . . . . . .9 C1
EGOSHAYLE 108 D6
Egret Cl PL10 . . . . .133 A6
Eider Wlk TR27 . . . . .77 E3
Eight Acre Cl **1** PL7 . . . . .131 C5
Elaine Cl PL7 . . . . .130 B5
Elbow La PL19 . . . . .147 C6
ELBURTON 136 B6
Elburton Prim Sch PL9 . . . . . .136 C7
Elburton Rd PL9 . . . . .136 B8
Eldad Hill PL1 . . . . .148 A3

Elder Cl **2** PL7 . . . . .131 B5
Elderfield Cl **7** PL24 . . . . . .60 D5
Eleanor Ho PL1 . . . . .148 A2
Electra Way **20** PL9 . . . . . .136 E8
Eleni Cl Carn Towan TR19 . . . . .86 E1
  Sennen Cove TR19 . . . . .96 C7
Elerkey Cl TR2 . . . . .83 F6
Elerkey La TR2 . . . . .83 F6
Eleven Doors PL25 . . . . .115 B2
Elford Cres PL7 . . . . .130 E7
Elford Dr PL9 . . . . .135 C7
Elford Pk PL20 . . . . .42 D2
Elgin Cres PL6 . . . . .124 E3
Elim Ct PL3 . . . . .128 E5
Elim Terr PL3 . . . . .128 E5
Eliot Cl PL15 . . . . .18 C2
Eliot Ct TR7 . . . . .110 F6
Eliot Dr PL12 . . . . .65 B8
Eliot Gdns TR7 . . . . .110 F6
Eliot Pl St Austell PL25 . . . . .114 A4
  Truro TR1 . . . . .137 C5
Eliot St PL5 . . . . .127 E8
Elizabeth Cl Bodmin PL31 . . . .109 D4
  Threemilestone TR3 . . . . . . .69 C3
Elizabeth Ct Bugle PL26 . . . . .47 C1
  2 Plymouth PL4 . . . . . . .149 A2
Elizabeth House Mus & Arts
  Gall★ PL4 . . . . .149 A2
Elizabeth Pl PL4 . . . . .149 A4
Elizabeth Rd Bude EX23 . . . . .104 F5
  St Austell PL25 . . . . .114 E3
Elizabeth Terr TR17 . . . . .89 B5
Ellbridge La PL12 . . . . .118 A3
Ellen Cl TR4 . . . . .68 C6
Ellenglaze Ct TR8 . . . . .55 D8
Ellenglaze La TR8 . . . . .55 D8
Ellenglaze Mdw TR8 . . . . .55 D8
Elliot Sq PL11 . . . . .127 B3
Elliot St PL1 . . . . .148 B2
Elliott Cl PL12 . . . . .122 D2
Elliott Terr PL1 . . . . .148 C1
Elliot Terrace La PL1 . . . . .148 C1
Ellis Cl TR27 . . . . .142 C5
Ellis Mdw TR27 . . . . .78 D6
Elliston Gdns **3** TR13 . . . . .98 C8
Ellis Way TR27 . . . . .142 C5
Elm Cl Callington PL17 . . . . . .39 F4
  Camborne TR15 . . . . .139 D6
  Newquay TR7 . . . . .110 F4
  Tavistock PL19 . . . . .147 C3
Elm Cotts PL12 . . . . .122 C3
Elm Court Gdns TR1 . . . . . . .137 D5
Elm Cres PL3, PL4 . . . . .129 A4
Elm Croft PL2 . . . . .128 B7
Elm Ct TR1 . . . . .137 D5
Elm Dr Bude EX23 . . . . .104 F6
  8 St Columb Major TR9 . . .45 D6
Elmgate Crossways PL12 . . . . .65 E8
Elm Gr Feock TR3 . . . . .82 C5
  Plymouth, Eggbuckland PL6 . .129 B8
  Plymouth, Plympton PL7 . . . .130 E5
Elmlea EX23 . . . . .82 C5
Elm Mdw TR3 . . . . .82 C5
Elm Meadow Dr PL13 . . . . . . .117 D4
Elm Pk PL10 . . . . .133 B6
Elm Rd
  Plymouth, Glenholt PL6 . . . . .125 D6
  Plymouth, Mannamead PL4 . .128 F4
Elms Close Terr **25** TR18 . . .143 C2
ELMSCOTT 2 E8
Elmsleigh PL25 . . . . .114 B3
Elmsleigh Rd PL27 . . . . .108 B6
Elms The Perranuthnoe TR20 . .89 D4
  Plymouth PL3 . . . . .128 A3
Elm Terr **8** Mullion TR12 . . . .99 A2
  1 Plymouth PL3 . . . . .128 F5
  St Austell PL25 . . . . .114 C4
Elm Terrace **21** PL26 . . . . . .85 D8
Elm Tree Rd PL13 . . . . .117 D4
Elm Villas TR11 . . . . .144 E1
Elmwood Cl PL6 . . . . .125 D5
Elowen Cl TR11 . . . . .144 E2
Elphinstone Rd PL2 . . . . .128 C7
Elspeth Sitters Ho **11** PL4 . .149 A2
Elwell Rd PL4 . . . . .123 A4
Elwick Gdns PL4 . . . . .129 B5
Embankment La PL4 . . . . . . .129 B2
Embankment Rd PL4 . . . . . . .129 B2
Embankment Road Lane N
  PL4 . . . . .129 B2
Emily Gdns PL4 . . . . .149 B4
Emlyn Fields PL25 . . . . .114 F6
Emma Pl PL1 . . . . .128 A1
Emma Place Ope PL1 . . . . . . .128 A1
EMPACOMBE 133 D6
Empire Way TR11 . . . . .144 E4
Empress Ave **23** TR18 . . . .143 E6
Empty La PL14 . . . . .37 B2
Emslie Rd TR11 . . . . .145 C2
Endeavour Ct PL1 . . . . .128 A3
Endsleigh Dr
  Dunterton PL15, PL19 . . . . . .28 F5
  Endsleigh PL19 . . . . .29 A5
Endsleigh Gdns **2** PL4 . . . .149 A4
Endsleigh Gdns Nursery★
  PL19 . . . . .29 B5
Endsleigh Park Rd PL3 . . . . . .128 D6
Endsleigh Pk EX23 . . . . .7 B6
Endsleigh Pl PL4 . . . . .149 A4
Endsleigh Rd PL9 . . . . .135 C7
Endsleigh Terr PL14 . . . . .113 C6
Engelly Rd TR4 . . . . .55 E4
Eningdale Rd PL19 . . . . .147 A4
Ennerdale Gdns PL6 . . . . .124 E5
ENNISCAVEN 46 D2

Ennis Cl TR4 . . . . .56 D1
Ennor's Rd TR7 . . . . .110 D6
Ensign Cl TR4 . . . . .56 D1
Ensign Way **7** TR20 . . . . . . .88 B7
Enterprise Dr PL5 . . . . .124 D2
Enys Cl Carbis Bay TR26 . . . . .141 D1
  Truro TR1 . . . . .137 B5
Enys Cotts TR19 . . . . .75 A2
Enys Hill TR3 . . . . .81 B4
Enys Quay **5** TR1 . . . . .137 D4
Enys Rd Camborne TR14 . . . . .138 D4
  Truro TR1 . . . . .137 B5
Enys Redenek TR14 . . . . .138 F5
Epping Cres PL6 . . . . .129 D7
Epworth Cl TR1 . . . . .137 E4
Epworth Terr **4** PL2 . . . . . .127 F5
Erdiston Ct EX23 . . . . .104 D6
Ergue-Gaberic Way EX23 . . . .104 D5
Eric Rd Calstock PL18 . . . . . . .41 B3
  Plymouth PL4 . . . . .149 C3
Erisey Terr TR11 . . . . .145 B4
Erith Ave PL2 . . . . .127 E7
Erle Gdns PL7 . . . . .130 F3
Erlstoke Cl PL6 . . . . .125 D1
Erme Gdns PL3 . . . . .129 C5
Ermington Terr PL4 . . . . .128 E4
ERNESETTLE 123 E3
Ernesettle Cres PL5 . . . . .123 E3
Ernesettle Gn PL5 . . . . .123 E4
Ernesettle La PL5 . . . . .123 D4
Ernesettle Prim Sch PL5 . . . . .123 F4
Ernesettle Rd PL5 . . . . .123 E3
Errow Glas TR10 . . . . .144 C8
Erskine Ct PL6 . . . . .125 F5
Esmonde Gdns PL5 . . . . .127 B8
Esmonde Rd TR13 . . . . .146 D4
Esperanza Ct TR11 . . . . .144 F6
Esplanade PL23 . . . . .116 C3
Esplanade Rd TR7 . . . . .110 A6
Esplanade The PL1 . . . . .148 C1
Essa Rd PL12 . . . . .122 F2
Essex Dr TR15 . . . . .139 B8
Essex St PL1 . . . . .148 B4
Esso Wharf Rd PL4 . . . . .149 C1
Eston Cl TR10 . . . . .93 C8
ESTOVER 125 E4
Estover Cl PL6 . . . . .125 F5
  Plymouth PL6 . . . . .125 F5
Estover Ind Est PL6 . . . . .125 E4
Estover Rd PL6 . . . . .125 F4
Estuary View
  2 Falmouth TR11 . . . . . . .145 B5
  Lelant TR26 . . . . .77 E3
  Newquay TR7 . . . . .110 D5
  12 Tremough TR10 . . . . . .81 C1
Estuary Way PL5 . . . . .127 C7
Eton Ave PL1 . . . . .148 C4
Eton Cl PL1 . . . . .148 C4
Eton Pl PL1 . . . . .148 C4
Eton St PL1 . . . . .148 C4
Eton Terr **3** PL1 . . . . .148 B3
Euny Cl TR15 . . . . .140 A4
Eureka Vale **7** TR6 . . . . . . .55 A5
Europa Ct TR8 . . . . .31 C2
Evans Ct PL1 . . . . .148 A3
Evans Pl PL2 . . . . .128 B5
Evans Way TR20 . . . . .90 C4
Evea Cl TR1 . . . . .69 F3
Evely Cl PL14 . . . . .113 D7
Evelyn Pl PL4 . . . . .149 A4
Evelyn St PL5 . . . . .123 D1
Evenden Ct PL11 . . . . .127 A3
Example Cross PL15 . . . . .27 B6
Exchange (Gall) The★ **37**
  TR18 . . . . .143 E5
Exchange St PL4 . . . . .149 A2
Exe Gdns PL3 . . . . .129 C7
Exeter Cl PL5 . . . . .123 C4
Exeter Ct **6** PL15 . . . . .106 C6
Exeter St Launceston PL15 . . .106 C6
  Plymouth, Barbican PL4 . . . . .149 A3
  Plymouth, St Jude's PL4 . . . . .149 B2
Exmouth Cl PL1 . . . . .127 F3
Exmouth Rd PL1 . . . . .127 F3
Explorer Cl PL2 . . . . .128 B5

F

Factory Cotts PL14 . . . . .51 F5
Fairbourne Rd PL25 . . . . .114 F4
Fair Cl TR8 . . . . .56 F5
Fair Cross TR2 . . . . .72 C6
Fairfax Rd TR2 . . . . .70 F5
Fairfax Terr **5** PL2 . . . . . . .127 F4
Fairfield Plymouth PL7 . . . . . .130 E7
  St Germans PL12 . . . . .65 A8
Fair Field TR9 . . . . .89 B8
Fairfield Ave PL2 . . . . .128 C7
Fairfield Cl Lelant TR26 . . . . . .77 E4
  St Austell PL25 . . . . .115 A4
Fairfield Pk PL15 . . . . .26 C7
Fairfield Rd Bude EX23 . . . . . .104 E5
  Falmouth TR11 . . . . .144 F4
Fairfields PL13 . . . . .117 D5
Fairing Cl **12** PL31 . . . . . . .109 A5
Fairlight PL14 . . . . .113 D5
Fairmantle St TR1 . . . . .137 D4
Fairmead Cl PL12 . . . . .53 E4
Fairmead Mews PL12 . . . . . . .122 C3
Fairmeadow TR10 . . . . .144 B7
Fairpark Rd Liskeard PL14 . . . .113 C5
  Wadebridge PL27 . . . . .108 B5
Fair Park View TR8 . . . . .56 F5
Fair Pk Cl **10** PL15 . . . . . . .106 C5
Fair St TR9 . . . . .45 E6
Fair View Bodmin PL31 . . . . . .109 B4
  Lanivet PL26 . . . . .47 E4
Fairview Ave PL3 . . . . .129 D5

Fairview Pk **5** TR9 . . . . . . .45 E2
Fairview Pl TR11 . . . . .145 B4
Fairview Terr TR7 . . . . .110 E6
Fair View Terr TR4 . . . . .55 D8
Fairview Way PL3 . . . . .129 E5
Fairway St Austell PL25 . . . . .115 D3
  Saltash PL12 . . . . .122 C2
Fairways The PL30 . . . . .48 C7
Fairway The PL11 . . . . .93 C2
FAIRY CROSS 49 B5
Falcon Terr EX23 . . . . .104 D5
FALMOUTH 145 A4
Falmouth Art Gall★ TR11 . . . .145 B4
Falmouth Bsns Pk TR11 . . . . .144 E3
Falmouth Docks Sta TR11 . . . .145 D3
Falmouth Hospl TR11 . . . . . . .144 F4
Falmouth Marine Sch **17**
  TR11 . . . . .145 A4
Falmouth Pl TR19 . . . . .86 F8
Falmouth Prim Sch TR11 . . . .145 A5
Falmouth Rd Helston TR13 . . .146 D7
  Penryn TR10 . . . . .144 E7
  Redruth TR15 . . . . .140 C4
  Truro TR1 . . . . .137 C3
Falmouth Road TR13 . . . . . . .146 E7
Falmouth Sch TR11 . . . . .144 D5
Falmouth Town Sta TR11 . . . .145 C4
Falmouth University (Penryn
  Campus) TR10 . . . . .144 A8
Falmouth University
  (Wellington Annexe)
  TR11 . . . . .145 B3
Falmouth University
  (Woodlane Campus)
  TR11 . . . . .145 B3
Falmouth Watersports Ctr **15**
  TR11 . . . . .145 C3
Falmouth Wharves TR11 . . . . .145 A6
Fanshawe Way PL9 . . . . .135 C6
Faraday Mill Bsns Pk PL4 . . . .129 B1
Faraday Rd PL4 . . . . .129 B1
Farfield Pl TR7 . . . . .110 E5
Faringdon Rd PL4 . . . . .129 B3
Farley Cl TR1 . . . . .137 C3
Farm Cl PL7 . . . . .130 C7
Farmers Cl PL14 . . . . .50 B6
Farmers Ct TR20 . . . . .89 B8
Farmer's La PL14 . . . . .50 B6
Farmers Mdw **8** PL28 . . . . .143 C2
Farmhouse La PL27 . . . . .21 E5
Farm La Gwealmayowe TR13 . .146 C7
  Plymouth PL5 . . . . .124 B2
  Saltash PL12 . . . . .122 D1
FARMS COMMON 79 F1
Farm Town TR15 . . . . .140 C3
Farnley Cl PL6 . . . . .125 B6
Farrar Cl TR27 . . . . .142 E8
Farriers Cotts PL7 . . . . .130 E7
Farriers Gn PL32 . . . . .105 B2
Farriers The PL19 . . . . .30 A3
Farrow Fordh PL26 . . . . .46 F3
Faugan La TR18 . . . . .143 B1
Faugan Rd TR18 . . . . .143 B1
Faukener Cl TR11 . . . . .144 E4
Fayre View PL12 . . . . .122 B1
Fearnside Way PL12 . . . . . . .122 C3
Federation Rd PL3 . . . . .129 C4
Feeding Field Cl **7** PL27 . . . .142 D6
Fegan Rd PL5 . . . . .123 B1
Feliskirk La TR17 . . . . .89 B6
Felixstowe Ave TR7 . . . . .111 E7
Fellowes La **4** PL4 . . . . . . .148 A4
Fellowes Pl PL1 . . . . .128 A2
Fenten Cl EX23 . . . . .104 E7
Fenten Pk PL12 . . . . .122 F3
Fenteroon Rd PL32 . . . . .105 C2
FENTONADLE 24 A5
Fentonluna La PL28 . . . . .107 D6
Fenwick Rd TR11 . . . . .145 B2
FEOCK 82 C5
Feock Rd TR3 . . . . .82 B3
Fern Cl PL7 . . . . .131 C5
Ferndale Ave PL2 . . . . .127 E5
Ferndale Cl PL15 . . . . .106 D8
Ferndale Rd Falmouth TR11 . . .145 A2
  Plymouth PL2 . . . . .127 F7
Ferndale Terr PL14 . . . . .113 B6
Fern Glen **18** TR26 . . . . . . .141 A5
Fernhill Rd TR7 . . . . .110 D6
Fern Lee Terr **19** TR26 . . . . .141 B5
Fernleigh Cres PL27 . . . . .108 C4
Fernleigh Gdns PL27 . . . . . . .108 C4
Fernleigh La PL27 . . . . .108 C4
Fernleigh Rd Plymouth PL3 . . .128 F5
  Wadebridge PL27 . . . . .108 C5
Fernleigh Terr
  Gunnislake PL18 . . . . .40 E5
  Nanpean PL26 . . . . .58 C6
Fern Mdw PL19 . . . . .147 D6
Fernside Pk PL14 . . . . .38 A3
Fernside Rd TR14 . . . . .138 B1
FERNSPLATT 81 C8
Ferrers Rd PL5 . . . . .123 E1
Ferretts Cross EX23 . . . . .11 A6
Ferris Town TR1 . . . . .137 C4
Ferris Way PL23 . . . . .116 E2
Ferry La PL11 . . . . .126 D5
Ferry Rd Braunder PL20 . . . . . .41 A2
  Plymouth PL1 . . . . .127 E3
Ferry St PL11 . . . . .126 D5
Festival Villas TR3 . . . . .69 D3
Fettling Lane **3** PL25 . . . . .115 A3
Feversham Cl PL7 . . . . .131 B6
FIDDLERS GREEN 56 B5
Field Cl PL22 . . . . .112 D2
Field Pl TR11 . . . . .93 D3
Field The TR20 . . . . .76 F2
Fifield Ho PL26 . . . . .58 B4

Fillace La **10** PL20 . . . . .42 C4
Fillace Pk PL20 . . . . .42 C4
Filtrick La TR16 . . . . .139 E1
Finch Cl PL3 . . . . .129 D4
Finches Cl PL9 . . . . .136 C7
Findon Gdns PL6 . . . . .125 C6
Finewell St PL1 . . . . .148 C2
Finnigan Rd PL4 . . . . .129 B1
Finn Vc Est **18** PL31 . . . . . .109 D5
Finnygook La PL11 . . . . .65 A4
Finsbury Rise PL26 . . . . .46 F3
Fir Cl Goonhavern TR4 . . . . . .55 C4
  Helston TR13 . . . . .146 B7
  St Austell PL25 . . . . .114 B3
Fir Cres PL26 . . . . .58 D5
Fircroft Rd PL2 . . . . .128 B7
Firestone Cl PL6 . . . . .125 C1
Fir Gr **8** TR3 . . . . .81 F7
Firsleigh Pk PL26 . . . . .46 F3
First Ave
  Plymouth, Billacombe PL9 . . .135 F8
  Plymouth, Stoke PL1 . . . . . .128 A2
Firs The 58 E8
Fisgard Way PL11 . . . . .126 D3
Fisher Cl PL27 . . . . .108 D6
Fisher Rd PL2 . . . . .128 A5
Fish Mkt PL4 . . . . .149 B2
Fish St **9** TR26 . . . . .141 B6
Fish Strand Hill TR11 . . . . . . .145 B4
Fish Strand Quay TR11 . . . . . .145 B4
Fistral TR7 . . . . .126 F4
Fistral Cres TR7 . . . . .110 A5
Fistral Ct TR7 . . . . .110 A5
Fistral Sands Apartments
  TR7 . . . . .110 A5
Fitch La PL15 . . . . .27 C4
Fitzford Cott PL19 . . . . .147 A4
Fitzroy Rd PL1 . . . . .128 A3
Fitzroy Terr **7** PL1 . . . . . . .128 A3
Fitzsimmons Cl **7** TR13 . . . .146 C5
Five Fields La TR11 . . . . .145 A5
Five Wells La TR13 . . . . .146 B5
Flamank Pk PL31 . . . . .109 C4
Flambards Experience The★
  . . . . .146 C5
Flamborough Rd PL6 . . . . .125 A7
Flamborough Way PL6 . . . . . .125 A6
Flamsteed Cres PL5 . . . . .123 E1
Flaxmoor Terr **17** PL31 . . . .109 D5
Fleet St PL2 . . . . .127 E6
Fleetwood Gdns PL6 . . . . .125 A7
Fletcher Cres PL9 . . . . .136 B6
FLETCHERSBRIDGE 48 F8
Fletchersbridge Hill
  Fletchersbridge PL30 . . . . . . .35 C1
  Tawnamoor PL30 . . . . .35 E1
Fletcher Way PL9 . . . . .136 A6
Fletemoor Rd PL5 . . . . .123 E1
Fletewood Sch PL4 . . . . .148 C4
FLEXBURY 104 E6
Flexbury Ave PL6 . . . . .104 E7
Flexbury Mews EX23 . . . . . . .104 E7
Flexbury Park EX23 . . . . .104 E7
Flexbury Park Rd EX23 . . . . . .104 E6
Flexbury Pk EX23 . . . . .104 E7
Flocksford PL30 . . . . .35 D4
Flora Cotts PL1 . . . . .148 B2
Flora Ct PL3 . . . . .148 B3
Flora Gdns **5** TR13 . . . . . . .146 C6
Flora St PL1 . . . . .148 B2
Florence Hill PL17 . . . . .39 F5
Florence Pl Falmouth TR11 . . .145 B3
  Newlyn TR18 . . . . .143 C3
  Plymouth PL4 . . . . .149 C3
Florence Rd PL4 . . . . .39 F5
Florence Road Bsns Pk
  PL17 . . . . .39 F6
Florence Road Ind Est PL17 . . .39 F6
Florence St PL5 . . . . .123 D1
Florence Terr TR11 . . . . .145 B3
Florida Gdns PL3 . . . . .129 C6
Floyd Cl PL7 . . . . .127 F7
FLUSHING Manaccan 101 B8
  Penryn 145 C6
Flushing CE Prim Sch
  TR11 . . . . .145 B6
Flushing Cove TR12 . . . . .101 B8
Focus Sch – Plymouth Campus
  PL5 . . . . .123 B1
Folders La PL30 . . . . .23 E7
Foliot Ave PL2 . . . . .128 A6
Foliot Rd PL2 . . . . .128 A6
Folkstone Cl PL26 . . . . .58 E6
FONSTON 11 C2
Forbes Cl TR18 . . . . .143 B1
Forbes Rd TR18 . . . . .143 B1
FORD 128 A5
Ford PL22 . . . . .49 E3
Fordbrook La PL9 . . . . .136 B6
Ford Cl PL14 . . . . .39 A2
FORDER Cawsand 132 F1
  Saltash 122 C1
Forder Hill PL10 . . . . .132 F1
Forder Hts PL6 . . . . .125 B1
Forder La PL10 . . . . .132 F1
Forder Valley Rd PL6 . . . . . . .129 D2
Fordh An Bal TR15 . . . . .139 B5
Ford Hill PL2 . . . . .128 A5
Fordh Talgarrek TR1 . . . . .137 B2
Fordh Tobmen TR5 . . . . .54 C1
FORD PARK 128 D4
Ford Park La PL4 . . . . .128 E4
Ford Park Rd PL4 . . . . .128 D4

Ford Pk PL4 . . . . .128 E4
Ford Prim Sch PL2. . . . . . . .127 F5
Fords Hill TR12. . . . . .100 D7
Ford's Row TR15 . . . . .140 B5
Ford St PL19 . . . . .147 B5
Foredown Pk PL14. . . . . .38 C3
Forest TR16 . . . . .80 A4
Fore St Ashton TR13 . . . . .90 E3
　Barripper TR14 . . . . .79 B5
　Bere Alston PL20 . . . . .41 B1
　Bere Ferrers PL20. . . . . . . .119 F3
　Bodmin PL31 . . . . .109 D5
　Boscastle PL35 . . . . .9 C1
　Bugle PL26 . . . . .47 C1
　6 Callington PL17 . . . . .39 E4
　Calstock PL18 . . . . .41 A3
　Camborne TR15 . . . . .139 B6
　Camelford PL32. . . . . .105 D4
　Cargreen PL12. . . . . .119 A2
　Carharrack TR16 . . . . .80 F8
　Chacewater TR4 . . . . .69 A3
　Constantine TR11 . . . . .92 F4
　Crumplehorn PL13. . . . . . . .62 D1
　Fowey PL23. . . . . .116 D4
　Golant PL23. . . . . .61 B5
　Goldsithney TR20. . . . . .89 E5
　Grampound TR2. . . . . .72 A7
　Grampound Road TR2 . . . . . .57 E1
　Gunnislake PL18 . . . . .40 F5
　Hayle TR27 . . . . .142 D6
　Herodsfoot PL14. . . . . .50 E3
　Kingsand PL10. . . . . .133 A2
　Lelant TR26 . . . . .77 E4
　Lerryn PL22. . . . . .61 C7
　Lifton PL16. . . . . .19 F4
　Liskeard PL14 . . . . .113 C6
　Looe PL13 . . . . .117 C3
　Lostwithiel PL22. . . . . .112 C2
　Madron TR20. . . . . .88 B7
　Marazion TR17. . . . . .89 C5
　Mevagissey PL26. . . . . .73 C3
　Millbrook PL10. . . . . .132 E5
　Milton Abbot PL19 . . . . .29 C6
　Mount Hawke TR4 . . . . .68 C6
　13 Mousehole TR19. . . . . . .88 C1
　Nanpean PL26. . . . . .58 D7
　Newlyn TR18 . . . . .143 C1
　Newquay TR7. . . . . .110 D6
　Par PL24 . . . . .60 B5
　Penponds TR14. . . . . .138 B1
　Pensilva PL14 . . . . .38 E4
　Plymouth, Devonport PL1 . .127 F2
　Plymouth, Plympton PL7 . . .130 E4
　Plymouth, Tamerton Foliot
　　PL5 . . . . .124 B6
　Polgooth PL26 . . . . .59 A1
　Polruan PL23. . . . . .116 D2
　4 Porthleven TR13. . . . . . . .98 B8
　Port Isaac PL29. . . . . .22 D7
　Praze-an-Beeble TR14. . . . .79 B2
　Probus TR2 . . . . .71 C6
　Redruth TR15. . . . . .140 B5
　Roche PL26 . . . . .46 F2
　St Austell PL25. . . . . .114 C3
　St Cleer PL14. . . . . .37 F3
　St Columb Major TR9 . . . . . . .45 E6
　St Day TR16 . . . . .68 D1
　St Dennis PL26. . . . . .58 C8
　St Erth TR27. . . . . .142 A1
　St Germans PL12. . . . . .65 A8
　St Ives TR26. . . . . .141 B6
　St Just TR19. . . . . .86 F6
　St Stephen PL26 . . . . .58 B4
　St Teath PL30. . . . . .23 E7
　Saltash PL12 . . . . .122 F2
　Sticker PL26 . . . . .58 E1
　7 Stratton EX23. . . . . .4 E1
　Tintagel PL34. . . . . .14 C7
　Torpoint PL11 . . . . .127 B3
　Tregony TR2. . . . . .71 F3
　Troon TR14. . . . . .79 E5
　9 Tywardreath PL24 . . . . . . .60 D5
Forest Ave PL2 . . . . .128 C7
Foresters Rd PL9 . . . . .135 D7
Forest Hos TR4. . . . . .70 D8
Forest View PL6. . . . . .125 D7
FORGE. 68 A4
Forge Ind Pk TR14 . . . . .138 E5
Forge La PL12 . . . . .122 C4
Forge The TR3 . . . . .82 A7
Forge Way TR4 . . . . .69 F6
Forlaze Rd PL27. . . . . .21 D2
Formal Ind Pk TR14 . . . . . . .138 B4
FORRABURY 9 C2
Forrabury Hill **5** PL35 . . . . . . .9 C1
Forreglos Dr **10** TR17 . . . . . . .89 C5
Forresters Dr PL6. . . . . .125 D7
Forsters Ct TR2. . . . . .72 A7
Forsythia Dr PL12. . . . . .122 C3
Fort Austin Ave PL6. . . . . . .125 C1
Fortescue Cl PL26 . . . . .58 D6
Fortescue Pl
　Lostwithiel PL22 . . . . .112 D3
　Plymouth PL3. . . . . .129 A6
Fortescue Terr PL19 . . . . . . .147 A6
Fortesque Ct **3** PL19 . . . . . . .30 A3
Forth an Cos TR3 . . . . .81 B4
Forth-an-Eglas TR16 . . . . . . .68 D1
Forth-an-Nance TR16 . . . . . . .67 C6
Forth-an-Praze
　Illogan TR15 . . . . .139 D8
　St Day TR16 . . . . .68 D1
Forth-an-Ryn TR15. . . . . . . .140 D4
Forth an Streth TR27 . . . . . . .142 E7
Forth an Tewennow TR27 . . .142 D7

Forth-an-Tre TR27 . . . . .142 D7
Forth an Ula TR27 . . . . .142 E7
Forth an Venegh PL31 . . . . .109 E3
Forth an Vre TR27 . . . . .139 A3
Forth Coth TR3 . . . . .82 A7
Forthcrom TR12. . . . . .92 C1
Forth Dall **21** TR16 . . . . .67 E4
Forth Gdns PL3. . . . . .129 D6
Forth Gwedhen TR13 . . . . .146 D8
Forth Kegyn TR15 . . . . .139 B4
Forthnoweth TR15. . . . . . . .140 B5
Forth Noweth **4** TR3 . . . . .81 F7
Forth Scol Camborne TR15 . .139 D7
　6 Porthleven TR13. . . . . . . .98 C8
Forthvean Camborne TR14. .138 D1
　Portreath TR16 . . . . .67 C5
Forth Vean TR13. . . . . .90 E6
Forthvean Cres TR4 . . . . .68 A6
Forthvean Rd TR4, TR16 . . . . .67 F7
Forth Veor TR15. . . . . .140 E7
Forthvras TR15 . . . . .139 B8
Fort Picklecombe PL10 . . . .133 F4
Fort Terr PL6 . . . . .124 F3
Fort The PL10 . . . . .133 A1
Fosbrooke Ct **10** PL3 . . . . . . .128 F6
FOSS 133 A5
Foster Dr PL31 . . . . .109 C3
Fosters La PL34 . . . . .14 C7
Fosters Mdw PL18 . . . . .40 D6
Fosters Way EX23 . . . . .104 F6
Foulston Ave PL5. . . . . .127 B8
Foulston Way PL31 . . . . . . .109 B4
FOUNDRY 142 B5
Foundry TR3 . . . . .80 F3
Foundry Cl **2** TR14. . . . . . . .138 E5
Foundry Dr PL25. . . . . .115 B3
Foundry Flats TR27 . . . . . . .142 B5
Foundry Gdns PL15. . . . . . . .106 B6
Foundry Hill Hayle TR27 . . . .142 B4
　Stithians TR3 . . . . .80 F3
Foundry Ho **3** TR27 . . . . . . .142 B5
Foundry La Hayle TR27 . . . . .142 B5
　Newlyn TR18 . . . . .143 C2
Foundry Mews PL19 . . . . . .147 D6
Foundry Rd Camborne TR14 138 E3
　Kennall Vale TR3 . . . . .81 A4
Foundry Row
　Marhamchurch EX23 . . . . .7 B6
　5 Redruth TR15 . . . . .140 B5
Foundry Sq TR27 . . . . .142 B5
Foundry St **6** PL27 . . . . .108 B5
Foundry Terr **14** PL27 . . . . . .108 B5
Fountain Ct **26** TR18 . . . . . . .143 E6
Fountains Cres PL2. . . . . . . .128 C8
Four Acres Rd TR2. . . . . .83 F6
Four Cross TR10 . . . . .81 C2
Fourgates PL14. . . . . .51 F5
FOUR LANES 80 A5
Four Lanes TR16. . . . . .80 B5
Four Lanes' End TR19 . . . . . . .97 F6
Fourlanesend Com Prim Sch
　PL10 . . . . .132 F3
Four Turnings PL23. . . . . .60 F3
Fowenn Ct **12** PL14 . . . . .113 B6
FOWEY 116 B4
Fowey Com Coll PL23 . . . . . .116 B4
Fowey Com L Ctr PL23 . . . . .116 B4
Fowey Cres **27** PL17. . . . . . . .39 F4
Fowey Gdns PL3. . . . . .129 D6
Fowey Hospl PL23 . . . . .116 C5
Fowey Mus **★** PL23 . . . . . . .116 B4
Fowey Prim Sch PL23. . . . . .116 C4
Fowlfield Row TR13 . . . . .90 F3
Foxdown PL27. . . . . .108 D5
Foxes Field TR18 . . . . .88 E6
Foxes La **5** TR19 . . . . .88 C1
Foxes Row TR16 . . . . .80 E8
Fox Field Cl PL3 . . . . .129 C5
Foxglove Cl PL26 . . . . .46 F3
　Launceston PL15. . . . . .106 E4
Foxglove Cres PL28. . . . . .31 F7
Foxglove End **8** PL20. . . . . . . .42 A2
Foxglove Rd **15** PL31 . . . . . .109 A5
Foxglove Way PL12 . . . . .122 B3
FOXHOLE 58 D5
Foxhole La PL26 . . . . .85 D5
Foxhole Prim Sch PL26 . . . . .58 D5
Fox's La TR11. . . . . .145 B5
Foxstanton Dr TR10. . . . . . .144 D7
Foxs Yd TR10 . . . . .144 A5
Foxtor Cl PL5. . . . . .124 B3
Foxwood Gdns
　Plymouth, Plymstock PL9 . . .135 F5
　Plymouth, Southway PL6. . . .124 E5
Foyle Cl PL7. . . . . .131 A5
FRADDAM. 78 D1
Fraddam Rd TR27 . . . . .78 D1
FRADDON. 45 E1
Fradgan Pl TR18. . . . . .143 C2
Fradgan The **12** TR18 . . . . . .143 C2
Frances St TR1 . . . . .137 C4
Francis La PL27. . . . . .21 D5
Francis Rd PL27 . . . . .21 D5
Francis St PL1. . . . . .148 A3
Frankfort Gate **9** PL1 . . . . . .148 B3
Frankland Cl TR11. . . . . .144 F1
Franklyn Cl PL25 . . . . .114 F5
Franklyns' PL6 . . . . .125 A4
Franklyns Cl PL14. . . . . .125 A4
Franwall Terr **16** TR18 . . . . . .143 C1
Fraser Pl PL5. . . . . .124 C7
Fraser Rd PL5 . . . . .124 C7
Fraser Sq PL5 . . . . .124 C7
FREATHY 65 C3
Frederick Street E PL1. . . . . .148 B3
Frederick Street W **6** PL1 148 B3
Fredington Gr PL2. . . . . .128 B6

Freedom Sq PL4. . . . . .149 B4
Freeman Collins Dr TR11 . .144 F4
Freemans Wharf PL1 . . . . . .134 A8
Fremantle Gdns **4** PL2 . . . .127 F4
Fremantle Pl PL2. . . . . .127 F4
Frenchman's La PL12. . . . . . .53 C4
Frensham Ave PL6. . . . . .125 C7
Frensham Gdns PL6. . . . . . .125 C7
Freshbrook Cl TR18 . . . . .88 E6
Freshford Cl PL6. . . . . .125 C1
Freshford Wlk PL6. . . . . .125 C1
Freshwater La TR2 . . . . .95 B6
Frewin Gdns PL6. . . . . .125 B6
Friars La TR12. . . . . .103 A6
Friar's La TR12 . . . . .102 F6
Friars' La PL1 . . . . .149 A2
Friars La TR12 . . . . .103 B5
Friars Wlk PL19. . . . . .147 E2
Friary Pk PL4. . . . . .149 B3
Friary St PL4 . . . . .149 B3
Frith Rd PL12. . . . . .122 D3
Frobisher App PL5. . . . . .124 D2
Frobisher Dr PL12 . . . . .122 E2
Frobisher Terr **9** TR11 . . . . . .145 A5
Frobisher Way
　Tavistock PL19. . . . . .147 B5
　Torpoint PL11 . . . . .126 D3
Frog La TR2 . . . . .71 F3
Frogmore Ave PL6. . . . . .129 B7
Frogmore Ct PL6. . . . . .129 B7
FROGPOOL. 81 C7
Frogwell Rd PL17. . . . . .39 E4
Frome Cl PL7. . . . . .131 A4
Frontfield Cres PL6. . . . . . . .124 E5
Front Rd PL11 . . . . .64 C4
Frost Ct TR11. . . . . .144 E5
Fuggoe Croft TR26 . . . . .141 C3
Fuggoe La TR26 . . . . .141 C2
Fullaford Rd PL17. . . . . .40 A4
Fuller Rd TR6. . . . . .55 A5
Fullerton Rd PL2 . . . . .128 A5
Fuller-Tre Cl PL26 . . . . .46 F3
Fulmar Rd **10** EX23. . . . . .7 B8
Furland Cl PL9 . . . . .135 C5
Furneaux Ave PL2 . . . . .128 B5
Furneaux Rd PL2 . . . . .128 B6
Furniss Cl **6** TR1. . . . . .137 D4
Furry The TR13 . . . . .146 B5
Furry Way TR13 . . . . .146 B5
Fursdon Cl PL9. . . . . .136 C6
Furse Pk PL5. . . . . .127 C7
Fursey La PL15 . . . . .27 B6
Furzeacre Cl PL7 . . . . .131 A7
Furze Cross EX22. . . . . .8 B5
Furzedown Terr PL13. . . . . .117 C4
Furze Gdns EX23 . . . . .2 D1
Furzehatt Ave PL9 . . . . .136 A6
Furzehatt Park Rd PL9. . . . .136 A6
Furzehatt Rd PL9 . . . . .135 F6
Furzehatt Rise PL9 . . . . .136 A6
Furzehatt Villas PL9 . . . . . . .135 F6
Furzehatt Way PL9 . . . . .136 A6
Furze Hill PL31 . . . . .109 E5
Furzehill Rd PL4. . . . . .128 F4
Furze Park Dr PL12 . . . . .52 F1
Furze Pk Polruan PL23 . . . . .116 D2
　St Issey PL27. . . . . .32 D5
　Trelights PL29 . . . . .22 D6
Furze Pk Dr PL12 . . . . .53 A1
Furze Vale PL25 . . . . .114 F2
FutureWorld@Goonhilly★
　TR12. . . . . .99 F4

G

Gabriel St **5** TR26 . . . . .141 B5
Gadiwall Rise TR27 . . . . .77 E3
Gainsborough Ct TR7. . . . . .110 D5
Gainsborough Ho PL19 . . . . .147 B6
Gains Cross EX22 . . . . .5 F3
Galgeth Rd PL30. . . . . .36 B2
Galileo Cl PL7 . . . . .130 E6
Galingale Dr **4** TR14 . . . . . .138 E5
Gallacher Way PL12. . . . . . .122 B3
Galland Rd TR1. . . . . .69 F4
Gallant's Dr PL23. . . . . .116 B3
Galleon Ct TR7. . . . . .110 D4
Galleries The **46** TR26 . . . . . .141 B6
Gallery La Landrake PL12. . . . .53 A1
　St Germans PL12 . . . . .65 A8
Galligan Cl TR19. . . . . .97 A6
Galligan La TR19 . . . . .97 A6
Gallopine La PL26 . . . . .73 B5
Gallops The PL12. . . . . .122 D4
Galsworthy Cl PL5. . . . . . . .124 C2
Galva Rd PL7 . . . . .131 C8
GAM. 24 A4
Gander La TR13 . . . . .146 B6
GANG. 38 F3
Ganges Cl TR11. . . . . .82 C2
Ganges Rd PL2 . . . . .128 A5
Ganna Park Rd PL3 . . . . .128 D6
Gannel Rd PL7 . . . . .110 E4
Gannel View Cl TR8. . . . . . . .111 B3
Gannet Dr PL25. . . . . .114 F4
Gants La PL9. . . . . .136 B6
Garage Field Pk EX23. . . . . . .5 A6
Garby La PL15 . . . . .140 C3
Garcia Terr PL15 . . . . .106 D4
Garden Cl PL7 . . . . .131 D5
Garden Cres PL1 . . . . .148 B1
Gardeners Way PL27. . . . . . .32 E6
Garden House The★ PL20 . . .42 A3
Garden Mdw TR11 . . . . .144 E3
Garden Park Cl PL9. . . . . . . .136 C7

Garden St PL2. . . . . .127 E4
Garden Village PL9 . . . . .135 F8
Garden Way TR8. . . . . .111 F3
Garden Wk PL26 . . . . .115 A1
Gards La PL5. . . . . .123 E2
Garfield Terr PL1, PL3. . . . . .128 A3
Garland Pl TR14. . . . . .138 D4
Garlidna **24** TR18 . . . . .143 E6
GARRAS 99 D6
Garras Com Prim Sch
　TR12. . . . . .100 A7
Garras Wharf TR1. . . . . .137 D3
Garrett St PL10 . . . . .133 A1
Garrick Cl PL5. . . . . .124 C2
Garris Cotts TR20. . . . . .88 E8
Garrison Cl PL1. . . . . .127 E1
Garro La TR12 . . . . .99 A1
Garston Cl PL9 . . . . .136 A8
Garth-an-Creet TR18. . . . . . .77 A7
Garth Besydhyans **6** TR8 111 D5
Garth Esels **3** TR8. . . . . . . .111 D5
Garth Glasneth **2** TR1 . . . . .137 B2
Garth Marhas TR14. . . . . . . .138 C3
Garth Mengleudh **6** TR7 . .111 E5
Garth Morcom PL14 . . . . . . .113 B5
Garth Rd TR18. . . . . .143 B3
Garth Woryan **7** TR7 . . . . . .111 E5
Gartland Dr **8** PL31 . . . . . . .109 A5
Gascoyne Cl PL4 . . . . .149 A3
Gascoyne Pl PL4. . . . . .149 A3
Gas Hill TR1. . . . . .137 C2
Gashouse La PL4. . . . . .149 B2
Gasking St PL4 . . . . .149 A3
Gas La **8** TR15 . . . . .140 B4
Gas St TR14 . . . . .138 D3
Gateway Ct TR27 . . . . .77 E2
GATHERLEY 19 E1
Gavercoombe Pk **2** PL34 . .14 F7
Gawton Way **5** PL19. . . . . . .147 B7
Gay's Hill TR12, TR13 . . . . . .146 E4
Gdynia Way PL4 . . . . .149 C2
GEAR 99 F7
Gear Hill Madron TR20 . . . . . .88 C8
　Mawgan TR12 . . . . .99 E8
Gear La TR20 . . . . .88 B8
Gears La TR17, TR20. . . . . . . .89 D6
Geasons La PL7 . . . . .130 E5
Gedon Way PL31 . . . . .109 A5
Geevor Cotts TR19. . . . . .86 F8
Geevor Tin Mine Mus★
　TR19. . . . . .74 F1
Geffery Cl PL12. . . . . .53 C3
Gemini Dr PL14. . . . . .113 E7
Gemini Rd PL3 . . . . .136 E8
Gems Bolitho Sch TR13 . . . .143 C5
Gendalls Way PL15 . . . . .106 B8
Gennys Cl PL18. . . . . .40 E6
George Ave PL7 . . . . .130 F6
George Cross PL7 . . . . .130 F5
George Downing Ho PL6. . . .125 A1
Georgel Fox Cl PL15. . . . . . .106 A4
George La PL7. . . . . .130 F5
George Pl PL1. . . . . .148 A2
Georges La PL11. . . . . .65 C6
Georges Paddock PL15 . . . . .27 B3
George Sq PL1 . . . . .127 F1
George St Plymouth PL1 . . . .127 F1
　Truro TR1. . . . . .137 C4
GEORGIA. 76 E3
Georgia Cres PL3. . . . . .129 C6
Georgia Hill TR20. . . . . .76 E3
Geraldine Terr PL12 . . . . . . .122 C1
GERMOE 90 C4
Germoe TR27. . . . . .90 C4
Germoe Com Prim Sch
　TR20. . . . . .90 C4
GERMOE CROSS ROADS 90 C3
Germoe La TR13. . . . . .90 C4
Gernick La TR14. . . . . .79 B3
GERRANS 83 B2
Gerrans Cl PL25 . . . . .115 B5
Gerrans Hill TR1 . . . . .83 B2
Gerrans Parish Her Ctr★
　TR2. . . . . .83 B2
Gerrans Sch TR2. . . . . .95 D7
Gerrans Sq TR2 . . . . .83 B2
Gewans Mdw PL25. . . . . . . .114 E2
Ghost Hill TR12. . . . . .99 A1
Gibbon La PL4. . . . . .149 A3
Gibbons Fields **9** TR12. . . . . .99 A2
Gibbon St PL4. . . . . .149 A3
Gibbs La PL35. . . . . .9 C1
Gibraltar Terr **6** TR2. . . . . . .95 A6
Gibralter Sq **6** EX23. . . . . . . .4 E1
Gibson Way TR13. . . . . .91 B1
Gifford Pl PL3 . . . . .128 D4
Gifford Terrace Rd PL3 . . . . .128 E5
Gig La TR3 . . . . .82 A7
Gilbert Cl PL26 . . . . .58 B4
Gilbert Ct PL7 . . . . .131 B6
Gilbert La PL2. . . . . .128 C5
Gilbert Rd PL31. . . . . .109 F4
GILBERT'S COOMBE. 140 A8
GILLAN. 101 C8
Gillan Cove TR12 . . . . .101 C7
Gill-an-Creet TR26. . . . . .77 A7
Gillbard Centenary Flats
　PL15 . . . . .106 B5
Gillbard Centenary Homes
　PL15 . . . . .106 B5
Gilley La PL26 . . . . .73 A4
Gilliflower Cres **4** PL31 . . . .109 A5
Gilliflower Pl **5** PL14. . . . . .113 D7
Gill Pk PL3 . . . . .129 B5
Gills Cl TR10. . . . . .144 B6
Gilly Fields TR15. . . . . .140 B3
Gilly Gabben Ind Est TR12. . .99 B7
Gilly Hill Cury TR12. . . . . .99 B5

Gilly Hill continued
　Redruth TR15. . . . . .140 C3
　Rosevear TR12 . . . . .99 B6
Gilly La TR26 . . . . .77 C1
Gilston Rd PL12 . . . . .122 D4
Gilwell Ave PL9. . . . . .136 B7
Gilwell Pl PL4. . . . . .149 A3
Gilwell St PL4 . . . . .149 A3
Gipsy La PL14 . . . . .113 A5
Gitchell La Crowlas TR20. . . . .89 C8
　St Erth TR26. . . . . .77 C1
Glade Cl PL6. . . . . .125 A4
Glade The PL6 Crapstone PL20 . . . .42 B2
　St Minver PL27. . . . . .22 A3
Gladstone Rd PL30 . . . . .109 C2
Gladstone Terr
　Longrock TR20. . . . . .88 F6
　3 Redruth TR15 . . . . .140 C5
Gladwell Gdns **10** EX23. . . . . .4 D1
Glamis Rd TR7. . . . . .111 B6
Glantis Cres TR9. . . . . .45 E2
Glanville Rd
　1 Higher Rosewarne
　　TR14. . . . . .138 E5
　Tavistock PL19. . . . . .147 B6
Glanville St PL1, PL4. . . . . . .148 C3
Glanville Terr PL12. . . . . . . .122 F3
Glasney Parc TR10. . . . . . . .144 A8
Glasney Pl TR10 . . . . .144 C7
Glasney Rd TR11. . . . . .145 A5
Glasney Terr TR10 . . . . .144 D7
Glasney View **2** TR10. . . . . .144 A8
Gleaner Cl **1** PL5. . . . . .124 D1
Glebe Ave PL12. . . . . .122 F3
Glebe Cl Mawgan TR12. . . . . .99 D7
　Pelynt PL13. . . . . .62 D5
　6 St Columb Major TR9 . . .45 E6
Glebe Cres PL27 . . . . .32 D6
Glebe Dr PL26 . . . . .46 F3
Glebe Est PL14 . . . . .38 F2
Glebelands Callington PL17. . .39 E5
　Looe PL13 . . . . .117 D5
Glebe Mdw PL17. . . . . .39 E5
Glebe Parc PL30. . . . . .23 E3
Glebe Pl TR12 . . . . .103 B5
Glebe Row TR27. . . . . .142 D7
Glebe Terr Constantine TR11. .92 F4
　Ruan Minor TR12. . . . . . . .103 B5
Glebe The Camborne TR14. . .138 C3
　Cubert TR8. . . . . .55 D8
　St Mellion PL12 . . . . .53 D8
　Tregony TR2 . . . . .71 F4
　Week St Mary EX22 . . . . . . .11 E8
Glenavon Rd PL3 . . . . .128 E5
Glenburn Cl PL3. . . . . .128 E7
Glencross Ct **3** PL14 . . . . . .113 C6
Glen-Dale Cl **3** PL25 . . . . . .115 A5
Glendale Cres TR4. . . . . .68 C6
Glen Dale Cres TR15 . . . . . .140 D4
Glen-Dale Cres PL25 . . . . . .115 A5
Glendorgal Pk **13** PL18. . . . . .40 F5
Glendower Rd PL3. . . . . .128 D5
Glendurgan Gdn★ TR11 . . . . .93 D2
Gleneagle Ave **4** PL3. . . . . .128 F6
Gleneagle Rd PL3 . . . . .128 F6
Gleneagle Villas **5** PL3. . . . .128 F6
Glenfeadon Terr TR16 . . . . . .67 C6
Glenfield Cl PL6. . . . . .125 D6
Glenfield Rd PL6. . . . . .125 C5
Glenfield Way PL6. . . . . .125 C5
GLENHOLT. 125 D6
Glenholt Cl PL6. . . . . .125 D6
Glenholt Rd PL6. . . . . .125 D6
Glenhurst Rd **5** PL3. . . . . . .128 E6
Glen Leigh TR15 . . . . .140 A6
Glenleigh Pk PL26 . . . . .58 E4
Glenmoor La TR12. . . . . .99 A1
Glenmore Ave PL2. . . . . .127 F5
Glenmore Terr
　7 Liskeard PL14. . . . . .113 C6
　Mabe Burnthouse TR10. . . . .81 A1
Glennaven Cl PL7. . . . . .131 C6
Glen Park Ave PL4. . . . . .148 C4
Glen Park Prim Sch
　Plymouth PL7. . . . . .130 E6
　6 Plymouth PL7 . . . . .131 B5
Glen Pk PL14 . . . . .38 D4
Glen Rd
　Plymouth, Mannamead PL3. .128 F5
　Plymouth, Plympton PL7 . . .130 E6
　Wadebridge PL27 . . . . .108 B5
Glenside Rise PL7. . . . . .130 E6
Glenthorne Rd TR3 . . . . .69 C3
Glentor Rd PL3 . . . . .128 E7
Glentowan Rd PL26. . . . . . . .73 C6
Glen Vale TR15 . . . . .139 E6
Glenview PL25 . . . . .114 E3
Glen View Callington PL17 . . . .39 E5
　Penryn TR10. . . . . .144 B8
　Tywardreath PL24. . . . . .60 D5
　Wadebridge PL27 . . . . .108 B4
Glenwood Rd PL3 . . . . .128 E6
Glew Hill TR26. . . . . .77 A4
Globerdon Rd PL14. . . . . .38 E4
Globe Sq TR16. . . . . .139 F2
Gloucester Ave PL25. . . . . . .115 C3
Gloucester Cres TR18. . . . . .143 B1
Gloucester Ct PL1 . . . . .148 C4
Gloucester Pl
　27 Newlyn TR18. . . . . .143 C2
　Plymouth PL1. . . . . .148 C4
Gloucester Rd TR18 . . . . . . .143 C2
GLOWETH. 69 E3
Gloweth View TR1. . . . . .69 E3
Gloweth Villas TR1 . . . . .69 E3
Glubhole La PL15 . . . . .27 B4
GLUVIAN. 45 E2
Gluyas The TR11. . . . . .144 E1

Glynn Ave **8** TR13 . . . . . .146 C5
Glynn Rd Liskeard PL14 . . . .113 A5
  Padstow PL28 . . . . .107 D5
Glynn Valley La **9** PL9 . . . .129 D1
Glyn Way TR3 . . . . .69 D3
Goad Ave Plymouth PL4 . . . .149 C2
  Torpoint PL11 . . . . .126 E3
Goad Cl PL11 . . . . .126 F3
Godding Gdns PL6 . . . . .124 E4
Godolphin Ave TR17 . . . . . . .89 B5
Godolphin Bridge TR27 . . . .90 D7
Godolphin Cl TR17 . . . . .89 B6
Godolphin Cres TR13 . . . . . .90 E6
GODOLPHIN CROSS 90 E6
Godolphin Cross TR13 . . . . .90 E6
Godolphin Ct **5** TR14 . . . .138 C3
Godolphin Dr TR17 . . . . .89 B5
Godolphin Est TR13 . . . . . . .90 E6
Godolphin Ho ★ TR13 . . . . . .90 E6
Godolphin Ho PL19 . . . . . . .147 C5
Godolphin Pk **11** PL17 . . . .39 E4
Godolphin Pl TR17 . . . . .39 E4
Godolphin Prim Sch TR13 . .90 E6
Godolphin Rd
  Falmouth TR11 . . . . .144 F5
  Helston TR13 . . . . .146 C6
  Longrock TR20 . . . . .88 F6
  Pengwedna TR13 . . . . .91 B6
Godolphin Terr TR17 . . . . . . .89 B5
Godolphin Way TR7 . . . . . . .111 B7
Godrevy Ct TR26 . . . . .141 D2
Godrevy Dr TR27 . . . . .142 E6
Godrevy Ho TR1 . . . . .69 C4
Godrevy Terr **28** TR26 . . . .141 B6
GODREVY TOWANS 66 B3
GOLANT 61 A5
GOLBERDON 39 C6
Golberdon Rd PL17 . . . . . . .39 A5
Goldbank Bglws PL30 . . . . . .34 C2
Golden Bank Pk TR11 . . . . .144 E1
Golden Sands **11** TR6 . . . . .55 A5
Goldfinch Cl PL15 . . . . .106 E4
Goldfinch Gdns PL19 . . . . .147 D2
Goldfinch Gr PL12 . . . . .122 D4
Goldmartin Cl TR11 . . . . . . .93 D3
Goldmartin Sq TR11 . . . . . . .93 D3
GOLDSITHNEY 89 D5
Goldsmith Gdns PL5 . . . . . .124 D3
Goldsworthy Dr EX23 . . . . .104 F5
Goldsworthy Way PL27 . . . .108 B5
Golf Course Hill PL21 . . . . . .22 D2
Golf House Rd EX23 . . . . . .104 D6
Golf Links Rd PL20 . . . . .42 A1
Golf Terr TR7 . . . . .110 C6
Golf View TR14 . . . . .79 B2
Golitha Falls National Nature
  Reserve ★ PL14 . . . . .37 D3
Golitha Rise PL14 . . . . .113 C6
GOLLAWATER 55 A1
Golva Cl TR13 . . . . .91 E4
GONAMENA 38 B5
GONVENA 108 C6
Gonvena Hill PL27 . . . . .108 D6
Gonvena Ho PL27 . . . . .108 C6
Gonwin Manor Dr TR26 . . . .141 E1
Goodern Drive TR3 69
Goodeve Cl PL9 . . . . .135 E6
Goodmans La PL14 . . . . .38 D4
Goodwin Ave PL6 . . . . .125 A6
Goodwin Cres PL2 . . . . .128 A6
Goonbarn Cotts PL26 . . . . . .58 C5
Goonabarn Rd PL26 . . . . . . .58 C5
Goonamarris PL26 . . . . .58 C6
Goonavean Pk PL26 . . . . . . .58 D5
Goonbarrow Mdw PL26 . . . . .47 C1
GOONBELL 68 D8
GOON GUMPAS 68 F1
Goongumpas La TR16 . . . . . .68 E1
GOONHAVERN 55 D4
Goonhavern Ind Est TR4 . . . .55 C4
Goonhavern Prim Sch TR4 . .55 D4
Goonhilly Cl TR4 . . . . .55 C4
Goonhilly Downs
  Trevassack TR12 . . . . .99 F4
  Trezise TR12 . . . . .100 C4
GOONHUSBAND 146 C1
Goonlaze TR5 . . . . .54 D1
Goonlaze Terr TR3 . . . . .80 D4
GOONOWN 54 D1
Goonown La TR5 . . . . .54 D1
Goonown Rd Goonbell TR5 . .68 D8
  St Agnes TR5 . . . . .54 D1
Goonrawe TR16 . . . . .67 F4
Goonrea PL13 . . . . .117 B4
Goonreeve TR10 . . . . .81 D3
Goonvean Hill PL26 . . . . .58 B5
Goonvean La TR12 . . . . .103 C7
GOONVREA 68 B8
Goonvrea TR3 . . . . .81 D5
Goonvrea Cl TR10 . . . . .110 F4
Goonvrea Ct TR7 . . . . .110 F4
Goonvrea Rd TR5 . . . . .54 C1
Goonwartha Cl PL13 . . . . . .117 C4
Goonwartha Rd PL13 . . . . . .117 B3
Gooseberry La Pensilva PL14 .38 E4
  Plymouth PL1 . . . . .148 B2
Gooseford La PL11 . . . . .132 C8
GOOSEHAM 2 E3
Goosewell Hill PL6 . . . . .129 C8
Goosewell Park Rd PL9 . . . .135 F6
Goosewell Prim Sch PL9 . . .135 F6
Goosewell Rd PL9 . . . . .135 F5
Goosewell Terr PL9 . . . . . . .135 F6
Gorbut Gdns PL9 . . . . .147 D4
Gordon Ct PL12 . . . . .122 D2
Gordon Pl **8** TR9 . . . . .45 E6
Gordons Cl TR3 . . . . .80 F3

Gordon Terr PL4 . . . . .128 E4
GORRAN CHURCHTOWN 73 B1
GORRAN HAVEN 85 D5
GORRAN HIGH LANES 72 F2
Gorran Sch PL26 . . . . .85 B5
Gorse Cl TR7 . . . . .111 A4
Gorsey Cl PL5 . . . . .124 E2
Gorvin Cross EX39 . . . . .3 E6
GOSS MOOR NATIONAL NATURE
  Reserve ★ PL26 . . . . .46 B2
Goswela Cl PL26 . . . . .135 F5
Goswela Gdns PL9 . . . . .135 F5
Gotch Gdns PL14 . . . . .50 B6
GOTHERS 46 D1
Gothers Hill Hendra PL26 . . .58 C8
  St Dennis PL26 . . . . .46 D1
Gothers Rd PL26 . . . . .46 D1
Goudges La PL26 . . . . .58 E8
Gounce The **14** TR6 . . . . . . .55 A5
Gover Cl TR7 . . . . .68 C5
Gover Hill TR4 . . . . .68 C6
Gover La TR7 . . . . .110 D6
Gover Rd PL25 . . . . .114 B4
Goverseth Hill PL26 . . . . .58 D6
Goverseth Rd PL26 . . . . .58 D6
Goverseth Terr PL26 . . . . . . .58 D6
GOVER VALLEY 59 A4
Govetts Field **5** PL15 . . . .106 D4
Gower Ridge Rd PL9 . . . . . .135 D6
Goyne's Field TR4 . . . . .68 A7
Gracca Terr PL26 . . . . .47 C1
Grade Rd TR12 . . . . .102 F4
Grade-Ruan CE Prim Sch
  TR12 . . . . .103 B5
Grafton Rd PL4 . . . . .128 E4
Graham Ave PL25 . . . . .114 E4
Graham Rd TR15 . . . . .140 C5
Grainge Rd PL6 . . . . .125 A1
Grammers Park PL15 . . . . . .106 A5
GRAMPOUND 72 B7
Grampound Hill TR2 . . . . . . .72 B7
GRAMPOUND ROAD 57 E1
Grampound Road Ind Est
  TR2 . . . . .57 E1
Grampound Road Village CE
  Sch TR2 . . . . .57 E1
Grampound-with-Creed CE
  Sch TR2 . . . . .72 A7
Granby Ct PL1 . . . . .127 E2
Granby Gn PL1 . . . . .127 E2
Granby Pl PL1 . . . . .127 E2
Granby St PL1 . . . . .127 E2
Granby Way PL1 . . . . .127 E2
Grand Hotel Rd PL1 . . . . . . .148 B1
Grand Par PL1 . . . . .148 B1
Grange Rd Helston TR13 . . .146 B5
  Plymouth PL7 . . . . .131 A4
  Yelverton PL20 . . . . .42 C3
Grange The **14** TR14 . . . . .138 D3
Granite Way Callington PL17 .39 F4
  Trembraze PL14 . . . . .113 D8
Grannery Ct EX23 . . . . .104 D5
Granny Polly La TR13 . . . . . .90 E5
Granny's Gn PL31 . . . . .109 E3
Granny's La TR5 . . . . .55 A4
Grantham Cl PL7 . . . . .130 B4
Grantley Gdns PL3 . . . . .129 A5
Grant's Ct PL25 . . . . .114 C3
Grant's Wlk **4** PL25 . . . . . .114 C3
Granville Terr EX23 . . . . . . .104 D5
Grasmere Cl PL6 . . . . .124 E5
Grasmere La PL14 . . . . .38 B5
Grassendale Ave PL2 . . . . . .127 F7
Grass La PL2 . . . . .128 C6
Grassmere Way PL12 . . . . . .122 D4
Grass Valley Pk PL31 . . . . . .109 F1
Grassy La PL14 . . . . .36 E1
Gratton Cross PL20 . . . . .42 D2
Gratton La PL20 . . . . .42 D2
Gratton Pl PL6 . . . . .125 A1
Gravellings La PL30 . . . . .22 F5
Gravesend Gdns PL11 . . . . .127 B3
Gravesend Wlk PL5 . . . . . . .123 D4
Graybridge Rd
  12 Horrabridge PL20 . . . . .42 C4
  Horrabridge PL20 . . . . .42 C4
Gray Cres PL5 . . . . .127 C8
GREAT BOSULLOW 87 D8
Great Berry Rd PL6 . . . . . . .124 F1
Great Charles Cl PL26 . . . . . .58 B4
Great Churchway PL9 . . . . . .136 A7
Greatfield Rd PL7 . . . . .129 B7
Greatlands Cres PL2 . . . . . .128 A6
Greatlands Pl **5** PL2 . . . . .128 A5
Great Mdw PL14 . . . . .36 F2
Great Mills Ind Parc PL25 . .115 E4
Great Mis Tor Cl **5** PL20 . . .42 C3
Great Orchard Cl PL9 . . . . . .135 E5
Great Park Cl **4** PL7 . . . . .131 C5
Great Western Commercial
  Village PL22 . . . . .112 D2
Great Western Rd PL1 . . . . .148 B1
Great Wheal Seton TR14 . . .138 F6
Greatwood PL11 . . . . .82 C3
Great Woodford Dr PL7 . . . .130 B6
Great Work TR13 . . . . .90 E5
Grebe Cl PL7 . . . . .130 F5
Greeb Way TR20 . . . . .89 D4
Green Acre PL15 . . . . .28 A5
Greenacres Bodmin PL30 . . .34 C2
  Plymouth PL9 . . . . .135 F8
Greenbank
  Connor Downs TR27 . . . . . .78 C6
  1 Penzance TR18 . . . . . . .143 D5
  Plymouth PL4 . . . . .149 A4
  Polruan PL23 . . . . .116 D2
  Whitehill TR13 . . . . .146 C4
Greenbank Ave PL4 . . . . . . .149 B3

Greenbank Cl TR2 . . . . .57 E1
Greenbank Cottages PL4 . . .149 B4
Greenbank Cres TR7 . . . . . .111 C7
Greenbank La PL14 . . . . . . .113 C6
Greenbank Rd Devoran TR3 . .81 F6
  Liskeard PL14 . . . . .113 C6
  Plymouth PL4 . . . . .149 B4
Greenbanks Rd PL27 . . . . . . .21 E2
Greenbank Terr
  1 Callington PL17 . . . . . . .39 F4
  Plymouth PL4 . . . . .149 B4
GREEN BOTTOM 69 B4
Greenbury TR20 . . . . .90 A4
Green Cl Feock TR3 . . . . .82 C5
  Truro TR1 . . . . .137 B3
Green Cres TR13 . . . . .146 D7
Greendale Rd PL2 . . . . .128 A7
Green Field Cl TR12 . . . . . . .102 F2
Greenfield Rd PL12 . . . . . . .122 D2
Greenfields Cl TR11 . . . . .93 D3
Greenfield Terr TR16 . . . . . . .67 D6
Greenfinch Cres PL12 . . . . .122 D4
Green Hill Lamerton PL19 . . .30 A3
  St Martin TR12 . . . . .100 D6
  Tavistock PL19 . . . . .147 D5
  Wadebridge PL27 . . . . . . .108 E5
Greenhill Cl PL9 . . . . .135 F5
Greenhill Rd PL9 . . . . .136 A5
Greenhills PL32 . . . . .105 C5
Green Hill Terr TR12 . . . . . .100 D6
Green Hill Villas PL7 . . . . . .108 E5
Greenla Treator PL28 . . . . . . .21 A2
  Treator PL28 . . . . .21 A2
Green La Bodmin PL31 . . . . .109 F2
  Boscastle PL35 . . . . .9 C1
  Crantock TR8 . . . . .43 D3
  Fowey PL23 . . . . .116 C5
  Gwithian TR27 . . . . .66 B2
  Kingsand PL10 . . . . .133 A2
  Lelant TR26 . . . . .77 E4
  Lizard TR12 . . . . .103 A4
  Marazion TR17 . . . . .89 B6
  Penryn TR10 . . . . .144 B8
  Porthleven TR13 . . . . .91 B1
  Portreath TR16 . . . . .67 C6
  Redruth, Plain-an-Gwarry
    TR15 . . . . .137 B3
  Redruth, Wheal Rose TR16 . .68 C4
  Rock PL27 . . . . .21 D2
  Tavistock PL19 . . . . .30 F1
  Tavistock PL19 . . . . .147 E5
  Tremough TR10 . . . . .81 D1
  Truro TR1 . . . . .137 B3
  Veryan TR2 . . . . .83 F6
  Yelverton PL20 . . . . .42 C1
Greenland PL10 . . . . .132 F5
Greenlands Est PL19 . . . . . .147 D5
Green Lane EX39 . . . . .3 A7
Green Lane Cl TR10 . . . . . . .144 B8
Green Lane Hill TR18 . . . . . .143 F8
Green Lane Vean TR15 . . . .140 B5
Green La The W TR17 . . . . . .89 B6
Green La The TR27 . . . . .77 F1
Greenlees Dr PL7 . . . . .131 B3
Greenmarket The **26** TR18 .143 E5
Green Mdws PL32 . . . . .105 C4
Green Parc Rd TR27 . . . . . . .142 D5
Green Park Ave PL4 . . . . . . .128 D4
Green Park Rd PL9 . . . . .135 D4
Green Pk PL10 . . . . .133 A2
Greenscoombe La PL17 . . . . .40 C8
GREENSPLAT 59 A6
Greensplat Rd PL25 . . . . . . .114 A6
Green St Penzance TR18 . . . .143 F4
  Truro TR1 . . . . .137 D4
Greens The TR19 . . . . .96 C7
Greensway Rd PL19 . . . . . . .147 A4
Green The Bridgerule EX22 . . .8 A5
  5 Horrabridge PL20 . . . . . .42 C5
  Kingsand PL10 . . . . .133 A2
  Meavy PL20 . . . . .42 F2
  Milton Combe PL20 . . . . . .120 F8
  Nancegollan TR13 . . . . .91 B7
  Plymouth, Ernesettle PL5 . .123 E3
  Plymouth, Hooe PL9 . . . . .135 B6
  Probus TR2 . . . . .71 C6
  St Buryan TR19 . . . . .97 A6
  St Martin TR12 . . . . .100 D6
  Saltash PL12 . . . . .122 C3
  6 Trewoon PL25 . . . . .59 A3
Greenvalley Rd PL31 . . . . . .109 A5
Greenway Ave PL7 . . . . .130 B6
Greenway Cl **2** PL20 . . . . . .42 E3
Greenwich Pl PL12 . . . . .122 F3
Greenwith Cl TR11 . . . . .137 B3
Greenwith Cres TR3 . . . . . . .81 D6
Greenwith Hill TR3 . . . . .81 D6
Greenwith Rd TR3 . . . . .81 D6
Greenwix Parc PL30 . . . . . . .34 D8
Greenwood Cres PL14 . . . . .144 A8
Greenwood Park Cl PL7 . . . .131 B6
Greenwood Park Rd PL7 . . .131 B6
Greenwood Rd TR10 . . . . . .144 A8
Gregor Rd TR1 . . . . .137 F5
Gregory's Ct **10** PL31 . . . .109 D5
Gregory's Mdw PL15 . . . . . .106 C4
Grenfell Ave PL12 . . . . .122 D3
Grenfell Gdns PL12 . . . . . . .122 C3
Grenfell St **13** TR14 . . . . . .88 C1
Grenifer Rd TR15 . . . . .139 D7
Grenna La TR3 . . . . .81 D7
GRENOFEN 42 A6
Grenofen Cl PL19 . . . . .42 A6
Grenville Cl Callington PL17 . .39 F4
  Nanpean PL26 . . . . .58 D6
Grenville Cres TR11 . . . . . . .144 F5
Grenville Ct Plymouth PL7 . .131 C6

Grenville Ct continued
  2 St Austell PL25 . . . . . . .114 C3
Grenville Dr **6** St Agnes TR5 .54 D1
  Tavistock PL19 . . . . .147 B3
Grenville Gdns TR14 . . . . . . .79 E5
Grenville Mdws
  Lostwithiel PL22 . . . . .112 E2
  St Austell PL25 . . . . .58 D7
Grenville Meadow PL19 . . . .147 B3
Grenville Pk PL20 . . . . .42 D2
Grenville Rd Falmouth TR11 .145 A5
  Helston TR13 . . . . .146 D5
  Lostwithiel PL22 . . . . .112 D2
  Padstow PL28 . . . . .107 C4
  Plymouth PL4 . . . . .149 C3
  Truro TR1 . . . . .137 B5
Grenville Road Lane S PL4 .129 B2
Grenville Wlk PL13 . . . . .62 D2
Gresham La Newquay TR7 . .110 F4
  Plymouth PL5 . . . . .124 C7
Greyfriars TR11 . . . . .145 C2
Grey Mare Hill PL27 . . . . . . .49 B7
Greys Terr **1** TR16 . . . . . . .140 F1
Greystoke Ave PL6 . . . . .129 C7
Greystone Ave PL26 . . . . . . .58 E5
Greystones TR9 . . . . .57 E8
Gribbas Cl TR3 . . . . .80 F3
Gribbas Cnr TR3 . . . . .80 F3
Gribben Cl PL25 . . . . .114 E6
Gribben Rd PL25 . . . . .114 E6
Gribbon Way PL24 . . . . .60 C4
Griffins The PL14 . . . . .113 D6
Griffin Way PL9 . . . . .136 C6
Griggs Cl PL7 . . . . .131 B4
Griggs Hill TR27 . . . . .77 E3
GRIMSCOTT 5 A2
Grimscott Est EX23 . . . . .5 B2
Grimspound Cl PL6 . . . . . . .129 E8
Grimstone Terr PL20 . . . . . . .42 B2
Grist La TR27 . . . . .78 C5
Grizedale Rd PL6 . . . . .129 D7
Grose Hill Cres **11** PL26 . . . .59 D7
Grose Mdws PL26 . . . . .58 B8
Grosvenor Ave TR7 . . . . . . .110 E6
Grosvenor Cotts **1** PL4 . . .128 F4
Grosvenor Pl PL25 . . . . .114 B4
Grosvenor Rd PL6 . . . . .124 F2
Grove Cl **2** PL6 . . . . .124 C6
Grove Cotts TR2 . . . . .57 C1
Grove Dr **4** PL14 . . . . .51 A7
Grove Hill
  Mawnan Smith TR11 . . . . . .93 D3
  St Mawes TR11 . . . . .95 A6
Grovehill Cres TR11 . . . . . . .145 C3
Grovehill Dr TR11 . . . . .145 C3
Grovehill Ho TR11 . . . . .145 B3
Grove La TR20 . . . . .89 F5
Grove Park Ct PL14 . . . . . . .113 B4
Grove Pk Par PL24 . . . . .60 C6
  Tavistock PL19 . . . . .147 D5
  Torpoint PL11 . . . . .126 E3
Grove Pl **3** TR11 . . . . .145 C3
Grove Rd Par PL24 . . . . .115 F6
  St Austell PL25 . . . . .59 F5
Grove The
  Plymouth, Plymstock PL9 . .135 D8
  Plymouth, Stoke PL3 . . . . .128 A4
Grovewood Ct TR9 . . . . .45 E1
Growan Rd PL25 . . . . .115 A6
GRUMBLA 87 C4
Grylls Parc TR13 . . . . .146 B6
Grylls Pk PL13 . . . . .62 A7
Guardian Ct **6** PL31 . . . . .109 E5
Guelder Way **4** PL6 . . . . . .124 C6
Gue The **2** TR13 . . . . .98 C8
GUILDFORD 142 E6
Guildford Cl Foxhole PL26 . . .58 D6
  Plymouth PL5 . . . . .124 E3
Guildford Rd TR27 . . . . .142 E7
Guildford Road Ind Est
  TR27 . . . . .142 E6
Guildford St PL4 . . . . .149 A3
Guildhall La PL22 . . . . .112 C2
Guildhall Sq PL1 . . . . .148 C2
Guineaport Parc PL27 . . . . .108 C5
Guineaport Rd PL27 . . . . . . .108 C5
Guipavas Rd PL17 . . . . .39 F4
Guissney Pl TR13 . . . . .91 B1
Gulland Rd PL27 . . . . .21 D6
Gull Rock Newquay TR7 . . . .110 A5
  Wadebridge PL27 . . . . .21 D2
GULVAL 88 E6
Gulval Almshouses TR18 . . .143 F8
Gulval Comm Prim Sch
  TR18 . . . . .88 E6
Gulval Cross TR18 . . . . .143 F8
GULWORTHY 41 B8
Gulworthy Cotts PL19 . . . . . .41 B7
Gulworthy Cross PL19 . . . . . .41 B7
Gulworthy Prim Sch PL19 . . .41 B7
Gun Hill Rd TR8 . . . . .43 B1
GUNNISLAKE 40 F5
Gunnislake Prim Sch PL18 . .40 F6
Gunnislake Rural Workshops
  PL18 . . . . .40 F6
Gunnislake Sta PL18 . . . . . . .40 E4
Gunpool La **9** PL35 . . . . . . .9 C1
Gunver PL28 . . . . .31 F7
GUNWALLOE 98 E5
Gunwalloe Rd TR12 . . . . .99 A7
Gunwennap PL32 . . . . .10 D2
Gunwin Ct PL26 . . . . .58 D8
Gurlyn Hill TR20 . . . . .90 A7
Gurnard Wlk PL3 . . . . .129 C6
Gurney Cl Bude EX23 . . . . . .104 E7
  Torpoint PL11 . . . . .126 F3
Gurney's La **2** TR14 . . . . . .138 D3
Gurneys Mews **6** TR14 . . . .138 D3

Gurnick Est TR18 . . . . .143 B2
Gurnick Rd TR18 . . . . .143 B1
Gurnick St **24** TR19 . . . . . . .88 C1
Gustavus Rd TR14 . . . . .138 D3
Gustory Rd TR8 . . . . .43 D3
Gutt Rd PL27 . . . . .22 C2
Guy Miles Way PL5 . . . . .124 B3
GWALLON 89 C6
Gwallon La TR17 . . . . .89 C6
Gwallon Rd PL25 . . . . .114 C5
Gwarak Agravayn **1** TR7 . .111 E6
Gwarak An Warak TR1 . . . . .137 B2
Gwarak Esels TR8 . . . . .111 D5
Gwarak Gwel An Mor
  Portscatho TR2 . . . . .83 B2
  9 Portscatho TR2 . . . . . . .95 D8
Gwarak Nansavalen **1**
  TR1 . . . . .137 B2
Gwarak Tewdar TR1 . . . . . . .137 B2
Gwarak Trystan **1** TR7 . . . .111 D6
Gwarder Pl **2** TR14 . . . . . .138 D4
Gwarnick Rd TR1 . . . . .137 B4
Gwartha Cl PL25 . . . . .115 C4
Gwarth an Drae TR13 . . . . .146 C8
Gwarth an Dre TR27 . . . . . .142 E8
GWAVAS 91 D4
Gwavas Bglws **4** TR18 . . . .143 C1
Gwavas La TR18 . . . . .88 C2
Gwavas Quay **7** TR18 . . . . .143 C2
Gwavas Rd TR18 . . . . .143 C1
Gwavas St **9** TR18 . . . . . . .143 C6
Gweal-an-Top TR15 . . . . . . .140 D5
Gweal Darras TR10 . . . . .81 C1
Gwealdues TR13 . . . . .146 C7
Gwealdues Ct TR13 . . . . . . .146 C7
GWEALFOLDS 146 C7
Gwealfolds Rd TR13 . . . . . .146 C7
Gweal Gollas TR27 . . . . .142 E8
Gweal Mellin TR11 . . . . .93 A3
Gweal Pawl TR15 . . . . .140 A4
Gweal Wartha TR13 . . . . . . .146 B8
Gweal Wollas Fields **3**
  TR12 . . . . .99 A4
Gwedhennek TR18 . . . . .143 F7
GWEDNA TR13 . . . . .90 F7
GWEEK 92 C1
Gweek Downs TR12 . . . . .92 B2
Gweek Dr Gweek TR12 . . . . .92 C1
  Mawgan TR12 . . . . .99 D8
Gweek La TR13 . . . . .92 A3
Gweek Quay TR12 . . . . .92 A1
Gwel an Garrek **2** TR12 . . . .99 A1
Gwel-an-mor
  1 Marazion TR17 . . . . .89 C5
  St Austell PL25 . . . . .115 A5
  Trenance TR8 . . . . .31 C2
Gwel-an-mor Apartments
  TR26 . . . . .141 C4
Gwelanmor Cl TR26 . . . . . . .141 D2
Gwelanmor Rd TR26 . . . . . .141 D2
Gwel-an-Nans Cl **2** PL14 .113 B5
Gwel-an-Scol TR3 . . . . .82 C5
Gwel-an-Skol TR14 . . . . . . .138 E5
Gwel an Wheal TR26 . . . . . .141 A4
Gwel an Wheal Cres TR26 . .141 A4
Gwel Avon Bsns Pk PL12 . . .122 C4
Gwelavon Cl PL27 . . . . .108 D5
Gwelenys Rd **3** TR19 . . . . .88 C1
Gwel Eryon **3** TR14 . . . . . .138 F2
Gwel Gwarthe TR16 . . . . . . .68 C3
Gwel Kann TR15 . . . . .139 C8
Gwel Ke **3** TR1 . . . . .137 B2
Gwell-an-Nans TR2 . . . . .71 C6
Gwel Lewern TR18 . . . . .88 E6
Gwel Marten Flats TR26 . . . .141 E2
Gwelmeneth TR13 . . . . .146 B4
Gwelmeneth Pk **8** PL14 . . .38 A3
Gwel Mengleth PL27 . . . . . .108 D5
Gwelmor TR14 . . . . .138 E2
Gwel-Mor **9** TR19 . . . . .75 A1
Gwel-Tek TR27 . . . . .142 D8
Gwel Trencrom TR27 . . . . . .142 B3
Gwendra La PL25 . . . . .58 E8
Gwendreath Gwente TR12 . .103 C7
  Trelan TR12 . . . . .100 C1
Gwendroc Cl TR1 . . . . .137 D3
Gwendroc Ho TR1 . . . . .137 D3
Gwendroc House Mews
  TR1 . . . . .137 D3
Gwendrona Cl TR13 . . . . . . .146 D8
Gwendrona Way TR13 . . . . .146 D8
GWENNAP 80 F7
Gwennap Pit ★ TR16 . . . . . .140 F4
Gwenter Rd TR12 . . . . .103 D7
Gwindra Ind Est PL26 . . . . . .58 C3
Gwindra Rd PL26 . . . . .58 B4
GWINEAR 78 D4
Gwinear Com Prim Sch
  TR27 . . . . .78 E4
Gwinear La TR27 . . . . .78 E4
Gwinear Rd TR27 . . . . .78 E5
GWITHIAN 66 B2
Gwithian Cl St Austell PL25 .114 C7
  Torpoint PL11 . . . . .126 F4
Gwithian Green Nature
  Reserve ★ TR27 . . . . .78 C8
Gwithian La **1** TR10 . . . . .144 A8
Gwithian Rd PL25 . . . . .114 C7
  Connor Downs TR27 . . . . . .78 D6
Gwithian Sands Chalet Pk
  TR27 . . . . .66 B1
GWITHIAN TOWANS 66 A2

Gwithian Towans TR27....78 C7
Gwithian Towans Nature Reserve★ TR27....78 B8
Gwyn Rd PL4....149 C4
Gwythian Way TR6....55 A4
Gyllyng Hall TR11....145 B3
Gyllyng St TR11....145 B4
Gyllyngvase Hill TR11....145 B2
Gyllyngvase Rd TR11....145 C2
Gyllyngvase Terr TR11....145 C2
Gypsy Corner Rd PL30....46 D7
Gypsy La Delabole PL33....14 C1
  St Elvan TR13....91 C2

H

Haddington Rd PL2....127 F4
Haddon Way PL25....115 D3
Haddy's Row PL14....39 A2
Haig Pl 6 TR18....143 C7
Hain Wlk TR26....141 C4
Halabezack TR13....92 C8
HALAMANNING....90 A6
Halbullock View TR1....69 E3
Halcyon Ct PL2....128 A6
Halcyon Rd PL2....128 A6
Haldon Pl PL5....124 A3
Halecombe Rd 10 PL9....129 D1
HALE MILLS....69 A1
Haley Barton 4 PL2....128 A5
HALGABRON....14 E7
Halgavor La Bodmin PL31....109 E2
  Little Kirland PL31....48 C8
Halgavor Pk PL31....109 F1
Halgavor Rd PL30, PL31....109 D2
Halgavor View PL31....109 F2
Halifax Rd PL27....31 F3
Halimote Rd PL26....58 C8
Hallane Rd PL25....115 A6
Hallan Vean TR19....96 A6
Hallaze Rd PL26....59 D7
Hallerton Cl PL6....125 E2
Hallett Cl PL12....122 B3
Hallett Way EX23....104 F7
HALLEW....47 C2
Hallew Rd PL26....58 C7
Halley Gdns PL5....123 E1
Hall for Cornwall (Theatre) The★ 21 TR1....137 D4
HALLIVICK....58 A4
Halloon Ave 9 TR9....45 E2
Hall Rd PL26....58 C8
Hall Terr PL23....116 E5
HALLWORTHY....16 D6
HALSETOWN....77 A5
Halsetown Rd TR26....77 A6
Halter Cl 2 PL5....124 C8
Halton Quay
  Bohetherick PL18....40 E1
  Greenbank PL20....118 D8
Halt Rd Goonhavern TR4....55 D4
  St Newlyn East TR8....56 B7
Halvana TR15....140 D3
Halvarras Pk TR3....82 B8
Halvarras Rd TR3....82 B8
Halvasso Herniss TR10....80 F1
  3 Longdowns TR10....81 A1
Halveor Cl 5 TR9....45 E6
Halveor Ct TR6....55 B5
Halveor La TR9....45 D6
HALVOSSO....93 A8
HALWIN....92 B8
Halwin Cres TR13....92 B8
Halwin La TR13....92 B8
Halwin Sch TR13....92 C8
Halwyn Ave Crantock TR8....110 A3
  Trevella TR8....43 E3
Halwyn Cl 12 TR3....81 F7
Halwyn Hill TR8....110 A3
Halwyn Pl TR1....137 B4
Halwyn Rd TR8....110 A3
Halwyn Terr TR1....137 B3
Halye Vw PL27....108 A6
HAM....128 A8
Hamble Cl PL3....129 D7
Ham Cl PL2....128 B8
Ham Dr PL2....128 B8
Ham Field PL27....21 D5
Ham Gn PL2....128 A7
Ham Green Ct PL2....128 A7
Ham Green La PL2....128 A7
Ham Ho PL2....128 A8
Hamilton Cl TR27....142 B4
Hamilton Gdns PL4....128 D4
Hamilton Pl TR11....145 D3
Ham La PL2....128 A8
Hammer Dr PL25....114 E7
Hammill's Cl 13 TR13....98 C8
Hammills Dr 12 TR13....98 C8
Hamoaze Ave PL5....127 D8
Hamoaze Pl PL1....127 D2
Hamoaze Rd PL11....127 B2
Hampton Cl TR7....110 D6
Hampton St PL4....149 A3
Hancock Cl PL6....124 D6
Hancock La 14 TR2....95 A6
Hangar La 4 PL6....125 B5
Hangmans Hill TR14....79 F3
Hangmans La 32 PL17....39 F4
Hangmans Wlk TR11....145 A1
Hannaford Rd PL16....19 F3
HANNAFORE....117 C2
Hannafore PL13....117 C3

Hannafore La PL13....117 D2
Hannafore Rd PL13....117 D2
Hanover Cl
  17 Perranporth TR6....55 A5
  Plymouth PL3....129 B5
Hanover Ct Camborne TR14....138 E4
  10 Penzance TR18....143 E5
  16 Plymouth PL1....149 A2
Hanover Ho EX23....4 D4
Hanover Parc TR9....45 F2
Hanover Pk TR9....45 F2
Hanover Rd PL3....129 C4
Hanson Dr PL23....116 C3
Hanson Rd PL14....113 D6
Harbour Ave Plymouth PL4....149 A2
  Plymouth, Camels Head PL5....127 E8
Harbour Ct Falmouth TR11....145 B4
  15 Penzance TR18....143 E5
  Portreath TR16....67 C6
Harbour Lights 11 TR18....143 C1
Harbour Mews
  2 Carn Towan TR19....86 D1
  Sennen Cove TR19....96 B7
Harbour Rd Par PL24....60 C4
  Wadebridge PL27....108 C5
Harbourside 12 TR13....98 B8
Harbour Side PL13....117 C3
Harbour St PL11....127 B3
Harbour Terr
  Falmouth TR11....145 B4
  Portreath TR16....67 C6
Harbour View Fowey PL23....116 C4
  Hayle TR27....142 B5
  Marazion TR17....89 B5
  Penryn TR10....144 B8
  Plymouth PL9....135 A7
  5 Porthleven TR13....98 B8
  Saltash PL12....122 E2
  Truro TR1....137 E3
Harbour View Cres TR18....143 E6
HARCOURT....82 B4
Harcourt Cl TR1....69 F3
Harcourt La TR3....82 B5
Harding Mdw PL13....63 F8
Hardings Cl PL12....122 E3
HARDISWORTHY....2 D7
Hardisworthy Cross EX39....2 E7
Hardwick Farm PL7....130 C3
Hardwick Cres PL5....124 E1
Hardy Ho TR3....80 F3
Harebell Cl PL12....122 D4
Hareston Cl PL7....131 B3
Harewood Cl PL7....130 E5
Harewood Cres PL5....124 E2
Harewood Rd PL18....41 A3
Hargood Terr 6 PL2....127 F4
Hargreaves Cl PL5....123 F2
Harlech Cl PL3....129 A7
Harleigh Rd PL31....109 E3
Harleigh Terr PL31....109 E3
Harlequins 27 TR26....141 B5
HARLYN....20 D2
Harlyn Barton PL28....20 D2
Harlyn Cotts PL28....20 D2
Harlyn Drive PL2....128 D8
Harlyn Rd PL28....20 D1
Harmer Cl PL31....109 D6
Harmony Cl Redruth TR15....140 B6
  Roche PL26....46 F3
Harmony Mdw PL26....46 F3
Harmony Rd PL26....46 F3
Harmony Terr
  4 Illogan TR16....67 E4
  Truro TR1....137 E2
Harnorlen Rd PL2....128 D7
Haroldsleigh Ave PL5....124 E2
Harpers Mdw PL15....27 B7
Harriet Gdns PL7....130 B6
Harriet Pl TR11....145 A5
Harris Cl PL17....39 F6
Harris Ct 1 Penryn TR10....144 C7
  Plymouth PL5....135 B6
Harris Mill TR16....67 F4
Harrison Gdns PL15....139 D7
Harrison St 7 PL2....127 F4
Harrison Terr TR1....137 B4
Harriss Hill TR3....82 A7
HARROWBARROW....40 D4
Harrowbarrow Sch PL17....40 D4
Hartland Cl PL6....125 E2
Hartland Forest Golf & Leisure Parc EX39....3 E6
Hartland Rd PL29....22 E7
Hartland Terr EX23....104 D6
HARTLEY....128 E7
Hartley Ave PL3....129 A6
Hartley Ct PL3....129 A6
Hartley Park Gdns PL3....128 F6
Hartley Rd PL3....128 E6
HARTLEY VALE....129 A8
Hartmeade PL4....52 A5
Hartwell Ave PL9....136 D7
Harvenna Cl TR9....45 E1
Harvenna Hts TR9....45 E1
Harvest Cl 1 PL5....124 C8
Harvest Moon TR7....110 D7
Harvey Ave PL4....129 B1
Harvey Rd PL3....137 D2
Harvey St PL11....127 B3
Harvey's Towans TR27....142 A7
Harvey's Way TR27....142 C5
Harwell Ct 8 PL1....148 B3
Harwell St PL1....148 B3
Harwood Ave PL5....124 C7
Hastings St PL1....148 B3
Hastings Terr PL1....148 B3

Haswell Cl PL6....129 A8
Hatch's Hill TR27....78 C5
Hatfield Cres TR7....110 B5
Hat La PL10....132 F2
HATT....53 E4
Havelock Terr PL2....127 F3
Haven Ct TR27....142 C5
Haven Pk PL14....39 A2
Haven Rd EX23....10 C6
Havett Cl PL14....50 E8
Havett Rd Dobwalls PL14....50 E8
  Dobwalls PL14....50 E8
Haviland Rd PL14....113 E4
Hawarden Cotts PL4....129 B1
Haweswater Cl PL6....124 E4
Hawke Cl TR7....110 D6
Hawkens Way 9 TR9....45 D6
Hawke Rd TR13....146 D4
Hawkers Ave PL4....149 A2
Hawkers Ct EX23....104 D7
Hawkers La PL3....128 E5
Hawkey Mews TR15....140 D2
Hawkinge Gdns PL5....123 E4
Hawkins Cl PL6....125 A5
Hawkins Ct 2 TR18....143 D5
Hawkins Way Newquay TR7....110 E5
  Padstow PL28....107 C5
  Penzance TR18....143 D5
Hawkins Way
  12 Falmouth TR11....145 A4
  Helston TR13....146 D6
Hawks Pk PL12....122 C4
Hawk's Tor Dr PL15....27 B7
Hawthorn Ave Bude EX23....104 E4
  Torpoint PL11....126 F3
Hawthorn Cl Bude EX23....104 E4
  Camelford PL32....105 D4
  Plymouth, Hooe PL9....135 C5
  Plymouth, Woolwell PL6....125 D7
  Redruth TR15....140 B6
  St Austell PL25....114 F4
  7 St Columb Major TR9....45 D6
Hawthorn Gr PL2....128 C7
Hawthorn Rd PL19....147 C2
Hawthorns PL12....122 D2
Hawthorn Way
  Plymouth PL3....129 B7
  Threemilestone TR3....69 C3
Haxter Cl PL6....121 B1
Haydon Gr PL5....123 C1
Haydown Cl PL30....24 B4
HAYE....39 D4
Haye Common Dr PL15....106 D3
Haye La PL17....39 E5
Haye Rd Callington PL17....39 D4
  Plymouth PL7, PL9....130 C1
Haye Rd S PL9....136 C7
Hayes Pl PL6....129 B8
Hayes Rd PL25....135 C7
Hay La Looe PL13....117 E4
  Sheviock PL11....65 B6
HAYLE....142 C6
Hayle Community School TR27....142 D5
Hayle Ind Pk TR27....142 F7
Hayle Rd Crowntown TR13....91 A6
  Fraddam TR27....78 C1
Hayle Sta TR27....142 B5
Hayle Terr TR27....142 C6
Hayman Way TR11....144 E5
Hayne Corfe Cres TR1....137 A4
Hayne Corfe Gdns TR1....137 A4
Haystone Pl PL1....148 B4
Haytor Pl PL5....124 B3
Hazel Cl Plymouth PL6....125 B6
  St Austell PL25....115 A6
Hazel Dr Pl 9....136 C7
Hazel Gr Plymouth PL9....136 C7
  Yelverton PL20....42 D3
Hazelmead PL14....113 B5
Hazelmere Dr PL25....115 B4
Hazel Rd PL19....147 C2
Hazelwood Cres PL9....136 D7
Hazelwood Dr PL6....125 D8
Hazelwood Rd PL14....39 F4
Heabrook Parc 2 TR18....143 C7
Hea Cl TR18....143 C7
Hea Cotts 5 TR18....143 C7
Head La TR5....68 D8
Headland Cl TR26....141 E2
Headland Cotts
  Coverack TR12....103 H7
  Newquay TR7....110 C8
Headland Ct TR26....141 E2
Headland Pk PL4....149 A4
Headland Point TR7....110 C7
Headland Rd
  Carbis Bay TR26....141 E2
  Newquay TR7....110 C7
Headlands The TR6....55 A5
Headleigh Rd TR7....110 F5
Headon Cross EX23....11 A5
Healy Ct 9 PL2....127 F4
Healy Pl PL2....127 F4
HEAMOOR....143 B7
Heamoor Com Prim Sch
  Heamoor TR18....88 B5
  Heamoor TR18....143 B6
Heanton Terr
  Millbrook PL10....132 E6
  Redruth TR15....140 C4
Heanton Villas TR15....140 C4
Hea Rd TR18....143 C7
Hearl Rd PL12....122 B3
Heatherbell Gdns TR26....141 E1
Heather Cl Heamoor TR18....143 B7
  Tavistock PL19....147 D4
Heather Gdns 16 PL31....109 A5

Heather La TR27....77 D2
Heather Mdw TR9....45 E1
Heathers The Foxhole PL26....125 D7
  Plymouth PL25....125 D7
Heather Vean TR3....69 D4
Heather Way TR20....89 F4
Heathfield Gdns TR15....140 E7
Heathfield Pk PL26....42 D3
Heathfield Rd PL4....129 B3
Heathlands Bsns Pk PL14....113 C5
  PL14....113 C5
Heathlands Ind Est 9
  PL14....113 C5
Heathlands Rd PL14....113 C5
Heath Terr PL18....40 F5
Heavitree Rd PL10....133 A2
Hedgerow Cl PL6....125 E8
Hedgerow La PL26....58 B4
Hedgerows The PL12....122 B3
Hedingham Cl PL7....131 C4
Hedingham Gdns PL6....125 B7
Helca Dr TR26....141 C3
HELE....13 C2
HELEBRIDGE....7 A6
Helebridge Rd EX23....7 B6
Hele Cross PL15....13 E3
Hele Gdns PL7....131 A4
Hele La PL6....121 F2
Helena Ct 7 PL26....59 D7
Hele Rd Bude EX23....104 F1
  Marhamchurch EX23....7 A6
Hele's Sch PL7....130 C6
Hele's Terr PL4....129 B2
HELFORD....93 B1
HELFORD PASSAGE....93 C2
Heligan Ho PL26....73 A5
Heligan La PL30....34 F7
HELLAND....35 A5
Helland TR10....93 B6
Helland Rd PL31....109 E6
Hellescoth Way
  Helston TR13....146 D8
  13 Tremenheere TR13....146 D8
Hellescott Rd PL15....18 B7
Hellesvean 2 TR26....77 A6
Hellesvean Cl 3 TR26....77 A6
HELLESVEOR....77 A7
Helleur 4 PL24....60 B4
Hellis Wartha TR13....146 D5
Helman Tor View PL31....109 E2
Helnoweth Cotts TR18....143 F8
Helnoweth Gdns TR18....143 F8
Helnoweth Hill TR18....143 F8
Helscott Rd EX23....7 A6
HELSTON....146 D6
Helston Business Pk TR13....146 D5
Helston Com Coll TR13....146 C7
Helston Com Hosp TR13....146 D3
HELSTONE....58 C8
Helston Folk Mus★ TR13....146 B5
Helston Relief Rd TR13....146 E6
Helston Sp Ctr TR13....146 C7
Hemball Cl 5 PL25....59 A3
Hemball La PL25....59 A3
Hembal Rd Burngullow PL26....58 F3
  4 Trewoon PL25....59 A3
HEMERDON....131 D7
Hemerdon Hts PL7....131 A6
Hemerdon La PL7....131 C8
Hemerdon Way PL7....130 D6
HENAFORD....2 F5
Hendergulling PL13....62 F4
Henders Cnr 6 PL2....128 F6
Henderson Pl PL2....127 F6
HENDRA Bodmin....46 F7
  Camelford....105 A4
  Mullion....102 F7
  St Dennis....58 C8
Hendra Barton TR1....137 B5
Hendraburnick Down PL32....15 E6
Hendra Cl Ashton TR13....90 E3
  Liskeard PL14....38 A4
  Stithians TR3....80 E4
  5 Truro TR1....137 C5
Hendra Garth PL15....17 C6
Hendra Gdns PL15....106 B5
Hendra Hts PL26....58 C8
Hendra La Ashton TR13....90 D2
  Hendra PL30....23 A2
  Trewethern PL27....22 F2
  Truro TR1....137 C5
Hendra Parc PL14....113 E7
Hendra Pk PL15....106 B5
Hendra Prazey PL26....58 B8
Hendra Rd St Dennis PL26....58 B8
  Stithians TR3....80 E4
  Truro TR1....137 C5
Hendra Road PL32....15 E7
Hendras Ct TR26....141 E2
Hendras Parc TR26....141 D2
Hendra Terr TR3....80 E4
Hendra Tor View PL15....26 C7
Hendra Vale PL15....106 B4
Hendra Vean
  Carbis Bay TR26....141 E1
  Truro TR1....137 B5
Hendrawna La TR6....55 B4
Hendrawna Mdws 1 TR6....55 B4
Hendwell Cl PL6....124 E6
Henfor Cl 12 TR17....89 C5
HENFORD....15 D7
Henford Grange PL14....113 A6
Henfor Mews 6 TR17....89 C5
Henfor Terr 13 TR17....89 C5

Hengar La PL30....23 F3
Henley Cl TR4....68 C6
Henley Cres TR4....68 C6
Henley Dr Mount Hawke TR4....68 C6
  Plymouth PL5....124 C7
Henliston Dr TR13....146 C4
Henry Avent Gdns PL9....136 C8
Henry Scott Tuke Ho 5
  TR11....145 A4
Henrys Croft 18 TR12....102 F2
Hensbarrow Hill PL26....59 A7
Hensbarrow Mdws PL26....58 D5
Hensbury La PL20....119 F4
Henscol TR16....80 C6
Henscol Praze TR16....80 D6
Henscol Vale PL14....113 A6
Henshorn Ct TR13....146 C7
Hental 3 TR6....55 A4
Henver Ct TR27....78 E3
Henver Ct TR7....111 C7
Henver Gdns TR27....78 E3
Henver La TR4....56 A3
Henver Rd TR7....111 B7
Henvor Ct TR15....140 D6
Henvor Terr TR15....140 E7
HENWOOD....38 B8
Henwood Cres TR7....111 C7
Hen Wythva TR14....138 E2
Herbert Pl PL2....127 E4
Herbert St PL2....127 E4
Hercules Rd Plymouth PL9....130 E1
  Plymouth PL9....136 D8
Hereford Rd PL5....124 B5
Heritage Cl PL12....122 C3
Heritage Pk PL19....147 D6
Herland Hill TR13....78 D4
Herland Pk TR13....90 D5
Herland Rd TR13....90 E6
Hermes Cl TR13....146 D5
Hermes Rd TR13....146 C4
Hermitage Ct 1 PL4....128 E4
Hermitage Rd
  Plymouth PL3....128 E5
  Roche PL26....46 F3
HERNISS....80 F1
Herniss La TR10....80 F1
HERODSFOOT....50 E3
Heron Cl Millbrook PL10....132 F6
  Tresillian TR2....70 C5
Heron Rd 9 PL18....40 F5
Herons Ct 13 TR6....55 A5
Heron Way TR1....137 E1
Herring Cl PL14....113 D7
Herring Rd PL14....113 D7
Herschel Gdns PL5....123 E1
Hersham Cross EX23....5 B2
Hertland Wlk PL27....128 A7
Heskyn View 3 PL12....52 F2
Hessary Dr PL6....121 C1
Hessary Ho 1 PL14....113 D6
Hessary View Saltash PL12....122 E4
  Tavistock PL19....147 B6
HESSENFORD....64 C6
Hessenford Rd PL13, PL11....64 B6
Hetling Cl PL1....148 B3
HEWAS WATER....72 D8
Hewer's Row PL4....149 A3
Hewitt Cl PL12....122 C1
Hexham Pl PL2....128 A8
Hexton Hill Rd PL9....135 D4
Hexton Quay PL9....135 C6
Heybrook Ave PL5....123 C1
Heybrook Mews PL7....110 D6
Hibernia Rd TR13....146 D4
Hibernia Terr PL5....127 E8
Hichens La TR11....145 A5
Hichens Rd TR13....146 D4
Hickory Dr PL7....131 B5
Hicks Cl TR2....71 C6
Hick's La PL4....124 D4
Hidden Valley Discovery Pk★
  PL15....18 A3
Hidderley Park TR14....138 E5
High Atlantic TR8....44 C6
Highbridge Ct PL7....130 E5
Highburrow 24 TR13....98 C8
Highburrow Ct TR15....139 C5
Highburrow La TR15....139 C5
Highbury PL17....38 E8
Highbury Cres PL7....130 D7
Highclere Gdns PL6....125 D8
Highcliff PL27....21 D5
Highcliffe PL27....21 D5
Highcombe La PL9....135 C4
High Cross Lanivet PL30....47 F5
  Porth Navas TR11....93 A4
  12 St Columb Major TR9....45 D6
  Treviades TR11....93 A4
  Truro TR1....137 D4
High Cross St PL25....114 C4
Higher Albion Row TR16....80 F4
Higher Anderton Rd PL10....132 F5
HIGHER BAL....54 B2
Higher Beech Terr PL13....117 C4
Higher Besore Rd TR3....69 C4
Higher Bodiniel Rd PL31....109 C7
Higher Bojewyan TR19....75 B1
Higher Bohenna 14 TR6....55 A4
Higher Bore St PL31....109 C5
HIGHER BOSCASWELL....75 A1
Higher Boskerris TR26....141 D1
HIGHER BREA....139 B3
Higher Bridge Pk PL27....108 D5
Higher Broad La TR15....139 D7
Higher Bugle Bugle PL26....47 C1
  Stenalees PL26....59 C8
Higher Burrow Cl TR26....141 A4
HIGHER CARNKIE....139 F2

Higher Chapel St PL13 . . . . . . .117 D3
Higher Church St **3** TR27 . 142 D6
Higher Churchway PL9 . . 136 A7
Higher Cl PL27 . . . . .108 E4
Higher Cleaverfield PL15 . 106 C7
HIGHERCLIFF 63 B8
HIGHER COMPTON 129 A6
Higher Compton Rd PL3 . 128 F6
HIGHER CONDURROW 139 A1
Higher Condurrow TR14 . 139 A1
Higher Cotts TR2 . . . . 57 C1
HIGHER CRACKINGTON. 10 C6
Higher Crill TR11 . . . . .114 E6
Higher Croft Parc **17** TR12 102 F2
Higher Cross PL32 . . . . . . 105 E4
Higher Daws La PL15 . . . . . 18 E2
HIGHER DOWNS 89 F5
Higher Drym TR27 . . . . 90 F8
Higher East St **9** TR9 . . . . . 45 E6
Higher Efford Rd PL3 . . . 129 B5
Higher Elms PL27 . . . . 21 F3
Higher Fernleigh Rd PL27 108 C4
Higher Fore St
  Marazion TR17 . . . . 89 C5
  Redruth TR15 . . . . 140 C5
Higher Glen Pk PL14 . . . . . 38 D4
Higher Goongumpas La
  TR16 . . . . 68 F1
Higher Green St TR18 . . . . 143 D1
Higher Grumbla TR20 . . . . 87 C4
Higher Gwavas Rd **3**
  TR18 . . . . 143 C1
Higher Kehelland
  Kehelland TR14 . . . . 79 A7
  Nancemellin TR14 . . . . 66 E1
  Nancemellin TR14 . . . . 79 A7
  Trehill PL18 . . . . 40 F4
Higher Kelly Calstock PL18 . 41 A3
Higher Kenneggy TR20 . . . 90 A3
Higher La Ashton TR13 . . . . 90 E3
  Clapper PL27 . . . . 108 E5
  Mawgan TR12 . . . . 99 D7
  Plymouth PL1 . . . . 148 C2
  Wadebridge PL27 . . . . . . 108 E4
Higher Lariggan TR18 . . . 143 D4
HIGHER LARRICK 27 E5
Higher Lavorrick PL26 . . . . 73 C4
Higher Lidden Rd PL14 . . .143 C3
Higher Lux St PL14 . . . . . . 113 C6
Higher Market St
  Looe PL13 . . . . .117 D3
  Penryn TR10 . . . . 144 C7
Higher Mdw PL14 . . . . 50 E4
Higher Medrose PL33 . . . . . 14 E3
Higher Middle Hill PL14 . . 38 D4
Higher Moor TR12 . . . . . . 103 A5
Highermoor Cross EX22 . . . 5 E1
Higher Mount Ambrose La
  TR15 . . . . 140 D6
Higher Mowles PL3 . . . . . 129 B6
Higher Newham La TR1 . . 137 D2
Higher Ninnis TR16 . . . . . 140 F4
Higher Park Cl PL7 . . . . . . 131 B3
Higher Park Stenak TR16 . . 80 F8
Higher Pengegon TR14 . . 138 F2
Higher Penponds Rd TR14 . 79 B5
Higher Pentire TR12 . . . . 146 A1
Higher Pentreath **4** TR20 . 90 B3
Higher Peverell Rd TR18 . 143 E7
Higher Polladras **3** TR13 . 90 F5
Higher Polsue Way TR2 . . . 70 F5
HIGHER PORTHPEAN 59 D1
Higher Port View PL12 . . 122 F2
Higher Pumpfield Row
  TR15 . . . . 139 B6
Higher Railway Terr TR16 . 80 F8
Higher Rd Breage TR13 . . . 90 F3
  Pensilva PL14 . . . . 38 D4
  Polmenna PL14 . . . . 36 E1
Higher Redannick TR1 . . . 137 B3
HIGHER ROSEWARNE 138 D5
Higher Row Ashton TR13 . . . 90 E3
  Kingsand PL10 . . . . 133 A2
Higher Silver Hill TR13 . . 146 C6
Higher Stennack TR26 . . . 141 A5
Higher Stert Terr PL4 . . . 149 C3
Higher Tamar Terr PL18 . . . 41 A7
Higher Terr TR3 . . . . 81 B4
HIGHER TOLCARNE 45 B8
Higher Tower Rd TR7 . . . .110 C6
HIGHERTOWN Camelford . . 24 E8
  Truro 69 F3
Highertown Portscatho TR2 . 83 B7
  Truro TR1 . . . . 69 F3
Highertown Pk PL12 . . . . . 53 C3
Higher Tregajorran TR15 . 139 C3
Higher Tregenna Rd TR26 141 B3
Higher Treglyn PL27 . . . . . 22 B3
Higher Trehaverne TR1 . . 137 C6
Higher Treluswell TR10 . . . 81 D2
Higher Tremena PL25 . . . .114 C4
Higher Trenant Rd PL27 . 108 D6
Higher Trengr TR11 . . . . . . 92 D6
Higher Trerank PL26 . . . . . 46 F2
Higher Tresavean Terr
  TR16 . . . . 80 C6
Higher Trevithick TR27 . . 142 D5
Higher Trevorian Barns
  TR19 . . . . 97 B7
Higher Trewidden Rd
  TR26 . . . . 141 B4
HIGHER TREWINCE 44 E6
Higher Trezaise PL26 . . . . . 47 A1
Higher Tristram PL27 . . . . . 21 D5
Higher Vicarage La **7**
  TR12 . . . . 99 A1
Higherwell Cl TR7 . . . . . . .111 A4
Higher Well La TR13 . . . . 146 C6

Higher Well Pk PL26 . . . . . 73 C3
Higher West End PL26 . . . . 73 C6
Higher Wharf EX23 . . . . . 104 D4
Higher Whiterock PL27 . . 108 B5
Higher Woodford La PL7 . 130 C7
Higher Woodside PL25 . . 114 A4
Highfield Ave
  St Austell PL25 . . . . 114 D3
  13 St Columb Major TR9 . . 45 D6
Highfield Cl Plymouth PL3 . 129 C5
  St Austell PL25 . . . . 114 D3
Highfield Ct **9** TR5 . . . . 54 D1
Highfield Est **9** TR14 . . . . . 38 E4
Highfield Park Rd PL15 . . 106 A5
Highfield Pk PL12 . . . . 122 B3
Highfield Rd
  Camelford PL32 . . . . 105 C3
  Falmouth TR11 . . . . 144 F4
  Mount Hawke TR4 . . . . 68 C6
Highfields Rd Ind Est PL32 105 C3
Highfields **19** TR18 . . . . . . 143 C2
Highfield View **3** PL5 . . . 124 C8
Highgate Hill **1** TR9 . . . . . 45 E1
Highglen Dr PL7 . . . . .131 B7
High La Higher Treslea PL30 . 36 A3
  Tregonwell TR12 . . . . 100 F7
  Trezance PL30 . . . . 35 F4
  Trudgwell TR12 . . . . .101 A8
Highland Pk Penryn TR10 . 144 B8
  Redruth TR15 . . . . 140 C5
Highlands PL9 . . . . 136 B3
HIGHLANES 32 B7
HIGH LANES 142 D5
High Lanes Cubert TR8 . . . 55 E8
  Hayle TR27 . . . . 142 D5
High Lanes Rd
  Leedstown TR27 . . . . 78 F1
  Tremayne TR14 . . . . 79 A2
Highmoor PL15 . . . . 12 B4
High Pk PL12 . . . . 52 F6
High St **14** PL15 . . . . 106 C6
  Boscastle PL35 . . . . 9 D1
  Camelford PL32 . . . . 105 C3
  Chacewater TR4 . . . . 68 F3
  Delabole PL33 . . . . 14 D3
  Falmouth TR11 . . . . 145 B5
  Launceston PL15 . . . . 106 C6
  Padstow PL28 . . . . 107 D5
  Penzance TR18 . . . . 143 E5
  3 Plymouth PL1 . . . . 149 A2
  Plymouth, Stonehouse PL1 . 128 A2
  Probus TR2 . . . . 71 C6
  St Ives TR26 . . . . 141 B6
  St Keverne TR12 . . . . 101 C4
HIGH STREET 58 D4
High Street Hill PL26 . . . . . 58 D2
High Street Ind Est PL26 . . 58 D3
High Street Prim Sch PL12 . 58 D4
High Street & Waterloo Street
  Flats PL1 . . . . 128 A1
Hightrip La PL17 . . . . 39 F7
High Trip La PL17 . . . . 40 A8
Highview TR4 . . . . 68 E5
Highview Cl PL14 . . . . 38 A2
Highview Cres TR4 . . . . 68 E5
High View Prim Sch PL3 . 129 D6
Highway PL14 . . . . 50 B6
Highway La PL15 . . . . 140 D7
Highwood Pk PL14 . . . . 50 E2
Higman Cl PL14 . . . . 50 E2
Hilda Row PL25 . . . . 114 E7
Hilgrove Rd TR7 . . . . .111 A6
HILL 10 B5
Hill Bunkers PL30 . . . . 47 E2
Hill Church TR4 . . . . 68 F2
Hill Cl Heamoor TR18 . . . . 143 B7
  Plymouth PL7 . . . . 130 D4
  St Breward PL30 . . . . 24 B3
Hillcrest Helston TR13 . . . 146 C7
  Shortlanesend TR4 . . . . 69 F6
Hill Crest PL3 . . . . 128 E5
Hillcrest Ave TR1 . . . . 137 A5
Hillcrest Cl Plymouth PL7 . 131 A5
  14 St Columb Major TR9 . . 45 E6
Hillcrest Dr PL7 . . . . 131 A4
Hillcrest Gdns **3** TR13 . . 146 C6
Hillcrest Rd TR27 . . . . 142 D6
Hilldale Rd PL9 . . . . 135 E6
Hilldean Cl PL5 . . . . 124 C7
Hill Gdns PL12 . . . . .119 A2
Hill Hay Cl PL23 . . . . .116 A4
Hillhead Gdns PL32 . . . . . 105 D4
Hillhead Rd TR11 . . . . 144 C5
Hillhead Rise TR11 . . . . . 144 C4
Hill La PL3 . . . . 128 F7
Hillocks The PL13 . . . . . . .117 D4
Hillpark Cotts PL15 . . . . . 106 D6
Hill Park Cres
  Plymouth PL4 . . . . 149 A4
  St Austell PL25 . . . . 114 A2
Hillpark La PL30 . . . . 35 E3
Hill Park Mews PL4 . . . . . 149 B4
Hill Path PL5 . . . . 123 F5
Hill Pk PL27 . . . . 108 D6
Hill Rd Hill EX23 . . . . 10 B5
  Wadebridge PL27 . . . . . . 108 C5
  Welltown PL30 . . . . 36 B2
Hillsborough **2** PL4 . . . . 128 F4
Hillsborough Cross EX22 . . 8 D7
Hillsdale Bglws TR13 . . . . . 90 F5
Hillsdunne Rd PL3 . . . . . . 128 E6
Hillside Grampound Road TR2 . 57 E1
  Lanivet PL30 . . . . 47 E3
  Portreath TR16 . . . . 67 C6

Hillside continued
  St Austell PL25 . . . . 115 B3
  Trewalland TR19 . . . . 86 F8
Hillside Ave Par PL24 . . . . . 60 B4
  Plymouth PL4 . . . . 128 D4
  Saltash PL12 . . . . 122 F3
Hillside Cl PL20 . . . . 41 F3
Hillside Cres PL9 . . . . 135 F8
Hillside Ct Angarrack TR27 . 78 C5
  21 Yelverton PL20 . . . . . . 41 B1
Hillside Gdns PL22 . . . . . . 112 C2
Hillside Ind Est TR16 . . . . 140 E8
Hillside Mdw TR10 . . . . . . 144 D7
Hillside Mdws PL26 . . . . . . 58 D5
Hillside Parc TR20 . . . . 88 B7
Hillside Pk PL31 . . . . 109 D5
Hillside Rd Boslowick TR11 . 144 F2
  Falmouth TR11 . . . . 144 F2
  St Austell PL25 . . . . 114 D5
  Saltash PL12 . . . . 122 E3
Hillside Terr
  Carharrack TR16 . . . . 80 E8
  Downderry PL11 . . . . 64 C5
  Looe PL13 . . . . .117 D4
  22 Newlyn TR18 . . . . 143 C2
  2 Redruth TR15 . . . . . . 140 C5
Hillside Villas PL13 . . . . . .117 F5
Hillson Cl PL29 . . . . 22 E7
Hill St Padstow PL28 . . . . 107 D5
  Plymouth PL4 . . . . 149 A3
Hillsview PL13 . . . . 62 D2
Hilltop Cotts PL8 . . . . 136 F5
Hill Top Crest PL5 . . . . . . 123 E2
Hill View PL20 . . . . 41 F3
Hilton Ave PL5 . . . . 124 D1
Hilton Rd EX23 . . . . 7 B6
Hingston Ct PL6 . . . . 129 A8
HINGSTON DOWN 40 B6
Hinton Ct PL6 . . . . 125 C1
Hirmandale Rd PL5 . . . . . 123 F3
Hirst Ho TR14 . . . . 139 A4
Hobart St PL1 . . . . 148 A2
Hobbacott La EX23 . . . . 7 B6
Hobbacott Rise EX23 . . . . . 7 B6
Hobbs Cres PL12 . . . . 122 C3
Hockens La PL23 . . . . 116 C2
Hockin Cl PL17 . . . . 39 E6
Hockings Gn **7** PL14 . . . .113 D7
Hockings Ho PL14 . . . . 37 F3
Hodders Way PL12 . . . . . .119 A2
Hodge Cl PL12 . . . . 122 C2
Hoe App PL1 . . . . 148 C2
Hoe Ct PL1 . . . . 148 C2
Hoegate Cl PL1 . . . . 148 C2
Hoegate Pl PL1 . . . . 148 C2
Hoegate St PL1 . . . . 149 A2
Hoe Gdns PL1 . . . . 148 C2
Hoe Rd PL1 . . . . 148 C1
Hoe St PL1 . . . . 148 C2
Hoe The PL1 . . . . 148 C1
Hogarth Cl PL9 . . . . 136 B6
Hogarth Ho **2** PL19 . . . . 147 B6
Hogarth Wlk PL9 . . . . 136 B6
Holberton La PL25 . . . . . .114 F7
Holbeton Gdns **3** PL28 . 107 C4
Holborn Pl PL7 . . . . 130 E6
Holborn St PL4 . . . . 149 B2
Holcombe Dr PL9 . . . . 135 F5
Holcroft Cl PL12 . . . . 122 D2
Holdsworth St PL4 . . . . . . 148 B4
Holebay Cl PL9 . . . . 136 A5
Hole Cross PL20 . . . . 119 E7
Hole La PL14 . . . . 36 E1
Hole Rd PL20 . . . . 120 A5
HOLESTROW 102 E2
Hollabury Rd EX23 . . . . . . 104 F7
Hollacombe Brake PL9 . . 136 C1
HOLLACOMBE HILL 136 A2
Holland Rd
  Plymouth, Chaddlewood
    PL7 . . . . 131 D5
  Plymouth, Peverell PL3 . . 128 E6
  Plymouth, Plymstock PL9 . 135 F6
  Widegates PL13 . . . . 63 E7
Hollies Cl PL15 . . . . 106 B7
Hollies Rd PL15 . . . . 106 C6
Hollies The TR27 . . . . 142 B6
Hollong Pk PL11 . . . . 65 E5
Holloway Gdns PL9 . . . . . 136 A5
Hollowell Ho **1** PL35 . . . . 9 C2
Hollow Hayes PL6 . . . . . . 129 B8
Hollow's Terr TR27 . . . . . 142 E7
Hollows The PL9 . . . . 136 B8
Holly Cl TR3 . . . . 69 C3
Hollycroft Rd PL3 . . . . 129 A7
Holly Ct PL6 . . . . 129 E7
Holly Park Cl PL5 . . . . 124 A5
Holly Park Dr PL5 . . . . . . 124 A5
Holly Terr **9** TR18 . . . . . 143 C7
Hollywood Head PL30 . . . . 35 C8
Hollywood Terr PL1 . . . . . 148 A3
Holman Ave TR14 . . . . . . 138 C4
Holman Ct PL2 . . . . 128 C8
Holman Rd PL14 . . . . .113 E6
Holmans Bldgs PL1 . . . . . 127 D2
Holmans Mdw PL15 . . . . . . 19 C1
Holmans Moor Rd TR26 . . 76 E4
Holman's Pl **1** TR13 . . . . . 98 C8
Holman's Terr TR16 . . . . . . 80 B5
HOLMBUSH 115 B4
Holmbush Arch Rd PL25 . 115 B3
Holmbush Hill PL17 . . . . . . 39 F7
Holmbush Ind Est PL25 . 115 B4
Holmbush Rd PL25 . . . . . .115 C4
Holmer Down PL6 . . . . . . 125 D7
Holmes Ave PL3 . . . . 129 B5
Holmes Way **4** PL31 . . . 109 F3
Holmwood Ave PL9 . . . . . 135 E5

Holne Chase PL6 . . . . 125 B7
Holnicote Rd EX23 . . . . . . 104 E5
Holt **5** PL7 . . . . 42 D3
Holt Cres TR7 . . . . 110 D5
Holtwood Rd PL6 . . . . 125 D6
Holwell Cl PL9 . . . . 136 A5
Holy Cross RC Prim Sch
  PL4 . . . . 149 A3
Holyrood La PL1 . . . . 148 C2
Holyrood Pl PL1 . . . . 148 C2
Holyway Cross PL15 . . . . . . 18 A1
HOLYWELL 43 B2
Holywell Bay Fun Pk★ TR8 . 43 C1
Holywell Ct TR3 . . . . 82 B8
Holywell Rd Cubert TR8 . . . 55 D8
  Holywell TR8 . . . . 43 B2
  Liskeard PL14 . . . . .113 E6
  Newquay TR7 . . . . 110 F6
  Playing Place TR3 . . . . 82 B8
Home Farm La TR14 . . . . 138 D8
Home Farm Rd PL9 . . . . . 135 E8
Homefield Pk PL31 . . . . . 109 F3
Home Park Ave PL3 . . . . . 128 E6
Home Park (Plymouth Argyle
  FC) PL2 . . . . 128 C5
Home Park Rd PL12 . . . . . 123 A3
Home Pk Kilkhampton EX23 . 5 A6
  Landrake PL12 . . . . 53 C3
  Plymouth PL2 . . . . 127 F4
Homer Park Lane S PL9 . . 135 C5
Homer Park Rd PL8 . . . . . . 20 F2
Homer Pk Plymouth PL9 . . 135 C5
  Saltash PL12 . . . . 122 D3
  13 Trewetha PL29 . . . . 22 D7
Homer Rise PL9 . . . . 136 B7
Homer Water Pk PL26 . . . . 58 B4
Homestead Ct TR11 . . . . . 144 F6
Home Sweet Home Terr
  PL4 . . . . 149 C2
Homeyard Homes The TR2 . 83 F6
Honcray PL9 . . . . 135 D8
Honeypin Gr **8** PL14 . . . .113 D7
Honeysuckle Cl
  Plymouth PL6 . . . . 125 D5
  Saltash PL12 . . . . 122 D4
Honeysuckle Gdns PL15 . 106 A4
HONICKNOWLE 124 B2
Honicknowle PL5 . . . . 124 B2
Honicknowle Gn PL5 . . . . 124 B2
Honicknowle La PL5 . . . . . 124 B1
Honicombe Cnr PL17 . . . . . 40 C5
Honicombe Pk PL17 . . . . . . 40 E5
Honiton Cl PL5 . . . . 124 B3
Honiton La PL15 . . . . 27 E7
Honiton Wlk PL5 . . . . 124 B4
Hood Hill TR14 . . . . 79 A6
HOOE 135 C5
Hooe Hill PL9 . . . . 135 D5
Hooe La PL9 . . . . 135 D3
Hooe Lake La PL10 . . . . . 133 C4
Hooe Manor PL9 . . . . 135 C5
Hooe Prim Sch PL9 . . . . . 135 B5
Hooe Rd PL9 . . . . 135 C5
Hooksbury Ave PL7 . . . . . 131 B3
Hooper Ct PL14 . . . . .113 C8
Hooper La TR14 . . . . 138 D2
Hoopers Cl PL12 . . . . 53 C3
Hoopers La PL18 . . . . 40 F6
Hooper St PL11 . . . . 127 C3
Hope Terr TR7 . . . . 110 D6
Hopton Cl Bude EX23 . . . . 104 F5
  Plymouth PL6 . . . . 128 F8
Hornapark Cl PL16 . . . . 19 F3
Hornbrook Gdns PL6 . . . . 124 D6
Hornby Ct PL1 . . . . 148 A3
Hornby St **2** PL2 . . . . . . 127 F4
Hornchurch La PL5 . . . . . 123 C4
Hornchurch Rd PL5 . . . . . 123 C5
Horn Cross PL9 . . . . 135 E7
Horn Cross Rd PL9 . . . . . 135 F7
Hornick Hill PL26 . . . . 58 E4
HORNINGTOPS 51 E3
Horn La Liskeard PL14 . . . .113 B6
  Plymouth PL9 . . . . 135 F7
Horn Lane Flats **4** PL9 . 135 F7
HORRABRIDGE 42 C5
Horrabridge Com Prim Sch
  PL20 . . . . 42 C4
HORSEBRIDGE 29 C1
HORSEDOWNS 78 E1
Horsedowns Rd TR27 . . . . 78 F1
Horse & Jockey La **2**
  TR13 . . . . 146 C5
Horsepool La PL11 . . . . . . 65 B6
Horsepool Rd
  Connor Downs TR27 . . . . . 78 E6
  Sheviock PL11 . . . . 65 B6
Horse Rd EX23 . . . . 2 C1
Horseshoe Cl PL26 . . . . . . 47 A3
Horsewhim Dr PL17 . . . . . 39 E6
Horse Whim Dr PL25 . . . . 115 B5
Horsham La
  Plymouth, Honicknowle
    PL5 . . . . 124 C7
  Plymouth, Tamerton Foliot
    PL5 . . . . 124 C7
Horslett Hill EX22 . . . . 13 B8
Horsley Rise PL25 . . . . . . 114 D3
Horswell Cl PL7 . . . . 131 B5
Horton Cross EX22 . . . . 3 F3
Horwell Dr TR27 . . . . 142 E6
Hosken's Mdw TR19 . . . . . 97 A6
Hosking's Row TR15 . . . . 140 B4
Hospital Rd Plymouth PL4 . 149 B4
  Stratton EX23 . . . . 4 D1
Hotham Pl PL1 . . . . 148 A4
Houldsworth Rd PL9 . . . . 135 C2

Houndiscombe Rd PL4 . . 128 E4
Hounster Dr PL10 . . . . . . 132 D4
Hounster Hill PL10 . . . . . 132 D4
House Field Mdw **6** PL15 106 D4
Housel Bay Rd
  Church Cove TR12 . . . . . 103 A2
  Lizard TR12 . . . . 102 F2
Housman Cl PL5 . . . . 124 D3
Howard Cl Plymouth PL5 . 123 F2
  Saltash PL12 . . . . 122 D3
  Tavistock PL19 . . . . 147 A5
Howard La EX23 . . . . 7 C8
Howard Rd PL9 . . . . 135 E8
Howards Way EX23 . . . . . 104 D5
Howe Downs TR14 . . . . 79 A2
Howell's Rd **10** EX23 . . . . . 4 E1
Howeson La PL6 . . . . 125 A4
How St PL4 . . . . 149 A2
HTP Apartments TR1 . . . . 137 E4
Hts The PL19 . . . . 147 A6
HUDDISFORD 3 F6
Hudson Cross EX22 . . . . 5 E4
Hudson Rd PL27 . . . . 31 F3
Hughville St TR14 . . . . . . 138 D4
Hugus Rd TR3 . . . . 69 D3
Hull Rd TR14 . . . . 138 F3
Hull's La TR11 . . . . 145 C3
Humber Cl PL3 . . . . 129 D6
Humphrey's Cl PL14 . . . . . 37 F3
Humphry Davy La PL12 . . 142 D5
Humphry Davy Sch TR18 . 143 E6
Hungerford Rd PL2 . . . . . 128 B5
Hunkin Cl TR1 . . . . 137 C5
Hunter Cl PL6 . . . . 124 F2
Huntersfield TR14 . . . . . . 138 F7
Hunter's Oak PL20 . . . . 41 D2
Huntfield Gdns **15** EX23 . . 4 E1
Huntingdon Gdns PL5 . . . 124 D4
Huntley Pl PL3 . . . . 129 C4
Hunts Crossing Sta★ PL15 . 18 E4
Hurdon Rd Landlake PL15 . . 28 B8
  Launceston PL15 . . . . 106 D2
Hurdon Way PL15 . . . . . . 106 C3
Hurdwick Rd PL19 . . . . . . 147 A5
Hurland Rd TR1 . . . . 137 D3
Hurlers Ct **11** PL14 . . . . . .113 C5
Hurlers The★ PL14 . . . . 38 A6
Hurlings The TR9 . . . . 45 E5
Hurling Way **5** TR9 . . . . . . 45 E5
Hurrabrook Cl PL6 . . . . . . 125 E2
Hurrabrook Gdns PL6 . . . 125 E2
Hurrell Cl PL3 . . . . 124 D6
Hurrell Ct PL3 . . . . 129 C5
Hursley Bsns Pk PL6 . . . . 121 D1
Hurst St PL9 . . . . 135 F5
Hustyns PL27 . . . . 33 D3
Hutchings Cl PL6 . . . . 124 D6
Huthnance Cl TR1 . . . . . . 137 F5
Hutton Hts TR1 . . . . 69 F3
Huxham Cl PL6 . . . . 129 A8
Huxley Cl PL7 . . . . 130 F7
Hyde Park Inf School **1**
  PL3 . . . . 128 E5
Hyde Park Junior School **2**
  PL33 . . . . 128 E5
Hyde Park Rd PL3 . . . . . . 128 E5

IDLESS 70 B6
Idless La TR4 . . . . 69 F6
Idless Wood Forest Walk★
  TR4 . . . . 70 B6
Ilbert Cotts PL7 . . . . 130 E4
Ilbert St PL1 . . . . 148 B4
Illand Rd PL15 . . . . 27 C5
ILLOGAN 67 E4
Illogan Churchtown TR16 . 67 D4
Illogan Downs TR15 . . . . 139 B8
ILLOGAN HIGHWAY 139 C6
Illogan Pk **8** TR16 . . . . 67 E4
Illogan Sch TR16 . . . . 67 D5
Imperial Ct TR11 . . . . 145 D3
Impham Cl **4** PL19 . . . . . 147 B7
Ince Cl PL14 . . . . 126 F4
Inchkeith Rd PL6 . . . . 124 F7
INDIAN QUEENS 45 E1
Indian Queens Ind Est TR9 . 45 F2
Indian Queens Prim Sch
  TR9 . . . . 45 E1
Indus Pl **3** PL9 . . . . 136 B8
Industrial Est The TR6 . . . . 55 B4
Infirmary Hill TR1 . . . . . . 137 C4
Ingra Rd PL3 . . . . 129 A6
Ingra Tor Cl **2** PL20 . . . . . 42 C3
Ingra Wlk PL6 . . . . 125 B8
Inner Tide La TR7 . . . . . . 110 F4
Innes Ho PL1 . . . . 148 B3
Inney Cl PL17 . . . . 39 F4
Inow Terr TR11 . . . . 93 A3
Institute Hill TR13 . . . . 98 B8
Instituteway PL30 . . . . 34 C2
Instow Wlk PL5 . . . . 124 A3
Inswell Ct PL19 . . . . 147 A6
INSWORKE 132 F2
Insworke Cl PL10 . . . . 133 A6
Insworke Cres PL10 . . . . . 132 F6
Insworke Pl PL10 . . . . 133 A6
Inverdene PL3 . . . . 128 D5
Ipswich Cl PL5 . . . . 124 C4
Iron Bars PL22 . . . . 48 D2
Iron Mine La PL20 . . . . 42 E3
Isacombe Oaks PL17 . . . . . 39 F6
Isambard Brunel Way PL1 148 A2

Island Cres TR7. . . . . .110 E6
Island Ct PL13 . . . . .117 D2
Island Lanes PL31 . . . . . . 109 F1
Island Rd **4** TR26. . . . . . 141 B6
Island Sq **8** TR26. . . . . . 141 B6
Islington Wharf TR10 . . . 144 D8
Ivanhoe **6** TR7. . . . . . . .110 F6
Ivanhoe Rd PL5. . . . . . . .123 D2
Ivey Terr PL14 . . . . .113 D7
Ivy CI PL28 . . . . 31 F8
Ivy Cotts PL18 . . . . 40 F6
Ivydale PL15. . . . . .106 B6
Ivydale Rd PL4. . . . . .128 F4
Ivydene Flats TR7. . . . . . .111 D7
Ivy Ho TR16. . . . . 80 C6
Ivy La TR18 . . . . .143 C5
Ivyleaf Hill EX23 . . . . 4 E3
Ivyleaf Holiday Pk EX23. . . .4 F3

J

Jack Bice CI PL14. . . . . . .113 E6
Jackett's Steps **6** TR11. .145 B5
Jack La TR18 . . . . .143 C2
Jackman's Mdw PL10. . . .133 A3
Jacks CI TR10 . . . . .144 D7
Jackson CI PL5. . . . . .127 F8
Jackson PI PL2. . . . . .127 F4
Jackson Way PL12. . . . . .122 E3
Jack Stephens Est TR18. . .143 D6
Jacobs La **39** TR18. . . . .143 E5
Jacob's Ladder TR11 . . . .145 B4
JACOBSTOW 11 B6
Jacobstow Com Prim Sch
  EX23. . . . . 11 A6
Jago Ave PL11. . . . . .127 B3
Jago CI PL31. . . . . .109 B3
Jago's Slip TR11. . . . . . . .145 B5
Jake's La **1** TR4. . . . . 69 A3
Jamaica Inn Mus★ PL15 . . 25 E3
Jamaica PI **14** TR18 . . . .143 C7
Jamaica Terr **13** TR18. . .143 C7
James CI PL9. . . . . .136 B6
James PI TR1. . . . . .137 D4
James Rd PL19 . . . . .147 E2
James's Cross EX23 . . . . 2 C2
James St Plymouth PL4. . .148 C4
  Plymouth, Mount Wise PL1 . .127 C1
Jane's Ct **9** TR11. . . . . .145 B5
Jan Luke Way **1** TR14. . .138 F3
Jasmine Gdns
  Plymouth, Chaddlewood
  PL7. . . . . .131 B5
  Plymouth, Glenholt PL6. .125 E6
Jasmine PI **7** TR14. . . . .138 E5
Jasmine Way St Merryn PL28 31 F7
  18 Tregolds PL28. . . . . . . 31 F7
Jasper Parc PL14. . . . . 37 F3
Jays Cross PL15 . . . . 19 C6
Jean Cres PL3. . . . . .129 B6
Jeanne Rees Ct **9** PL14. .113 B5
Jedburgh Cres PL2 . . . . .128 A8
Jeffery CI PL6. . . . . .124 D6
Jelbert Way TR18. . . . . . . 88 E6
Jellicoe Rd PL5. . . . . .124 E1
Jenkins CI PL9 . . . . .136 A5
Jenkins Terr **5** TR15 . . .140 C5
Jenner Gdns TR9 . . . . 45 D6
Jenner Parc TR9 . . . . 45 D6
Jennings Rd TR10 . . . . . .144 A6
Jennings St TR18. . . . . . .143 E5
Jenns Cross EX22. . . . . .5 F7
Jennycliff La PL9 . . . . . . .135 A6
Jennys Combe CI PL9. . . .135 F4
Jephson Rd PL4 . . . . .129 B3
Jericho La Polhilsa PL17 . . 39 D7
  St Erth TR27. . . . . .142 D1
Jeryon CI PL25 . . . . .114 E6
Jessops PL7. . . . . .130 D7
Jethan Dr TR14. . . . . .138 E4
Jetty St PL26 . . . . 73 C3
Jewell's Terr TR16. . . . . . . 80 B5
JEWEL'S CROSS 7 F6
Jinkin Ave PL4 . . . . .149 B4
Jobs Water Treverva TR10. . . 93 A6
  Treworvack TR10. . . . . . . 92 F6
Jodel CI **1** PL6. . . . . . . .125 B5
John Ellis Ct TR27. . . . . . .142 C5
John La PL4. . . . . .148 C4
John's Cnr TR20 . . . . 89 F5
Johnson CI **2** PL20. . . . . 41 B1
John Sparke Ho **17** PL1. .149 A2
Johns Pk TR15 . . . . .140 B6
John St Plymouth PL1 . . . .127 E3
  Truro TR1. . . . . .137 C4
JOLLY'S BOTTOM 69 A4
Jon Davey Dr TR16 . . . . .140 C7
Jopes CI **2** PL14. . . . . . . 38 A3
JOPPA Hayle. 142 E4
  St Just. 87 A4
Jordan La PL20. . . . . 42 C5
Jorys Mdw PL30 . . . . 23 E3
Joseph's Ct **27** TR6 . . . . 55 A5
Joseph's La TR18. . . . . . .143 D8
Jubilee Bglws **20** TR18. .143 C1
Jubilee CI Cubert TR4. . . . 55 D8
  Duloe PL14 . . . . 51 A1
  8 Kilkhampton EX23. . . . .5 A6
  Saltash PL12. . . . . 1 A1
Jubilee Cotts Landrake PL12 .53 C3
  Saltash PL12. . . . . .122 C1
Jubilee Ct **15** TR26. . . . . 77 A6

Jubilee Hill PL13. . . . . 62 D5
Jubilee Mdw PL25. . . . . .115 C5
Jubilee PI Camborne TR14. .138 E2
  Plymouth PL3. . . . . .129 C4
Jubilee Poll TR18. . . . . . .143 F4
Jubilee Rd Falmouth TR11. .145 A5
  Pensilva PL14. . . . . 38 D4
  Plymouth PL5. . . . . .123 F3
  Threemilestone TR3 . . . . . 69 C3
  Wadebridge PL27 . . . . . .108 C5
Jubilee St TR7. . . . . .110 D6
Jubilee Terr Bodmin PL31 . .109 F1
  3 Camborne TR14 . . . . .138 E2
  Goonhavern TR4. . . . . 55 D5
  Helston TR13. . . . . .146 C4
  Plymouth PL4. . . . . .129 B2
Julian St PL4 . . . . .149 C2
Julian Wlk PL6 . . . . .125 E6
Jump CI PL6. . . . . .121 C1
Junction Gdns PL4 . . . . .149 C3
Juniper CI **14** PL31 . . . .109 A5
Juniper Gdns **2** PL14. . . 50 D7
Juniper Way PL7 . . . . . . .131 B5
Juniper Wlk **6** PL14 . . . .113 D8

K

Kailem CI TR9. . . . . 45 D5
Kaolin Hts PL25. . . . . . . .114 E8
Karenza Ct TR26. . . . . . . .141 E2
Kargel Gdns TR11. . . . . . .144 D1
Kathleaven St PL5. . . . . . .123 D1
Kay CI PL7. . . . . .130 F7
Kay Cres PL31. . . . . .109 B3
Kay Gdns PL27. . . . . .108 E5
Kays Mews **7** PL34. . . . . 14 C7
Kea Com Prim Sch TR3. . . 70 A1
Keason Est PL14. . . . . 39 A2
Keason Hill PL12 . . . . 53 C8
Keast CI **2** TR9. . . . . 45 E1
Keat St PL2. . . . . .127 E4
Keay Heights PL25. . . . . .114 E6
Kedlestone Ave PL5 . . . . .124 A3
Keeble Pk TR3. . . . . 81 E6
Keep The PL12 . . . . .122 C2
KEHELLAND 66 F2
Kehelland Village Prim Sch
  TR14. . . . . 66 F1
Keigwen PI TR19. . . . . 88 C1
Keiro La Pityme PL27 . . . . . 21 F3
  St Minver PL27 . . . . 22 A3
Kel Avon CI TR1 . . . . .137 F5
Kellaway Pk TR13. . . . . . .146 D6
Kelley Rd TR11 . . . . .144 E5
Kelliwith TR3. . . . . 82 B6
Kellow Hill PL13 . . . . 62 D2
Kellow Pk PL11. . . . . 65 A7
Kellow Rd PL26. . . . . 58 C8
KELLY 29 B8
KELLY BRAY 39 F6
Kelly CI PL5 . . . . .127 C7
Kelly Coll PL19 . . . . .147 D7
Kelly Coll Prep Sch PL19. .147 D7
Kelly Pk PL30. . . . . 34 C8
Kelvin Ave PL4 . . . . .149 C4
Kelwyn Ct TR26. . . . . .141 C2
Kemp CI TR1 . . . . .137 D4
Kempe CI PL2 . . . . .127 F6
Kemp's CI **7** TR5. . . . . . 54 C1
Kempton Terr PL11. . . . . .127 B2
Kemyell PI PL2 . . . . .127 E4
Kendal Gn TR2. . . . . 57 C1
Kendall Park PL23 . . . . . . 61 B3
Kendall Pk PL23 . . . . .116 D2
Kendall PI PL5 . . . . .124 F4
Kenidjack Ct TR26 . . . . . .141 E1
Kenilworth Rd PL2. . . . . .128 B7
Kenilworth Way PL26. . . . 58 E5
Kenley Gdns PL5. . . . . . . .123 F4
Kenmare Dr PL7. . . . . . . .131 A5
Kennack Sands TR12. . . . .103 C6
Kennall Pk TR3. . . . . 81 B4
Kennall Vale TR3. . . . . 81 B4
Kennall Vale SchTR3. . . . . 81 B4
Kennall Valley TR3 . . . . . . 81 A4
Kenna Pk TR1. . . . . 69 F3
KENNARDS HOUSE. 18 B2
Kenn CI PL5 . . . . .124 B3
Kennedy CI TR15. . . . . . . .139 B8
KENNEGGY. 90 A3
KENNEGGY DOWNS 90 B4
Kennel Hill Carwen PL30. . .35 D8
  Plymouth PL7. . . . . .130 D4
Kennel Hill CI PL7 . . . . . .130 C4
Kennerley Terr **16** TR2. . .95 A6
Kennet CI PL3 . . . . .129 B6
Kenneth Launder Ct **10**
  PL14 . . . . .113 B5
Kensa Way TR27 . . . . 78 E6
Kensey Ct PL15. . . . . .106 D6
Kensey PI **3** PL25. . . . . .106 D6
Kensey Valley Mdw PL15. .106 D6
Kensey View PL15. . . . . . .106 D5
Kensington PI **8** PL4. . . .128 F4
Kensington Rd PL4 . . . . . .149 B4
Kenstella Rd TR18 . . . . . .143 C2
Kent Ave PL25. . . . . .115 D3
Kent CI PL26. . . . . 58 C8
Kent Rd PL2. . . . . .127 F5
KENTS 10 F6
KENWYN. 137 C6
Kenwyn Church Rd TR1. . .137 B6
Kenwyn CI Bude EX23. . . .104 D7
  Truro TR1. . . . . .137 B6
Kenwyn Hill TR1. . . . . . . .137 B6
Kenwyn Mews TR1. . . . . .137 C6

Kenwyn Pk
  St Kew Highway PL30. . . . 23 B2
  Truro TR1. . . . . .137 B6
Kenwyn Rd TR1. . . . . .137 C5
Kenwyn St TR1 . . . . .137 C4
Kenython La TR19 . . . . 86 F7
Keppel PI PL2 . . . . .127 F4
Keppel St PL2 . . . . .127 F4
Keppel Terr **8** PL2. . . . . .127 F4
Kerensa Gdns **13** TR5 . . . 54 D1
  St Agnes TR5. . . . . 68 D8
Kerensa Gn TR1. . . . . . . .144 E5
Kergillack CI TR11. . . . . . .144 C4
Kergilliack Rd TR11. . . . . .144 D5
Kerhuon Ct PL31 . . . . . . .109 D5
Kerkin CI **1** TR4. . . . . . . 55 E4
Kerley Gr TR1. . . . . 69 F3
Kerley Hill TR4 . . . . 69 A3
Kerley Vale TR4. . . . . 69 A3
Kernick Bsns Pk TR10. . . .144 A6
Kernick Gdns TR10. . . . . .144 A6
Kernick Ind Est TR10. . . . .144 A7
Kernick Rd TR10. . . . . . . .144 A6
Kernick Rd Penryn TR10. . .144 B7
  Tregonetha PL30. . . . . . . 46 D6
Kernick Way TR27 . . . . . .142 E8
Kernow CI Bodmin PL31 . .109 F5
  Torpoint PL11. . . . . .126 E3
  Wadebridge PL27 . . . . . .108 B5
Kernow Cres EX23. . . . . .104 E4
Kernow Ct Newquay TR7. . .110 E6
  Torpoint PL11. . . . . .126 E3
Kernyk Lowen TR14. . . . . .138 F5
Kernyk Parc **4** TR13. . . .146 C6
Kerrier Way TR14. . . . . . . .138 E3
  Tuckingmill TR14. . . . . . .139 A4
KERRIS 97 E8
Kerris Gr TR1. . . . . .137 B5
Kerrow La PL26. . . . . 59 D8
KERROW MOOR. 59 D8
Ker St Ope PL1 . . . . .127 E2
Kersbrook Cross PL17 . . . . 27 F2
Kersey CI TR11 . . . . .145 C1
Kersey Rd Flushing TR11. . .145 B7
  Flushing TR11. . . . . .145 C7
Ker St TR1. . . . . .127 E1
Keryor CI PL25. . . . . .114 F3
Kestell Pk PL31. . . . . .109 E2
Kestenenn **16** PL31. . . .109 D5
KESTLE 73 A4
Kestle Ct PL31. . . . . .109 C5
Kestle Dr TR1. . . . . 69 F3
Kestle La PL15. . . . . 18 C2
KESTLE MILL 111 F1
Kestle Rd PL26. . . . . 73 A4
Keston Gdns PL27. . . . . . .108 A6
Kestor CI PL2. . . . . .128 A7
Kestral Units PL5 . . . . . . .124 A1
Kestral Way **10** TR16. . . 67 E4
Kestrel CI **2** Guildford TR27 142 E6
  Plymouth PL6. . . . . .125 D8
  7 Porthleven TR13. . . . . .98 B8
Kestrel Pk PL19. . . . . .147 D2
Keswick Cres PL6 . . . . . . .125 D2
Keveral La PL11 . . . . 64 B5
Kew Hal An Tow TR13. . . .146 A6
Kew Klavji **11** PL31. . . . .109 E5
Kew Lastanen TR1. . . . . . .137 F5
Kew Noweth TR14 . . . . . .138 D2
Kew Pendra TR19. . . . . 97 A6
Kew Pendra TR19 . . . . 97 A6
Kew Vean TR26. . . . . .141 C2
KEYBRIDGE 35 B8
Keyes CI PL1 . . . . .127 F2
KFYHAM. 127 E5
Keyham Barton RC Prim Sch
  PL2. . . . . .127 E6
Keyham Ct PL2. . . . . .127 E6
Keyham Rd PL2. . . . . .127 E6
Keyham St PL5 . . . . .127 E8
Keyham Sta PL2. . . . . . . .127 E6
Khyber CI PL11. . . . . .127 A3
Kibbiscombe Terr PL14. . . .63 A8
Kidwelly CI PL7. . . . . .131 C4
Kiel PI PL3 . . . . .129 D5
Kiel Pla PL3 . . . . .129 D5
Kilhallon PL24. . . . . 60 C5
Kilhallon Woodlands PL24. .60 C5
KILKHAMPTON 5 A6
Kilkhampton Junior and Infant
  Sch EX23. . . . . 5 A6
Killaganogue Rd PL30 . . . . 46 B8
KILLATOWN. 37 B1
Killatown Hill PL14 . . . . . . 37 B1
Killatree Cross EX22. . . . . . . 8 F7
Killerton La PL9. . . . . .129 D1
Killerton Rd EX23. . . . . . .104 E5
Killicourt TR3 . . . . 82 A7
Killiers Ct TR15. . . . . .139 C7
Killiersfield TR15. . . . . . . .139 C6
Killigrew Ave PL12. . . . . .122 D1
Killigrew Gdns TR4. . . . . . 70 B8
Killigrew PI **9** TR11. . . . .145 A4
Killigrew Rd PL14. . . . . . .113 D6
Killigrew St TR11. . . . . . . .145 A4
KILLIVOSE 79 C5
Killivose Beacon TR14. . . .138 D1
  Shorts Hill TR14. . . . . 79 C5
Killivose Gdns TR14. . . . . .138 D1
Killivose Rd TR14. . . . . . . .138 D1
Killyvarder Way PL25. . . . .115 B6
Kilmar CI PL14. . . . . 37 F3
Kilmar Rd PL14. . . . . .113 E6
Kilmar St PL9. . . . . 135 D6
Kilmar Stkillerton La PL9 .129 D1
Kilmar Way PL14 . . . . 37 F3

Kilminorth Woods Nature
  Reserve★ PL13. . . . . . . .117 A4
Kilna La PL12. . . . . 53 A2
Kiln CI Cawsand PL10. . . .133 A1
  Mevagissey PL26. . . . . . . 73 C4
  Plymouth PL5. . . . . .127 C8
Kiln Mdws TR12 . . . . 92 C1
Kilnpark Wlk PL12. . . . . . .126 E6
Kilworthy House Chelfham
  Senior Sch PL19. . . . . . . 30 E3
Kilworthy Hill PL19 . . . . .147 D6
Kilworthy Rd Tavistock PL19. .30 F3
  Tavistock PL19. . . . . .147 C6
Kimber Ct TR11. . . . . .145 B2
Kimberley Ct TR7. . . . . . .110 D6
Kimberley Foster CI PL11. . 65 B5
Kimberley Park Rd TR11. . .145 A4
Kimberley Pk PL14 . . . . . . 38 A3
Kimberley PI TR11. . . . . . .145 A4
Kimberley Rd PL27. . . . . .108 D5
Kimberly CI TR7. . . . . . . .110 D6
Kimberly Dr PL6. . . . . . . .125 B1
Kiming EX23. . . . . .104 E4
Kimlers Way PL13 . . . . . . .117 D6
King Arthurs Terr **5** PL34. .14 C7
KINGBEARE 27 A1
King Charles Prim Sch
  TR11. . . . . .145 A3
King Charles St TR11 . . . .144 F2
King Edward Cres TR7 . . . .110 D7
King Edward Mine Mus★
  TR14. . . . . 79 E5
King Edward Rd PL12. . . .122 F2
Kingfisher CI Plymouth PL6 .125 E6
  Tavistock PL19. . . . . .147 D2
Kingfisher Dr PL25 . . . . . .115 A4
Kingfisher Way PL9. . . . . .135 C7
King George V Memorial Wlk
  PL27. . . . . .142 C6
KINGSAND. 133 A2
King's Ave Falmouth TR11 . .144 F4
  St Austell PL25. . . . . .114 D3
Kingsbury Ho TR11. . . . . .145 A6
Kings Cross EX39. . . . . .2 E5
Kings Ct PL1 . . . . .128 A3
King's Hill EX23 . . . . .104 E4
Kings Hill CI EX23. . . . . . .104 E4
King's Hill Ind Est EX23 . .104 F3
Kings Hill Mdw EX23. . . . .104 E3
Kingsland Gardens CI PL3 . 128 E6
Kingsley Ave PL11 . . . . . .127 B2
Kingsley CI TR1. . . . . 69 E3
Kingsley Cove TR4. . . . . . . 68 A7
Kingsley Ct TR9 . . . . 57 E8
Kingsley Meade TR8. . . . .111 B5
Kingsley Rd PL4. . . . . . . .128 E4
Kingsley Terr TR16 . . . . . . 67 C6
Kingsley Way TR13. . . . . .146 C5
Kingsmill Rd PL12 . . . . . .122 C5
Kings Pippin PL26. . . . . . . 58 E5
Kings Rd Marazion TR17. . . 89 B5
  Plymouth, Devonport PL1. .127 F2
  Plymouth, West Park PL5. .123 F3
  4 St Mawes TR2. . . . . . . 95 A6
King's Rd Camborne TR14. .138 D4
  Penzance TR18. . . . . . . .143 D5
  Plymouth PL1. . . . . .128 A2
  Plymouth Sch & Nur PL3. .128 E6
King's St PL22 . . . . .112 C2
King St Bude EX23. . . . . . .104 E5
  Gunnislake PL18. . . . . 41 A6
  Millbrook PL10. . . . . .132 C5
  Newquay TR7. . . . . .110 D6
  Plymouth PL1. . . . . .148 B3
  Redruth TR15. . . . . .140 B5
  Tavistock PL19. . . . . .147 B6
  Torpoint PL11. . . . . .127 C3
  Truro TR1. . . . . .137 D4
KING'S TAMERTON. 123 F2
King's Tamerton Rd PL5. . .123 F2
Kingston CI PL7. . . . . .131 A5
Kingston Dr PL7. . . . . . . .131 B5
Kingston Rd PL17. . . . . . . 28 E1
Kingston Way **9** TR10 . . . 81 C1
Kingston Way Rd **10** TR10 . . 81 C1
Kingsway PL10 . . . . .133 B2
Kingsway Gdns PL6. . . . . .124 F3
Kingswear Cres PL6. . . . . .125 B1
Kings Wood★ PL26 . . . . . . 73 B7
Kingswood Est PL14. . . . . 38 C1
Kingswood Park Ave PL3 . .128 D6
Kingswood Rd PL18. . . . . 41 A6
Kinnard Cres PL6. . . . . . .124 F7
Kinross Ave PL4 . . . . .129 A4
Kinsale Rd PL5 . . . . .123 F3
Kinsman Est PL31 . . . . . . .109 C3
Kinterbury Rd PL5. . . . . . .127 B8
Kinterbury St PL1. . . . . . .149 A2
Kinterbury Terr PL5 . . . . .127 B8
Kinver CI PL5. . . . . .125 D4
Kipling Gdns PL5. . . . . . . .124 D2
Kirby Rd TR1. . . . . .137 A4
Kirkby PI PL4. . . . . .148 C4
Kirkby Terr PL4. . . . . .148 C4
Kirkdale Gdns PL2. . . . . . .128 B7
Kirkella Rd PL20. . . . . 42 D2
Kirkland CI PL7. . . . . .131 B5
Kirkwall Rd PL5. . . . . .124 E3
Kirland Bower PL30. . . . . . 48 B7
Kirland Rd PL30. . . . . .109 B2
Kirthen Wood TR27. . . . . . 90 C8
Kirton PI PL3. . . . . .129 B5
Kitchen Gdns TR11 . . . . . .144 E5
Kit Hill Cres PL5. . . . . . . .127 C8
Kit Hill Ctry Pk★ PL17. . . . 40 A6
Kit Hill Rd PL17. . . . . 40 B6

Kit Hill Vw PL15. . . . . . . .106 D4
Kitley Way PL5. . . . . .123 D1
Kitter Dr PL9. . . . . .136 A5
Kittiwake CI TR27. . . . . 77 E3
Kitts Ct **17** TR18. . . . . . .143 E5
Kleinfontein Terr PL14. . . . 38 D4
Knapmedown PL15. . . . . . 11 B1
Knapps CI PL9. . . . . .136 C6
Knave-Go-By TR14. . . . . . . 79 D5
Kneele Gdns PL3 . . . . . . .128 E8
Knighton Rd PL4. . . . . . . .149 C3
Knighton Terr **3** PL20. . . 42 C5
Knightor CI PL26 . . . . 59 E6
Knights CI **1** PL34. . . . . . 14 C7
Knights Ct PL22 . . . . .112 B3
Knights Hill TR1 . . . . .137 B6
Knights Mdw TR3. . . . . . . 81 F7
Knight's Mdws TR3. . . . . . 81 F7
KNIGHTSMILL. 23 F7
Knights Mill Hill
  St Teath PL30. . . . . 23 E7
  Tregreenwell PL30 . . . . . . 23 F7
Knights Way TR15. . . . . . .140 D7
Knill CI TR26. . . . . .141 C2
Knill Cross PL10. . . . . .132 E5
Knill Cross Cotts PL10. . . .132 E5
Knoll Pk TR1. . . . . .137 F4
Knoll The PL7. . . . . .130 B6
Knowland CI PL1 . . . . . . .127 F3
Knowle Ave PL2 . . . . .127 E6
Knowle Terr PL20. . . . . . . 42 E4
Koth Karrji PL30 . . . . 23 E7
KUGGAR 103 B6
Kyl Cober Parc PL17. . . . . . 28 E1
Kynance CI PL11. . . . . . . .126 F4
Kynance Cove TR12. . . . . .102 E3
Kynance Ho TR1. . . . . 69 E4
Kynance Terr TR12. . . . . . .102 F2

L

Labatt CI PL6. . . . . .125 D3
Labernum Terr **1** EX23. . . . 5 A6
Labour In Vain TR19 . . . . . 87 A5
Laburnam CI TR11. . . . . . .144 F5
Laburnum Cotts PL19. . . .147 C6
Laburnum Ct TR11. . . . . . .144 F6
Laburnum Dr TR11 . . . . . .144 F5
Lacey CI TR14 . . . . 79 E5
Ladder La PL30. . . . . 35 F2
LADOCK 57 C1
Ladock CE SchTR2 . . . . . . 57 C2
Ladock Rd Ladock TR2. . . . 57 C1
  Probus TR2. . . . . 71 C7
Lady Beam Ct PL17 . . . . . . 39 F6
Ladybird La **6** PL20 . . . . 42 D3
Ladycross PL15. . . . . 18 F7
Ladyfern Rd PL6. . . . . . . .121 C1
Lady La **2** TR2. . . . . 84 A8
Lady Modiford's CE Prim Sch
  PL20. . . . . 42 E4
LADY NANCE 44 F3
Ladysmith Ct PL4. . . . . . .149 C4
Ladysmith Rd PL4. . . . . . .129 B3
Lady St TR13 . . . . .146 B5
Ladywell PL28. . . . . .107 D5
Ladywell PI PL4 . . . . .149 B3
Laflouder Fields TR12 . . . . 99 A2
Laflouder La TR12 . . . . 99 A2
Lafrowda CI TR19. . . . . 86 E6
Lafrowda Terr TR19 . . . . . . 86 F6
Laguna Ct TR15. . . . . .140 B5
LAIRA. 129 C4
Laira Ave PL3. . . . . .129 C4
Laira Bridge Rd PL4 . . . . .129 B1
Laira Gdns PL3. . . . . .129 C4
Laira Green Prim Sch PL3 . 129 C4
Laira Park Cres PL4. . . . . .129 B4
Laira Park PI PL4. . . . . . . .129 B4
Laira Park Rd PL4. . . . . . .129 B4
Laira PI PL4. . . . . .149 C2
Laira St PL4. . . . . .149 C3
Laity TR13. . . . . 92 B5
Laity Dr TR14 . . . . .138 F3
Laity Fields TR14. . . . . . . .138 F3
Laity La Carbis Bay TR26. . . 77 C4
  Withen TR26. . . . . .141 B1
Laity Moor Burnthouse TR3. . 81 B3
  Forge TR16. . . . . 68 A4
Laity Rd TR14. . . . . 79 E4
Laity Wlk PL6. . . . . .124 D6
LAKE. 42 E3
Lake La Dousland PL20. . . . 42 E3
  Liskeard PL14 . . . . .113 D5
Lake Mews PL10. . . . . . . .132 E5
Lake Rd PL9. . . . . .135 B6
Lakeside PL19. . . . . .147 B6
Lakeside Dr PL5. . . . . .123 E5
Lake View PL12. . . . . 53 C8
Lake View Ct PL15. . . . . . .124 B6
Lakeview Dr PL5. . . . . .124 B5
Lalebrick Rd PL9. . . . . . . .135 B5
LAMANVA 93 C6
Lamanva CI **16** TR16. . . . 67 E4
Lamanva Rd **17** TR16. . . . 67 E4
Lambert Rd PL5. . . . . .124 B6
Lambert Terr **4** TR11. . . .145 A5
Lambhay Hill PL1. . . . . . . .149 A1
Lambhay St PL1 . . . . .149 A1
LAMBOURNE. 55 B2
Lambourne Ave **7** TR5 . . 54 C1
Lamb Pk **5** PL24. . . . . . . 60 C4
Lambs La PL15 . . . . .144 E5
LAMELLION. 113 A4
Lamellyn Dr TR1. . . . . 69 F3
Lamellyn Rd PL24. . . . . . . 60 B4
Lamerhooe Cross PL19 . . . 29 C1

Lamerhooe Dr
  Horsebridge PL19 ....29 C1
  Luckett PL19 ....40 C8
LAMERTON 30 B3
Lamerton CE Prim Sch
  PL19 ....30 B3
Lamerton Cl PL5 ....124 B3
Lametton Gn PL14 ....51 B4
Lamledra Hill PL26 ....85 D5
Lamorak Cl PL26 ....73 B3
LAMORICK 47 E7
LAMORNA 97 E5
Lamorna Cl TR27 ....78 D6
Lamorna Ct TR16 ....67 D6
Lamorna Dr **11** PL17 ....39 F4
Lamorna Parc **12** PL17 ....39 F4
Lamorna Pk St Austell PL25 ....114 E7
  Torpoint PL11 ....126 E4
Lamorne Cl **4** TR6 ....55 A4
LAMORRAN 83 C8
Lampen Rd PL14 ....36 F2
Lampen Terr PL14 ....36 F2
LANA 13 D7
Lana Cotts EX22 ....13 C7
Lanadwell St PL28 ....107 C5
Lanaton Rd TR10 ....144 A8
Lancashire La TR20 ....89 F5
Lancaster Cres PL27 ....31 F3
Lancaster Gdns PL5 ....124 D4
Lanchard Cl PL14 ....113 B5
Lanchard Rd PL14 ....113 B5
Lanchard Rise PL14 ....113 B5
Landaviddy La PL13 ....62 D2
Lander Ct TR1 ....137 D3
Lander Rd PL12 ....122 F3
Landers Hill PL27 ....32 F5
Landerslake PL15 ....27 B7
Landeryon Gdns TR18 ....143 D5
Landewednack Com Prim Sch
  TR12 ....102 F2
Landithy TR20 ....143 A8
Landlake Cross PL15 ....28 A8
Landlake Rd Landlake PL15 ....28 A8
  Launceston PL15 ....106 B2
Landlooe La PL14 ....51 C2
LANDRAKE 53 B3
Landrake Cl PL5 ....127 C8
Landreath Pl PL24 ....60 B5
Landrew Rd PL25 ....114 F6
LANDREYNE 27 C2
Land's End Airport TR19 ....86 F3
Lands End Rd TR19 ....97 A6
Lands Pk PL9 ....135 F7
LANDULPH 123 A7
Landulph Cross PL12 ....118 F1
Landulph Gdns PL5 ....127 C8
Landulph Sch PL12 ....118 F1
LANE 111 B3
LANEAST 17 B2
Lanepark La EX39 ....2 D5
Lane Reddin Terr **21** TR18 143 C2
LANESCOT 60 D6
Lane The PL7 ....130 D6
Langage Cross PL7 ....131 F6
Langage Ind Est PL7 ....131 D4
Langage Pk PL7 ....131 C4
Langage Science Pk PL7 ....131 D5
Langage S Rd PL7 ....131 E4
Langarth Cl TR3 ....69 D4
Langdale Cl PL6 ....125 D1
Langdale Gdns PL6 ....125 D1
LANGDON 11 C3
Langdon Cross PL15 ....18 D8
Langdon Ct PL9 ....136 B6
Langdon Down Way PL11 ....126 E3
Lang Dr **1** PL27 ....108 C5
Langerwell Cl PL12 ....122 C3
Langerwell La PL12 ....122 C3
Langford Pl **6** PL28 ....107 C4
Langfords Mdw **4** PL35 ....9 C1
Lang Gdns PL18 ....41 A3
Lang Gr Plymouth PL9 ....136 C7
  Tavistock PL19 ....147 D5
Langham Pl PL4 ....149 C3
Langhill Rd PL3 ....128 D5
Langley Cl PL6 ....125 A7
Langley Cres PL6 ....124 F7
Langman Ct **3** PL20 ....41 B1
Langmead Cl PL6 ....129 C8
Langmead Rd PL6 ....129 C8
Langmore Cl PL6 ....129 A7
LANGORE 18 D5
Langore Rd PL15 ....18 D5
Langorran Rd TR14 ....138 B3
Lang Rd PL14 ....113 B4
Langreek Bglws PL13 ....62 C2
Langreek Rd PL13 ....62 C2
Langstone Rd PL12 ....128 C2
Langstone Terr PL2 ....128 C7
Langston Hiill PL15 ....27 C4
Langton Rd Falmouth TR11 ....145 A6
  8 Yelverton PL20 ....42 C3
Langton Terr **8** TR11 ....145 A5
Langurroc Rd TR8 ....110 A3
Langurtho Rd PL23 ....116 B4
Langweath Est TR12 ....99 D7
Langweath Gdns TR27 ....77 E3
Langweath La TR12 ....99 D7
Langwedh TR16 ....67 D4
Lanhenvor Ave TR7 ....110 E5
Lanherne Ave TR8 ....45 A8
Lanheverne Parc **4** TR12 101 C4
Lanhydrock Ho & Gdns★
  PL30 ....48 D6
Lanhydrock Rd PL4 ....129 B2
Lanhydrock View PL31 ....109 D3
Laninval Hl PL30 ....47 F8

LANIVET 47 F6
Lanivet Prim Sch PL30 ....47 E7
LANJETH 58 E3
LANJEW 46 F7
LANK 24 B2
Lankelly Cl PL23 ....116 B4
Lankelly La PL23 ....116 A4
LANLIVERY 48 C1
Lanlivery Prim Sch PL30 ....48 D2
Lanlovie Mdw TR8 ....55 D8
Lanmoor Est TR16 ....80 D6
Lannarth Glas TR16 ....140 E1
LANNER 80 D6
Lanner Gn TR16 ....140 E1
Lanner Hill Redruth TR15 ....140 D2
  Redruth, Pennance TR16 ....140 E1
Lanner Moor Terr TR16 ....80 E6
Lanner Prim Sch TR16 ....80 D6
Lanner Sq TR16 ....80 D6
Lannoweth Rd TR18 ....143 F6
Lanoweth TR10 ....81 D2
Lanow La PL30 ....23 A4
Lanoy Rd PL15 ....27 D5
LANREATH 62 B7
LANSALLOS 62 A2
Lansallos St PL13 ....62 D1
Lansdown Cl EX23 ....104 D5
Lansdowne PL26 ....141 B4
Lansdowne Cl TR18 ....143 C5
Lansdowne Rd TR26 ....141 B4
Lansdowne Pl TR18 ....143 C4
Lansdown Rd
  Callington PL17 ....39 E4
  Falmouth TR11 ....145 C3
  Penzance TR18 ....143 C5
  Plymouth PL6 ....124 F2
  Wadebridge PL27 ....108 B5
LANSTEPHAN 106 C8
Lansweden La EX23 ....10 C6
Lantallack Cross PL12 ....53 A3
LANTEGLOS 14 F1
LANTEGLOS HIGHWAY 61 E4
Lantoom Way **8** PL14 ....50 E7
Lanuthnoe Est TR27 ....77 F1
Lanwithan Cl PL22 ....112 D2
Lanwithan Rd PL22 ....112 E1
Lanxon Cres PL30 ....48 C2
Lanxon Rd PL30 ....35 C8
Lanyon Cl PL14 ....37 F3
Lanyon Rd Bosiliack TR20 ....87 F8
  Playing Place TR3 ....82 B8
Lappa Valley Steam Railway★
  TR8 ....56 C7
Lapthorn Cl PL9 ....135 C7
Larch Cl PL12 ....122 C3
Larch Dr PL6 ....125 E7
Larcombe Rd PL25 ....115 A6
Laregan Hill TR18 ....143 D4
Lariggan Cres TR18 ....143 D4
Lariggan Rd TR18 ....143 D4
Larkfield Cl PL26 ....58 E5
Larkfield Rise **13** TR2 ....95 A6
Larkhall Rise PL3 ....129 B5
Larkham Cl PL7 ....130 C6
Larkham La PL7 ....130 C6
Lark Hill PL2 ....128 A6
LATCHLEY 40 D8
Latchley Plain PL18 ....40 D7
Latham Cl PL6 ....129 A7
Latimer Cl PL7 ....131 B5
Latimer Wlk PL6 ....124 E7
Launcells Cross EX23 ....5 B1
LAUNCESTON 106 D5
Launceston Cl Bodmin PL31 ....109 F4
  Plymouth PL6 ....125 B7
Launceston Coll PL15 ....106 C4
Launceston Comm Prim Sch
  PL15 ....106 C5
Launceston Community Hospl
  PL15 ....106 C4
Launceston Rd Bodmin PL31 ....35 B1
  Holton PL31 ....35 B3
  Kelly Bray PL17 ....39 E6
  Newtown PL15 ....27 C5
  St Clether PL15 ....17 A3
  Treraven PL15 ....16 F3
Launceston Ret Pk PL15 ....106 C4
Launceston Sta★ PL15 ....106 B6
Launceston Steam Rly★ PL15 ....18 E3
Laura Cl PL34 ....14 D7
Laura Dr PL25 ....115 A5
Laurel Ct PL2 ....128 A7
Laurel Dene PL2 ....128 A7
Laurel Dr PL6 ....125 E5
Laurel La PL17 ....39 E6
Laurel Rd PL2 ....128 A7
Laurels The PL18 ....40 E6
La Vague TR3 ....82 C5
Lavington Cl PL7 ....131 B5
Lavinia Dr PL7 ....130 C5
Lavorrick Orchs PL26 ....73 C4
Lawellan La PL30 ....47 B8
LAWHITTON 19 C1
Lawn Cl **2** PL7 ....131 C5
Lawn Steps TR11 ....145 B4
Lawns The Plymouth PL5 ....124 F1
  Torpoint PL11 ....127 A4
  Tavistock PL19 ....147 D6
Lawrence House Mus★
  PL15 ....106 C6
Lawrence Rd Plymouth PL9 ....135 A6
  St Agnes TR5 ....54 C1
Lawry Cl **6** PL14 ....113 B5

Lawson Gr PL9 ....135 C7
Lawton Cl TR7 ....110 B5
Law Wlk PL6 ....124 D6
Leader Rd TR7 ....111 E7
Leafield PL31 ....35 B2
Leander Way PL5 ....124 D2
Leanway PL12 ....122 E2
Leap Pk TR3 ....69 C3
Leas The TR1 ....137 E5
Leat Cl PL20 ....42 E3
Leatfield PL26 ....73 C3
Leatfield Dr PL6 ....124 F4
Leatherby Cl PL6 ....124 C1
Leathern Bottle Hill PL30 ....24 A5
Leather Tor Cl **4** PL20 ....42 C3
Leat Rd Lifton PL16 ....19 F3
  Pendeen TR19 ....75 A1
Leatside PL6 ....121 C1
Leats The TR1 ....137 C4
Leat The **9** EX23 ....4 E1
Leat View PL12 ....122 B3
Leat Wlk Plymouth PL3 ....128 E6
  Roborough PL6 ....121 D1
  Saltash PL12 ....122 D4
Leaves Yd PL3 ....129 B7
Lea Way EX23 ....104 F6
Le Ball Hill Bellasize PL30 ....49 B8
  Tawnamoor PL30 ....35 F1
LEBURNICK 28 D8
Leburnick Cross PL15 ....28 D8
Lecudden Rd PL30 ....34 F5
Ledgate La PL7 ....131 F8
Ledra Cl TR12 ....103 A4
Ledrah Gdns PL25 ....114 B3
Ledrah Rd PL25 ....114 B3
LEEDSTOWN 78 E1
Leedstown Com Prim Sch
  TR27 ....78 E1
Leeside Ct **7** PL2 ....128 A4
Lefra Orch TR19 ....97 B6
Legendry Land's End★ TR19 ....96 A5
Leggos Ct **10** TR15 ....140 B5
Legion Hall La **12** PL18 ....40 F5
Legion La **3** PL24 ....60 D5
Legis Wlk PL6 ....125 B8
Leg O Mutton Corner **13**
  PL20 ....42 C3
Le Hayes Hill PL30 ....35 F4
LEIGHAM 129 E8
Leigham Ct PL1 ....148 B1
Leigham Manor Dr PL6 ....129 F8
Leigham Prim Sch PL6 ....125 E1
Leigham St PL1 ....148 B1
Leigham Terrace La PL1 ....148 B2
Leigham Terr La W PL1 ....148 B2
Leigh Ct PL6 ....129 A8
Leigh La Hatt PL12 ....53 D6
  Roborough PL6 ....121 D2
Leighton Rd PL3 ....128 F8
LELANT 77 E4
LELANT DOWNS 77 D2
Lelant Mdws TR26 ....77 E3
Lelant Saltings Sta TR26 ....77 E3
Lelant Sta TR26 ....77 E4
Lemellen Gdns PL30 ....23 B2
Lemin Parc TR27 ....78 E3
Lemin's Ct TR15 ....140 B5
Lemon Hill TR11 ....82 A3
Lemon Hill Gdns TR11 ....82 A3
Lemon Mews TR1 ....137 D4
Lemon Quay TR1 ....137 D4
Lemon Row TR1 ....137 D5
Lemon St St Keverne TR12 ....101 D3
  19 Truro TR1 ....137 D4
Lemon Terr TR4 ....81 D8
Lender La **5** TR12 ....99 A2
Lendra La PL17 ....39 D4
Leo Ave **12** PL9 ....136 E8
LERRYN 61 D8
Lerryn CE Prim Sch PL22 ....61 D8
Lerryn Rd PL22 ....49 A1
Lerryn View PL22 ....61 C8
Lerwick Rd PL27 ....31 F3
LESCROW 116 B6
Lescudjack Cres TR18 ....143 F6
Lescudjack Rd TR18 ....143 F6
Lescudjack Terr TR18 ....143 F6
Lesingey La TR18 ....88 A5
Leskinnick Pl **14** TR18 ....143 E6
Leskinnick Terr TR18 ....143 E6
Leslie Ct TR13 ....146 B6
LESNEWTH 10 A1
Lesnewth **18** PL24 ....60 B4
Lester Cl PL3 ....129 B6
Lestraynes La TR10 ....92 E8
Lethlean Cl TR27 ....142 D7
Lethlean La TR27 ....142 D7
Lethlean Towans TR27 ....142 D8
LEVALSA MEOR 73 B8
Levant Cl TR19 ....86 F1
Levant Mine & Beam Engine★
  TR19 ....74 E1
Levant Rd TR19 ....86 F1
Leven Cotts EX23 ....104 D5
Leverlake Rd EX23 ....6 F4
Levine View TR11 ....144 E1
LEWANNICK 27 B7
Lewannick Cl PL15 ....27 B7
Lewannick Com Prim Sch
  PL15 ....27 B7
Lewannick Rd TR8 ....43 D1
Lewarne Cres TR7 ....111 C7
Lewarne Hill PL14 ....36 E1
Lewarne Rd TR7 ....111 C8
Lewes Gdns PL5 ....124 C4
Lewis Way PL25 ....114 E6
Lewman Cl TR2 ....71 C6

Lewman Rd TR2 ....71 C6
Leworthy Cross EX22 ....8 E4
LEY 36 E1
Leyford La PL9 ....135 F3
Ley La PL20 ....119 D6
Leypark Ct PL6 ....125 C2
Leypark Dr PL6 ....125 C2
Leypark Wlk PL6 ....125 C2
Leys La TR17 ....89 B5
LEZANT 28 B6
Libby Ct PL12 ....122 C5
Liberator Row **4** PL27 ....31 F3
Libra Ave **5** PL9 ....136 E8
Lidden Cl TR18 ....143 C3
Lidden Cres TR18 ....143 C3
Lidden Rd TR18 ....143 C3
Liddicoat Rd PL22 ....112 D3
Liddle Way PL7 ....131 B6
Lifeboat Hill **32** TR26 ....141 B6
LIFTON 19 F3
Lifton Comm Prim Sch
  PL16 ....19 F4
LIFTONDOWN 19 D4
Liftondown Cross PL16 ....19 D4
Liggars Dr **9** PL14 ....50 E7
Liggars Farm Rd PL14 ....50 F5
Lighterage Hill TR1 ....137 E2
Lighthouse Hill TR16 ....67 C6
Lighthouse La PL26 ....85 C5
Lighthouse Rd
  19 Lizard TR12 ....102 F2
  Lizard TR12 ....102 F2
Lilac Cl PL2 ....135 C5
Lily Way PL28 ....31 F7
Lime Cl TR8 ....44 F6
Limerick Pl PL4 ....149 C3
Limes La Liskeard PL14 ....113 B5
  Tavistock PL19 ....147 A6
Limes The PL6 ....124 F2
Limetree Rd PL3 ....128 D7
Lime Tree Way PL15 ....27 D4
Limmicks Rd PL13 ....117 D6
Lincoln Ave PL4 ....149 C4
Lincoln Row **6** PL27 ....31 F3
Linden Ave TR7 ....110 E5
Linden Cres TR7 ....110 E5
Linden Terr PL4 ....149 C3
Lindsay Fields TR9 ....45 E1
Lingard Cl PL4 ....113 A6
Lingfield Ave PL26 ....58 E1
Linhay Cl PL25 ....115 D6
Linhay La **4** PL9 ....129 D1
Linkadells PL7 ....130 D6
Link Cl TR11 ....144 F4
Linketty La E PL6 ....130 C5
Linketty Lane E PL6 ....125 A1
LINKINHORNE 39 B3
Link Rd PL15 ....106 B3
Links The Falmouth TR11 ....144 F1
  Praa Sands TR20 ....90 C4
Links View EX23 ....104 F6
Linley Cl TR3 ....69 D3
Linnet Cl TR12 ....122 C2
Linton Cl PL5 ....124 C8
Linton La EX39 ....2 E5
Linton Rd PL5 ....124 C7
Linton Sq PL5 ....124 C8
Lippell Dr PL9 ....135 E6
Lipson Co-operative Academy
  PL4 ....129 A4
LIPSON 149 C4
Lipson Ave PL4 ....149 C4
Lipson Ct PL4 ....149 B3
Lipson Rd PL4 ....149 B4
Lipson Sp Ctr PL4 ....129 A4
Lipson Terr PL4 ....149 C4
LIPSON VALE 129 A4
Lipson Vale PL4 ....129 A4
Lipson Vale Prim Sch PL4 ....129 C4
Lipstone Cres PL4 ....149 C4
Lisburne Terr TR19 ....97 A6
Liscawn Terr PL11 ....127 B3
Liscombe Cl PL18 ....41 A7
Lishaperhill Cross EX22 ....5 E2
LISKEARD 113 E6
Liskeard Bsns Pk PL14 ....113 E6
Liskeard Com Hospl PL14 ....113 E7
Liskeard & District Mus★
  PL14 ....113 C6
Liskeard Hill PL14 ....36 F2
Liskeard Hillfort Prim Sch
  PL14 ....113 A6
Liskeard Rd Callington PL17 ....39 E4
  Newtown PL15 ....27 C4
  Saltash PL12 ....122 B3
  Trematon PL12 ....53 E3
Liskeard Sch & Com Coll
  PL14 ....113 C7
Liskeard Sta PL14 ....113 B4
Liskerrett Rd PL14 ....113 D5
Liskey TR6 ....55 A4
Liskey Hill TR6 ....55 A4
Liskey Hill Cres **1** TR6 ....55 A4
Liskey Tourist Pk TR3 ....69 C4
Lisson Gr PL4 ....128 F4
Lister Cl PL7 ....130 F6
Lister Hill **10** TR11 ....145 A4
Lister St PL11 ....145 A3
Listowel Dr PL13 ....117 D4
Listry Rd TR7 ....110 E5
Litchaton Cres PL7 ....130 D7
Litchaton Way PL7 ....130 D7
Litchfield Cl PL7 ....131 B6
Little Ash Gdns PL5 ....123 B1
Little Ash Rd PL5 ....123 B1
LITTLE BOSULLOW 75 D1
Little Bridge Cross EX22 ....8 A5
Littlebridge Mdw EX22 ....8 A5

Little Bridge Pk PL27 ....108 D6
LITTLE BRYNN 46 E5
Little Butts PL9 ....135 C6
Little Castle St **7** TR1 ....137 C4
LITTLE COMFORT 28 C7
Little Dean PL14 ....113 A5
Little Dinas PL28 ....107 E4
Little Dock La PL5 ....124 B2
Little Down La PL6 ....121 E3
Little Down Pk TR7 ....111 A4
Little Downs PL30 ....36 A2
LITTLE FALMOUTH 145 B7
Little Falmouth TR11 ....145 B7
Little Fancy Cl PL6 ....125 C7
Little Field Ct PL19 ....147 E5
Little Gilly Hill **3** TR15 ....140 C4
Little Gregwartha TR16 ....80 A5
Little Hill PL13 ....62 D1
Little-in-sight **19** TR26 ....141 B6
LITTLE KIRLAND 109 C1
Little La Hayle TR27 ....142 E7
  Kingsand PL10 ....133 A2
  Staddiscombe PL9 ....135 D3
Little Laney PL13 ....62 D1
Little Mdw Bodmin PL31 ....109 D5
  Pyworthy EX22 ....8 E5
Little Nanteague TR4 ....69 E7
Little Oaks TR10 ....144 B6
Little Orch PL12 ....53 C3
LITTLE PETHERICK 32 C6
Little Point Cres PL10 ....132 F5
LITTLE PRIDEAUX 60 B7
Little Sinns TR16 ....68 A3
Little Stark Cl PL26 ....58 B4
Littleton Pl PL2 ....127 F4
Little Trelower Pk PL26 ....58 E1
Little Treloweth TR15 ....139 B6
Little Trelyn PL27 ....21 E2
Little Trenethick **15** TR13 146 D8
Little Treslea Hill PL30 ....36 A3
Little Trethewey Est TR19 ....96 E4
Little Trethiggey TR8 ....111 F2
Little Treverrow PL27 ....21 E2
Little Treviscoe PL26 ....58 B7
Little Western Rly★ TR7 ....110 F5
Little Woburn Cl PL15 ....106 C4
Littlewood Cl PL7 ....131 A4
Littlewood Mill La PL30 ....23 C1
LIZARD 102 F2
Lizard Cl PL6 ....124 F7
Lizard Head La TR12 ....102 F2
Lizard Lighthouse Her Ctr★
  TR12 ....102 F1
Lizard Nature Reserve The★
  TR12 ....100 F2
Lizard Point TR12 ....102 F1
Lizard Point Holiday Park★
  TR12 ....102 F8
Lizard Point Holiday Pk★
  TR12 ....99 D1
Lizard Wlk PL6 ....125 A7
Llantillio Dr PL7 ....128 B8
Llawnroc Cl TR14 ....138 E2
Llewellyn Cl TR32 ....105 C3
Lloyds Rd TR12 ....103 A2
Loatmead Cross EX22 ....3 E3
LOCKENGATE 47 E4
Lockeridge Rd PL20 ....41 B1
Lockington Ave PL3 ....128 F7
Locks Wlk PL1 ....127 E1
Lockyer Ct PL1 ....148 C2
Lockyer Mews PL19 ....147 C6
Lockyer Rd PL3 ....128 E5
Lockyers Quay PL4 ....149 B2
Lockyer St PL1 ....148 C2
Lodenek Ave PL28 ....107 D4
Lodge Dr TR1 ....137 F6
Lodge Gdns PL6 ....124 E3
Lodge Hill PL14 ....113 A3
Lodge La PL8 ....136 F5
Lodge Way TR9 ....45 F2
Loe Bar Rd TR13 ....98 C8
Loe Hill TR11 ....82 C5
Loe Valley Rd TR13 ....146 B1
Lofotin Cl PL1 ....127 E2
Loftus Gdns PL5 ....123 C2
Logans Ct TR26 ....141 D2
Loggans Cl TR27 ....142 E8
Loggans Rd TR27 ....142 E8
Loggans Way TR27 ....142 E8
Loggans Wlk TR27 ....142 E8
Lollabury Rd PL12 ....122 E3
Lomond Hall PL31 ....141 D1
LONDON APPRENTICE 59 B1
Longacre
  Harrowbarrow PL17 ....40 C4
  Plymouth PL7 ....130 B7
Long Acre PL12 ....122 B4
Long-A-Row Cl EX23 ....10 C6
Long Barn The TR20 ....89 D8
LONGBRIDGE 129 F7
Longbridge Cl PL6 ....129 F6
Longbridge Rd
  Plymouth, Laira PL3 ....129 C4
  Plymouth, Longbridge PL6 ....129 C4
Longbrook Barton PL7 ....130 D5
Longbrook St PL7 ....130 F4
Longcause PL7 ....130 F4
Longcause Specl Sch PL7 ....130 F4
Long Croft Rd **11** TR27 ....142 D6
LONGCROSS 29 F6
Long Cross PL29 ....22 C6

Longcross Victorian Gdns★ PL29 ....22 C6
LONGDOWNS 81 A1
Longdowns Ind Est 6 TR10 81 A1
Longdowns Trad Est TR10 .81 A1
Longfield TR11 ....144 E4
Longfield Cl 25 PL17 .....39 F4
Longfield Dr PL32 ......105 C3
Longfield Pl PL4 ....149 B4
Longfield Rd PL32 ......105 C3
Long Field Rd PL15 ....106 D4
Longfield Villas PL9 ....135 D8
Longhouse La PL27 ......21 E3
Long La High Street PL26 .58 C4
  Ludgvan TR20 ....89 A7
  St Erth TR20,TR27 .....89 E8
  Tregurrian TR8 ....44 F8
LONGLANDS 122 A1
Longlands PL9 ....135 D8
Longlands La PL12 ......122 B1
Long Lanes TR20 ....89 F7
Long Ley PL3 ....129 B6
Longman's La 3 PL17 ....39 E4
Long Mdw Chapel PL15 ..106 A5
  Plymouth PL4 ....130 D7
Long Mdw La 1 TR11 ...144 D5
Long Mdw View PL23 ...116 B5
Longmeadow Cl PL7 ....130 E7
Longmeadow Rd PL12 ..122 E3
Long Moor TR12 ....103 A5
Long Orch PL20 ....41 B1
Long Park Cl PL9 ......135 F5
Longpark Dr EX23 ....6 F5
Long Park Dr PL6 ......125 D7
Long Park Rd PL12 .....122 D2
Longpark Way PL25 ....114 F5
Long Pk PL15 ....18 D2
Long Rd PL12 ....122 B4
LONGROCK 88 F6
Long Rock Business Park TR20 ....88 F6
Long Rock Industrial Estate TR20 ....88 F6
Long Row TR19 ....97 F7
Long Rowden PL3 ......128 E6
Long Steps PL23 ....116 C4
LONGSTONE Carbis Bay ..141 E1
  St Mabyn 34 F8
Longstone Ave PL6 .....125 A6
Longstone Cl TR26 .....141 E1
Longstone Downs TR13 ..91 E6
Longstone Hill TR26 ....141 E1
Longstone Rd PL30 ......34 E8
Long Terrace Cl 5 PL7 ..131 C5
Longview Rd PL12 ......122 D3
Longview Terr PL3 ......129 B7
Longwood Cl PL7 ....131 A4
Longwool Mdw EX23 .....7 B6
LOOE 117 D3
Looe Com Academy PL13 .117 D6
Looe Hill Looe PL13 ......63 F5
  Seaton PL13,PL11 ....64 A5
Looe Prim Sch PL13 ....117 D4
Looe St PL4 ....149 A2
Looe Sta PL13 ....117 C4
Lookout The 7 TR11 ...145 B5
Looseleigh Cl PL6 ......125 A4
Looseleigh La PL6 ......124 F5
Looseleigh Pk PL6 ......124 E5
Lopes Dr PL6 ....121 C1
Lopes Rd Dousland PL20 ..42 E3
  Plymouth PL2 ....128 B6
Lopwell Cl PL6 ....124 F5
Lord Louis Cres PL9 ....134 F6
Lords Mdw TR2 ....71 F3
Lorrimore Ave PL2 ......127 F5
Loscombe Ct TR16 ......80 A5
Loscombe La TR16 ......80 A5
Lost Gdns of Heligan The★ PL26 ....73 B5
LOSTWITHIEL 112 E1
Lostwithiel Mus★ PL22 .112 C2
Lostwithiel Prim Sch PL22 112 C2
Lostwithiel Rd PL30,PL31 ..48 C7
Lostwithiel St PL23 .....116 C4
Lostwithiel Sta PL22 ....112 D2
Lostwood Rd PL25 ......114 E4
Lotherton Cl PL7 ....131 B3
Loughboro Rd PL5 ......123 C1
LOVATON 42 F1
Love La Bodmin PL31 ...109 F5
  Hayle TR27 ....142 E7
  Mousehole TR19 ....88 C1
  Penryn TR10 ....144 D8
  Penzance TR18 ....143 C4
  Saltash PL12 ....122 E2
  24 St Ives TR26 ....141 B6
Lovell Rd PL3 ....128 F6
Lovely La PL12 ....65 A8
Loveny Cl 1 Bodmin PL31 .109 A4
  St Neot PL14 ....36 F2
Loveny Rd PL14 ....36 F2
Lovering Rd PL25 ......114 E4
Lovers La EX23 ....10 B7
Lovibond Wlk PL27 .....108 C5
Lowarth Cl TR13 ....146 B6
Lowarth Elms 13 TR15 ..140 B5
Lowarthow Marghas TR15 140 D5
Lowenac Cres TR27 ......78 E6
Lowenac Gdns TR14 ....138 C2
Lowen Bre TR1 ....69 E3
Lowen Cl 7 TR1 ....137 D4
Lowenek Cl TR11 ......144 E5
Lowenna Fields TR11 ....93 D4

Lowenna Gdns PL13 ....117 C4
Lowenna La 3 TR6 ......55 B4
Lowenna Manor PL27 ....21 E3
Lowen Way TR3 ....69 C3
Lower Anderton Rd PL10 .132 F5
Lower Balwest TR13 .....90 D4
Lower Barncoose TR15 ..139 F6
Lower Biteford Cross EX39 ..3 E6
LOWER BODINNAR 87 E7
Lower Bore St PL31 .....109 D5
LOWER BOSCASWELL 74 F2
Lower Boscaswell Parc TR19 ....74 F1
Lower Bostraze TR20 ....87 A6
LOWER BREA 139 A3
Lower Broad La TR15, TR16 ....139 C8
Lower Cardrew La TR15 ..140 B6
Lower Carnkie TR16 ....140 A1
Lower Castle Rd TR2 .....95 A5
Lower Chapel St PL13 ...117 D3
Lower Church St 2 TR27 .142 D6
Lower Cleaverfield PL15 .106 C7
LOWER CLICKER 51 F4
Lower Clicker Rd PL14 ...51 F4
LOWER COMPTON 128 F5
Lower Compton Rd PL3 ..128 F5
Lower Condurrow TR14 ..139 A1
Lower Coronation Terr 9 PL17 ....39 F4
Lower Eastcliff TR4 .....68 A7
Lower East Street 1 TR9 ..45 E6
Lower Elms PL27 ....21 F3
Lower Fairfield PL12 .....65 A8
Lower Farm Rd PL7 .....131 A4
Lower Fore St PL12 .....123 A2
Lower Glen Pk PL14 .....38 D4
Lower Goongumpas La TR16 ....68 F1
Lower Goonrea PL13 ....117 B4
LOWER GREEN 146 A5
Lower Greenbanks PL27 ..21 E2
Lower Green St TR18 ...143 D1
Lower Grumbla Rd TR20 ..87 C4
Lower Gurnick Rd TR18 .143 B3
Lower Hill TR13 ....146 C6
Lower Hillcrest
  Helston TR13 ....146 C6
  9 Perranporth TR6 ......55 A4
Lower Hillside PL14 ......50 B6
Lower Hugus Rd TR3 .....69 C3
Lower Kelly PL18 ....41 A3
Lower Kenneggy TR20 ....90 A3
Lower La Mawgan TR12 ...99 D7
  6 Plymouth PL1 ....149 A2
Lower Lux St 5 PL14 ...113 C6
Lower Market St
  Looe PL13 ....117 D3
  Penryn TR10 ....144 C7
Lower Mdw 5 TR4 ....69 A3
Lower Merritts Hill 22 TR16 67 E4
Lower Middle Hill PL14 ...38 E4
Lower Molinnis PL26 .....47 D2
LOWER NINNES 76 B1
Lower Ninnis TR16 ......140 F5
Lower North Country TR16 .67 F4
Lower Parc TR12 ....92 C2
Lower Park Dr PL9 .....135 F4
Lower Pengegon TR14 ...138 F3
Lower Pentreath 5 TR20 ..90 B3
Lower Peverell Rd PL18 .143 E7
Lower Pk TR2 ....70 F5
Lower Polstain Rd TR3 ....69 D3
LOWER PORTHPEAN 59 E1
Lower Port View PL12 ...122 F2
LOWER PROSPIDNICK 91 C6
Lower Pumpfield Row TR15 ....139 B6
Lower Quay PL12 ....92 C1
Lower Quay Rd TR3 ......81 F6
Lower Rd Downderry PL11 ..64 A7
  Welltown PL30 ....36 A2
Lower Redannick TR1 ..137 C4
Lower Ridings PL7 ......131 B7
LOWER ROSE 55 D5
Lower ROSEWARNE 138 B3
Lower Rosewin Row 9 TR1 ....137 D5
Lower Row PL10 ....133 A2
Lower Rowes Terr PL26 ..58 D5
Lower Saltram PL9 .....135 C2
Lower Sheffield TR19 ....97 F7
Lowerside PL2 ....128 A8
Lower Sladesmoor Cres PL15 ....13 F1
Lower Sq EX22 ....11 E8
Lower St Looe PL13 .....117 D3
  Plymouth PL4 ....149 A3
Lower Tamar Terr PL18 ...41 A7
Lower Terr TR3 ....81 B4
Lower Tokenbury Rd PL14 .38 E5
LOWERTOWN Helston 91 E4
  Lostwithiel 48 A4
Lowertown TR13 ....146 C8
Lowertown Town PL17 ...28 E1
Lowertown Cl PL12 ......53 C3
Lowertown La TR13 ....146 C7
LOWER TREBULLETT 28 A4
Lower Trecuilliacks TR15 ..93 C8
Lower Tregongeeves PL26 .59 A1
Lower Treloweth Rd PL26 .59 A1
Lower Treluswell TR10 ...81 D2
Lower Trevance TR7 ......32 E7
Lower Tywarnhayle 18 TR6 .55 A5
Lower Well La TR13 ....146 C6
Lower Well Pk PL26 .....73 C3
Lower Wesley Terr PL14 ..38 D4

Lower Woodside PL25 ...114 A4
Lowery Cross PL20 ....42 F4
Low Lee Rd TR19 ....88 D1
Lowley Rd PL15 ....18 E2
Lucas Cl PL31 ....109 E3
Lucas La PL7 ....130 D6
Lucas Terr PL4 ....129 B2
LUCKETT 40 B8
Lucknow Hill PL17 ....40 B7
Lucknow Rd PL31 ....48 D8
Lucknow Road S 2 PL31 ..48 D8
LUDGVAN 89 A7
Ludgvan Com Prim Sch TR20 ....89 B8
Ludlow Rd 2 PL3 ....128 E6
LUFFINCOTT 13 C5
Luffman Cl PL13 ....62 D6
Lugger The TR2 ....83 B2
Lukes Cl TR1 ....137 F5
Luke's La TR20 ....89 F6
Lulworth Dr PL6 ....125 B7
Lundy Cl PL6 ....124 F7
Lundy Dr EX23 ....10 C6
Lundy Rd PL29 ....22 E7
Luney La PL26 ....72 E8
Lusart Dr TR12 ....102 F2
Luscombe Ave 1 PL19 ..147 B7
Luson Cl 4 PL28 ......107 C4
Lusty Glaze Adventure Ctr TR7 ....111 A8
Lusty Glaze Rd TR7 ....111 A7
LUTSFORD 3 A6
Lutsford Cross EX39 ......3 A6
Lutyens Fold PL19 ....29 C6
Luxland View TR7 ......110 F3
Luxmore Cl PL6 ....125 E1
Luxon Dr TR7 ....110 F4
Lux Park L Ctr PL14 ....113 C7
Luxstowe Dr 1 PL14 ...113 C6
Luxstowe Gdns PL14 ...113 C6
LUXULYAN 48 A1
Luxulyan Rd PL24 ......115 F7
Luxulyan Sch PL30 ......48 A1
Luxulyan Sta PL30 ......47 F1
Lych Cl PL9 ....135 A6
Lychgate Dr TR1 ....137 C6
Lydcott Cl PL13 ....63 F8
Lydcott Cres PL13 ......63 F8
Lydcott La PL13 ....64 A8
Lydcot Wlk PL6 ....125 A1
Lydford Park Rd PL3 ....128 D5
Lyd Gdns PL19 ....147 D5
Lydia Way PL4 ....149 B4
Lympne Ave PL5 ....123 F5
Lynbridge Ct 5 PL19 ...147 B5
Lyndhurst Ave PL25 ....115 A4
Lyndhurst Cl PL2 ....128 C6
Lyndhurst Rd PL2 ....128 C6
Lyndon Ct PL12 ....122 D4
Lyndrick Rd PL3 ....128 E7
Lynes Cotts 2 PL14 .....51 A7
Lynher Cl PL15 ....27 B3
Lynher Ct PL12 ....122 F1
Lynher Dr PL12 ....122 F1
Lynher La PL15 ....27 B2
Lynher St PL5 ....123 D2
Lynher View 2 PL17 ....38 E8
Lynher Way
  28 Callington PL17 ......39 F4
  North Hill PL15 ....27 A4
Lyn-Meynek TR15 ......140 D4
Lynmouth Cl PL7 ......130 C7
LYNSTONE 104 D3
Lynstone Cotts EX23 ...104 D3
Lynstone Rd EX23 ......104 D4
Lyn Terr 7 TR18 ....143 C1
Lynwood Ave PL7 ......130 B6
Lynwood Bungalows TR13 .91 A1
Lynwood Cl 3 PL31 ....109 E4
Lynwood Cotts 1 TR19 ..88 C1
Lynwood Flats PL13 ....91 A1
Lynx La 2 PL9 ....136 E8
Lyons Rd PL25 ....115 A4
Lysander La 2 PL25 ....125 B5
Lytton Pl PL25 ....114 F4

M

MABE BURNTHOUSE 93 C8
Mabena Cl PL30 ....34 C8
Mabe Prim Sch TR10 ....81 C1
Macadam Rd PL4 ....149 C1
Macaulay Cres PL5 .....124 C1
Macey St PL11 ....127 C3
Mackenzie Pl PL5 ......123 C2
Mackerel Cl PL25 ......114 E7
Madden Rd PL1 ....127 F2
Maddever Cres PL14 ....113 C5
Maddock Cl PL7 ....131 A4
Maddock Dr PL7 ....131 B4
Maddocks Cross EX22 ....3 F2
Madeira Dr EX23 ....6 F5
Madeira Rd
  Falmouth TR11 ....145 A1
  Plymouth PL1 ....149 A1
Madeira Villas 1 PL20 ...42 C5
Madeira Wlk TR11 .....145 A2
MADERS 39 D6
Madford La PL15 ......106 C5
Madge Cl 3 PL19 ......147 B6
Madge La PL19 ....147 B6
Madison Terr PL27 .....142 E7
Madison Vean TR27 ....142 E7
MADRON 143 B8
Madron Rd PL18 ....143 C7
MAENPORTH 93 E4
Maenporth Est TR11 ....93 E4

Maenporth Rd
  Maenporth TR11 ....93 E4
  Maenporth TR11 ....94 B3
  Tregedna TR11 ....94 B3
Maen Valley Pk TR11 ....93 E5
Maenwennel Rd PL7 ....130 C5
Maer Down Rd EX23 ...104 C7
Maer La EX23 ....104 D8
Magdalen Gdns PL7 ....130 F3
Magistrates Gr PL14 ....113 C8
Magnificent Music Machines Mus★ PL14 ....51 C3
Magnolia Cl 3 PL7 .....131 B5
Magnolia Cl 3 PL9 .....135 F7
Magor Ave TR14 ....79 E5
Magor Hill TR14 ....67 B3
Maida Vale Terr PL4 ....128 F4
Maiden St 1 EX23 ....4 E1
Maidenwell Rd PL7 ....130 C5
Maidstone Pl PL5 ....123 E4
Maine Gdns PL2 ....127 F7
Mainlay TR12 ....99 B7
Main Rd Crumplehorn PL13 .62 D2
  Downderry PL11 ....64 C5
Mains Bridge Rd PL30 ...34 D7
MAINSTONE 125 F2
Mainstone Ave PL4 ....149 C2
Maitland Dr PL3 ....128 F8
Maker Cl PL10 ....133 B4
Maker Rd PL11 ....127 A2
Maker View PL3 ....128 B4
Maker View Rd PL10 ...133 A6
Malabar Ho TR1 ....69 F3
Malabar Rd TR1 ....69 F3
Mallard Cl PL7 ....130 F5
Mallets Cl PL27 ....108 C6
Malletts Hill PL14 ....36 E2
Mallory Dr TR7 ....111 B5
Malmesbury Cl PL2 ....128 B8
Malory Cl PL5 ....124 D2
MALPAS 70 D2
Malpas Ho TR1 ....137 E4
Malpas Rd TR1 ....137 E2
Malthouse Cl 16 TR3 ....81 B4
Malt House Ct 1 TR27 ..142 D6
Malt House Gdns 2 TR18 .143 C2
Malthouse La TR17 .....89 C5
Malt House The 3 TR18 .143 C2
MANACCAN 101 A8
Manaccan TR12 ....101 A8
Manaccan Prim Sch TR12 101 A8
MANADON 124 D1
Manadon Cl TR13 ......146 D8
Manadon Dr PL5 ....124 E1
Manadon Football Ctr PL2 124 D2
Manadon Hill PL5,PL6 ..124 E1
Manadon Vale Prim Sch 1 PL5 ....128 E8
Manaton Cl TR13 ......146 D8
Manaton Dr PL15 ......106 C5
Manby Gdns PL5 ....123 F5
Mandalay Villas 8 TR9 ..45 E1
Mandeley Cl PL5 ....14 D2
Maneley Wy PL17 ....40 C4
Manely Way PL17 ....40 C4
Manewas Way TR7 .....111 B7
Manfield Way PL25 ....115 C4
Manhay TR13 ....92 B5
Manifold Gdns PL3 ....129 D5
Manley Cl PL14 ....113 B5
Manley Rd PL14 ....113 B5
Manley Terr 5 PL14 ...113 B5
MANNAMEAD 128 F5
Mannamead Ave PL3 ..128 F5
Mannamead Ct 9 PL3 ..128 F6
Mannamead Rd PL3 ....128 F6
Man of War View TR12 ..102 F2
Manor Bourne Rd PL9 ..135 C1
Manor Cl Blisland PL30 ...35 D8
  Crackington Haven EX23 ..10 C6
  Falmouth TR11 ....144 C5
  Heamoor PL18 ....143 D7
  Helston TR13 ....146 D8
  St Austell PL25 ....114 C5
  Tavistock PL19 ....147 A6
Manor Cotts PL11 .....145 D3
Manor Cres TR11 ......144 C5
Manor Ct 1 TR2 ....95 A6
Manor Dr TR26 ....141 C3
Manor Est PL20 ....42 B4
Manor Farm PL20 ....42 E3
Manor Farm Cl 7 TR20 ..89 E5
Manor Farm Rd PL26 ...115 A1
Manor Gdns
  Camelford PL32 ....105 D4
  Horrabridge PL20 ....42 B4
  Millbrook PL10 ....132 F6
  Plymouth PL1 ....148 B2
  Redruth TR15 ....140 B6
  St Erth TR27 ....142 A1
  Truro TR1 ....137 E5
Manor La PL3 ....129 D5
Manor Park Cl PL7 .....130 F5
Manor Park Dr PL7 ....131 A4
MANOR PARSLEY 68 B5
Manor Pk Dousland PL20 ..42 E3
  Duloe PL14 ....51 A1
  Saltash PL12 ....122 A1
Manor Pl PL1 ....148 A3

Manor View PL24 ....60 B4
Manor Way Heamoor PL18 .143 D7
  Helston TR13 ....146 D8
  Tavistock PL19 ....147 B6
Manse Rd 6 TR3 ....81 F7
Mansion Ho The PL1 ...134 A8
Manson Pl PL26 ....58 C8
Manston Cl PL5 ....123 E5
Mantle Gdns PL5 ......127 D8
Maple Ave Camelford PL32 .105 E5
  Torpoint PL11 ....127 A3
Maple Cl Bodmin PL31 ..109 B4
  23 Callington PL17 .....39 F4
  Plymouth PL6 ....125 E7
  5 St Columb Major TR9 ..45 D6
  St Dennis PL26 ....58 B8
  Tavistock PL19 ....147 C3
Maple Ct 2 PL9 ....135 F7
Maple Gr
  Plymouth, Mutley PL4 ..128 D4
  Plymouth, Plympton PL7 .130 B5
Maple Leaf Cl PL27 ....108 C7
Maple Way PL6 ....125 E7
MARAZION 89 B6
Marazion Mus★ TR17 ...89 B5
Marazion Sch TR17 .....89 C5
Marazion Way PL2 .....128 D8
Marchant's Cross PL20 ..42 F1
Marchant's Way PL20 ...42 F2
Marconi Centre (Mus)★ TR13 ....98 F2
Marconi Cl TR13 ....146 B6
Marcus Hill TR7 ....110 E6
Marcwheal Dr TR19 .....88 C1
Mardon Cl PL6 ....125 D4
Marett Rd PL5 ....123 F3
Margaret Ave PL25 ....114 E3
Margaret Cnr PL31 ....109 C4
Margaret Cres PL31 ...109 C4
Margaret Gdns PL27 ...108 D5
Margaret Pk PL3 ......128 E8
Margaret Pl TR11 .....144 F3
Margate La PL30 ....35 C1
MARHAMCHURCH 7 B6
Marhamchurch CE Prim Sch EX23 ....7 B6
Maria's La TR19 ....96 B7
Maribou Ct PL28 ....31 F7
Marina Ct TR16 ....67 C5
Marina Rd PL5 ....123 F3
Marina Terr 7 PL4 .....128 F4
Marine Academy PL5 ..123 E1
Marine Cres 5 TR11 ...145 C3
Marine Ct Falmouth TR11 .145 D3
  26 Perranporth TR6 .....55 A5
  Torpoint PL11 ....127 B2
Marine Dr Looe PL13 ...117 D1
  Torpoint PL11 ....127 B2
  Widemouth Bay EX23 ...6 E4
  Widemouth Bay EX23 ...6 E5
Marine Par PL2 ....95 A5
Marine Rd PL9 ....135 B7
Marine Terr Boscastle PL35 ..9 C2
  7 Penzance TR18 ......143 E4
Maristow Ave PL2 ......127 F5
Maristow Cl PL6 ....124 F5
Maristow La PL12 ......122 F3
Maritime House Discovery Quay 16 TR11 ....145 C3
Marjorie Cl PL12 ......122 C4
Market Ave PL1 ....148 B3
Market Cl PL1 ....123 C1
Market Ct 4 Hayle TR27 .142 D6
  9 Launceston PL15 ....106 C6
Market Hill PL25 ....114 C4
Market House Arc
  3 Bodmin PL31 ....109 E5
  10 Launceston PL15 ...106 C6
Market Inn PL24 ....60 B5
Market Jew St TR18 ...143 E5
Market Pl Camelford PL32 .105 D4
  Helston TR13 ....146 B5
  Marazion TR17 ....89 B5
  Padstow PL28 ....107 D5
  25 Penzance TR18 ....143 E5
  St Columb Major TR9 ...45 E6
  33 St Ives TR26 ....141 B6
  Week St Mary EX22 ....11 E8
Market Rd Plymouth PL7 .130 B6
  Tavistock PL19 ....147 C5
Market Sq 18 Callington PL17 39 E4
  Hayle TR27 ....142 D6
  Plymouth PL1 ....148 C3
  St Day TR16 ....68 D1
  St Just TR19 ....86 F6
Market St Bodmin PL31 ..109 E5
  Devoran TR3 ....81 F6
  Falmouth TR11 ....145 B4
  Fowey PL23 ....116 D4
  Hayle TR27 ....142 D6
  Kingsand PL10 ....133 A1
  11 Launceston PL15 ...106 C6
  Liskeard PL14 ....113 C6
  Plymouth PL1 ....128 A1
  6 St Austell PL25 .....114 C3
  St Just TR19 ....86 F6
  3 Stratton EX23 ....4 E1
  Tavistock PL19 ....147 C5
Market Strand
  Falmouth TR11 ....145 B4
  Padstow PL28 ....107 D5
  7 Redruth TR15 ....140 B5
  31 St Ives TR26 ....141 B6
Market Way Plymouth PL1 .148 C3
  5 Redruth TR15 ....140 B4
Marks Dr PL31 ....109 E3
Mark's Way TR7 ....110 D4
Markwell La PL12 ....53 C1

Marlborough Ave TR11 . . .145 A3
Marlborough Cl
 1 Falmouth TR11 . . . . .145 A3
 Saltash PL12 . . . . .122 F1
Marlborough Cres TR11 . .145 A3
Marlborough Ct **5** TR11 . .145 A3
Marlborough Gr **2** TR11 . .145 A3
Marlborough Prim Sch
 PL1 . . . . .127 E2
Marlborough Rd
 Falmouth TR11 . . . . .145 A3
 Plymouth PL4 . . . . .149 A4
Marlborough Row PL1 . . .127 E2
Marlborough Sch TR11 . . .145 A3
Marlborough St PL1 . . . . .127 E2
Marlborough Way PL26 . . .58 E1
Marldon Cl PL5 . . . . .124 B3
Marlow Cres PL16 . . . . . . .29 F8
Marlow Gdns PL20 . . . . . .135 F5
Marriotts Ave TR14 . . . . .138 B4
Marrowbone Slip PL4 . . . .149 B2
Marryat Gdns PL5 . . . . . .124 E1
Marshall Ave PL27 . . . . . .108 D5
Marshall Cl Roche PL26 . . . .46 F3
 Tavistock PL19 . . . . .147 D2
Marshallen Rd TR4 . . . . . .68 C6
Marshall Rd Bodmin PL31 .109 D3
 Bodmin, Nanstallon PL30 . .34 C2
 Plymouth PL7 . . . . .130 A5
 Tavistock PL19 . . . . .147 D2
Marshalls Way PL29 . . . . .22 D6
Marsh Cl PL6 . . . . .129 F6
Marshfield Cl **4** TR4 . . . . .55 D4
Marshfield View PL11 . . . .64 B5
MARSHGATE 10 C2
Marsh La Angarrack TR27 .142 F7
 Calstock PL18 . . . . .41 A3
 Hayle TR27 . . . . .142 E7
Marshlands PL27 . . . . . . .34 A6
Marsh Lane Ind Est TR27 .142 F7
MARSH MILLS 130 A6
Marsh Mills PL6 . . . . .129 F7
Marsh Mills Pk PL6 . . . . .129 F6
Marsh Mills Ret Pk PL6 . .129 E7
Marsh Mills Sta* PL7 . . . .130 A7
Marthas Mdw TR9 . . . . . .45 E1
Marthus Ct **10** PL14 . . . . .113 C5
Martin Cl TR15 . . . . .140 D5
Martin Ho **11** TR15 . . . . . .140 B4
Martin La PL4 . . . . .149 A2
Martins Cl PL14 . . . . .113 E7
Martin's Ct **2** PL31 . . . . .109 D5
Martin's La TR15 . . . . . . .139 C8
Martin Sq **6** PL17 . . . . . . .39 F4
Martin St PL1 . . . . .148 B2
Martinvale Ave TR15 . . . .140 E7
Martinvale Parc TR15 . . . .140 E7
Martlesham Pl PL5 . . . . .123 F4
Martyn's Cl TR4 . . . . .55 D4
Mary Dean Ave PL5 . . . . .124 C7
Mary Dean Cl PL5 . . . . . .124 C7
Mary Dean's CE Prim Sch
 PL5 . . . . .124 C7
Maryland Gdns PL2 . . . . .127 F7
Mary Moon Cl PL12 . . . . .53 B7
Mary Newman's Cottage*
 PL12 . . . . .123 A2
Mary Seacole Rd PL1 . . . .148 A3
Marys Well TR16 . . . . .67 D4
Marythorne Rd **15** PL20 . . .41 B1
Masefield Gdns PL5 . . . . .124 B1
Masons Row PL18 . . . . . . .40 F6
Masterman Rd PL2 . . . . . .127 F4
Matela Cl **10** TR13 . . . . . . .98 C8
Matthews Way PL14 . . . . .51 F6
Maudlin Cl PL14 . . . . . . .113 D4
Maudlins La PL15 . . . . . . .147 A5
Maudlins Pk **7** PL19 . . . . .147 A5
Maunsell Cl PL2 . . . . . . .127 F7
Mavisdale PL2 . . . . .127 F6
Mawes Ct PL18 . . . . .40 D5
Mawgan Garras TR12 . . . .100 A6
 Mawgan TR12 . . . . .99 D6
Mawgan Cross TR12 . . . . .99 D7
Mawgan-in-Pydar Com Prim
 Sch TR8 . . . . .45 A8
MAWGAN PORTH 31 B2
Mawgan Porth Hill TR8 . .31 C1
Mawgan Vu TR9 . . . . .57 E8
MAWLA 68 B4
MAWNAN 93 E2
Mawnan Church of England
 (Voluntary Aided) Primary
 School TR11 . . . . .93 D3
MAWNAN SMITH 93 E3
Maxwell Rd PL4 . . . . . . .135 B8
MAXWORTHY 12 A3
Maxworthy Cross PL15 . . .12 B4
Maxworthy Rd PL15 . . . . .12 B4
Maybank Rd PL4 . . . . . . .149 C3
Maybrook Dr PL12 . . . . . .122 D2
Mayers Way PL9 . . . . . . .135 D6
Mayfair Cres PL6 . . . . . . .125 B1
Mayfair Ho PL4 . . . . .149 A3
Mayfield Cl Bodmin PL31 . .35 B2
 Port Isaac PL29 . . . . .22 D7
 St Austell PL25 . . . . .115 A4
Mayfield Cres TR7 . . . . . .110 E5
Mayfield Dr
 Port Isaac PL29 . . . . .22 E7
 Roche PL26 . . . . .47 A3
Mayfield Rd
 Falmouth TR11 . . . . .144 F4
 Newquay TR7 . . . . .110 E4
 Port Isaac PL29 . . . . .22 D7
Mayflower Cl
 19 Bere Alston PL20 . . . . .41 B1
 Plymouth PL9 . . . . .135 F7

Mayflower Community
 Academy & Nursery **1**
 PL2 . . . . .128 A7
Mayflower Dr PL2 . . . . . .128 B5
Mayflower L Ctr PL2 . . . .128 C5
Mayflower St PL1 . . . . . . .148 C3
May Gdns TR16 . . . . .80 D6
May La PL13 . . . . .117 F5
Maymear Terr PL30 . . . . . .23 E3
Mayna Parc PL15 . . . . . . .18 B8
Maynarde Cl PL7 . . . . . . .131 B5
Maynard Pk PL20 . . . . . . .41 B1
Mayne Cl PL15 . . . . .106 B7
Maynes Row TR14 . . . . . .139 A5
MAYON 96 B6
Mayon Green Cres TR19 . .96 B7
Mayon Farm TR19 . . . . . .96 B6
May Terr PL4 . . . . .149 B3
McCarthy Dr PL26 . . . . . . .58 B4
Mclean Dr PL26 . . . . .58 D5
MEAD 2 D4
Mead Cnr EX39 . . . . .2 D4
Meadfoot Terr **2** PL4 . . . .128 F5
Mead Gdns **11** PL31 . . . . .109 A5
Mead Hos The TR18 . . . .143 F8
Meadowbank TR11 . . . . . .82 A3
Meadowbank Rd TR11 . . .145 A6
Meadow Brook PL19 . . . . .147 A4
Meadow Cl Gloweth TR1 . .69 E3
 Newquay TR7 . . . . .111 A4
 Plymouth PL7 . . . . .131 D4
 Polruan PL23 . . . . .116 D2
 St Austell PL25 . . . . .114 F6
 St Stephen PL26 . . . . .58 B4
 Saltash PL12 . . . . .122 F3
Meadow Ct Mevagissey PL26 .73 C3
 Padstow PL28 . . . . .107 B4
 St Mabyn PL30 . . . . .34 C8
 Stithians TR3 . . . . .80 E4
Meadow Dr Bude EX23 . . .104 F6
 Camborne TR14 . . . . .138 C4
 Looe PL13 . . . . .117 D5
 Par PL24 . . . . .115 F5
 Saltash PL12 . . . . .122 D4
Meadowfield Pl PL7 . . . . .131 B3
Meadow Flats **27** TR26 . .141 B6
Meadowhead PL27 . . . . . .108 C4
Meadow La TR1 . . . . .137 D3
Meadowlands PL26 . . . . . .125 D7
Meadowlands Leisure Pool
 PL19 . . . . .147 B5
Meadow Pk
 7 Liskeard PL14 . . . . . . .113 B5
 Plymouth PL9 . . . . .135 C5
 Trewoon PL25 . . . . .59 A3
Meadow Pl PL31 . . . . . . .109 D4
Meadow Plash PL30 . . . . .35 C8
Meadow Rd PL13 . . . . .62 A7
Meadow Rise Foxhole PL26 .58 D6
 1 Penwithick PL26 . . . . . .59 D7
 Plymouth PL7 . . . . .131 A4
 12 St Columb Major TR9 . . .45 E6
Meadowside
 Launceston PL15 . . . . . . .106 A4
 Newquay TR7 . . . . .111 A4
 Plymouth PL9 . . . . .135 F7
 St Austell PL25 . . . . .115 C6
 Whitstone EX22 . . . . .12 B8
Meadowside Cl Hayle TR27 142 A3
 St Kew Highway PL30 . . . . .23 B2
Meadowside Rd TR11 . . . .144 F2
Meadow St PL26 . . . . .73 C3
Meadows The
 St Dennis PL26 . . . . .58 C8
 St Dominick PL12 . . . . . . .40 D2
 St Teath PL30 . . . . .23 E7
 Torpoint PL11 . . . . .126 E4
Meadowsweet Cl **6** PL14 .113 D8
Meadowsweet Pk PL12 . . .122 C2
Meadow Terr PL14 . . . . . . .37 F3
Meadow The Illogan TR16 . .67 D4
 Polgooth PL26 . . . . .59 A1
 47 St Ives TR26 . . . . .141 B6
 Truro TR1 . . . . .137 B5
Meadow View
 Camborne TR14 . . . . .138 E1
 8 Goldsithney TR20 . . . . .89 E5
 St Minver PL27 . . . . .21 F3
 St Tudy PL30 . . . . .23 E3
Meadow View Rd PL7 . . . .130 D5
Meadow Villas **8** TR13 . .143 C1
Meadow Way Plymouth PL7 130 D7
 St Issey PL27 . . . . .32 E6
Meadow Wlk PL23 . . . . . .116 D2
Mead The PL7 . . . . .130 D7
Meadway Looe PL13 . . . . .117 E4
 St Austell PL25 . . . . .114 F5
 Saltash PL12 . . . . .122 E1
MEADWELL 29 C8
Mearwood La TR11 . . . . . .144 F4
Meaver La **3** TR12 . . . . . . .99 B2
Meaver Rd TR12 . . . . .99 B1
MEAVY 42 F2
Meavy Ave PL5 . . . . .124 E2
Meavy Bourne PL20 . . . . . .42 D2
Meavy CE Prim Sch PL20 . .42 F2
Meavy La PL20 . . . . .42 D2
Meavy Villas PL20 . . . . . . .42 D2
Meavy Way Plymouth PL5 .124 E2
 Tavistock PL19 . . . . .147 D5
MEDDON 3 C4
Meddon Cross Edistone EX39 . .3 C4
 Welcombe EX39 . . . . .3 C4
Medland Cres PL6 . . . . . .124 D6
Medland Gdns PL26 . . . . .114 C4
Medlyn Carnkie TR13 . . . . .80 C1
 Halwin TR13 . . . . .92 C8
Medlyn Ct **3** TR13 . . . . . .146 B5

Medrose PL27 . . . . .21 D2
Medrose St PL33 . . . . .14 E3
Medrose Terr **21** TR18 . . .143 E6
Medrow PL15 . . . . .27 A8
Medway Pl PL3 . . . . .129 D6
Melbourne Cotts PL1 . . . .148 B3
Melbourne Gn **2** PL1 . . . .148 B3
Melbourne Pl PL1 . . . . . .148 B4
Melbourne Rd PL14 . . . . .113 B5
Melbourne St PL1 . . . . . .148 B3
Melbourne Terr **17** TR18 .143 C7
MELBUR 57 F5
Melin Dr TR1 . . . . .137 B6
Mellanear Cl TR27 . . . . . .142 B4
Mellanear Ct TR27 . . . . . .142 B4
Mellanear Rd TR27 . . . . . .142 B3
Mellangoose TR13 . . . . . .146 A8
Mellanvrane La TR7 . . . . .110 F4
Melliars Way EX23 . . . . . .104 F6
MELLINGEY 32 D6
Mellingey Rd PL27 . . . . . .32 D6
Mellingey Valley **5** TR3 . .81 D6
Melrose Ave PL2 . . . . . . .128 C8
Melrose Terr **6** TR9 . . . . .45 E1
Melvill Cres TR11 . . . . . . .145 B3
Melvill Ct TR11 . . . . .145 B2
Melville Pl **1** PL2 . . . . . .128 A5
Melville Rd Plymouth PL2 .128 A5
 Threemilestone TR3 . . . . . .69 D3
Melville Terr PL22 . . . . . .112 C2
Melville Terrace La PL2 . . .128 A5
Melvill La TR11 . . . . .145 B2
Melvill Rd TR11 . . . . .145 C2
Melyn Cl TR27 . . . . .142 E8
Memory La PL9 . . . . .135 E7
Menabilly Cl PL17 . . . . . . .39 E3
Menabilly Rd PL25 . . . . . .114 E6
Mena Chinowyth **3** TR11 .144 F2
Menacuddle Hill PL25 . . .114 C4
Menacuddle La PL25 . . . .114 C4
MENADARVA 66 E2
Menadue Ct TR27 . . . . . . .78 E3
Menage St TR13 . . . . . . .146 C5
MENAGISSEY 68 C5
Menague PL7 . . . . .21 E3
Menakarne TR16 . . . . .80 F8
Menallack Cheese Farm*
 TR10 . . . . .93 A6
Mena Park Cl PL9 . . . . . .136 B7
Mena Park Rd PL9 . . . . . .136 B7
MENDENNICK 132 C7
Mendennick Hill
 Freathy PL11 . . . . .65 F4
 Mendennick PL11 . . . . . . .132 C7
Meneage Cotts **3** TR13 . .146 C5
Meneage Ho **4** TR13 . . . .146 C5
Meneage Parc TR13 . . . . .146 C5
Meneage Rd TR13 . . . . . .146 C4
Meneage St TR13 . . . . . . .146 C5
Meneage Villas PL25 . . . .114 B3
Menear Rd PL25 . . . . . . .115 A6
Menehay Farm TR11 . . . .144 D3
Menerdue La TR16 . . . . . .80 E1
Meneth TR12 . . . . .92 C1
Meneth Rd TR14 . . . . . . .138 F2
Menhaye Gdns TR15 . . . .139 D7
Menhay View TR11 . . . . .144 C3
MENHENIOT 52 A5
Menheniot Cres PL15 . . . .18 D5
Menheniot Prim Sch PL14 .52 A5
Menheniot Sta PL14 . . . . .51 F4
Menhinick Cl PL12 . . . . . .53 C3
Menhyr Dr TR26 . . . . . . .141 C2
Menhyr Pk TR26 . . . . . . .141 C2
Menna La Ladock TR2 . . . .57 E5
 St Dennis PL26 . . . . .46 C1
Mennaye Ct TR18 . . . . . .143 D4
Mennaye Rd TR18 . . . . . .143 D4
Merafield Cl PL7 . . . . . . .130 B5
Merafield Dr PL7 . . . . . . .130 C4
Merafield Farm Cotts PL7 130 B4
Merafield Rd PL7 . . . . . . .130 C4
Merafield Rise PL7 . . . . . .130 C4
Merbein Cotts TR8 . . . . . .44 E8
Merchant's House (Mus)*
 PL1 . . . . .148 C2
Merchants Quay PL15 . . . .18 E2
Meredith Rd PL2 . . . . . . .128 C6
Meres Valley TR12 . . . . . .99 A3
Meridian Ho PL4 . . . . . . .149 A3
Merlin Cl PL6 . . . . .125 E8
Merlin Pl TR20 . . . . .88 D1
Merlins Way TR34 . . . . . . .14 D7
Mermaid Ct TR7 . . . . . . .111 C8
Merrick Ave TR1 . . . . . . .137 E6
MERRIFIELD 7 F4
Merrifield Cl TR1 . . . . . . .137 B5
Merrifield Cross EX22 . . . . .7 F4
Merrill Pl TR11 . . . . .145 A3
Merritts Hill TR16 . . . . . . .67 E4
Merritts Way TR15 . . . . . .139 C7
Merrivale Rd
 Plymouth, Ham PL2 . . . . . .128 B7
 Plymouth, Honicknowle PL5 .124 B3
Merrivale View Rd PL20 . . .42 E3
MERRYMEET 38 C1
Merry Meeting TR4 . . . . . .78 F6
Merry Meet La TR11 . . . .144 C3
Merry Mit Mdw TR11 . . . .144 C3
Merryn Hts **20** PL28 . . . . .31 F7
Mersey Cl PL3 . . . . .129 D6
Merthen TR11 . . . . .92 C1
MERTHER 70 F3
Merther Cl TR11 . . . . .91 B3
Merther Collyn TR2 . . . . . .83 B3
Merther La TR13 . . . . .91 B3
MERTHER LANE 70 F1

Messack Cl TR11 . . . . . . .144 E2
Metha Pk TR8 . . . . .56 C7
Metha Rd TR8 . . . . .56 C7
METHERELL 40 D4
Metherell Cl TR18 . . . . . . .40 D4
Metheleigh Bottoms TR13 .91 A1
Methleigh Parc TR13 . . . . .91 A1
MEVAGISSEY 73 D3
Mevagissey Aquarium*
 PL26 . . . . .73 C3
Mevagissey Com Prim Sch
 PL26 . . . . .73 C4
Mevagissey Ho TR1 . . . . . .69 E4
Mevagissey Mus* PL26 . . .73 C3
Mews Ct PL14 . . . . .51 F6
Mews The Launceston PL15 106 A8
 Par PL24 . . . . .60 B5
 3 Penzance TR18 . . . . . .143 E6
 Plymouth, Devonport PL1 . .128 A3
 Plymouth, Stonehouse PL1 .148 A3
Mexico La TR27 . . . . .142 C7
Mexico Terr TR27 . . . . . . .142 C8
Michael Rd PL3 . . . . .129 A5
MICHAELSTOW 24 A5
Michell Ave TR7 . . . . .110 C6
Michell Ct TR7 . . . . .110 D6
Michigan Way PL3 . . . . . .129 C6
Mid Churchway PL9 . . . . .136 A7
Mid Cornwall Bsns Ctr
 PL25 . . . . .115 E4
MIDDLE CRACKINGTON . . .10 B6
Middle Down Cl PL9 . . . .136 A5
Middlefield Rd PL6 . . . . . .124 D6
Middlefield Cl PL12 . . . . .122 B2
Middlegates **5** TR5 . . . . . .54 D1
MIDDLE GREADOW 48 B1
MIDDLEHILL 38 D3
Middle Market St PL33 . . .117 D3
MIDDLEMOOR 147 F2
Middle Rd TR15 . . . . .140 E7
Middle Rosewin Row **8**
 TR1 . . . . .137 D5
Middle Row TR13 . . . . . . .90 E3
Middle St Padstow PL28 . .107 D5
 Port Isaac PL29 . . . . .22 D7
Middle Stennack Cotts **13**
 TR26 . . . . .141 A5
Middleton Cres TR7 . . . . .110 F4
Middletons Row **6** TR15 .140 C5
Middleton Wlk PL5 . . . . . .123 D4
Middleway PL24 . . . . .60 B5
Middlewell Parc PL27 . . . .108 B4
Middle Wharf PL1 . . . . . . .73 C3
Middle Wlk **1** PL26 . . . . .115 A1
MIDDLEWOOD 27 B2
Midella Rd PL20 . . . . .42 D2
Mid Moor PL14 . . . . .38 B6
Midway Dr TR1 . . . . .137 D5
Midway Rd PL31 . . . . . . .109 A5
Miers Cl PL5 . . . . .127 C8
Miers Ct PL5 . . . . .127 C8
Milch Pk PL12 . . . . .122 C2
MILCOMBE 62 F6
Mildmay St PL4 . . . . .149 A4
Mile End Grochall PL12 . . .102 F4
 Lizard TR12 . . . . .102 F4
Mile Hill TR4 . . . . .68 A5
Milehouse Rd PL2 . . . . . .128 A5
Miles Mitchell Ave PL6 . . .125 A1
Milestone Ct TR3 . . . . .69 D4
Milford La PL5 . . . . .124 D5
Military Rd Millbrook PL10 .132 C3
 Plymouth PL3 . . . . .129 C6
 Rame PL10 . . . . .64 C2
 St Mawes TR2 . . . . .95 B4
Milladon La PL12 . . . . . . .64 D8
Mill Ball Hill EX23 . . . . . .10 B7
Millbank Mdw TR27 . . . . .78 E1
MILLBAY 148 B2
Millbay Rd PL1 . . . . .148 A2
Mill Bridge PL1 . . . . .148 A3
MILLBROOK 132 E5
Millbrook Bsns Ctr PL11 .132 C6
Millbrook CE VA Prim Sch
 PL10 . . . . .132 E5
Mill Cl Porthleven TR13 . . .91 A1
 Wadebridge PL27 . . . . . . .108 E5
Mill Cotts TR13 . . . . .146 A6
Millefleur TR11 . . . . .144 F3
MILLENDREATH 117 F5
Millennium Appartments
 TR10 . . . . .81 D2
Millennium Way TR13 . . .146 D8
Miller Bsns Pk PL14 . . . . .113 B4
Miller Ct Liskeard PL14 . . .113 B4
 Plymouth PL1 . . . . .148 A2
Miller Way PL6 . . . . .125 C4
Millet Cl TR17 . . . . .89 D5
Millfield TR18 . . . . .88 E6
Millfields TR17 . . . . .89 B6
Mill Flats TR13 . . . . .146 B6
Mill Ford Sch PL5 . . . . . .123 F4
Mill Gdns PL22 . . . . .112 C2
Millham La PL22 . . . . . . .112 E3
MILLHILL 30 B1
Mill Hill Crumplehorn PL13 .62 D1
 Lelant TR27 . . . . .77 E3
 Lostwithiel PL22 . . . . .112 D2
 St Just in Roseland TR2 . . .82 F3
Mill Hill Cotts PL19 . . . . . .30 B1
Mill Hill La Millhill PL19 . . .30 C1
 Tavistock PL19 . . . . .147 A6
Millhouse Pk PL11 . . . . . .127 A4
Mill La Camelford PL32 . . .105 D5
 Coad's Green PL15 . . . . . . .27 C1
 Grampound TR2 . . . . .72 A7
 Helston TR13 . . . . .146 B6
 Middlewood PL15 . . . . .27 B2

Mill La continued
 20 Mousehole TR19 . . . . . . .88 C1
 Porthleven TR13 . . . . .91 A1
 St Breward PL30 . . . . .24 B3
 St Germans PL12 . . . . .65 A8
 Torpoint PL11 . . . . .127 A2
 Tregony TR2 . . . . .71 F3
 Truro TR3 . . . . .137 C1
MILLOOK 6 D2
Millpond Ave TR27 . . . . . .142 B4
MILLPOOL Cardinham 35 F5
 Praa Sands 90 B5
Millpool Lostwithiel PL22 .112 F3
 Newtown TR20 . . . . .90 B4
 Rilla Mill PL17 . . . . .38 E8
Millpool Head PL10 . . . . .132 E4
Millpool Hill PL30 . . . . . . .35 F5
Millpool Rd PL10 . . . . . . .133 A6
Mill Rd Millbrook PL10 . . .133 A5
 Otterham Mill PL32 . . . . . .10 L1
 Padstow PL28 . . . . .107 D5
 Penhallick PL12 . . . . .101 C1
 Penponds TR14 . . . . .79 B5
 Perranporth TR6 . . . . .55 B4
 Tideford PL12 . . . . .52 F2
Mill Rd Est PL12 . . . . .52 F2
Mill Rise PL27 . . . . .108 E5
Mills Gdns TR16 . . . . .68 E1
Mill Sq PL28 . . . . .107 D5
Mills Rd PL1 . . . . .127 F2
Mills' St TR16 . . . . .68 E1
Mill St PL31 . . . . .109 E4
MILLTOWN Cardinham 35 E3
 Lostwithiel 60 F8
Milltown Gdns PL15 . . . . .18 E6
Milltown La PL14 . . . . . . .36 F2
Mill View Gdns PL30 . . . .132 F5
Mill View Rd PL10 . . . . . .132 F5
Millway Pl PL9 . . . . .135 D8
Millwood Dr PL6 . . . . . . .125 E1
Mill Yard **17** TR3 . . . . . . .81 B4
Milne Pl PL1 . . . . .127 F3
MILTON ABBOT 29 D6
Milton Abbot Sch PL19 . . .29 D5
Milton Cl PL5 . . . . .124 D2
MILTON COMBE 120 F8
Milton Cres PL19 . . . . . . .147 D5
Milton Ct
 Plymouth, Cattedown PL4 .149 C2
 Plymouth, Prince Rock PL4 .129 B1
MILTON GREEN 29 D5
Minack Open Air Theatre*
 TR19 . . . . .96 E2
Mine Hill PL14 . . . . .51 F6
Mine La PL30 . . . . .47 E7
Miners Ct Perranporth TR6 . .55 A4
 Redruth TR15 . . . . .140 C5
Miners Row TR15 . . . . . . .140 C5
Miners Way **12** TR5 . . . . . .54 D1
 Liskeard PL14 . . . . .113 D7
Minerva Cl PL7 . . . . .131 A6
MINGOOSE 68 C7
Miniatura Park* TR4 . . . . .55 E4
MINIONS 38 B6
Minions Heritage Ctr*
 PL14 . . . . .38 B6
Minions Row PL14 . . . . . .145 B3
Minnie Pl TR11 . . . . .145 B3
Minorca La PL26 . . . . .47 D2
Minses Cl PL9 . . . . .136 C7
Minster Ave EX23 . . . . . . .104 F4
Minster Mdw TR12 . . . . . .101 A8
Minster Rd PL35 . . . . .9 E1
Minster Terr TR12 . . . . . .101 A8
Minton Cl PL25 . . . . .115 A4
Mirador Pl PL4 . . . . .129 C3
Mission The TR18 . . . . . .143 F4
Misterton Cl PL9 . . . . . . .136 B8
MITCHELL 56 F5
Mitchell Cl Lizard TR12 . .102 F2
 Plymouth PL9 . . . . .135 C5
Mitchell Ct **11** TR1 . . . . . .137 D5
Mitchell Hill TR1 . . . . . . .137 D5
Mitchell Hill Terr **4** TR1 .137 D5
 Mitchell TR8 . . . . .56 E5
Mitchell Mews **17** TR1 . . .137 D5
Mitchell Rd Camborne TR14 138 C3
 St Austell PL25 . . . . .114 F4
Mitchell's Boatyard PL26 . .73 C2
Mitchells Cnr **24** TR6 . . . . .55 A5
MITHIAN 54 F1
MITHIAN DOWNS 68 F8
Mithian Prim Sch TR5 . . . .54 E1
Mitre Cl PL19 . . . . .147 A3
Mitre Ct **16** PL1 . . . . .149 A2
MIXTOW 116 D7
Moat Pk PL6 . . . . .125 C1
Mob La PL14 . . . . .37 B2
Modbury Cl PL5 . . . . .124 B3
Modus La PL26 . . . . .58 E1
Modyford Wlk PL20 . . . . . .41 F3
Mohun's Cl PL19 . . . . . . .147 C4
Mohun's Pk PL19 . . . . . . .147 C3
Molenick La PL12 . . . . . . .52 E3
Molesworth Ct **4** PL27 . . .108 B5
Molesworth Rd
 Plymouth, Plympton PL7 . .130 C6
 Plymouth, Stoke PL1, PL3 .128 A3
Molesworth St Tintagel PL34 14 C7
 Wadebridge PL27 . . . . . . .108 B5
Molesworth Terr PL10 . . .132 F5
MOLINNIS 47 C2
Molinnis PL26 . . . . .47 C2

Molinnis Rd PL26 . . . . .47 C2
Mollison Rd PL5 . . . . .123 E2
Molyneaux Pl 10 PL1 . . . . . .127 F3
Monastery Cl TR12 . . . . . . .101 D4
MONGLEATH 144 E4
Mongleath Ave TR11 . . . . . .144 E3
Mongleath Cl TR11 . . . . . . .144 E3
Mongleath Rd TR11 . . . . . . .144 E3
Monica Wlk PL4 . . . . .149 B4
Monkey Sanctuary The★
  PL13 . . . . .63 F5
Monks Hill PL15 . . . . .28 C4
Monksmead PL19 . . . . .147 A4
Monks Park Cotts PL15 . . . .106 D6
Monmouth Gdns PL5 . . . . . .124 C4
Monmouth La PL22 . . . . . . .112 D2
Monroe Gdns PL4 . . . . .148 B4
Montacute Ave PL2 . . . . . . .124 E2
Montague Ave TR15 . . . . . .140 A6
Monterey Cl EX23 . . . . .104 E4
Monterey Gdns TR1 . . . . . .137 E5
Montgomery Cl PL12 . . . . . .122 D3
Montgomery Dr PL19 . . . . . .147 A6
Montgomery Rd 2 PL26 . . . . .59 D7
Montpelier Prim Sch PL2 . .128 B6
Montpelier Rd PL2 . . . . . . .128 C7
Montrose Way 2 PL5 . . . . . .124 D2
Monument Rd TR13 . . . . . . .146 B5
Monument St PL1 . . . . .127 E1
Monument Way PL31 . . . . . .109 C4
Moonrakers TR26 . . . . .141 D2
Moonsfield 5 PL17 . . . . .39 F4
Moon St PL4 . . . . .149 A3
Moorcroft Cl PL9 . . . . .136 A7
Moor Cross EX22 . . . . .8 D3
Moor Cross Cotts EX23 . . . . .4 C3
Moorfield PL16 . . . . .19 F4
Moorfield Ave 4 PL6 . . . . . .129 C7
Moorfield Rd
  Camborne TR15 . . . . .139 C6
  St Giles on the Heath PL15 . .13 F1
Moor Hill PL15 . . . . .26 E4
Moor La PL5 . . . . .123 E1
Moorland Ave PL7 . . . . .130 F6
Moorland Cl Liskeard PL14 .113 D7
  Pendeen TR19 . . . . .74 F1
  Yelverton PL20 . . . . .121 D8
Moorland Ct
  1 St Austell PL25 . . . . . . .114 C3
  Yelverton PL20 . . . . .42 C2
Moorland Dr PL7 . . . . .130 E6
Moorland Gdns PL7 . . . . . .130 F6
Moorland Rd
  Indian Queens TR9 . . . . . . .45 F2
  Launceston PL15 . . . . .106 A4
  Plymouth PL7 . . . . .130 E5
  St Austell PL25 . . . . .114 C3
  Tywardreath PL24 . . . . .60 C4
Moorland Road Ind Est TR9 .45 F2
Moorlands La PL12 . . . . . . .122 C4
Moorlands Trad Est PL12 . .122 C4
Moorland View
  Golberdon PL17 . . . . .39 B6
  Liskeard PL14 . . . . .113 D7
  Plymouth, Derriford PL6 . . .125 A5
  Plymouth, Plymstock PL9 . .136 B7
  Saltash PL12 . . . . .122 F4
Moorland Villas 13 PL20 . . . .42 D2
Moorland Way PL18 . . . . . . .40 F5
Moorlan Mdws PL26 . . . . . . .47 A3
Moor Parc TR12 . . . . .100 D6
Moor St TR14 . . . . .138 D3
Moorstone Pl 15 PL26 . . . . . .59 D7
Moorswater Ind Est PL14 . . .51 A7
Moor The TR11 . . . . .145 B4
MOORTOWN Tavistock 42 D8
  Tetcott 13 C7
Moor View Bodmin PL31 . . .109 F2
  Plymouth PL9 . . . . .135 D7
  Plymouth, Keyham PL2 . . . .127 F5
  Plymouth, Laira PL3 . . . . . .129 C4
  Torpoint PL11 . . . . .127 B3
Moorview Ct PL6 . . . . .125 F5
Moorview Terr PL14 . . . . . . .38 D7
Moor View Terr
  Plymouth PL4 . . . . .128 E4
  Yelverton PL20 . . . . .42 D2
Morcom Cl PL25 . . . . .115 A5
Moresk Cl TR1 . . . . .137 D5
Moresk Gdns TR1 . . . . .137 D5
Moresk Rd TR1 . . . . .137 D5
Moreton Ave PL6 . . . . .124 F1
Moreton La EX23 . . . . .5 B2
Morice Sq PL1 . . . . .127 E2
Morice St PL1 . . . . .127 E2
MORICE TOWN 127 D3
Morice Town Prim Sch
  PL2 . . . . .127 E4
Morlaix Ave TR1 . . . . .137 D3
Morlaix Dr PL6 . . . . .125 B4
Morla La TR15 . . . . .140 A6
Morleigh Cl PL25 . . . . .114 F3
Morley Cl PL7 . . . . .130 A5
Morley Ct PL1 . . . . .148 B3
Morley Dr PL20 . . . . .42 A2
Morley View Rd PL7 . . . . . .130 C6
MORNICK 39 B7
Morrab Cl 8 TR7 . . . . .110 F6
Morrab Gdns 40 TR18 . . . . .143 E5
Morrab Pl 34 TR18 . . . . . . .143 E5
Morrab Rd Camborne TR14 .143 E5
  Penzance TR18 . . . . .143 E5
Morrab Terr 35 TR18 . . . . . .143 E5
Morris Gdns TR7 . . . . .110 D4

Morrish Pk PL9 . . . . .135 F6
Morshead Rd PL6 . . . . .124 F2
Mortain Rd PL12 . . . . .122 D4
Mortimore Cl PL12 . . . . . . .122 D2
MORVAH 75 C2
Morvah Hill TR20 . . . . .75 C2
MORVAL 63 D7
Morvan Trad Est PL25 . . . . .114 F3
Morven Rd PL25 . . . . .114 F3
Morview Rd PL13 . . . . .63 F8
Morwell Gdns PL2 . . . . . . .128 A6
MORWELLHAM 41 B4
Morwellham Cl PL5 . . . . . . .127 C8
Morwellham Quay★ PL19 . . .41 B4
Morwenna Gdns TR6 . . . . . .55 B5
Morwenna Pk EX23 . . . . .5 A6
Morwenna Rd EX23 . . . . .2 D1
Morwenna Terr EX23 . . . . .104 D6
MORWENSTOW 2 B2
Morweth Cotts PL11 . . . . . . .64 C5
Morweth Ct PL11 . . . . .64 C5
Moses Cl PL6 . . . . .124 E7
Moses Ct PL6 . . . . .124 E7
Mosquito Cres 3 PL21 . . . . .31 F3
Moss Side Ind Est 30 PL17 . .39 F4
Moss Terr PL23 . . . . .116 D3
Mostyn Ave PL4 . . . . .129 A4
Mote Pk PL12 . . . . .122 C3
Mothecombe Wlk PL6 . . . . .125 E1
Moulton Cl PL7 . . . . .131 B5
Moulton Wlk PL7 . . . . .131 B4
MOUNT Cardinham 36 B2
  Cubert 55 C7
MOUNT AMBROSE 140 E2
Mount Agar Rd TR3 . . . . . . .81 F7
MOUNT AMBROSE 140 E2
Mount Ambrose TR15 . . . . .140 E7
Mountbatten Cl
  Plymouth PL9 . . . . .135 D6
  St Columb Minor TR7 . . . . .111 E7
Mount Batten Ctr★ PL9 . . . .134 F7
Mountbatten Rd 5 PL26 . . . .59 D7
Mountbatten Way PL9 . . . . .135 E6
Mount Bennett Rd 5 PL24 .60 D5
Mount Bennett Terr 4
  PL24 . . . . .60 D5
Mount Camel PL32 . . . . . . .105 C4
Mount Carbis Gdns TR15 . .140 C3
Mount Carbis Rd TR15 . . . .140 D3
MOUNT CHARLES 114 E4
Mount Charles Prim Sch
  PL25 . . . . .114 F3
Mount Charles Rd PL25 . . . .114 F3
Mount Cres PL24 . . . . .60 C4
Mount Edgcumbe House &
  Country Pk★ PL10 . . . . . .133 E6
Mount Edgcumbe Terr
  TR11 . . . . .145 B4
Mountfield Terr 6 PL24 . . . .60 C4
Mount Folly TR27 . . . . .142 C6
Mount Folly Sq PL31 . . . . . .109 E4
Mount Ford PL19 . . . . .147 A5
Mount George Rd TR3 . . . . .82 B7
MOUNT GOULD 129 B3
Mount Gould Ave PL4 . . . . .129 B2
Mount Gould Cres PL4 . . . .129 B3
Mount Gould Hospl PL4 . . .129 B3
Mount Gould Rd PL4 . . . . . .129 B3
Mount Gould Way PL4 . . . . .129 B3
MOUNT HAWKE 68 C6
Mount Hawke Academy
  TR4 . . . . .68 C6
Mount Ho PL11 . . . . .64 C5
Mount House Sch PL19 . . . .147 E7
MOUNTJOY 45 A3
MOUNT LANE 13 E6
Mountlea Dr 9 PL24 . . . . . . .60 C4
Mount Lidden TR18 . . . . . . .143 C6
Mount Pleasant
  Bodmin PL31 . . . . .109 E5
  Boscastle PL35 . . . . .9 D1
  Falmouth TR11 . . . . .144 E1
  Hayle TR27 . . . . .142 C6
  Lelant TR26 . . . . .77 E3
  Millbrook PL10 . . . . .132 E5
  Newlyn TR18 . . . . .143 C4
  Par PL24 . . . . .60 B6
  Plymouth PL5 . . . . .124 B2
  38 St Ives TR26 . . . . .141 B6
Mount Pleasant Cl PL18 . . .138 E1
Mount Pleasant Gdns
  TR27 . . . . .138 D1
Mount Pleasant Pl PL22 . . .112 C3
Mount Pleasant Rd
  Camborne TR14 . . . . .138 D1
  11 Porthleven TR13 . . . . . .98 B8
  Threemilestone TR3 . . . . . .69 D3
Mount Pleasant Terr PL2 . .128 A4
  Mousehole TR19 . . . . .88 C1
  Redruth TR15 . . . . .140 E7
Mount Pleasure TR14 . . . . .138 D1
Mount Prospect Terr
  TR18 . . . . .143 C3
Mount Rant Hill PL14 . . . . . .50 A8
Mount Rd Mount PL30 . . . . .36 A3
  Par PL24 . . . . .60 C4
Mount Royal Cl TR18 . . . . . .143 F6
Mount's Bay Academy
  TR18 . . . . .143 B7
Mounts Bay Rd TR18 . . . . . .143 C4
Mounts Bay Terr TR13 . . . . .90 E3
Mount's Bay Terr 21 TR13 . .98 C8
Mount's Rd 20 TR13 . . . . . .98 C8
Mount St Mevagissey PL26 . .73 C3
  Penzance TR18 . . . . .143 E6
  Plymouth, Ford PL2 . . . . . .127 E1
  Plymouth, Mutley PL4 . . . . .149 A4
Mount Stamper Rd PL25 . . .114 D7
Mountstephen PL25 . . . . . .114 B3

Mount Stephens La TR11 . .144 F4
Mount Stone Rd PL1 . . . . . .134 A8
Mount Street Prim Sch
  PL4 . . . . .149 A4
Mount Tamar Cl PL5 . . . . . .123 E2
Mount Tamar Sch PL5 . . . . .123 E2
Mount Tavy Rd PL19 . . . . . .147 E6
Mount Terr 9 PL24 . . . . .60 B4
Mount View Lane TR8 . . . . .111 B3
  Madron TR20 . . . . .88 A7
Mount View Cl 15 TR2 . . . . . .83 B2
Mount View Cotts TR20 . . . .89 A7
Mount View Terr
  5 Madron TR17 . . . . .89 C5
  24 Newlyn TR18 . . . . .143 C2
Mount Whistle Rd TR14 . . . .138 F7
MOUNT WISE 127 F1
Mount Wise
  Launceston PL15 . . . . .106 C5
  Newquay TR7 . . . . .110 D5
Mount Wise Com Prim Sch
  PL1 . . . . .127 E1
Mount Wise Cotts TR7 . . . . .110 E5
Mount Wise Ct PL1 . . . . . . .127 F1
Mount Zion 52 TR26 . . . . . .141 B6
Mourne Villas PL9 . . . . . . .135 F8
MOUSEHOLE 88 C1
Mousehole Com Prim Sch
  TR19 . . . . .88 C1
Mousehole La TR19 . . . . . . .88 C1
Mowbray Mews PL32 . . . . . .10 B2
Mowhay Cl TR2 . . . . .111 A4
Mowhay Cotts PL26 . . . . . . .85 C5
Mowhay La 1 PL17 . . . . .39 E4
Mowhay Mdw TR9 . . . . .45 E1
  St John PL11 . . . . .132 B8
  Wadebridge PL27 . . . . . . .108 B4
Mowhay Rd PL5 . . . . .124 A2
Mowie The 13 TR9 . . . . .45 E2
Moyle Rd PL28 . . . . .107 E4
MUCHLARNICK 62 E7
Mudgeon TR12 . . . . .100 D7
Mudgeon Vean TR12 . . . . . .100 D8
Mudges Terr PL18 . . . . .41 A6
Mudge Way PL7 . . . . .130 E5
Mulberry Cl PL6 . . . . .125 E7
Mulberry Ct 12 TR11 . . . . . .145 B5
Mulberry Gr PL19 . . . . .147 C2
Mulberry Quay 11 TR11 . . . .145 B5
Mulberry Rd PL12 . . . . .122 E1
MULFRA 76 B1
Mulgrave St PL1 . . . . .148 C2
Mullet Ave PL3 . . . . .129 C4
Mullet Cl PL3 . . . . .129 C4
Mullet Rd PL3 . . . . .129 C4
MULLION 99 A1
Mullion Cl PL25 . . . . .114 E7
  Torpoint PL11 . . . . .126 F4
Mullion Cove Mullion TR12 . .98 F1
  Mullion TR12 . . . . .102 B7
Mullion Junior & Infant Sch
  TR12 . . . . .99 A1
Mullion Rural Workshops
  TR12 . . . . .99 A1
Mullion Sch TR12 . . . . .99 B1
Mundys Field TR12 . . . . . . .103 A5
Muralto Ho PL19 . . . . .147 A4
Murdoch Cl Redruth TR15 . .140 B6
  Truro TR1 . . . . .137 C6
Murdoch Flyer The★ 12
  TR15 . . . . .140 B4
Murdoch House & St Rumon's
  Gdn★ 13 TR15 . . . . .140 B4
Murdock Rd PL11 . . . . .126 F3
Murhill La 1 PL9 . . . . .129 D1
Murray Villas TR19 . . . . . . .86 E6
Murtons Terr TR16 . . . . .80 E7
Mus of Witchcraft★ PL35 . . . .9 C2
MUTLEY 128 F4
Mutley Ct PL4 . . . . .149 A4
Mutley Plain PL4 . . . . .128 E4
Mutley Plain La PL4 . . . . . .128 E4
Mutley Rd PL3 . . . . .128 E5
Mutton Hill TR27 . . . . .78 D6
Mutton Row PL10 . . . . .144 C8
MYLER CHURCHTOWN 82 C2
MYLOR BRIDGE 82 A3
Mylor Bridge Prim Sch
  TR11 . . . . .82 A3
Mylor Cl PL2 . . . . .128 D8
My Lords Rd TR9 . . . . .57 E8
Mylor Yacht Harbour
  TR11 . . . . .145 D8
Myrtle Cl PL20 . . . . .42 E3
Myrtle Ct PL26 . . . . .73 C3
Myrtles Ct PL2 . . . . .122 D4
Myrtle Terr 10 PL18 . . . . . . .40 F5
Myrtleville PL2 . . . . .128 A6
Mythyon Ct 4 TR18 . . . . . . .143 C7

N

Nailzee Ho PL13 . . . . .117 D2
Nailzee Point PL13 . . . . . . .117 D2
Nalder's Ct 10 TR1 . . . . . . .137 C4
Nampara Cl TR26 . . . . .141 E2
Nampara Ct 7 TR6 . . . . .55 A4
Nampara Row 21 TR6 . . . . . .55 A4
Nampara Way TR1 . . . . .137 F4
Nancarrow Ct 6 PL25 . . . . .114 F2
Nancarrows PL12 . . . . .122 C2
Nancealverne Specl Sch
  TR20 . . . . .143 C6
Nancedden Farm TR20 . . . . .89 A8
NANCEGOLLAN 91 C7
Nancegollan Ind Est TR13 . .91 B7
Nancekuke Cambrose TR16 . .67 F6

Nancekuke continued
  Porthtowan TR16 . . . . .68 A5
NANCEMELLIN 66 D1
Nancemellin Cl 3 TR3 . . . . .81 D6
Nancemere Rd TR1 . . . . . . .137 D6
Nancevallon TR14 . . . . .139 B3
Nancherrow Hill TR19 . . . . .86 F6
Nancherrow Row TR19 . . . . .86 F6
NANCLEDRA 76 F2
Nancledra Bottoms TR20 . . .76 F2
Nancledra Hill TR20 . . . . . . .76 F2
Nancledra Prim Sch TR26 . .76 F2
Nangitha Cl TR11 . . . . .144 C3
Nangitha Terr TR11 . . . . . . .144 C3
Nanhayes Row TR8 . . . . . . .56 B7
Nanjivey Pl 8 TR26 . . . . . . .141 A5
Nanjivey Terr 9 TR26 . . . . .141 A5
NANPEAN 58 D7
Nanpean Com Prim Sch
  PL26 . . . . .58 D6
Nanpusker Cl TR27 . . . . . . .142 E6
Nanpusker Rd TR27 . . . . . . .78 C4
Nansalsa Ct TR7 . . . . .111 A6
Nansavallon Rd TR1 . . . . . . .69 F3
Nanscober Pl TR13 . . . . . . .146 B8
Nanscothan TR15 . . . . .140 B4
Nanseglos Hill Madron TR20 88 B6
  Madron TR20 . . . . .143 A8
Nans Kestenen TR13 . . . . .146 B5
NANSLADRON 73 B7
Nansloe Academy TR13 . . .146 C4
Nansloe Cl TR13 . . . . .146 D4
Nansmellyon Rd
  Henscath TR12 . . . . .102 B7
  Mullion TR12 . . . . .99 A1
Nanstallo Com Prim Sch
  PL30 . . . . .34 C1
NANSTALLON 34 C1
Nanterrow Dr 6 PL31 . . . . . .109 A5
Nanterrow La TR27 . . . . . . .66 D1
NANTITHET 99 B5
Nanturras Parc TR20 . . . . . .89 F5
Nanturras Row TR20 . . . . . .89 E5
Nanturras Way TR20 . . . . . .89 F5
Napier St 1 PL1 . . . . .127 F3
Napier Terr PL4 . . . . .128 E4
Napps La PL15 . . . . .17 A4
NARKURS 64 D6
Narkurs Cross PL11 . . . . . . .64 D7
Narrowcliff TR7 . . . . .111 A7
Narrow La
  Botusfleming PL12 . . . . . . .122 C7
  Davidstow PL15 . . . . .16 A6
  Summercourt TR8 . . . . .57 C8
Nash Cl PL7 . . . . .131 A5
Nathan Cl PL11 . . . . .111 B5
National Lobster Hatchery★
  PL28 . . . . .107 E5
National Marine Aquarium★
  PL4 . . . . .149 A2
National Maritime Mus
  Cornwall★ TR11 . . . . . . .145 C3
National Seal Sanctuary The★
  TR12 . . . . .92 C1
NAVARINO 18 B8
Navy Inn Ct 10 TR18 . . . . . .143 C1
Neal Cl PL7 . . . . .131 B4
Neath Rd PL4 . . . . .149 C4
Neeham Rd TR8 . . . . .56 B7
Negus Gdns 5 PL31 . . . . . .109 A5
Nelson Ave PL1 . . . . .127 F3
Nelson Gdns 6 PL1 . . . . . . .127 F3
Nelson St PL4 . . . . .149 A4
Nelson Terr PL6 . . . . .125 E6
Nepean St 1 PL2 . . . . .127 F3
Neptune Ave PL27 . . . . .31 F3
Neptune Pk PL9 . . . . .135 B8
Neswick St PL1 . . . . .148 B3
Neswick Street Ope PL1 . . .148 A3
NETHERCOTT 13 E7
Nethercott Cross EX21 . . . . .13 F7
NETHERTON 38 D7
Netherton Est PL20 . . . . . . .42 A3
Netherton Rd PL28 . . . . . . .107 D4
Netley Mdw PL26 . . . . .47 C1
Nettell's Hill TR15 . . . . .140 B5
Nettlehayes PL9 . . . . .136 D7
Netton Cl PL9 . . . . .136 B6
Nevada Cl PL3 . . . . .129 D6
Nevada Pl 16 TR18 . . . . . . .143 C7
Nevada St TR18 . . . . .143 C7
Nevada Villas 8 PL24 . . . . . .60 C4
Newacott Cross EX22 . . . . . .7 F5
New Barn Hill PL7 . . . . .130 F3
New Bglws PL30 . . . . .36 B3
NEWBRIDGE Callington 39 D2
  Penzance 87 E6
  Truro 69 F3
Newbridge Hill PL18 . . . . . . .41 A6
Newbridge La TR1, TR3 . . . .69 F3
New Bridge St 9 TR1 . . . . . .137 D4
Newbridge Vw TR1 . . . . . . .69 F3
Newbridge Way TR1 . . . . . . .69 F3
Newbury Cl PL5 . . . . .124 B4
Newcastle Gdns PL5 . . . . . .124 B5
New Connection St 4
  TR14 . . . . .138 D3
New Cotts Gunnislake PL18 . .41 A6
  2 Kilkhampton EX23 . . . . . .5 A6
New Ct TR11 . . . . .145 B4
New Cut PL15 . . . . .140 B5
New Dairy La TR19 . . . . .89 B6
NEW DOWNS St Agnes 54 B2
  St Just 86 E6
New George St PL1 . . . . . . .148 C3
Newham Est TR1 . . . . .137 D3
Newham Ind Est TR1 . . . . . .137 D2
Newham La Helston TR13 . .146 A7

Newham La continued
  Lostwithiel PL22 . . . . .49 A1
Newham Rd TR1 . . . . .137 E2
Newhams La PL15 . . . . .27 B4
New Hill Est TR2 . . . . .72 A7
New Hos TR14 . . . . .139 B3
Newhouses 3 PL17 . . . . . . .38 E8
New La TR15 . . . . .140 E7
New Launceston Rd PL19 .147 A5
NEWLYN 143 D2
Newlyn Art Gall★ TR18 . . . .143 C3
Newlyn Halt Sta★ TR8 . . . . .56 C6
Newlyn Rd TR19 . . . . .97 B6
Newlyn Sch TR18 . . . . .143 C3
Newman Rd Plymouth PL5 . .123 E2
  Saltash PL12 . . . . .122 F3
NEWMILL Penzance 76 B1
  Poundstock 7 A1
Newmills Cl TR1 . . . . .137 B6
New Mills Farm Pk★ PL15 . .18 D4
Newmills Hill PL15 . . . . .18 C4
New Mills La TR1, TR4 . . . . .137 B6
Newmills Sta★ PL15 . . . . . . .18 D4
New Molinnis PL26 . . . . .47 C2
Newnham Ind Est PL7 . . . . .130 F6
Newnham Rd PL7 . . . . .130 F7
Newnham Way PL7 . . . . . . .130 F6
New Northernmayne 2
  PL15 . . . . .106 C6
New Park Rd Plymouth PL7 .131 A4
  Wadebridge PL27 . . . . . . .108 C5
New Passage Hill PL1 . . . . .127 E3
New Pk Horrabridge PL20 . . .42 C4
  Wadebridge PL27 . . . . . . .108 C4
NEW POLZEATH 21 E6
NEWPORT 106 B7
Newport Callington PL17 . . .39 E4
  St Germans PL12 . . . . .65 A8
Newport Cl 8 PL17 . . . . .39 E4
Newport Ind Est PL15 . . . . .106 C6
Newport Industrial Est
  PL15 . . . . .106 C6
New Portreath Rd
  Illogan TR16 . . . . .67 F5
  Redruth TR16 . . . . .140 A7
Newport Sq PL15 . . . . .106 B7
Newport St Millbrook PL10 .132 E5
  Plymouth PL1 . . . . .128 A1
Newport Terr 3 PL17 . . . . . .39 F4
NEWQUAY 110 E7
Newquay Adult Ed Ctr TR7 110 F6
Newquay Airport TR8 . . . . . .44 F8
Newquay Hospl TR7 . . . . . .110 F5
Newquay Junior Academy
  TR7 . . . . .110 F6
Newquay Rd
  Goonhavern TR4 . . . . .55 D4
  Roche PL26 . . . . .46 F3
  St Columb Major TR9 . . . . .45 D6
  Truro TR1 . . . . .137 F7
Newquay Sports & Com Ctr
  TR7 . . . . .111 B4
Newquay Sta TR7 . . . . .110 F6
Newquay Tretherras Sch
  TR7 . . . . .111 B6
Newquay Zoo TR7 . . . . .111 A5
New Rd Barripper TR14 . . . .79 B5
  Bere Alston PL20 . . . . .41 B2
  Bodelva PL24 . . . . .60 A6
  Boscastle PL35 . . . . .9 C2
  Cadgwith TR12 . . . . .103 A4
  Callington PL17 . . . . .39 E4
  Camborne TR14 . . . . .139 B3
  Cawsand PL10 . . . . .133 A1
  Coldvreath PL26 . . . . .46 F1
  Kingsand PL10 . . . . .133 B2
  Lifton PL16 . . . . .19 F4
  Liskeard PL14 . . . . .113 B5
  Newlyn TR18 . . . . .143 C3
  Perranporth TR6 . . . . .55 B4
  Port Isaac PL29 . . . . .22 D7
  Portscatho TR2 . . . . .83 B2
  Roborough PL6 . . . . .121 D2
  St Columb Major TR9 . . . . .45 E6
  St Hilary TR20 . . . . .89 F6
  St Just TR19 . . . . .86 F6
  Saltash PL12 . . . . .122 E3
  Stithians TR3 . . . . .80 F3
  Stratton EX23 . . . . .4 D1
  Summercourt TR8 . . . . .57 D7
  Tregony TR2 . . . . .71 F3
  Tregurrian TR8 . . . . .44 F8
  Troon TR14 . . . . .79 E4
New Road Cl PL10 . . . . . . .133 A2
New Road Hill PL23 . . . . . .116 C4
New Road Terr PL12 . . . . . . .53 C3
New Row Gweek TR12 . . . . .92 C1
  Mylor Bridge TR11 . . . . . . .82 A3
  Nancledra TR20 . . . . .76 F2
  Redruth TR16 . . . . .139 D1
  Summercourt TR8 . . . . .57 B6
New St Bugle PL26 . . . . .47 C1
  Falmouth TR11 . . . . .145 B4
  Millbrook PL10 . . . . .132 E5
  Padstow PL28 . . . . .107 D5
  Penryn TR10 . . . . .144 D7
  Penzance TR18 . . . . .143 E5
  Plymouth PL1 . . . . .149 A2
  Troon TR14 . . . . .79 E4
Newtake Rd PL19 . . . . .147 E2
Newton Ave PL5 . . . . .123 E2
Newton Ct Dobwalls PL14 . .50 E8
  Redruth TR15 . . . . .140 B6
Newton Farm Cotts PL13 . . .62 E3
Newton Gdns PL5 . . . . .123 E2
Newton Moor Tolcarne TR14 79 E5
  Treskillard TR14 . . . . .139 B1
Newton Pk 12 TR2 . . . . .95 A6

Newton Rd Newton PL30 . . . . 35 F8
St Mawes TR2 . . . . 95 A6
Treswigga TR22 . . . . 24 E1
Troon TR14 . . . . 79 E5
Newton's Margate Ind Est
PL31 . . . . 35 B1
NEWTOWN Coad's Green . . 27 D5
Praa Sands 90 B4
Newtown Fowey PL23 . . . . . 60 F3
Newtown TR20 . . . . 90 B4
Tregidden TR12 . . . . 100 E5
Trevegean TR19 . . . . 86 F4
NEWTOWN-IN-ST
MARTIN 100 E6
New Town La TR18 . . . . . . 143 E5
Newtown La PL15 . . . . 27 D5
New Windsor Terr **11**
TR11 . . . . 145 A4
New Wood Cl PL6 . . . . 125 E8
New Zealand Ho PL3 . . . . . 128 B4
Nicholas Ave TR16 . . . . 80 A5
Nicholas Holman Rd **2**
TR14 . . . . 138 E3
Nicholas Mdw PL17 . . . . . . 40 E4
Nicholas Parc **3** TR18 . . . 143 C7
Nicholson Rd PL5 . . . . 124 E2
Nicolls Flats PL15 . . . . 106 B5
Nightingale Cl PL9 . . . . . . 136 C8
Nine Maidens TR16 . . . . . . 80 A4
Nine Maidens Short Stay Sch
TR16 . . . . 80 A4
Nine Oaks Est TR20 . . . . . . 42 F3
Ninnesbridge Rd TR27 . . . . 77 B3
NINNIS BRIDGE 77 B2
No Go By Hill TR19 . . . . 86 F7
NO MAN'S LAND 63 E7
No Mans' Land Rd TR11 . . . 93 D5
Nook The PL19 . . . . 147 D6
NOONVARES 90 E7
Noonvares La TR13 . . . . . . 90 D7
Norfolk Cl PL3 . . . . 129 C5
Norfolk Rd Falmouth TR11 . 145 B4
Plymouth PL3 . . . . 129 C4
Norman Cotts PL5 . . . . 106 C7
Normandy Hill PL5 . . . . . . 123 B2
Normandy Way
Bodmin PL31 . . . . 109 F2
Plymouth PL5 . . . . 123 C2
Norman's Way PL30 . . . . . . 23 E3
NORRIS GREEN 40 E4
Northampton Cl PL5 . . . . . 124 B5
NORTH BEER 12 F3
NORTH BRENTOR 30 E8
North Carnmarth
Busveal TR16 . . . . 80 D8
Busveal TR16 . . . . 140 E8
North Cl EX23 . . . . 5 A6
North Cliff **12** TR19 . . . . . 88 C1
North Cliffs Churchtown TR14 67 F5
Coombe TR14 . . . . 66 F3
North Cnr **1** TR18 . . . . . . 143 C2
NORTH CORNER 101 C2
North Cornwall Mus & Gall★
PL32 . . . . 105 C4
NORTHCOTT Bude 4 C3
St Giles on the Heath 13 D3
Northcott Mouth Rd EX23 104 F8
NORTH COUNTRY 140 B8
NORTH DARLEY 38 D8
North Dimson PL18 . . . . . . 40 F6
North Down Cres PL2 . . . . 127 F6
North Down Gdns PL2 . . . 127 F6
North Down Rd PL2 . . . . . 128 B6
Northesk St PL2 . . . . 128 A4
Northey Cl TR4 . . . . 69 F6
Northey Rd Bodmin PL31 . . 109 D4
Bodmin PL31 . . . . 109 D4
Northfield Cl TR16 . . . . 68 E1
Northfield Dr TR1 . . . . 137 D3
Northgate Pl **1** PL15 . . . . 106 C6
North Grange Ind Est TR3 . 81 F6
NORTH HILL 27 B3
North Hill Blackwater TR4 . . 68 A5
Carharrack TR16 . . . . 80 F8
Chacewater TR4 . . . . 68 F3
6 Plymouth PL4 . . . . . . 149 A4
North Hill Pk PL25 . . . . . . 114 D4
North La PL14 . . . . 49 E7
NORTHMOOR 3 F3
North Moor Cross EX22 . . . . 3 F3
Northolt Ave PL5 . . . . 123 D4
North Orchard Ct **1** TR20 . 89 E5
North Par Camborne TR14 . 138 E3
Falmouth TR11 . . . . 145 A6
Penzance TR18 . . . . 143 E5
Portscatho TR2 . . . . 83 B2
North Parade Rear TR14 . . 138 D3
North Park Villas PL12 . . . 122 C4
NORTH PETHERWIN 18 A8
North Petherwin Ind Est
PL15 . . . . 18 A8
North Petherwin Prim Sch
PL15 . . . . 12 B1
North Pier TR18 . . . . 143 C2
North Pl **15** TR26 . . . . . . 141 B6
North Pool Cl TR15 . . . . . 139 C7
North Pool Rd TR15 . . . . . 139 C7
NORTH PROSPECT 128 A6
North Prospect Rd PL2 . . . 128 A6
North Quay Hayle TR27 . . 142 B6
Padstow PL28 . . . . 107 D6
Plymouth PL4 . . . . 149 A4
North Quay Hill TR7 . . . . . 110 D7
North Quay Par PL28 . . . . 107 D6
North Rd Camborne TR14 . 138 D3
Goldsithney TR20 . . . . . . 89 E5
Landrake PL12 . . . . 53 C3

North Rd *continued*
Lifton PL16 . . . . 19 F4
Looe PL13 . . . . 117 C3
Pentewan PL26 . . . . 73 C6
Plymouth PL12 . . . . 123 A2
Redruth TR16 . . . . 140 E1
St Teath PL30 . . . . 23 E7
Saltash PL12 . . . . 122 F3
Torpoint PL11 . . . . 127 B3
Whitemoor PL26 . . . . 58 E8
Yelverton PL20 . . . . 42 C3
North Road E PL4 . . . . . . 148 C4
North Road W PL1 . . . . . . 148 B4
North Roskear TR14 . . . . . 138 F5
North Roskear Mdw TR14 . 138 E5
North Roskear Rd TR14 . . 138 F5
North Row TR19 . . . . 86 F6
North St Fowey PL23 . . . . 116 D4
Launceston PL15 . . . . . . 106 A8
Lostwithiel PL22 . . . . 112 C2
Marazion TR17 . . . . 89 B5
14 Mousehole TR19 . . . . 88 C1
Plymouth PL4 . . . . 149 A3
Redruth TR15 . . . . 140 B6
St Austell PL25 . . . . 114 C4
Tavistock PL19 . . . . 147 C5
Tywardreath PL24 . . . . . . 60 D5
NORTH TAMERTON 12 F8
North Terr
2 Penzance TR18 . . . . . 143 E4
12 St Ives TR26 . . . . . . 141 B5
Whitemoor PL26 . . . . 58 E8
Northumberland St PL5 . . 127 E8
Northumberland Terr PL1 148 B1
North View PL13 . . . . 117 D4
North Way TR8 . . . . 111 F4
North Weald Gdns PL5 . . . 123 E5
Norton Ave PL5 . . . . 124 C4
Norton Ct **2** PL31 . . . . . 109 E5
Norway La TR3 . . . . 81 D5
Norwich Ave PL5 . . . . 124 B5
Notley Gdns PL2 . . . . 128 A8
Notre Dame Cl PL1 . . . . . 124 F5
Notre Dame Ho PL1 . . . . . 148 B3
Notre Dame RC Sch PL6 . . 124 F5
Notte St PL1 . . . . 148 C2
Novorossisk Rd PL6 . . . . . 125 E2
Noweth Pl TR11 . . . . 144 E5
N Polmenor Downs TR14 . . 78 F5
Nuffield Health Plymouth
Hospl PL6 . . . . 125 B4
NUMPHRA 87 A4
Nunnery Hill PL26 . . . . . . 72 F7
Nurseries The TR11 . . . . . 144 D5
Nursery Cl Plymouth PL5 . . 124 B7
Truro TR1 . . . . 137 D5
11 Tywardreath PL24 . . . 60 D5
Nut La TR27 . . . . 77 E3
Nut Tree Hill PL12 . . . . . . 65 B8
Nutwell Cl **2** PL28 . . . . . 107 C4

O

Oakapple Cl PL7 . . . . 130 B7
Oak Apple Cl PL12 . . . . . . 122 D4
Oak Ave PL12 . . . . 40 A1
Oakcroft Rd PL2 . . . . 128 B6
Oakdene Rise PL9 . . . . . . 135 F6
Oakdene Villas **7** TR9 . . . 45 E1
Oak Dr **8** Liskeard PL14 . 113 E5
Plymouth PL6 . . . . 124 F3
Oakey Orch PL17 . . . . 40 D4
Oakfield PL15 . . . . 27 D3
Oakfield Cl PL7 . . . . 131 C6
Oakfield Dr PL15 . . . . 106 D3
Oakfield Pl PL4 . . . . 129 B1
Oakfield Rd Falmouth TR11 144 F5
Plymouth PL7 . . . . 130 C6
Oakfield Terrace Rd PL4 . . 129 B1
Oak Ford PL30 . . . . 48 C7
Oakham Rd PL5 . . . . 124 B5
Oakhill PL30 . . . . 47 C6
Oak La Truro TR1 . . . . 69 E4
Whitstone EX22 . . . . 7 F1
Oakland Pk TR11 . . . . 144 D5
Oaklands PL7 . . . . 147 D2
Oaklands Bsns Pk PL13 . . . 63 D8
Oaklands Cl PL6 . . . . 125 C7
Oaklands Ct TR9 . . . . 45 E6
Oaklands Dr PL12 . . . . . . 122 C3
Oaklands Gn PL12 . . . . . . 122 D3
Oaklands Ind Est PL14 . . . 113 E6
Oaklands Rd PL14 . . . . . . 113 E6
Oakleigh Terr TR7 . . . . . . 110 F6
Oak Moor Dr PL5 . . . . 106 D3
Oak Park Terr PL14 . . . . . 113 A6
Oak Pk PL30 . . . . 23 E3
Oak Rd PL19 . . . . 147 C2
Oakridge PL12 . . . . 53 C7
Oak Ridge PL16 . . . . 19 F4
Oaks The **12** Par PL24 . . . 60 C4
Quintrell Downs TR8 . . . . 111 F3
St Austell PL25 . . . . 114 B3
Oak Tree Cl PL25 . . . . 115 B3
Oaktree Ct PL6 . . . . 124 F1
Oak Tree La
Godolphin Hill TR27 . . . . . 90 C6
Tavistock PL19 . . . . 147 C3
Oak Tree Pk PL6 . . . . 125 D6
Oak Tree School **9** TR4 . . 69 C3
Oak Vale TR2 . . . . 72 A7
Oak Way TR1 . . . . 137 D5
Oakwood Cl PL6 . . . . 125 D7
Oakwood Pk PL31 . . . . . . 109 F4
Oakwood Prim Sch PL6 . . 125 A6
Oakwood Rise PL32 . . . . . 105 E5

Oates Rd Helston TR13 . . . 146 C6
Marazion TR17 . . . . 89 C5
Plymouth PL2 . . . . 128 B5
Observer Cl TR1 . . . . 137 C3
Ocean Cres **22** TR13 . . . . 98 C8
Ocean Ct Plymouth PL1 . . 133 F8
Porthtowan TR4 . . . . 68 A7
Ocean St PL2 . . . . 127 E6
Ocean View
Indian Queens TR9 . . . . . 45 E1
Newquay TR7 . . . . 110 B5
Polruan PL23 . . . . 116 D2
St Austell PL25 . . . . 114 E7
Ocean View Rd EX23 . . . . 104 D7
Ocean View Terr TR26 . . . 141 B6
Octagon St PL1 . . . . 148 B3
Octans Way **6** PL9 . . . . . 136 E8
Okehampton Cl PL7 . . . . . 131 B4
Old Bakehouse Flats The
TR18 . . . . 143 F6
Old Barn Ct TR7 . . . . 110 D4
Old Barns The TR14 . . . . . . 66 F2
Old Boat Yard The PL28 . . 107 E6
Old Boys School TR16 . . . . 67 E5
Old Brewery Yd **4** TR18 . 143 E5
Old Bridge St TR1 . . . . . . 137 C4
Old Butchers Shop The
TR20 . . . . 89 B8
Old Cable La TR19 . . . . . . 96 E3
Old Callywith Rd PL31 . . . . 35 B2
Old Canal Cl EX23 . . . . 7 B6
Old Cardinham La PL30 . . . 35 F2
Old Carnon Hill TR3 . . . . . 81 F6
Old Chapel The TR4 . . . . . 68 F5
Old Chapel Way PL10 . . . . 132 F6
Old Chough Flats TR7 . . . . 111 B7
Old Church Rd TR11 . . . . . 93 E2
Old Church The TR18 . . . . 143 D4
Old Coach Rd
Lanivet PL26, PL30 . . . . . 47 D6
Playing Places TR3 . . . . . . 82 B8
Truro TR3 . . . . 70 A1
Old Coastguard Cotts PL11 65 A4
Old Coastguard Row TR19 . 96 B7
Old Corn Mill The TR12 . . . 92 C1
Old Cottage La PL27 . . . . . 22 E1
Old Dairy The Plymouth PL3 129 B6
Sancreed TR20 . . . . 87 E4
Old Drovers Way EX23 . . . . 4 E1
Old English Ind Est PL20 . . 42 E3
Old Exeter Rd PL19 . . . . . 147 D7
Old Falmouth Rd TR1 . . . . 137 C1
Old Farm Rd PL5 . . . . 127 C8
Old Ferry Rd PL12 . . . . . . 123 A3
Old Fore St Cl TR19 . . . . . . 86 F6
Old Foundry The
Menheniot PL14 . . . . 51 E6
Tavistock PL19 . . . . 147 D6
Old George St PL1 . . . . . . 148 C2
Old Grammar School Ct
PL22 . . . . 112 C2
Old Grammar School, The
PL32 . . . . 105 C4
Old Greystone Hill PL15,
PL19 . . . . 28 F6
Old Guildhall Mus★ PL13 117 D3
Old Hill Falmouth TR11 . . 144 F6
Grampound TR2 . . . . 72 A7
Helston TR13 . . . . 146 A6
Lewannick PL15 . . . . 27 B7
Trethevey PL30 . . . . 34 C8
Old Hill Cres TR11 . . . . . 144 F5
OLD KEA 82 E8
Old La PL26 . . . . 46 F3
Old Laira Rd PL3 . . . . 129 C4
Oldlands Cl PL6 . . . . 125 B6
Old Launceston Rd PL19 . 147 B6
North Petherwin PL15 . . . 18 B8
St Erth TR27 . . . . 77 E2
Old Laundry The PL1 . . . . 148 A3
Old Lawn School La PL25 . 114 B3
Old Market Pl PL31 . . . . . 109 C4
Old Mill Ct PL7 . . . . 130 E6
Old Mill Herbary The★
PL30 . . . . 34 F6
Old Mill La Camborne TR14 . 78 F6
Penponds TR14 . . . . 79 A6
Old Mill The
3 Boscastle PL35 . . . . . . 9 C2
Lerryn PL22 . . . . 61 D8
Old Mine La PL18 . . . . 40 E6
Old Nursery Cl TR13 . . . . . 91 A1
Old Orchard Cl EX23 . . . . . 7 B6
Old Park Rd PL3 . . . . 128 D6
Old Paul Hill TR18 . . . . . 143 C2
Old Plymouth Rd PL3 . . . 129 E5
Old Portreath Rd
Illogan TR16 . . . . 67 F5
Redruth TR15 . . . . 67 F4
Old Post Office Hill **8** EX23 4 E1
Old Pound PL26 . . . . 58 E6
Old Priory PL7 . . . . 130 D5
Old Priory Jun Sch PL7 . . 130 D5
Old Quarry Rd PL20 . . . . . 42 A3
Old Quay La PL12 . . . . . . 65 B8
Old Rail Rd TR14 . . . . 79 C2
Old Rectory Dr TR9 . . . . . 45 E6
Old Roselyon Cres PL24 . . 60 B5
Old Roselyon Rd PL24 . . . . 60 C4
Old Sandy La TR16 . . . . . 140 D3
Old School Cl PL27 . . . . . . 21 F3
Old School Ct
Padstow PL28 . . . . 107 C4
Wadebridge PL27 . . . . . 108 B5
Old School Ho The PL10 . . 133 A1
Old Schoolhouse The
TR11 . . . . 145 B4

Old School La PL30 . . . . . . 34 D4
Old School Rd Pityme PL27 . 21 F3
Plymouth PL5 . . . . 127 C8
Old School The **10** TR5 . . 54 D1
Old Smithy Cl **4** TR17 . . . 89 C5
Old Smithy Cotts EX39 . . . . 2 E4
Old Sta La TR17 . . . . 89 A6
Old Station Rd
Horrabridge PL20 . . . . . . 42 C4
1 Liskeard PL14 . . . . . . 51 A7
Old Station The PL20 . . . . 42 B4
Old Tannery Bsns Pk The **4**
PL4 . . . . 149 A4
Old Tannery La TR2 . . . . . 72 A7
Old Temple Rd
Merrifield PL30 . . . . 36 B8
Sprey Moor PL18 . . . . . . 25 C1
Old Town Hall The PL24 . . 60 B5
Old Town St PL1 . . . . 148 C3
Old Tram Rd
Carnon Downs TR3 . . . . . 82 A5
Devoran TR3 . . . . 81 F6
Stencoose TR16 . . . . 68 B4
Old Truro Rd TR4 . . . . 55 E3
Old Vicarage Cl TR3 . . . . . 80 F4
Old Vicarage Pl **11** PL25 . 114 C3
Old Vicarage The TR26 . . . 76 E5
Old Warleigh La PL5 . . . . 124 B7
Old Well Gdns TR10 . . . . 144 C8
Old Wharf The PL30 . . . . . 23 C1
Old Wheel Rd PL30 . . . . . . 23 C1
Old Woodlands Rd PL5 . . 124 D3
Old Workhouses The TR15 140 B8
Oliver Ct Liskeard PL14 . . . 50 E8
St Mellion PL12 . . . . 40 A1
Oliver's Terr TR13 . . . . . . 146 C5
Olive Villas TR3 . . . . 81 F6
Olivey Pl TR11 . . . . 82 A3
Olivia Ct PL4 . . . . 149 B4
Oll An Gwella **10** PL18 . . . 40 D6
Olympic Way PL6 . . . . . . 125 C6
Omaha Rd PL31 . . . . 109 F3
Onslow Rd PL2 . . . . 128 C7
Ope's Ct **13** TR11 . . . . . 145 B5
Opies La TR3 . . . . 109 C5
Opie's Row TR16 . . . . 80 B5
Opie's Terr TR16 . . . . 80 A5
Orange La TR26 . . . . 141 A6
Orchard Ave PL6 . . . . 129 B7
Orchard Cl PL15 . . . . 106 B7
Helston TR13 . . . . 146 B7
3 Plymouth PL7 . . . . . . 131 C5
Poughill EX23 . . . . 4 D2
St Austell PL25 . . . . 114 E4
St Giles on the Heath PL15 . 13 F1
St Mellion PL12 . . . . 53 C8
Tavistock PL19 . . . . 41 D8
Tideford PL12 . . . . 52 F2
Truro TR1 . . . . 69 F3
Orchard Cotts
Lamerton PL19 . . . . 30 B3
St Austell PL25 . . . . 114 F5
Orchard Cres PL9 . . . . . . 135 C7
Orchard Ct PL25 . . . . 114 B4
Orchard Ho **11** TR18 . . . 143 C2
Orchard La Helford TR12 . . 93 B1
Plymouth PL7 . . . . 130 E6
Tregonhaye TR11 . . . . . . 144 C5
Orchard Mdw **4** PL12 . . . 53 E4
Orchard Pk PL26 . . . . 47 C2
Orchard Pl **10** TR18 . . . . 143 C2
Orchard Terr **20** TR16 . . 143 C2
Orchard The Gunnislake PL18 41 A6
Lerryn PL22 . . . . 61 D8
Newquay TR7 . . . . 111 B7
Orchard Way
6 Goldsithney TR20 . . . . 89 E5
2 St Austell PL26 . . . . . 115 A1
Orchard Wlk **13** PL27 . . . 108 B5
Orch Wy EX23 . . . . 104 E5
Orch The PL13 . . . . 117 D4
Ordnance St PL1 . . . . 127 E2
Ordulf Rd PL19 . . . . 147 A5
Oregon Way PL3 . . . . 129 D6
ORESTON 135 C7
Oreston Com Academy
PL9 . . . . 135 C7
Oreston Rd PL9 . . . . 135 C8
Orion Dr PL27 . . . . 31 F3
Osborne Ct PL1 . . . . 148 C2
Osborne Parc TR13 . . . . . 146 B7
Osborne Pl PL1 . . . . 148 C2
Osborne Rd PL3 . . . . 128 A3
Osborne Villas
10 Falmouth TR11 . . . . 145 C3
2 Plymouth PL3 . . . . . . 128 A3
Osprey Gdns PL9 . . . . . . 136 C7
OTTERHAM 10 D1
Otterham Com Prim Sch
PL32 . . . . 10 C1
Otterham Pk PL32 . . . . . . 16 A8
OTTERHAM STATION . . . 16 A8
OTTERY 30 A2
Ottery Cotts PL19 . . . . . . 30 A2
Ottery Park Ind Est PL19 . . 30 A2
Outer Down PL19 . . . . 30 A3
Outer Slip Dr **4** PL15 . . . 106 C4
Outland Rd PL2 . . . . 128 C7
Outta Sight Ct **7** PL31 . . 109 A5
Overcliff PL29 . . . . 22 D8
Overton Gdns **3** PL3 . . . 128 F5

Overtonn Villas **6** PL15 . . 106 C5
Owen Dr PL7 . . . . 130 C7
Owen Sivell Cl PL14 . . . . . 113 E6
Oxford Ave PL3 . . . . 128 E5
Oxford Gdns PL3 . . . . 128 E5
Oxford Pl PL1 . . . . 148 C3
Oxford St PL1 . . . . 148 B3
Oxford Terr **4** PL1 . . . . . 148 B3
Ox La TR8 . . . . 31 E1
Oxland Rd TR16 . . . . 67 E5
Oxley Vale TR7 . . . . 111 B5

P

Paardeburg Rd **1** PL31 . . . 48 D8
Packet La TR20 . . . . 89 F5
Packington St PL2 . . . . . . 128 A4
Packsaddle **1** TR10 . . . . . 81 D2
Packsaddle Cl TR10 . . . . . 81 D2
Paddock Cl Plymouth PL9 . 135 E5
Saltash PL12 . . . . 122 D4
Paddock The Helston TR13 146 C2
Redruth TR15 . . . . 140 D2
Sticker PL26 . . . . 58 E1
Paddons Row PL19 . . . . . 147 C6
Padnover Terr **22** TR26 . . 141 B5
PADSTOW 107 C4
Padstow Harbour Ind Est
PL28 . . . . 107 E4
Padstow Mus★ PL28 . . 107 C5
Padstow Sch PL28 . . . . . . 107 C4
Padstow Workshop Units
PL28 . . . . 107 B4
Page's Cross PL15 . . . . . . 106 D4
Pagoda Dr PL26 . . . . 115 A1
Paiges Farm PL2 . . . . 135 C1
Painton Water EX39 . . . . . . 3 A8
Palace Rd PL25 . . . . 114 D4
Palace St PL1 . . . . 149 A2
Palm Ct TR1 . . . . 137 D3
Palm Dr PL28 . . . . 31 F7
PALMERSBRIDGE 25 E4
Palmers Terr TR34 . . . . . . 14 C6
Palmerston St PL1 . . . . . . 148 A4
Palmers Way PL27 . . . . . 108 D6
PANCRASWEEK 8 C3
Pannier La TR26 . . . . 141 C2
Pannier Mkt PL15 . . . . . . 147 C5
Panson Cross PL15 . . . . . . 13 E3
PANTERSBRIDGE 36 D3
PAR 60 C4
Parade PL1 . . . . 149 A2
Parade Bsns Pk **4** PL19 . 147 B4
Parade Hill TR19 . . . . 88 D1
Parade Ope PL1 . . . . 149 A2
Parade Pass **29** TR18 . . . 143 E5
Parade Rd PL5 . . . . 124 A3
Parade Sq PL22 . . . . 112 C2
Parade St TR18 . . . . 143 E5
Parade The Helston TR13 . 146 C5
Liskeard PL14 . . . . 113 C6
Lostwithiel PL22 . . . . . . 112 D2
Millbrook PL10 . . . . 132 E5
Milton Abbot PL19 . . . . . . 29 C6
Mousehole TR19 . . . . 88 C1
Truro TR1 . . . . 137 E4
Paradise Park & The World
Parrot Trust★ TR27 . 142 A4
Paradise Pk EX22 . . . . 7 F1
Paradise Pl PL1 . . . . 128 A2
Paradise Rd Boscastle PL35 . 9 C1
Plymouth PL1 . . . . 128 A2
PARAMOOR 72 E3
Par Beach & St Andrews Rd
Nature Reserve★ PL24 . 60 D4
Parc-Abnac TR20 . . . . 88 B7
Parc-an-Bal Ct TR14 . . . . 138 E4
Parc-an-Bre Dr PL26 . . . . 58 C8
Parc-an-Cady Est TR19 . . . 97 A6
Parc-an-Challow TR10 . . . 144 B8
Parc-an-Creet TR26 . . . . . 77 A7
Parc-an-Dillon Rd TR2 . . . 83 B2
Parc-an-Dix La TR27 . . . . 142 C7
Parc-an-Dower TR13 . . . . 146 C6
Parcandowr TR7 . . . . 57 E1
Parc-an-Forth **6** TR26 . . . 77 A6
Parc an Gate TR19 . . . . . . 88 C1
Parc An Gew TR13 . . . . . . 146 C6
Parc-an-Gwarry **7** TR3 . . 81 F7
Parc-an-Ithan TR12 . . . . . 102 F2
Parc-an-Maen **11** TR13 . . 98 C8
Parc an Manns TR11 . . . . . 93 D3
Parc-an-Peath TR19 . . . . . 97 A6
Parc-an-Stamps **4** TR26 . 77 A6
Parc an Yorth TR19 . . . . . . 86 F8
Parc-Askell Cl TR12 . . . . . 98 E5
Parc Bean Terr TR26 . . . . 141 A6
Parc Behan Cl TR2 . . . . . . 83 F6
Parc Bottom TR12 . . . . . . 92 C1
Parc Bowen TR13 . . . . 92 A3
Parc-Bracket St TR14 . . . 138 D3
Parc Brawse TR12 . . . . . . 102 F2
Parc Briwer TR10 . . . . . . 144 D7
Parc Eglos Helston TR13 . 146 B6
St Merryn PL28 . . . . 31 F8
Parc Eglos Sch TR13 . . . . 146 C6
Parc Enys TR12 . . . . 99 B4
PARC ERISSEY 68 A3
Parc Erissey Ind Est TR16 . 68 A3
Parc Fer Cl EX23 . . . . 4 E1
Parc Garland **15** TR12 . . 102 F2
Parc Godrevy TR7 . . . . . . 110 C5
Parc Holland TR13 . . . . . 146 D8

Parc Ledden TR13 . . . . 146 C6
Parc Ledrak TR13 . . . . 146 B8
Parc Letta TR18 . . . . 143 C7
Parc Mellan TR18 . . . . 143 D7
Parc Merys TR2 . . . . 83 B2
Parc Monga Dr TR11 . . . . . 92 F3
Parc Monga Rd TR11 . . . . . 92 F3
Parc Morrep TR20 . . . . 90 B3
Parc Owles TR26 . . . . 141 D2
Parc Peneglos TR11 . . . . . . 82 A3
Parc Pennkarn PL33 . . . . . . 14 E3
Parc Pordic TR2 . . . . 142 D5
Parc Shady TR26 . . . . 77 C1
Parc Stephney TR11 . . . . . 144 C2
Parc Terr **19** TR18 . . . . . . 143 C1
Parc Trenance PL28 . . . . . . 31 F7
Parc Trethias PL28 . . . . 31 F7
Parc Vean TR30 . . . . 34 C1
Parc Venton Cl **2** TR14 . . 138 F2
Parc Villas **17** TR18 . . . . 143 C1
Parc Wartha Ave TR18 . . . 143 D6
Parc Wartha Cres TR18 . . 143 D6
Par Gn PL24 . . . . 60 C4
Pargolla Rd TR7 . . . . 110 F6
Park 30 PL15 . . . . 106 A3
Parka Cl **12** TR9 . . . . 45 E2
Park-an-Bans TR14 . . . . . 138 E1
Parkancreeg **9** TR3 . . . . . 81 F7
Park An Dreas **4** TR2 . . . . 83 F6
Park An Fenten TR13 . . . . 146 E7
Park an Gonwyn TR26 . . . 141 E2
Park an Gorsaf TR14 . . . . 138 D2
Park An Gwarry **7** TR3 . . . 81 F7
Park an Harvey TR13 . . . . 146 C6
Park An Keres PL14 . . . . . . 52 A5
Park-an-Mengleth TR15 . . 140 D4
Park-an-Pyth **2** TR19 . . . . 75 A1
Park-an-Tansys TR14 . . . . 138 E2
Parka Rd Indian Queens TR9 . 45 E1
  8 St Columb Road TR9 . . . 45 E2
Park Ave
  Plymouth, Devonport PL1 . . 127 E3
  Plymouth, Plymstock PL9 . . 135 D7
  St Ives TR26 . . . . 141 B5
PARK BOTTOM 139 B8
Park Bottom TR15 . . . . 67 D3
Park Cl Illogan TR15 . . . . . 139 B8
  Nancegollan TR13 . . . . 91 B7
  Plymouth PL7 . . . . 130 B7
Park Cnr TR18 . . . . 143 E5
Park Cres Falmouth TR11 . 145 A4
  Helston TR13 . . . . 146 B5
  Plymouth PL6 . . . . 135 C7
  Ponsanooth TR3 . . . . 81 B4
Park Ct Chillaton PL16 . . . . 29 F8
  28 Penzance TR18 . . . . 143 E5
Park Dr PL31 . . . . 109 B4
Parkenbutts TR7 . . . . 111 D7
Parkengue Vean TR2 . . . . . 71 D6
Parkengue TR10 . . . . 144 A7
Parkenhead La PL28 . . . . . 20 F2
Park Enskellaw **6** TR12 . . 99 A2
Park en Venton TR12 . . . . 99 A2
Park-en-Vine PL27 . . . . . . 32 D6
Park En Vine PL27 . . . . 32 D7
Parker Cl PL7 . . . . 130 B5
Parker Rd PL2 . . . . 128 B6
Parkers Cross PL13 . . . . . . 63 A4
Parker's Gn PL18 . . . . 40 F6
Parkesway PL12 . . . . 122 D2
Park Fenton PL14 . . . . . . 113 D5
PARKFIELD 39 A2
Parkfield Dr PL6 . . . . 125 F1
Park Gwyn PL26 . . . . 58 B4
Park Hill TR11 . . . . 145 A4
Park Ho PL25 . . . . 114 B3
Park Holly TR14 . . . . 138 B3
Parkins Terr **7** TR1 . . . . 137 D5
Park La Bere Alston PL20 . . 41 B1
  Bugle PL26 . . . . 47 C1
  Camborne TR14 . . . . 138 E2
  Plymouth PL9 . . . . 135 C7
Parklands **14** TR5 . . . . . . 54 D1
  Nanpean PL26 . . . . 58 C7
Parklands Cl TR7 . . . . . . 111 D6
Park Leder TR16 . . . . 68 C3
Park Leven TR16 . . . . 139 C8
Park Lowen TR26 . . . . . . 141 C2
Parknoweth TR12 . . . . 99 A4
Parknoweth Cl TR8 . . . . . . 56 B6
Park Pl Grampound Road TR2 . 57 E1
  Wadebridge PL27 . . . . . 108 B5
Park Place La **12** PL3 . . . 128 A4
Park Rd Camborne TR14 . . 138 E4
  Fowey PL23 . . . . 116 C4
  Illogan TR15 . . . . 139 B7
  Lifton PL16 . . . . 19 F3
  Liskeard PL14 . . . . 113 C6
  18 Newlyn TR18 . . . . . 143 C1
  Plymouth PL3 . . . . 129 A6
  Ponsanooth TR3 . . . . 81 B4
  Redruth TR15 . . . . 140 C4
  St Austell PL25 . . . . 114 C3
  St Dominick PL12 . . . . . . 40 D2
  Torpoint PL11 . . . . 127 B3
  Wadebridge PL27 . . . . . 108 B5
  Whitemoor PL26 . . . . 58 E8
Park Rd Hos PL22 . . . . . . 112 C2
Park Rise TR11 . . . . 145 A4
Parkryn Rd **4** TR19 . . . . . 88 C1
Parkside PL3 . . . . 127 F5
Park St PL3 . . . . 128 A5
Park Stenak TR16 . . . . 80 F8
Parkstone La PL7 . . . . 130 F6
Park Street Ope PL3 . . . . 128 A4

Park Terr Falmouth TR11 . 145 A4
  Truro TR1 . . . . 70 D1
Park The Penryn TR10 . . . 144 B7
  Tregony TR2 . . . . 71 F4
Parkvedras Ho **5** TR1 . . . 137 B4
Parkvedras Terr **4** TR1 . . 137 B4
Parkventon PL26 . . . . 47 C2
Park View Lifton PL16 . . . . 19 F4
  Liskeard PL14 . . . . 113 C6
  Perranarworthal TR3 . . . . . 81 E6
  Plymouth PL4 . . . . 149 C3
  Summercourt TR8 . . . . 57 B7
  Truro TR1 . . . . 137 C3
Parkview Apartments TR7 110 F5
Park View Cl TR3 . . . . 82 A7
Park View Rd TR13 . . . . . 146 B5
Park View Terr PL27 . . . . 108 B5
Park Villas TR3 . . . . 81 B4
Park Way PL25 . . . . 114 F5
Parkway Ct PL6 . . . . 129 E7
Parkway Ind Est The PL6 . . 129 E7
Parkway The PL3, PL5, PL6 124 B1
Park Wise Penryn TR10 . . 144 C7
  Penryn TR10 . . . . 144 C8
Parkwood Cl PL6 . . . . 121 B2
Parkwood Ct PL19 . . . . . 147 D6
Parkwood Rd PL19 . . . . . 147 D6
Park Wood Rise PL16 . . . . . 19 F4
Parkwoon Cl PL26 . . . . . . 46 F3
Par La PL24 . . . . 60 B4
Par Moor Rd Par PL24, PL25 . 60 B3
  St Austell PL24, PL25 . . . 115 F4
PARNACOTT 8 E8
Parnell Cl PL6 . . . . 129 A8
Parr La PL4 . . . . 149 B2
Parr St PL4 . . . . 149 B2
Parsonage Ct PL16 . . . . . . 19 F4
Parsonage Way PL4 . . . . 149 B2
Parsons Cl PL9 . . . . 136 A4
Parsons Ct PL10 . . . . 132 F6
Parsons Gn PL17 . . . . 39 E6
Par Sta PL24 . . . . 60 C5
Partwayes PL19 . . . . 30 A3
Pascoe Cl TR3 . . . . 69 D4
Pasley Cl St E PL2 . . . . . . 127 F4
Pasley St PL2 . . . . 127 F4
Pasmore Road TR13 . . . . 146 D6
Passage La PL23 . . . . 116 B5
Passage St PL23 . . . . 116 D5
Passmore Cl Blackwater TR4 . 68 E5
  Liskeard PL14 . . . . 113 D6
Pathfields EX23 . . . . 104 E5
Pathway Fields The TR27 . 142 C5
Patience Cl PL27 . . . . 31 C4
Patna **1** PL1 . . . . 148 B4
Pato Point PL11 . . . . 127 A5
Patterdale Cl PL6 . . . . . . 125 D3
Patterdale Wlk PL6 . . . . . 125 D3
Pattern Cl **1** PL25 . . . . . 115 A3
Pattinson Cl PL6 . . . . 125 E2
Pattinson Ct PL6 . . . . 125 E2
Pattinson Dr PL6 . . . . 125 F2
PAUL 88 C2
Paull Rd PL31 . . . . 109 B4
Paulls Row **4** TR15 . . . . 140 C5
Paul's Row PL1 . . . . 137 D5
Paul's Terr TR1 . . . . 137 D5
Paviland Grange **6** PL1 . 128 A3
Pavilion Pk TR14 . . . . 138 F4
Pavilion Rise **5** PL26 . . . 115 A1
Pavlova Cl TR14 . . . . 113 C5
Pavlova Ct **6** PL14 . . . . . 113 C5
Pavo St **10** PL9 . . . . 136 E8
Paynter's Cross PL12 . . . . 53 E7
Paynter's Cross Cotts PL12 53 E7
Paynters La TR16 . . . . 67 E4
PAYNTER'S LANE END 67 E4
Paynter's Lane End Est
  TR16 . . . . 67 D4
Paynter Wlk **5** PL7 . . . . 131 B5
Peachys Hill PL30 . . . . 35 E3
Peachys Rd PL30 . . . . 35 F3
Peacock Ave PL11 . . . . . . 127 A3
Peacock Cl PL7 . . . . 130 F7
Peacock La PL4 . . . . 149 A2
Pearce's La **12** TR26 . . . 141 A5
Pearce's Row **3** PL24 . . . 60 C4
Pearn Cotts **3** PL3 . . . . 128 F6
Pearn Gdns PL3 . . . . 129 A7
Pearn Rd PL3 . . . . 129 A7
Pearn Ridge PL3 . . . . 129 A7
Pearson Ave **3** PL4 . . . . 128 F4
Pearson Rd PL4 . . . . 128 F4
Pebble Ct TR7 . . . . 111 C7
Pedlars Cl PL15 . . . . 18 B8
Pedlars Orchard PL15 . . . . 18 A8
Pedna Carne TR9 . . . . 57 E8
Pedna Carne Mobile Home Pk
  TR9 . . . . 57 E8
Pednandrea TR19 . . . . 86 E6
Pednavounder PL12 . . . . . 103 F7
Pedn-m'n-du TR19 . . . . . . 96 A7
Pedn-Moran TR2 . . . . 95 B6
Pedn-y-ke **1** TR12 . . . . . 99 A1
Peek Moor Cross EX22 . . . . 13 E4
Peeks Ave PL9 . . . . 135 F7
Peel St PL1 . . . . 128 A1
Pegasus PL7 . . . . 136 E8
Peguarra Cl PL28 . . . . 20 E1
Peguarra Ct PL28 . . . . 20 E1
Pelean Cross
  Ponsanooth TR3 . . . . 81 B5
  Trebost TR3 . . . . 81 A5
Pelham Ct **11** TR11 . . . . 145 C3
Pellew Cl **7** Falmouth TR11 145 A5
  Padstow PL28 . . . . 107 C5

Pellew Cres TR13 . . . . . . 146 C4
Pellew Pl PL2 . . . . 127 F4
Pellew Rd TR11 . . . . 145 A5
Pellor Fields TR13 . . . . 90 F3
Pellor Rd TR13 . . . . 90 F3
Pellymounter Rd PL25 . . . 114 F2
PELYNT 62 D5
Pelynt Sch PL13 . . . . 62 D6
Pemboa La Tregarrick TR13 146 F4
  Trewennack TR13 . . . . . . 92 A2
  Whitehill TR13 . . . . 91 F1
Pembrey Wlk PL5 . . . . . . 123 E4
Pembroke Cl **7** PL24 . . . . 60 C4
Pembroke La PL1 . . . . 127 E1
Pembroke Rd PL7 . . . . . . 111 E7
Pembroke St PL1 . . . . 127 E1
Pemros Rd PL5 . . . . 123 C1
Penair Cres TR1 . . . . 137 F6
Penair Sch TR1 . . . . 70 C4
Penair View TR1 . . . . 137 F4
Penally Cl PL35 . . . . 9 D2
Penally Hill PL35 . . . . 9 D2
Penally Terr PL35 . . . . 9 C2
Penalverne Ave TR18 . . . . 143 D5
Penalverne Cres TR18 . . . 143 D5
Penalverne Dr TR18 . . . . . 143 D5
Penalverne Pl TR18 . . . . . 143 D5
Penameyne Ct **5** TR26 . . 141 B6
Pen-an-Gwel TR11 . . . . . 141 A4
Pen-An-Vre **11** TR10 . . . . 81 C1
Penare Gdns **2** TR18 . . . 143 E6
Penare Rd TR18 . . . . 143 E6
Penare Terr TR18 . . . . . . 143 E6
Penarrow Cl TR11 . . . . . . 144 E2
Penarrow Rd TR11 . . . . . . 145 C8
Penarth PL13 . . . . 117 B3
Penarth Rd TR11 . . . . 145 A5
Penarvon TR2 . . . . 93 B1
Penarwyn Cres TR18 . . . . 143 B7
Penarwyn Rd PL24 . . . . . . 60 B4
Penarwyn Woods **6** PL24 . 60 B4
PENBEAGLE 141 A4
Penbeagle Cl **17** TR26 . . . 77 A6
Penbeagle Cres **8** TR26 . . 77 A6
Penbeagle Ind Est TR26 . . . 77 A6
Penbeagle La TR26 . . . . . . 77 A6
Penbeagle Terr **7** TR26 . . . 77 A6
Penbeagle Way TR26 . . . . 141 A4
PENBERTH 97 A3
Penberthy Cross TR27 . . . . 89 F7
Penberthy Rd Helston TR13 146 C5
  Portreath TR16 . . . . 67 D6
Penbothidno TR11 . . . . 92 F3
Pen Brea Cl TR2 . . . . 95 B6
Penbrea Rd TR18 . . . . . . 143 E7
Penbro Way **4** TR13 . . . . 91 A3
Penbugle La PL31 . . . . . . 109 E7
Pencair Ave PL11 . . . . . . 126 E2
Pencalenick Sch TR1 . . . . . 70 E4
Pencarn Parc TR16 . . . . . . 80 A5
Pencarrick Cl TR1 . . . . . . 137 B6
PENCARROW 105 D1
Pencarrow * PL30 . . . . 34 D6
Pencarrow Rd **13** TR16 . . 67 E4
Pencavo Hill PL12 . . . . 53 A3
Pencoys Prim Sch TR16 . . . 80 A5
Pencrebar La PL17 . . . . . . 39 E3
Pencreber Rd **3** PL20 . . . . 42 C4
PENCUKE 10 D5
Pencuke La EX23 . . . . 10 D5
Pendale Sq TR1 . . . . 137 B4
Pendarves St Merryn PL28 . . 31 F7
  Tresillian TR2 . . . . 70 F5
Pendarves Est TR14 . . . . . 79 C5
Pendarves Rd
  Camborne TR14 . . . . 138 C1
  Falmouth TR11 . . . . 144 F6
  Penzance TR18 . . . . 143 D6
  Truro TR1 . . . . 137 C6
Pendarves St
  Camborne, Beacon TR14 . . 138 F1
  Troon TR14 . . . . 79 C4
Pendarves View TR14 . . . . 138 C1
Pendean Ave PL14 . . . . . . 113 B6
Pendean Cl PL14 . . . . 113 B6
Pendean Ct PL14 . . . . 113 B6
Pendean Dr PL14 . . . . 113 B6
PENDEEN 75 A1
Pendeen Cl Plymouth PL6 . 124 F6
  Threemilestone TR3 . . . . . 69 D3
Pendeen Cres
  Plymouth PL6 . . . . 125 A6
  Threemilestone TR3 . . . . . 69 D3
Pendeen Ho TR1 . . . . 81 C5
Pendeen Pk TR13 . . . . . . 146 C8
Pendeen Rd PL7 . . . . 110 F6
Pendeen Rd Porthleven TR13 91 B1
  Threemilestone TR3 . . . . . 69 D3
  Truro TR3 . . . . 137 E3
Pendeen Sch TR19 * 75 A1
Pendennis Castle * TR11 . 145 E2
Pendennis Cl
  Penzance TR18 . . . . 143 E7
  Plymouth PL3 . . . . 128 F8
  Torpoint PL11 . . . . 126 F3
Pendennis Pl TR18 . . . . . . 143 E7
Pendennis Rd
  Falmouth TR11 . . . . 145 D3
  Looe PL13 . . . . 117 D5
  Penzance TR18 . . . . 143 E7
Pendennis Rise TR11 . . . . 145 D3
Pender's La TR15 . . . . 140 B5
Pendilly Ave PL11 . . . . . . 126 F2
Pendilly Dr PL25 . . . . 114 E2
Pendinnes Gdns PL15 . . . 106 B8

PENDOGGETT 23 A6
Pendoggett Rd
  Treharrock PL30 . . . . 22 F5
  Trewiggett PL30 . . . . 23 C8
Pendola Wlk TR26 . . . . . . 141 B5
Pendour Pk PL22 . . . . 112 E2
Pendower Ct TR1 . . . . 83 D5
Pendower Rd Looe PL13 . . 117 E4
  Veryan TR2 . . . . 83 F6
Pendower Terr TR1 . . . . . 138 E1
Pendragon Cres TR7 . . . . 111 A4
Pendragon Ho TR11 . . . . . 145 D3
Pendragon Rd **3** PL14 . . . 113 D6
Pendra Loweth TR11 . . . . 144 D1
Pendray Gdns PL14 . . . . . . 50 E7
Pendrea Cl TR18 . . . . 143 F7
Pendrea Pk TR14 . . . . 138 F5
Pendrea Pl TR18 . . . . 143 F7
Pendrea Rd TR18 . . . . 143 F7
Pendrea Wood TR1 . . . . . . 69 F3
PENDRIFT 24 B1
Pendrim Rd PL13 . . . . 117 D4
Pendruccombe Ct PL15 . . . 106 D5
Pen-Eglos **8** TR2 . . . . . . 95 A6
PENELEWEY 82 C7
Penforth TR1 . . . . 138 E2
Penfound Gdns EX23 . . . . 104 F5
Pengannel Cl TR7 . . . . . . 110 D4
Pengarrock Hill TR12 . . . . 101 D5
Pengarth **1** TR5 . . . . 54 D1
Pengarth Cl TR1 . . . . 137 C2
Pengarth Rd TR11 . . . . . . 145 A3
Pengarth Rise TR11 . . . . . 145 A3
PENGEGON 138 F2
Pengegon Moor TR14 . . . . 138 F2
Pengegon Parc
  Camborne TR14 . . . . 138 F2
  Pengegon TR14 . . . . 138 F2
Pengegon Way TR14 . . . . 138 F2
PENGELLY 14 E2
Pengelly **24** Callington PL17 . 39 F4
  Delabole PL33 . . . . 14 E2
Pengelly Cl PL11 . . . . 126 F5
Pengelly Cross
  Godolphin Cross TR27 . . . . 90 F7
  Wadebridge PL27 . . . . . 108 C1
Pengelly Hill Pengelly PL14 . 50 B8
  Torpoint PL11 . . . . 127 A5
Pengelly Pk PL11 . . . . . . 126 F5
Pengelly Pl TR11 . . . . 144 E5
Pengellys Row TR14 . . . . 139 A5
Pengelly Way TR3 . . . . 69 D3
Pengeron Ave **1** TR14 . . 138 F7
Pengersick Est TR20 . . . . . 90 C3
Pengersick La TR20 . . . . . . 90 C3
Pengersick Parc TR20 . . . . 90 C3
Pengliddon PL27 . . . . 33 B7
PENGOLD 10 A5
Pengover Cl PL14 . . . . . . 113 D6
Pengover Gn PL14 . . . . 51 E8
Pengover Hts PL14 . . . . . 113 D6
Pengover Parc TR15 . . . . 140 C6
Pengover Pk PL14 . . . . . . 113 D6
Pengover Rd PL14 . . . . . . 113 E6
Pengrowyn PL26 . . . . 59 D6
Pengwarras Rd TR14 . . . . 138 C3
Pengwel **16** TR18 . . . . . . 143 C2
PENHALE Indian Queens . . . 57 D8
  Millbrook 132 D7
  Mullion 99 D1
Penhale Crowntown TR13 . . 91 A5
  1 Perranporth TR6 . . . . . 55 A5
Penhale Cl **10** Dobwalls PL14 50 E7
  St Cleer PL14 . . . . 37 E7
Penhale Cotts TR3 . . . . 82 D6
Penhale Est TR15 . . . . . . 140 B6
Penhale Gdns TR7 . . . . 57 D8
Penhale La St Cleer PL14 . . 38 F3
  Treworrick PL14 . . . . 37 F3
Penhale Mdw PL14 . . . . . . 38 F3
Penhale Rd Barripper TR14 . 79 A4
  Carnhell Green TR14 . . . . . 78 F4
  Falmouth TR11 . . . . 144 F1
  Penhale PL32 . . . . 10 D2
  Penwithick PL26 . . . . 59 D7
Penhaligon Cl TR15 . . . . . 140 D4
Penhaligon Ct TR1 . . . . . . 137 E5
Penhaligon Way PL25 . . . . 114 F2
PENHALLICK 139 C4
Penhallick TR12 . . . . 101 A2
Penhall La TR4 . . . . 68 C6
PENHALLOW 55 B2
Penhallow TR15 . . . . 139 B8
Penhallow Ho
  Mount Hawke TR4 . . . . . . 68 C6
  Veryan TR2 . . . . 83 C5
Penhallow Ct TR7 . . . . . . 111 C7
Penhallow Parc PL33 . . . . . 14 D2
Penhallow Rd TR7 . . . . . . 111 C7
Penhalls Way TR3 . . . . 82 B8
PENHALVEAN 80 C4
Penharget Cl PL14 . . . . . . 38 D5
Penhaven Cl TR8 . . . . 56 B7
Penhaven Ct TR7 . . . . 110 E6
Penhellaz Hill TR13 . . . . . 146 B6
Penhellaz Rd TR13 . . . . . 146 B6
Penhole Cl PL15 . . . . 27 D3
Penhole Dr PL15 . . . . 106 D3
Penhole Rd PL15 . . . . 27 C3
Penina Ave TR7 . . . . 110 F4
Peninsula Coll PL2 . . . . . . 127 F2
Peninsular Pk PL12 . . . . . 122 C4
Penisker Rd PL25 . . . . 58 F4
Penjerrick Gdns * TR11 . . . 93 D5
Penjerrick Hill
  Budock Water TR11 . . . . . 144 C1
  Falmouth TR11 . . . . 93 E5
Penkenna Cl EX23 . . . . 10 C6

Penkernick Cl TR18 . . . . . 143 B1
Penkernick Way TR9 . . . . . 45 E6
Penknight La PL22 . . . . . . 112 A2
Penlean Ct TR15 . . . . 140 E7
Penlea Rd TR10 . . . . 144 B8
Penlee Apartments PL23 . . 116 C3
Penlee Cl **13** Callington PL17 . 39 F4
  Praa Sands TR20 . . . . 90 C3
  Tregony TR2 . . . . 71 F4
Penlee Cotts PL10 . . . . 64 C2
Penlee Gdns PL3 . . . . 128 A4
Penlee Ho TR1 . . . . 69 E4
Penlee House Gall & Mus *
  TR18 . . . . 143 E5
Penlee Manor Dr TR18 . . . 143 E4
Penlee Pk PL11 . . . . 126 E4
Penlee Pl **4** PL4 . . . . . . 128 F4
Penlee Rd PL3 . . . . 128 A4
Penlee St **10** TR18 . . . . . 143 E5
Penlee View Terr **3** TR18 143 E4
Penlee Villas TR3 . . . . 82 B8
Penlee Way PL3 . . . . 128 B4
Penlu TR14 . . . . 138 F5
Penlu Ho TR14 . . . . 138 F5
Penluke Cl TR16 . . . . 80 A5
Penmare Cl TR27 . . . . 142 F2
Penmare Ct TR27 . . . . 142 F2
Penmare Terr TR27 . . . . . 142 F2
PENMARTH 80 C2
Penmayne Parc TR16 . . . . 140 F1
Penmayne Villas PL27 . . . . 21 E3
Penmead Rd PL33 . . . . 14 E2
Penmelen PL32 . . . . 105 C4
Penmellyn Gdns **2** TR9 . . . 45 E6
Penmeneth TR13 . . . . 146 F8
Penmenner Est **7** TR12 . . 101 C4
Penmenner Gdns **14** TR12 102 F2
Penmenner Rd TR12 . . . . . 102 F2
Penmere Cl Helston TR13 . 146 B7
  Penzance TR18 . . . . 143 E5
Penmere Cres TR11 . . . . . 144 F3
Penmere Ct **4** TR11 . . . . 145 A3
Penmere Dr Newquay TR7 . 110 C5
  Swanvale TR11 . . . . 144 F3
Penmere Hill **7** TR11 . . . 145 A4
Penmere Pl
  3 Falmouth TR11 . . . . . 145 A3
  Penzance TR18 . . . . 143 E7
Penmere Rd Penzance TR18 143 E7
  St Austell PL25 . . . . 115 A3
Penmere Sta TR11 . . . . . . 144 F3
Penmeva View PL26 . . . . . 73 C3
Penmorvah TR11 . . . . 82 A2
Penmorvah Pl TR14 . . . . . 138 E2
Penmorvah Rd TR15 . . . . 137 F6
PENNANCE 140 F1
Pennance Field TR11 . . . . . 94 B3
Pennance Ho TR11 . . . . . . 145 A4
Pennance La TR16 . . . . . . 140 F1
Pennance Parc TR16 . . . . 140 F1
Pennance Rd
  Falmouth TR11 . . . . 145 A3
  Falmouth TR11 . . . . 145 B2
  Lanner TR16 . . . . 80 E7
  Redruth TR16 . . . . 140 F1
Pennance Terr TR16 . . . . . 140 F1
Penn an Drea Helston TR13 146 D4
  14 Tremenheere TR13 . . 146 D8
Pennant Farm PL29 . . . . . . 22 B4
Pennant Hill PL30 . . . . 48 C2
Pennard Villas PL27 . . . . . 33 B5
Pennare TR12 . . . . 101 C4
Penn Kernow PL15 . . . . . . 106 E4
Pennor Dr PL25 . . . . 114 D3
Pennoweth Prim Sch
  TR15 . . . . 140 C5
PENNYCOMEQUICK 148 B4
Pennycomequick Hill PL4 148 B4
PENNYCROSS 128 C8
Pennycross Cl PL2 . . . . . . 128 D8
Pennycross Park Rd PL2 . . 128 C7
Pennycross Prim Sch PL2 128 C8
Pennygillam Ind Est PL15 106 C4
Pennygillam Way PL15 . . . 18 E2
Pennys La PL24 . . . . 115 F5
Penny's La PL9 . . . . 136 C4
PENNYTINNEY 23 A4
Penoweth TR11 . . . . 82 A2
PENPETHY 14 F5
PENPILLICK 60 D7
PENPOL 82 B6
Penpol Ave TR27 . . . . 142 C5
Penpol Hill Crantock TR8 . . 110 B4
  Devoran TR3 . . . . 82 B6
PENPOLL 61 D5
Penpol Prim Sch TR27 . . . 142 C5
Penpol Rd TR27 . . . . 142 B5
Penpol Terr TR27 . . . . 142 C5
Penpol Vean TR27 . . . . . . 142 C5
PENPONDS 138 B2
Penponds Prim Sch TR14 . . 79 B5
Penponds Rd TR13 . . . . . . 91 A3
Penpons Cl TR18 . . . . 143 C4
PENPONT 24 A1
Penpont TR8 . . . . 31 E1
Penpont Rd TR15 . . . . 140 D6
Penpont View PL15 . . . . . . 26 C7
Pen Pont Ave TR26 . . . . . . 77 A7
Penpraze TR16 . . . . 67 C5
Penquite Dr PL31 . . . . . . 109 F5
Penquite La PL22 . . . . 112 A4
Penrice Com Coll PL25 . . . 115 A3
Penrice Parc PL25 . . . . . . 115 A3
Penrith Cl PL6 . . . . 125 D3
Penrith Gdns PL6 . . . . . . 125 D3
Penrith Wlk PL6 . . . . 125 D3

PENROSE St Breward.........24 A3
St Eval.................31 E5
Penrose Ct Penzance TR18 .143 F6
2 South Tehidy TR14........138 F7
Penrose Est Degibna TR13..98 D8
Nansloe TR12.............146 A3
Whitehill TR13.............91 E1
Penrose La Penrose PL15 ..17 E8
Penrose PL27.............31 F5
Trevengenow PL27........32 A4
Penrose Mdws 3 TR4 .....55 E4
Penrose Parc TR13........91 B1
Penrose Rd Falmouth TR11.145 A4
Helston TR13............146 C6
Penrose St PL1...........148 B3
Penrose Terr TR18........143 F6
Penrose Villas 5 PL4....128 F4
Penruan La TR2...........95 B6
PENRYN.................144 B7
Penryn Campus TR10.....144 A8
Penryn Coll TR10.........144 A8
Penryn Com Inf Sch TR10 .144 B7
Penryn Jun Sch TR10.....144 B8
Penryn Mus ★ TR10......144 C7
Penryn St TR15..........140 B4
Penryn Sta TR10.........144 B8
Pensans Com Prim Sch
TR18..................143 D6
Penscombe Cross PL15...28 C6
Penscott La TR12........114 C1
Penscowen Rd 6 TR14 ..138 D4
PENSILVA................38 E5
Pensilva Ind Est PL14 ....38 E4
Pensilva Prim Sch PL14...38 E5
Pensilva Rd TR1.........137 E6
Penstowe Pk EX23.........4 A7
Penstowe Rd 5 EX23......5 A6
Penstrasse Pl 1 PL24.....60 D5
PENSTRAZE.............69 A4
Penstraze Bsns Ctr TR4 ..69 A5
Penstraze La PL26........47 A4
Penstruthal Carvannel TR16..80 C6
Pennance TR16..........80 C6
Pennance TR16..........140 D1
Pensylva PL25...........114 E3
Pentalek Rd TR14........138 E1
Pentamar St PL2.........127 E4
Pentargon Rd 1 PL35......9 C1
PENTEWAN...............73 C6
Pentewan Hill PL26.......73 D6
Pentewan Rd
St Austell PL24, PL26......59 C1
Tregorrick PL26..........114 C1
Pentidna La TR27.........66 B2
Pentillie PL26............73 C4
Pentillie Cl 22 PL20......41 B1
Pentillie Cres PL4.......128 D4
Pentillie Gdns
14 Callington PL17.........39 E4
St Austell PL25..........114 F6
Pentillie Rd Bere Alston PL20 41 B1
Plymouth PL4............128 E4
Pentillie View 28 PL20 ...41 B1
Pentillie Way PL26........73 C4
PENTIRE.................43 D4
Pentire 15 PL28...........31 F7
Pentire Ave TR7.........110 A5
Pentire Cres TR7.........110 B5
Pentire Ct TR7...........110 B6
Pentire Gn TR8...........43 D3
Pentire Hts TR7.........110 A5
Pentire Rd Newquay TR7 .110 C5
Penryn TR10............144 B8
Torpoint PL11...........126 F3
Pentland Cl PL6.........124 F7
Pen Tor PL30.............35 C8
Pentor Ct PL30...........35 C8
Pentour 3 PL24...........60 B4
Pentowan Ct TR26.......141 E2
Pentowan Gdns TR27....142 E8
Pentowan Rd TR27.......142 E8
Pentreath Cl Fowey PL23 .116 B5
Lanner TR16.............80 E7
Penzance TR18..........143 D7
Pentreath La Lizard TR12 .102 F2
Praa Sands TR20.........90 B3
Pentreath Terr TR16......80 E7
Pentre Cl PL26...........46 F3
Pentre Ct EX23............4 D4
Pentrevah Ct TR7........110 D6
Pentrevah Rd 8 PL26.....59 D7
Pen-Tye TR27............78 E3
Pentyre Ct PL4..........149 C4
Pentyre Terr PL4.........149 C4
Penvale 3 Pensilva PL14..38 E4
Treluswell TR10..........81 D3
Penvale Cl TR14..........79 B5
Penvale Cres TR10......144 B8
Penvale Ct 8 TR11......145 A4
Penvale Villas TR10......81 D3
Penvean Cl TR10.........93 C8
Penvean La TR11.........144 E5
Penvenen 2 TR26........55 A5
Penventinnie La TR1......69 E4
Penventinue La PL23 ....116 B7
Penventon TR16..........80 B6
Penventon Terr
Four Lanes TR16.........80 B6
Redruth TR15...........140 A4
Penventon View TR13 ...146 B5
Penview Cres TR13......146 B5
Penvorder Cotts PL30....24 B2
Penvorder La PL30.......24 B2
Penvose La TR10.........81 C2
Penware Parc TR14......138 C1
Penwarne Cl Penjerrick TR11 93 D5

Penwarne Cl continued
South Tehidy TR14........138 F7
Sparnon TR11............144 A1
Penwarne La PL26.........73 C3
Penwarne Rd TR11........93 D5
Penwartha TR12..........101 B2
Penwartha Cl
Constantine TR11.........92 F3
St Columb Minor TR7.....111 D7
PENWARTHA COOMBE 55 B3
Penwartha Ct TR11........92 F3
Penwartha Rd
15 Illogan TR16..........67 E4
Perranporth TR6..........55 B4
Penwartha Vean 14 TR16 .67 E4
PENWEATHERS...........69 F2
Penwerris Ct TR11.......145 A6
Penwerris Farm TR11....144 F5
Penwerris La TR11......145 A6
Penwerris Rd TR1.........69 F3
Penwerris Rise TR20......90 B3
Penwerris Terr
Falmouth TR11..........145 A5
10 Falmouth TR11......145 A5
Penwethers La TR1.......69 F3
Penwinnick Cl 9 TR5.....54 C1
Penwinnick Parc 4 TR5 ..54 D1
Penwinnick Rd St Agnes TR5 68 D8
St Austell PL25..........114 B3
Penwith Bsns Ctr TR20...88 F6
Penwith Cl TR26.........141 A4
Penwithick Rd PL26.......59 D7
Penwithian Cl TR27......142 E6
PENWITHICK.............59 E7
Penwithick Pk 6 PL26....59 D7
Penwith Rd TR26........141 A4
Penworth Cl PL15.......106 C5
Penwyth TR12............92 C1
Pen y Bryn PL27.........108 D6
Pen Y Morfa Cl TR27......45 A8
Penyoke La PL12.........119 A2
PENZANCE..............143 F5
Penzance L Ctr TR18.....143 D6
Penzance Rd Helston TR13 146 A6
St Buryan TR19...........97 C7
Penzance School of Art
TR18..................143 E5
Penzance Sta TR18......143 F6
Pepo La TR2..............72 A7
Pepper Cl PL12...........40 C2
Pepper La PL9...........136 D7
Peppers Ct PL12..........40 C2
Peppers Hill Cl PL15......18 F7
Peppers Park Rd PL14 ...113 E6
Pepper St PL19.........147 C6
Pepys Pl PL5...........124 E1
PERCUIL................83 A1
Percy Davy Cl TR6........55 A5
Percymews PL28........107 C4
Percy Mews PL28.......107 C4
Percy St PL5...........123 D1
Percy Terr PL4..........129 A4
Pergolla Ct 9 TR7.......110 F6
Perhaver Pk PL26........85 D5
Perhaver Way PL26.......85 D5
Periwinkle Dr PL7.......131 C5
Periwinkle Gr 7 PL14 ...113 D8
Per Kithen TR11.........102 F2
Permarin Rd TR10......144 C8
PERRANARWORTHAL
Prim Sch TR3............81 D6
Perran Cl Devoran TR3 ....81 F6
Perran Downs TR20.......89 F5
Perrancombe Garden Ct
TR6....................55 A4
PERRANCOOMBE..........55 A4
Perran Crossroads TR20...89 F5
PERRAN DOWNS..........89 E5
Perran Downs Lane TR20 .89 F5
Perran Foundry TR3.......81 D5
Perran La TR20..........89 E4
PERRANPORTH...........55 B5
Perranporth Cl
3 Penryn TR10.........144 A8
Plymouth PL5...........123 E4
Perranporth Com Prim Sch 18
TR6....................55 A4
PERRANUTHNOE.........89 D4
PERRANWELL Goonhavern..55 C3
Perranarworthal.........81 C5
Perranwell Rd TR4........55 D4
Perranwell Sta TR3.......81 E6
PERRANZABULOE.........55 B3
Perranzabuloe Mus ★ TR6..55 A5
Perrily Mount EX23.....104 E4
Perry Cl PL9.............147 B6
Perryfield Pl PL9........129 D1
Perryman Cl PL7.........130 E7
Perseus Cres 17 PL9 ...136 E8
Perseverance Cotts 1
PL7...................130 E7
Peryn Rd PL19...........147 B6
Peter Hopper's Hill PL5...120 C2
Peter's Ct PL9...........136 C7
Petersfield Cl PL3.......129 B3
PETER'S FINGER.........19 C7
Peters Hill PL26..........58 E4
Peters Park Cl PL5......123 E1
Peter's Park La PL5......123 E1
Peters Row 1 TR19......75 A1
PETERVILLE..............54 D1
Petes Pl 24 TR26.......141 B5
Petherick Rd EX23......104 E7
PETHERWIN GATE.........18 B7
Pethick Cl PL6..........124 D6
Pethill PL6.............125 F2

Pethybridge Dr PL31.....109 B3
Petroc Ct PL18...........40 D6
PEVERELL..............128 D6
Peverell Park Rd PL3....128 D6
Peverell Rd Penzance TR18 143 E7
7 Porthleven TR13.......98 C8
Peverell Terr Plymouth PL3 128 D5
Porthleven TR13..........98 B8
Pew Tor Cl 3 PL20........42 C3
Phernyssick Rd PL25 ....114 F6
Philgray Cl TR27........142 E7
Philip Cl PL9............136 A6
Philip Gdns PL9.........135 F6
PHILLACK..............142 D7
Phillack Hill TR27.......142 D7
PHILLEIGH...............83 B6
Phillimore Cl PL26........58 D5
Phillimore St 8 PL2.....127 F4
Philpott La PL19.........147 B2
Phoebe Cl 2 PL18........40 E5
Phoenix Cl 8 PL20........42 C4
Phoenix L Ctr PL15......106 C4
Phoenix St PL1.........148 A2
Piala Pl PL27...........142 E7
Piazza 14 PL26.........141 B6
Piazza The 5 PL31......109 E5
Pickard Way PL25.......104 D7
Pickering Villas TR4......69 A3
Pickle Cl 11 TR11......144 F2
Picklecombe Dr PL5.....124 E4
Pick Pie Dr PL6.........125 E8
PIECE..................139 D2
Pier La PL10...........133 A1
Pier St PL1.............148 B1
Pigmeadow La PL14.....113 C6
Pike Rd PL3............129 D5
Pikes Hill PL23.........116 C4
Pike's Hill TR11.........145 B3
Pike St PL14...........113 C6
Pilchard Works The ★
TR18..................143 C3
Pilgrim Cl PL2..........128 B6
Pilgrim Ct 11 PL20.......41 B1
Pilgrim Dr PL20..........41 B1
Pilgrim Prim Sch PL1....148 B3
Pilgrims Way TR27........78 C1
Pillars Cl TR8............56 F5
Pillars Rd Flushing TR11 .145 B8
Mylor Bridge TR11........82 A2
Pillar Wlk PL6...........124 E7
PILLATON................53 B6
PILLATONMILL............53 B6
Pill La Saltash PL12.....122 E4
Trevilla TR3.............82 C5
Pillmere Dr PL12........122 D4
Pilot Cotts PL28.........21 B4
Pinch Hill Bude EX23....104 F2
Marhamchurch EX23......7 B7
Pinder Ct PL19.........147 B5
Pine Cl TR13...........146 D5
Pine Ct Par PL24.......115 D4
Perranworthal TR3.......81 D6
Pinehurst Cl PL31.......109 E3
Pine Lodge Gdns ★ PL25 .115 D4
Pine Rd TR18...........143 B4
Pine Trees on the Lizard ★
TR12..................99 F5
Pine View Gunnislake PL18 .41 A6
St Dennis PL26..........46 D1
Pinewood Cl PL7........130 F6
Pinewood Dr PL6........125 E7
Pinewood Flats PL27......21 D5
Pinkhams Cotts PL12 ...122 B6
Pink Moors TR16.........68 D1
Pin La PL1.............149 A2
Pinnacle Quay PL4......149 B2
Pinsla Garden & Nursery ★
PL30...................35 E1
Pinslow Cross PL15.......19 C8
Pintail Ave TR27.........77 E3
Pintail Way PL6.........125 B2
Pipers Cl PL15...........18 E2
Pipers Ct TR8............56 F5
PIPERS POOL............17 F3
Pipers Pool Rd PL15......17 F4
Piper St PL6............125 B5
Pipit Cl TR27...........142 E7
Pippin Ave Addington PL14 .113 D7
Addington PL14.........113 D7
Piran Cl PL18............40 D6
Piran Hts EX23.........104 C2
Piran View 2 TR6........55 B4
Pitick Terr TR11........145 B6
Pitland Cnr PL19.........30 D4
Pit Mdw TR11...........144 E3
Pits La PL12.............64 B2
Pitts Cleave Ind Est PL19..30 F3
Pittsmingle Hill PL26.....46 E2
PITYME.................21 F3
Pityme Bsns Ctr PL27....21 F3
Pityme Farm Rd PL27.....21 F3
Pityme Inst PL27.........21 F3
Pixie's Hall ★ TR11.......92 E4
Pixon La PL19..........147 B4
Pixon Trad Ctr 2 PL19 ...147 B4
Place de Brest PL1......148 C3
Place Hill PL28.........107 C5
Place Parc TR7..........111 D7
Place Rd PL23..........116 C4
Place Stables PL23......116 C4
Place View PL23........116 C4
Place View Rd 15 TR2.....95 A6
PLAIDY................117 E5
Plaidy La PL13..........117 E4
Looe PL13..............117 E4

Plaidy Park Rd PL13.....117 E4
PLAIN-AN-GWARRY......140 B6
Plain-an-Gwarry TR15 ..140 B5
Plain St PL27.............22 B5
Plaistow Cl PL5.........123 E2
Plaistow Cres PL5.......123 E2
Plaistow Hill Inf & Nur Sch
PL5...................123 E2
Planet Pk PL33...........14 D2
Plantation TR14..........79 D3
Plantation La TR27......142 B5
Plantings Sch PL3.......128 E6
Plashford Bridge PL13....63 B8
Plas Jowan PL26.........46 F2
Platt The PL27.........108 C5
PLAYING PLACE..........82 B8
Pleasant Pl 16 TR18.....143 C7
Pleasure Hill Cl PL9.....135 D8
Plestin Cl PL15.........106 C7
Pleyber Christ Way PL22 .112 C2
Pleydon Cl PL13..........62 E2
Plintona View PL7.......130 E7
Plough Ct TR10...........81 C2
Plough Gn PL12.........122 C3
Plover Avenue TR13.....146 D6
Plovers Field TR13........91 B5
Plumer Rd PL6..........124 F2
PLUSHABRIDGE...........38 F7
Plymbridge Gdns PL7....130 C7
Plymbridge La PL6......125 B4
Plymbridge Rd
Plymouth, Eggbuckland
PL6...................125 C1
Plymouth, Estover PL6....125 C1
Plymouth, Mainstone PL6 .125 F2
Plymouth, Plympton PL7 .130 C7
Plym Cres PL19.........147 D5
PLYMOUTH..............148 C1
Plymouth Arts Ctr ★ PL4..149 A2
Plymouth Athenaeum &
Theatre ★ PL1.........148 B2
Plymouth Business Sch
PL4...................149 A3
Plymouth City Mkt PL1 ..148 B3
Plymouth City Mus & Art Gal ★
PL4...................149 A3
Plymouth Coll PL4.......128 C4
Plymouth Coll Inf Sch 1
PL3...................128 F5
Plymouth Coll of Art & Design
PL4...................149 A3
Plymouth Coll of Art & Design
(Sutton Annexe) PL4 ...149 A3
Plymouth Coll Prep Sch
PL1...................148 A3
Plymouth Discovery Ctr ★
PL3...................129 F6
Plymouth Eggbuckland Com
Coll PL6...............129 A8
Plymouth Girls High Sch
PL4...................149 A4
Plymouth Knowle Prim Sch
PL5...................124 A4
Plymouth Medical & Tech Pk
PL6...................125 A3
Plymouth Pavilions PL1..148 B2
Plymouth Rd
Bolitho PL14...........113 D4
Horrabridge PL20........42 B4
Liskeard PL14..........113 D5
Plymouth PL7...........130 B6
Tavistock PL19.........147 B4
Plymouth Road Ind Est
PL19..................147 C3
Plymouth St Joseph's RC Prim
Sch PL1...............127 E2
Plymouth Sch of Creative Arts
PL1...................148 A2
Plymouth Ski & Snowboard
Ctr ★ PL6.............129 E7
Plymouth Sta PL4.......148 C4
Plymouth Sta PL4.......148 C4
Plymouth Trade Pk PL4 .149 C1
Plymouth Univ Marine Station
PL4...................149 B1
PLYMPTON.............130 E5
Plympton Hill PL7.......130 F3
Plympton St Mary CE Inf Sch
PL7...................130 E5
PLYMPTON ST MAURICE..130 E3
Plympton St Maurice Prim Sch
PL7...................130 F3
Plym St PL4............149 A3
PLYMSTOCK............135 E6
Plymstock Rd PL9.......135 D7
Plymstock Sch PL9......135 F8
Plymstock Sp Ctr PL9...135 F8
Plymtree Dr PL7........130 C7
Plym Valley Rly ★ PL7...130 A7
Poadsmill Hill PL15.......27 B8
Poad's Trust PL14.........51 F5
Pochin PL25............114 F7
Pocklington Rise PL7....130 E5
Pocohontas Cres 4 TR9 ..45 E1
Pode Dr PL7............131 B4
Poets Corner 1 PL5......124 C1
POINT..................82 B5
Point Neptune PL23.....116 B3
Point Rd TR3............82 A6
Polapit Tamar PL15.......19 A4
Polaris Mews 2 PL9.....136 E7
POLBATHIC..............64 F8
Polbathic Rd PL15......140 C6
POLBORDER.............53 D7
Polbreen Ave 12 TR5.....54 C1
Polbreen La 11 TR5.......54 C1
POLBROCK..............34 A4

Polcoverack
Penhallick TR12.........101 A2
Penhallick TR12.........103 F8
Poldark Gdns 7 PL24.....60 B4
Poldark Mine ★ TR13 ....92 A6
Poldark Rd 12 TR16......67 E4
Poldark Way 2 TR14 ...138 F3
Poldhu Cl TR26.........141 D1
Poldhu Rd Liskeard PL14 .113 D6
Mullion TR12............99 A2
Poldice La TR16..........68 E1
Poldice Terr TR16........68 E1
Poldory TR16............81 A8
Poldown TR13...........91 A4
Poldrea PL24............60 D5
Poldrissick Hill PL12......53 C2
Poldrissick La PL12.......53 C2
Poldue Cl TR15.........140 D6
Polean La PL13.........117 B4
Polean Trad Est PL13....117 B4
Polecoverack La TR12...101 C1
Polgarth 1 Camborne TR15 139 C6
Newlyn TR18............143 B3
Polgarth Cl TR26........141 D1
Polgaver Ho PL25.......115 E3
Polgear TR16............80 A4
POLGIGGA...............96 D4
Polgine Cl TR14..........79 E5
Polgine La TR14..........79 E5
Polglase Wlk TR4........70 D8
Polglaze Ct TR18.......143 D7
Polglist PL26............58 D5
POLGOON Cl TR18.......143 C5
POLGOOTH...............59 A1
Polgooth Cl TR15.......140 D6
Polgover Way 5 PL24....60 B4
Polgrain Hill PL30........46 C7
Polgrain Rd TR14.......138 F6
Polgrean Pl PL24........60 B5
Polhigey TR16............80 C1
Polhigey Terr TR16.......80 C2
Polhorman La TR12.......99 A2
Police Ho TR11.........145 B4
Polisken Way TR4........56 D1
Polkanugga
Lesneague TR12........101 A4
Tregeague TR12........100 F4
Polkanuggo La TR10......80 F1
POLKERRIS..............60 E3
Polkerris Pk PL24........60 E3
Polkerris Rd TR16........80 F8
Polkirt Hill
Gorran Haven PL26.......73 B1
Mevagissey PL26.........73 C3
Polkirt Hts PL26..........73 C3
Polkyth L Ctr PL25......114 E4
Polkyth Par PL25.......114 E4
Polkyth Rd PL25........114 E4
POLLADRAS..............90 F5
Polladras TR13...........91 A5
Pollard Cl Plymouth PL9 .135 B5
Saltash PL12...........122 B2
Pollard Rd 7 PL11........39 F4
Pollards Cl Goonhavern TR4 55 C4
Pensilva PL14............38 E4
Pollards Way PL12......122 E3
Polmark Dr PL28.........20 D2
Polmarth Cl PL25.......114 F6
POLMASSICK............72 E4
Polmassick Vineyard ★
PL26..................72 E4
POLMEAR...............60 E4
Polmear Ct 9 PL27.....108 B5
Polmear Hill PL24........60 E4
Polmear Rd St Austell PL25 114 F4
Tywardreath PL24........60 D4
Polmeere Ho TR18......143 E7
Polmeere Rd TR18......143 E7
Polmena La PL22.......112 E1
Polmenna Hill PL14......36 F1
Polmenna La TR4........36 E1
Polmennor Dr TR26.....141 D1
Polmennor Rd
Falmouth TR11.........144 F1
Heamoor TR18..........143 C8
Polmenor Downs N TR14,
TR27.................78 F5
Polmenor Downs S TR14..78 F4
Polmeor Cl TR26........141 D1
Polmewan Flats PL26.....59 A1
POLMORLA.............108 A4
Polmorla Mews 10 PL27..108 B5
Polmorla Rd PL27.......108 B5
Polmorla Wlk PL27......108 B5
Polmor Rd TR20.........89 B8
Polpennic Dr PL28......107 C4
POLPEOR...............77 B3
Polpeor La TR12........102 F1
Polpeor Row TR27.......77 A3
POLPERRO...............62 E1
Polperro Com Prim Sch
PL13..................62 E2
Polperro Heritage Mus of
Smuggling & Fishing ★
PL13..................62 E2
Polperro Model Village ★
PL13..................62 D1
Polperro Pl PL2.........128 D8
Polperro Rd PL13.......117 B4
Polpey La PL24..........60 D5
POLRUAN..............116 C2
Polruan Cl TR26.........77 C4
Polruan Ct TR1.........137 E2
Polruan Prim Sch PL23 ..116 D2

Polruan Rd Redruth TR15. . . .**140** D6
  Truro TR1. . . . . **137** E2
Polruan Terr PL1. . . . . **148** A3
POLSCOE **112** E3
Polscoe Rd PL22. . . . . **112** F3
Polsethow Penryn TR10. . . . **144** B7
  Tremough TR10. . . . . **81** D1
Polsethow Vale TR10. . . . . . . **144** B7
Polstain Cres TR3 . . . . **69** D3
Polstain Rd TR3 . . . . **69** D3
Polstain Villas TR3 . . . . **69** D3
Polstrong Kehelland TR14 . . . **66** F1
  Treswithian TR14. . . . . **79** B7
  Treswithian TR14. . . . . **138** A3
Polsue Way TR2. . . . . **70** F5
Poltair Ave PL25. . . . . **114** E4
Poltair Cl TR18 . . . . **143** C7
Poltair Cres PL25. . . . . **114** D4
Poltair Ct PL25 . . . . **114** E4
Poltair Dr TR10. . . . . **144** B7
Poltair Rd Penryn TR10 . . . . . **144** B7
  St Austell PL25. . . . . **114** D4
Poltair School PL25. . . . . **114** D4
Poltair Terr 7 TR18 . . . . **143** C7
Poltamar PL15. . . . . **106** D5
Pol-Tec Lane PL23. . . . . **61** D3
POLTESCO **103** B5
Poltesco La TR12. . . . . **103** B5
Poltisco Cl TR1. . . . . **137** E3
Poltisco Wharf TR1. . . . . **137** E4
Poltisko Rd TR10. . . . . **144** B7
Poltisko Terr TR10. . . . . **144** B7
Poltreen Cl TR26 . . . . **141** D1
Polurrian Cliffs
  3 Henscath TR12. . . . . **98** F1
  Mullion TR12. . . . . **102** B8
Polurrian Rd TR12. . . . . **99** A1
Polvarth Es 3 TR2. . . . . **95** B6
Polvarth Est TR2. . . . . **95** B6
Polvarth La 4 TR2. . . . . **95** B6
Polvarth Rd TR2. . . . . **95** A6
Polvean Cross TR14. . . . . **51** A1
Polvean Terr PL14. . . . . **51** A1
Polvella Cl TR7 . . . . **110** B5
Polvellan Manor PL13. . . . . . **117** C4
Polvellan Terr PL13. . . . . **117** C4
Polvelyn Parc TR27. . . . . **142** E7
Polventon 17 PL28. . . . . **31** F7
Polventon Cl
  Falmouth TR11. . . . . **144** E4
  Heamoor TR18. . . . . **143** C7
Polventon Hill PL14. . . . . **37** A1
Polventon Parc 6 TR12. . . . . **101** C4
Polvillion Rd PL23. . . . . **116** B4
Polweath Cl TR18. . . . . **143** E7
Polweath Rd TR18. . . . . **143** E7
Polwhaveral Terr 6 TR11 . . . **145** A5
Polwheal Rd TR14. . . . . **138** F6
Polwhele House Sch TR4 . . . **70** C6
Polwhele Rd Newquay TR7 . . . **111** A3
  Truro TR1. . . . . **137** F6
Polwithen Ct TR26. . . . . **141** C2
Polwithen Dr TR26 . . . . **141** C1
Polwithen Gdns TR26. . . . . . **141** C1
Polwithen Rd
  Falmouth TR11. . . . . **145** A4
  Penryn TR10 . . . . **144** B7
  Penzance TR18 . . . . **143** D5
Polwrath Terr PL14. . . . . **38** A3
Polwyn Cl TR18. . . . . **143** B7
Poly Arts & Science TR11 . . . **145** B4
Polyear Cl PL26. . . . . **59** A1
Polyne Cotts PL13. . . . . **62** F3
POLYPHANT. **17** F1
POLZEATH. **21** E5
Polzeath Ct PL27 . . . . **21** D6
Polzeath Gdns PL2 . . . . **128** D8
Pomarine Cl 1 EX23. . . . . **7** B8
POMPHLETT **135** E8
Pomphlett Cl PL9. . . . . **135** D8
Pomphlett Farm Ind Est
  PL9. . . . . **129** E1
Pomphlett Gdns PL9. . . . . . . **135** D8
Pomphlett Prim Sch PL9. . . . **135** E8
Pomphlett Rd PL9. . . . . **135** E8
Ponchin Dr PL25 . . . . **114** E7
  St Austell PL25. . . . . **114** E7
Pondbridge Hill 1 PL14. . . . . **113** C5
Pondfield Rd PL12. . . . . **122** B3
Pondhu Cres PL25. . . . . **114** B3
Pondhu Prim Sch PL25 . . . . . **114** B2
Pondhu Rd PL25. . . . . **114** C3
Pond La TR15. . . . . **140** A6
Ponds Hill TR19 . . . . **75** B1
Pond View Terr PL26 . . . . **58** D5
Pond Wlk TR27 . . . . **142** D7
PONIOU. **76** A5
Poniou La TR20. . . . . **88** F6
Poniou Rd TR20. . . . . **88** F6
Poniou Way TR20. . . . . **88** F6
Ponsandane Farm Mews
  TR18 . . . . **143** F7
PONSANOOTH. **81** B5
PONSHARDEN. **144** F6
Ponsharden Cotts TR11. . . . . **144** F6
Ponsharden Ind Est TR11. . . **144** F6
Ponsmere Ct 9 TR6. . . . . **55** A5
Ponsmere Rd TR6. . . . . **55** A5
Ponsonby Rd PL3. . . . . **128** B4
PONSONGATH. **103** D7
Ponsongath
  Penhallick TR12. . . . . **101** A1
  Trelan TR12. . . . . **100** F1
Ponstantual Hill TR12. . . . . . **99** D7

Ponsvale TR3. . . . . **81** B4
PONT. **61** D3
Pont Bottom PL23. . . . . **61** D3
Pontsmill Rd PL24. . . . . **60** C6
POOL. **139** B5
Pool Academy TR15. . . . . . . **139** B6
Pool Bsns Pk TR15. . . . . **139** B4
Poole Park Rd PL5. . . . . **127** C8
Poolfield Way TR11. . . . . **144** D3
Pool Hall PL4. . . . . **51** F5
Pool Ind Est TR15. . . . . **139** C5
Pool La Milltown PL30. . . . . . . **35** F2
  Welltown PL30. . . . . **36** A2
Pool Rd PL15. . . . . **17** E2
Pool's Ct TR27. . . . . **142** D6
Pool St PL31. . . . . **109** E5
Poorhouse Hill PL15. . . . . . . **12** B2
Poor House Hill TR10. . . . . . . **81** E3
Poplar Cl PL7. . . . . **131** B5
Poplars Ct 16 TR6. . . . . **55** A5
Poplar Terr TR11 . . . . **145** B7
Popplestone Pk PL8 . . . . **136** F5
Porcupine Rd PL24. . . . . **60** C6
Pordenack Cl TR26 . . . . **141** E2
Porfell Wildlife Park &
  Sanctuary ★ PL14. . . . . **50** A2
Porhan Gn TR11. . . . . **144** E6
PORKELLIS. **92** B8
Pork St TR12. . . . . **100** D6
Porsham Cl PL6. . . . . **121** B1
Porsham La PL5. . . . . **124** E8
Porsnoder Pl PL10. . . . . **133** A2
Portbigham PL13. . . . . **117** C3
Portbyhan Rd PL13. . . . . **117** C3
PORTEATH. **22** A6
Porteath Bee Ctr ★ PL27. . . . **22** A6
Porteath Rd PL27. . . . . **21** F6
Porteous Cl PL1. . . . . **127** F3
Porter Way PL12. . . . . **122** C3
PORT GAVERNE. **22** E7
PORTH. **111** C8
PORTHALLOW Looe. **62** F2
  St Keverne. **101** D6
Porth Beach Rd TR7. . . . . . . **111** B8
Porth Bean Ct TR7. . . . . **111** C7
Porth Bean Rd TR7. . . . . **111** C7
Porthcollum La TR27. . . . . . . **78** A1
PORTHCOTHAN. **31** C6
PORTHCURNO. **96** E3
Porthcurno Telegraph Mus ★
  TR19. . . . . **96** E3
Portheast Cl PL26. . . . . **85** C5
Portheast Way PL26. . . . . . . **85** C5
Portherras Cross TR19. . . . . . **75** A1
Portherras Terr 11 TR19 . . . . **75** A1
Portherras Villas 10 TR19. . . **75** A1
Porthgwidden TR3 . . . . **82** C4
Porthgwidden Studios
  TR26 . . . . **141** C6
Porthia Cl TR26. . . . . **141** A4
Porthia Cres TR26 . . . . **141** A4
Porthia Rd 12 TR26. . . . . **77** A6
PORTHILLY. **21** D3
Porthilly Cvn Site PL27. . . . . **21** D2
Porthilly La PL27. . . . . **21** D2
Porthilly View PL28. . . . . . . **107** E4
PORTH KEA. **70** B1
Porthkerris TR12. . . . . **101** E5
Porthkerris Divers ★ TR12. . **101** E5
PORTHLEVEN. **98** B8
Porthleven Com Prim Sch
  TR13. . . . . **91** B1
Porthleven Rd TR13 . . . . **146** A5
Porthmellon Gdns PL17. . . . . **39** F4
PORTHMEOR. **75** F4
Porthmeor Ct 51 TR26. . . . . **141** B6
Porthmeor Hill TR26. . . . . . . **141** A6
Porthmeor Rd
  St Austell PL25. . . . . **115** B3
  6 St Ives TR26. . . . . **141** B6
Porthmeor Sq 21 TR26. . . . . **141** B6
Porthmeor Studios 50
  TR26 . . . . **141** B6
Porthminster Terr 23
  TR26 . . . . **141** B5
Porthmissen 16 PL28. . . . . . . **31** F7
PORTH NAVAS. **93** B2
PORTHOUSTOCK. **101** E4
Porth Par TR7. . . . . **111** C8
Porthpean Beach Rd
  PL26 . . . . **59** E1
Porthpean Rd PL24, PL26. . . . **114** F2
Porthrepta Rd TR26. . . . . . . **141** E1
Porth Sawle Flats TR2 . . . . . **83** B2
PORTHTOWAN. **68** A6
Porth View TR26. . . . . **95** B6
Porth Way TR7. . . . . **111** B7
PORTINGTON. **29** E3
PORT ISAAC. **22** D8
Port Isaac Prim Sch PL29 . . . **22** E7
Port La PL15. . . . . **27** B2
Portland Cl PL14. . . . . **113** D7
Portland Ct 9 PL1. . . . . **127** F3
Portland Gdns TR11. . . . . . . **144** F4
Portland Pl 23 TR19. . . . . **88** C1
Portland Rd PL1. . . . . **127** F3
Portland Sq PL4. . . . . **148** C4
Portland Square Lane N
  PL4. . . . . **149** A4
Portland Terr PL14. . . . . **113** C7
Portland Villas PL4. . . . . **148** C4
PORTLOE. **84** B3
PORTLOOE. **117** A2
PORTMELLON. **73** C3
Portmellon Pk PL26. . . . . **73** C3
Portmellon Rd PL26 . . . . **73** C3
PORT QUIN. **22** B7
PORTREATH. **67** C6

Portreath Com Prim Sch
  TR16. . . . . **67** D6
PORTSCATHO. **83** B2
Portuan Rd PL13. . . . . **117** D1
Portway Cl PL9. . . . . **136** D7
PORTWRINKLE. **65** B4
Posses La TR18 . . . . **88** E6
Possession La PL12. . . . . **53** C3
Post Box Row TR14 . . . . **139** B3
Potters La PL35. . . . . **9** C1
Potters Mews TR4. . . . . **55** B4
Potters Way PL7. . . . . **130** D5
Pottery Est PL10. . . . . **132** E6
Pottery Rd PL1. . . . . **127** D3
POUGHILL. **4** D2
Poughill Rd EX23. . . . . **104** F7
Poultney Cl PL7. . . . . **131** A5
Pounda PL14. . . . . **51** B4
Pound Dean PL14. . . . . **113** A5
Poundfield Cl 2 EX23. . . . . . . **4** D1
Poundfield Hill 1 EX23. . . . . . **4** D1
Poundfield La EX23. . . . . **4** D1
Pound Hill PL12. . . . . **53** C3
Pound La Bodmin PL31. . . . . . **109** E5
  Stoke Climsland PL17. . . . . **28** E1
  Threemilestone TR3 . . . . **69** E1
Pound Pk PL14. . . . . **51** F5
Pound Rd PL20. . . . . **42** B3
Pound's Cross PL6 . . . . **120** E5
Pounds Park Rd
  1 Bere Alston PL20. . . . . **41** B1
  Plymouth PL3. . . . . **128** D7
Pounds Pk PL12 . . . . **122** F3
Pound St Liskeard PL14 . . . . . **113** C6
  Plymouth PL1. . . . . **134** A8
POUNDSTOCK. **6** E2
Poundstock Cl PL30 . . . . **35** F3
Powderham Rd PL3 . . . . **128** F7
Powis Gdns PL5. . . . . **124** B2
Powisland Dr PL6 . . . . **125** A5
PRAA SANDS. **90** C3
Praa Sands Holiday Pk 6
  TR20. . . . . **90** B3
Praed Pl TR26. . . . . **77** E4
Praed's La TR17. . . . . **89** C5
Pras An Fer La 4 PL32. . . . . . **105** C3
Pras Coth TR16. . . . . **68** C3
Pras Gwartha 5 PL14. . . . . . . **51** A1
Pras Meynek TR12. . . . . **99** A2
PRAZE-AN-BEEBLE. **79** C2
Praze-an-Creet TR26. . . . . . . **77** A7
Praze-an-Cronor TR9 . . . . . . **45** E5
Praze Bsns Pk TR14. . . . . **79** B2
Prazegooth La TR12. . . . . . . **103** A4
Praze La PL30. . . . . **35** E5
Praze Mdw TR10. . . . . **144** C8
Praze Rd Leedstown TR27 . . . **78** E1
  Newquay TR7. . . . . **111** B7
Praze The TR10. . . . . **144** C8
Predannack Airfield ★
  TR12. . . . . **102** D6
Predannack Holiday Village
  TR12 . . . . **102** E6
Predannack Rd
  Henscath TR12 . . . . **102** C7
  4 Mullion TR12. . . . . **99** A1
Preeze Cross PL30 . . . . **35** E6
Prestonbury Cl PL6 . . . . **125** B7
Prevenna Rd 2 TR19 . . . . **88** C1
Prickly Post La PL23 . . . . **116** A5
Prideaux Cl PL12 . . . . **122** C5
Prideaux Rd PL24. . . . . **60** B6
Pridham La PL2. . . . . **128** D7
Pridmouth Rd PL25. . . . . **114** E6
Priestacott Pk 6 EX23 . . . . . . **5** A6
Priesthood Terr PL10. . . . . . . **132** E5
Priestley Ave PL5. . . . . **123** E2
Primelin Pl 8 TR10. . . . . **81** C1
Primitive Row TR14. . . . . . . **139** A5
Primrose Cl Camborne TR14 **138** B4
  9 Goldsithney TR20 . . . . **89** E5
  Roche PL26 . . . . **47** A3
  Torpoint PL11 . . . . **126** E4
Primrose Cotts TR2. . . . . **71** C6
Primrose Ct TR26. . . . . **141** B4
Primrose Dr PL28. . . . . **31** F7
Primrose Gdns Illogan TR16 **67** D4
  Tavistock PL19. . . . . **147** A4
Primrose Hill TR20 . . . . **89** E5
Primrose La 4 TR20. . . . . **89** E5
Primrose Rd EX23 . . . . **104** F5
Primrose Terr
  Newlyn TR18 . . . . **143** D1
  Portreath TR16. . . . . **67** D6
  Tresillian TR2 . . . . **70** F5
Primrose Valley TR26. . . . . . **141** C4
Primrose Wlk PL12. . . . . **122** D7
Prince Charles Cl PL15. . . . . **106** C7
Prince Charles Ho PL25. . . . . **114** E5
Prince Charles Pk PL25. . . . . **114** E5
Prince Charles Rd PL25. . . . . **114** E5
Prince Maurice Cl PL4. . . . . . **149** B3
Prince Maurice Rd PL4. . . . . **128** F4
PRINCE ROCK. **129** B1
Prince Rock Prim Sch PL4 **129** B2
Princes Rd PL6 . . . . **125** E6
Princes Row PL14 . . . . **38** B6
Princess Ave
  Plymouth, Plymstock PL9 . . . **135** E6
  Plymouth, West Park PL5. . . . **124** A3

Princess Cres PL9. . . . . **135** E6
Princess Ct 12 TR18. . . . . . . **143** E5
Princess Parc TR9. . . . . **45** E1
Princess Sq PL13. . . . . **117** C3
Princess Rd PL14. . . . . **38** E4
Princess St PL1. . . . . **148** C2
Princess Street Ope PL1. . . . **148** C2
Princes St Bude EX23. . . . . . **104** D6
  Looe PL13. . . . . **117** C3
  Penzance TR18 . . . . **143** E5
Prince's St TR1. . . . . **137** D4
Princess Terr 7 PL14. . . . . . . **38** E4
Princess Villas PL17. . . . . **28** B1
Princess Way PL1. . . . . **148** C2
Princetown Rd PL20. . . . . **42** E3
Prior's Barn PL31. . . . . **109** F4
Priors Cl 10 TR26. . . . . **77** A6
Priors Row TR13. . . . . **146** C5
Priory Cl Par PL24. . . . . **60** C5
  Tavistock PL19. . . . . **147** D3
Priory Cotts PL15. . . . . **106** B6
Priory Dr PL7. . . . . **130** D5
Priory Gdns PL19 . . . . **147** D3
Priory La PL15. . . . . **106** B7
Priory Lawn Terr PL3 . . . . . . **129** A6
Priory Mews PL15. . . . . **106** B7
Priory Mill PL7. . . . . **130** D5
Priory Park Rd PL15. . . . . . . **106** B6
Priory Rd Bodmin PL31. . . . . . **109** F4
  Plymouth PL3. . . . . **129** A6
  St Austell PL25. . . . . **114** C4
  St Columb Minor TR7, TR8 . . . **111** E7
Priory Ridge PL7. . . . . **130** D5
Prislow Cl TR11. . . . . **144** E2
Prislow Fields TR11 . . . . **144** E2
Prislow La TR11. . . . . **144** E2
Proad La PL30. . . . . **23** F6
PROBUS. **71** C6
Probus Com Prim Sch TR2 . . **71** C6
Promised Land TR5. . . . . **54** D1
Prospect Bldgs TR7 . . . . **110** E6
Prospect Cl 6 TR27. . . . . **142** D6
Prospect Gdns TR1 . . . . **137** E6
Prospect La PL12 . . . . **122** C3
Prospect Pl Ashton TR13. . . . . **90** E3
  3 Falmouth TR11. . . . . **145** B5
  Hayle TR27. . . . . **142** D5
  Helston TR13 . . . . **146** C5
  Mevagissey PL26. . . . . **73** C4
  25 Penzance TR18 . . . . **143** E6
  Plymouth PL1. . . . . **148** B2
  8 Porthleven TR13. . . . . **98** B8
  5 Truro TR1. . . . . **137** D5
Prospect Row PL1. . . . . **127** E1
Prospect St PL4. . . . . **149** A3
Prospect Terr Bodmin PL31 **109** E4
  Gunnislake PL18. . . . . **41** A6
  Gunnislake, St Ann's Chapel
  PL18. . . . . **40** E5
  Mevagissey PL26. . . . . **73** C4
Prospect Wlk PL12. . . . . **122** C3
Prosper Cl PL26 . . . . **47** A2
Prosper Hill TR27. . . . . **66** B1
Prosper Rd Roche PL26. . . . . . **47** A2
  Trezaise PL26 . . . . **47** A2
Protector Rd 1 PL5. . . . . **124** D2
Prouse Cres PL2. . . . . **128** C8
Prouse Rise PL12. . . . . **122** C2
Prouts Ct 4 PL15. . . . . **106** C6
Prout's La PL27 . . . . **78** D6
Prouts Mews 5 PL15 . . . . . . **106** C6
Prouts Way PL15 . . . . **18** C2
Providence Pl Calstock PL18 **41** A3
  Plymouth PL1. . . . . **128** A3
Providence St PL4. . . . . **149** A4
Provis Rd TR18 . . . . **143** C4
Prussia Cove PL26. . . . . **89** F4
Prussia Cove Rd TR20. . . . . . . **89** F4
Prynne Cl PL1 . . . . **148** B3
Puckator La PL14. . . . . **38** A2
Puffin Close EX23 . . . . **104** F5
Puggis Hill TR14. . . . . **138** A5
Pulla Cross TR4 . . . . **81** B6
Pulsack TR27. . . . . **78** C6
Pump La TR20. . . . . **88** A5
Putnam Cl PL14 . . . . **113** D5
Pydar Cl TR7 . . . . **111** B5
Pydar Mews 8 TR1. . . . . **137** C4
Pydar St TR1 . . . . **137** C5
Pym St Plymouth PL1. . . . . . . **127** F3
  Tavistock PL19. . . . . **147** C6
Pyramid Cl PL25. . . . . **58** F4
Pyrite Gdns 4 PL14 . . . . **113** D8
PYWORTHY. **8** E5
Pyworthy CE Prim Sch EX22. **8** E5
PZ Gall ★ TR18. . . . . **143** F4

Q

Quakers Rd Polzeath PL27. . . . **21** F5
  Ponsanooth TR4, TR3. . . . . **81** B6
Quant Pk PL19. . . . . **147** C6
Quarry Cl EX23 . . . . **104** E7
Quarry Cl Rd PL26 . . . . **58** C7
Quarry Cnr PL20. . . . . **41** C2
Quarry Cotts Plymouth PL1. . **148** A3
  Plymouth, Honicknowle PL5 . . **124** B2
Quarry Cres PL15. . . . . **106** A3
Quarry Ct TR11 . . . . **145** B4
Quarry Gdns TR18 . . . . **143** D5
Quarry Hill Falmouth TR11. . . **145** B4
  Gulval TR18. . . . . **88** E7
  Landreyne PL15. . . . . **27** C2
  Tregellist PL30. . . . . **22** F3
Quarry House Flats TR1. . . . **137** E3
Quarry La Gunnislake PL18. . . **40** F6

Quarry La continued
  Landrake PL12. . . . . **53** D3
  Launceston PL15. . . . . **18** E2
  11 Pensilva PL14. . . . . **38** E4
  St Germans PL12. . . . . **65** A8
  Sheffield PL19. . . . . **97** F7
Quarrymans Cotts PL27. . . . . **33** B7
Quarry Park Ave PL9. . . . . . **135** D7
Quarry Park Rd
  Newquay TR7. . . . . **110** F5
  Plymouth, Peverell PL3. . . . . . **128** D5
  Plymouth, Plymstock PL9. . . . **135** D7
Quarry Park Terr PL31. . . . . **109** C4
Quarry Pk 6 TR13. . . . . **146** B5
Quarry Rd Pensilva PL14. . . . . **38** E4
  Perranporth TR6 . . . . **55** B4
Quarry St St Germans PL12. . . **65** A8
  Torpoint PL11 . . . . **127** C3
Quarterdeck The PL1. . . . . . **134** A8
Quartz Cl PL14. . . . . **113** D8
Quay Hill Falmouth TR11. . . . **145** C4
  Penryn TR10 . . . . **144** D7
Quay La PL12. . . . . **53** D1
Quay Mews 8 TR1. . . . . **137** D4
Quay Rd Crumplehorn PL13. . . **62** D1
  Devoran TR3. . . . . **81** F6
  Landrake PL12. . . . . **53** A2
  Looe PL13. . . . . **117** C3
  Mylor Bridge TR11. . . . . **82** B4
  Plymouth PL1. . . . . **149** A2
  St Agnes TR5 . . . . **54** C2
  St Austell PL25. . . . . **115** B2
  St Germans PL12. . . . . **65** B8
  Tideford PL12 . . . . **52** F2
  Trenarth TR11. . . . . **93** B2
Quayside 6 PL19. . . . . **147** B5
Quay St Falmouth TR11. . . . . **145** C4
  Looe PL13. . . . . **117** C3
  Lostwithiel PL22. . . . . **112** C2
  11 Mousehole TR19. . . . . **88** C1
  Penzance TR18 . . . . **143** F4
  St Ives TR26. . . . . **141** C6
  20 Truro TR1. . . . . **137** D4
Quay The Pentewan PL26. . . . **73** C6
  Penzance TR18 . . . . **143** F5
  Plymouth PL9. . . . . **135** C4
  Polruan PL23. . . . . **116** D3
  Portscatho TR2 . . . . **83** B2
  St Germans PL12. . . . . **65** B8
  St Mawes TR2 . . . . **95** A6
Queen Anne Gdns TR11. . . . **144** B3
Queen Anne's Quay PL4 . . . **149** B2
Queen Elizabeth Rd PL15. . . **106** C7
Queenie Dr 2 PL14. . . . . **113** D8
Queen Mary Ct TR11 . . . . . . **145** B2
Queen Mary Rd TR11 . . . . . **145** B2
Queens Cl
  5 Indian Queens TR9. . . . . . . **45** E1
  Plymouth PL6. . . . . **125** E6
  St Austell PL25. . . . . **46** F3
Queen's Cres PL31. . . . . **109** B3
Queen's Ct 6 TR18 . . . . **143** E4
Queen's Gate
  Plymouth, Lipson PL4 . . . . **149** A4
  Plymouth, Stoke PL3. . . . . **148** A4
Queen's Gate Mews PL4 . . . **149** B4
Queen's Gate Villas PL4 . . . . **149** B4
Queen's Gate Villas Rd
  PL4 . . . . **149** B4
Queens Pk PL27. . . . . **108** C4
Queens Rd Plymouth PL5 . . . **123** F3
  St Austell PL25. . . . . **114** E3
Queen's Rd PL4. . . . . **149** B4
Queen's Sq 24 TR18. . . . . . . **143** E5
Queen St Bude EX23. . . . . . . **104** D6
  Goldsithney TR20. . . . . **89** E5
  Lostwithiel PL22. . . . . **112** C2
  Penzance TR18 . . . . **143** E5
  Plymouth PL1. . . . . **127** D2
  St Just TR19. . . . . **86** E6
Queen's Way
  2 Goldsithney TR20. . . . . **89** E5
  Hayle TR27. . . . . **142** C5
Queen Terr PL17. . . . . **40** C4
Quenchwell Rd TR3. . . . . **81** F7
QUETHIOCK. **52** C7
Quethiock La Parkfield PL14 **39** A1
  Quethiock PL14. . . . . **52** C8
Quethiock Prim Sch PL14. . . **52** C7
Quilkin Av TR15. . . . . **139** B5
Quillet Cl PL26. . . . . **114** F2
Quillet Rd TR18. . . . . **143** B3
Quilver Cl PL26. . . . . **85** D5
Quimperle Way PL14. . . . . . **113** C6
Quintrell Cl TR8 . . . . **44** E3
QUINTRELL DOWNS. **44** E3
Quintrell Downs Sta TR8. . . **111** F3
Quintrell Gdns TR8 . . . . **44** E3
Quintrell Rd TR7, TR8. . . . . . **111** E5
QUITHER. **30** A3
QUOIT. **45** F4

R

Rabys Row TR16. . . . . **140** D6
Race Course Rd PL31. . . . . . . **35** B4
Race Hill Launceston PL15. . . **106** C5
  Truro TR4. . . . . **81** C8
Race Hill Terr PL15. . . . . **106** C5
Rachel's Way 17 TR9. . . . . . . **45** E6
Radar Rd PL6. . . . . **125** B5
Radcliffe Cl PL6 . . . . **124** E6
Radford Ave PL4. . . . . **129** B1
Radford La PL10. . . . . **132** D4
Radford Park Dr PL9. . . . . . . **135** D6
Radford Park Rd PL9 . . . . . . **135** D6
Radford Rd PL1. . . . . **148** B1

Radford View PL9 . . . . .135 D6
Radiant Ho PL1 . . . . .148 B2
Radland Cross PL12 . . . . . .40 C3
Radnor Cl PL31 . . . . .109 F4
Radnor Hall PL4 . . . . .149 A3
Radnor Pl PL4 . . . . .149 A3
Radnor Rd
  Redruth, North Country
  TR16 . . . . .140 C8
  Redruth, Scorrier TR16 . . . . .68 D3
Radnor St PL4 . . . . .149 A3
Raginnis Hill 25 TR19 . . . . . .88 C1
Raglan Ct PL1 . . . . .127 F2
Raglan Gdns PL1 . . . . .127 F2
Raglan Rd PL1 . . . . .127 F2
Rail Way PL15 . . . . .17 F5
Railway Cotts
  Camborne TR14 . . . . .139 A3
  Falmouth TR11 . . . . .145 D3
  6 Plymouth, Ford PL2 . . . . .127 F5
  Plymouth, Plymstock PL9 . .135 D7
  Tavistock PL19 . . . . .147 B6
Railway Cres PL14 . . . . .38 A4
Railway Terr Bodmin PL31 . .109 D5
  Carharrack TR16 . . . . .80 E4
Railway Villas TR15 . . . . . .139 F6
Rainham Cl TR15 . . . . .139 C8
Rainyfields PL28 . . . . .107 D5
Rainy Fields Cl PL28 . . . . . .107 D5
Raleigh Cl PL28 . . . . .107 C4
Raleigh Ct PL7 . . . . .131 B6
Raleigh Gdns 5 PL31 . . . . .109 F3
Raleigh Rd PL28 . . . . .107 C5
Raleigh Pl 13 TR11 . . . . . . .145 A4
Raleigh St PL1 . . . . .148 B3
Ralph's Ct PL19 . . . . .147 B5
Ramage Cl PL6 . . . . .125 F3
RAME Cawsand 64 B2
  Stithians 92 E8
Rame Comm TR13 . . . . .80 E1
Rame Croft TR10 . . . . .80 E1
Ramehead Cotts PL10 . . . . .64 B1
Ramehead La PL10 . . . . .64 B1
Rame La Cawsand PL10 . . . .132 F1
  Rame PL10 . . . . .64 B2
Rame Terr PL10 . . . . .80 E1
Rame View PL13 . . . . .117 E5
Ramillies Ave PL5 . . . . .124 A4
Ramoth Way TR6 . . . . .55 B5
Ramsey Gdns PL5 . . . . .124 D1
Ramsgate TR14 . . . . .79 B5
Ranch View PL15 . . . . .106 A5
Randwick Park Rd PL9 . . . .135 D7
Ranelagh Ct TR7 . . . . .111 C7
Ranelagh Mews PL31 . . . . .109 D5
Ranelagh Rd PL25 . . . . .114 F4
Range Rd PL30 . . . . .35 F4
Ranneys Cl PL13 . . . . .117 D6
Ransum Way PL19 . . . . .147 B4
Raphael Cl PL9 . . . . .136 B5
Raphael Dr PL9 . . . . .136 A6
Raphael Rd PL13 . . . . .62 C1
Rapson Rd PL14 . . . . .113 D6
Rashleigh Ave
  Plymouth PL7 . . . . .130 F7
  Saltash PL12 . . . . .122 D1
Rashleigh Ct PL25 . . . . .115 C3
Rashleigh La PL23 . . . . .116 A4
Rashleigh Mews PL25 . . . . .115 A3
Rashleigh Pl PL25 . . . . .114 F4
Rashleigh Road 6 PL26 . . .115 A1
Rashleigh Vale TR1 . . . . . . .137 E4
Ratcliffes La TR13 . . . . .146 A5
Rattle St PL26 . . . . .85 D5
Rawley Ct TR7 . . . . .110 E5
Rawley La TR7 . . . . .110 E5
Rawlin Cl PL6 . . . . .129 C8
Rawlings La PL23 . . . . .116 D5
Raymond Rd TR15 . . . . .140 C4
Raymond Way PL7 . . . . .130 D6
Raynham Rd PL3 . . . . .128 B4
Read Cl TR10 . . . . .144 B7
Reading Wlk PL5 . . . . .124 C4
READYMONEY 116 B3
Readymoney Rd PL23 . . . . .116 B3
REAWLA 78 E3
Reawla La TR27 . . . . .78 E3
Rebecca Cl PL24 . . . . .60 B6
Recreation Rd PL2 . . . . .128 C7
Recreation Road Ind Est
  PL2 . . . . .128 C7
Rectory Gdns
  Camborne TR14 . . . . .138 C2
  Lanreath PL13 . . . . .62 B8
  St Stephen PL26 . . . . .58 B4
Rectory La PL30 . . . . .34 D7
Rectory Rd Camborne TR14 .138 C2
  Lanivet PL30 . . . . .47 F6
  Plymouth PL1 . . . . .128 A2
  St Buryan TR19 . . . . .97 B6
  St Dennis PL26 . . . . .46 B1
  St Stephen PL26 . . . . .58 B4
Rectory The TR1 . . . . .137 C5
Redannack Est 11 TR12 . . . .99 A2
Redannack N 1 TR12 . . . . . .99 A2
Redannick Cres TR1 . . . . . .137 B3
Redannick La TR1 . . . . .137 B4
Redbrooke Rd TR14 . . . . . . .138 C2
Redbrooke Terr TR14 . . . . .138 C2
Red Cove Cl 10 PL27 . . . . . .31 F3
Reddicliff Cl PL9 . . . . .135 E5
Reddicliff Rd PL9 . . . . .135 D5
Red Down Cl PL15 . . . . .17 F5
Redfern Ct 2 TR26 . . . . . . .141 B5
Redhill Cl PL5 . . . . .123 E4
Redinnick Gdns 4 TR18 . . .143 E4
Redinnick Pl TR18 . . . . .143 D4

Redinnick Terr 1 TR18 . . .143 E4
Red La Bugle PL26 . . . . .47 C2
  Rosudgeon TR20 . . . . .89 F5
REDMONSFORD 3 F2
Redmoor Cl PL19 . . . . .147 A2
Redmoor Rd PL17 . . . . .39 E6
Redmore Cl PL17 . . . . .39 E6
RED POST 7 F8
Red River Valley Nature
  Reserve ★ TR27 . . . . .66 D2
REDRUTH 140 D5
Redruth Cl PL5 . . . . .124 A5
Redruth Highway TR15 . . . .140 E7
Redruth Old Cornwall Society
  Mus ★ TR16 . . . . .67 F5
Redruth Rd Helston TR13 . . .146 D7
  Lowertown TR13 . . . . .91 E4
Redruth Sch & Tech Coll
  TR15 . . . . .140 A5
Redruth Sta TR15 . . . . .140 C5
Redvale Rd PL30 . . . . .23 E3
Redvers Gr PL7 . . . . .130 E4
Redvers Hts TR15 . . . . .140 B3
Redwing Dr PL6 . . . . .125 D8
Redwood Cl EX23 . . . . .104 E5
Redwood Dr PL7 . . . . .131 B5
Redwood Gr EX23 . . . . .104 E5
Reeds Pk PL22 . . . . .112 D2
Reeds Way TR7 . . . . .110 D5
Reen Cross Rd TR4 . . . . .55 D4
Reen Hill TR6 . . . . .55 B4
Reen La TR6 . . . . .55 B5
Reens Cres TR18 . . . . .143 D7
Reens Rd TR18 . . . . .143 C7
Reeshill Rd PL26 . . . . .46 F2
Reeves Cl TR13 . . . . .91 B1
Regal Ct PL12 . . . . .122 F2
Regal Theatre ★ 11 TR15 . .140 B5
Regan Ct TR10 . . . . .144 A7
Regency Ho PL25 . . . . .115 E3
Regent Bldgs 38 TR18 . . . . .143 E5
Regent Ct PL4 . . . . .149 A3
Regent Sq 21 TR18 . . . . . . .143 E5
Regent St PL4 . . . . .149 A3
Regent Terr Penzance TR18 .143 E4
  St Just TR19 . . . . .86 E6
Regulator Rd PL30 . . . . .23 A5
Reigate Rd PL9 . . . . .135 E8
Rejarden TR27 . . . . .90 B5
REJERRAH 55 F7
Relistian La TR27 . . . . .78 E3
Relistian Pk TR27 . . . . .78 E3
RELUBBUS 90 A7
Relubbus Hill TR20 . . . . . . .90 A6
Relubbus La TR20 . . . . .90 A6
Renaissance Gdns PL24 . . .128 C7
Rendlesham Gdns PL6 . . . .125 E3
Rendle St Delabole PL33 . . . .14 E3
  Plymouth PL1 . . . . .148 B3
Renney Rd PL9 . . . . .135 C1
Rennie Ave PL5 . . . . .123 C1
Renoir Cl PL9 . . . . .136 A6
Renown St PL2 . . . . .127 E6
Reperry Cross PL30 . . . . .47 F6
Reppersfield Row TR13 . . . .90 F3
RESCASSA 72 F1
RESCORLA 59 D8
Rescorla Ct TR27 . . . . .142 C5
Research Way PL6 . . . . .125 C4
Reservoir Cres PL9 . . . . . . .136 B7
Reservoir La 1 PL3 . . . . . . .128 F6
Reservoir Rd
  Plymouth, Hartley PL3 . . . . .128 F6
  Plymouth, Plymstock PL9 . .136 B7
Reservoir Way PL9 . . . . .136 B7
RESKADINNICK 138 B5
Reskadinnick Rd TR14 . . . .138 B4
Reskadinnick Streams
  TR14 . . . . .138 B6
RESKIVERS 71 F3
Resolution Ho PL4 . . . . .149 B3
Respryn Cl PL14 . . . . .113 D6
Respryn Rd PL31 . . . . .48 D8
RESTORMEL 112 C5
Restormel Castle ★ PL22 . .112 C5
Restormel Ind Est PL22 . . . .112 D2
Restormel Rd Looe PL13 . . .117 D4
  Lostwithiel PL22 . . . . .112 C4
  Newlyn TR18 . . . . .143 C3
  Plymouth PL4 . . . . .148 C4
Restormel Terr
  Falmouth TR11 . . . . .145 B3
  Plymouth PL4 . . . . .148 C4
Restronguet TR11 . . . . .82 B3
Restronguet Barton TR11 . .82 B3
Restronguet Hill TR11 . . . . .82 B4
RESTRONGUET PASSAGE . .82 A4
RESUGGA GREEN 59 F7
Resugga Green La 13 PL26 .59 D7
Resugga Green Residential
  Homes Pk PL26 . . . . .59 D7
Reswythen Wlk 4 TR14 . . .138 F7
Retallack Gdns 3 TR20 . . . .89 E5
Retallick Mdws PL25 . . . . . .115 B5
Retanning La PL26 . . . . .58 E1
Retreat The
  8 Chacewater TR4 . . . . . . .69 A3
  Plymouth PL3 . . . . .129 B7
  St Columb Major TR9 . . . . . .45 E4
Revell Park Rd PL7 . . . . .130 D6
Revel Rd PL3 . . . . .129 A6
Reynolds Gr PL5 . . . . .127 C8
Reynolds Rd PL7 . . . . .130 C6
REZARE 28 E4
Rheola Gdns PL6 . . . . .125 D3
Rhind St PL31 . . . . .109 E5
Rhodes Cl PL7 . . . . .130 E7

Rhubarb Hill TR8 . . . . .43 B1
Rhude Cross EX23 . . . . .5 B3
Rialton Hts TR7 . . . . .111 E7
Rialton Rd TR7, TR8 . . . . . . .111 E6
Ribble Gdns PL3 . . . . .129 D7
Rice La PL26 . . . . .85 C5
Richard Lander Sch TR3 . . . .69 D3
Richards Cres TR1 . . . . .69 F3
Richards La TR16 . . . . .67 E4
Richards Row PL3 . . . . .128 F7
Richards Terr PL10 . . . . .132 E5
Richmond Hill TR1 . . . . .137 B4
Richmond Pl
  40 St Ives TR26 . . . . .141 B6
  3 Truro TR1 . . . . .137 B4
Richmond Rd Pelynt PL13 . . .62 D6
  Plymouth PL6 . . . . .125 A2
Richmond St
  Heamoor TR18 . . . . .143 C7
  Penzance TR18 . . . . .143 E6
Richmond Terr
  Buckland Monachorum PL20 . . .14 C2
  Truro TR1 . . . . .137 B4
Richmond Way TR26 . . . . . .141 D1
Richmond Wlk PL1 . . . . .127 F1
Ricketts Rd PL26 . . . . .59 A1
Rick Mdw PL15 . . . . .18 E6
Ride The PL7, PL9 . . . . .129 D2
Ridge Cross PL9 . . . . .136 A3
Ridgegrove Hill PL15 . . . . .106 D6
Ridgegrove La PL15 . . . . . . .106 C7
Ridge Ho PL4 . . . . .129 A4
Ridgeley Cl 2 PL27 . . . . . . .108 C5
Ridge Park Ave PL14 . . . . . .128 D4
Ridge Park Rd PL7 . . . . .130 E5
Ridge Pk PL7 . . . . .130 E5
Ridge Rd PL7 . . . . .130 E3
Ridgevale Cl TR18 . . . . .143 F8
Ridgevale La TR18 . . . . .143 F8
Ridgeway
  28 Perranporth TR6 . . . . . . .55 A5
  Plymouth, Plympton PL7 . . . .130 D5
  Plymouth, Plympton St Maurice
  PL7 . . . . .130 F5
  Probus TR2 . . . . .71 C6
Ridgeway Sch PL7 . . . . .130 E5
Ridgeway Sp Ctr PL7 . . . . .130 E5
Ridgewell Terr TR9 . . . . .57 E8
Ridgewood Cl PL26 . . . . . . .114 F1
Riflemans Walk PL6 . . . . . . .125 B7
Riga Terr PL3 . . . . .129 C4
Rigdale Cl PL6 . . . . .129 A7
RILLA MILL 38 E8
Ringmore Way PL5 . . . . .124 B3
Ringway Flats 8 PL31 . . . . .109 D5
Ringwell Hill TR3 . . . . .81 E7
RINSEY 90 D2
Rinsey La TR13 . . . . .90 D2
Risdon Ave PL4 . . . . .129 B1
Rivendell PL27 . . . . .108 C4
River Ct Saltash PL12 . . . . . .122 D5
  Tavistock PL19 . . . . .147 D6
Riverford PL6 . . . . .125 F5
Riverford La PL6 . . . . .125 D7
River Pk 11 PL20 . . . . .42 C4
Riversdale Pl 8 PL27 . . . . .108 B5
RIVERSIDE 123 A1
Riverside Angarrack TR27 . . .78 C5
  Lelant TR26 . . . . .77 E4
  Padstow PL28 . . . . .107 E5
Riverside Ave TR1 . . . . .110 A5
Riverside Bsns Pk PL1 . . . .127 E3
Riverside Cl 1 PL20 . . . . . . .42 C4
Riverside Com Prim Sch
  PL5 . . . . .127 C8
Riverside Cott PL12 . . . . . . .122 C1
Riverside Cres TR7 . . . . .110 A5
Riverside Ct PL22 . . . . .112 C2
Riverside Ho TR1 . . . . .137 D1
Riverside Mews
  Angarrack TR27 . . . . .78 C5
  Saltash PL12 . . . . .123 A3
Riverside Mills
  Launceston PL15 . . . . .106 B7
  6 Newport PL15 . . . . .106 A4
Riverside Pl PL1 . . . . .127 D2
Riverside Terr TR1 . . . . .137 E3
Riverside Wlk PL5 . . . . .124 B6
River St Mevagissey PL26 . . .73 C3
  Portscatho TR2 . . . . .83 B2
  Truro TR1 . . . . .137 C4
Rivers The PL12 . . . . .122 E1
Riverview TR11 . . . . .145 A6
River View Flushing TR11 . .145 B7
  Gunnislake PL18 . . . . .40 E5
  Lerryn PL22 . . . . .61 C7
  Plymouth PL4 . . . . .129 B1
  Saltash PL12 . . . . .122 F3
  Tresillian TR2 . . . . .70 E4
River View La PL4 . . . . .129 B1
River Wlk PL25 . . . . .114 B3
Riviera Apartments TR26 .141 D2
Riviera Cl
  8 Helston TR12 . . . . .99 A1
  3 Mullion TR12 . . . . .99 A1
Riviera Est TR1 . . . . .70 D1
Riviera La TR2 . . . . .95 A6
RIVIERE TOWANS 142 B7
Riviere Towans TR27 . . . . . .142 B7
Rix Hill PL19 . . . . .41 F6
Roach's Ct TR26 . . . . .141 E1
Roach's Row TR15 . . . . .140 B5
Road From Prazegooth La To
  Ingewidden TR12 . . . . .103 A4
Robartes Ace Acad PL31 . .109 D4
Robartes Ct 13 TR1 . . . . . . .137 C4

Robartes Gardens Flats
  PL25 . . . . .114 E4
Robartes Gdns PL25 . . . . . .114 E4
Robartes Pl PL25 . . . . .114 E5
Robartes Rd Bodmin PL31 . .109 D4
  Newquay TR7 . . . . .110 F5
  St Dennis PL26 . . . . .58 C8
Robartes Terr
  3 Illogan TR16 . . . . .67 E4
  Lostwithiel PL22 . . . . .112 C3
Robert Adams Cl PL7 . . . . .130 B5
Robert Eliot Ct PL25 . . . . . .114 B3
Robert Hichens Rd TR11 . .145 A5
Roberts Ave PL11 . . . . .127 B3
Roberts Rd PL5 . . . . .127 D8
Robin Dr PL15 . . . . .106 E4
Robins Cl 13 PL24 . . . . .60 B4
Robins Rd PL15 . . . . .139 B5
Robins Way PL9 . . . . .135 E8
ROBOROUGH 121 D1
Roborough Ave PL6 . . . . . . .125 B5
Roborough Cl PL16 . . . . . . .125 B5
Roborough Down La PL6 . .121 F5
Roborough La PL5 . . . . .124 D8
Robyns Cl PL7 . . . . .131 B5
ROCHE 46 F3
Roche Com Prim Sch PL26 .46 F2
Roche Rd Bugle PL26 . . . . . .47 C2
  Stenalees PL26 . . . . .59 C7
  Trezaise PL26 . . . . .47 A2
Roche Rural Workshops
  PL26 . . . . .47 A4
Roche Sta PL26 . . . . .47 A4
Rochester Rd
  3 Plymouth PL4 . . . . .128 C4
  7 Plymouth PL4 . . . . .149 A4
Rochford Cres PL5 . . . . .123 F5
ROCK 21 D2
Rock Cl 1 TR14 . . . . .138 F2
Rock Close Ho TR27 . . . . . .142 A1
Rockfield Ave PL6 . . . . .124 F6
Rock Gdns PL9 . . . . .129 D1
Rockhaven Gdns PL27 . . . . .21 F3
ROCKHEAD 14 E3
Rockhead St PL33 . . . . .14 E3
Rock Hill PL5 . . . . .124 C7
Rockingham Rd PL3 . . . . . .129 A5
Rock La PL31 . . . . .109 C4
Rock Rd Newlyn TR18 . . . . . .143 C3
  St Minver PL27 . . . . .21 E2
Rock Terr Heamoor TR18 . . .143 C7
  Plymouth PL7 . . . . .130 D4
Rock Twrs PL13 . . . . .117 D2
Rock View Parc PL26 . . . . . .47 A3
Rock Villas PL27 . . . . .21 D2
Rockville Pk PL9 . . . . .135 E8
Rockwood Rd PL6 . . . . .125 E8
Rocky Hill PL19 . . . . .147 B5
Rocky La Gweek TR12 . . . . . .92 A1
  Praa Sands TR20 . . . . .90 C6
  St Agnes TR5 . . . . .54 C2
  Veryan TR2 . . . . .83 D5
Rocky Park Ave PL9 . . . . . . .135 E8
Rocky Park Rd PL9 . . . . .135 E8
Rodda Cl PL18 . . . . .41 A7
Rodda's Rd TR8 . . . . .68 C6
Roddick Way 3 PL7 . . . . . .131 C5
Rodings The PL14 . . . . .51 F5
Rodney St PL5 . . . . .127 D8
Rodwell Cl TR15 . . . . .140 D5
Rodwill Cl TR27 . . . . .78 E1
Roebuck Villas TR11 . . . . . .145 D3
Roekindale Cl TR15 . . . . . . .139 D6
Roeselare Ave PL11 . . . . . . .127 A3
Roeselare Cl PL11 . . . . .127 A3
Rogate Dr PL6 . . . . .125 D4
Rogate Wlk PL6 . . . . .125 D4
Rogers Dr PL12 . . . . .122 D5
Roland Bailey Gdns PL19 . .147 A6
Rollis Park Cl PL9 . . . . .135 C8
Rollis Park Rd PL9 . . . . .135 C8
Rolston Cl PL6 . . . . .124 D6
Roma Cl 7 TR27 . . . . .111 C7
Roma Ct TR27 . . . . .142 B5
Roman Bridge PL13 . . . . . . .62 D1
Roman Dr PL31 . . . . .109 F2
Roman Rd PL5 . . . . .123 E2
Roman Way PL5 . . . . .123 E2
Romilly Gdns PL7 . . . . .130 B5
Romney Cl PL5 . . . . .124 B1
Ronald Terr PL2 . . . . .127 E5
Ronsdale Cl PL9 . . . . .135 D8
Rooke Rd PL27 . . . . .22 D2
Roope Cl PL5 . . . . .127 C7
Ropehaven Cl PL25 . . . . . . .114 E6
Ropehaven Rd PL25 . . . . . . .114 E6
Roper Ave PL9 . . . . .135 D8
Ropewalk 9 TR2 . . . . .95 A6
Ropewalk Ct 2 TR11 . . . . . .145 C3
Ropewalk Rd TR3 . . . . .137 C1
Ropewalk The TR18 . . . . . . .143 E4
Rope Wlk Mount Hawke TR4 . .68 C6
  Padstow PL28 . . . . .107 D5
  3 St Austell PL25 . . . . .115 A1
Rope Wlk The 3 TR26 . . . . .141 B6
Rorkes Cl PL1 . . . . .127 F2
Roscadghill Parc 1 TR18 . .143 C7
Roscadghill Rd TR18 . . . . . .143 C6
Roscarrack Cl TR11 . . . . . . .144 E2
Roscarrack Rd TR11 . . . . . .144 D1
Roscarrick Villas TR11 . . . .93 D3
Roscarrock Hill PL29 . . . . . .22 D7
ROSCROGGAN 138 D7
Roscroggan TR14 . . . . .79 C8
Roscrow Dr 1 TR14 . . . . . . .138 D7
ROSE 55 C5

Rad – Ros 173

Rose Acre Dr 8 TR15 . . . . .140 C5
ROSE-AN-GROUSE 77 D2
Roseannon TR11 . . . . .93 D3
Rosebery Ave PL4 . . . . .149 C4
Rosebery La PL4 . . . . .149 C4
Rosebery Rd PL4 . . . . .149 C4
ROSECARE 10 D6
Roseclave Cl PL7 . . . . .131 C6
Rose Cottage PL27 . . . . .21 F5
Rosecott Pk 4 EX23 . . . . .5 A6
Rose Cotts Camborne TR14 .138 E3
  Plymouth PL6 . . . . .129 B8
  Stithians TR3 . . . . .80 E3
Rosecraddoc View PL14 . . .38 A2
Rose Ct PL25 . . . . .115 A5
Rosedale Ave PL2 . . . . .128 D7
Rosedale Gdns PL31 . . . . . .35 B2
Rosedale Rd TR1 . . . . .137 C5
Rosedene Farm TR3 . . . . . . .69 C4
ROSEDINNICK 45 E3
Rosedown Ave PL2 . . . . . . .128 A7
Rose Eglos TR11 . . . . .144 C2
Rose Eglos Cl TR11 . . . . . . .144 C2
Rose Gdns PL6 . . . . .125 E6
ROSEHILL Goonhavern 55 D5
  Lostwithiel 112 C1
Rosehill Heamoor TR20 . . . .88 A5
  Ladock TR2 . . . . .57 C1
  Lanivet PL30 . . . . .47 C6
  Marazion TR17 . . . . .89 B5
  Mylor Bridge TR11 . . . . .82 A2
  Tregolls PL27 . . . . .32 C6
Rose Hill Altarnun PL15 . . . .26 C8
  Fowey PL23 . . . . .116 C4
  Par PL24 . . . . .60 B5
  Porthtowan TR4 . . . . .68 A6
  Port Isaac PL29 . . . . .22 D7
  Redruth TR15 . . . . .140 B5
  Sticker PL26 . . . . .58 F1
Rose Hill Cl PL22 . . . . .112 C2
Rosehill Gdns TR18 . . . . . . .143 B6
Rosehill Mdw TR18 . . . . . . .143 B6
Rose Hill Terr PL17 . . . . .41 A3
Rosehip Cl PL6 . . . . .125 E7
Rose In The Bush PL12 . . . .99 B8
Rose In The Bush Pk TR12. .99 B8
Rose La 23 TR26 . . . . .141 B6
Roseladden TR13 . . . . .91 A3
ROSELAND 51 E6
Roseland Cres
  6 Chacewater TR4 . . . . . . .69 A3
  Tregony TR2 . . . . .71 F3
Roseland Flats TR2 . . . . . . .82 E1
Roseland Gdns
  Bodmin PL31 . . . . .109 E6
  Redruth TR15 . . . . .140 D6
  Veryan TR2 . . . . .83 F6
Roseland Parc 8 TR2 . . . . .84 A8
Roseland Pk TR14 . . . . .138 D4
Roselands La PL31 . . . . .35 A2
Roselands Rd PL31 . . . . . . .109 F6
Roseland Terr TR4 . . . . .55 F2
Roselare Cl 5 PL25 . . . . . . .114 E7
Roselidden Parc TR13 . . . . .146 B7
Roseline Est TR13 . . . . .80 D1
Roselyon Pl PL24 . . . . .60 C5
Roselyon Preparatory School
  PL24 . . . . .60 C4
Rosemaber TR13 . . . . .90 F4
Rose Mdw TR3 . . . . .80 F3
Rose Mdws TR4 . . . . .55 D4
Rosemellen Terr PL14 . . . . .113 B4
Rosemellin TR14 . . . . .138 C4
Rosemellin Com Prim Sch
  TR14 . . . . .138 C4
ROSEMELLING 59 E8
ROSEMERGY 75 D3
Rosemerryn Bareppa TR11 . .93 C4
  Carlidnack TR11 . . . . .94 A2
Rosemorran 28 TR26 . . . . .141 B6
Rosemullion 4 TR6 . . . . . . .55 A5
Rosemullion Gdns 9
  TR14 . . . . .138 F7
Rose Mullion Gdns PL17 . . .39 F5
Rosemullion Ho TR1 . . . . . . .69 E4
Rosemundy TR5 . . . . .54 D1
ROSENANNON 33 A1
Rosenannon La TR15 . . . . . .139 B8
Rosenannon Rd TR15 . . . . .139 B8
Rose Row TR15 . . . . .140 D5
ROSERROW 21 E5
Rose Terr Gunnislake PL18 . .40 E5
  Mitchell TR8 . . . . .56 F5
  22 Penzance TR18 . . . . . . .143 E6
Rosevale TR18 . . . . .143 D4
Rosevale Cres TR14 . . . . . . .138 C4
Rosevale Gdns PL30 . . . . . . .59 F8
Rosevalley TR3 . . . . .69 D3
Rose Valley TR19 . . . . .75 B2
Rosevallon La PL31 . . . . . . .109 C5
ROSEVEAN 47 D1
Rosevean Ave TR14 . . . . . . .138 E3
Rosevean Cl TR14 . . . . .138 E3
Rosevean Ct 8 PL3 . . . . . . .128 F6
Rosevean Gdns PL3 . . . . . . .128 F6
Rosevean Ho 7 PL3 . . . . . .128 F6
Rosevean Rd TR18 . . . . .143 E6
Rosevean Terr TR18 . . . . . . .143 E6
ROSEVEAR 99 C7
Rosevere Cl PL9 . . . . .136 A8
Rosevere Dr PL26 . . . . .46 D1
Rosevere Mobile Home Pk
  PL26 . . . . .46 D1
Rosevear Hill TR12 . . . . .99 C7
Rosevear Rd PL26 . . . . .47 C1

ROSEVINE...83 B3
Rosevine Way 4 TR14...138 D4
Rosewall Cotts 16 TR26...141 A5
Rosewall Terr 17 TR26...141 A5
ROSEWARNE...78 F3
Rosewarne TR13...91 A1
Rosewarne Cl TR14...138 D4
Rosewarne Downs
　Reskadinnick TR14...79 C8
　Reskadinnick TR14...138 C5
Rosewarne Gdns TR14...138 D3
Rosewarne Mews TR14...138 D4
Rosewarne Pk TR14...138 E4
Rosewarne Rd
　1 Camborne TR14...138 D3
　Carnhell Green TR27...78 F4
Rosewarne Terr TR14...138 D5
Rosewarne (Trng Ctr)
　TR14...138 D5
Rosewin Bridge Rd PL27...22 A4
Rosewin Mews 3 TR9...45 E6
Rosewin Row
　2 St Columb Major TR9...45 E6
　Truro TR1...137 D5
Rosewithian Cl TR27...78 E6
Rosewood Cl PL9...135 F5
ROSEWORTHY Camborne...78 F6
　Shortlanesend...69 E6
ROSEWORTHY BARTON...78 F6
Roseworthy Hill TR14...78 F6
Rosina Way PL26...59 D7
Roskear TR14...138 E6
ROSKEAR CROFT...138 E6
Roskear Croft TR14...138 E6
Roskear Fields TR14...138 E4
Roskear Parc TR14...138 F5
Roskear Prim & Nur Sch
　PL9...135 B5
Roskear Rd TR14...138 E3
Roskear Sch TR14...138 F3
Roskilling TR13...146 D7
Roskilling Wartha TR13...146 D7
Roskilly Cotts TR19...88 C2
Roskilly La TR14...79 B5
Roskilly's Ice Cream & Organic
　Farm★ TR12...101 D3
Roskrow TR10...81 C2
Roskrow Cl TR16...80 A5
Roskruge Cl TR13...146 D8
Ros Lyn TR26...141 C1
Roslyn Cl St Austell PL25...114 F5
　2 St Austell PL25...115 A5
Rosparc TR2...71 D6
Rosparvah Gdns TR18...143 C7
Rospeath Cres PL2...128 D8
Rospeath La TR20...89 C7
Rossett Gdns PL31...35 B1
Rossiter Ho TR19...96 B6
Rosslyn Park Rd PL3...128 D5
Ross St PL1...127 E4
Rossventon TR4...69 A1
Rostalek PL30...24 B2
Rostigan Hill PL30...46 E7
ROSUDGEON...89 F4
Rosudgeon Downs 3 TR20...89 F4
Rosva Morgowr TR11...144 F2
Rotair Rd 1 TR14...138 E3
Rothbury Cl PL6...125 E4
Rothbury Gdns PL6...125 D4
Rothesay Gdns PL5...124 D3
Rougemont Cl PL3...129 B7
Rough La TR3...81 B4
Rough St TR16...80 D6
Roughtor Dr PL32...105 C3
Roughtor Rd PL32...15 D1
Roughtor View PL33...14 D2
Rounders Rise 10 TR27...142 D6
Roundhayes Farm Cotts
　EX23...10 C5
Roundhouse Way TR13...146 B4
Round Ring TR10...144 D8
Round Ring Gdns 3 TR10...94 A8
Round's La PL34...14 D7
Rous Rd PL12...40 C2
ROW...24 B3
Rowan Cl Bodmin PL31...109 B4
　Plymouth PL7...131 B5
　Tavistock PL19...147 C3
Rowan Ct PL12...122 C2
Rowan La 6 Lamellion PL14...51 A7
　Lamellion PL14...113 A6
Rowans The Bude EX23...104 E4
　Lifton PL16...19 F4
　St Mellion PL12...53 C8
Rowan Way PL6...125 E7
Rowan Wood Rd PL19...30 F3
Rowden St PL3...128 E5
Rowdown Cl PL7...131 D4
Rowe Ct PL14...50 E8
Rowe's La TR13...146 E8
Rowe St PL11...127 B3
Rowes Terr PL26...58 D5
Row La PL5...123 E2
Rowland Cl PL9...135 E5
Rowse Gdns PL18...41 A3
Row The Launceston PL15...17 F1
　Pillaton PL12...53 B7
　Portloe TR2...84 A4
Royal Cornwall Hosp TR1...69 E4
Royal Cornwall Mus★ TR1...137 C4
Royal Cornwall Showground★
　Pl27...33 C6
Royalist Ct 14 TR11...145 C3
Royal Navy Ave PL2...127 F6
Royal Par PL1...148 C2

Royal Talbot PL22...112 C2
Royal William Rd PL1...134 A8
Royal William Yard PL1...134 A8
Roydon Cl PL15...106 B8
Roydon La PL15...106 B8
Roydon Rd PL15...106 B8
Royffe Way PL31...109 F3
RUAN HIGH LANES...83 B6
RUAN LANIHORNE...83 E8
RUAN MAJOR...102 F6
RUAN MINOR...103 B5
Ruan Minor Treleague TR12 103 A5
　6 Treleague TR12...103 B4
Rubble La TR7...110 B5
Ruby Terr TR13...92 B8
RUDDLEMOOR...59 B6
Rudyerd Wlk PL3...129 D6
Rufford Cl PL2...128 A7
Rule Cross EX23...2 E2
RUMFORD...32 A5
Ruminella View TR12...103 A4
Rumours Apartments TR7 111 B7
Rundle Ct PL14...113 B4
Rundles Ct TR1...137 E3
Runnymede Ct PL6...125 E2
Ruscullion La PL27...32 B6
Ruses Mill La PL15...27 D4
RUSHFORD...30 A3
Rush Park Terr PL18...40 F7
Ruskin Cres PL5...124 D2
Ruskin Ct TR9...45 D5
Russell Ave PL3...128 F7
Russell Cl Gunnislake PL18...41 A7
　Plymouth PL9...136 B7
　Saltash PL12...122 C3
Russell Court Gdns PL19...147 B6
Russell Ct Plymouth PL1...148 C2
　Saltash PL12...122 C3
　Tavistock PL19...147 C5
Russell Mews PL31...109 C5
Russell Pl PL1...148 B4
Russell Ct 7 Liskeard PL14 113 C5
　Tavistock PL19...147 C5
Russell Way 4 TR10...144 C7
Russet Wood PL5...123 F4
Rutger Pl PL1...148 A4
Ruthdower TR13...90 F7
RUTHERNBRIDGE...34 A1
Ruthern Valley PL30...34 A1
Ruthven Cl PL6...128 F8
RUTHVOES...45 F3
Ruthy's La PL28...107 D5
Rutland Pl PL4...128 F4
Rydal Cl PL6...125 D2
Ryder Rd PL2...127 F4
Rydon La EX22...8 F7
Rye Hill Ponsanooth TR3...81 B4
　Saltash PL12...122 C2
Rylands Terr PL30...24 B3

S

Saffron Cl PL23...116 C4
Safron La PL23...61 D2
Sail Loft Flats 2 TR26...141 B6
ST AGNES...54 D1
ST AGNES BEACON...54 B1
St Agnes Mus★ TR5...54 C1
St AgneS Sch TR5...54 C1
St Albans Pk PL20...42 D2
St Ambrusca Rd TR8...110 A3
St Andrew's CE Prim Sch
　PL20...41 F3
St Andrew's CE VA Prim Sch
　PL1...148 B2
St Andrews Cl
　12 Bere Alston PL20...41 B1
　Ponsanooth TR3...81 B4
　Saltash PL12...122 C2
St Andrew's Cl PL18...41 A3
St Andrew's Cross 1 PL1 149 A2
St Andrew's Pl PL15...133 A1
St Andrews Rd PL19...147 D2
St Andrew's Rd Par PL24...60 C5
　12 Stratton EX23...4 D1
St Andrew's St
　Cawsand PL10...133 A1
　1 St Ives TR26...141 B5
St Andrew St
　Millbrook PL10...132 E5
　Plymouth PL1...148 C2
St Andrews Terr TR3...81 B4
St Andrew's Terr PL24...60 C5
St Annes TR11...93 D3
St Annes Cl Lelant TR26...77 E4
　Whitstone EX22...7 F1
St Annes Rd 17 TR24...60 B4
St Anne's Rd Newquay TR7 111 A7
　Plymouth PL6...125 D6
　Saltash PL12...122 C3
　3 Trewoon PL25...59 A3
ST ANN'S CHAPEL...40 E6
St Ann's Hill EX23...104 F3
St Anta Rd TR26...141 E1
ST ANTHONY...95 B5
St Anthony TR12...101 B8
ST ANTHONY-IN-
　MENEAGE...101 C8
St Anthony Rd TR12...101 B8
St Anthony Way TR11...145 A2
St Aubyn TR16...140 E5
St Aubyn Ave PL2...127 F5
St Aubyn Cres TR7...111 A6
St Aubyn Est TR14...79 B2
St Aubyn Rd PL1...127 E3
St Aubyns TR20...89 E5

St Aubyn's Rd TR1...137 D3
St Aubyn St PL1...127 E2
St Aubyn's Vean TR1...137 D3
ST AUSTELL...114 B5
St Austell Bay Bsns Pk
　PL25...115 E4
St Austell Brewery Visitor
　Ctr★ PL25...114 B4
St Austell Com Hospl PL26 114 E1
St Austell Rd PL24...115 C5
St Austell Row 2 TR2...95 A6
St Austell St
　Summercourt TR8...57 C6
　Truro TR1...137 D4
St Austell Sta PL25...114 D4
St Barnabas Ct PL1...148 A4
St Barnabas Hospl PL12...122 F2
St Barnabas Terr PL1...148 A4
St Benedicts Cl 13 PL24...60 D5
St Benets Cl PL30...47 E6
ST BLAZEY...60 B5
ST BLAZEY GATE...115 F6
St Blazey Rd PL24...60 C4
St Boniface Cl PL2...128 C7
St Boniface Dr PL2...128 C7
St Boniface RC Coll PL5...124 E1
St Breaca Cl TR13...91 A3
ST BREOCK...33 C6
St Breock Prim Sch PL27...108 B5
ST BREWARD...24 B3
St Breward Prim Sch PL30...24 B3
St Bridget Ave PL6...124 F1
ST BUDEAUX...123 D2
St Budeaux Bypass
　Honicknowle PL5...124 A1
　St Budeaux PL5...123 F1
St Budeaux Ferry Rd Sta
　PL5...127 D8
St Budeaux Foundation CE (A)
　Jun Sch PL5...123 F2
St Budeaux Victoria Rd Sta
　PL5...123 D1
ST BURYAN...97 B6
St Buryan Hill TR19...96 F4
St Buryan Prim Sch TR19...97 B6
St Cadocs PL28...31 F7
St Carantoc Way TR8...43 D3
St Catherine's Castle★
　PL23...116 B2
St Catherine's CE Prim Sch
　PL15...106 C4
St Catherines Ct PL23...116 C3
St Catherine's Parade
　PL23...116 B4
St Clare Flats TR18...143 D6
St Clare St Heamoor TR20...88 C5
　Penzance TR18...143 D6
　2 Rosehill TR18...143 D6
ST CLEER...37 E2
St Cleer Dr PL27...108 D6
St Cleer Prim Sch PL14...38 A3
St Cleer Rd PL14...113 C7
ST CLEMENT...70 D2
St Clement's Cl TR1...137 E4
St Clement's Hill TR1...137 E4
St Clements Parc TR1...137 E4
St Clement St TR1...137 D5
St Clement's Terr 3 TR1 137 D5
St Clement Vean TR1...137 F6
ST CLETHER...17 A3
St Columb Bsns Ctr TR9...45 E6
ST COLUMB MAJOR...45 E6
St Columb Major Academy
　TR9...45 D6
St Columb Major Bsns Pk
　TR9...45 E5
St Columb Major Ind Est
　TR9...45 D5
ST COLUMB MINOR...111 E7
St Columb Minor Academy
　TR7...111 D7
ST COLUMB ROAD...45 D2
St Columb Road Ind
　Workshops TR9...45 D2
St Columb Road Sta TR9...45 D2
St Crewenna Terr TR27...78 E1
St Cuthbert Cl PL15...106 B7
St Cuthbert's Rd TR7...110 D6
St Cyriac PL30...47 F1
St Davids Cl EX23...4 C8
St David's Rd PL19...147 E5
ST DAY...68 E1
St Day & Carharrack Com Sch
　TR16...68 E1
St Day Rd TR15...140 C5
ST DENNIS...58 C8
St Dennis Com Prim Sch
　PL26...58 C8
St Dennis Ind Est PL26...58 B8
St Dominic Cl PL31...109 E5
ST DOMINICK...40 D3
St Dominick CE Prim Sch
　PL12...40 D2
St Dominic Pk PL7...40 C4
St Dominic Sq 4 TR1...137 C4
St Dominic St
　8 Penzance TR18...143 E6
　5 Truro TR1...137 C4
St Dunstan's Terr PL4...149 C3
St Edmunds La PL28...107 D5
St Edward Gdns PL6...125 B1
St Edward's CE Prim Sch
　PL7...135 C6
St Eia St TR26...141 C6
St Elizabeth Cl PL7...130 F3
St Elvan Cres TR13...91 A1
St Elwyns Rise TR27...142 B6
ST ENDELLION...22 D5

St Endellion Rd PL30...22 E5
ST ENODER...57 B7
St Enodoc Cl PL27...108 D6
ST ERME...70 E8
St Erme with Trispen Com
　Prim Sch TR4...70 D8
ST ERNEY...53 B2
ST ERTH...142 A1
St Erth Com Prim Sch
　TR27...142 A1
St Erth Hill TR27...77 F1
St Erth Ind Est TR27...77 E2
ST ERTH PRAZE...142 F1
St Erth Rd PL2...128 D7
St Erth Sta TR27...77 E2
ST EVAL...31 F3
St Eval Pl PL5...123 E4
St Eval Rd PL8...31 C2
ST EWE...72 E5
St Fimbarrus Rd PL23...116 C3
St Francis CE Sch TR11...144 E3
St Francis Ct PL5...124 B3
St Francis Mdw TR8...56 F5
St Francis Rd TR8...45 E2
St Francis St 5 TR18...143 E6
St Gabriel's Ave PL3...128 D5
ST GENNYS...10 C8
St George's Arc TR11...145 B4
St George's Ave PL2...128 C7
St George's CE Prim Acad
　PL1...148 A1
St George's Cres PL31...109 C4
St Georges Ct Looe PL13...117 D2
　1 Plymouth PL1...127 F4
St George's Hill TR6...55 A4
St Georges Hill Cl 13 TR6...55 A4
St George's Pk PL22...112 C3
St Georges Rd
　Nanpean PL26...58 D6
　Saltash PL12...122 D3
St George's Rd Hayle TR27 142 C5
　Looe PL13...117 D2
　Newquay TR7...110 D5
　Saltash PL12...122 E3
　Truro TR1...137 B5
St George's Terr
　Perranporth TR6...54 F4
　Plymouth PL2...127 F4
ST GERMANS...65 A8
St Germans Prim Sch PL12...65 A8
St Germans Rd PL17...39 F3
St Germans Sta PL12...65 B8
St Giles Dr PL27...108 C6
St Giles Mews PL27...108 C6
ST GILES ON THE HEATH...13 E1
St Giles-on-the-Heath
　Sch PL15...13 F1
ST GLUVIAS...144 D8
St Gluvias Parc TR10...144 D8
St Gluvias St TR10...144 D7
St Golder Rd TR18...143 B3
St Gothian Sands Nature
　Reserve★ TR27...66 B2
St Grace's Ct TR2...71 C6
St Helens Wlk PL5...124 C5
St Henry St 4 TR18...143 E6
ST HILARY...89 E6
St Hilary Sch TR20...89 F6
St Hilary Terr PL4...149 C3
St Ia Sch TR26...141 D1
St Ingunger La PL30...48 B6
ST ISSEY...32 E6
St Issey CE Prim Sch PL27...32 D6
St Issey Hill PL27...32 D7
ST IVE...38 F2
ST IVE CROSS...39 A1
St Ivc Rd PL14...38 E4
ST IVES...141 C6
St Ives Jun & Inf Schs
　TR26...141 A5
St Ives La TR27...66 B1
St Ives L Ctr TR26...141 A5
St Ives Mus★ TR26...141 C6
St Ives Mushroom Farm
　TR26...70 C6
St Ives Rd Carbis Bay TR26 141 D1
　Pendeen TR19...75 A1
　St Ives Sch TR26...141 B3
St Ives Sta TR26...141 B5
St James Cl Delabole PL33...14 E2
　Plymouth PL1...148 B2
　Torpoint PL11...127 B3
St James Mews PL1...148 B2
St James' Place E PL1...148 B2
St James' Place W PL1...148 B2
St James Rd PL11...127 B2
St James's Terr TR10...144 B7
St James View TR9...57 D8
ST JIDGEY...32 F4
ST JOHN...132 C8
St JOHNS...146 A6
St Johns PL19...147 C5
St John's Bridge Rd PL4...149 B2
St Johns Bsns Pk TR13...146 B6
St John's Catholic Prim Sch 4
　TR14...138 C2
St Johns Cl PL6...125 D4
St John's Cl Helston TR13...146 A6
　Millbrook PL10...132 E5
St Johns Ct 7 TR18...143 E5
St John's Ct
　7 Falmouth TR11...145 A4
　Hayle TR27...142 D6

St John's Rd Helston TR13 ...146 B6
　Horrabridge PL20...42 C4
　Millbrook PL10...132 F5
　Newquay TR7...110 D5
　Plymouth PL4...149 B2
St John's St
　Plymouth, Turnchapel PL9...135 A6
　3 St John's TR13...81 F6
St John's Terr 8 TR19...75 A1
St Johns Wlk TR26...77 A7
St Joseph's Cl PL6...124 F1
St Joseph's Rd PL15...106 B8
St Joseph's Sch PL15...106 B7
ST JUDE'S...149 B3
St Jude's Rd PL4...149 B2
St Julians Cres PL10...133 E7
St Julitta PL30...48 A1
ST JUST...86 E6
ST JUST IN ROSELAND...82 F2
St Just Prim Sch TR19...86 E6
St Keri Ct PL15...18 A5
ST KEVERNE...101 C4
St Keverne Com Prim Sch
　TR12...101 D4
St Keverne Pl PL2...128 D8
St Keverne Rd TR12...99 D7
St Keverne Rural Workshops
　TR12...101 C3
ST KEW...23 A4
ST KEW HIGHWAY...23 A2
St Kew Prim Sch PL30...22 F3
St Kew Rd PL30...23 A2
ST KEYNE...51 A3
St Keyne Cl TR1...137 C5
St Keyne Wishing Well Halt
　PL14...51 C3
ST LAWRENCE...34 D1
St Lawrence Mews PL4...149 A4
St Lawrence Rd
　Bodmin PL30, PL31...109 A4
　Plymouth PL4...149 A4
St Leonards PL31...109 C5
St Leonard's Rd
　Launceston PL15...106 B8
　Plymouth PL4...149 C2
St Leonards Terr PL31...109 C5
St Leo Pl PL2...127 E4
ST LEVAN...96 B3
St Levan Cl 8 TR17...89 C5
St Levan Prim Sch TR19...96 B5
St Levan Rd
　8 Marazion TR17...89 C5
　Plymouth PL2...127 E4
ST MABYN...34 C8
St Mabyn CE Prim Sch
　PL30...34 D8
St Mabyn Hill PL27...34 A8
St Madderns CE Sch TR20 143 A8
St Margarets La PL26...59 A1
St Margarets Rd PL7...130 B7
St Mark's CE Prim Sch EX23...2 E7
St Marks Rd PL6...125 D4
St Marnarch's PL13...62 B8
St Marnarch's Rd PL13...62 B8
ST MARTIN Looe...117 D7
ST MARTIN
　Mawgan...100 C6
St Martin-in-Meneage Com
　Prim Sch TR12...100 D6
St Martin's Ave PL3...128 C6
St Martin's CE Prim Sch
　PL14...113 C6
St Martins Cl Lewannick PL15 127 B7
　Looe PL13...117 D5
St Martin's Cl 2 TR14...138 C3
St Martin's Cres TR14...138 C3
St Martins Ct PL14...113 C5
St Martins Green 4 TR2...100 D6
St Martins Rd EX23...7 B8
St Martin's Rd PL13...117 D6
St Martin's Terr TR14...138 C4
St Marwenne Cl EX23...7 B6
St Maryhaye PL19...147 A5
St Mary's PL13...117 D2
St Mary's CE Prim Sch
　TR18...143 E4
　St Mary's CE Sch TR1...137 C6
St Marys Cl PL31...130 C5
St Mary's Cl PL31...109 C4
St Mary's Cres PL31...109 C4
St Marys Ct PL7...130 C5
St Mary's Ct 2 TR7...110 D5
St Mary's Gdns PL31...109 C4
St Mary's RC Prim Sch
　Bodmin PL31...109 C4
　Falmouth TR11...144 E3
St Mary's RC Sch TR18...143 E2
St Marys Rd Callington PL17...39 F5
　Par PL24...60 B4
St Mary's Rd Bodmin PL31...109 B4
　Launceston PL15...106 C8
　Newquay TR7...110 D5
　Plymouth PL7...130 C6
St Mary's St 5 Penzance TR18 143 E6
　12 Truro TR1...137 D4
St Mary's Street Mews 10
　TR1...137 D4
St Mary's Terr
　Penzance TR18...143 E5
　4 Truro TR1...137 C5
St Matthews Hill PL27...108 D5
St Maurice Ct PL7...130 F4
St Maurice Mews PL7...130 E4
St Maurice Rd PL7...130 F3
St Maurice View PL7...131 B4
ST MAWES...95 B6
St Mawes Castle★ TR2...95 A5

St Mawes Prim Sch TR2....95 A6
St Mawes Terr **8** PL2....127 F5
ST MAWGAN....45 A8
St Mawgan Cl PL31....109 F5
St Mellans Terr **5** TR12....99 A1
ST MELLION....53 E8
St Mellion CE School PL12.53 D8
ST MELLION PK....53 C8
St Meriadoc CE Infant
  Academy TR14....138 C2
St Meriadoc CE VA Junior
  Academy TR14....138 B2
St Meriadoc Rd TR14....138 C3
ST MERRYN....31 F8
St Merryn Airfield PL28...31 F6
St Merryn Sch PL28....31 E8
ST MEWAN....59 A2
St Mewan Com Prim Sch
  PL26....59 A2
St Mewan La PL24, PL26...59 A3
ST MICHAEL CAERHAYS....72 D1
ST MICHAEL PENKEVIL....70 F1
St Michael's CE Prim Sch
  TR13....146 C5
St Michaels Cl PL15....19 C1
St Michael's Cl Hayle TR27..144 B4
  Plymouth PL1....127 F5
St Michael's Cotts **11** TR18 143 E5
St Michaels Ct
  Mawnan Smith TR11....93 D3
  18 Penzance TR18....143 E5
St Michael's Ct **7** PL1...127 F3
St Michael's Hospl TR27...142 B4
St Michael's Mount ★ TR17. 89 B4
St Michael's RC Small Sch **17**
  TR1....137 C4
St Michaels Rd TR3....81 B4
St Michael's Rd
  Newquay TR7....110 D5
  Perranporth TR6....55 A4
  3 Ponsanooth TR3....81 C4
  9 Stratton EX23....4 D1
St Michael's St TR18....143 E6
St Michael's Terr
  Penzance TR18....143 D6
  Plymouth PL4....148 C4
  8 Plymouth, Devonport PL1 127 F3
St Michaels Way
  Marazion TR17....89 C5
  St Austell PL26....47 A2
St Michaels Wy PL26....46 F2
ST MINVER....22 A4
St Minver Sch PL27....21 F3
St Modwen Rd PL6....129 F7
St Moritz Ct PL27....21 D5
St Moritz Villas PL27....21 D5
St Nazaire App PL1....127 F2
St Nazaire Cl
  3 Boslowick TR11....144 F1
  Plymouth PL1....127 E2
ST NEOT....36 F2
St Neot Com Prim Sch PL14 36 F2
ST NEWLYN EAST....56 C7
St Newlyn East Prim Sch
  TR8....56 B4
St Nicholas' CE Prim Sch
  PL11....64 C4
St Nicholas Cl TR27....78 C6
St Nicholas Ct **1** TR26...141 B6
St Nicholas Pk PL22....116 C3
St Nicholas St Bodmin PL31 109 E4
  14 Truro TR1....137 C4
St Nonna's Cl PL15....26 C8
St Olaf's Rd **18** EX23....4 D1
St Pancras Ave PL2....128 C8
St Paternus Cl PL15....27 E8
St Pauls Cl PL3....129 C5
St Paul's RC Prim Sch PL5 123 D1
St Paul St PL1....134 A8
St Peter Cl PL7....130 F4
St Peters CE VA Prim Sch &
  Nur PL1....148 B3
St Peters Ct PL1....148 A3
St Peter's Hill TR18....143 C1
St Peter's RC Prim Sch
  PL5....124 B5
St Peters Rd
  Plymouth PL5....124 C2
  11 Stratton EX23....4 D1
St Peters St **16** TR26....141 B6
St Peters Way TR13....98 C8
St Petrocs CE VA Prim Sch
  PL31....109 E4
St Petrocs Cl PL31....109 E4
St Petrocs Mdw PL28....107 C5
St Petroc's Sch EX23....104 D7
St Petry TR20....89 E5
St Philip St **7** TR18....143 E6
ST PINNOCK....50 D6
St Piran Cl PL31....109 B4
St Pirans Cl **2** TR1....137 D4
St Piran's Cl PL25....114 F6
St Pirans Ct
  Camborne TR14....138 D3
  13 Penzance TR18....143 E5
  Tintagel PL34....14 E8
St Pirans Hill TR3....81 D6
St Pirans Ho **15** TR6....55 A5
St Pirans Par **10** TR6....55 A5
St Pirans Parc **14** TR13...98 C8
St Piran's Rd TR6....55 A5
St Piran's Rd TR7....110 C4
St Piran's St TR27....142 B4
St Pirans Way TR20....89 D4
St Pol de Leon View TR19..88 C2
ST RUAN....103 A4

St Rumon's CE Inf Sch
  PL19....147 C6
St Sampsons Cl **6** PL24...60 D5
St Sampson's Terr PL23....61 B5
St Saviour's Hill PL23....116 D2
St Saviour's La PL28....107 D6
St Simon's La PL4....129 B3
St Smithwick Way TR11...145 C3
ST STEPHEN....58 B4
St Stephen Churchtown Prim
  Sch PL26....58 B4
St Stephen Rd PL7....130 F3
ST STEPHENS Launceston..106 A8
  Saltash....122 D2
St Stephens Community Prim
  Sch
  Launceston PL15....106 B8
  Saltash PL12....122 E2
St Stephen's Hill
  Launceston PL15....106 B7
  Saltash PL12....122 C1
St Stephens Rd PL26....58 E1
St Stephen's Rd PL12....122 E2
St Stephen St PL1....127 F1
St Sulien PL30....48 A1
ST TEATH....23 E7
St Teath Com Prim Sch
  PL30....23 E7
St Teresa Ho PL4....149 A3
St Therese **20** PL17....39 F4
St Therese's Ct PL1....127 F2
ST THOMAS....106 B6
St Thomas Cl Plymouth PL7 130 F3
  Truro TR1....69 F3
St Thomas Hill PL15....106 B6
St Thomas Rd PL15....106 B6
St Thomas' Rd TR7....110 F5
St Thomas St TR10....144 F7
St Tinney Farm PL32....10 D1
ST TUDY....23 E3
St Tudy CE Prim Sch PL30..23 E3
St Tudy Rd Cross Hill PL30..23 C1
  Treveglos PL30....34 D8
St Uny CE Sch TR26....141 D1
St Uny Cl TR26....77 E3
St Uny Cres TR15....139 F5
ST VEEP....61 C6
St Vincent St PL2....127 E4
St Warren St **6** TR18....143 E6
ST WENN....46 D7
St Wenn Sch PL30....46 D7
St Winnolls Pk PL13....117 D4
ST WINNOW....61 A8
St Winnow Barton Farm Mus★
  PL22....61 A8
St Winnow CE Prim Sch
  PL22....112 F2
Salamanca St PL11....127 B3
Salcombe Rd PL4....149 C4
SALEM....68 F3
Salisbury Ope PL3....128 B5
Salisbury Rd Plymouth PL4 149 C4
  Truro TR1....137 B4
Salisbury Road Jun Sch
  PL4....149 C3
Salmon Row **3** TR1....137 D4
SALTASH....122 B1
Saltash Bsns Pk PL12....122 C4
Saltash Com Sch PL12....122 E1
Saltbox Cl TR11....82 A2
Saltbox Rd TR11....82 A2
Saltburn Rd PL5....123 C1
Salt Cellar Hill **10** TR13...98 B8
Saltings Cl TR26....77 E3
Saltings Reach TR26....77 E3
Saltings The TR26....77 E4
Salt Mill PL12....122 F4
Saltmill Cl PL12....122 F3
Saltponds **27** PL19....88 C1
Saltram House ★ PL7....130 A4
Salts Mdw PL14....50 B6
Sam Bonds Nip PL27....22 E3
Sampford Gdns PL20....42 D5
SAMPFORD SPINEY....42 E7
Sampford Terr **8** PL20....42 C5
Sampson Cl PL18....40 D6
Sampson Gdns TR3....81 B4
Sampson's Ct TR27....78 C6
Sampson Way TR3....69 D3
Sampys Hill TR11....93 D3
Sams La PL24....60 C5
Samuel Bassett Ave PL6...125 B7
Samuel Bone Cl PL14....113 D6
SANCREED....87 E4
Sancreed La TR20....87 D4
Sancreed Rd TR20....87 E4
Sanctuary Cl TR14....138 C2
Sanctuary La Helston TR13 146 C6
  12 Stratton EX23....4 E1
Sanctuary Lane Flats
  TR13....146 C6
Sand Bay TR11....145 C2
Sandercock Cl PL17....39 F7
Sanderling Cl **7** EX23....7 B8
Sanders Hill Rosken PL28...32 A8
  Tregolls PL28....31 F7
Sandfield Cres **3** TR14...138 C2
Sandford Rd PL9....135 F8

Sand Hill PL18....41 A6
Sand Hill Pk PL18....40 F5
Sandhole Cross EX39....2 D8
Sandhurst Terr **1** TR1....137 C5
Sand La PL18....41 A3
Sandon Wlk PL6....125 A1
Sandows La **15** TR26....141 A5
Sandpiper Rd
  9 Binham EX23....7 B8
  Plymouth PL6....125 B2
Sandpiper Road EX23....104 F5
SANDPLACE....63 C7
Sandplace Rd Looe PL13...117 C6
  Looe, Sandplace PL13....63 B7
Sandplace Sta PL13....63 B8
Sandra Way PL31....109 C5
Sandyacres TR27....78 B6
Sandy Acres TR27....142 B6
SANDY BOTTOM....114 F4
Sandy Cl PL4....51 B3
Sandy Cove TR4....68 A7
Sandy Ct TR8....31 B2
Sandy Hill PL25....114 F4
Sandy Hill Academy PL25.114 F4
Sandyhills PL27....21 E2
Sandy La Harlyn PL28....20 D2
  Redruth TR15, TR16....140 D5
  Trevone PL28....20 F2
Sandylake La PL22....112 F3
Sandymoor TR14....139 B3
Sandy Rd Plymouth PL7...131 C4
  Porthtowan TR4....68 A7
Sandy Way Colcerrow PL24...60 C8
  Kerrow PL30....24 C1
Sango Ct PL10....132 F6
Sango Rd PL11....127 A2
San Sebastian Sq PL1....148 C2
Saracen Cl TR10....144 C7
Saracen Cres TR10....144 C7
Saracen Ho **5** TR10....144 C7
Saracen Pl TR10....144 C7
Saracen Way TR10....144 C7
Sarah Cl PL20....41 B1
Sarahs Cl PL28....107 D4
Sarah's Ct PL28....107 D4
Sarah's La PL28....107 D4
Sarah's Mdw PL28....107 D4
Sarah's View PL28....107 D4
Sargents Mdw EX23....2 D1
Sarum Cl PL3....128 F7
Saud La PL17....40 B7
Saunders La PL11....65 A5
Saunders Wlk PL6....124 D6
Savage Rd PL5....127 D7
Savath La PL26....47 D4
SAVEOCK....69 B3
Savery Terr PL4....129 A4
Savoy Bldg **3** PL25....114 C3
Sawles Rd PL25....114 B2
Sawmills Cl **8** PL31....109 A5
Sawmills La TR16....68 D3
Sawrey St PL1....148 A2
Sawyers Ct TR13....92 A6
Saxon Rd PL19....147 A6
Scannell Cl PL12....122 D1
SCARCEWATER....57 E5
Scarletts Well Pk PL31....109 C6
Scarletts Well Rd PL31....109 B5
Scarlett's Well Rd PL31....109 B5
Scarne Ind Est PL15....106 D3
Scarne Lake Gdns PL15...106 D3
Scarne Mill Ind Est PL15..106 D3
Scarne Side Gr PL15....106 D3
Scawns St **11** PL14....50 E7
Scholars Cl PL14....38 F2
Scholar's La TR13....91 C3
School Cl Par PL24....60 B4
  Plymouth PL7....130 D7
  St Columb Minor TR7....111 E6
  Tavistock PL19....147 D5
School Dr PL6....125 D7
School Hill Golant PL23....61 B5
  Herodsfoot PL14....50 E3
  Lanjeth PL26....58 E4
  Mevagissey PL26....73 C4
  Padstow PL28....107 D5
  Penhallick PL26....59 D7
  Perranworthal TR3....81 D6
  St Keverne PL12....101 D4
  St Keverne, Porthallow TR12 101 D4
  St Neot PL14....36 F2
  Shortlanesend TR4....69 F6
  South Petherwin PL15....27 E8
School La
  Budock Water TR11....144 C3
  Gulval TR18....88 E6
  Harrowbarrow PL17....40 C4
  Jacobstow EX23....11 A6
  Marazion TR17....89 C5
  Plymouth PL7....130 E4
  Polruan PL23....116 D2
  Redruth TR15....140 D5
  St Austell PL25....115 C6
  St Erth TR27....142 A1
  St Hilary TR20....89 F6
  Summercourt TR8....57 C7
  Tregellist PL30....22 F4
  Troon TR14....79 E4
  Truro TR1....137 C3
School Rd
  Harrowbarrow PL17....40 D4
  Landrake PL12....53 C4
  Pensilva PL14....38 E5
  Summercourt TR8....57 B7
  Tavistock PL19....147 D2
School Wlk PL27....108 D6

Sclerder La PL13....62 E4
Scoble's Terr TR1....70 D1
Sconner Rd PL11....127 A3
Scoria Cl TR16....68 D3
SCORRIER....68 D3
Scorrier House Workshops
  TR16....68 D2
Scorrier Rd Treleigh TR16...68 E1
  Treleigh TR16....140 F8
Scorrier St TR16....68 E1
Scott Ave PL5....127 C8
Scott Bsns Pk PL2....128 A6
Scott Cl **2** PL14....38 E4
Scott Hospl PL2....128 A6
Scott Rd PL2....128 A6
Scowbuds TR14....138 F5
Scrations La PL22....112 C2
SCREDDA....114 D8
Screech Owl Sanctuary★
  TR9....46 A3
Sculptor Way **11** PL9....136 E8
Seabank TR11....145 B2
Sea Breeze Cl PL34....14 C6
Seabank TR11....145 B2
Seacroft Rd PL5....123 C2
Sea Front Ct PL13....117 D3
Seaholme Ct TR11....145 A5
Sea La TR27....142 D6
Seapoint Ho TR7....110 E6
Sea Rd PL25....115 D2
SEATON....64 B5
Seaton Ave PL4....128 E4
Seaton Bsns Pk PL6....125 B3
Seaton La PL4....128 E4
Seaton Pk PL11....64 B5
Seaton Pl PL2....127 F5
Seaton Valley North Nature
  Reserve ★ PL13, PL13....64 B6
Seaton Way PL20....42 A2
Sea Urchin TR26....141 E2
Seaureaugh TR3....80 F4
Sea View
  Crackington Haven EX23....10 C6
  Gunnislake PL18....40 E5
Sea View Ave PL4....149 C4
Sea View Cl EX23....5 A6
Seaview Cotts **10** TR11...145 B5
Sea View Cotts PL26....73 C3
Sea View Cres **11** TR2....95 A6
Sea View Ct TR11....145 B3
Sea View La TR8....43 C1
Sea View Rd Falmouth TR11 145 B2
  St Mawes TR2....95 A6
Seaview Terr TR8....57 E6
Sea View Terr
  Camborne TR14....138 D5
  Carn Towan TR19....96 C7
  Helston TR13....146 B6
  6 Newlyn TR18....143 C1
  Par PL24....60 B6
  Penwithick PL26....59 D7
  Plymouth PL4....149 B4
  Redruth TR15....140 C5
  20 St Ives TR26....141 B5
Seawell Rd EX23....104 F7
Second Ave
  Plymouth, Billacombe PL9....130 A1
  Plymouth, Devonport PL1...128 A2
  Plymouth, Weston Mill PL2..127 E7
Sedley Way PL5....124 D3
Sefton Ave PL4....129 B3
Sefton Cl PL4....149 C4
Segrave Rd PL2....128 B6
Seiners Ct **10** TR6....55 A4
Seleggan Hill Carnkie TR16...80 B7
  Pennance TR16....140 A1
Selkirk Ho **5** PL9....135 F7
Selkirk Pl PL5....124 E2
SELLAN....87 E5
Selsden Cl PL9....136 C6
Sendall's Way PL6....124 F4
Seneschall Pk TR13....146 D8
SENNEN....96 B6
Sennen Cl PL11....126 F4
SENNEN COVE....96 B7
Sennen Cty Prim Sch TR19..86 E1
Sennen Hts TR19....96 B7
Sennen Pl PL11....127 E5
Sentry Cl PL27....32 D6
Sergeants Hill TR4....68 F3
Serpell Cl PL6....124 E6
Serpells Mdw PL15....17 F1
Serpens Vale **1** PL9....136 E7
Sethnoe Way TR13....91 A3
Seton Gdns TR14....138 B4
Setons The **6** TR14....138 F7
Seven Stars La PL5....124 C6
Seven Trees Ct PL4....149 B4
Severn Pl PL3....129 C5
Sewell Ct PL3....128 E5
SEWORGAN....92 C6
Seymour Ave Newquay TR7 110 E6
  Plymouth PL4....149 B4
Seymour Cl TR3....69 C3
Seymour Dr PL3....128 F5
Seymour Mews PL4....149 C4
Seymour Pl PL1....148 A4
Seymour Rd
  Plymouth, Mannamead PL3..128 F5
  Plymouth, Plympton PL7....130 C6
Seymour St PL4....149 A3
Shackleton Cres **9** PL4....31 F3
Shackleton Cl PL5....124 E1
Shackleton Dr TR7....111 B5
Shaft Downs La TR27....78 F3
Shaftesbury Cotts PL4....149 A4
Shaftesbury Ct **8** PL4....149 A4

Shakespeare Prim Sch
  PL5....124 B2
Shakespeare Rd PL5....124 C2
Shaldon Cres PL5....124 B3
Shallowford Cl PL6....129 C8
Shallowford Rd PL6....129 C8
Shapleys Gdns PL9....136 A5
Shapters Rd PL4....149 C2
Shapters Way PL4....135 B8
Sharaman Cl PL25....115 A5
Sharlands Rd EX23....7 B6
Sharon Way PL6....125 A5
Sharpitor Gdns PL2....128 A7
Sharpitor Row PL20....42 E4
Sharrose Rd PL9....135 B5
Shaw Way PL9....135 A7
Shearwater Dr **1** EX23....7 B8
Shearwood Cl PL7....130 C6
Sheep Fair Mdw **14** PL17...39 F4
Sheepstor Rd PL5....125 D1
SHEFFIELD....97 F7
Sheila's Ct TR26....141 D1
Shelburne Ct TR11....144 F3
Shelburne Rd TR11....144 F3
Shell Cl PL25....125 E1
Shellduck Cl **5** EX23....7 B8
Shelley Ave PL19....147 D5
Shelley Rd PL25....115 A4
Shelley Way PL5....123 D1
Shepherds Hill PL30....34 C5
Shepherds La PL4....149 B2
Sherborne Cl PL9....136 C6
Sherford Cres
  Plymouth, Elburton PL9....136 C5
  Plymouth, West Park PL5....124 A3
Sherford Rd PL9....136 D7
Sherford Wlk PL9....136 E7
Sheridan Rd PL5....124 C1
Sherrell Pk PL20....41 B1
Sherril Cl PL9....135 F4
Sherwell La PL4....149 A4
Sherwood Dr PL31....109 C5
SHEVIOCK....65 B6
Sheviock La PL11....65 B5
Shilla Pk PL32....24 A8
Shilson Terr **7** PL15....106 C5
Shipbuilder Cl PL26....73 C4
Shipley Wlk PL5....125 A1
Shippen Wlk **5** PL5....114 F2
Ships & Castles L Ctr TR11 145 E4
Shirburn Rd PL6....129 B8
Shire Horse Farm & Carriage
  Mus The ★ TR16....79 F5
Shires Way PL6....46 F3
Shirley Gdns PL5....124 C1
Shoemaker's La PL12....122 E2
Shoemakers Row PL13....63 B7
Shoot Row TR15....140 C5
SHOP Morwenstow....2 D1
  St Merryn....31 E8
Shop Hill **3** TR17....89 C5
Shop La PL30....35 F3
Shop Pk PL14....38 A2
Shoreline TR7....111 B8
Shores La PL27....21 E3
Short View TR11....145 A1
Short Cotts PL11....127 A3
Short Cross Mews TR4....68 C6
Short Cross Rd TR4....68 C6
Shortlands EX22....8 E5
SHORTLANESEND....69 F6
Shortlanesend Com Prim Sch
  TR4....69 F6
Short Park Rd PL3....128 D5
Short Stone Rd PL30....34 C7
Shortwood Cres PL9....136 A7
Shrewsbury Rd PL5....124 C4
Shrubberies Hill TR13....98 C3
Shuffley TR15....139 E8
Shute Hill Breage TR13....90 F3
  Carharrack TR16....80 E8
  Lostwithiel PL22....112 C2
  Mawnan Smith TR11....93 D3
  Pelynt PL13....62 D5
Shute La Penryn TR10....144 C8
  Pensilva PL14....38 E4
  6 Porthleven TR13....98 B8
Shute Mdw TR10....144 C7
Shute Park Rd PL9....135 F6
SHUTTA....117 C4
Shutta Rd PL13....117 C4
Siding Rd PL4....148 C4
Sidings The Bugle PL26....47 C2
  Delabole PL33....14 E2
Sidmouth Cotts **9** PL4....128 F4
Sidney Terr **7** TR15....140 C5
Sika Dr TR13....146 D6
Silvanus Jenkin Ave PL14 113 E5
Silver Birch Cl PL6....125 C7
Silver Birch Cres **13** PL31 109 A5
Silver Ct **1** TR15....140 B4
Silverdale Ct TR7....110 E6
Silverdale Rd TR11....145 A2
Silver Hill
  Perranarworthal TR3....81 D6
  Trebarvah TR11....92 E5
Silvershell Rd PL29....22 D7
Silvershell View PL29....22 D7
Silver St Bere Ferrers PL20...120 A3
  Saltash PL12....123 A2
Silver Terr PL10....133 A6
Silverton Rd EX23....104 E5
Silver Way TR3....69 C3
SILVERWELL....68 F7

Simms Terr PL18 . . . . 41 A6
Simon Cl PL9 . . . . 135 E6
Simpsons Ct TR18 . . . . . 143 E5
Sina Hill PL30 . . . . 36 B1
Singlerose Rd PL26 . . . . 59 C7
Sinns Common TR16 . . . . 68 B4
Sir James Smith's Com Sch
  PL32 . . . . 105 C4
Sir John Hunt Com Sports Coll
  PL5 . . . . 124 D4
Sir Robert Geffery's CE Prim
  Sch PL12 . . . . 53 C3
Sir Williams Morles
  Almshouses PL12 . . . . 65 A8
Sisna Park Rd PL6 . . . . 125 E5
SITHNEY 91 B3
SITHNEY COMMON 91 B3
Sithney Common Hill TR13 . 91 C2
Sithney Com Prim Sch
  TR13 . . . . 91 B5
SITHNEY GREEN 91 C4
Sithney Old Hill
  Helston TR13 . . . . 146 A6
  St Elvan TR13 . . . . 91 C2
Sithney St PL5 . . . . 123 C1
Six O Clock La PL7 . . . . 130 E3
Six Turnings TR11 . . . . 82 A2
Skardale Gdns PL6 . . . . 129 D8
Skardon Pl PL4 . . . . 149 A4
Skerries Rd PL6 . . . . 124 F7
Skewes Rd PL30 . . . . 46 E8
Skidden Hill 18 TR26 . . . . . 141 B5
Skimmel Hill TR20 . . . . 87 E5
Skinnard La PL18 . . . . 40 F5
SKINNERS BOTTOM 68 D5
Skitches Cnr EX23 . . . . 4 D1
Skitta Cl PL17 . . . . 39 F5
Skyburriowe Burnoon TR12 100 A5
  Trevassack TR12 . . . . 99 D5
  Trevassack TR12 . . . . 100 A5
Skyburriowe La TR12 . . . . . . 99 C6
Skyburriowe Mill TR12 . . . . . 99 C5
Skylark Rise Plymouth PL6 . 125 E8
  Tavistock PL19 . . . . 147 D1
Slade Cl PL9 . . . . 136 A5
Slade Park Rd PL14 . . . . 38 E5
SLADESBRIDGE 34 A6
Slades La 2 TR10 . . . . 144 C7
Slades Rd PL25 . . . . 114 E5
Slate Ave 3 PL14 . . . . 113 D8
Slate Cl PL33 . . . . 14 D2
Slate La PL1 . . . . 148 A2
Slatelands Cl PL7 . . . . 131 B3
SLAUGHTERBRIDGE 105 D7
Slemans La Milland PL30 . . . 36 A4
  Trezance PL30 . . . . 35 F4
Slipway PL27 . . . . 21 D2
Slipway Quay PL12 . . . . 119 B2
Smallack Cl PL6 . . . . 124 F2
Smallack Dr PL6 . . . . 124 F2
Smallridge Cl PL9 . . . . 135 F5
Smallridge La EX23 . . . . 4 F1
Small Side 3 TR27 . . . . 142 D6
Smeaton Sq PL3 . . . . 129 D6
Smeaton's Twr ★ PL1 . . . . . 148 C1
Smithfield Ct TR8 . . . . 111 B3
Smithfield Dr PL12 . . . . 122 B3
Smithick Hill TR11 . . . . 145 B4
Smiths Way PL12 . . . . 122 B3
Smithy Cl PL12 . . . . 122 C4
Smithy Ct PL32 . . . . 105 D3
Smithy La TR3 . . . . 81 F7
Smugglers Ct 2 TR18 . . . . 143 D6
Smugglers Row 3 TR11 . . 145 B5
Snell Dr PL12 . . . . 122 B3
Snowdrop Cres PL15 . . . . . . 106 E4
Snow Hill Lanlivery PL30 . . . 48 C2
  Trelill PL30 . . . . 23 C5
Snow's Pas TR11 . . . . 145 B4
Soap St Ferryport PL1 . . . . . 134 C8
  Millbay PL1 . . . . 148 A2
Socotra Dr 7 PL25 . . . . 59 A3
Solar Row 6 TR1 . . . . 137 D5
Soldon Cl PL28 . . . . 107 C4
Somer Ct TR11 . . . . 145 B4
Somerset Cotts 10 PL3 . . . 128 A4
Somerset Pl PL3 . . . . 128 A4
Somerset Place La 11 PL3 128 A4
Somerville Rd TR6 . . . . 55 A4
Sona Merg TR18 . . . . 143 C7
Sonnet Cl PL5 . . . . 124 C2
Sopers Hill PL6 . . . . 121 A2
Soper's Hill PL5 . . . . 120 E1
Sorrell St 3 TR27 . . . . 142 E6
Sortridge Cl 3 PL19 . . . . . 147 B7
Sourton Sq 8 PL9 . . . . 129 D1
South Albany Rd TR15 . . . . 140 C3
Southbourne Cl PL26 . . . . . . 58 E6
Southbourne Rd PL25 . . . . . 114 E2
South Calvadnack TR16 . . . . 80 B2
South Carn Brea
  Bosleake TR16 . . . . 67 F1
  Carnkie TR16 . . . . 80 A7
  Carnkie TR16 . . . . 139 F3
  Pennance TR16 . . . . 140 A1
Southcliff TR11 . . . . 145 C2
South Cliff 18 TR16 . . . . 88 C1
South Coombe La PL17 . . . . 39 F8
SOUTHCOTT 11 A6
Southcott Mdws EX23 . . . . . 11 A6
South Crofty Way TR15 . . . 139 B7
SOUTHDOWN 133 B6
Southdown Cl PL26 . . . . 58 E1
Southdown Cotts PL10 . . . . 133 B6

Southdown Quay PL10 . . . . 133 B6
Southdown Rd
  Millbrook PL10 . . . . 133 A6
  Sticker PL26 . . . . 58 E1
South Down Rd PL2 . . . . . . 128 B6
South Downs TR15 . . . . 140 D2
Southdown Terr PL10 . . . . . 133 A6
South Dr Redruth TR15 . . . . 140 D2
  South Tehidy TR14 . . . . . . 138 E8
Southella Rd PL20 . . . . 42 D2
Southern Cl PL2 . . . . 127 F7
Southernhaye 8 PL15 . . . . 106 C5
Southern Rd 31 PL17 . . . . . . 39 F4
Southern Terr PL14 . . . . 128 F4
Southernway PL9 . . . . 136 A8
Southern Way PL27 . . . . . . 108 C5
Southfield PL12 . . . . 122 C3
Southfield Rd EX23 . . . . 104 E5
Southfields EX22 . . . . 8 A5
Southfields Pl 3 TR26 . . . . 141 A5
Southgate Ave PL6 . . . . 135 E4
Southgate Cl PL6 . . . . 135 E4
Southgate Pl 4 PL15 . . . . . 106 C5
Southgate St
  Launceston PL15 . . . . 106 C5
  Redruth TR15 . . . . 140 C3
South Harbour TR10 . . . . . . 144 D7
SOUTH HILL 39 C7
South Hill
  Plymouth, Hooe PL9 . . . . . 135 C4
  Plymouth, Stoke PL1 . . . . . 128 A3
South Hill Rd PL7 . . . . 39 E5
SOUTH HOLE 2 D7
Southlea Terr TR3 . . . . 80 F3
Southleigh Ho 15 TR1 . . . . 137 C4
Southleigh Mews 14 TR1 . . 137 C4
South Milton St PL4 . . . . . . 149 C2
South Par 33 TR18 . . . . 143 E5
South Park Cl TR15 . . . . 140 A4
Southpark Rd PL24 . . . . 60 C5
SOUTH PETHERWIN 27 E8
South Petherwin Prim Sch
  PL15 . . . . 27 E8
SOUTH PILL 122 E3
South Pk Jacobstow EX23 . . 11 A6
  Redruth TR15 . . . . 139 F6
  16 St Columb Major TR9 . . 45 E6
South Pl TR19 . . . . 86 E6
South Place Folly 5 PL18 143 E4
South Place Gdns TR19 . . . 86 E6
South Quay PL28 . . . . 107 D5
South Quay Hill TR7 . . . . . 110 D6
South Rd Goldsithney TR20 . 89 E5
  Stithians TR3 . . . . 80 F3
South Roskear Terr TR14 . . 138 F4
Southside Ope 14 PL1 . . . . 149 A2
Southside St PL1 . . . . 149 A2
South St Fowey PL23 . . . . . 116 D4
  Grampound Road TR2 . . . . 57 E1
  Lostwithiel PL22 . . . . 112 C2
  St Austell PL25 . . . . 114 C4
SOUTH TEHIDY 138 E7
South Terr Camborne TR14 . 138 D2
  12 Penzance TR18 . . . . . . 143 E4
South Towan TR4 . . . . 68 A6
Southview PL10 . . . . 133 A6
South View
  9 Horrabridge PL20 . . . . . . 42 C4
  Liskeard PL14 . . . . 113 D7
  Penryn TR10 . . . . 144 C8
  Plymouth, Crownhill PL5 . . 124 E2
  Plymouth, Elburton PL9 . . 136 B6
  Porthleven TR13 . . . . 91 A1
South View Cl PL7 . . . . 130 D7
Southview Dr PL31 . . . . 109 E5
South View Parc TR4 . . . . . . 68 A6
South View Pk PL7 . . . . 130 D7
Southview Rd 15 PL24 . . . . 60 B4
Southview Terr 8 TR19 . . . . 88 C1
South View Terr
  Nancegollan TR13 . . . . 91 B7
  Plymouth PL4 . . . . 149 C3
SOUTHWAY 124 F6
Southway PL28 . . . . 20 F2
South Way TR8 . . . . 111 F3
Southway Dr PL6 . . . . 124 E6
Southway La
  Plymouth, Southway PL6 . . 125 B6
  Plymouth, Tamerton Foliot
  PL6 . . . . 124 C6
Southwell Rd PL6 . . . . 124 E1
SOUTH WHEATLEY 11 F3
Sovereign Ct PL7 . . . . 130 C5
Sowton Rd PL20 . . . . 121 D8
Spargo Ct TR10 . . . . 93 C8
Spargo's La TR1 . . . . 137 E5
Sparkatown La PL20 . . . . . . 42 E3
Sparke Cl PL7 . . . . 131 B4
SPARKWELL 131 F8
Spar La TR15 . . . . 67 D4
Sparnock Grove TR1 . . . . . . 69 E3
SPARNON 96 F5
Sparnon Cl Redruth TR15 . . 140 C4
  St Austell PL25 . . . . 114 B4
Sparnon Cross TR13 . . . . . . 90 F5
Sparnon Ct TR15 . . . . 140 C4
SPARNON GATE 67 F4
Sparnon Gate TR16 . . . . 67 F4
Sparnon Hill 1 TR15 . . . . . 140 C4
Sparnon Terr 2 TR15 . . . . . 140 C4
Sparrow Cl 1 TR27 . . . . . . 142 E6
Sparry La TR16 . . . . 80 E8
Spaven Mor TR14 . . . . 138 F5
Speares The PL12 . . . . 122 B2
Spear's Terr TR11 . . . . 144 F1
Speech La TR3 . . . . 81 C4
Speedwell Cl Bude EX23 . . 104 F5
  Millbrook PL10 . . . . 132 F5

Speedwell Cres PL6 . . . . . . 129 B7
Speedwell Wlk PL6 . . . . 129 B7
Spencer Gdns PL12 . . . . . . 122 F1
Spencer Rd PL9 . . . . 135 E8
Spernen Cl TR26 . . . . 141 C2
Spernen Wyn Rd TR11 . . . . 145 B2
Spicers La 11 EX23 . . . . 4 E1
Spindrift TR8 . . . . 44 C6
Spinnaker Dr TR2 . . . . 95 A6
Spinnaker Quay PL9 . . . . . . 134 F7
Spinney The PL7 . . . . 131 A4
Spire Ct PL3 . . . . 129 B5
Spire Hill Pk PL12 . . . . 122 C2
Spires The PL1 . . . . 137 C6
Spitfire Row PL27 . . . . 31 F3
Splash Pool EX23 . . . . 104 F5
SPLATT Rock. 21 E3
  Warbstow Cross 17 B7
Sportmans Cl PL15 . . . . 28 C4
Sportsmans PL32 . . . . 105 C3
Sportsmans Rd PL32 . . . . . 105 C3
Sprey Rd 2 PL31 . . . . 109 A4
SPRIDDLESTONE 136 C4
Springfield Horrabridge PL20 42 C4
  Portscatho TR2 . . . . 83 B2
  12 Yelverton PL20 . . . . 42 C4
Springfield Ave PL9 . . . . . . 136 B6
Springfield Bsns Pk PL15 . . 18 E2
Springfield Cl Dobwalls PL14 50 E7
  Lostwithiel PL22 . . . . 112 C2
  Phillack TR27 . . . . 142 D7
  Plymouth PL9 . . . . 136 B7
  Polgooth PL26 . . . . 59 A1
  St Austell PL25 . . . . 114 F5
Springfield Dr PL3 . . . . 128 A4
Springfield Gate PL13 . . . . 117 D5
Springfield La PL9 . . . . 136 B7
Springfield Pk
  Barripper TR14 . . . . 79 B5
  Mylor Bridge TR11 . . . . 82 A3
  Widegates PL13 . . . . 63 E7
Springfield Pl 15 TR9 . . . . . 45 E6
Springfield Rd
  Falmouth TR11 . . . . 144 E5
  Goldsithney TR20 . . . . 89 E5
  Liskeard PL14 . . . . 113 C6
  Looe PL13 . . . . 117 D5
  Newquay TR7 . . . . 110 F6
  Plymouth PL9 . . . . 136 B6
Springfield Rise PL9 . . . . . . 136 B7
Springfields PL26 . . . . 47 C2
Springfields Fun Pk & Pony
  Ctr ★ TR9 . . . . 45 E4
Springfield Way Roche PL26 46 F3
  St Day TR16 . . . . 68 D1
  Threemilestone TR3 . . . . . . 69 C3
Springhill PL2 . . . . 128 C8
Spring Hill PL19 . . . . 147 B5
Springhill Gn PL2 . . . . 128 C8
Spring Pk PL6 . . . . 125 E7
Springwell View PL31 . . . . . 109 F5
Springwood Cl PL7 . . . . 131 A3
Spurway Rd PL14 . . . . 113 D5
Square The
  16 Bere Alston PL20 . . . . . . 41 B1
  Cawsand PL10 . . . . 133 A1
  2 Chacewater TR4 . . . . 69 A3
  Grampound Road TR2 . . . . 57 E1
  Gunnislake, St Ann's Chapel
  PL18 . . . . 40 E5
  3 Kilkhampton EX23 . . . . . . 5 A1
  Landrake PL12 . . . . 53 C3
  Lizard TR12 . . . . 102 F2
  Ludgvan TR20 . . . . 89 A8
  Manaccan TR12 . . . . 101 A7
  Marazion TR17 . . . . 89 B5
  7 Pendeen TR19 . . . . 75 A1
  Penryn TR10 . . . . 144 D7
  Pentewan PL26 . . . . 73 C6
  Plymouth, Stonehouse PL1 . 128 A2
  Portreath TR16 . . . . 67 C6
  Portscatho TR2 . . . . 83 B2
  Praze-an-Beeble TR14 . . . . 79 B2
  Probus TR2 . . . . 71 C6
  Redruth TR16 . . . . 80 B5
  St Keverne TR12 . . . . 101 D4
  3 St Mawes TR2 . . . . 95 A6
  St Stephen PL26 . . . . 58 B4
  St Teath PL30 . . . . 23 E7
  Saltash PL12 . . . . 122 C3
  Tregony TR2 . . . . 71 F3
  Veryan TR2 . . . . 83 F4
  Week St Mary EX22 . . . . . . 11 E8
Squire La TR16 . . . . 80 F8
Squires La TR13 . . . . 91 C2
Stable Cotts PL7 . . . . 130 F5
Stable Ct PL27 . . . . 108 C6
Stable Hobba TR20 . . . . 143 A3
Stable Hobba Ind Est TR14 143 B3
Stables The TR14 . . . . 67 B4
STADDISCOMBE 135 F3
Staddiscombe Rd PL9 . . . . . 135 F4
Staddon Cres PL9 . . . . 135 E6
Staddon Gn PL9 . . . . 135 D6
Staddon La PL9 . . . . 135 B4
Staddon Park Rd PL9 . . . . . 135 E6
Staddon Terrace La PL1 . . . 148 B4
Stafford Cl TR7 . . . . 111 A5
Staggy La TR3 . . . . 81 F7
Stag La
  Plymouth, Elburton PL9 . . 136 B8
  Plymouth, Plympton PL9 . . 130 B1
Stamford Cl PL9 . . . . 135 A6
Stamford Fort Cotts PL9 . . . 135 A6
Stamford Hill EX23 . . . . 4 D1
Stamford La PL9 . . . . 135 A6
Stamps Hill Fraddon PL26 . . 57 F8

Stamps Hill continued
  Indian Queens TR9 . . . . 45 F1
Stamps La TR15 . . . . 139 D6
Stamps The PL17 . . . . 40 D5
Stanborough Cross PL9 . . . 136 C7
Stanborough Rd PL9 . . . . . . 136 B7
Stanbury Ave PL6 . . . . 124 F1
Stanbury Cl PL15 . . . . 13 F1
Stanbury Cross EX23 . . . . . . 2 C1
Stanbury Hill PL15 . . . . 27 B6
Stancombe La PL15 . . . . 12 B2
Standarhay Cl PL9 . . . . 136 C7
Standarhay Villas PL9 . . . . 136 C7
Stanford Cl 5 TR18 . . . . . . 143 D5
Stanford Mews TR9 . . . . 45 E6
Stanford Terr TR18 . . . . 143 D5
Stangray Ave PL4 . . . . 128 D4
Stanharver Cl TR7 . . . . 111 E6
Stanhope Rd PL5 . . . . 123 C1
Stanley Ct 4 PL31 . . . . 109 D5
Stanley Pl PL4 . . . . 129 B2
Stanley Terr 1 TR15 . . . . . 140 B5
Stanley Way PL5 . . . . 140 C6
Stannary Bridge Rd PL19 147 D6
Stannary La PL7 . . . . 130 D5
Stannary Rd Pengegon TR14 138 F3
  Stenalees PL26 . . . . 59 C8
Stantons Row PL14 . . . . 38 A3
Stanways Rd TR7 . . . . 111 D7
Staple Cl PL21 . . . . 121 C1
Stapleford Gdns PL5 . . . . . 123 F5
Stapleton Rd EX23 . . . . 104 F4
Star Pk PL18 . . . . 41 A6
START 77 E3
Statham Rd PL31 . . . . 109 D4
Station App
  3 Newquay TR7 . . . . 110 F6
  3 St Columb Road TR9 . . . 45 E2
  St Erth TR27 . . . . 77 E2
Station Hill Badharlick PL15 . 17 F5
  Hayle TR27 . . . . 142 B5
  Lelant TR26 . . . . 77 E4
  Praze-an-Beeble TR14 . . . . 79 B2
  Redruth TR15 . . . . 140 B4
Station La PL18 . . . . 41 A3
Station Par TR7 . . . . 110 F6
Station Rd
  20 Bere Alston PL20 . . . . . . 41 B1
  Bere Ferrers PL20 . . . . 119 E3
  Bugle PL26 . . . . 47 C2
  Camborne TR15 . . . . 139 C5
  Carnhell Green TR14 . . . . . 78 F4
  Chacewater TR4 . . . . 68 F4
  Fowey PL23 . . . . 116 C5
  Grampound Road TR2 . . . . 57 E1
  Gunnislake PL18 . . . . 40 F6
  Helston TR13 . . . . 146 C7
  Horrabridge PL20 . . . . 42 C4
  Kelly Bray PL17 . . . . 39 F6
  Launceston PL15 . . . . 106 C6
  Liskeard PL14 . . . . 113 B4
  Looe PL13 . . . . 117 C4
  Marazion TR17 . . . . 89 A6
  Mary Tavy PL19 . . . . 30 F5
  North Brentor PL19 . . . . . . 30 E8
  Padstow PL28 . . . . 107 D5
  Par PL24 . . . . 60 C5
  Penryn TR10 . . . . 144 B8
  Penzance TR18 . . . . 143 F6
  Perranarworthal TR3 . . . . . 81 E6
  Perranporth TR6 . . . . 55 B5
  Plymouth, Elburton PL9 . . 136 C7
  Plymouth, Keyham PL2 . . . 127 E5
  Plymouth, Plympton PL7 . . 130 E5
  Plymouth, Tamerton Foliot
  PL5 . . . . 124 A6
  Redruth TR15 . . . . 140 C5
  St Columb Major TR9 . . . . 45 E5
  St Mabyn PL30 . . . . 34 C8
  St Newlyn East TR8 . . . . . . 56 B7
  Saltash PL12 . . . . 123 A2
  Truro TR1 . . . . 137 B4
  Yelverton PL20 . . . . 42 D2
Station View PL19 . . . . 30 E8
Station Yd 6 PL31 . . . . 109 D5
Steamers Hill TR27 . . . . 78 C5
Steamers Mdw TR27 . . . . . . 78 C5
Steeple Cl Plymouth PL9 . . 135 E4
  St Ives TR26 . . . . 141 B3
Steeple La TR26 . . . . 141 B3
Steeple View Cl TR26 . . . . . 141 C1
Steeple Woodland Nature
  Reserve ★ TR26 . . . . 141 B3
Steer Park Rd PL7 . . . . 131 C5
Steer Point Cotts PL8 . . . . . 136 F2
Steer Point Rd PL8 . . . . 136 F3
Stefan Cl PL9 . . . . 135 B5
STENALEES 59 B8
Stenalees Hill PL26 . . . . 59 C7
Stenhill Hill PL15 . . . . 18 C8
Stenlake Pl PL4 . . . . 129 B2
Stenlake Terr PL4 . . . . 129 B2
STENNACK 79 D4
Stennack Gdns 14 TR26 . . 141 A5
Stennack Parc TR19 . . . . . . 86 F8
Stennack Rd PL25 . . . . 115 B4
Stennack The TR26 . . . . 141 B5
Stentaway Cl PL9 . . . . 135 E6
Stentaway Dr PL9 . . . . 136 A8
Stentaway Rd PL9 . . . . 135 E6
STEPASIDE 58 B5
Stephens Rd PL14 . . . . 113 E7
Stephney Cl TR11 . . . . 144 C2
Steppy Downs Rd TR27 . . . . 78 A1
Stewart Ct 2 TR11 . . . . . . 144 F1
Stewarts Rd Kitleigh EX23 . . . 7 D2

Stewarts Rd continued
  Week St Mary EX22 . . . . . . 11 E8
STIBB 4 D5
STICKER 58 F1
Stiles The TR8 . . . . 56 B7
Stillman Ct 7 PL4 . . . . 149 A2
Stillman St PL4 . . . . 149 A4
Stippy Stappy 11 TR5 . . . . 54 D1
Stirling Cl PL5 . . . . 123 C1
Stirling Rd PL5 . . . . 123 C1
STITHIANS 80 F3
Stithians Com Prim Sch
  TR3 . . . . 80 F4
Stithians Row TR16 . . . . 80 B5
Stockadon Farm Barns
  PL12 . . . . 118 B4
Stocks La PL30 . . . . 24 A5
Stoggy La PL7 . . . . 131 A6
STOKE 128 A3
STOKE CLIMSLAND 28 E1
Stoke Climsland Sch PL17 . 28 D1
Stoke Damerel Bsns Ctr 9
  . . . . 128 A4
Stoke Damerel Com Coll
  PL3 . . . . 128 B4
Stoke Damerel Prim Sch
  PL1 . . . . 128 A3
Stoke Hill PL17 . . . . 28 D1
Stoke Hill La PL20 . . . . 42 B2
Stoke Rd Bray Shop PL17 . . 28 A1
  Kelly Bray PL17 . . . . 39 E6
  Linkinhorne PL17 . . . . 39 A8
  Plymouth PL1 . . . . 148 A3
Stokesay Ave PL6 . . . . 125 A5
Stokes Rd PL1 . . . . 149 A2
Stoke Terr PL17 . . . . 39 E6
Stokingway Cl PL9 . . . . 135 E5
Stonebarton Cl PL7 . . . . . . 130 C6
Stonebarton Rd PL7 . . . . . . 130 C6
Stone Chair La TR19 . . . . . . 96 B7
Stone Cross PL16 . . . . 19 F5
Stonehall Flats PL1 . . . . . . 128 A1
Stone Hill EX23 . . . . 4 E2
STONEHOUSE 128 A1
Stonehouse Bridge PL1 . . . 128 A1
Stonehouse St PL1 . . . . 148 A2
Stonerock Flats PL13 . . . . . 117 C1
Stones Ct 30 TR26 . . . . 141 B5
Stonewood Ct 4 TR9 . . . . . 45 E6
Stoney Hill PL25 . . . . 59 A4
Stoney La
  2 Goonhavern TR4 . . . . . . 55 E4
  Illand PL15 . . . . 27 C6
  Polgooth PL26 . . . . 59 A1
  St Austell PL25 . . . . 114 C4
Stoney Lands PL12 . . . . 53 C3
Stony La Bodmin PL31 . . . . . 34 D1
  Gunnislake PL18 . . . . 40 F5
Stopford Pl PL1 . . . . 127 F3
STOPTIDE 21 E2
Stott Cl PL3 . . . . 129 D5
Stour Cl PL3 . . . . 129 D5
STOURSCOMBE 106 F4
Stourscombe PL15 . . . . 106 F3
Stourscombe Wood PL15 . 106 F4
Stowe Gdns PL5 . . . . 124 B2
STOWFORD 5 E8
Stowford Cl PL20 . . . . 42 E3
Stowford Cross EX22 . . . . . . 5 F1
Stracey Rd TR11 . . . . 145 B2
Strafford Cl EX23 . . . . 104 C3
Strand TR18 . . . . 143 C2
Strand Sh Ctr The EX23 . . . 104 C5
Strand St Padstow PL28 . . . 107 D5
  Plymouth PL1 . . . . 134 A8
Strand The Bude EX23 . . . . 104 C5
  Falmouth TR11 . . . . 145 C2
  Padstow PL28 . . . . 107 D5
Strangways Terr TR1 . . . . . 137 D3
Strangways Villas TR1 . . . . 137 D3
STRATTON 4 E1
Stratton Hospl EX23 . . . . . . 4 D1
Stratton Pl TR11 . . . . 145 A6
Stratton Prim Sch EX23 . . . . 4 D1
Stratton Rd Bude EX23 . . . 104 F4
  Stratton EX23 . . . . 4 D1
Stratton Ter TR11 . . . . 94 C6
Stratton Terr
  Falmouth TR11 . . . . 145 A6
  Flushing TR11 . . . . 145 A6
  Truro TR1 . . . . 137 B4
Stratton Wlk PL2 . . . . 128 D8
Strawberry Cl TR15 . . . . . . 140 B6
Strawberry Cres TR15 . . . . 140 B6
Strawberry Fields
  Crowlas TR20 . . . . 89 B7
  Mitchell TR8 . . . . 56 F5
  Redruth TR15 . . . . 140 E1
Strawberry Gdns TR16 . . . . 140 E1
Strawberry La Hayle TR27 . 142 D4
  Lelant TR26 . . . . 77 E4
  Redruth TR15 . . . . 140 B6
Stray Park Ct TR14 . . . . . . 138 E2
Stray Park Rd TR14 . . . . . . 138 E2
Stray Park Way TR14 . . . . . 138 F2
Street-an-Garrow 17
  TR26 . . . . 141 B5
Street-an-Pol 3 TR26 . . . . 141 B5
Stret Caradoc TR7 . . . . 110 D5
Stret Constantine TR7 . . . . 110 C5
Stret Dor Wartha 3 TR7 . . 111 D4
Stret Euther Penndragon 1
  TR7 . . . . 111 E5
Stret Goryan
  Trencreek TR8 . . . . 111 D5
  5 Trencreek TR8 . . . . 111 D5
Stret Grifles TR7 . . . . 111 E5

Stret Kosti Veur Woles TR7 111 D6
Stret Lugan TR7 111 E5
Stret Myghtern Arthur TR8 111 D5
Stret Rosemelin TR1 137 F6
Stret Trystan TR7 111 E5
Stretyn 5 TR3 81 F7
Strickland Cotts 6 TR18 143 C2
Stringers Hill TR20 88 A5
Strode Rd PL7 130 F6
Stroma Cl PL6 124 F7
Stroud Park Rd PL2 128 C7
Stuart House Arts & Heritage Ctr★ PL14 113 C5
Stuart Rd PL3 148 A4
Stuart Road Prim Sch PL1 148 A4
Stuarts Way PL12 53 E5
Stucley Rd EX23 4 D1
Sturdee Rd PL2 128 A5
Stursdon Cross EX23 5 A8
Sturta La PL30 48 D4
Sugar Mill Bsns Pk PL9 129 C1
SUMMERCOURT 57 C7
Summercourt TR10 144 D7
Summercourt Prim Sch TR8 57 C7
Summerfield Cl PL26 73 B3
Summerfields PL12 122 D1
Summer Gn 2 PL19 30 A3
Summerheath TR10 81 C1
Summerhill Rd PL15 106 A5
Summer La PL13 62 D6
Summerlands Cl PL7 131 C5
Summerlands Gdns PL7 131 C5
Summerlane Pk PL13 62 D6
Summerleaze Ave EX23 104 D7
Summerleaze Cres EX23 104 D6
Summers Cl PL6 129 B7
Summers La PL24 60 B8
Summers St PL22 112 C2
Summerville Cross EX39 3 C6
Suncrest PL14 38 A4
Suncrest Est TR9 45 E1
Sunderland Cl PL9 135 A6
Sunderland Rd PL27 31 F3
Sun Girt La PL14 113 C5
Sunningdale TR1 137 A4
Sunningdale Rd PL12 122 C2
Sunnybank 23 TR13 98 C8
Sunny Bank Bodmin PL30 48 E8
Liskeard PL14 113 A4
Sunnybanks PL12 53 E4
Sunny Cnr Goldsithney TR20 89 F5
Truro TR4 81 B7
Sunny Corner La TR19 96 C7
Sunnycroft PL13 117 C3
Sunny Dene PL5 123 D1
Sunnyside PL11 64 F7
Carnkie TR13 80 D1
Crantock TR8 110 A3
Menheniot PL14 51 F5
Menheniot PL14 52 B5
2 Perranporth TR6 55 A4
Portscatho TR2 83 B2
7 Redruth TR15 140 B4
Sunnyside Mdw PL32 105 D4
Sunnyside Parc TR15 139 C8
Sunnyside Rd PL4 129 B2
Sunny Terr TR18 143 B2
Sunnyvale Cl TR16 67 C6
Sunnyvale Rd TR16 67 D6
Sunrise Hill TR16 80 E8
Sunrising Est PL13 117 D5
Sunset Dr 8 TR13 98 C8
Sunset Gdns 9 TR13 98 C8
Sun Valley Pk TR9 45 E6
Sunway Cl PL19 147 A6
Sunwell La Antony PL11 65 E4
St John PL11 132 A8
Surf View TR7 110 A6
Sussex Pl PL1 148 C2
Sussex Rd PL2 127 F5
Sussex St PL1 148 C2
Sussex Terr 5 PL2 127 F5
Sutherland Rd PL4 149 A4
Sutton Ct PL1 127 F1
Sutton Mews 22 PL4 149 A2
Sutton Pl PL4 149 B2
Sutton Rd PL4 149 B2
Sutton Wharf PL4 149 A2
Swaindale Rd 3 PL3 128 E6
Swale Cl PL3 129 B6
Swallow Cl EX23 104 D5
Swallowfield Cl PL24 60 D5
Swallow Ho 13 TR11 145 C3
Swallows End PL9 135 E8
Swan Cl PL10 133 A6
Swan Gdns PL7 130 F5
Swanpool Ave TR10 144 A8
Swanpool Ct TR11 145 A1
Swanpool Hill TR11 145 A2
Swanpool Nature Reserve★ TR11 145 A2
Swanpool Rd TR11 144 F1
Swanpool St TR11 145 C3
Swans Reach 1 TR11 144 F1
SWANVALE 144 F3
Swanvale Rd TR11 144 F3
Sweet Briar Cres TR7 111 A4
Sweetshouse Rd PL22 112 A2
Swift Gdns PL5 124 C2
Swinburne Gdns PL5 124 C1
Swingate Cross EX22 13 E8
Sycamore Ave
Plymouth PL4 149 C2
St Austell PL25 114 E5
Tavistock PL19 147 C2
Sycamore Cl Bodmin PL31 109 B4
Polgooth PL26 59 A1
Praze-an-Beeble TR14 79 B2
Rock PL27 21 E3
Sycamore Dr Illogan TR15 139 D7
Plymouth PL6 125 C7
Redruth TR15 140 D5
Torpoint PL11 127 A3
Trispen TR4 56 D1
Sycamore Gdns TR8 57 B7
Sycamore Rd PL12 122 B3
Sycamores The PL25 114 C4
Sycamore Way PL6 125 E6
Sydenham Cross PL19 29 C2
SYDENHAM DAMEREL 29 D2
Sydney Cl Plymouth PL7 130 E4
St Austell PL25 114 C3
Sydney Rd Newquay TR7 110 D6
Torpoint PL11 127 B3
Sydney St PL1 148 B4
Sylvan Cl PL25 114 E6
Sylvan Ct PL1 128 A3
Sylverton Pl 12 TR18 143 C7
Symons Cl Blackwater TR4 68 E5
St Austell PL25 115 A5
Symons Hill TR11 145 A5
Symons Rd PL12 122 F2
Symons Row PL14 37 F3
Symons Terr TR15 140 B5
Syra Cl PL30 23 B2

T

Tabernacle St TR1 137 D4
Tackbear Rd EX22, EX23 7 E4
Tailyour Rd PL6 124 F2
Talbot Gdns PL5 127 D7
Talexandra Terr PL15 106 D5
Talgarrek Wartha 4 TR1 137 B2
Talgos Cl TR16 140 E8
TALLAND 62 F2
Talland Ct 20 TR26 141 B5
Talland Hill PL13 62 E2
Talland Rd TR26 141 B5
Talland St PL13 62 D1
Tall Ships Cl 2 TR11 144 F2
Tally Ho 6 TR20 88 B7
Talmena Ave PL27 108 A5
TALSKIDDY 45 E8
Talveneth Camborne TR14 138 F3
Pendeen TR19 75 A1
Redruth TR15 140 C6
Talvenydh Ct PL31 109 D5
Tamar Ave Plymouth PL2 127 E5
Tavistock PL19 147 D5
Tamar Bridge PL5 123 A2
Tamar Bsns Pk PL15 18 E2
Tamar Cl 18 Bere Alston PL20 41 B1
29 Callington PL17 39 F4
Tamar Ho PL1 127 E1
Tamarisk Cl PL28 31 F7
Tamarisk La TR7 111 A4
Tamar Otter & Wildlife Ctr★ PL15 18 B8
Tamar Science Pk PL6 125 C4
Tamarside Sp Complex PL5 123 F2
Tamar St Plymouth PL1 127 E3
Saltash PL12 123 A2
Torpoint PL11 127 C3
Tamar Terr Calstock PL17 41 A3
Horsebridge PL19 29 C1
Launceston PL15 106 D5
Saltash PL12 123 A2
Tamar Valley Ctr★ PL18 40 F5
Tamar Valley Discovery Trail★ Pl20 41 C1
Tamar Valley Donkey Pk★ PL18 40 D5
Tamar View
Launceston PL15 106 D5
Milton Abbot PL19 29 C6
St Dominick PL12 40 D2
Tamar View Ind Est PL12 122 D5
Tamar Villas PL9 135 D7
Tamar Way PL18 41 A6
Tamar Wharf PL1 127 D3
Tamblin Ave PL14 50 E7
Tamerton Ave PL5 123 D1
Tamerton Cl PL5 124 A6
TAMERTON FOLIOT 124 B7
Tamerton Foliot Rd PL6 124 D5
Tamerton Hill EX22 13 A8
Tamerton Rd PL6 121 B2
Ta Mill Rd PL15 16 D4
Tangmere Ave PL5 123 E5
Tangye Cl TR16 67 E5
Tangye Rd TR15 139 C6
Tanhouse Rd PL22 112 C2
Tanners La TR3 81 C5
Tanwood La Bodmin PL31 34 E2
Bodmin PL31 109 A6
Tanwood View PL31 109 C5
Tanyard La 19 PL17 39 E4
Tapson Dr PL9 135 A6
Taranto Rd TR13 146 D4
Taroveor Rd TR18 143 E6
Taroveor Terr 3 TR18 143 E5
Tarr PL22 49 E3
Tarrandean La TR3 81 E6
Tarten Cross PL12 53 B4
Tate St Ives (Gall)★ TR26 141 B6
Taunton Ave PL5 124 B5
Taunton Pl PL5 124 B5
Taurus St PL9 136 E8
Tavern Barn PL23 116 C5
TAVISTOCK 147 E5
Tavistock Coll PL19 147 A3
Tavistock Community Hospital PL19 147 B5
Tavistock Com Prim Sch PL19 147 B4
Tavistock Cross PL20 41 C2
Tavistock Mus★ PL19 147 C5
Tavistock Pl PL4 149 A3
Tavistock Rd Callington PL17 39 F4
Launceston PL15 106 D5
Launceston, Stourscombe PL15 106 E3
Plymouth PL6 125 B5
Plymouth Manadon PL5 124 E1
Yelverton PL20 42 C3
Tavistock St Peter's CE Jun Sch PL19 147 D5
Tavy Pl PL4 128 F4
Tavy Rd Saltash PL12 123 A3
Tavistock PL19 147 D5
Taw Cl PL3 129 D6
Tawna La PL30 36 B2
Tayberry Dr TR16 140 F1
Tay Gdns PL3 129 D7
Taylor Cl PL12 122 C3
Taylor Rd PL12 122 C4
Taylor's Cross EX23 5 B7
Taylors La Legonna TR8 44 C2
Legonna TR8 111 C2
Taylor Sq PL19 147 B6
Teason Hill Trezance PL30 35 F4
Trezance PL30 35 F4
Teats Hill Flats PL4 149 B1
Teats Hill Rd PL4 149 B1
Tedder Rd 4 PL26 59 D7
Tees Cl PL3 129 C7
Teetotal St TR26 141 C6
Tehidy Cl TR14 138 F7
Tehidy Copse TR14 67 B4
Tehidy Country Park★ TR14 67 B4
Tehidy Gdns TR14 138 F7
Tehidy Mill TR14 138 E7
Tehidy Rd Camborne TR14 138 D4
Tywardreath PL24 60 D5
Tehidy Terr TR11 145 A6
Teign Rd PL3 129 B6
Telcarne Cl TR27 78 D6
Telegraph Hill TR16 68 E1
Telegraph St TR16 68 D1
Telegraph Wharf PL1 134 A8
Telephone La PL26 59 C8
Telford Cres PL5 123 F2
Temeraire Rd PL5 124 D2
TEMPLE 36 B8
Tenacres La PL14 38 E4
Tenby Rd PL5 123 C1
TENCREEK 63 A3
Tencreek Ave TR18 143 E5
Tenderah Ct TR13 146 C7
Tenderah Rd TR13 146 C6
Tennyson Gdns PL5 124 B1
Tern Gdns PL7 130 F5
Terrace The Chacewater TR4 68 F3
Crafthole PL11 65 B5
Dobwalls PL14 50 D7
Downderry PL11 64 C5
East Portholland PL26 84 E5
Harrowbarrow PL17 40 D5
Penryn TR10 144 C7
Pentewan PL26 73 D6
Port Isaac PL29 22 E7
Portwrinkle PL11 65 A4
Rock PL27 21 D2
St Ives TR26 141 B5
Yeolmbridge PL15 18 E6
Terra Nova Gn PL2 128 B5
TERRAS 58 A4
Terras Hill PL22 112 C3
Terras Rd PL26 58 A4
TETCOTT 13 C7
Tethadene PL30 23 E7
Tewedh Pl 4 PL27 21 E3
Tewington Pl PL25 114 B4
Tewkesbury Cl PL2 128 A8
Tewynn Ct TR27 142 E8
Teyla Tor Rd TR26 141 D1
Thackeray Gdns PL5 124 B1
Thames Gdns PL3 129 D5
Thanckes Cl PL11 127 A3
Thanckes Dr PL11 127 A4
The All Saints CE Academy PL5 124 B1
Theatre Ope PL1 127 F1
Theatre Royal Plymouth PL1 148 C2
The Bank TR27 71 C6
The Bay Holiday Complex★ PL13 63 A2
The Beeches PL18 40 D5
The Bishops CE Prim Sch TR7 110 F4
The Carn TR14 79 D1
The Coach Ho 14 TR10 144 D7
The Crescent PL25 114 E4
The Cross 10 PL14 38 E4
The Drive PL26 114 F1
The Glebe 11 PL14 37 F3
The Hayes TR1 137 E6
The Level Ponjeravah TR11 92 F4
Treviades TR11 93 A4
The Lizard TR12 102 F3
The Meadow TR3 81 D5
The Moors TR13 98 B8
The Oaks 3 PL15 27 B7
The Quarry 13 TR2 83 B2
The Quay TR5 54 D2
Therlow Rd PL3 129 B6
The Roseland Com Coll TR2 72 A4
The Shrubberies 26 TR13 98 C8
The Sidings PL25 114 E3
Nancegollan TR13 91 B7
The Straight Billacott PL15 12 C1
Navarino PL15 18 A8
Thetford Gdns PL6 129 D8
The Village PL19 29 C6
The Wharf EX23 104 D5
Theydon Rd TR11 144 F3
Third Ave
Plymouth, Billacombe PL9 130 A1
Plymouth, Camels Head PL2 127 E7
Plymouth, Stoke PL1 128 A2
Thirlmere Gdns PL6 124 F4
Thistle Cl PL6 125 E7
Thomas Bullock Cl PL30 48 C2
Thomas Johnson Ct 6 TR1 137 C4
Thomas La PL4 149 B4
Thomas St 4 TR13 98 C8
Thomas Terr 5 TR13 98 C8
Thornberry Terr TR18 143 F6
Thornbury Park Ave PL3 128 D6
Thornbury Prim Sch PL6 125 D4
Thornbury Rd PL6 125 E4
Thorn Cl PL15 26 C7
Thorndon Cross EX22 8 F5
Thorne Cross EX23 4 F2
THORNE MOOR 19 F8
Thorney Wlk 1 PL27 108 C6
Thornhill Rd PL3 128 E6
Thornhill Way PL3 128 E6
Thorn La PL12 122 C3
Thorn Moor Cross PL15 19 F7
Thornpark Rd PL25 114 E5
Thorn Pk PL3 128 F5
Thorn Terr PL14 113 B5
Thornton Ave PL4 149 B4
Thornton Cl PL26 46 F3
Thornville Terr PL9 135 C7
Thornwell La PL12 53 E2
Thornyville Cl PL9 135 C8
Thornyville Dr PL9 135 D8
Thornyville Villas PL9 135 C8
Three Bridges Specl Sch 1 TR10 144 C8
THREE BURROWS 68 F5
Three Corners Cl PL32 105 B2
Three Cross TR13 91 F5
THREE HAMMERS 17 C6
Three Holes Cross PL27 34 A8
THREEMILESTONE 69 D4
Threemilestone Ind Est TR4 69 C3
Threemilestone Ret Pk TR3 69 C4
Threemilestone Sch TR3 69 D3
THREEWATERS 34 C1
THURDON 5 D5
Thurlestone Wlk PL6 129 D8
Tichbarrow Rd
Davidstow PL15 16 A6
Hendra PL32 15 F7
Tiddy Brook Rd
Tavistock PL19 147 E2
Whitchurch PL19 147 E2
Tiddy Cl St Germans PL12 65 B8
Tavistock PL19 147 B3
TIDEFORD 52 F2
Tideford Cross La PL12 52 F3
Tideford Dr Landrake PL12 53 A2
St Germans PL12 65 B8
Tideford Rd PL12 53 C3
Tidemill Ho TR11 145 C3
Tides Reach TR7 111 B7
Tillard Cl PL7 131 C5
Tillie St 5 PL17 39 E4
Tilly Cl PL9 135 F4
Timber Cl PL25 114 B4
Tincombe PL12 122 C2
Tincroft Rd TR15 139 B4
Tin Hut La EX23 10 E7
Tin La PL4 149 A2
Tinners Croft TR8 56 B7
Tinners Dr PL27 21 D6
Tinners La PL14 36 F3
Tinners Way
Boslowick TR11 144 F2
Callington PL17 39 F5
New Polzeath PL27 21 D6
16 St Ives TR26 77 A6
Tinners Wlk TR11 145 D3
Tinney Dr TR1 137 F5
Tinney Hall La PL15 27 B7
Tinside Lido PL1 148 C1
TINTAGEL 14 D7
Tintagel Castle★ PL34 14 B8
Tintagel Cres PL2 128 C8
Tintagel Hts PL34 14 D6
Tintagel Old Post Office★ PL34 14 C7
Tintagel Prim Sch PL34 14 C6
Tintagel Rd PL35 9 C1
Tintagel Terr PL29 22 D7
Tintagel Toy Mus★ PL34 14 C7
Tintagel Visitor Ctr★ PL34 14 C7
Tintern Ave PL4 149 C2
Tiny Mdws Launceston PL15 18 E1
South Petherwin PL15 27 F8
Tipple Cross PL15 19 C6
Titan Ave 19 PL9 136 E8
Titchsborough Hill PL15 16 A8
Tithe Rd PL7 130 B7
TITSON 7 D4
Tiverton Cl PL6 125 B8
Toads Hole PL26 46 D2
Tobruk Rd PL12 122 E3
Toby Way TR7 110 D7
Todda Cl PL15 25 E3
Toddington Lea PL26 58 E5
TODPOOL 68 F2
TOLBOROUGH 25 E4
TOLCARNE Camborne 79 D5
Newlyn 143 C3
Tolcarne TR16 80 E8
Tolcarne Cl PL25 114 E3
Tolcarne La Tolcarne TR13 80 A1
Tregurrian TR8 44 E8
Trevarrian TR8 31 C1
Tolcarne Mews 7 TR7 110 F6
Tolcarne Rd Camborne TR14 79 D5
Newquay TR7 110 F6
St Day TR16 68 D1
Tolcarne PL15 26 F5
Tolcarne St TR14 138 D2
Tolcarne Terr TR18 143 C3
Tolcrows Ct TR7 111 C7
TOLDISH 45 F2
Toldish La TR9 45 E2
Tolgarrick Rd TR14 138 F5
Tolgus Illogan TR15 67 F3
Tolskithy TR15 139 F8
Tolgus Hill TR15 140 A5
TOLGUS MOUNT 139 E8
Tolgus Mount TR15 139 F8
Tolgus Pl TR15 140 A6
Tolgus Tin★ TR16 67 F5
Tolgus Vean TR15 140 A5
Tolgus Wartha TR15 140 A6
Tollgate Cl PL14 113 B4
Tollgate Rd PL31 35 B1
Tollox Pl PL3 129 B4
Tollyfrank Hill TR2 83 F6
Tolmennor TR13 90 F4
Tolpedn Flats TR26 141 E2
Tolponds Rd TR13 91 A1
Tolroy Rd TR27 142 D1
TOLSKITHY 139 E7
Tolskithy La TR15 139 E6
Tolticken Hill TR16 67 E6
Toltuff Cres TR18 143 C4
Toltuff Rd TR18 143 C4
TOLVADDON 138 F6
Tolvaddon Reskadinnick TR14 79 D8
Tolvaddon TR14 138 F6
Tolvaddon Bsns Pk TR14 139 A7
TOLVADDON DOWNS 139 A7
Tolvaddon Energy Pk TR14 138 F7
Tolvaddon Rd TR15 139 A5
Tolvan Cross TR12 92 C2
Tolver Pl TR18 143 E6
Tolver Rd TR18 143 E6
Tolverth Terr TR20 88 F6
Tolview Terr TR27 142 B4
Tom Lyon Rd PL14 113 E5
Tom Nicolls Cl 7 PL14 38 A3
Tom Putt Mews 6 PL14 113 D7
Top Hill TR2 57 E1
Top of the Town Ctyd PL12 122 F2
Top Rd PL11 64 C5
Torbridge Cl PL12 122 D2
Tor Bridge High PL6 125 D2
Tor Bridge Prim Sch PL6 125 D2
Torbridge Rd
6 Horrabridge PL20 42 C4
Plymouth PL7 130 E6
Torbryan Cl PL6 129 E8
Tor Cl Plymouth, Hartley PL3 128 E7
Porthleven TR13 91 B1
Tor Cres PL3 128 E7
Torland Rd PL3 128 E7
Torleven Rd TR13 91 B2
TORPOINT 127 C3
Torpoint Com Coll PL11 127 A4
Torpoint Nur & Inf Sch PL11 127 B3
Tor Rd Newquay TR7 110 E6
Plymouth PL3 128 E7
Torridge Cl PL7 131 A6
Torridge Rd PL7 130 F6
Torridge Way PL3 129 C5
Torr La PL3 128 E7
Torr Rd PL3 128 E7
Torr View Ave PL3 128 D7
Tors View Cl PL17 39 F4
Torver Cl PL6 125 D2
Tor View Bugle PL26 47 C2
Camelford PL32 105 C2
7 Horrabridge PL20 42 C4
Tregadillett PL15 18 C2
Torwood Cl PL31 109 D4
Tory TR3 81 A3
Tory Brook Ave PL7 130 E6
Tory Brook Ct PL7 130 E6
Tory Way PL7 130 D6
TOSBERRY 3 B8
Tosberry Cross EX39 3 B8
Tothill Ave PL4 149 B3
Tothill Rd PL4 149 B3
Totnes Cl PL7 131 B4
Tottertown La Lampen PL14 36 F2
Polventon PL14 37 A1
Touch Me Pipes TR12 101 B3
Tovey Cres PL5 124 D2
Towan Blystra Rd TR7 111 A5
TOWAN CROSS 68 B7
Towan Ct PL28 31 E8
Towan Rd Pentewan PL26 73 D8
Porthtowan TR4 68 A7
Trevear PL28 31 E8

Towans The PL28.........20 D1
Towans View TR27 .....78 D6
TOWEDNACK 76 E5
Towednack Rd TR26 .....77 A6
Tower Cl Pelynt PL13 .....62 D6
  Sennen TR19 ....96 B6
Tower Ct PL12.........122 C2
Towerfield Dr PL6.....125 C8
Tower Hill Looe PL13 .....117 D3
  Wadebridge PL27 ....108 E5
Tower Hill Gdns **12** PL31 ..109 E5
Tower Hill Rd PL15 .....13 F1
Tower Mdws TR19.........97 A6
Tower Park Est PL13.....62 E6
Tower Park Rd PL13 .....62 C6
Tower Pk Fowey PL23.....116 B3
  Lanivet PL30 ....47 E7
  Pelynt PL13 ....62 D6
Tower Rd Newquay TR7 .....110 D6
  St Erme TR4 ....70 D8
Towers Cl PL6 ....125 F2
Tower St PL15.........106 C6
Tower View PL12.........122 D1
Town Arms Pas PL31 .....109 E5
Town End PL31.........109 C5
Town Farm TR15 ....140 C3
Town Farm Cl **5** PL20 .....42 C4
Townfield PL15.........139 C6
Town Hill TR5 ....54 D1
TOWNLAKE 29 C1
Town Mill Gdns PL19 .....147 C6
Town Mills Cl **7** PL15.....106 A7
Town Mills Flats PL15.....106 B7
Town Quay 137 D4
Townsend Polruan PL23....116 D2
  14 Stratton EX23 ....4 E1
TOWNSHEND 90 D7
Townshend Ave PL2 .....127 E5
Townswell Cl PL12 .....53 E2
Townswell La PL12 .....53 E2
TRABOE 100 E4
Traboe Cross TR12 ....100 D3
Tracey Ct PL1 ....148 B3
Track Pot Rd PL30 ....22 E4
Tradewinds Cl **10** PL31.....109 A5
Trafalar Fields TR20 ....88 B7
Trafalgar Cl PL5.........127 D8
Trafalgar Fields TR20.........88 B7
Trafalgar Pl **3** PL1.....127 F3
Trafalgar Place La PL1.....127 F3
Trafalgar Sq TR1 ....137 D4
Trafalgar St PL4 ....149 A3
Traine Brake PL9 ....136 C1
Traine Rd PL9 ....136 B1
Traly Cl EX23 ....104 F4
TRAMAGENNA 105 A1
Tram Cross La TR16 ....140 D1
Tram La TR16.........140 E1
Tramway Rd PL6 ....125 E7
TRANNACK 91 D5
Trannack Com Prim Sch
  TR13 ....91 E5
Trannack Mill Ind Est TR13 .91 E5
Trannack Rd TR20 ....87 D5
Trannack Terr TR18 ....143 E7
Tranquil La PL31 ....109 C5
Transit Way PL5.........124 C3
Trasdeves Orch **18** PL17... 39 F4
Travers Cl PL14.........113 A6
Treago Gdns PL6 ....125 C8
Treago Rd TR8 ....43 D3
TREAL 103 A6
Trease **3** TR19 ....75 A1
Treassowe Mews TR20.....88 F8
Treassowe Rd TR18.........143 E6
Treassowe Riding TR20.....88 F8
TREATH 93 C1
TREATOR 107 A5
Treator Cotts PL28.........107 A5
Trebah TR11 ....93 D2
Trebah Gdns ✱ TR11.........93 C2
Treban Rd TR18 ....143 C4
TREBARBER 44 F5
TREBARTHA 27 A4
Trebartha Cl PL17 ....39 E3
Trebartha Rd TR1 ....137 F5
Trebarthen Terr TR4.........55 D5
Trebarva Cl TR15 ....140 A6
TREBARVAH.........89 E4
Trebarvah Cl **1** TR11 .....92 E4
Trebarvah Ct **2** TR11 .....92 E4
Trebarvah La TR11 ....92 E4
  3 Brill TR11 ....92 E4
  Rosudgeon TR20 ....89 E4
Trebarvah Rd TR11 ....92 E4
Trebarvah Woon TR11.....92 C4
TREBARWITH 14 C5
Trebarwith Cres TR7 ....110 E6
Trebarwith Rd PL33 ....14 D4
TREBEATH 17 F6
Trebeath Ln PL15.........17 E6
Treberran Gdns TR14.....138 F6
TREBETHERICK 21 D4
Trebost La TR12 ....81 A5
  Trembroath TR16.........80 F5
Treboul Cross PL12.........64 F8
Treboul Way PL12 ....65 B8
Trebray Rd PL15 ....16 E1
TREBUDANNON 45 C4
TREBULLETT 28 A5
Treburdon Dr PL26 ....46 F3
TREBURGETT 23 D6
Treburgie Water PL14.....50 D7
Treburick La PL27 ....32 B7
TREBURLEY 28 C4

Treburley Cl PL15 ....28 C4
Treburley Ind Est PL15 .....28 C4
TREBURRICK 31 D5
Tebursye Rd PL15 ....18 E3
TREBYAN 48 C6
Trebyan Bsns Pk PL30.........48 C6
Trebyhan Parc TR3 ....80 F3
Treby Rd PL7 ....130 F4
Trecarn Cl PL15 ....106 B5
Trecarne TR1 ....137 E5
Trecarne Cl Polgooth PL26 ...59 A1
  St Austell PL25.........115 B5
  Truro TR1.........137 E5
Trecarne Gdns PL33.........14 E3
Trecarne La **10** PL14.........38 A3
Trecarne View PL14.........37 F3
Trecarrack Rd TR14 ....138 F3
Trecarrell Launceston PL15 106 C4
  1 Scarne PL15.........106 D4
Trecerus Ind Est PL28.........107 B4
Treclago View PL32.........105 C2
Trecombe TR11 ....93 C4
TRECROGO 27 E7
Treculliacks TR11 ....92 D6
Tredanek Cl PL31.........109 B5
Tredannick Hill PL27 ....34 A6
Tredarrup Cross PL15.........11 A1
Tredarvah Dr TR18 ....143 C5
Tredarvah Rd TR18 ....143 C5
TREDAVOE 143 A2
Tredavoe La TR18 ....143 B1
Tredenham Cl **4** PL24.....60 C4
Tredenham Rd TR2 ....95 B6
TREDETHY 34 F6
Tredethy Hill PL30.........34 E6
Tredethy Rd PL30.........34 F6
TREDINNICK Looe 63 A8
  Penzance.........76 A1
  St Issey.........32 D5
Tredinnick Cotts TR20.........76 A1
Tredinnick La PL12 ....53 B2
Tredinnick Lane-End PL13. 64 A8
Tredinnick Rd PL27.........32 E4
Tredinnick Way **12** TR6.....55 A4
Tredinnick Wood Cl TR13 146 D8
Tredis Vw PL11 ....65 B5
Tredore La PL27 ....32 D7
Tredour Rd TR7 ....110 E4
Tredova Cres TR11 ....145 B2
TREDOWN 2 E5
Tredragon Cl TR8 ....31 C2
Tredragon Rd TR8.........31 C2
Tredrea Gdns TR3 ....81 D5
Tredrea La TR27 ....77 E2
Tredrea Manor TR3.........81 D5
TREDRIZZICK 21 F4
Tredrizzick Cl PL27 ....21 F3
Tredruston Rd PL27 ....33 B6
Tredydan Rd PL15.........106 B6
Tredynas Rd TR11 ....145 D3
Tredyson Pl TR11 ....145 A3
Tre-el-Verne Cl TR1.........137 A4
TREEN Porthcurno 96 F3
  Zennor.........75 F4
Treen Cotts TR26 ....75 F4
Treen Flats TR14 ....138 F3
Treen Hill TR19.........96 F4
TREESMILL 60 D6
Treetop Cl PL12 ....122 D4
Treetops Hill PL13 ....117 A3
Treeve La TR27 ....78 C6
Treeve Lane Ind Est TR27....78 C6
TREFANNY HILL 62 D8
Treffry Ct TR7 ....110 D6
Treffry La PL30 ....48 C6
Treffry Rd TR1 ....137 E7
Treffry Way **12** PL24.....60 B4
Trefinnick Rd PL17 ....39 B8
Trefleur Cl **3** PL35 ....9 C1
Trefloyd Cl PL17.........39 E6
TREFOFDA 24 A8
Treforda Rd TR4 ....110 F4
Treforest Rd PL27 ....108 A6
Treforthlan **7** TR16 ....67 E4
Treforthlan Cl **6** TR16.....67 E4
Trefrank Rd PL15.........16 F4
TREFREW 105 D6
Trefrew Rd PL32.........105 D5
TREFRIZE 27 E3
Trefrize La PL15 ....27 E3
Trefula Redruth TR16 ....68 C1
  Trefula TR16.........140 E5
Trefusis Cl TR1 ....137 F5
Trefusis Ct TR1 ....145 A6
Trefusis Gdns PL3.........129 A5
Trefusis Rd Falmouth TR11 .144 E2
  Flushing TR11.........145 C6
  Redruth TR15.........140 C4
Trefusis Terr
  Millbrook PL10.........132 E6
  Redruth TR15.........140 C5
Tregaddock La PL30 ....34 E8
TREGADILLETT 18 C2
Tregadillett Comm Prim Sch
  PL15 ....18 C2
Tregaer TR11.........145 C3
Tregainlands Pk PL30.........34 D3
TREGAJORRAN 139 D4
Tregalister Gdns PL12 .....65 B8
Tregaller La PL15.........18 E1
Tregallon Rd PL30.........34 C7
TREGAMERE 45 F7
Treganoon Rd TR15.........140 D7
Tregargus View PL26.........58 B4
TREGARLAND 63 C8
Tregarland Cl
  Camborne TR14.........138 E2

Tregarland Cl continued
  Coad's Green PL15 ....27 D4
Tregarne Terr PL25.........114 C4
Tregarrek Cl PL26 ....46 F3
Tregarrian Rd TR14.........138 F7
Tregarrick Cl TR13 ....117 B3
Tregarrick Cl TR13 ....146 D6
Tregarrick Ct PL13 ....117 B3
Tregarrick La PL13 ....62 D6
TREGARRICK MILL 62 D7
Tregarrick Rd PL26 ....46 F3
Tregarrick View TR13.........146 D6
Tregarrick Way PL13 .....62 D6
Tregarth **12** PL26 ....59 D7
Tregartha Way PL14.........113 D6
Tregarthen **2** St Ives TR26 141 A5
  Tregarthen TR20 ....88 F7
  Varfell TR20.........89 A7
Tregarth Pl TR18 ....143 C4
Tregaskes Parc EX23 ....104 F5
Tregassack Rd TR1 ....137 C5
Tregassick Rd TR2 ....83 B1
Tregastick La PL13 ....51 F2
TREGASWITH 45 C5
Tregaswith Rd TR8 ....45 C5
Tregatherall La PL35 ....15 C7
TREGATTA 14 C6
TREGAVARRAS 85 A5
Tregavarras Row PL26.........85 A5
Tregavethan View TR3.........69 C4
Tregay La PL14 ....113 C7
Tregeagle Rd PL26 ....47 A2
Tregea Hill TR16.........67 C6
Tregear Cl TR12 ....99 D6
TREGEARE 17 D5
Tregeare Rd PL15 ....17 E5
Tregear Gdns TR1 ....137 C4
Tregear Hill Polmassick PL26 72 F4
  Treworrick TR2.........84 F8
Tregease Rd TR5 ....54 C1
Tregea Terr TR16.........67 C6
Tregeath La PL34 ....14 D6
Tregella La Tregella PL28 ...32 B8
  Tregella PL28.........107 A2
Tregellas Cl **10** TR15 ....54 C1
Tregellas Rd TR12 ....99 B1
Tregellas Tapastry The ✱ **12**
  TR15.........140 B4
Tregellast Cl TR12.........101 D4
Tregellast Parc TR12 ....101 D4
Tregellast Rd TR12.........101 D3
TREGELLIST 22 E4
Tregembo Hill TR20 ....90 A7
Tregender La TR20 ....89 B8
Tregender Rd TR20.........89 B8
Tregenna Cl Plymouth PL7. .131 C4
  Wainhouse Corner EX23 ...10 F6
Tregenna Ct
  Camborne TR14.........138 C2
  Falmouth TR11.........145 C3
Tregenna Fields TR14 ....138 C2
Tregenna Hill **16** TR26 .....141 B5
Tregenna La TR14 ....138 C2
Tregenna Parc TR26 ....141 C3
Tregenna Pl **4** TR26 ....141 B5
Tregenna Rd PL30.........35 C8
Tregenna Terr TR26 ....141 B5
Tregenver La TR11 ....144 F4
Tregenver Rd TR11 ....144 F4
Tregenver Terr TR11 ....144 F4
Tregenver Villas TR11 ....144 F4
TREGESEAL 86 F7
Tregeseal Hill TR19.........86 F7
Tregeseal Row TR19.........86 F6
Tregeseal Terr TR19 ....86 F6
TREGFGW 145 B8
Tregew Cl TR11.........145 B7
Tregew Ct **3** TR14.........138 D4
Tregew Rd Flushing TR11.....145 B8
  Penryn TR10, TR11.........81 F2
Treggoddick Cotts TR20 .....143 A8
Tregian Cl TR1 ....137 F5
Tregidden TR12 ....100 E5
Tregidden Hill
  Lesneague TR12.........101 A5
  St Martin TR12.........100 F5
Tregie TR18 ....143 B3
Tregildry La TR12.........101 C1
Tregirls La Trethellick PL28 ..21 B3
  Trethillick PL28.........107 C6
TREGISKEY 73 C5
Tregiskey Cotts PL26 ....73 C5
Tregisky La TR1.........101 C1
Treglenwith Rd TR14 ....138 C4
Treglines La Gunnverna PL27 .22 A6
  Polzeath PL27.........21 F5
Treglisson Rural Workshops
  TR27.........78 C3
Treglyn Cl TR18 ....143 B1
Treglyn Farm Cotts PL27....22 B3
Tregoddick St TR20.........88 B7
Tregoide La PL30.........23 C3
Tregolds La St Merryn PL28...31 F7
  Tregolds PL27.........32 C6
  Tregolds PL28.........31 F7
TREGOLE 6 E1
TREGOLLS 80 F3
Tregolls Cl TR1.........137 E5
Tregolls Hill PL30.........33 C2
Tregolls Rd Tregustick PL30 .33 D1
  Truro TR1.........137 E5
Tregolls Sch TR1.........137 E5
TREGONCE 107 F2
TREGONETHA 45 D5
Tregoney Ct **13** PL26.........85 D8
Tregoney Hill PL26 ....73 C3
Tregongeeves La PL26.........59 A2

TREGONHAWKE 132 B4
Tregonhay PL14 ....38 C7
Tregonhayne Ct TR2.........72 A4
Tregoniggie Ind Est TR11. .144 D4
Tregoning Rd PL11 ....126 F2
Tregonissey Cl PL25.........114 D5
Tregonissey Rd PL25 ....114 E5
Tregonissy La End PL25....114 E6
TREGONNA 32 C7
Tregonna Hill Tregonna PL27 32 C7
  Tregonna PL27.........32 C7
Tregonnett La PL17 ....39 B5
Tregonning Cl TR13 ....90 E3
Tregonning Ct **8** TR6.........55 A5
Tregonning Hill TR13 ....90 E4
Tregonning La TR13.........90 E3
Tregonning Parc **10** TR12 .101 C4
Tregonning Rd TR3.........80 F3
Tregonning Terr TR13.........90 F5
Tregonning View **17** TR13 ..90 F5
TREGONY 71 F4
Tregony Com Prim Sch TR2 71 F4
Tregony Hill TR2 ....71 F3
Tregony Ind Est TR2.........71 E3
Tregony Rd TR2 ....71 D6
TREGOODWELL 105 F4
Tregorden La Bodieve PL27 .33 F8
  Tregorden PL27.........22 E1
  Trevarner PL27.........108 F8
Tregorden Mine La
  Bodieve PL27.........33 F8
  Trevarner PL27.........108 E8
TREGORRICK 114 D1
Tregorrick Pk (St Austell RFC)
  PL26.........114 D1
Tregorrick Rd PL26.........114 E1
Tregos Rd TR26 ....141 C2
TREGOSS 46 D3
Tregoss Moor PL26 ....46 E3
Tregoss Rd TR7 ....110 F6
Tregothnan Rd
  Falmouth TR11.........145 A5
  Truro TR1.........137 E3
Tregowris Court Cotts
  TR12 ....101 B5
Tregrea TR14.........138 E1
TREGREENWELL 23 F7
Tregreenwell Hill 23 F7
Tregrehan Gdns ✱ PL24.....115 E6
TREGREHAN MILLS 115 D6
Treguddick La PL15 ....18 A1
Treguddock Dr PL27.........108 D5
Tregue PL15.........16 E2
Tregullan TR15 ....139 C8
Tregulland Rd PL15.........16 E5
Tregullan View PL31.........109 D3
Tregullon La PL30 ....48 A7
Tregullow Rd TR11 ....144 F5
Tregundy Cl **21** TR6 ....55 A5
Tregundy Ct **20** TR6.........55 A5
Tregundy La TR6 ....55 A5
Tregundy Rd TR6.........55 A5
TREGUNE 10 F4
TREGUNNA 33 B8
Tregunna Cl TR13 ....91 B1
Tregunnel Hill TR7 ....110 D4
Tregunnick La PL11.........64 B6
Tregunnus La PL11 ....64 D5
Tregunter Mews TR11.........145 D3
Tregunwith TR11 ....82 A4
Tregurra La TR1 ....137 E6
TREGURRIAN 44 E8
Tregurrian Hill TR8.........44 E8
Tregurtha Farm Cotts TR17 89 D6
Tregurtha View TR20 ....89 E5
Tregurthen Cl TR14.........138 C2
Tregurthen Rd TR14 ....138 C2
TREGUSTICK 33 D1
Tregustick Rd PL30.........33 E1
Treguth Cl TR8 ....43 B1
Tregwary Rd TR14 ....141 B1
Tregwina La PL27 ....32 A3
Tregye Rd TR3.........82 A7
Trehaddle TR4 ....81 B7
TREHAN 122 A1
Trehane Rd TR14 ....138 B3
Trehannick Cl PL30.........23 E7
Trehannick Rd PL30.........23 E6
Trehaverne Cl TR1.........137 C5
Trehaverne La TR1 ....137 C5
Trehaverne Terr **3** TR1.....137 C5
Trehaverne Vean TR1.........137 C5
Trehawke La PL14 ....38 C1
Trehayes Mdw TR27 ....77 E2
Trehayes Parc TR27 ....142 E7
Trehaze-Na Cl PL32.........10 C3
Treheath Rd PL14 ....50 E7
Trehill Cross PL12.........40 C2
Trehill La Newbridge PL17...39 E3
  Rame PL10.........64 B2
TREHUNIST 52 C6
Trehunsey Cl TR11.........93 C2
Trehurst TR18 ....143 D4
Trekeek Rd PL32 ....15 C6
Trekee La PL30 ....23 C7
Trekeen Rd TR10.........144 B8
TREKENNER 28 B5
Trekenner Com Prim Sch
  PL15 ....28 C5
TREKENNING 45 D5
Trekenning Rd TR9.........45 D5
Trekernell Rd Tolcarne PL15. 26 F5
  Trebartha PL15.........27 A5
Trekestle Pk PL15 ....18 C2
TREKNOW 14 C5
Trekye Cl TR16 ....80 B5
Trelake La PL34 ....14 D5

Trelake Rd PL25 ....114 B4
TRELAN 100 E1
Trelan TR12 ....138 F3
Trelander Barton TR1 ....137 E5
Trelander E TR1.........137 E5
Trelander Highway TR1.....137 E4
Trelander N TR1.........137 E5
Trelander S TR1 ....137 E5
Trelander Vean TR1 ....137 E4
Trelantis PL28.........20 E1
Trelantis Est **4** PL28.........31 F8
TRELASH 10 F1
Trelaske La Lewannick PL15 . .27 C7
  Pelynt PL13.........62 F4
Trelavour Prazey PL26.........58 B8
Trelavour Rd PL26.........58 C8
Trelavour Sq PL26.........58 C8
Trelawne Cl **10** TR3 ....81 F7
Trelawne Cottage Gdns
  PL13 ....62 E4
Trelawne Gdns PL13.........62 E5
Trelawne Rd TR3 ....81 F7
Trelawney Apartments
  TR7 ....110 F6
Trelawney Ave
  Falmouth TR11.........145 B3
  Plymouth PL5.........123 D1
  Poughill EX23.........4 C3
  Redruth TR15.........140 E7
  St Ives TR26.........141 A5
Trelawney Cl Bodmin PL31 .109 C4
  Maenporth TR11.........93 E3
  Torpoint PL11.........126 E3
  Warbstow Cross PL15.........11 B1
Trelawney Cotts PL15.........106 C5
Trelawney Ct PL27.........21 E3
Trelawney Est
  Madron TR20.........143 A8
  Ponsanooth TR4.........81 B7
Trelawney Gdns PL14.........38 D4
Trelawney Hts **19** PL17.....39 F4
Trelawney Parc
  St Columb Major TR9 ....45 D5
  Warbstow Cross PL15.........11 B1
Trelawney Pl Hayle TR27....142 C6
  Penryn TR10.........144 C8
  Plymouth PL5.........123 D1
Trelawney Rd
  Bodmin PL31.........109 C3
  Callington PL17.........39 F4
  Camborne TR14.........138 D3
  Chacewater TR4.........69 A3
  Helston TR13.........146 C5
  Newquay TR7.........110 E5
  Padstow PL28.........107 D4
  Plymouth PL3.........128 C3
  Ponsanooth TR3.........81 B4
  St Austell PL25.........114 C5
  St Ives TR26.........141 A5
  St Mawes TR2.........95 A4
  Saltash PL12.........122 E2
  Truro TR1.........137 B5
Trelawney Rise
  18 Callington PL17.........39 F4
  Torpoint PL11.........126 E3
Trelawney Terr Cury TR12 ...99 B4
  Looe PL13.........117 C4
Trelawney Way Hayle TR27 142 C6
  Torpoint PL11.........126 E3
Trelawny Ct TR14.........138 C3
Trelawny Rd Falmouth TR11 145 B4
  Menheniot PL14.........52 A6
  Plymouth PL7.........130 C6
  St Agnes TR5.........54 C1
  Tavistock PL19.........147 C6
Treleague TR12 ....101 C4
Treleaver Crossroads
  TR12.........103 A5
Trelean Vean PL26.........72 F6
Treleaver Way TR1 ....69 F3
Trelee Cl TR27.........142 E7
TRELEIGH 140 D8
Treleigh Ave TR15 ....140 B6
Treleigh Com Prim Sch
  TR16.........140 C8
Treleigh Downs TR16.........140 D8
Treleigh Ind Est TR16 ....140 C7
Treleigh Terr TR15 ....140 A5
Trelevan Cl PL25 ....114 C3
Treleven Rd EX23.........104 F4
TRELEW 82 B2
Treliddon La PL11 ....64 C5
Treliever Cross TR10.........81 C1
Treliever Cross TR10.........81 C1
Treliever Layby TR10 ....81 C2
Treliever Rd
  Mabe Burnthouse TR10 ....81 C1
  Penryn TR10.........144 B8
TRELIGGA 14 C3
Treligga Downs Rd PL33.....14 C2
Treligga Rd PL33.........14 C2
Treliggon Bottoms PL30.....48 C6
TRELIGHTS 22 C6
Trelil Cvn Site TR13.........146 E7
TRELILL 23 C5
Trelil La TR11 ....144 C2
Trelill Rd PL30.........23 C4
Trelindon PL15.........27 E8
Trelinnoe Cl PL15 ....27 E8
Trelinnoe Gdns PL15.........27 E8
Treliske Ind Est TR1.........69 E4
Treliske La TR1, TR4.........69 F4
Treliske La PL16 ....140 D6
Trelispen Park Dr PL26 .....85 C5
Trelispen Pk PL26 ....85 C5
Trelissick Fields TR27.........142 B3
Trelissick Gdns PL17 ....39 E3
Trelissick Gdns ✱ TR3 ....82 D6

Trelissick Rd
  Falmouth TR11 . . . . 144 F5
  Hayle TR27 . . . . 142 B3
Trelissick Woodland Wlk★
  TR3 . . . . 82 D6
TRELIVER 46 E8
Treliver Hill PL30 . . . . 46 F8
Treloan La TR2 . . . . 83 B1
Treloar Terr PL15 . . . . 106 B6
Treloggan Ind Est TR7 . . . 111 B4
Treloggan Rd TR7 . . . . 111 A4
Trelorrin Gdns PL3 . . . . . . 128 E5
Trelowarren★ TR12 . . . . 99 F6
Trelowarren Ct 13 PL17 . . . 39 E4
Trelowarren Est
  Garras TR12 . . . . 100 A7
  Halliggye TR12 . . . . 99 E6
Trelowarren St TR14 . . . . . 138 D3
Trelowen Dr TR10 . . . . 144 A6
Treloweth Cl Plymouth PL2 128 D8
  St Erth TR27 . . . . 77 E2
Treloweth Com Prim Sch
  TR15 . . . . 139 D6
Treloweth Gdns TR15 . . . . 139 C6
Treloweth La TR27 . . . . 77 E2
Treloweth Rd TR15 . . . . . . 139 C6
Treloweth Terr TR15 . . . . . 139 B7
Treloweth Way TR15 . . . . . 139 C7
Trelowth Rd PL26 . . . . 59 A1
Treloyan TR12 . . . . 101 E4
Treloyhan Cl TR26 . . . . 141 C3
Treloyhan Manor Dr TR26 141 C3
Treloyhan Park Rd TR26 . . 141 C3
Treluswell Roundabout
  TR10 . . . . 81 D3
Trelyn PL27 . . . . 21 E3
Trelyn Rd TR12 . . . . 101 D4
TRELYON 141 B3
Trelyon TR2 . . . . 57 F3
Trelyon Ave TR26 . . . . 141 C4
Trelyon Cl TR19 . . . . 97 B6
Tremabe La Dobwalls PL14 . 50 E7
  Tremabe PL14 . . . . 38 A2
Tremabe Pk PL14 . . . . 50 E7
Tremadart Cl PL14 . . . . 51 A1
Tremadart Farm Barns
  PL14 . . . . 51 A1
Tremaddock Cotts PL14 . . 36 F3
Tremaddock Council Hos
  PL14 . . . . 36 F3
TREMAIL 16 B5
Tremaine Cl TR18 . . . . 143 C7
Tremalic PL13 . . . . 117 B3
Tremall Parc TR3 . . . . 80 F3
Tremanor Way TR11 . . . . . 144 D5
TREMAR 38 A2
Tremar Cl PL14 . . . . 38 A2
Tremar La St Cleer PL14 . . . 37 F3
  Tremar PL14 . . . . 38 A3
Tremar Rd TR26 . . . . 77 A7
Tremarren Rd PL27 . . . . . . 108 B5
TREMATON 53 E2
Trematon Cl PL11 . . . . 126 E4
Trematon Terr PL4 . . . . . . 128 E4
TREMAYNE 79 C2
Tremayne TR27 . . . . 79 C2
Tremayne Cl TR3 . . . . 81 F6
Tremayne Ho PL31 . . . . . . 109 B4
Tremayne Pk TR14 . . . . . . 138 F2
Tremayne Rd
  Carharrack TR16 . . . . 80 F8
  St Austell PL25 . . . . 114 E4
  Truro TR1 . . . . 137 C5
Tremayne Rise PL19 . . . . . 147 B5
Tremayne Terr PL13 . . . . . . 63 F8
Trembath Cres TR7 . . . . . . 110 E5
Trembear Rd PL25 . . . . . . 114 A4
Trembel La Mullion TR12 . . 99 B1
  Mullion TR12 . . . . 102 D8
Trembel Rd PL12 . . . . 99 B2
Trembleath Rd TR9 . . . . 45 B8
Trembrase TR19 . . . . 96 C7
TREMBRAZE 113 D7
Trembraze La PL14 . . . . . . 113 D7
Tremeadow Terr
  Hayle TR27 . . . . 142 B4
  Liskeard PL14 . . . . 113 D7
Tremeale PL15 . . . . 18 E2
Tremear Gn TR9 . . . . 45 E2
Tremearne Rd 16 TR13 . . . . 98 C8
Tremeddan Ct 2 PL14 . . . 113 C6
Tremeddan La PL14 . . . . . . 113 C6
Tremeddan Terr PL14 . . . . 113 B4
Tremeer La PL30 . . . . 23 E3
Tremellin La TR27 . . . . 77 F1
Tremena Gdns PL25 . . . . . 114 C4
Tremena Rd PL25 . . . . 114 C4
Tremenheere Ave TR13 . . . 146 E8
Tremenheere Ct TR13 . . . . 146 F8
Tremenheere Rd TR18 . . . 143 E6
Tremenva Ct 1 TR13 . . . . 146 C5
TREMETHICK CROSS 88 A5
Tremewan 1 PL25 . . . . 59 A3
Tremodrett La PL26 . . . . . . 47 B4
Tremodrett Rd
  Bawdens PL26 . . . . 47 B4
  Roche PL26 . . . . 46 F3
Tremoh Ct TR2 . . . . 71 C6
TREMOLLETT 27 D2
Tremollett Cotts PL17 . . . 28 B1
Tremollett Rd PL15 . . . . . . 27 D3
TREMORE 47 C7
Tremore Rd TR15 . . . . 140 D6
Tremorva TR27 . . . . 142 C6
Tremorvah Barton TR1 . . . 137 E5

Tremorvah Cres TR1 . . . . . 137 E5
Tremorvah Ct
  Falmouth TR11 . . . . 144 F1
  Truro TR1 . . . . 137 F5
Tremorvah Pk TR11 . . . . . 144 F1
Tremorvah Way 4 TR11 . . . 144 F1
Tremorvah Wood La TR1 . 137 E5
Tremough Barton Cotts
  TR10 . . . . 81 C1
Tremoughdale
  Penryn TR10 . . . . 144 B8
  Treliever TR10 . . . . 81 D2
Trenale La PL34 . . . . 14 D7
Trenalt Terr TR1 . . . . 137 B5
TRENANCE Newquay 110 E5
  Roche 46 F7
  St Issey 32 D5
  Tregurrian 31 C2
Trenance Ave TR7 . . . . 110 F5
Trenance Cl TR13 . . . . 146 B7
Trenance Ct TR7 . . . . 110 E4
Trenance Dr PL19 . . . . 30 A3
Trenance Hill PL25 . . . . . . 114 A5
Trenance La TR7 . . . . 110 E4
Trenance Learning Academy
  TR7 . . . . 110 E5
Trenance Leisure Park &
  Gdns★ TR7 . . . . 111 A5
Trenance Pl PL25 . . . . 114 B4
Trenance Rd
  Camborne TR14 . . . . 138 E4
  Newquay TR7 . . . . 110 E5
  St Austell PL25 . . . . 114 B4
  Trenance TR27 . . . . 32 D5
TRENANT 37 C3
Trenant TR16 . . . . 68 D1
Trenant Cl PL27 . . . . 21 E5
Trenant Cross PL14 . . . . . . 63 A6
TRENANT GIRT 108 C5
Trenant Ind Est PL27 . . . . 108 D6
Trenant Rd Looe PL13 . . . . 117 D5
  2 Tywardreath PL24 . . . . . 60 D5
Trenant Vale PL27 . . . . . . 108 D6
TRENARREN 73 E7
Trenarren View PL25 . . . . 115 A6
Trenarth TR10 . . . . 144 C8
Trenarth Rd TR7 . . . . 110 E5
Trenawin La TR27 . . . . 78 E5
TRENCREEK 111 C4
Trencreek Cl TR4 . . . . 56 D1
Trencreek La TR8 . . . . 111 B4
Trencreek Rd TR7, TR8 . . . 111 B4
TRENCROM 77 B3
Trencrom La TR26 . . . . 141 D1
Trencrom Rd TR27 . . . . 77 C3
Trencrom Row TR20 . . . . . 77 B3
TRENDEAL 57 C3
Trendeal Gdns 1 TR18 . . . 143 E5
Trendeal La TR8 . . . . 57 C5
Trendlewood Rd PL6 . . . . . 125 D7
Trendreath Cl TR26 . . . . . . 77 E3
Treneague Pk PL27 . . . . . . 108 B4
TRENEAR 92 A6
Trenear Trenear TR13 . . . . . 92 A7
  Wendron TR13 . . . . 91 F6
Trenear Ct TR15 . . . . 140 D6
TRENEERE 143 E7
Treneere La TR18 . . . . 143 D7
Treneere Rd TR18 . . . . 143 D6
TRENEGLOS 16 F7
Treneglos TR4 . . . . 81 C7
Treneglos Terr Gulval TR18 . 88 E6
  Newlyn TR18 . . . . 143 C3
Trenerry Cl TR1 . . . . 137 D6
TRENERTH 78 D2
Trenerth Rd TR27 . . . . 78 E2
Trenethick Ave TR13 . . . . . 146 D8
Trenethick Bsns Pk TR13 . 146 C8
Trenethick Cl TR13 . . . . . . 146 D7
Trenethick Farm TR13 . . . 146 B8
Trenethick Parc TR13 . . . . 146 D8
TRENEWAN 62 A4
TRENGALE 37 C2
Trengove Cross TR11 . . . . . 92 D5
Trengove Ave PL11 . . . . . . 126 F3
Trengrouse Way TR13 . . . . 146 C5
TRENGUNE 11 A4
Trengwainton Gdns★ TR20 88 A6
Trenhaile Terr TR1 . . . . 70 D1
Trenhayle La TR27 . . . . 142 B2
Treniffle La
  Stourscombe PL15 . . . . . 106 F3
  Treniffle PL15 . . . . 19 C2
Treningle Hill PL30 . . . . . . 47 F7
Treningle View PL31 . . . . . 109 C3
TRENINNICK 111 A4
Treninnick Hill TR7 . . . . . . 110 F5
Treninnow & Wiggle Chalets
  PL10 . . . . 132 C2
Trenithick Mdw TR4 . . . . . . 68 C6
Trenithon La TR8 . . . . 57 C6
Trennal La TR27 . . . . 90 C5
Trennance Ct 6 TR12 . . . . 99 A1
Trennick La TR1 . . . . 137 E3
Trennick Row TR1 . . . . 137 E3
Trennick Villas Ct TR1 . . . 137 E3
Trenode CE Prim Sch PL13 . 51 F1
Trenouth Cl 5 PL14 . . . . . . 38 A3
Trenouth La PL27 . . . . 32 B5
Trenovissick Rd PL24 . . . . 60 B4
Trenowah Rd PL25 . . . . . . 115 C5
Trenower La PL26 . . . . 47 B4
TRENOWETH 93 B8
Trenoweth TR4 . . . . 79 B3
Trenoweth Ave TR14 . . . . 138 B3
Trenoweth Cres TR18 . . . . 143 B4
Trenoweth Ct TR12 . . . . . . 102 F2

Trenoweth Est TR15 . . . . . 140 A8
Trenoweth La TR10 . . . . . . 93 B8
Trenoweth Mdw TR12 . . . . 102 F2
Trenoweth Rd
  Falmouth TR11 . . . . 144 F2
  Penzance TR18 . . . . 143 B5
Trenoweth Terr TR10 . . . . 93 B8
Trenoweth Vean TR10 . . . . 81 B1
Trenow La TR20 . . . . 89 D5
Trenowth Terr TR2 . . . . 57 E1
Trent Cl PL3 . . . . 129 B6
Trentham Cl PL6 . . . . 125 B6
Trentworthy Cross EX22 . . . 3 E2
TRENWHEAL 90 F7
Trenwheal TR13 . . . . 90 F7
Trenwith La TR26 . . . . 141 A4
Trenwith Pl 14 TR26 . . . . . 141 B5
Trenwith Rd TR14 . . . . 138 B3
Trenwith Sq TR26 . . . . 141 A5
Trenwith Terr 11 TR26 . . . 141 B5
Trenython Rd 10 PL24 . . . . 60 B4
Treore Cl PL30 . . . . 23 A6
Treore La Hendra PL29 . . . . 23 A7
  Tregavarne PL29 . . . . 22 F7
Treovis Cross PL14 . . . . 38 C8
Tre-Pol PL26 . . . . 58 F1
TREQUITE 23 B3
Treraven La PL27 . . . . 108 C3
Treraven Rd PL15 . . . . 16 E2
Trerew Rd TR18 . . . . 143 C4
Trerice★ TR8 . . . . 44 D1
Trerice Cl 15 PL17 . . . . 39 E4
Trerice Dr TR7 . . . . 111 B5
Trerice Fields TR14 . . . . . . 79 B2
Trerice Holdings TR8 . . . . . 44 C1
Trerice Pl TR26 . . . . 141 A5
Trerice Rd 6 TR26 . . . . 141 A5
Trerice Terr PL26 . . . . 58 A8
TRERIEVE PL11 . . . . 64 C5
TRERISE 103 A7
Trerise Rd TR14 . . . . 138 C3
Treroosel Rd PL30 . . . . 23 D8
Trerose Coombe PL11 . . . . 64 C5
Treruffe Hill TR15 . . . . 140 B4
Treruffe Terr 9 TR15 . . . . 140 B4
TRERULEFOOT 52 D2
Treryn Cl PL24 . . . . 60 B5
Tresaderns Rd TR15 . . . . . 140 A6
Tresahar Rd TR11 . . . . 145 A3
Tresamble Hill TR4, TR3 . . 81 B6
TRESARRETT 35 B8
Tresavean Est TR16 . . . . . . 80 B8
Tresavean Hill TR16 . . . . . . 80 E6
Tresavean Terr TR16 . . . . . 80 E6
Tresawla Ct TR14 . . . . 138 F6
TRESAWLE 71 C5
Tresawle Rd TR11 . . . . 145 A6
Tresawls Ave TR1 . . . . 69 F3
Tresawls Rd TR1, TR4 . . . . 69 E4
Tresawna Terr TR11 . . . . . 145 B4
Tresawya Dr TR1 . . . . 137 C4
Trescobeas Rd
  Falmouth TR11 . . . . 144 E5
  4 Mongleath TR11 . . . . . 144 D5
  Mongleath TR11 . . . . 144 E4
Trescoe Rd TR20 . . . . 88 F6
Tresco Gdns PL6 . . . . 124 F7
Tresco Pl TR11 . . . . 144 F4
Trescore PL28 . . . . 31 F7
TRESCOWE 90 B5
Trescowe TR27 . . . . 90 B5
Trescowe Comm TR27 . . . . 90 C6
Trescowe Rd TR20 . . . . 89 F5
Tresdale Parc TR27 . . . . . . 78 D6
Treseder's Gdns TR1 . . . . 137 D5
Tresevern Cl TR3 . . . . 80 D4
Tresevern Hill TR3 . . . . 80 D4
Tresidder Cl TR11 . . . . 144 E4
TRESILLIAN 70 F5
Tresillian Ho TR1 . . . . 69 E4
Tresillian Rd TR11 . . . . 144 F6
Tresillian St PL4 . . . . 149 C2
TRESINNEY 24 C8
Tresithney Rd TR16 . . . . . . 80 F8
Treskerby TR16 . . . . 140 F7
Treskewes Est 1 TR12 . . . 101 C4
Treskewes Ind Est 1
  TR12 . . . . 101 C3
TRESKILLARD 139 C1
Treskilling PL30 . . . . 59 F8
TRESKINNICK CROSS 6 F1
Treslothan 79 D4
Treslothan Rd TR14 . . . . . . 79 D4
Tresluggan Rd PL5 . . . . . . 123 D1
Tresmarrow Rd PL15 . . . . . 18 E3
Tresooth Ct TR10 . . . . 144 D7
Tresooth La TR10 . . . . 144 D8
Tresooth Terr TR10 . . . . . 144 D7
Tresowes TR13 . . . . 90 D4
TRESOWES GREEN 90 D4
Tresowes Hill TR13 . . . . . . 90 E4
Tresowgar La TR12 . . . . . . 71 B6
TRESPARRETT 10 B2
TRESPARRETT POSTS 10 C4
Tresprison Tregarrick TR13 146 E5
  Whitehill TR13 . . . . 91 F2
Tresprison Ct TR13 . . . . . . 146 E5
Tressa Dowr La TR1 . . . . . 137 F5
Tressennack TR20 . . . . 88 A5
Treswigga Rd PL30 . . . . . . 24 E1
TRESWITHIAN 138 A4
Treswithian Barns TR14 . . 138 A3
Treswithian Downs
  Kehelland TR14 . . . . 66 F1

Treswithian Downs continued
  Kehelland TR14 . . . . 79 A7
  Reskadinnick TR14 . . . . . 138 A5
Treswithian Park Rd TR14 138 B3
Treswithian Rd TR14 . . . . . 138 B3
Tretawn Cl PL30 . . . . 23 B2
Trethannas Gdns TR14 . . . 79 B2
Tretharrup Rd TR16 . . . . . . 80 D6
TRETHELLAN 110 C6
Trethellan TR16 . . . . 80 D5
Trethellan Hill TR7 . . . . . . 110 C5
Trethern Cl TR14 . . . . 79 E4
Tretherras Cl TR7 . . . . 111 A6
Tretherras Rd TR7 . . . . . . 111 A6
TRETHEVEY 14 F8
Trethevy Cl PL14 . . . . 37 F3
Trethevy Quoit★ PL14 . . . . 38 A3
TRETHEWEY 96 E4
Trethewey Cl 10 TR9 . . . . . 45 E6
Trethewey Way TR7 . . . . . . 110 D5
Trethew Gdns TR14 . . . . . 138 E4
Trethiggey Cres TR8 . . . . . 111 F3
Trethillick La
  Trethillick PL28 . . . . 21 B2
  Trethillick PL28 . . . . 107 C6
Trethill La PL11 . . . . 65 C5
Trethorne Leisure Farm★
  PL15 . . . . 18 B2
Trethorns Ct TR20 . . . . 89 A8
TRETHOSA 58 A5
Trethosa Downs PL26 . . . . 58 B5
Trethosa Hill PL26 . . . . 58 A5
Trethosa Rd PL26 . . . . 58 B4
Trethowan Hts TR1 . . . . . . 69 F3
TRETHOWEL 114 C6
Trethurffe TR2 . . . . 57 C1
Trethurffe Terr TR9 . . . . . . 45 E5
Trethurffe Villas TR1 . . . . . 57 C1
TRETHURGY 59 F6
Trethurgy Gdns 17 PL17 . . 39 E4
Tretoil Hill PL30 . . . . 48 B7
Tretoil View PL31 . . . . 109 E2
Tretorvic TR18 . . . . 143 C8
Tretower Cl PL6 . . . . 124 F5
TREVADLOCK 27 A6
Trevadlock Hall Pk PL15 . . 27 A6
TREVAIL 43 D1
Trevail Cotts TR8 . . . . 43 D1
Trevail Way PL25 . . . . 114 E4
Trevale TR18 . . . . 143 C5
Trevales TR3 . . . . 81 A2
TREVALGA 9 B1
Trevalga Cl 5 TR6 . . . . 55 C4
Trevalga Hill PL35 . . . . 14 F8
Trevalga Rd PL35 . . . . 15 A8
Trevallack Cl 9 TR12 . . . . 101 C4
Trevallack Parc 8 TR12 . . 101 C4
Trevallack View 2 TR12 . . 101 C4
Trevallett La PL15 . . . . 18 A3
Trevallion Pk TR3 . . . . 82 B5
Trevallyn Rd PL15 . . . . 106 B4
TREVANCE 32 E6
Trevance TR10 . . . . 144 A8
Trevance Pk TR24 . . . . 60 D5
Trevance Rd PL27 . . . . 32 E6
Trevaney TR11 . . . . 93 A4
TREVANGER 21 F4
Trevanger La PL27 . . . . 21 F4
Trevanion Cl PL27 . . . . 108 B4
Trevanion Ct
  Mawnan Smith TR11 . . . . 93 D3
  1 Newquay TR7 . . . . 110 F6
  Truro TR1 . . . . 69 F3
Trevanion La PL25 . . . . 59 A3
Trevanion Pk PL27 . . . . . . 108 C4
Trevanion Rd
  Liskeard PL14 . . . . 113 D5
  St Austell PL25 . . . . 114 D2
  2 Trewoon PL25 . . . . 59 A3
  Wadebridge PL27 . . . . . . 108 B4
Trevanion Terr PL27 . . . . . 108 C4
Trevannion Cl PL6 . . . . 129 A8
TREVANSON 33 C7
Trevanson Rd
  Wadebridge PL27 . . . . . . 108 B4
  Whiterock PL27 . . . . 108 A4
Trevanson St PL27 . . . . . . 108 B6
Trevanson Street PL27 . . 108 B6
Trevarner Mdw PL27 . . . . 108 D6
Trevarner Way PL27 . . . . . 108 D6
Trevarno TR13 . . . . 91 C4
Trevarno Estate & Gdns★
  TR13 . . . . 91 C5
TREVARNON 78 D6
Trevarnon Cl PL27 . . . . 78 D6
Trevarnon La TR27 . . . . . . 78 D5
Trevarnon Moor PL27 . . . . 78 D6
Trevarrack Cl TR18 . . . . . . 143 F8
Trevarrack La TR18 . . . . . . 143 F8
Trevarrack Pl TR18 . . . . . . 143 F8
Trevarrack Rd Gulval TR18 143 F8
  Trythogga TR18 . . . . 143 F8
Trevarrack Row TR18 . . . . 88 E6
TREVARREN 45 E3
Trevarren Ave TR16 . . . . . . 80 A5
TREVARRIAN 31 C1
Trevarrian Hill TR8 . . . . . . 44 D8
TREVARRICK 72 F2
Trevarrick Ct TR26 . . . . . . 141 C1
Trevarrick Dr PL25 . . . . . . 114 B4
Trevarrick Rd PL25 . . . . . . 114 B4
TREVARTH 80 E7
Trevarth 22 PL26 . . . . 85 D8
Trevarthen Ct PL27 . . . . . . 73 C4
Trevarthian Ho TR17 . . . . . 89 B5
Trevarthian Rd PL25 . . . . 114 C4

Trevarth Rd TR11 . . . . 144 F5
Trevarth Terr TR16 . . . . . . 80 E7
Trevarweneth Rd 8 PL24 . . 60 B4
Trevassack Ct TR27 . . . . . 142 D6
Trevassack Gdns TR14 . . . 79 B2
Trevassack La TR27 . . . . . 142 E6
Trevassack Manor Pk 6
  TR27 . . . . 142 D6
Trevassack Parc TR27 . . . 142 E6
Trevaunance Cl TR5 . . . . . 54 C2
Trevaunance Cove TR5 . . . 54 D2
Trevaunance Cove★ TR5 . . 54 D2
Trevaunance Rd TR5 . . . . . 54 C2
Trevaylor Cl TR1 . . . . 137 E5
Trevaylor Rd TR11 . . . . 144 F5
Trevean Cl TR14 . . . . 138 D3
Trevean Gdns 3 TR18 . . . . 143 D5
Trevean La Rosudgeon TR20 89 F4
  Trevean PL27 . . . . 31 E7
Trevean Rd Penzance TR18 143 D5
  Truro TR1 . . . . 69 F3
Trevean Way Newquay TR7 110 C5
  Rosudgeon TR20 . . . . 89 F4
Trevear Cl TR25 . . . . 114 D3
Trevear Rd PL26 . . . . 58 B4
Trevease TR10 . . . . 92 D7
Trevecca Cotts PL14 . . . . . 113 C8
Trevedras Rd TR8 . . . . 31 F1
Trevegean TR19 . . . . 86 E4
Treveglos TR27 . . . . 142 B6
Treveglos Rd TR11 . . . . . . 144 E1
TREVEIGHAN 23 F6
Trevelga Ct TR7 . . . . 111 A7
Trevelgue Ct TR8 . . . . 44 C6
Trevelgue Rd TR7, TR8 . . . 44 C6
Trevellance La TR6 . . . . . . 55 B4
Trevellan Rd TR11 . . . . 82 A3
Trevella Rd EX23 . . . . 104 E7
TREVELLAS 54 E2
Trevella Vean TR4 . . . . 70 D8
Trevell La PL15 . . . . 26 F7
TREVELMOND 50 D6
Trevelthan Rd 18 TR16 . . . 67 E4
Trevelva Rd TR1 . . . . 137 E2
Trevelveth Rd TR8 . . . . 110 B3
Trevelyan Cl 10 TR20 . . . . 89 F5
Trevelyan Gr TR20 . . . . 89 F5
Trevelyan Holiday Homes
  TR12 . . . . 102 E6
Trevelyan Rd TR15, TR16 . 67 E4
Trevelyan Way 5 TR20 . . . 89 F5
TREVEMPER 110 E2
Trevemper Rd TR7, TR8 . . 110 F3
TREVEN 14 C6
Trevena Cl TR18 . . . . 143 C4
Trevena Cross Breage TR13 90 F3
  Trevena TR13 . . . . 90 F4
Trevena Dr 8 PL34 . . . . 14 C7
Trevena Gdns TR11 . . . . . . 93 D3
Trevena La TR13 . . . . 90 F4
Trevena Lodge 6 PL34 . . . . 14 C7
Trevena Rd TR18 . . . . 143 C4
Trevena Terr TR7 . . . . 110 D6
Trevendon PL17 . . . . 28 D1
Treveneague Gdns PL2 . . . 128 D8
Trevenen TR13 . . . . 92 A4
Trevenen Bal TR13 . . . . . . 91 F4
Trevenen Rd TR13 . . . . . . 146 C5
Treveneth Cres TR18 . . . . 143 C1
Treveneth Pl 11 TR18 . . . . 143 C1
Treven La TR27 . . . . 78 B1
Trevenna Cross TR8 . . . . . 45 A8
Trevenner Ho 8 TR15 . . . . 140 B5
Trevenner La TR17 . . . . 89 C5
Trevenner Mews 6 TR15 . 140 B5
Trevenner Sq TR17 . . . . . . 89 C5
TREVENNING 23 F5
Trevenna La PL15 . . . . 17 A3
Treven Noweth TR16 . . . . . 68 C3
Trevenson Ct TR15 . . . . . . 139 B6
Trevenson La
  Camborne TR14 . . . . 138 D2
  Camborne, Pool TR15 . . . 139 A6
Trevenson Moor TR14 . . . . 139 A7
Trevenson Rd
  Camborne TR15 . . . . 139 B5
  Newquay TR7 . . . . 111 B6
Trevenson St TR14 . . . . . . 138 D2
Treventon Cl
  Falmouth TR11 . . . . 144 E4
  Portscatho TR2 . . . . 83 B2
Treventon Rd TR2 . . . . 83 B2
Treventon Rise 11 TR9 . . . 45 E6
TREVERBYN Penwithick . . . 59 C7
  St Cleer 37 B2
Treverbyn Academy PL26 . 59 C8
Treverbyn Cl Liskeard PL14 113 E6
  Plymouth PL7 . . . . 130 D6
Treverbyn Gdns PL25 . . . . 114 F4
Treverbyn Rd
  Falmouth TR11 . . . . 144 E1
  Padstow PL28 . . . . 107 E4
  Plymouth PL7 . . . . 130 D6
  St Austell PL25 . . . . 141 A5
  Stenalees PL26 . . . . 59 C8
  Truro TR1 . . . . 137 E6
Treverbyn Rise TR10 . . . . 144 A8
Trevere Cl TR27 . . . . 78 C6
Treverno Rd TR14 . . . . 138 E6
Treverry La TR12 . . . . 99 B3
TREVERVA 93 B6
Treveryn Parc TR11 . . . . . . 144 C2
TREVESCAN 96 B5
Trevessa Cl PL2 . . . . 128 D8
Trevethan Cl TR6 . . . . 55 B4

Trevethan Cl continued
  Falmouth TR11............145 A4
Trevethan Ct **2** TR11.......145 A5
Trevethan Gdns **2** TR11...145 A4
Trevethan Hill **1** TR11.....145 B5
Trevethan Pk PL20........119 F4
Trevethan Rd
  Falmouth TR11............145 A4
  Falmouth TR11............145 A4
Trevethan Rise TR11........145 A4
Trevethenick Rd TR1.......137 C6
Treveth La TR13...........146 D8
TREVETHOE................77 D3
Treveth Tean TR9..........57 E8
Treveth Ylyn TR14.........138 F5
TREVIA...................105 B4
TREVIADES................93 A3
Trevia La PL32............105 B4
Trevian Cl **6** TR6........55 A4
Trevia Pk Terr PL32........105 C3
Treviglas Cl TR7..........111 D7
Treviglas Com Coll TR7....111 D7
Treviglas La TR2...........71 C6
Treviglas Rise TR2.........71 C6
TREVIGRO.................39 C4
TREVILLA.................82 C6
Trevilla Hill TR3..........82 C6
Trevilla Rd TR3...........82 C6
Trevillet Rd PL32.........15 A6
Trevilley La PL30, PL33....23 E8
Trevillick La PL30.........23 F6
Trevilling Rd PL27........108 B6
Trevillis Pk PL14.........113 B4
TREVILSON................56 D6
Trevilson Cl TR8..........56 C7
Trevince Parc TR16........80 F8
Trevingey Cl TR15........140 A3
Trevingey Cres TR15......140 A3
Trevingey Parc TR15......140 A4
Trevingey Rd TR15........140 A3
Trevinnick Rd PL30........22 F4
TREVISCOE................58 B7
Trevisker Com Prim Sch
  PL27...................31 F3
Trevisker Dr TR13.........91 A1
Treviskey Hill TR2.........84 B3
Trevisquite La PL30........23 D1
Trevissome Bissom TR11...81 F1
  Bissom TR11.............94 B7
  Bissom TR11............144 F8
Trevissome Ct TR11.......144 F6
Trevithick Ave PL11.......126 F4
Trevithick Cl Newquay TR7 110 F4
  St Merryn PL28...........31 F8
  1 St Merryn PL28......31 F8
  Truro TR1...............137 E6
Trevithick Cres TR27......142 D5
Trevithick Ct
  Camborne TR14..........138 C3
  3 Camborne, Illogan Highway
  TR15...................139 C6
  Truro TR1...............137 E6
Trevithick Est **7** PL28.....31 F8
Trevithick Hill PL26.........72 D4
Trevithick Learning Academy
  TR14..................138 D1
Trevithick Rd
  Camborne TR14..........138 D3
  Camborne, Illogan Highway
  TR15...................139 C6
  Chacewater TR4..........69 A3
  Falmouth TR11..........144 E5
  Plymouth PL5...........123 E2
  St Austell PL25.........114 E3
  Truro TR1..............137 E5
Trevitho La **4** TR12........99 B2
Trevoarn TR27............142 B5
Trevol Bsns Pk PL11......126 D3
TREVOLLARD...............53 D1
Trevollard PL13...........61 F7
Trevollard La PL12.........53 D1
Trevol Pl PL11...........126 E3
Trevol Rd PL11...........126 E3
TREVONE..................20 E2
Trevone Cres PL25........114 A4
Trevone Gdns PL2.........128 D8
Trevone Rd PL28...........20 F2
Trevoney TR11............144 C2
Trevonnen Cl TR13.........90 E3
Trevonnen Rd TR3..........81 B4
Trevorder Cl PL11.........126 F2
Trevorder Dr PL25.........114 E7
Trevorder Rd PL11........126 F2
Trevorgans Cross TR19.....96 F8
TREVORRICK..............107 E1
Trevorrick Rd PL27.........32 D7
Trevose Ave TR7..........110 C6
Trevose Cl
  Constantine Bay PL28.....20 C1
  St Agnes TR5............54 C1
Trevose Ho TR1............69 E4
Trevose Rd TR1............69 F4
Trevose Way PL3..........129 C6
Trevothen Penhallick TR12..101 A1
  Penhallick TR12.........103 F8
Trevowah Mdws TR8.......110 A3
Trevowah Rd TR8...........43 D3
TREVOWHAN...............75 C2
Trevowhan Hill TR20.......75 D2
Trevozah Cross PL15........28 B8
Trevu Ho TR1.............138 E1
Trevu Rd TR14............138 E2
Trevurvas La TR13..........90 C3
TREW.....................90 F4

Trew TR13.................90 F4
TREWALDER................14 E1
Trewalder Rd PL33.........14 D1
Trewall Hill PL11..........64 D5
Trewan Hall TR9...........45 E7
Trewans Terr TR15........140 A6
Trewardreva Cross TR11....92 E4
Trewarlett Cross PL15......28 A7
TREWARMETT...............14 D5
Trewarmett La PL33........14 D5
Trewarne La TR8..........111 F3
Trewartha Ct TR26.........141 D1
Trewartha Ct **4** PL14.....113 C6
Trewartha Est TR26........141 D1
Trewartha Flats TR26......141 D1
Trewartha Rd TR20.........90 C3
Trewartha Terr **12** TR18..143 E6
Trewarton Rd TR10.........81 D2
Trewarveneth Farm Cotts
  TR18...................88 C2
Trewarveneth St TR18.....143 C2
TREWASSA................15 F5
Trewassa Flats PL32.......15 F5
Trewavas TR13.............90 D2
Trewavas Cres TR13.......146 C5
Trewavas Rd TR18.........143 C1
Treweath TR16............80 C2
Treweath Rd TR18.........143 D7
Trewedna La TR3..........81 C5
Treweeks Rd TR19..........75 A1
Treweese Cross PL14.......52 B7
Treweese Rd Menheniot PL14 52 B7
  Quethiock PL14..........52 B8
TREWELLARD...............86 F8
Trewellard Hill TR19.......87 A8
Trewellard Ind Est TR19....86 F8
Trewellard Rd TR19........86 F8
Trewelloe Rd TR20.........90 C3
Trewelm La TR16...........68 E1
TREWEN..................17 E2
Trewen Farm La
  Menehay TR11..........144 C1
  Sparnon TR11............93 D6
  Tregedna TR11..........94 A4
Trewen Hill PL15..........17 E1
TREWENNACK..............146 F8
Trewennack
  Treloquithack TR13.......92 A4
  Tremenheere TR13........91 F4
  Trewennack TR13........146 F8
TREWENNAN..............23 E8
Trewennan Hill PL30.......23 E8
Trewen Rd TR11...........144 C2
Trewen Terr TR11.........144 C2
Trewern La TR20...........87 E6
TREWETHA................22 E7
Trewetha Farm Lodges
  PL29...................22 E7
Trewetha La PL29.........22 D7
Trewethen La PL30.........23 C5
TREWETHERN..............22 E3
TREWEY..................76 B5
Trewey Hill TR26..........76 B4
Trewhella La TR20.........89 F7
Trewhiddle Rd PL25.......114 C2
Trewidden Cl TR1.........137 E5
Trewidden Ct TR1.........137 E5
Trewidden Gdn★ TR20......88 A4
Trewidden Rd TR26.......141 B5
TREWIDLAND..............51 C2
Trewidland Prim Sch PL14 .51 C3
Trewiggett La PL30.........23 B6
Trewince TR11............93 B3
Trewince La
  Grampound Road TR2......57 E1
  Lostwithiel PL22........112 C3
  Porth Navas TR11........93 B3
Trewince Manor TR2.......95 C6
Trewince Terr **2** TR18...143 C1
Trewince Villas PL27.......32 E6
Trewinnard Ct TR1........137 B6
Trewinnard Gr TR1........137 B6
Trewinnard La TR27........77 E1
Trewinnard Rd TR3.........81 D5
Trewinnick Council Hos
  PL27...................32 A5
Trewinnick Rd PL27........32 A5
Trewinnow Cross PL15......27 D6
Trewin Rd **2** PL31.......109 A5
TREWINT.................10 F8
Trewint Cres PL13........117 D4
Trewint Est PL14...........52 A5
Trewint Hill PL27..........21 D4
Trewint La Landrake PL12..53 B2
  Rock PL27...............21 D3
Trewint Rd PL14...........52 A6
Trewirgie Gdns TR15......140 B4
Trewirgie Hill TR15.......140 B3
Trewirgie Jun & Inf Schs
  TR15..................140 B4
Trewirgie Rd TR15........140 B3
Trewirgie Vean TR15......140 B4
Trewiston La PL27..........21 E3
Trewithan Parc PL22......112 D2
Trewithen Rd TR3..........80 E4
Trewithen Gdns★ TR2......71 E6
Trewithen La PL28..........32 A8
Trewithen Parc TR8........56 B7
Trewithen Rd TR18.......143 D5
Trewithen Terr TR13.......90 D5
Trewithey La PL15.........27 C4
TREWITHIAN..............83 B4
Trewithick Hill PL15.......18 C4
Trewithick La PL15........18 C4
Trewithick Rd TR13.........90 F2
Trewithy Ct PL6..........124 F1
Trewithy Dr PL6..........124 F1
TREWOLD.................9 E1

Trewollack Rd St Wenn PL30 46 D8
  Trewollack PL30.........33 B1
Trewollack Cl PL26.........85 C5
Trewollock Cl PL26.........85 C5
TREWOODLOE.............39 B6
Trewoolsta Terr **5** PL14..38 E4
TREWOON Mullion.........99 B2
  St Austell..............59 A3
Trewoon Rd TR12..........99 B2
Treworden Cl EX23.........4 E1
Treworder La
  7 Treleague TR12.....103 B5
  Wadebridge PL27........108 F5
Treworder Rd TR1.........137 B3
TREWORGA................83 D7
Treworgan View TR4........56 D1
Treworgie La TR12........100 F6
TREWORLAS...............83 D5
Treworlis Cl TR13.........146 D8
TREWORNAN................22 C1
TREWORRICK..............37 E3
TREWORTHAL..............83 C5
Treworthal Rd TR3.........81 D5
Treworval TR11............90 A3
Treworvenneth Dr **9** TR17 89 C5
Trewrickle La PL11.........65 A5
Trewyn Flats **4** TR26...141 B6
Treyarnon La PL28..........31 D8
Treyew Pl TR16............80 F8
Treyew Prim Sch TR1......137 A4
Treyew Rd TR1............137 B3
TREZAISE.................47 A2
Trezaise Ave PL26..........47 A2
Trezaise Cl PL26...........47 A2
Trezaise Rd PL26...........46 F2
Trezaise Sq PL26...........47 A2
Treza Rd TR13.............91 A1
Trezebel Hill TR12........101 A6
Trezela Rd TR13...........143 D6
Triangle, The **16** TR12...102 F2
Trillacott Rd Billacott PL15 .12 B1
  Navarino PL15...........18 A8
  Trillacott PL15..........17 F8
Trinity Bldgs TR19.........96 B6
Trinity Cl Bere Alston PL20..41 B1
  Carnkie TR16............80 C2
Trinity Praze TR16.........80 C2
Trinity St PL25...........114 C3
Trinity Way PL19.........147 A4
Tripp Hill PL14...........36 F2
TRISPEN.................56 D1
Trispen Hill TR4...........56 D1
Tristan Rd TR1...........137 F5
Triumphal Cres PL7.......130 A6
TROAN...................57 C8
Trolver Hill TR3...........82 B6
Trolvis TR10..............81 A1
Trolvus Vean TR10.........81 A1
Troods Mill PL15.........106 B7
TROON...................79 E5
Troon CP Sch TR14........79 E4
Troon Moor TR14..........79 E4
Troon Row TR13...........90 F3
Trossell Rd PL15..........11 F1
Troswell Hill
  Caudworthy Bridge PL15...11 F3
  Webworthy PL15.........12 A3
Troubridge Rd TR13.......146 C4
Trowan La TR26............76 F7
Trowbridge Cl PL5........124 C4
Troy Ct PL23.............116 C4
Truck Hill TR2............71 B6
Trungle Parc **3** TR19....88 C2
Trungle Terr TR19.........88 C2
TRURO...................137 E3
Truro Bsns Pk TR3.........69 C3
Truro Dr PL5............124 A5
Truro High Sch TR1.......137 C3
Truro Hill TR10..........144 C8
Truro L Ctr TR10.........144 C8
Truro L Ctr TR1...........69 E3
Truro & Penryn Coll
  TR1...................69 E3
  22 Truro TR1........137 D4
Truro Prep Sch TR1........69 F4
Truro Rd Lanivet PL30......47 F7
  St Austell PL25.........114 A2
Truro Sch TR1...........137 E3
Truro Sta TR1...........137 B4
Truro Vean Terr TR1.......137 D5
TRUSCOTT................18 D4
Truscott La PL15..........18 C4
Trussall TR13.............92 B4
TRUTHAN.................56 C2
Truthan View TR4..........56 D1
TRUTHWALL Marazion......89 D7
  St Just...............86 E7
Truthwall La TR19.........86 F7
Tryelyn PL31............109 F2
Tryhornek TR26............77 D4
Trythall Prim Sch TR20....76 B1
TRYTHOGGA..............143 F8
Trythogga Rd TR18........143 F8
Tubbon Hill Ponsanooth TR3 .81 A4
  Trebost TR3............81 A4
TUBBS MILL...............72 D2
TUCKER PL5..............127 F8
TUCKERMARSH............41 B2
Tuckers Cl TR18.........111 B4
TUCKINGMILL Camborne...139 D2
  St Breward............24 B4
Tuckingmill TR13..........91 D4
Tuckingmill Terr TR13-.....91 E4
Tucoyse Hill PL26.........72 D4
Tucoyse La TR11...........92 D4
Tudor Cl PL9............135 E5
Tudor Ct PL12...........123 A2

Tudor Lodge Pk TR20.......89 C7
Tuke Cl TR11............144 E5
Tunnels Through Time★
  TR7...................110 D5
Turbill Gdns **4** PL7.....131 B5
TURFDOWN................48 E8
Turfdown Rd PL30..........48 E8
Turf St PL31.............109 E5
Turnavean Rd PL25........114 A5
Turnaware Rd TR11.......144 E2
TURNCHAPEL.............135 B7
Turnpike
  Gunnislake/Calstock PL18...40 E5
  Helston TR13...........146 C7
  Trebyan PL30............48 D5
Turnpike Hill **2** TR17....89 C5
Turnpike Pl PL14.........113 B4
Turnpike Rd
  Connor Downs TR27......78 D6
  Marazion TR17..........89 C5
Turnpike The TR19.........86 F6
Turnquay PL9............135 C7
Turnstone Way EX23......104 F4
Turret Gr PL4...........128 F4
TUTWELL.................29 A2
Tuxton Cl PL7............131 C3
TWELVEHEADS.............69 B1
Twelvewoods Bsns Pk **3**
  PL14...................50 D7
Twelvewoods Cl PL14.......50 E8
Twelvewoods Pl PL14.......50 E8
Twiggy La TR27............90 C6
Twinbrook Pk TR11........93 B3
TWO BURROWS.............68 E5
Two Chimneys Caravan Pk **7**
  TR20...................90 B3
Two Hills Pk PL12.......122 C2
Two Trees PL27..........108 B4
Two Trees Rd PL22.......112 F1
Tyacke Rd TR13..........146 B5
Tybesta TR2..............72 A7
  Grampound TR2..........72 A7
Tye Hill Cl PL25...........59 A3
Tyland Rd PL32...........105 F4
Tylney Cl PL6...........125 B6
Tyndale Cl PL5..........124 B1
Tyringham Pl TR26.........77 E4
Tyringham Rd TR26.........77 E4
Tyringham Row TR26.......77 E4
Tyshute La PL26...........59 A1
Tything Wlk **4** PL3.....128 E6
TYWARDREATH.............60 E5
Tywardreath Highway PL24 60 C6
Tywardreath Hill PL24......60 D5
Tywardreath Sch PL24......60 D5
Tywarnhale Way TR4........68 A6
Tywarnhayle Rd TR6........55 A5
Tywarnhayle Sq **23** TR6..55 A5

U

Uglow Cl TR14...........138 C3
Ualia Rd TR7............110 F6
Ullswater Cres PL6.......124 E4
Umfulla Pl **18** TR26....141 B5
Under Chapel Yd TR18.....143 F4
Undercliff TR27..........142 D7
Undercliff Rd PL9........135 B7
Underhayes La PL15.......106 A8
Underhill Rd PL3.........128 A4
Underhill Villas **1** PL3..128 A3
Underla TR13.............92 D8
Under La Cross Hill PL30....23 C1
  Haywood PL30...........34 C8
  Launceston PL15.........18 C3
Underlane Boyton PL15.....13 A3
  Marhamchurch EX23........7 B6
  Plymouth, Plympton PL7...130 C5
  Plymouth, Plymstock PL9..135 C6
Under Rd Boscastle PL35....9 C1
  Bridgerule EX22..........8 A5
  Gunnislake PL18.........41 A6
Underways PL20...........41 B1
UNDERWOOD.............130 C5
Underwood Rd PL7........130 D4
Unicorn Cl PL7..........130 B6
Union Hill
  St Columb Major TR9......45 E6
  6 Stratton EX23.......4 D1
Union Pl Fowey PL23......116 D4
  Plymouth PL1...........148 A2
  Truro TR1..............137 D5
Union Rd TR11...........144 D6
Union Sq TR9.............45 E6
Union St Camborne TR14...138 D2
  27 Penzance TR18.....143 E5
  Plymouth PL1...........148 A2
  Truro TR1..............137 C5
UNITED DOWNS............81 A8
United Downs Ind Pk
  Truro TR16.............81 A8
  United Downs TR16.......81 A8
United Rd Carharrack TR16..80 F8
  United Downs TR16.......81 A8
Unit Hos PL27.............33 B5
Unity Cl PL6............125 D5
Unity Rd TR13............98 C8
University of Plymouth Bsns
  Sch PL4...............148 C4
University of Plymouth
  (Cookworthy Bldg) PL4..149 A3
Univ of St Mark & St John
  PL6...................125 C4
UPCOTT..................2 F4
Upcott Cross EX39.........2 F5

Upland Cl TR1...........137 F6
Upland Cres TR1.........137 E6
Upland Dr PL6...........125 A5
Uplands Lostwithiel PL22...112 B2
  Saltash PL12...........122 E1
  Tavistock PL19.........147 A4
Uplands Vean TR1........137 F5
Upper Castle Rd TR2.......95 A6
Upper Chapel PL15.......106 A4
Upper Dobbin Cl PL28......20 F2
Upper Dobbin La PL28......20 F2
Upper Eastcliffe Rd PL24...60 D4
Upper Hillcrest **8** TR6....55 A4
Upper Knollys Terrace La
  PL3...................128 C4
Upper Lemon Villas TR1...137 C3
Upper Ridings PL7........131 B7
Upper School La TR1......137 C3
Upperton La PL6.........121 F3
Upper Tredrea TR3.........81 D5
UPTON Bude.............104 C2
  Upton Cross............38 C7
Upton Cl PL3............129 B7
UPTON CROSS.............38 D6
Upton Cross EX23........104 C2
Upton Cross Prim Sch PL14 38 C7
Upton Mdws EX23.........104 C3
Upton Terr EX23.........104 C2
UPTON TOWANS............78 B6
Upton Towans
  Gwithian TR27..........66 B1
  Upton Towans TR27......78 C7
Upton Twrs Nature Reserve★
  TR27...................78 B6
Urban Terr PL17..........39 F5
Ursa Gdns **21** PL9......136 E8
UTC Plymouth PL19.......127 E3
Uxbridge Dr PL5.........123 E4
Uzella Pk PL22..........112 C2

V

Vaagso Cl PL1...........127 E2
Valency Row PL35..........9 C2
Valentine Row **4** PL17...39 E4
Valiant Ave PL5.........124 A4
Vallard's La PL12.........53 E4
Valletort Flats PL1.......128 A2
Valletort Ho PL1.........148 C3
Valletort La PL1.........128 A3
Valletort Pl PL1.........128 A2
Valletort Rd PL1, PL3.....128 A3
Valletort Terr PL1.......148 A4
Valley Bglws PL13........117 F5
Valley Cl Goonhavern TR4..55 C3
  Truro TR1...............69 F3
Valley Gdns **20** TR16....67 E4
Valley La TR3............81 F7
Valley Park La PL26........73 C3
Valley Pk **20** PL26.......85 D8
Valley Rd Bude EX23......104 F5
  Carbis Bay TR26........141 C2
  Mevagissey PL26.........73 C4
  Plymouth PL7...........130 B5
  Saltash PL12...........122 E2
Valley The TR19...........96 E3
VALLEY TRUCKLE..........105 C2
Valley View Bodmin PL31..109 E3
  19 Illogan TR16......67 E4
  Plymouth PL6...........125 D7
  Redruth TR16...........140 E1
  St Keyne PL14...........51 A4
  St Teath PL30............23 E7
  Wadebridge PL27........108 C4
Valley View Cl PL3.......129 B6
Valley View Dr TR1........69 F3
Valley View Pk Bodmin PL31 34 D2
  St Austell PL26..........47 C2
Valley View Rd PL3.......129 B6
Valley View Terr TR3......81 B5
Valley Wlk PL6..........125 E6
Vanguard Cl PL5.........124 D1
Vapron Rd PL3...........128 F6
Varfell La TR20...........89 A7
Varley La PL14...........113 A5
Varley Terr **1** PL14.....113 B5
Vauban Pl PL2...........127 F4
Vaughan Cl PL2..........128 C7
Vauxhall Ct **10** PL4....149 A2
Vauxhall Quay PL4........149 A2
Vauxhall St PL4.........149 A2
Vauxhall Street Flats **19**
  PL4...................149 A2
Vean Rd TR14...........138 C2
Vean Terr TR14..........138 E2
Vear Ho TR14...........138 D2
Vellan Cl TR14...........79 B5
Vellan Dreath TR19........86 E1
Vellan Rd TR3............80 F3
Vellandrucia TR3..........80 F3
Vellanhoggan Mews TR18...58 E6
VELLANOWETH.............89 A8
Vellan Parc Ave TR27......78 C5
Vellan Vrane TR27.........78 C5
Venetian Views TR9........57 D8
Venland Cl **9** PL14......38 A3
Venn Cl **6** PL3.........128 E6
Venn Cres PL3...........128 E6
Venn Ct PL3.............128 E6
Venn Gdns PL3...........128 E7
Venn Gr PL3............128 E6
Venn Hill PL19...........29 C6
Venn La PL30.............36 A2
Venn Way PL3...........128 E6
Vensloae Hill PL14........113 B7
VENTERDON..............28 D2
Ventnor Terr TR26.......141 B4
Venton East Sq TR19......86 F6

VENTONGIMPS 55 C2
Venton Lace Rd TR2 . . . . . .57 E1
VENTONLEAGUE 142 F7
Ventonleague Hill TR27 . .142 E7
Ventonleague Row TR27. .142 E7
Ventonraze TR16 . . . . .67 E4
Ventonraze Terr **2** TR16. .67 E4
Venton Rd Falmouth TR11 . .144 E4
St Ives TR26 . . . . .141 D3
Ventonvase **5** TR6. . . . . . . .55 A5
Venton Vision Rise TR26 . . .77 A7
Veor Rd TR7. . . . . .111 C7
Verden Cl PL3 . . . . .128 E5
Verdun Terr PL14. . . . . .113 B5
Vermont Gdns PL2 . . . . . . .127 F7
Verna Pl PL5 . . . . .123 D2
Verna Rd PL5. . . . . .123 E2
Vernigo Cross PL12. . . . . . . .40 B1
Vernon Pl TR11. . . . . .145 B4
Vernon Villas PL24 . . . . .60 B4
Vernon Way TR10. . . . . .144 B7
VERYAN 83 F6
Veryan CE Prim Sch TR2 . .83 F6
VERYAN GREEN 83 F7
Viaduct Hill TR27 . . . . .142 E6
Viaduct La TR14. . . . . .138 A1
Vicarage Cl
  Budock Water TR11. . . . . .144 C3
  Menheniot PL14. . . . . .51 F5
Vicarage Gate TR27. . . . . . .142 A1
Vicarage Gdns
  Milton Abbot PL19. . . . . . . .29 C6
  Plymouth PL5. . . . . .123 B1
Vicarage Hill
  Budock Water TR11. . . . . .144 C3
  Mevagissey PL26. . . . . .73 C4
  10 St Austell PL25. . . . . . .114 C3
  St Day TR16 . . . . .68 L1
  9 Tintagel PL34. . . . . .14 C7
Vicarage La Lelant TR26 . . .77 E4
  Manaccan TR12. . . . . .101 A8
  Poundstock EX23. . . . . .6 F2
Vicarage Mdw PL23 . . . . . .116 C4
Vicarage Rd Bude EX23 . .104 D5
  Plymouth PL7. . . . . .130 C6
  Porthleven TR13 . . . . .91 A1
  St Agnes TR5 . . . . .54 D1
  Torpoint PL11 . . . . .127 B2
  Tywardreath PL24. . . . . .60 D5
Vicarage Row TR13. . . . . . . .90 F3
Vicarage Terr TR11. . . . . . . .92 F4
VICTORIA Lostwithiel 112 B2
  Roche 46 F4
Victoria Ave PL14. . . . . . . .148 A4
Victoria Bsns Pk PL26. . . . .47 A4
Victoria Cl PL14 . . . . .113 C6
Victoria Cotts
  Budock Water TR11. . . . . .144 C3
  Falmouth TR11. . . . . .145 B3
  Plymouth PL6. . . . . .129 B8
Victoria Ct **15** TR18. . . . .143 E6
Victoria Gdns
  2 St Columb Road TR9 . . . .45 E2
  Threemilestone TR3 . . . . . . .69 D3
Victoria La PL12. . . . . .122 F2
Victoria Mews **17** TR18. .143 E6
Victoria Pk PL27. . . . . .108 D6
Victoria Pl
  31 Penzance TR18. . . . . . .143 E5
  Plymouth PL1. . . . . .148 A2
  Plymouth, Devonport PL2 . .127 F4
  Ponsanooth TR3. . . . . .81 B4
  9 St Austell PL25. . . . . . .114 C3
  12 St Ives TR26 . . . . .141 B6
Victoria Quay
  5 Falmouth TR11. . . . . . .145 B5
  Truro TR1. . . . . .70 D1
Victoria Rd Bude EX23 . . .104 D7
  Camelford PL32. . . . . .105 E4
  Plymouth PL5. . . . . .123 D2
  Roche PL26 . . . . .46 F3
  St Austell PL25. . . . . .114 F3
  11 St Ives TR26 . . . . .141 B6
  Saltash PL12. . . . . .122 F2
  Threemilestone TR3 . . . . . . .69 D3
Victoria Road Prim Sch **1**
  PL5. .123 D1
Victoria Row TR19. . . . . . . .86 E4
Victoria Sq Bodmin PL31 . .109 F3
  16 Penzance TR18. . . . . . .143 E6
  Truro TR1. . . . . .137 C4
Victoria St Camborne TR14 .138 D2
  St Columb Major TR9 . . . . . .45 E6
  Torpoint PL11 . . . . .127 B3
Victoria Terr
  4 Liskeard PL14. . . . . . . .113 B5
  Plymouth PL4. . . . . .148 A4
  Portscatho TR2 . . . . .83 B2
  St Breward PL30 . . . . .24 B3
Victory Cl **8** TR20 . . . . . . .88 B7
Victory Rd EX22 . . . . .13 A8
Victory St PL2. . . . . .127 E6
Vigo Bridge Rd PL19 . . . . .147 C6
Vigo Mews PL19 . . . . .147 C6
Village Dr PL6. . . . . .121 C1
Village Farm Cl EX23 . . . . . .7 B6
Village The
  Buckland Monachorum PL20 . .41 F3
  Duloe PL14. . . . . .51 A1
Villa Marina TR17. . . . . .89 B5
Villiers Cl PL9 . . . . .135 D7
Vincent Way PL12. . . . . . . .122 F2
Vine Cres PL2 . . . . .128 B6
Vine Gdns PL2. . . . . .128 B6
Vine Pl **10** PL24. . . . . .60 D5
Vinery La PL7, PL9. . . . . . . .130 E1
Vineyard The TR3 . . . . .80 F3
Vingoe's La TR20 . . . . .88 B7

Vinstone Way PL5 . . . . .123 D1
Violet Dr PL6. . . . . .125 E8
Violet La PL19. . . . . .147 E6
Virgin Hill TR17. . . . . .89 C6
Virginia Gdns PL2. . . . . . . .127 F7
Virgin Pl **16** TR19 . . . . .88 C1
Virgin St **26** TR26 . . . . . . .141 B6
Visicks Works TR3 . . . . .81 E6
Vivian Cl TR7. . . . . .110 E5
Vivian Cl TR1. . . . . .137 D3
Vivian Pk TR14 . . . . .138 F2
Vivian Rd PL31. . . . . .109 B4
Vivid App PL1 . . . . .127 E2
Vixen Tor Cl PL20. . . . . .42 C3
VOGUE 68 D1
Vogue Hill TR16. . . . . .68 D1
Volans La **8** PL19. . . . . . . .136 E8
Vollards La **5** PL12. . . . . . .53 E4
Vorfield Cl TR15. . . . . .140 B6
Vosporth Hill TR8 . . . . .110 A3
Voss Rd PL12. . . . . .53 E1
Vounder Glaze TR19 . . . . . . .86 E6
Voundervour La **20** TR18 . .143 E5
Vyvyan Dr TR8. . . . . .44 E3
Vyvyan Pl TR13. . . . . .146 C5
Vyvyan's St TR14. . . . . .138 D3
Vyvyan's Terr TR14. . . . . . . .79 B2

W

Waddon Cl PL7. . . . . .130 E7
WADEBRIDGE 108 A6
Wadebridge L Ctr PL27 . . .108 C7
Wadebridge Prim Academy
  PL27. . . . . .108 C6
Wadebridge Rd
  St Mabyn PL30. . . . . .34 C8
  St Tudy PL30. . . . . .23 E3
Wadebridge Sch PL27 . . . .108 D6
Wadeland Terr **3** PL14. . . .51 A7
Wadham Cl **4** PL14. . . . . . .113 D5
Wadham Dr PL14. . . . . .113 D5
Wadham Ho **5** PL14. . . . . .113 C5
Wadham Rd PL14. . . . . .113 D5
Wadham Terr **6** PL2 . . . . .128 A5
Wagg La TR2. . . . . .71 C6
Waggon Hill PL7. . . . . .131 A4
Wagtail Cl **8** EX23. . . . . .7 B8
Wagtail Way **4** TR27 . . . . .142 E6
WAINHOUSE CORNER 10 E6
Wain Pk PL7. . . . . .130 F4
Wainsway **19** TR6. . . . . .55 A4
Wainways EX23. . . . . .10 F6
Wakefield Ave PL5 . . . . . . .123 E1
Wake St PL4. . . . . .148 B4
Walcot Cl PL6 . . . . .125 E3
Waldon Cl PL7. . . . . .131 B6
Walker Lines Ind Est **3**
  PL31. .48 D8
Walker Terr PL1. . . . . .148 B1
Walkham Bsns Pk PL5 . . . .124 B1
Walkham Cl PL19. . . . . .147 D5
Walkham Mdws PL20. . . . . .42 C4
WALKHAMPTON 42 D4
Walkhampton Rd PL20. . . . .42 C4
Walkhampton Wlk PL6 . . . .125 E1
Walkham Terr **4** PL20. . . . . .42 C5
Walk Terr PL23. . . . . .116 C2
Walk The PL15 . . . . .106 C6
WALL .78 E3
Wallace Mews **1** PL31. . . .109 D5
Wallace Rd Bodmin PL31. . .109 D5
  Plymouth PL7. . . . . .131 A4
Walled Gdn The TR10. . . . .144 A6
Wall Gdns PL27. . . . . .78 E3
Wallpark Cl PL7. . . . . .130 E7
Wall Rd TR27 . . . . .78 E3
Wallsend Ind Est PL4 . . . . .149 C1
Wall Vean TR27. . . . . .78 E3
Walnut Cl PL7. . . . . .131 B5
Walnut Dr PL7. . . . . .131 C5
Walnut Gdns PL7. . . . . .131 C5
Walreddon Cl PL19. . . . . . .147 B4
Walsingham Ct PL7. . . . . . .131 B6
Walsingham Pl **18** TR1. . . .137 D4
Walters La PL15 . . . . .18 D5
Walters Rd PL5. . . . . .123 C2
Walters Way
  3 Pengegon TR14. . . . . . .138 F3
  4 Rosudgeon TR20. . . . . . .89 F4
Waltham Pl PL2 . . . . .128 A8
Walton Cres PL5. . . . . .124 C1
Wandle Pl PL3. . . . . .129 D5
Wansford Mdws PL26. . . . . .85 C5
WANSON. 6 F3
Wanstead Gr PL5. . . . . .124 A2
Wantage Gdns PL1 . . . . . . .148 A3
WARBSTOW. 11 B1
Warbstow Com Sch PL15 . .11 B1
WARBSTOW CROSS 11 B2
Warburton Gdns PL5 . . . . .123 C1
Ward Cl **4** EX23. . . . . .4 D1
Wardlow Cl PL6. . . . . .128 F8
Wardlow Gdns PL6. . . . . . . .128 F8
Wardour Wlk PL6. . . . . .125 B7
Ward Pl PL3. . . . . .129 B5
Warfelton Cres PL12. . . . . .122 E2
Warfelton Gdns PL12. . . . . .122 E2
Warfelton Terr PL12. . . . . . .122 E2
Waring Rd PL6. . . . . .124 D7
WARLEGGAN 36 C4
Warleigh Ave PL2. . . . . .127 E5
WARLEIGH BARTON 123 F8
Warleigh Cres PL6. . . . . . . .124 F5
Warleigh La PL2. . . . . .127 E5
Warleigh Rd **2** PL4. . . . . .128 E4
Warmwell Rd PL5 . . . . .123 E4

Warne Cl TR2 . . . . .71 F3
Warran La PL19. . . . . .147 C3
Warraton Cl PL12. . . . . .122 D3
Warraton Gn PL12. . . . . . . .122 D3
Warraton La PL12. . . . . .122 D3
Warraton Rd PL12. . . . . . . .122 D3
Warren TR26. . . . . .141 B5
Warren Cl **18** TR13. . . . . . . .98 C8
Warren La PL5 . . . . .124 A8
Warren Pk PL6. . . . . .125 D7
Warren Rd TR9 . . . . .45 F2
Warrens Field PL32. . . . . . .105 D5
Warren St PL2. . . . . .127 E4
Warren The PL13 . . . . .62 E1
Warspite Gdns PL5 . . . . . . .124 D2
Warton Cl PL5. . . . . .124 D3
Warwick Ave Illogan TR16.. .67 D4
  Plymouth PL5. . . . . .124 D3
Warwick Cl PL28 . . . . .31 F8
Warwick Cres **5** PL27 . . . .31 F3
Warwick Dr PL5. . . . . .115 B5
Warwick Orchard Cl PL5. . .124 B3
Warwick Rd EX23. . . . . .104 E4
Warwick Cl PL6. . . . . .125 D2
Wasdale Gdns PL6. . . . . . . .125 D2
WASHAWAY. 34 C4
Washbourne Cl PL1 . . . . . . .127 E3
Wassa La PL32. . . . . .15 F5
Watch Hill PL26 . . . . .58 E5
WATERGATE 24 E8
Watergate TR16. . . . . .67 E5
Watergate La PL30. . . . . . . .34 C8
Watergate Rd TR8. . . . . .44 C6
Watering Hill Cl PL25. . . . .114 E3
Waterings Rd TR11. . . . . . . .82 A2
Water La Crantock TR8 . . . .110 A3
  Delabole PL33. . . . . .14 E3
  Golant PL23. . . . . .61 B5
  Hayle TR27. . . . . .142 B3
  St Agnes TR5 . . . . .54 D1
  Tresuck PL35. . . . . .9 D2
WATERLOO. 35 D7
Waterloo TR1 . . . . .137 E4
Waterloo Cl Plymouth PL1 . .128 A2
  St Mawes TR2 . . . . .95 A6
Waterloo Ct PL1. . . . . .128 A2
Waterloo Hill PL30. . . . . . . .35 D7
Waterloo Pl TR11. . . . . .145 B4
Waterloo Rd TR11 . . . . .145 B4
Waterloo St Plymouth PL4 . .149 A4
  Plymouth, Stoke PL1 . . . . . .128 A3
Waterloo Yard Flats PL1. . .128 A2
Water-ma-Trout TR13. . . . .146 C8
Water-ma-Trout Ind Est
  TR13. . . . . .146 C8
Waters Ct TR15. . . . . .140 E7
Waters Edge Newquay TR7 .110 A6
  Tavistock PL19. . . . . .147 D6
Water's Edge PL28. . . . . . . .107 E6
Watersedge Cl PL25. . . . . .114 B4
Waterside Lane PL30. . . . . .47 E7
Waterside Mews PL1 . . . . .127 D3
Watersmead Parc TR11. . . .144 C3
Waterwheel Cl **4** PL25 . . .115 A3
Watery La Bodmin PL31 . . .109 D5
  Milton Combe PL6 . . . . .120 D6
Watery Pk PL30. . . . . .36 A3
Watson Gdns PL4. . . . . .149 B3
Watson Pl PL4. . . . . .149 B2
Watts Park Rd PL2. . . . . . . .128 C7
Watts Rd PL19. . . . . .147 B5
Watt's Rd PL4 . . . . .149 C3
Waveney Gdns PL5 . . . . . . .124 C3
Waverley Cl PL25. . . . . .115 A5
Waverley Hts **4** TR13. . . .146 B5
Waverley Rd PL5 . . . . .123 C2
Wavish Pk PL11. . . . . .126 E3
Waycott Wlk PL6 . . . . .124 D6
Way Cross PL15. . . . . .27 B3
Wayfield Rd TR11. . . . . .82 B2
Wayfields PL30. . . . . .23 B2
Wayside Ct TR7. . . . . .111 A4
Wayside Folk Mus ★ TR26 . .76 B5
WEARDE. 122 F2
Wearde Rd PL12. . . . . .122 E1
Webber Hill TR11. . . . . .145 B4
Webber Rd TR11. . . . . .145 B4
Webbs Ct **9** PL14. . . . . . . .113 C6
Webb St PL23 . . . . .116 D4
Wedgewood Rd PL25 . . . . .115 A4
WEEK GREEN 11 E8
WEEK ST MARY 11 E8
Weeks Rise PL32. . . . . .105 B2
Weekstone Cross EX22 . . . .8 C8
Weeth Cl TR14 . . . . .138 C3
Weeth Com Prim Sch
  TR14. . . . . .138 C4
Weethes Cotts **6** TR18. . .143 D5
Weeth La TR14 . . . . .138 C3
Weeth Rd TR14. . . . . .138 C4
Weir Cl PL6. . . . . .125 F2
Weir Gdns PL6. . . . . .125 F2
Weir Rd PL6. . . . . .125 F2
Welbeck Ave PL4. . . . . .148 C4
WELCOMBE 2 D5
Welcombe Cross EX39. . . . .3 B4
Welcome Cl TR4. . . . . .56 D1
Welland Gdns PL3. . . . . . . .129 C5
Weller Ct TR11. . . . . .145 B3
Wellfield Cl
  Coad's Green PL15 . . . . .27 D3
  Plymouth PL7. . . . . .131 C5
Wellhay Cl PL9. . . . . .136 D5
Wellhouse The **8** PL14. . .113 C6
Wellington Cl TR14 . . . . . . .138 C3
Wellington Ct TR2. . . . . .72 A7
Wellington Gdns TR11. . . . .145 B4

Wellington Pl
  Falmouth TR11. . . . . .145 B4
  Penzance TR18 . . . . .143 D5
  Wadebridge PL27 . . . . .108 C4
Wellington Plantation TR3. .82 B7
Wellington Rd
  Camborne TR14. . . . . .138 D3
  Porthleven TR13 . . . . .91 B1
  St Dennis PL26. . . . . .58 C8
  2 St Eval PL27. . . . . .58 C8
Wellington St Plymouth PL4 .149 A4
  Plymouth, Stoke PL1 . . . . . .128 A3
  Torpoint PL11 . . . . .127 B3
Wellington Terr
  Falmouth TR11. . . . . .145 B4
  Porthleven TR13 . . . . .91 B1
  14 Portscatho TR2. . . . . . .83 B2
  2 Truro TR1. . . . . .137 C4
Well La TR11 . . . . .92 F3
  Constantine TR11 . . . . .92 F4
  Falmouth TR11. . . . . .145 B4
  Goldsithney TR20. . . . . .89 F5
  Lamorna TR19. . . . . .97 E5
  Liskeard PL14. . . . . .113 C6
  Polmenna PL14. . . . . .36 E1
  16 Portscatho TR2. . . . . . .83 B2
  St Cleer PL14. . . . . .37 F3
  St Keverne TR12 . . . . .101 D4
  Tregony TR2. . . . . .71 F3
  Tremar PL14. . . . . .38 A3
  Welcombe EX39 . . . . .2 E5
Well Mdw PL15. . . . . .18 A5
Wellpark Rd PL18. . . . . .40 F5
Well Park Rd TR11. . . . . . . .127 B3
Wellsbourne Pk PL3 . . . . . .129 A6
Wells Ct PL10. . . . . .132 E4
Well St Callington PL17. . . .39 E4
  22 Callington PL17. . . . . .39 E4
  Delabole PL33. . . . . .14 E3
  Tregony TR2. . . . . .71 F3
  Tywardreath PL24. . . . . .60 D5
Well Way TR7. . . . . .111 C7
Welman Rd PL10 . . . . .132 F6
Welsby Terr PL14. . . . . .37 F3
WELSFORD. 3 C8
Welsford Ave PL2 . . . . .127 F5
Welway TR6. . . . . .55 A4
WEMBURY 136 B1
Wembury Park Rd PL3. . . . .128 D6
Wembury Rd PL9 . . . . .136 A4
WENDRON 91 F6
Wendron Trenear TR13 . . . .92 A5
  Wendron PL15. . . . . .91 F5
Wendron CE Prim Sch TR13 .91 F6
Wendron St TR13 . . . . .146 C6
WENFORDBRIDGE 24 A2
Wenlock Gdns PL2 . . . . . . .128 B8
WENMOUTH CROSS 37 A3
Wensum Cl PL1. . . . . .131 A4
Wentwood Gdns PL6 . . . . .125 C3
Wentwood Pl PL6 . . . . .125 C3
Wentworth Cl
  Lynstone EX23. . . . . .104 C3
  Polzeath PL27 . . . . .21 D5
  Redruth TR15. . . . . .140 C3
Wentworth Pl PL4 . . . . .129 B2
Wentworth Way PL12. . . . .122 C2
WERRINGTON 18 F6
Werrington Comm Prim Sch
  PL15. .18 F7
Werrington Dr PL17. . . . . . .39 E4
Wesley Ave PL3 . . . . .128 E5
Wesley Cl Kelly Bray PL17. . .39 F6
  Stenalees PL26. . . . . .59 C8
Wesley Ct Penryn TR10. . . .144 C8
  Pensilva PL14. . . . . .38 D4
  25 Porthleven TR13. . . . . .98 C8
  18 Portmellon PL26. . . . . .85 D8
  Torpoint PL11 . . . . .127 C3
Wesley La PL12. . . . . .122 F2
Wesley Pl **5** Newlyn TR18. .143 C2
  Plymouth, Mutley PL3 . . . . .128 E5
  1 Plymouth, Stoke PL2. . .128 A4
  St Austell PL25. . . . . .114 F3
  7 St Ives TR26 . . . . .141 B5
Wesley Rd Cubert TR8 . . . . .55 D8
  Pensilva PL14. . . . . .38 D4
  Saltash PL12. . . . . .122 F2
  Trevail PL14. . . . . .43 D1
Wesley St Camborne TR14 .138 E3
  11 Heamoor TR18. . . . . . .143 C7
  Redruth TR15. . . . . .140 C5
Wesley Terr Bugle PL26. . . .47 C2
  Looe PL13. . . . . .117 D4
Wesley Way PL15. . . . . .26 B7
Wesley Yd TR7. . . . . .110 C6
West Ave **4** PL19. . . . . . . .147 B5
West Bay TR11 . . . . .93 F4
West Beach Rd TR4. . . . . . . .68 A6
West Beckon Cl EX23 . . . . . .2 D1
WEST BLACKDOWN 30 F8
Westborne Hts TR15. . . . . .140 B3
Westborne Rd TR14 . . . . . .138 B4
Westbourne Dr PL25. . . . . .114 B3
Westbourne La PL14. . . . . .113 B6
Westbourne Rd PL3. . . . . . .128 D5
Westbourne Terr
  Fraddon TR9. . . . . .57 D8
  Saltash PL12. . . . . .122 F2
Westbridge Cotts PL19 . . .147 B4
Westbridge Ind Est **3**
  PL19. . . . . .147 B4
Westbridge Rd PL25 . . . . . .59 A3
West Bridge Rd PL15 . . . . .106 B7
Westbury Cl PL5. . . . . .124 B4
Westby Rd EX23 . . . . .104 E5
West Camps Bay PL11 . . . . .64 C4

Ven–Wes 181

West Charles St TR14. . . . .138 D2
West Cl TR13. . . . . .146 D7
West Cliff TR4. . . . . .68 A6
Westcliff Flats EX23. . . . . .104 D6
West Cnr **1** TR3. . . . . .81 F7
Westcombe Cres PL9 . . . . .135 D5
West Cornwall Hospl
  TR18. . . . . .143 D6
Westcott PL27. . . . . .108 A6
Westcott Cl PL6. . . . . .129 A8
Westcott Mdw PL27. . . . . . .108 A6
Westcountry Cl PL2 . . . . . .127 F7
Westcove Ho **2** TR7. . . . . .110 F6
Westcroft Rd PL5. . . . . .123 C1
West Ct TR7. . . . . .110 C5
WEST CURRY 12 D4
West Devon Bsns Pk PL19 .147 B3
Westdown Rd PL33. . . . . . . .14 D2
West Down Rd PL2 . . . . . . .128 B6
WESTDOWNS 14 C1
Westella Rd **12** Gratton PL20 .42 D2
  Yelverton PL20. . . . . .42 D2
West End Goldsithney TR20 . .89 E5
  Marazion TR17. . . . . .89 B5
  18 Methleigh TR13 . . . . . .91 A1
  Pentewan PL26. . . . . .73 C5
  Porthleven TR13 . . . . .98 B8
  15 Porthleven TR13. . . . . .98 B8
  Redruth TR15. . . . . .140 B4
  St Day TR16 . . . . .68 D1
West End Cl TR10. . . . . .144 C8
West End Cotts PL11. . . . . .64 B8
West End Ct **2** TR15. . . . . .140 B4
West End Ind Est TR10 . . . .144 B8
West End Sq **7** PL17. . . . . .39 E4
Westend Terr TR10 . . . . . . .144 C8
Westeria Terr PL2 . . . . .128 C7
Westerlands Rd PL27. . . . . .108 B6
Western App PL1. . . . . .148 B2
Western Ave PL14. . . . . .51 A7
Western College Rd PL4 . .128 F5
Western Dr PL3 . . . . .129 B4
Western Pl TR10. . . . . .144 B8
Western Promenade Rd
  TR18. . . . . .143 E4
Western Rd PL15. . . . . .106 B5
Western Side
  Higher Horslett EX22. . . . . . .13 B8
  iron bars EX22. . . . . .8 F1
Western Terr Bodmin PL31 .109 C4
  Falmouth TR11. . . . . .145 A3
  Launceston PL15 . . . . .106 C5
Western Wood Way PL7 . . .131 D5
West Fairholme Rd EX23. .104 E7
Westfield PL7. . . . . .131 A6
Westfield Ave PL9 . . . . .135 C6
Westgate Mews **2** PL15 . .106 C5
Westgate St PL15. . . . . .106 C5
Westground Way PL34. . . . .14 D7
Westhampnett Pl PL5. . . . .123 F4
Westhaul Pk PL25 . . . . .115 E4
Westhays Cl PL9. . . . . .135 F4
Westhead Rd PL10. . . . . . . .64 B2
Westheath Ave PL30, PL31 .109 B3
Westheath Rd PL31. . . . . . .109 B3
West Hill St Austell PL25. . .114 C3
  Wadebridge PL27 . . . . .108 A6
West Hill Ct **16** PL25 . . . . .114 C3
West Hill Rd PL4. . . . . .128 F4
WEST HOE 148 B1
West Hoe Rd PL1 . . . . .148 B1
West Kitty TR5 . . . . .54 C1
West La Crafthole PL11. . . .65 B5
  Delabole PL33. . . . . .14 E2
  Landrake PL12. . . . . .53 B3
Westlake Cl PL11. . . . . .126 F3
Westleigh Way PL9. . . . . . . .129 D1
WEST LOOE 117 C3
West Looe Hill PL13 . . . . . .117 B3
West Looe Sq PL13 . . . . . . .117 C3
West Malling Ave PL5. . . . .123 E5
Westmoor Cl PL7. . . . . .131 C6
Westmoor Cres TR3 . . . . . . .81 D6
Westmoor Pk PL19 . . . . . . .147 C3
WESTON MILL. 127 E8
Weston Mill Dr PL5. . . . . . .127 F8
Weston Mill Hill PL5. . . . . .123 F1
Weston Mill La PL5 . . . . . . .124 A1
Weston Mill Prim Sch PL2 .127 E7
Weston Mill Rd PL5. . . . . . .123 E1
Weston Park Rd PL3. . . . . .128 D6
Westover Rd PL17 . . . . .39 E4
WEST PANSON 13 D2
West Park PL27. . . . . .108 D5
West Park Dr PL7. . . . . .131 C5
West Park Hill PL7. . . . . . . .131 B7
Westpark Rd PL27. . . . . . . .108 E4
West Park Rd EX23 . . . . . . .104 D7
West Penrest Farm PL15. . .28 B4
WEST PENTIRE 43 C3
West Pentire Rd TR8. . . . . .43 D3
West Pk Egloshayle PL27 . . .33 E7
  Perranarworthal TR3. . . . . . .81 D6
  Redruth TR15. . . . . .139 F6
  13 St Columb Major TR9 . .45 E6
  Tideford PL12. . . . . .52 F2
  Trewidland PL14. . . . . .51 C3
Westpoint Falmouth TR11. .145 A3
  45 St Ives TR26 . . . . .141 B6
West Point TR8. . . . . .111 C4
West Porthmear Cotts
  PL25. . . . . .115 B2

West Porthmear Ct PL25 . . 115 B2
WEST PORTHOLLAND . . 84 D5
West Quay PL10 . . 132 E5
West Rd Looe PL13 . . 117 C4
  Quintrell Downs TR8 . . 111 E3
West Rise TR11 . . 144 F3
West Seton
  Higher Rosewarne TR14 . . 138 D5
  Reskadinnick TR14 . . 79 C8
West Seton Rd **6** TR14 . . 138 E5
West St Grimscott EX23 . . 5 B1
  Liskeard PL14 . . 113 B6
  Millbrook PL10 . . 132 E5
  Penryn TR10 . . 144 C8
  Polruan PL23 . . 116 C2
  St Columb Major TR9 . . 45 E6
  Tavistock PL19 . . 147 B5
  Torpoint PL10 . . 132 E4
WEST TAPHOUSE . . 49 E6
West Tehidy TR14 . . 138 F7
West Terr Hayle TR27 . . 142 B6
  Newlyn TR18 . . 143 C3
WEST TOLGUS . . 139 D8
West Tolgus TR15 . . 139 D8
West Trevingey TR15 . . 140 A3
West Trewirgie Rd TR15 . . 140 B4
Westview TR6 . . 55 B5
West View Porthleven TR13 . . 91 A1
  Tavistock PL19 . . 147 E2
  Trevone PL28 . . 20 E2
West View Rd **5** PL20 . . 41 B1
West Villas TR8 . . 57 B7
Westward PL27 . . 21 D5
Westward Rd TR26 . . 141 A6
WEST WATERGATE . . 62 E4
Westway PL9 . . 135 B5
West Week Cl EX22 . . 11 E8
West Wharf TR26 . . 73 C3
Westwinds PL32 . . 16 A8
Westwood PL14 . . 113 B6
Westwood Ave PL6 . . 125 C6
WEST YOULSTONE . . 3 B2
Wetherham La PL30 . . 23 E3
Wet La PL30 . . 48 B8
Whalesborough Parc EX23 104 F1
Wharf Rd Penzance TR18 . . 143 F5
  St Ives TR26 . . 141 B6
Wharfside **8** TR18 . . 143 E5
Wharfside Sh Ctr TR18 . . 143 E5
Wharfside Village **9** TR18 143 E5
Wharf The
  22 Mousehole TR19 . . 88 C1
  St Ives TR26 . . 141 B6
Wharf Theatre & Gall The ★
  PL19 . . 147 B5
Whatley Mews **3** PL9 . . 129 D1
Wheal Agar **4** TR14 . . 138 F7
Wheal Agar TR15 . . 139 C6
WHEAL ALFRED . . 142 F4
Wheal Alfred Rd TR27 . . 142 F5
Wheal-an-Wens TR17 . . 89 C5
Wheal Ayr Ct **1** TR26 . . 141 A5
Wheal Boys TR16 . . 140 E8
Whealbrake Lodge PL26 . . 58 D6
Whealbrothers La PL17 . . 40 C4
Wheal Bull PL26 . . 58 D5
Wheal Buller Carnkie TR16 . . 80 C7
  Pennance TR16 . . 140 A1
WHEAL BUSY . . 68 F3
Wheal Busy La TR4 . . 68 F3
Wheal Butson Rd TR5 . . 68 D8
Wheal Catherine Cl TR6 . . 55 B5
Wheal Cl TR8 . . 56 B7
Wheal Damsel Rd TR16 . . 80 E8
Wheal Dance TR16 . . 140 D3
Wheal Dream TR26 . . 141 C6
Wheal Eliza Cl PL25 . . 115 E5
Wheal Fortune TR13 . . 91 A3
Wheal Fortune La TR15 . . 139 D6
WHEAL FRANCES . . 55 D3
Wheal Friendly La TR5 . . 54 C2
Wheal Gerry TR14 . . 138 E4
Wheal Golden Dr TR8 . . 43 C1
Wheal Gorland Rd TR16 . . 68 D1
Wheal Harmony Terr TR15 140 B7
Wheal Jane Mdws TR3 . . 69 C3
Wheal Jewel (Gipsy Site)
  TR16 . . 68 E1
Wheal Kitty TR5 . . 54 D1
Wheal Kitty La TR5 . . 54 D2
Wheal Kitty Rd TR27 . . 77 A3
Wheal Kitty Workshops
  TR5 . . 54 D2
Wheal Leisure TR6 . . 55 A5
Wheal Leisure Cl **25** TR6 . . 55 A5
Wheal Margery TR26 . . 141 C3
Wheal Maria PL19 . . 29 D1
Wheal Maria Cotts PL19 . . 29 D1
Wheal Martyn Mus ★ PL26 . . 59 B6
Wheal Montague TR16 . . 140 B7
Wheal Northey PL25 . . 115 B5
Wheal Oak TR13 . . 146 D8
Wheal Prussia TR16 . . 140 D8
Wheal Quoit Ave TR5 . . 54 C1
Wheal Ramoth **3** TR6 . . 55 A5
Wheal Regent Pk PL25 . . 115 D3
Wheal Rodney Holiday Pk ★
  TR20 . . 89 C6
WHEAL ROSE . . 68 C3
Wheal Rose **19** TR13 . . 146 D8
Wheal Silver TR15 . . 140 B5
Wheal Speed Rd TR16 . . 141 C2
Wheal Sperries Way TR1 . . 69 E3
Wheal Tehidy La TR15 . . 139 E6
Wheal Trefusis TR15 . . 140 D2

Wheal Trelawney TR16 . . 140 D3
Wheal Venture Rd TR26 . . 141 C3
Wheal View PL26 . . 58 B4
Wheal Virgin Ho TR26 . . 77 A6
WHEAL VOR . . 91 A5
Wheal Vor TR15 . . 140 D3
Wheal Vrose Business Pk **12**
  TR13 . . 146 D8
Wheal Vyvyan TR11 . . 92 F4
Wheal Whidden TR26 . . 141 C2
Wheatfield Cl **3** PL15 . . 106 D4
Wheatfield Cres TR7 . . 111 A4
Wheatley Rd EX22 . . 11 F4
Wheatridge PL7 . . 130 B7
Wheal Ayr Terr TR26 . . 141 A5
Wheelage House Sch TR8 . . 43 D2
Wheelwright Ct PL20 . . 42 E4
Wherry Pl PL23 . . 116 D2
WHERRY TOWN . . 143 D4
Wherry Way PL14 . . 50 E7
Wheildon Rd PL25 . . 115 A4
Whimbrel Way PL9 . . 136 C8
Whimple St PL1 . . 148 C2
Whin Bank Rd PL5 . . 124 E2
WHIPSIDERRY . . 44 C6
Whipsiderry Cl TR7 . . 44 C6
Whistley Down PL20 . . 42 B2
Whitby Cres PL6 . . 125 A1
Whitby Rd PL6 . . 125 A1
WHITCHURCH . . 147 D3
Whitchurch Com Prim Sch
  PL19 . . 147 D2
Whitchurch Rd
  Horrabridge PL20 . . 42 C5
  Tavistock PL19 . . 147 C3
  Tavistock PL19 . . 147 C4
Whitcross Hill TR15 . . 139 C3
Whitebarrow Cotts PL14 . . 37 A4
Whitecroft Way EX23 . . 5 A6
WHITECROSS Crowlas . . 77 C1
  Wadebridge . . 33 B7
Whitecross Blisland PL30 . . 35 D7
  Bodinnick PL23 . . 116 F6
WHITE CROSS Mullion . . 99 B4
  St Columb Road . . 45 C2
White Cross Cury TR12 . . 99 B4
  Redruth TR16 . . 68 D3
White Cross Ct PL4 . . 149 A3
Whitecross Hill PL23 . . 61 D3
Whitecross Ind Est TR8 . . 45 B2
Whitefield Terr PL4 . . 149 B4
Whiteford Cl **16** PL17 . . 39 E4
Whiteford Rd PL3 . . 128 C6
White Friars La PL4 . . 149 B3
Whitegate Mdws PL26 . . 58 B8
Whitegate PL26 . . 58 B8
Whitegate Rd TR7 . . 111 A6
Whitegate Sh Complex
  TR7 . . 111 A7
Whitehall Dr
  9 Bere Alston PL20 . . 41 B1
  Plymouth PL9 . . 136 B7
Whitehall Est PL30 . . 23 B2
White Hart Arc The **3**
  PL15 . . 106 C5
Whitehaven Way PL6 . . 125 A7
WHITEHILL . . 146 C4
Whitehill Cross PL15 . . 19 C6
Whitehill Terr TR13 . . 146 C4
White Horse
  Crowntown TR13 . . 91 A6
  Nancegollan TR13 . . 91 A6
White House Cl TR26 . . 141 C2
Whitehouse Villas **5**
  TR10 . . 81 A1
White La Philleigh TR2 . . 83 B6
  Plymouth PL1 . . 149 A2
White Lady Rd PL9 . . 135 D5
White Lodge EX23 . . 10 C7
WHITEMOOR . . 58 E8
Whitemoor Inf & Jun Sch
  PL26 . . 58 E8
White River Pl TR13 . . 114 C3
White River Pl Sh Ctr
  PL25 . . 114 C3
WHITEROCK . . 108 A5
Whiterock Cl PL27 . . 108 B5
Whiterock Rd PL27 . . 108 B5
Whiterocks Pk PL18 . . 40 D6
Whiterock Terr PL27 . . 108 B5
White's Cl **3** TR5 . . 54 D1
White Smock Mdw **7** PL35 . . 9 C1
Whitestone Cres PL31 . . 109 C3
Whitestone Rd PL31 . . 109 C3
White Walls Ct **16** TR6 . . 55 A4
Whitewater Ct PL7 . . 130 E6
WHITEWELL . . 23 D7
Whitewell Rd PL30 . . 23 D7
Whitham Pk PL19 . . 147 C4
WHITLEIGH . . 124 C5
Whitleigh Ave PL5 . . 124 E2
Whitleigh Com Prim Sch
  PL5 . . 124 D4
Whitleigh Cotts PL5 . . 124 E2
Whitleigh Ct PL5 . . 124 D4
Whitleigh Gn PL5 . . 124 C4
Whitleigh Vale PL5 . . 124 E2
Whitleigh Way PL5 . . 124 C4
Whitley Cl TR1 . . 137 D4
Whitley Grange PL14 . . 113 A6
Whitlieburn Terr PL13 . . 117 C3
Whitpot Hill PL12 . . 64 F8
Whitsam Cross PL20 . . 41 A1
Whitsand Bay View PL11 . . 65 A4
Whitson Cross PL5 . . 124 C7
Whitsoncross La PL5 . . 124 C7
WHITSTONE . . 7 F1

Whitstone Cty Prim Sch
  EX22 . . 7 F1
Whitstone Head Sch EX22 . . 7 F1
Whittington St PL3 . . 148 B4
Whitworth Cl TR5 . . 54 C1
Whity Cross PL12 . . 122 A4
Widegate Nursery PL9 . . 136 D8
WIDEGATES . . 63 F8
WIDEMOUTH BAY . . 6 F5
Widewell La PL6 . . 125 C7
Widewell Prim Acad PL6 . . 125 B7
Widewell Rd PL6 . . 125 B7
Widey Court Prim Sch PL6 124 F1
Widey Cross PL6 . . 124 F1
Widey Ct PL6 . . 124 F1
Widey La PL6 . . 124 F1
Widey View PL3 . . 128 F6
Widgeon Way TR27 . . 77 E3
Wigeon Rd **6** EX23 . . 7 B8
Wilcove PL11 . . 127 A6
Wilcove La PL11 . . 126 E5
Wildebeest Rd **7** PL27 . . 31 F3
Wilderness Rd PL3 . . 128 E5
Wilderness Trail ★ PL30 . . 48 C5
Wildflower La TR7 . . 111 A6
Wilkes Wlk TR1 . . 137 D4
Wilkinson Cl PL17 . . 39 E6
Wilkinson Rd PL5 . . 127 D8
Willapark View PL35 . . 9 C1
Willas Rd PL16 . . 19 F4
William Edwards Cl EX23 . . 104 E6
William Evans Cl PL6 . . 124 D5
William Laundry Cl PL14 . . 52 A5
William Prance Rd PL6 . . 125 A3
Williams Ave PL4 . . 129 B1
Williams Ho PL31 . . 109 B4
William St Camborne TR14 . . 138 D2
  Truro TR1 . . 137 D4
William Young Mews
  PL14 . . 113 E5
Willis Vean PL12 . . 99 A1
Willoughby Pl PL17 . . 39 E4
Willoughby Way TR27 . . 78 D6
Willowby Pk PL20 . . 42 D2
Willow Cl **22** Callington PL17 . . 39 F4
  Mylor Bridge TR11 . . 82 A3
  Plymouth PL3 . . 129 A5
  Quintrell Downs TR8 . . 44 E3
Willow Cotts PL7 . . 130 D4
Willow Ct PL6 . . 129 E2
Willow Dr TR14 . . 138 B4
Willowfield PL18 . . 143 C5
Willow Gn PL12 . . 122 D2
Willow Rd PL19 . . 147 C3
Willows The Bugle PL26 . . 47 C1
  Whipsiderry TR7 . . 44 C6
Willow Way PL14 . . 113 B5
Willow Wlk PL6 . . 125 D5
Wills Cl PL6 . . 124 E7
Wills La **53** PL26 . . 141 B6
Wills Moor PL26 . . 85 C5
Will's Row TR15 . . 139 C8
Willsworthy Dr **2** PL19 . . 147 B7
WILMINSTONE . . 30 F3
Wilmington Ind Est PL19 147 E7
Wilmot Gdns PL5 . . 124 A3
Wilsey View St Clether PL15 . . 17 B7
  Splatt PL15 . . 17 B7
Wilson Cres PL2 . . 128 B5
Wilson Way
  Camborne TR15 . . 139 D5
  14 Par PL24 . . 60 B4
Wilsworthy Cross EX22 . . 12 C7
Wilton Cl PL14 . . 128 A3
Wilton St PL1 . . 148 A4
Wilton Terr PL13 . . 62 D6
Wiltshire Cl PL4 . . 128 F4
Winchester Gdns PL5 . . 124 A5
Windermere Cres PL6 . . 124 F4
Winding Terr PL10 . . 81 A1
WINDMILL . . 20 F1
Windmill PL23 . . 116 C4
Windmill Hill TR2 . . 57 E1
  Launceston PL15 . . 106 C5
  St Just in Roseland TR2 . . 82 F2
  Saltash PL12 . . 122 C2
Windmill Hill Terr PL15 . . 106 C5
Windmill Ho PL23 . . 116 C4
Windmill Ind Est PL23 . . 116 C4
Windmill La PL15 . . 106 C5
Windmill Park PL15 . . 106 C5
Windmill Rd PL27 . . 22 A5
Windsbatch La **7** PL9 . . 129 D1
Windsor Ct Falmouth TR11 . . 145 B4
  Newquay TR7 . . 110 D5
Windsor Dr PL25 . . 115 C3
Windsor Gr PL31 . . 109 F5
Windsor Hill **8** TR26 . . 141 B5
Windsor Ho **9** PL31 . . 109 E5
Windsor La Kelly Bray PL17 . . 39 F6
  Saltash PL12 . . 122 E2
Windsor Mews PL31 . . 109 C5
Windsor Pl Liskeard PL14 . . 113 C5
  28 Penzance TR18 . . 143 E6
  Plymouth PL1 . . 148 C2
Windsor Terr
  Falmouth TR11 . . 145 B4
  Penzance TR18 . . 143 D6
  4 St Ives TR26 . . 141 A5
Windsor Villas PL1 . . 148 C2
Windsworth PL24 . . 115 F7
Windy Ridge PL26 . . 46 D1
Wingfield PL31 . . 35 B2
Wingfield Mans PL3 . . 128 A3
Wingfield Rd PL3 . . 148 A4

Wingfield Way PL3 . . 148 A4
Winifred Baker Ct **5** PL4 . . 149 A4
Winnard's Perch TR9 . . 32 D1
Winnicott Cl PL6 . . 124 E7
Winnow Cl PL9 . . 135 F4
Winns Row
  Gwealmayowe TR13 . . 146 C6
  Helston TR13 . . 146 C6
Winsbury Ct PL6 . . 125 A1
Winsor Cotts PL15 . . 106 B7
Winsor Est PL13 . . 62 D5
Winsor La TR11 . . 31 E1
Winstanley Wlk PL3 . . 129 D6
Winston Ave PL4 . . 148 C4
Winstowe Terr TR8 . . 110 A3
Winwell Field PL27 . . 108 D6
Wireless Rd PL26 . . 47 B5
Wishing Well La TR20 . . 88 A7
Witham Gdns PL3 . . 129 C5
WITHEVEN . . 11 D3
WITHIEL . . 47 A8
WITHIELGOOSE MILLS . . 47 C8
Withies St **5** PL9 . . 129 D1
WITHNOE . . 11 D3
Withnoe La PL10 . . 132 B6
Withnoe Terr PL10 . . 65 E3
Withnoe Way Cl PL15 . . 106 D3
Wixenford Ct PL9 . . 135 F8
Woburn Rd PL15 . . 106 B4
Woburn Terr PL9 . . 135 C7
Wodehouse Terr TR11 . . 145 B4
Wolcocke Cl TR17 . . 89 D5
Wollaton Gr PL5 . . 123 F3
Wolrige Ave PL7 . . 131 B5
Wolrige Way PL7 . . 131 A5
Wolsdon Pl PL1 . . 148 A3
Wolsdon St PL1 . . 148 B3
Wolseley Bsns Pk **2** PL2 . . 128 A5
Wolseley Cl PL2 . . 128 A5
Wolseley Rd
  Plymouth, Camels Head
    PL5 . . 127 F6
  Plymouth, St Budeaux PL5 . . 127 F6
Wolseley Road Flats PL2 . . 127 F6
Wolverwood Cl PL7 . . 131 C3
Wolverwood La PL7 . . 131 B3
Wombwell Cres PL2 . . 127 E7
Wood Acre PL12 . . 122 B4
Woodacre Ct PL12 . . 122 B4
Wooda La PL15 . . 106 B6
Wooda Rd PL15 . . 106 C6
Woodbine Cotts PL7 . . 130 E4
Woodbine La TR16 . . 67 D4
Woodbury Gdns PL5 . . 124 A3
Woodchurch PL20 . . 42 B3
Wood Cl
  17 Resugga Green PL26 . . 59 D7
  Saltash PL12 . . 122 B3
Woodcock Cl PL10 . . 133 A6
Woodend Rd PL6 . . 125 D7
Woodfield Prim Sch PL5 . . 124 C5
Woodfield Rd EX23 . . 104 E7
WOODFORD Plymouth . . 130 C7
  Shop . . 4 D8
Woodford Ave PL7 . . 130 A6
Woodford Cl PL7 . . 130 A7
Woodford Cres PL7 . . 130 A6
Woodford Cross EX23 . . 2 C1
Woodford Gn PL7 . . 130 B6
Woodford Prim Sch PL7 . . 130 B6
Woodford Rd PL6 . . 125 D6
Woodgate Rd PL14 . . 113 A5
Woodgrove Pk PL26 . . 59 A1
Woodhill TR10 . . 81 B2
Wood La Landrake PL12 . . 53 D2
  Truro TR1 . . 137 D3
  Tywardreath PL24 . . 60 D5
Woodland Ave Penryn TR10 144 B6
  Plymouth PL9 . . 136 A8
  12 Tywardreath PL24 . . 60 D5
Woodland Cl
  Gunnislake PL18 . . 40 F6
  Lanivet PL30 . . 47 E7
  St Austell PL25 . . 114 E3
Woodland Dr PL7 . . 130 B4
Woodland Glade PL30 . . 47 F7
Woodland Hill
  Doublebois PL14 . . 50 B8
  Polmenna PL14 . . 36 F1
Woodland Hts TR1 . . 137 E5
Woodland Rd Plymouth PL7 130 C6
  St Austell PL25 . . 114 E3
Woodland Rise
  Penryn TR10 . . 144 B7
  Rilla Mill PL17 . . 38 B1
Woodlands Dousland PL20 . . 42 E3
  4 Mullion TR12 . . 99 A2
  10 Par PL24 . . 60 C4
  Plymouth PL9 . . 135 F6
Woodlands Ct PL5 . . 124 A3
Woodlands End PL6 . . 125 D5
Woodlands La Coombe PL26 . . 58 C2
  Plymouth PL6 . . 125 F1
Woodlands Sch PL5 . . 124 B4
Woodlands Terr **3** TR16 . . 140 C1
Woodlands The TR14 . . 67 B4
Woodlands View PL13 . . 117 B4
Woodland Terr
  Plymouth PL4 . . 149 B4
  4 St Columb Road TR9 . . 45 E2
Woodland Terr La PL4 . . 149 B4
Woodland View **7** PL26 . . 115 A1
  Coombe PL26 . . 58 C2
  Lanivet PL30 . . 47 E6
Woodland Way
  Gunnislake PL18 . . 41 A7
  Torpoint PL11 . . 126 F3

Woodland Way Cl **2** PL18 . . 40 F6
Woodlane TR11 . . 145 B3
Woodlane Cl TR11 . . 145 B3
Woodlane Cres TR11 . . 145 B3
Woodlane Dr TR11 . . 145 B3
Woodley Cl **8** EX23 . . 4 D1
Woodman's Cnr PL20 . . 42 D3
Woodpecker Way PL19 . . 147 D2
Woodridge Cl TR27 . . 78 E1
Woods-Browning Ind Est
  PL31 . . 109 F2
Woodside Penryn TR10 . . 144 B7
  Plymouth PL4 . . 149 B4
Woodside Ave PL9 . . 135 C6
Woodside Ct PL7 . . 130 E4
Woodside La PL4 . . 149 B4
Woodstock Gdns PL5 . . 123 D1
Woodvale Terr PL15 . . 106 C5
Wood View TR10 . . 144 B7
Woodview Pk PL9 . . 136 A6
Woodville Cl PL2 . . 127 F7
Woodville Rd
  Morwenstow EX23 . . 2 C1
  Plymouth PL2 . . 127 F6
  Woodford EX23 . . 4 D8
Woodway Penryn TR10 . . 144 B7
  Plymouth PL9 . . 136 A7
Woolacombe Cross PL20 . . 41 C1
Woolacombe Rd PL20 . . 41 C1
Woollcombe Ave PL7 . . 130 F4
WOOLLEY . . 3 A3
Woolster Ct **8** PL4 . . 149 A2
WOOLSTON . . 38 E3
WOOLWELL . . 125 C7
Woolwell Cres PL6 . . 125 C5
Woolwell Dr PL6 . . 125 C7
Woolwell Rd PL6 . . 125 D7
Woon La **3** TR3 . . 81 F7
Worcester Rd PL25 . . 115 A4
Wordsworth Cres PL2 . . 127 F7
Wordsworth Rd PL2 . . 127 F7
Worvas La TR12 . . 102 F5
Wotton Cross PL12 . . 53 B4
Wreford Cl **11** TR9 . . 45 D6
Wren Gdns PL7 . . 130 C6
Wren Ind Est TR1 . . 69 E4
Wrens Gate PL9 . . 135 E8
Wrey Ave PL14 . . 113 C7
Wright Cl PL1 . . 127 E3
WRINGSDOWN . . 18 E6
Wrinklets Rd PL30 . . 23 A4
Wyatts La PL19 . . 147 B6
Wych Hazel Way TR7 . . 110 F4
Wycliffe Rd PL3 . . 129 B4
Wye Gdns PL3 . . 129 C7
Wykeham Dr PL2 . . 128 A7
Wyndham La PL1 . . 148 A3
Wyndham Mews PL1 . . 148 A3
Wyndham Pl PL1 . . 148 A3
Wyndham Sq PL1 . . 148 A3
Wyndham Street E PL1 . . 148 B3
Wyndham Street W PL1 . . 148 B3
Wyndhurst Orch PL27 . . 108 B2
Wyoming PL3 . . 129 C6
Wythburn Gdns PL6 . . 125 D3

Y

Yardley Gdns PL6 . . 125 C5
Yarrow Mead PL9 . . 136 D7
Yealmpstone Cl PL7 . . 131 B4
Yealmpstone Dr PL7 . . 131 B3
Yealmpstone Farm Prim Sch
  PL7 . . 131 B3
Yeats Cl PL5 . . 124 C2
Yellowmead Rd PL2 . . 128 A4
Yellow Tor Ct PL12 . . 122 C2
Yellow Tor La PL12 . . 122 C2
Yellow Tor Rd PL12 . . 122 B2
Yellow-Wort TR16 . . 80 C3
YELVERTON . . 42 D3
Yelverton Bsns Pk PL20 . . 42 B2
Yelverton Cl PL5 . . 123 D4
Yelverton Paperweight Mus ★
  PL20 . . 42 C2
Yelverton Terr
  Tavistock PL19 . . 147 D4
  Yelverton PL20 . . 42 D2
Yeo Cl PL3 . . 129 B5
Yeoland Down PL20 . . 121 E4
Yeoland La PL20 . . 42 C1
YEOLMBRIDGE . . 18 F6
Yeomadon Cross EX22 . . 8 E4
Yeomans Cl PL14 . . 113 D5
Yeomans Way PL7 . . 131 A4
Yeoman Way TR8 . . 44 B4
Yewdale Gdns PL6 . . 125 D2
Yew Tree Ct TR1 . . 137 F6
Yonder St PL9 . . 135 B6
York Pl PL2 . . 127 F4
York Rd Plymouth PL5 . . 127 E4
  Torpoint PL11 . . 127 B3
York St Penzance TR18 . . 143 E6
  Plymouth PL1 . . 127 E4
York Terr **7** PL2 . . 127 F5
Youldon Way PL20 . . 42 C2

Z

Zaggy La PL17 . . 39 E4
ZELAH . . 56 A2
ZENNOR . . 76 B5
Zennor/Truro & Penwith Coll
  TR18 . . 143 D2
Zion St PL1 . . 148 C2
Zodiac Ho TR19 . . 96 E3